HANDBOOK OF
Psychoeducational Assessment

This is a volume in the Academic Press
EDUCATIONAL PSYCHOLOGY SERIES

Critical comprehensive reviews of research knowledge, theories, principles, and practices

Under the editorship of Gary D. Phye

Handbook of Psychoeducational Assessment

Ability, Achievement, and Behavior in Children

EDITED BY

Jac J. W. Andrews
Division of Applied Psychology
University of Calgary

Donald H. Saklofske
Department of
Educational Psychology and Special Education
University of Saskatchewan

Henry L. Janzen
Department of
Educational Psychology
University of Alberta

ACADEMIC PRESS

A Harcourt Science and Technology Company

San Diego   San Francisco   New York   Boston   London   Sydney   Tokyo

The sponsoring editor for this book was Nikki Levy, the editorial coordinator was Barbara Makinster, and the production editor was Theresa Moran. The cover was designed by Cathy Reynolds. Composition was done by G & S Typesetters, Austin, Texas

Cover photo credit: © 2001 PhotoDisc, Inc.

This book is printed on acid-free paper. ∞

Academic Press
A Harcourt Science and Technology Company
525 B Street, Suite 1900, San Diego, California 92101-4495, USA
http://www.academicpress.com

Academic Press
84 Theobalds Road, London WC1X 8RR, UK
http://www.academicpress.com

Library of Congress Catalog Card Number: 2001086089

International Standard Book Number: 0-12-058570-7

PRINTED IN THE UNITED STATES OF AMERICA
02   03   04   05   06   MB   9   8   7   6   5   4   3   2

This book is dedicated to
Deb (JWA)
Vicki (DHS)
Sue (HLJ)

Contents

INVITED FOREWORD AND INTRODUCTION
Moshe Zeidner

Ability Assessment

3. ASSESSMENT WITH THE DIFFERENTIAL ABILITY SCALES

Bruce Gordon and Colin D. Elliott

4. BRIEF COGNITIVE ASSESSMENT OF CHILDREN: REVIEW OF INSTRUMENTS AND RECOMMENDATIONS FOR BEST PRACTICE

Rex B. Kline

5. ASSESSMENT WITH THE WOODCOCK–JOHNSON III

Nancy Mather and Noel Gregg

II

Achievement Assessment

6. WECHSLER INDIVIDUAL ACHIEVEMENT TEST

Donna Rury Smith

7. ASSESSMENT FOR READING AND WRITING INTERVENTION: A THREE-TIER MODEL FOR PREVENTION AND REMEDIATION

Virginia W. Berninger, Scott A. Stage,
Donna Rury Smith, and Denise Hildebrand

8. ASSESSMENT FOR MATH TALENT AND DISABILITY: A DEVELOPMENTAL MODEL

Julie Busse, Virginia W. Berninger, Donna Rury Smith,
and Denise Hildebrand

Behavior Assessment

9. BEHAVIOR ASSESSMENT SYSTEM FOR CHILDREN (BASC): TOWARD ACCURATE DIAGNOSIS AND EFFECTIVE TREATMENT

Gail S. Matazow and R. W. Kamphaus

10. THE ACHENBACH SYSTEM OF
EMPIRICALLY BASED ASSESSMENT

Stephanie H. McConaughy

11. ASSESSMENT OF SOCIAL SKILLS IN CHILDREN AND ADOLESCENTS

Frank M. Gresham

12. ASSESSMENT WITH BRIEF
BEHAVIOR RATING SCALES

Robert J. Volpe and George J. DuPaul

Recent Advances in Psychological and Educational Assessment

15. DYNAMIC ASSESSMENT OF LEARNING POTENTIAL

David Tzuriel

Contributors

Numbers in parentheses indicate the pages on which the authors' contributions begin.

Jac J. W. Andrews (xxi), Division of Applied Psychology, University of Calgary, Calgary, Alberta, T2N 1N4, Canada

Alfredo Ardila (391), Memorial Regional Hospital, Hollywood, Florida 33021

Virginia Berninger (195, 225), Multidisciplinary Learning Disabilities Center, University of Washington, Seattle, Washington 98195

Julie Busse (225), Multidisciplinary Learning Disabilities Center, Educational Psychology, University of Washington, Seattle, Washington 98195

J. P. Das (33), J. P. Das Developmental Disabilities Centre, University of Alberta, Edmonton, Alberta, T5G 2E5, Canada

George J. DuPaul (357), College of Education, Lehigh University, Bethlehem, Pennsylvania 18015

Ruben Echemendía (391), Department of Psychology, Pennsylvania State University, University Park, Pennsylvania 16802

Colin D. Elliott (65), Graduate School of Education, University of California, Santa Barbara, California 93106

Bruce Gordon (65), Alvin Buckwold Child Development Program, Royal University Hospital, Saskatoon, Saskatchewan, S7N 2Z1, Canada

Noel Gregg (133), Department of Educational Psychology, University of Georgia, Athens, Georgia 30602-5875

Frank M. Gresham (325), Graduate School of Education, University of California–Riverside, Riverside, California 92521

Josette Harris (391), Departments of Psychiatry and Neurology, University of Colorado School of Medicine, Denver, Colorado 80262

Denise Hildebrand (13, 195, 225), The Psychological Corporation, San Antonio, Texas 78204

Henry L. Janzen (xxi), Department of Educational Psychology, University of Alberta, Edmonton, Alberta, T5J 2JM, Canada

R. W. Kamphaus (257), Department of Educational Psychology, University of Georgia, Athens, Georgia 30606

Rex B. Kline (103), Department of Psychology, Concordia University, Montreal, Quebec, H4B 1R6, Canada

Mark F. Ledbetter (13), Trinity Clinical Associates, San Antonio, Texas 78229

Gail Matazow (257), Alberta Hospital, Edmonton and Department of Educational Psychology, University of Alberta, Edmonton, Alberta, T6R 2J5, Canada

Nancy Mather (133), Department of Special Education, Rehabilitation, and School Psychology, University of Arizona, Tucson, Arizona 85750-1309

Stephanie H. McConaughy (289), Department of Psychiatry, University of Vermont, Burlington, Vermont 05401

Jack A. Naglieri (33), Center for Cognitive Development, Psychology Department, George Mason University, Fairfax, Virginia 22030-4444

Mónica Rosselli (391), Department of Psychology, Florida Atlantic University, Boca Raton, Florida 33314

Donald H. Saklofske (xxi), Department of Educational Psychology and Special Education, University of Saskatchewan, Saskatoon, Saskatchewan, S7N 0X1, Canada

Donna Rury Smith (169, 195, 225), The Psychological Corporation, San Antonio, Texas 78204

Scott A. Stage (195), School Psychology Program, University of Washington, Seattle, Washington 98195

H. Gerry Taylor (415), Department of Pediatrics, Case Western Reserve University, and Rainbow Babies and Children's Hospital, Cleveland, Ohio 44106

David Tzuriel (451), School of Education, Bar-Ilan University, Ramat-Gan 52900, Israel

Robert J. Volpe (357), College of Education, Lehigh University, Bethlehem, Pennsylvania 18015

Keith Owen Yeates (415), Department of Pediatrics, Ohio State University, and, Children's Hospital, Columbus, Ohio 43205

Moshe Zeidner (1), Center for the Interdisciplinary Research of Emotions, University of Haifa, Mt. Carmel 31905, Israel

Preface

INTRODUCTION

Handbook of Psychoeducational Assessment: Ability, Achievement, and Behavior in Children is composed of an introductory chapter followed by 15 chapters distributed across 4 sections. The challenge of creating this book was to present some of the most frequently used and most recently published empirically validated tests within the context of clinical practice, thereby addressing the realities of today's psychoeducational assessment environment while guiding the reader toward a consideration of emerging developments. When we first proposed this book to Academic Press, several of the tests we wanted to include were under revision. We felt it imperative to describe these new tests as much as possible, even as they were still moving toward final completion. We think our goals have been achieved because of the expertise and extensive experience that the authors bring to their respective chapters. All of the contributors either have authored or been actively involved in the construction of the assessment instruments highlighted in this book or have played key roles in the evolution of the theoretical and empirical foundations, as well as practice, of psychological testing. This combination of psychological knowledge, psychometric expertise, and clinical sensitivity is reflected throughout the chapters of this book. Thus, while all of the chapters focus on one or more tests, the intent is to go beyond a summary overview of the test or a technical review of the research literature. It is here that the authors also share their rich insights and knowledge, which certainly contributes to our understanding of why these tests have become so important in the psychological and educational assessment of children and youth. Although the critical importance of other methods (e.g., observation, interviews) is recognized, there is little disagreement that psychologists make extensive use of tests in the assessment process.

PRESENT TRENDS AND PARADIGM SHIFTS

Over the past decade, advances occurring concurrently in the theories, research, and practice of psychology have culminated in substantial changes in the processes and products of psychoeducational assessment. Cognitive psychologists have demonstrated that we can measure and, in turn, effect positive changes in children's and youth's processing ability and acquired skills to learn and think. Recent developments in testing have focused on improving the examiner's resources for evaluating psychological and educational factors, as well as the determinants and processes underlying a wide range of individual differences, and to do this much more effectively and efficiently. Thus, current tests are now serving a needed and important role in linking assessment to diagnosis and program development at the primary, secondary, and tertiary levels.

Second, psychologists and educators recognize the complex interaction between intelligence, behavior, and achievement. For example, socially competent individuals engage successfully in interpersonal relationships and tend to have academic and vocational success. An underachieving child of average or above-average intelligence might also be manifesting some indications of social and behavioral difficulties (e.g., aggression, withdrawal, depression). The kind and severity of these problems may be better recognized, monitored, and acted upon with the use of sensitive behavior rating scales. There has been a growing use of instruments that can provide objective and meaningful information about the nature and scope of behavioral maladjustment within children and adolescents, as well as on adaptive behavior functioning and well-being. In a related vein, intelligence and achievement tests are more often being statistically and clinically linked during the standardization phase in order to facilitate the diagnostic assessment process.

Third, as we have moved forward into the new millennium, the limitations of static and fragmented assessment approaches continue to be heard. There has been a shift toward the view that psychoeducational assessment is integral to intervention. Assessment and intervention are more commonly thought of as reciprocal and interactive processes that require the use of several methods to better describe and understand the complexity of thinking, learning, and behaving. Moreover, it has become increasingly recognized that the education and social–emotional development of children and youth requires the coordinated and collaborative efforts of psychologists and educators. Psychologists are spending a greater amount of time consulting with teachers and other community specialists to design and implement procedures for maximizing the development of children and adolescents. This has expanded the role of psychologists and clinicians in serving children and youth in today's schools and communities. Hence, it is critical that psychologists improve their knowledge and skills relative to assessment to be able to make insightful and meaningful recommendations in consultation with teachers, parents, and other professionals.

Finally, there has been a shift in the way psychologists and clinicians approach testing and report writing. At present, they are taking an approach that goes beyond the reporting of test results and places a far greater premium on the *interpretation* of test results, particularly with respect to learning, thinking, and behavior. This has resulted in the demand for wide-ranging yet, at the same time, selective assessment techniques. Psychologists and clinicians are seeking test instruments and procedures that not only focus on the more traditional assessment of intelligence and achievement but also address, among other things, developmental level, memory, cognitive structures, cultural variance, and situational context. Moreover, there is much more interest in determining the types of strategies that children and youth use in their learning, thinking, academic accomplishments, and social decision making, which, in turn, can provide teachers and parents the types of knowledge they require to design proactive and preventative programs and interventions.

The above trends and paradigm shifts have required transformations in psychoeducational assessment practices. Clinicians must become more flexible and adaptive in order to respond to current psychological and educational assessment demands. Our challenge has been to put together a resource that provides psychologists and clinicians in practice as well as those in training with practical knowledge, guidance, and insight with respect to current psychoeducational tests and practices associated with the use of these tests. Our hope is that we achieved this goal.

FEATURES OF THE BOOK

- The chapter authors are recognized leaders in psychoeducational test development, research, and practice.
- The tests selected for inclusion are among the instruments used most often in psychological and educational assessment.
- The most recent versions of previously published tests are highlighted.
- Throughout the book, the authors present historical, theoretical, and empirical foundations that serve as bases for the use of tests in educational and clinical settings.
- Each chapter describes the nature and scope of the tests and presents the salient psychometric properties (i.e., reliability and validity) of the tests.
- Each chapter gives critical information on administration, scoring, and interpretation guidelines of the tests.
- Throughout the text, the authors draw upon their professional experiences as well as from the published literature in discussing the usefulness of the tests.

- Empirical findings regarding the use of the tests are summarized together with evidence of various patterns of performance with tested populations.
- Case studies provided in each chapter highlight the utility of the respective tests and exemplify the critical features and assets of the tests.
- Throughout the text, figures and tables illustrate some of the properties of the tests as well as their clinical significance.
- A list of references is provided at the end of each chapter to enhance the reader's awareness of research and clinical practice of relevance to the test(s) under review.
- Each chapter points out the new developments in instrumentation and the unique features of the tests that help identify and address the problems experienced by children and youth.

ORGANIZATION OF THE TEXT

As mentioned earlier, this book is composed of 15 chapters that are distributed among 4 sections. In his foreword and introduction, Moshe Zeidner overviews key issues related to the assessment of intelligence, behavior, and achievement. He attests to the need and importance of placing psychological tests solidly within the framework of theory, research, and best practices.

Part 1: Ability Assessment. Intelligence tests have been a cornerstone of both academic and professional psychology for more than a century. Intelligence tests continue to be among the instruments used most often for the psychological and educational assessment of children and adolescents. In Chapter 1, Denise Hildebrand and Mark Ledbetter begin with a practical overview of intellectual assessment using the Wechsler Intelligence Scale–Third Edition (WISC-III). They pay particular attention to the hierarchical analysis of the WISC-III results and the use of the General Ability Index for summarizing overall performance. The authors also discuss the relationship between intellectual functioning and memory as well as the assessment of memory with the use of the Children's Memory Scale (CMS). In Chapter 2, intellectual assessment is examined with a relatively new test, the Cognitive Assessment System (CAS) developed by J. P. Das and Jack Naglieri. In addition to overviewing both the underlying theory and the CAS as a measure of attention, planning, and information processing, the authors present a reading enhancement program based on the PASS theory. Chapter 3 by Bruce Gordon and Colin Elliott offers an in-depth description of the Differential Ability Scales (DAS). A unique feature of the DAS is the analysis of subtest profile patterns to gain a better understanding of a child's cognitive abilities, and this chapter focuses on profiles of children with dyslexia and other learning disabilities to illustrate the diagnostic utility of the DAS. Chapter 4 addresses the assessment of intelligence with brief ability scales. In addition to provid-

ing the contexts for using brief cognitive testing and a discussion of the necessary properties of these tests, Rex Kline focuses on several contemporary
tests specifically constructed as brief measures of intelligence, as well as on
short forms of full-battery IQ tests. Moreover, the author addresses issues
regarding brief inteligence testing and guidelines for best practice. This
section closes with Chapter 5 by Nancy Mather and Noel Gregg, which also
sets the stage for the next section. One of the best examples of building a
comprehensive assessment battery for the assessment of both intelligence
and achievement is the Woodcock–Johnson Tests of Cognitive Abilities and
Achievement (WJ-III). This chapter forms a nice bridge between the first and
second sections because it reports on an instrument that is a co-normed
comprehensive battery of individually administered tests designed to measure ability and achievement. The chapter also presents discrepancy options
for determining individual strengths and weaknesses along with special clinical clusters that can help evaluators measure different cognitive aspects of
attention, phonological awareness and skill, cognitive and academic speed
of processing, executive processing, and basic academic skills, fluency, and
problem solving.

Part 2: *Achievement Assessment.* Here, achievement testing is discussed in
three comprehensive chapters. While authentic assessment, the use of portfolios, and standardized achievement tests assessing both basic skills and
curricular areas are widely used in schools as part of the everyday assessment of achievement, the tests and processes described here focus much
more on individual diagnostic assessment. As previously shown in Chapter 5,
linking cognitive abilities with achievement measures is so important in the
assessment of children and youth presenting with learning difficulties. In
Chapter 6, Donna Smith discusses assessment with the Wechsler Individual
Achievement Test (WIAT). This chapter points out that a distinct advantage of
this instrument is that it is the only achievement battery that is linked with
the WISC-III. Moreover, it is noted that the WIAT is distinguished by its coverage of all of the areas of learning disability as specified by U.S. federal law.
Importantly, this chapter describes the changes made to the second edition
to enhance the WIAT II's diagnostic utility, resulting in a stronger link between assessment and intervention. Chapter 7 by Virginia Berninger, Scott
Stage, Donna Smith, and Denise Hildebrand and Chapter 8 by Julie Busse,
Virginia Berninger, Donna Smith, and Denise Hildebrand together describe
an assessment-for-intervention model that is designed to translate research
on prevention and treatment of reading, writing, and math disabilities into
practice. A three-tier model forms the basis from which diagnostic and treatment approaches are presented and illustrated in both chapters. Here the
Process Assessment of the Learner (PAL) is brought to the fore. The components that contribute to effective reading, writing, and mathematical problem
solving are outlined together with an approach to assessment that promotes
a more useful and expanded role by psychologists in their collaboration and
consultation with educators.

Part 3: Behavior Assessment. The systematic assessment of behavior requires the use of self-report and other report questionnaires to complement observation, interview, and case history information. Descriptions of behavior are important not only in the assessment of children and youth presenting with behavioral problems but also in a comprehensive assessment of all children and youth referred for psychological services. We elected to focus on two of the more frequently used broad-based questionnaires before turning to an examination of brief measures and the assessment of social skills. Gail Matazow and Randy Kamphaus in Chapter 9 describe the Behavior Assessment System for Children (BASC). They review the BASC in relation to the assessment of clinical constructs, adaptive behavior functioning, and self-perceptions of children and youth. In addition, the authors pay particular attention to a new variant of the original BASC that is designed to comprehensively assess the primary symptoms of ADHD. In Chapter 10, Stephanie McConaughy provides an in-depth description of the new Achenbach System of Empirically Based Assessment and discusses its use for behavior assessment, intervention planning, and outcome evaluation. Among other areas, this chapter highlights the kinds of cross-informant data that are often sought in such contexts as school settings, mental health services, residential treatment, child custody and placement decisions, evaluations of child abuse, and delinquency adjudications. In Chapter 11, Frank Gresham surveys the assessment of social skills and examines the conceptual and practical relationship between social competence and social skills and methods that can provide information about prosocial and competing behavior problems. A useful aspect of this chapter is its practical guidance on naturalistic observations of social behavior and the use of functional assessment interviews in conjunction with behavior rating systems. Chapter 12 by Robert Volpe and George DuPaul turns to behavior asessment with the use of brief scales. The uses of brief scales are placed in the context of the varying stages of assessment. The authors then give more specific information about the use of brief scales in the assessment of ADHD, anxiety, and depression.

Part 4: Recent Advances in Psychological and Educational Assessment. This last section has been included to ensure that the relevance and importance of tests are fully understood and appreciated in the wider and ever-changing context of psychological and psychoeducational assessment. While all of the previous 12 chapters recognize the critical importance of context- and person-sensitive assessment practices, the final three chapters highlight these considerations. We decided to focus on three topics that are particularly germane to this theme and to the assessment practices of psychologists: cross-cultural assessment, neuropsychological assessment, and dynamic assessment. Chapter 13, written by Josette Harris, Ruben Echemendía, Alfredo Ardila, and Mónica Rosselli, discusses salient factors and issues concerning the cognitive and neuropsychological assessment of culturally and linguistically diverse children and youth. The interplay and interaction of language and culture in the diagnostic assessment process are illustrated in two case studies. The rapid growth of knowledge regarding brain–behavior relationships has placed increasing demands on the assessment skills of psychologists. In Chapter 14, Keith Yeates and Gerry Taylor report on research and practices relative to neuropsychological assessment. The multimodal methods required for a comprehensive neuropsychological assessment are placed in the context of several principles that guide practice. Chapter 15 completes Part 4 with a discussion by David Tzuriel on the relevance and usefulness of dynamic assessment for program planning and intervention delivery. In this chapter, the reader is reminded of the importance of evaluating the cognitive strategies that can facilitate learning performance and how dynamic assessment can be effective in better understanding clinical groups of children and youth as well as in the evaluation of intervention programs aimed at improving their learning potential.

ACKNOWLEDGMENTS

We are indebted to the contributing authors for their diligence and commitment to the project and for sharing their clinical expertise about psychological tests. This is truly their book. We are very grateful to Professor Moshe Zeidner for writing the introduction. His exceptional knowledge of this field is also found in his many books and journal articles. The publication of this book was made possible by the efforts of two people at Academic Press. We thank Nikki Levy, Publisher, for her acceptance of this handbook as part of the Educational Psychology Series, and Barbara Makinster, Senior Editorial Coordinator, for her support and guidance. We would like to thank Theresa Moran, who greatly enhanced the quality of this book in her role as Production Coordinator. This project was partially funded by the John Ranton McIntosh Research/Fellowship and a publication grant from the University of Saskatchewan.

Finally, for their help and encouragement, we share this book with our families, who encourage us to do our work and make us feel that it is worthwhile. This book is dedicated to them.

Jac Andrews
Don Saklofske
Hank Janzen

Invited Foreword and Introduction

MOSHE ZEIDNER

University of Haifa, Israel

Contemporary society may be described as test-oriented and test-consuming (Zeidner & Most, 1992). A wide array of tests and assessment procedures are currently used by psychologists, special education teachers, and counselors to help in making important decisions about children and youth. Tests of students' abilities, achievements, and behaviors are invaluable tools for understanding children's intellectual and social strengths and weaknesses and essential for making accurate diagnoses and valid predictions and for tailoring appropriate programs and treatments to clients' needs. With the current interest in student performance and the heightened emphasis on school accountability, the time spent in testing school children is on the rise. As the Information Age continues to evolve, test scores will become of increasing importance in admission into highly competitive educational programs.

This handbook, focusing on the psychoeducational assessment of students' achievements, abilities, and behaviors, provides psychological practitioners and researchers with state-of-the-art theory, research findings, psychometric data, and test applications. The tests most often used by psychologists are placed within a framework of contemporary best practices. The handbook's focus on cognitive and behavioral assessments presumably rests on the notion that the level and quality of a student's achievements and adaptation to the classroom environment are based on three crucial and broad determinants: the student's store of acquired knowledge, cognitive aptitudes (verbal, numerical, spatial, etc.) and efficiency (speed of processing, access to short-term memory), and myriad noncognitive factors (social, emotional, motivational) that facilitate or inhibit student learning.

This very timely and practical handbook provides readily accessible information on some of the most prominent and widely employed individual cognitive, achievement, and behavioral assessment devices and tests in the field today—information that would be hard for practitioners to compile on their own. The chapters provide handy information designed to help professionals better understand the goals, key features, and quantitative and qualitative uses of the psychological instruments presented. In addition, the illustrative and rich case study materials presented serve as excellent guides in interpreting test scores and profiles and in making diagnostic decisions based on the assessment data.

CURRENT DIRECTIONS AND TRENDS IN PSYCHOEDUCATIONAL ASSESSMENT

The chapters in this handbook reflect a number of contemporary currents and trends in the domain of psychoeducational assessment. Some of these salient and prominent currents, which express the current *zeitgeist* in the field, are briefly delineated below.

Emphasis on Theory-Based Assessments

As suggested in various chapters throughout the handbook, in order for a cognitive or behavioral test to be intelligible and interpretable, a sound and tenable theory needs to guide the instrument's construction or revision. When assessment is guided by a coherent theoretical framework, the results can more readily be analyzed, interpreted, and communicated to clients, thus rendering the test easier for school psychologists to work with. The recent appearance of a plethora of new, theoretically grounded cognitive instruments (or revised batteries) has the effect of challenging practitioners' comfortable reliance on some of the old, better known atheoretical or pragmatically oriented instruments.

The chapters focusing on the assessment of intelligence or ability reflect a shift from unifactorial conceptions of ability (g-based models) to multifactorial models of intelligence. Accordingly, the various tests described in the chapters reflect multiple perspectives, ranging from the conventional psychometric ability tradition (e.g., the Woodcock-Johnson Tests of Cognitive Ability, based on the psychometric model of Cattell-Horn), through biologically or neuropsychologically based instruments (e.g., The Das-Naglieri Assessment Battery for Children, based on Luria's functional theory of the brain), through dynamic assessment (e.g., Feurstein's Learning Propensity Assessment Device [LPAD]). Yet, the shift toward a multifactorial model has not been accompanied by a general rejection of the concept of general ability, still so predominant in measures such as the Wechsler Intelligence Scale for Children—Third Edition (WISC-III). It is noted, in passing, that the long-standing argument over general intelligence versus multiple abilities gives way to a broad acceptance of a hierarchical model in which abilities are nested under a higher-order general factor, each level having a substantial amount of explanatory power.

Focus on Cognitive Process in Assessment

Various chapters give testimony to the recent upsurge of interest among researchers in unraveling the cognitive and neuropsychological processes that determine test performance. Indeed, the focus of cognitive assessment has shifted from deriving global scores of ability or achievement to identifying specific cognitive processes and operations that underlie intellectual functioning (Daniel, 1997). Experts now realize that those prevalent conventional tests, viewing intelligence as a unidimensional and often undifferentiated mass of general ability, are not very useful for understanding the variety of intellectual abilities that characterize students. Neither are these approaches informative in establishing a profile of children's cognitive processing for purposes of diagnosis of difficulties in student learning and attention. The process approach, by contrast, is claimed to facilitate the identification of strategies employed by examinees to solve a cognitive task as well as facilitating identification of the nature of the errors made. By understanding the process underlying performance and the interrelations among the different processing components contributing to performance, psychologists are better prepared to troubleshoot—to discover which components are underdeveloped and thus interfere with the functioning of student problem solving and consequently require intervention or further practice. Advances in both cognitive psychology and neuropsychology are reflected not only in our contemporary test instruments but also in our approach to assessment and the use of assessment information.

Assessing Learning Potential via Dynamic Procedures

The handbook includes a chapter presenting recent developments in a novel breed of assessment procedures that offer a new option for the measurement of abilities (i.e., dynamic assessment). The model used in dynamic assessment is that of a clinical interview of the examinee, aimed at revealing deficient cognitive processes in the child and identifying effective intervention methods to improve cognitive processes. In comparison with traditional psychometric ability tests, dynamic assessment is less concerned with uncovering the examinee's level and pattern of abilities and more interested in uncovering the ability to learn and degree of cognitive modifiability. In dynamic tests, examinees receive test problems with a twist: If they fail to answer the question correctly, they are given guided successive feedback to help them solve the problem. The idea is that examinees' abilities to profit from guided feedback convey a sense of the differences between their latent capacity and observed proficiency, or "zone of proximal development." Dynamic assessment claims to provide better classification and diagnosis of a student's learning potential because test performance followed by intervention is thought to be a more valid indication of true ability. The particular brand of dynamic assessment described in the handbook is the LPAD proposed by Israeli psychologist Reuven Feurstein, an international leader in this area.

Broadening the Domain of Abilities Measured

The content domain of conventional tests of ability and achievement is frequently claimed to be too narrow. Accordingly, published instruments fail to represent key theoretical and research advances in our understanding of such cognitive attributes as creativity, social and emotional abilities, practical intelligence, wisdom, and the like. Most conventional tests assess only a particular subset of the ability domain, being heavily biased in favor of linguistic and logical-mathematical abilities (Gardner, 1992). Current tests favor individuals who possess a blend of linguistic and logical intelligence and who are comfortable in being assessed in a decontextualized setting under timed and impersonal conditions. Since current tests do not exhaust the domain, and often lack "ecological validity," they tend to mask individual strengths and differences on a variety of dimensions (e.g., interpersonal understanding, social competence, creativity, and practical ability). Thus, some individuals often fail on formal measures of intelligence but can show precisely these skills in the course of ordinary work (e.g., defending rights in a dispute, providing leadership in a peer group, demonstrating expertise in a sport).

A number of chapters reflect recent developments in the measurement of relatively neglected cognitive constructs, which have typically not been included in earlier cognitive batteries. A case in point is that of declarative *episodic memory*, a key facet of long-term memory. This ubiquitous cognitive ability, which assesses novel contextually bound information that the examinee has recently acquired, has typically been ignored and has not been assessed. This ability is now included in one test protocol (i.e., the Children's Memory Scale [CMS]) and introduced to the readers of the handbook. Another attribute that traditional assessment devices have avoided until recently is self-regulation (see the chapter by Das & Naglieri). This important component of executive function is now included in scales such as the Woodcock-Johnson.

Behavioral Measures as an Essential Part of the Psychoeducational Assessment of Children and Youth

Few people would question the significance of social and emotional competencies in classroom adaptation and student development. Social competence is crucial because it adequately predicts long-term social adjustment and is a key factor in the development of behavioral malfunction in the classroom. While interventions and treatment strategies based on behavioral principles have a long and rich tradition in school psychology, assessment procedures based on these principles have lagged behind significantly. In recent years this gap has been addressed and filled, as evidenced by the coverage of this area in the handbook. Volpe and DuPaul point out in their chapter that a wide variety of instruments are now available for obtaining information on how the behavior of youngsters is viewed by various referents, including parents, teachers, and children. Behavioral assessments can be used to formulate and evaluate specific intervention procedures that facilitate positive classroom behaviors and remediate behavioral problems, as demonstrated in the chapters on the Behavior Assessment System for Children and the Achenbach System of Empirically Based Assessment. Indeed, many students, particularly those with high incidences of disabilities, do not meet the model behavioral profile expected by teachers, such as the presence of positive academic behavior and the absence of disruptive behavior.

Focus of Interpretive Efforts on Students' Profiles of Strengths and Weaknesses

Practitioners could improve interpretation of the scores yielded by conventional ability and achievement measures by taking the test profile and scatter into serious account. As noted by a number of handbook authors, rather than relying on composite ability test scores, the most defensible procedure is to strive to create a profile of an examinee's strengths and weaknesses across a range of behaviors. By analyzing the varied patterns of strengths and weaknesses exhibited by a student's profile, an evaluator can deduce the types of tasks that will be easy and difficult for that student. This will be achieved if each of the subtests in the battery has specificity and reliability sufficiently high to allow the clinician to interpret the pattern of subtest scores and their scatter.

Using Test Score Profiles as an Aid to Test Interpretation

Although profile analysis may not aid in the assignment of children to different diagnostic categories, it may be valuable in delineating and interpreting a child's personal strengths and weaknesses. This in itself may be useful in in-dividualizing instruction and treatment and may also be helpful as a method of generating hypotheses about the origins of intellectual functioning.

Improved Psychometric and Statistical Technology in Test Construction and Validation of Current Measures

The new generation of cognitive measures described in various chapters at-tests to improved test construction procedures, including more sophisti-cated sampling, item analyses, and validation procedures. With respect to most of the new ability and achievement measures detailed in the handbook, or the revised versions of older instruments, test norms are typically derived from large normative samples, based on such stratification variables as age, grade, gender, race, geographical session, and parental education level. Cur-rent norms, available for a wide range of age groups, allow the examiner to follow the student's performance at different periods in development. Fur-thermore, items on a number of current tests described in the handbook (e.g., the Wechsler Individual Achievement Test [WIAT] and the Woodcock-Johnson battery) underwent extensive field testing at the test development stage, including the use of both conventional and modern IRT item analysis. Also, a number of tests provide evidence of construct validity based on mod-ern confirmatory factor analytic procedures as well as discriminant criterion-group validity. In addition, the co-norming of ability and achievement tests (e.g., the WIAT and the Woodcock-Johnson Psychometric Battery) on the same standardization sample offers a distinct advantage when employing discrepancy scores for diagnostic purposes (e.g., to detect underachieve-ment, lack of motivation, or learning disabilities).

Using Qualitative Measures to Supplement Test Scores

A number of qualitative methods, including error analysis and diagnostic in-terviews, are frequently used to supplement quantitative testing in practice. For example, as pointed out in the handbook, in the area of math achieve-ment testing, students may be asked to show their work on assessment mea-sures so that the examiner may observe the process they go through in gen-erating the answers, such as using think-aloud or similar procedures. Error analysis on these work samples may provide a vital link between ongoing as-sessment and intervention. Thus, by analyzing several incorrect answers to the same or similar items, the examiner may be able to determine if the stu-dent failed the items because of lack of knowledge of basic math facts, a systematic procedural error, or a lack of basic concepts. A further step in re-vealing a student's problem-solving strategies is interviewing, in which inter-viewers simply ask the student to explain the way they solved a problem; if a student finds it difficult to provide an after-the-fact explanation, use of a think-aloud technique while solving a new, similar problem may be helpful.

Assimilating Data from Various Sources

As evidenced throughout the handbook, authorities currently hold that a simple composite test score, be it in the domain of ability or achievement measurement, should not be used alone in describing, predicting, or explaining an examinee's behavior. Sound test interpretation involves integrating various sources of data and assimilating them into an exposition that describes the examinee's functioning. Thus, poor performance on a math achievement test may be due to memory problems, poor instruction, limited schooling, distractibility, anxiety, and so on, rather than to low quantitative ability. Intellectual competence is always intertwined with motivation and adjustment. Consequently, whenever we are measuring a subject's cognitive functioning, we are also measuring cooperation, attention, persistence, and social responsiveness to the test situation.

By necessity, psychologists and educational practitioners will be responsible for a considerable amount of integration of cognitive and affective variables in practice. Thus, the psychologist working in the schools may not only assess a student's intelligence, achievements, and behaviors but also gather data from multiple sources (tests, interviews with the child's teachers and parents, observations, clinical interviews) on motivation, learning styles, self-concept, anxiety, coping strategies, and moods as well as health and physical status and home environment and adaptations. The integration of information from multiple assessment sources will help the practitioner arrive at a diagnosis and prescription of the most appropriate interpretations. As stressed by Most and Zeidner (1995), the psychological practitioner's task is to develop a comprehensive integration of the person by employing precise measurement strategies and continuously referencing theory and research that describe the relationships among the various examined factors. Given that such an integration is not always explicit from theory or from the available literature, clinicians may be required to make the integration on their own.

Focus on Assessments' Practical Benefits for the Client

Psychoeducational testing is now faced with increasing pressure to demonstrate practical applications and benefits within school settings. The tests reviewed and considered in this handbook are seen to be aids to stimulating personal development, and some claim they deserve to be evaluated largely in terms of their constructive potential. The various chapters show how current assessment instruments are to be used for myriad practical purposes, such as screening students, monitoring progress in response to educational interventions, and making educational recommendations for students based on assessment results. In addition, a number of handbook authors emphasize matching instruction to cognitive profiles and remediating processing deficits.

This handbook reflects the recent shift from static psychometric perspectives guiding psychoeducational assessments to treatment-oriented ones. It is commonly held that the ultimate purpose of psychoeducational assessment is to assist the child in some way. This means that tests and assessment procedures should be seen as a means by which children can be helped, although many of the earlier cognitive tests were not designed for that purpose. Considering the prominence of testing in contemporary schools, it is really amazing how useless and irrelevant some of the currently used ability and achievement tests seem to be to teachers, counselors, and psychologists. Many standardized tests give little assistance or clue to what should be done to eradicate deficiencies or take advantage of a student's skills and talents. As clearly stated by Das and Naglieri in Chapter 2: "Assessment without an implication for what to do next with the child who was assessed is no longer enough."

Sensitivity to Cultural Context

If conventional tests and assessment procedures are to be used soundly in a culturally different context, then the user must be sensitive to a number of issues. For one, the practitioner must realize that tests are not universally valid and reliable instruments. Tests are specific cultural genres, reflecting the values, knowledge, and common strategies of the culture in which the test was developed and normed. One needs to be aware of culture-specific meanings, ways of knowing, and communication modes that enhance the validity of cross-cultural tests. Because cultures provide specific models for ways of behaving, feeling, thinking, and communicating, cultural values and expectations have a significant influence on both the process and the outcome of cognitive, neuropsychological, and behavioral assessment.

As pointed out by several authors, a first step in the assessment of culturally different or ethnically diverse examinees is to make an honest attempt to understand and appreciate the examinee's culture. This includes an understanding of the cognitive abilities that are valued, developed, and trained in the culture, knowledge of the cultural values and traditions and beliefs that can impact both the process and the outcome of assessment, and developmental expectations for acquisition of various cognitive competencies. Some of the materials presented in the handbook chapters nicely demonstrate how cultural context shapes the manner in which individuals approach cognitive or behavioral assessment and the culturally indigenous ways they respond to test stimuli. Furthermore, test authors are increasingly aware of the need to test for any sign of cultural bias on newly constructed measures, using internal, external, and ecological validity criteria.

Assessment within Context

The various chapters provide ample evidence in support of the notion that test scores need to be understood within the context of a person's life and ecosystem. Thus, assessment of test performance requires appreciation of the possible multiple influences on test scores, interactional influences, and multiple relations. This includes the subject's past history and current social, emotional, vocational, and economic adjustments, as well as behavior during the exam. In fact, the kind of life one leads is itself a pretty good test of a person's intellectual ability. When a life history is in disagreement with the test results, the practitioner should pause before attempting classification on the basis of the test alone, as the former is generally a more reliable criterion. Thus, interpretation should only be made after the relevant information beyond test scores has been examined.

In sum, the editors are to be commended for pulling together a valuable resource for state-of-the-art and state-of-the-science information on cognitive and behavioral assessment of school children. A careful reading of each of the chapters should aid professionals in narrowing the gap that currently exists between contemporary theory and research on intelligence, achievement, and socioemotional behavior, on one hand, and applied psychoeducational assessment of school children, on the other hand. Students undergoing assessment, as well as their parents and teachers, should expect professionals to use tools that are based on the best evidence of current science and to make interpretations of the testing data that are supported by contemporary theory and research. This handbook is designed to offer professionals the theoretical knowledge, research data, psychometric properties, and accumulated experience of experts in testing and assessment to help them meet this expectation.

I am confident that practitioners will find this information of much value as they use these tests in their own practice or research in the schools.

References

Daniel, H. (1997). Intelligence testing: Status and trends. *American Psychologist*, 52, 1038–1045.

Gardner, H. (1992). Assessment in context: The alternative to standardized testing. In B. R. Gifford & M. C. O'Conner (Eds.), *Changing assessments: Alternative views of aptitude, achievement, and instruction* (pp. 77–119). Boston: Kluwer Publishers.

Most, B., & Zeidner, M. (1995). Constructing personality and intelligence test instruments: Methods and issues. In D. Saklofske & M. Zeidner (Eds.), *International handbook of personality and intelligence* (pp. 475– 503). New York: Plenum.

Zeidner, M., & Most, R. (Eds.). (1992). An introduction to psychological testing. In M. Zeidner & R. Most (Eds.), *Psychological testing: An inside view* (pp. 2–47). Palo Alto, CA: Consulting Psychologists Press.

PART

I

Ability Assessment

Assessing Children's Intelligence and Memory: The Wechsler Intelligence Scale for Children— Third Edition and The Children's Memory Scale

DENISE K. HILDEBRAND

The Psychological Corporation

MARK F. LEDBETTER

Trinity Clinical Associates

INTRODUCTION

The assessment of intellectual functioning has been a critical component of the psychologist's mandate in the schools. Traditionally, school psychologists have evaluated intellectual functioning in order to provide information for the assessment of mental retardation, giftedness, and learning disabilities. Although IQ scores offer the clinician a general overview of a child's performance relative to his or her peers, these scores do not provide specific information regarding appropriate intervention or remedial activities. The absence of direct intervention outcomes or treatment validity has traditionally been a criticism of intelligence measures that provide global IQ scores. Within the past few years, however, the focus of cognitive assessment has

Handbook of Psychoeducational Assessment

shifted from primarily an IQ score derivation to an identification of cognitive processes that underlie intellectual functioning. This shift in assessment focus has prompted the development of test instruments that facilitate the examination of processes or problem-solving strategies. The Wechsler Intelligence Scale for Children—Third Edition as a Process Instrument (WISC-III PI; Kaplan, Fein, Kramer, Delis, & Morris, 1999) and The Children's Memory Scale (CMS; Cohen, 1997) are examples of tests that help facilitate the evaluation of cognitive and memory processes.

Within this chapter, the focus will be primarily centered upon the Wechsler Intelligence Scale for Children—Third Edition (WISC-III; Wechsler, 1991); however, in keeping with the current emphasis on process assessment, the discussion will also include the WISC-III PI and the CMS. The case study provided at the end of the chapter will provide an examination of a child's performance on both the WISC-III and the CMS. While the emphasis within this chapter will be on the decontextualized "science" of test interpretation, there is the recognition that the "art" of test interpretation lies with the clinician whose task it is to construct the assessment picture within the context of the child.

THE WISC-III

Historical Development of the WISC-III

Historically, the conceptualization of intellectual functioning has been closely aligned with measures that were designed to provide information about children's and adults' functioning on a global basis (g), such as the Wechsler scales (e.g., WISC-III; Wechsler, 1991). The children's version of the test, the Wechsler Intelligence Scale for Children (WISC; Wechsler, 1949), was developed by David Wechsler as a downward extension of the adult version of the test, the Wechsler-Bellevue Intelligence Scale (Wechsler, 1939). Although essentially atheoretical in their origination, the Wechsler scales have proven to be sound psychometric instruments over time. Each subsequent revision of the Wechsler scales has resulted in improved psychometric properties and has lent itself to interpretation within current theoretical models of intelligence, for example, information processing models and the Gf-Gc model (Flanagan, McGrew, & Ortiz, 2000; Kaufman, 1994). The current WISC-III is no exception to this trend. According to Kaufman (1994), the WISC-III incorporates the input (e.g., sensory input), integration (e.g., processing information), storage, and output (e.g., expression of information) components of information processing. For example, "Verbal Comprehension and Perceptual Organization refer to cognitive processes and are best interpreted as measures of integration. The new Processing Speed factor is intended as an output factor. And the Freedom from Distractibility factor can fill several slots, depending on how it is interpreted" (Kaufman, 1994, p. 11). Flanagan et al. (2000), on the other hand, have analyzed the WISC-III's fit within contemporary Gf-Gc theory. They contend that the Wechsler scales have strong representation in the Gc (Crystallized Intelligence) and Gv (Visual Processing) domains; in addition, "the WISC-III adequately represents the construct of Gs [Processing Speed]" (Flanagan et al., p. 66). Overall, however, the WISC-III does not represent all of the Gf-Gc domains, particularly the Gf (Fluid Intelligence), Ga (Auditory Processing), and Glr (Long-term Storage and Retrieval) areas.

Psychometric Properties of the WISC-III

A plethora of research attests to the robust psychometric properties of the WISC-III with normal, clinical, and culturally diverse populations (cf. Grice, Krohn, & Logerquist, 1999; Puente & Salazar, 1998; Spruill, 1998; Wechsler, 1996). According to reliability estimates calculated on the WISC-III standardization sample data, internal consistency reliability coefficients for all three scales (Full, Verbal, and Performance) are .89 and greater (Wechsler, 1991). Test-retest reliability (median time interval = 23 days) is reported as .86 or greater for all three scales. The long-term stability (i.e., test-retest) of the WISC-III has also been demonstrated across demographic subgroups such as gender, race/ethnicity, and age (Canivez & Watkins, 1999). Using the standardization data, the validity of the WISC-III was assessed along three dimensions: concurrent validity, predictive validity, and construct validity (Wechsler, 1991). All validity studies reported in the WISC-III Manual suggest that the test has adequate validity within these domains. For a more in-depth discussion of the psychometric properties of the WISC-III, the reader is referred to Sattler (1992). Flanagan et al. (2000) have also summarized the validity studies that have been conducted on the Wechsler scales.

WISC-III Subtests and Subscales

The development of the WISC-III (Wechsler, 1991), a revision of the Wechsler Intelligence Scale for Children—Revised (WISC-R; Wechsler, 1974), was prompted by the need for current normative information, updated stimulus materials, improvement in the fairness of the test, and an enhanced factor structure (Prifitera, Weiss, & Saklofske, 1998).

The WISC-III contained several changes to the WISC-R, including the addition of several new subtests. The addition of these subtests enhanced the interpretive structure of the test to include not only Full Scale, Verbal, and Performance IQ scores but also four factor-based Index scores: Verbal Comprehension, Perceptual Organization, Freedom from Distractibility, and Processing Speed (Wechsler, 1991).

Currently, the WISC-III is composed of 13 subtests, 3 of which are supplemental or optional. Following the WISC-R model, the WISC-III is organized into two primary scales: Verbal and Performance. The Verbal Scale contains subtests that provide a measure of verbal reasoning skills that are primarily reflective of acquired knowledge: Information, Similarities, Arithmetic, Vocabulary, Comprehension, and Digit Span (optional). The Performance Scale, on the other hand, provides a measure of nonverbal reasoning and perceptual-motor skills: Picture Completion, Coding, Picture Arrangement, Block Design, Object Assembly, Symbol Search (optional), and Mazes (optional). (See Table 1.1.)

The four factor-based indexes contain different compositions of the Verbal and Performance scales. The Verbal Comprehension Index is composed of subtests that provide a purer measure of verbal reasoning skills: Information, Similarities, Vocabulary, and Comprehension. Those subtests that are also part of the Verbal Scale but load on another factor, Freedom from Distractibility, are Arithmetic and Digit Span. The Perceptual Organization Index contains several Performance Scale subtests that are purer measures

TABLE 1.1
WISC-III Subtests and Description

Verbal scale	Construct	Performance scale	Construct
Subtest		Subtest	
Information	Factual knowledge	Picture Completion	Ability to differentiate salient from nonsalient visual information
Similarities	Verbal concept formation	Coding	Psychomotor speed
Arithmetic	Auditory memory and attention Mental computation	Picture Arrangement	Planning ability and attention to detail
Vocabulary	Fund of information	Block Design	Spatial visualization and visual-motor coordination
Comprehension	Use of practical judgment in social situations	Object Assembly	Ability to synthesize concrete parts into meaningful wholes
Digit Span	Short-term auditory memory	Symbol Search	Attention and processing speed
		Mazes	Planning ability and visual-motor coordination

Source: From *Assessment of Children: Revised and Updated Third Edition*, by J. M. Sattler, 1992, San Diego, CA: Author.

of nonverbal reasoning skills: Picture Completion, Picture Arrangement, Block Design, and Object Assembly. The subtests Coding and Symbol Search, which constitute the Processing Speed Index, are also part of the Performance Scale.

WISC-III Scores and Interpretive Paradigms

WISC-III Hierarchical Analysis

The WISC-III Full Scale, Verbal Scale, and Performance Scale IQ (FSIQ, VIQ, and PIQ, respectively) scores as well as the four index scores have a mean of 100 and a standard deviation of 15. Each of the 13 subtests has a mean of 10 and a standard deviation of 3.

The derivations of the IQ and Index scores lend themselves to a hierarchical interpretive sequence: FSIQ, VIQ-PIQ, index scores, and individual subtests (Kaufman, 1994). According to Kaufman (1994), the recommended procedure for analyzing a child's performance can be summarized in seven steps.

Step One involves the interpretation of the FSIQ. The FSIQ provides a measure of overall functioning; however, large discrepancies between a child's performance on the Verbal and Performance scales, or large fluctuations on subtest performance within each of these scales, may lessen the weight that is given to the FSIQ as an indication of global performance. To illustrate, if a child obtains a Verbal IQ score of 85 and a Performance IQ score of 115, the FSIQ score of 99 would not adequately represent the functioning of the child given the 30-point disparity between the child's verbal and nonverbal reasoning skills.

Step Two involves the analysis of statistically significant discrepancies between Verbal and Performance IQ scores (i.e., VIQ-PIQ). The base rate (cumulative percentage of students in the standardization sample obtaining that VIQ-PIQ difference or lower) should also be examined in order to determine whether the statistical difference is clinically significant. For example, if 32% of the standardization sample obtained a 13-point or lower difference between the VIQ and PIQ scores, a statistically significant difference would be less meaningful in its clinical interpretation because this difference was obtained by a large percentage of the standardization sample. In fact, the clinician may wish to deemphasize the difference because this discrepancy is fairly common within the normal population.

Step Three involves the determination of whether the VIQ-PIQ discrepancy should be forfeited in favor of the more factorial pure verbal and performance factors, Verbal Comprehension (VC) and Perceptual Organization (PO). In order to assess whether this kind of interpretation is warranted, the four factors should be analyzed within their respective scales. For instance, as described earlier in the chapter, VC and Freedom from Distractibility (FD) constitute the Verbal Scale. If these two factor scores are markedly discrepant from each other, the VIQ does not provide a representative picture of the child's performance in this domain; VC may be a better indicator of verbal reasoning in this regard. On the other hand, if a child's performance is variable across the two factor scores that constitute the PIQ, PO and Processing Speed (PS), PO should be reported in lieu of the PIQ. In fact, both the VC and PO factors are purer measures of each of the verbal and performance domains than the VIQ and PIQ, respectively. As a result, the clinician may wish to describe student performance within the context of these larger factors only.

Step Four involves the additional analysis of VC and PO discrepancies; this analysis is similar to the VIQ-PIQ discrepancy analysis in the determination of statistically and clinically significant differences.

Step Five includes the interpretation of the global verbal and performance domains in light of the two smaller factors: PS and FD. In instances in which the VIQ and PIQ are forfeited in favor of the two larger and two smaller factors, the factor scores should be used for interpretive purposes in lieu of reporting the VIQ, PIQ, or FSIQ. Practically, this situation may present a dilemma for the clinician because most diagnostic and placement decisions (e.g., diagnosis of mental retardation) are made on the basis of an overall IQ score. However, from the standpoint of meaningful interpretation regarding the cognitive processing strengths and weaknesses of the child, the description of performance within factor domains is the most defensible.

Steps Six and Seven address the interpretation of individual subtests and any fluctuations in subtest performance within each of the factor indexes as well as within the more global Verbal and Performance scales. As a general interpretive rule, individual subtest scores can be compared to the mean scaled score within their respective Verbal and Performance scales. Again, both statistical and clinical considerations must be taken into account in the interpretation of significantly discrepant scores. In cases in which the performance of the child varies greatly across the Verbal and Performance scales as well as factor domains, the most appropriate interpretation of the child's strengths and weaknesses lies in a subtest by subtest analysis. For example, if the child has subtest scores that are statistically significantly different from each other within a factor (e.g., Comprehension, Similarities, and Information in the Verbal Comprehension factor), the child's performance would suggest that there is significant variability within this domain. If a child obtains an above average score on Information, an average score on Comprehension, and a below average score on Similarities, the clinician may conclude that the child has a good fund of factual knowledge and can make reasonable judgments within a social context, but is experiencing difficulty with more abstract verbal reasoning tasks. This level of interpretation (at the subtest level) would be more appropriate than describing the child's performance at the factor level (e.g., the child demonstrates verbal reasoning skills within the average range).

In an analysis of the correlations of the individual subtests with overall IQ,

Kaufman (1994) further recommends that the optional subtest, Symbol Search, be substituted for Coding because Symbol Search correlates more highly with Performance IQ (Symbol Search, .58; Coding, .32) and has higher loadings on the Perceptual Organization factor than Coding (.54 vs. .39). Subsequent research studies (Reynolds, Sanchez, & Willson, 1996; Saklofske, Hildebrand, Reynolds, & Willson, 1998) have substituted Symbol Search for Coding in the calculation of norms and have provided normative tables for the calculation of Performance and Full Scale IQ scores for both the American and Canadian standardization data.

The hierarchical analysis (as recommended by Kaufman, 1994) is readily expedited through the use of computer scoring assistants and interpretive software (e.g., WISC-III Writer, 1994, and Scoring Assistant for the Wechsler Scales [SAWS], 1992). These computer programs include both statistical and base rate analyses. The WISC-III Writer also provides interpretive clinical and parent reports that can serve as a basis for the clinician's assessment reports.

General Ability Index

Overall, the addition of the third and fourth factor indexes on the WISC-III has facilitated the shift from an overreliance on the three IQ scores (FSIQ, VIQ, and PIQ) to more of a factor-based interpretation of performance. In fact, Prifitera, Weiss, and Saklofske (1998; see also Weiss, Saklofske, Prifitera, Chen, & Hildebrand, 1999) have proposed an alternative way of summarizing overall performance using a composite score, the General Ability Index (GAI), based upon the Verbal Comprehension Index and the Perceptual Organization Index. The GAI is recommended for use rather than the FSIQ under any one of the following conditions: (a) when the VC is reported in favor of the VIQ (e.g., when Arithmetic is significantly different from the average of the other Verbal scaled scores), (b) when the PO is interpreted in favor of the PIQ (e.g., when Coding is significantly discrepant from the mean of the other Performance scaled scores), and (c) when the VC and PO factor indexes are reported in lieu of the VIQ and PIQ. The utility of the GAI is comparable to that of the FSIQ in determining eligibility for services and placement decisions; however, the GAI may result in a higher estimate of overall functioning if the child has obtained Arithmetic and/or Coding scores that are significantly lower than the other subtest scores—these scores would contribute to a lower FSIQ score (Prifitera, Weiss, and Saklofske).

A Priori and A Posteriori Hypothesis Testing

According to Kamphaus (1993, 1998), test interpretation based upon the four factors of the WISC-III has greater scientific support than interpretation based upon individual subtests. Empirical evidence and theoretical considerations can drive both a priori and a posteriori hypothesis generation and testing. Test interpretation can begin at the early stages of the assessment process and involves the generation of theoretically and research-driven hypotheses prior to the calculation of test scores. The hypotheses can then be tested against the data that are derived. Alternatively, a posteriori hypotheses allow the review of obtained scores within the context of supporting evidence based upon both research and theoretical information. Both nomethetic and idiographic approaches may be taken in the generation of a posteriori hypotheses. For example, the child's pattern of performance may be compared to his or her peers' within the standardization sample, or alternatively may be assessed within the context of his or her individual strengths and weaknesses. Testing of limits (e.g., administering items in a nonstandardized fashion after the completion of the initial test administration) allows generation of hypotheses based upon an idiographic approach.

A caveat should be noted, however, in the interpretation of the four factors on the WISC-III. The third and fourth factors, Freedom from Distractibility and Processing Speed, each consist of only two subtests. As a result, these factor scores break down more readily than the larger factors due to the small number of subtests that contribute to each. Also, the third factor's descriptor, Freedom from Distractibility, is a misnomer, because scores on the third factor do not necessarily correlate with other measures of attention (Lowman, Schwanz, & Kamphaus, 1996; Riccio, Cohen, Hall, & Ross, 1997).

THE WISC-III PI

The WISC-III PI was developed to supplement the standard test administration of the WISC-III (Kaplan et al., 1999). As stated in the introduction to this chapter, the WISC-III PI takes a process approach to the interpretation of a child's performance on the WISC-III tasks. Its purpose is to serve as "a means of identifying the strategies that are employed to solve a task as well as a means of examining the nature of the errors made, the particular context in which they occurred, and the nature of the stimulus parameters" (Kaplan et al., p. 4).

The WISC-III PI incorporates several approaches to obtaining information on a child's strategies: Current WISC-III subtests are given with alternative or supplemental procedures for scoring, current WISC-III subtests are given with add-on procedures, subtests equivalent to the WISC-III are administered with alternative formats, and new subtests are administered with administration formats similar to those of the WISC-III but with different content (Kaplan et al., 1999). Current WISC-III subtests that have additional scoring procedures include Picture Completion, Information, Coding, Arithmetic, Block Design, Vocabulary, Digit Span, and Picture Arrangement. Subtests with add-on administration procedures are Coding and Arithmetic. Supplemental components of current WISC-III subtests include Information Multiple Choice, Coding-Symbol Copy, Written Arithmetic, Block Design Multiple Choice, Vocabulary Multiple Choice, and Picture Vocabulary. New subtests on the WISC-III PI are Letter Span, Spatial Span, Elithorn Mazes, and Sentence Arrangement.

Alternative administration and scoring formats and parallel subtests allow additional analyses of a child's cognitive processing strengths and weaknesses. For example, the Block Design subtest on the WISC-III PI is a multiple choice task (rather than a block manipulation task); the motor component is removed to allow assessment of visual-perceptual skills without the confound of visual-motor coordination difficulties.

The newness of the WISC-III PI has precluded a review of the test's properties and applications in independent research studies; however, the test authors have identified several applications of the WISC-III PI in the test manual:

1. Investigation of reasons for low WISC-III subtest scores.
2. Systematized observation of a child's problem-solving approaches.
3. Derivation of a detailed profile of a child's strengths and weaknesses.
4. Analysis of a child's performance for the purposes of diagnostic decision making (e.g., determination of neurodevelopmental disorders).
5. Establishment of a baseline for evaluating improvement or decline in functioning over time.
6. Implementation of the test as a research tool in the areas of neurological and developmental disorders.

THE CMS

The Relationship between Intellectual Functioning and Memory

While the WISC-III is primarily a measure of prior or past learning and information processing, the CMS is a novel measure of new learning and memory. The concept of memory is closely associated with learning because memory is the natural outcome of learning. Squire (1987) provides an excellent definition of learning and memory: "Learning is the process of acquiring new information, while memory refers to the persistence of learning in a state that can be revealed at a later time" (p. 3). The traditional or most common memory distinction is short- versus long-term memory. Short-term memory refers to a temporary storage (usually from only seconds to 1–2 minutes), whereas long-term memory refers to the permanent or more stable storage of memories. The process by which information is transformed into mental representations is referred to as encoding. The process of bringing stored information into conscious awareness, or remembering, is referred to as retrieval.

A further categorization of delayed or long-term learning and memory is into either procedural or declarative memory. Procedural memory effects a change in a person's behavior on the basis of experiences without the person necessarily having conscious access to the events that produced the change in behavior. These behaviors, such as riding a bicycle, are performed automatically. In contrast, declarative memory is the ability to store and retrieve specific elements of information or knowledge. Declarative memory can be further divided into semantic and episodic memory. Semantic memory involves memories for general facts and concepts. Episodic memory involves information that is situation- and context-specific. Within this conceptual framework, the CMS is primarily a measure of declarative episodic memory. In other words, the information that is presented in the CMS is novel and contextually bound by the testing situation (i.e., situation/context specific) and requires the examinee to retrieve newly learned information.

Discrepancies between general intellectual ability and memory can be used to evaluate an individual's current memory functioning. Because of the relatively high correlation between IQ and memory (e.g., FSIQ–General Memory Index $r = .58$) (Cohen, 1997), the individual's IQ scores become an index or estimate of his or her probable level of memory ability. Discrepancies between the estimated memory performance based on IQ scores and the individual's actual memory performance form the foundation for the discrepancy analysis. The discrepancy score then provides a global indication of whether the examinee's ability to learn and remember new material is commensurate with what would be expected on the basis of his of her intellectual functioning. The interpretation of differences between intellectual and memory functioning follows the same logic and methodology used in the interpretation of ability-achievement discrepancies. An essential criterion for the appropriateness of score comparisons is the comparability of the normative data for the two test measures. That is, they should be highly comparable or identical. Because the CMS was directly linked to the WISC-III, direct comparisons based on the same normative data can be made.

Historical Development of the CMS

The CMS was developed to fill the previous void of comprehensive and well-normed instruments in the area of learning and memory in children (Cohen, 1997). According to Cohen, traditional psychoeducational assessment protocols included tests for intellectual functioning, achievement, and behavior, but did not assess the area of new learning and memory despite the fact that most referrals were related to the inability of the child to learn and remember school-related content. As a result, most of the diagnostic information gleaned from the test data was limited in scope (e.g., Digit Span on the WISC-III) or inferential in nature (e.g., clinical observations).

The CMS was designed to address five issues:

1. The development of an instrument that was predicated on current theoretical models of learning and memory.

2. The development of an instrument that was sensitive to developmental changes over time.
3. The evaluation of the relationship between memory and intellectual functioning.
4. The development of tasks that had relevance to clinical and educational settings.
5. The development of tasks that could be administered within a standardized testing situation (Cohen, 1997).

Psychometric Properties of the CMS

The CMS was standardized on a representative U.S. sample of 1000 children. The sample was stratified according to age (10 age groups ranging from 5 to 16 years of age), sex (equal number of males and females), race/ethnicity (White, African American, Hispanic, and Other), geographic region (northeast, north central, south, west), and parent education (5 categories ranging from less than 8th grade to university degree).

Reliability coefficients were calculated on the standardization data: split-half and test-retest. As reported in the CMS Manual, average split-half reliability estimates for the subtests ranged from .71 (Faces Immediate) to .91 (Word Pairs Learning). For the indexes, split-half reliability estimates ranged from .76 (Visual Immediate and Visual Delayed) to .91 (General Memory). Test-retest reliability was assessed using a subsample of 125 students across 3 age bands. The average reliability estimates across subtests ranged from .54 (Dot Locations) to .86 (Word Lists). Across each of the 3 age bands, test-retest reliability estimates for the indexes ranged from .29 (Visual Immediate—13 to 16 years age band) to .89 (Attention/Concentration—9 to 12 years age band).

Given the nature of the learning and memory construct, additional analyses were conducted to further assess score stability over time. Decision consistency reliability coefficients were calculated for each of the subtests, and index scores were calculated for each of the three age bands. Results indicated that a general practice effect of up to one standard deviation was apparent; this practice effect was similar to those on the WISC-III Performance IQ (Cohen, 1997). Interrater reliability was also assessed on those subtests requiring more subjective scoring (e.g., Stories, Family Pictures); interrater reliability was found to be high.

Content, construct, and concurrent validity were examined using the standardization sample. Content reviews on the CMS test items were conducted by expert pediatric neuropsychologists and school psychologists. Construct validity was assessed using confirmatory factor analysis; results of the factor analysis provided strong support for the three-factor model: attention/concentration and delayed subtests of the verbal and visual subtests. Concurrent validity studies were conducted with intelligence and achievement tests (e.g., the Wechsler Intelligence Scale for Children—Third Edition [WISC-III], the Wechsler Individual Achievement Test [WIAT], and the Otis-Lennon School Ability Test [OLSAT]). Correlations between the CMS and these measures indicated that the General Memory Index is moderately correlated with general, verbal, and nonverbal intellectual abilities. The Attention/Concentration Index correlated highly with other measures of complex attention. Verbal intellectual ability correlated higher with auditory/verbal measures than with visual/nonverbal measures. CMS and measures of achievement correlated moderately; the strongest relationship was exhibited between the Attention/Concentration Index and total academic achievement.

CMS Subtests and Subscales

The CMS is designed for children ages 5 through 16 years and includes the assessment of learning and memory in three areas: (a) auditory/visual learning and memory (verbal), (b) visual/nonverbal learning and memory (visual), and (c) attention/concentration. Each of the three areas is measured by two core subtests and one supplemental subtest. Both the auditory/verbal and visual/nonverbal areas include subtests that have both an immediate and a delayed memory portion. Auditory/visual subtests include Stories, Word Pairs, Word Lists (supplemental); visual/nonverbal subtests include Dot Locations, Faces, and Family Pictures (supplemental); and Attention/Concentration area is composed of the Numbers, Sequences, and Picture Locations (supplemental) subtests. (See Table 1.2.)

CMS Scores and Interpretation

All of the subtests are reported in scaled scores with a mean of 10 and a standard deviation of 3. Index scores (mean = 100; standard deviation = 15) can be derived for each area/domain: auditory/verbal, visual/nonverbal, and attention/concentration. A General Memory Index score (mean = 100; standard deviation = 15) that includes the immediate and delayed memory indexes from both the visual/nonverbal and auditory/verbal areas can also be calculated.

The steps recommended for the interpretation of the CMS are similar to the interpretive steps on the WISC-III. The first step involves the interpretation of the General Memory Index as a measure of global memory functioning. The General Memory Index can be compared to the WISC-III FSIQ score as an indication "of whether or not a child's ability to learn and remember new material is commensurate with what one would expect based upon his/her intellectual potential" (Cohen, 1997, p. 156). The CMS Manual provides tables for both predicted difference and simple difference methods. The CMS offers two methods of IQ-memory discrepancy analysis: the simple-difference method and the predicted-difference method. Although both methods are presented, the predicted-difference method is generally pre-

TABLE 1.2
CMS Subtests and Description

Domain	Subtest	Description
Auditory/Verbal	Stories	Ability to recall meaningful and semantically related verbal information
	Word Pairs	Ability to learn a list of word pairs over a series of learning trials
	Word Lists	Ability to learn a list of unrelated words over a series of learning trials
Visual/Nonverbal	Dot Locations	Ability to learn the spatial location of an array of dots over a series of learning trials
	Faces	Ability to remember and recognize a series of faces
	Family Pictures	Ability to remember scenes of family members doing various activities
Attention/Concentration	Numbers	Ability to repeat random digit sequences of graduated length
	Sequences	Ability to manipulate and sequence auditory/verbal information rapidly
	Picture Locations	Immediate visual/nonverbal memory for spatial location of pictured objects

Source: From *The Children's Memory Scale*, by M. J. Cohen, 1997, San Antonio, TX: The Psychological Corporation.

ferred because of two primary considerations. The formula for the predicted-difference method not only takes into account the reliabilities and the correlations between the two measures but also corrects for regression to the mean. In general, FSIQ should be used as the best estimate of overall intellectual ability. If the difference between an examinee's VIQ and PIQ scores is 11–15 points or more ($p < .05$), however, the higher of these two IQ scores could be used instead of the FSIQ score as the best estimate of intellectual ability. Similarly, the General Memory Index score is usually the best estimate of a child's memory functioning. When there are meaningful differences between the measures that make up the General Memory Index, other CMS measures may be used.

The second step involves the interpretation of the Attention/Concentration Index; a child's performance on this index should be compared to that on the WISC-III FSIQ using the predicted discrepancy model. A discrepancy that is deemed statistically and clinically significant should be examined further. For example, a difference of 25 points between the actual CMS Attention/Concentration Index and the predicted index score based on the WISC-III FSIQ is obtained by only 2% of children in the CMS–WISC-III linking sample. These results should be investigated further to determine the nature and extent of these attention difficulties across settings (e.g., home/school).

The third step involves the interpretation of the Verbal and Visual Memory Indexes; this step allows comparison between material that is learned and remembered aurally and material learned and remembered visually. To illustrate, a 19-point difference or less between the Visual Immediate Index and the Verbal Immediate Index is found in about 31% of children in the CMS standardization sample. Put another way, almost one of every three children in the standardization sample had a discrepancy of 19 points or lower, suggesting that it is rather common to see verbal-visual differences of this magnitude in children. Comparisons can also be made between the child's ability to hold material in working memory and the child's ability to store and retrieve learned material from delayed memory (i.e., Working Memory Index versus the visual/verbal immediate and delayed indexes).

Subtest interpretation is included in the fourth step. Similar to the WISC-III subtest interpretive format, the individual subtest scores can be compared to other scores within their respective indexes.

The fifth step includes the comparison between the Verbal Delayed Index and the Delayed Recognition Index. Discrepancies between the two indexes allow comparison between encoding/storage aspects of memory and retrieval of material. For example, a large difference between the Verbal Delayed Index (a recall measure) and the Verbal Delayed Recognition Index may provide valuable clinical information. The retrieval of information via recall is more demanding than the recognition condition because the child is required to impose an organizational structure on the stored information. The ability to access the previously learned information during the recognition condition is enhanced because the child is exposed to the actual material and is simply required to identify the information. If the child has significantly greater access to memories under the recognition condition than under the recall condition, the assumption is made that the child has actually learned the material but is unable to access the information under the more demanding recall process. This type of retrieval difficulty can be remediated by having the child provide self-cues and structure in order to facilitate remembering.

The sixth step involves the interpretation of the Learning Index. In order to interpret this index score, a large discrepancy between the predicted Learning Index (based on the WISC-III FSIQ and the actual Learning Index—with the actual index being lower) may be indicative of a generalized learning impairment.

THE WISC-III AND THE CMS
AND CLINICAL POPULATIONS

The WISC-III and, to a lesser extent, the CMS, have been administered to specific clinical populations (e.g., learning disabled, attention-deficit/hyperactivity disorder [ADHD]) in an effort to determine if there are subtest/factor profiles that define these individuals as a group (see Prifitera & Saklofske, 1998). To date, profile analysis has received mixed reviews; most researchers caution against such an analysis given the heterogeneity within each of these groups and the potential for misinterpretation based upon a single test administration (Daley & Nagle, 1996). On the other hand, this kind of analysis can enhance clinical decision making in determining strengths and weaknesses. Children referred for psychological assessment often present with less than easily diagnosed conditions. Both subtest and factor profiles may serve a most important role in both a priori and a posteriori hypothesis testing, and eventually contribute to a diagnosis.

Research conducted with children with learning disabilities suggests that particular subtypes of learning disabilities in older children (e.g., nonverbal learning disability; basic phonological processing disorder) are identifiable using the WISC-III VIQ-PIQ discrepancies (Rourke, 1998). As well, studies using the CMS with children with learning disabilities (e.g., phonological processing deficits) have demonstrated that these children exhibit mild to moderate impairments in attention/immediate working memory and auditory/verbal memory (Cohen, 1997).

Children with ADHD have been assessed with the WISC-III, resulting in mixed findings. Some research studies suggest that children with ADHD demonstrate significant deficits on the Freedom from Distractibility factor, a factor that measures attentional and memory processes (e.g., Prifitera & Dersh, 1993; Schwean, Saklofske, Yackulic, & Quinn, 1993). Other studies, however, have not replicated these results (e.g., Semrud-Clikeman & Lorys-Vernon, 1988). Also, lower scores on the Processing Speed factor (a measure of the rapidity with which simple or routine information can be processed without making errors) relative to both the WISC-III FSIQ and the Perceptual Organization Index have been reported (Prifitera & Dersh, 1993; Schwean et al., 1993).

On the CMS, however, children with ADHD have been shown to demonstrate lower scores on the Attention/Concentration Index and the Verbal Immediate Index. A small percentage of children with ADHD (i.e., approximately 10%) may also demonstrate verbal memory dysfunction (Cohen, 1997).

CRITIQUE OF THE WISC-III AND THE CMS

The WISC-III and the CMS represent two measures in the assessment of cognitive processing that have been subjected to intense study and review. The diagnostic strength of these two instruments lies in the comparisons that can be drawn between the intellectual and memory components of cognitive processing. However, the diagnostic utility has been hampered in the past by the limitations regarding direct treatment outcomes. These criticisms have, in part, been addressed by the reconceptualization of the WISC-III as a process instrument. An analysis of processing strengths and weaknesses is more amenable to skill remediation than the mere description of subtest scores.

The WISC-III continues to provide the basis for diagnostic decision making; for example, a diagnosis of a learning disability is predicated upon a significant discrepancy between aptitude (e.g., IQ score) and achievement. Although the development of interventions is based upon both quantitative and qualitative information, funding and placement decisions continue to be based upon IQ and achievement composite scores. The WISC-III has proven to be a reliable and valid instrument for these purposes.

Both the WISC-III and the CMS require considerable clinical skill in order to be utilized most effectively. These instruments are complex and multidimensional and do not lend themselves readily to direct interpretation. For example, the WISC-III subtests themselves assess multiple constructs. The clinician must have sufficient clinical skill in first identifying the constructs being measured and then comparing performance across subtests measuring comparable constructs within the WISC-III and between the WISC-III and the CMS. The standardized or norm-referenced comparisons provide a nomethetic paradigm for test interpretation; however, the clinician must also be able to develop hypotheses regarding performance based upon idiographic considerations. Again, these kinds of comparisons require specialized skills and practice.

CASE STUDY

John is a 9-year-old male who was referred for assessment due to a history of academic difficulties. A review of John's developmental and medical history indicated that John was born full-term after a normal pregnancy. Developmental gross motor milestones were attained within normal limits; fine motor development was slightly delayed. Developmental language milestones were also obtained within normal limits.

John's educational history indicated that he began experiencing reading difficulties in kindergarten. During the primary grades, John continued to have difficulty with reading; he demonstrated poor phonetic and word attack skills and displayed number and letter reversals. During grade 4, John's grades tended to be inconsistent across subjects. The teacher noted that John also had difficulty following spoken directions and appeared inattentive.

John was a willing participant during the testing sessions; his use of language was fluent and prosodic but was marked by mild word-finding difficulties. He also experienced difficulty expressing himself orally when the material was complex. Although his comprehension at the sentence level was good, he appeared to have difficulty retaining directions and had to repeat them to himself frequently. In general, John's attention span, activity level, and impulsivity appeared to be age-appropriate within the context of the testing session. He displayed good motivation and task persistence throughout testing.

Among others, the following tests were administered during the session: WISC-III, CMS, WIAT, and Woodcock-Johnson Tests of Achievement—Revised. (See Table 1.3 for tests administered and accompanying scores.) Intellectual functioning, as measured by the WISC-III, was found to be in the high average range. John obtained an FSIQ of 116 (CI = 110–121); VIQ of 112 and PIQ of 119. In general, John's verbal and visual-spatial reasoning abilities were uniformly developed. Analysis of factor/index scores revealed a relative strength in speed of processing and a relative weakness in focused auditory attention/working memory (VC = 113; PO = 113; FD = 96; PS = 126).

In order to assess learning and memory, John was administered the CMS. Analysis of his performance on the subtests constituting the Attention/Concentration Index indicated that John exhibited focused auditory attention/working memory skills that were discrepant from his measured intellect. He also demonstrated reduced working memory for material presented orally.

TABLE 1.3
Student Scores on Assessment Protocols

WISC-III IQ and factor scores		WISC-III subtest scores			
FSIQ	116	Information	13	Picture Completion	11
VIQ	112	Similarities	14	Coding	16
PIQ	119	Arithmetic	11	Picture Arrangement	11
VC	113	Vocabulary	11	Block Design	12
PO	113	Comprehension	11	Object Assembly	14
FD	96	Digit Span	7	Symbol Search	14
PS	126				

CMS Index scores	
Visual Immediate	128
Visual Delayed	131
Verbal Immediate	112
Verbal Delayed	122
General Memory	133
Attention/Concentration	94
Learning	122
Delayed Recognition	97

Source: From case study data provided courtesy of Dr. M. J. Cohen.

Further, he had difficulty reciting the alphabet during the Sequences subtest. Comparison of John's superior General Memory Index (GMI = 133) with his best estimate of intellectual potential (FSIQ = 116) indicated that his ability to learn and remember was above expectancy. However, a more detailed analysis of John's performance indicated that he was demonstrating significant variability in his ability to learn and remember. Comparison of John's auditory/verbal and visual/nonverbal index scores indicated that his visual learning and memory were superior overall. In contrast, his verbal learning and memory ranged from average to superior. John demonstrated above average ability to learn concise rote verbal material (Word Pairs) presented three times and superior ability to recall the material after a 30-minute delay. However, his ability to learn lengthy verbal material presented once (Stories) was average. John had difficulty encoding material presented at the beginning of the paragraphs.

On the Woodcock-Johnson Tests of Achievement—Revised, John demonstrated low average phonetic word attack skills and average reading comprehension. As a measure of written expression, John was administered the Written Expression subtest from the WIAT. John performed in the low average range on this subtest.

In summary, the results of the assessment indicated that John was currently functioning within the high average range of intellectual ability. He demonstrated relative strengths in areas of visual-spatial perception/construction, sustained attention, and visual learning and memory. These were contrasted by relative weaknesses in phonological processing, focused auditory attention/working memory, and verbal learning and memory for lengthy material presented once. During testing, John was also noted to exhibit reduced auditory working memory, having to repeat directions to himself before completing tasks. Academically, John demonstrated relative strengths in arithmetic contrasted by relative weaknesses in basic reading and written expression that were of learning disability proportion. It is likely that the inattention noted at home and school was due to his reduced auditory processing as opposed to an attention deficit disorder per se, given his average performance in sustained attention for visual material. Taken together, this pattern of test performance was consistent with a diagnosis of Specific Learning Disability in Reading and Written Expression. As a result, it was recommended that John receive special education services designed for children with learning disabilities. John's teachers were made aware that his word attack skills and knowledge of sight words were weak, given his measured intellect. Because his visual learning and memory were superior and his phonological processing skills were poor, it was recommended that reading/writing instruction should emphasize visual and multisensory approaches. Further, it was recommended that John would benefit from approaches that relied heavily on tactile input and experiential learning. Given his learning disabilities and reduced auditory attention, a reduction in the amount, but not the difficulty level, of assignments was recommended in order to assist John in completing classroom tasks and homework in a timely manner.

Acknowledgment

The authors gratefully acknowledge Morris J. Cohen of the Medical College of Georgia for contributing the case study for this chapter.

References

Canivez, G. L., & Watkins, M. W. (1999). Long-term stability of the Wechsler Intelligence Scale for Children—Third Edition among demographic subgroups: Gender, race/ethnicity, and age. *Journal of Psychoeducational Assessment, 17,* 300–313.

Cohen, M. J. (1997). *The Children's Memory Scale.* San Antonio, TX: The Psychological Corporation.

Daley, C. E., & Nagle, R. J. (1996). Relevance of WISC-III indicators for assessment of learning disabilities. *Journal of Psychoeducational Assessment, 14*(4), 320–333.

Flanagan, D. P., McGrew, K. S., & Ortiz, S. O. (2000). *The Wechsler Intelligence Scales and Gf-Gc theory: A contemporary approach to interpretation.* Boston: Allyn & Bacon.

Grice, J. W., Krohn, E. J., & Logerquist, S. (1999). Cross-validation of the WISC-III factor structure in two samples of children with learning disabilities. *Journal of Psychoeducational Assessment, 17,* 236–248.

Kamphaus, R. W. (1993). *Clinical assessment of children's intelligence.* Boston: Allyn & Bacon.

Kamphaus, R. W. (1998). Intelligence test interpretation: Acting in the absence of evidence. In A. Prifitera & D. Saklofske (Eds.), WISC-III *clinical use and interpretation.* San Diego, CA: Academic Press.

Kaplan, E., Fein, D., Kramer, J., Delis, D., & Morris, R. (1999). WISC-III *as a Process Instrument.* San Antonio, TX: The Psychological Corporation.

Kaufman, A. S. (1994). *Intelligent testing with the* WISC-III. New York: Wiley.

Lowman, M. G., Schwanz, K. A., & Kamphaus, R .W. (1996). WISC-III third factor: Critical measurement issues. *Canadian Journal of School Psychology, 12*(1), 15–22.

Prifitera, A., & Dersh, J. (1993). Base rates of WISC-III diagnostic subtest patterns among normal, learning-disabled, and ADHD samples. *Journal of Psychoeducational Assessment monograph series, Advances in psychological assessment: Wechsler Intelligence Scale for Children—Third Edition,* 43–55.

Prifitera, A., & Saklofske, D. (Eds.). (1998). WISC-III *clinical use and interpretation.* San Diego, CA: Academic Press.

Prifitera, A., Weiss, L. G., & Saklofske, D. (1998). The WISC-III in context. In A. Prifitera & D. Saklofske (Eds.), WISC-III *clinical use and interpretation.* San Diego, CA: Academic Press.

Puente, A. E., & Salazar, G. D. (1998). Assessment of minority and culturally diverse children. In A. Prifitera & D. Saklofske (Eds.), WISC-III *clinical use and interpretation.* San Diego, CA: Academic Press.

Reynolds, C .R., Sanchez, S., & Willson, V. L. (1996). Normative tables for calculating WISC-III Performance and Full Scale IQs when Symbol Search is substituted for Coding. *Psychological Assessment, 8*(4), 378–382.

Riccio, C. A., Cohen, M. J., Hall, J., & Ross, C. M. (1997). The third and fourth factors of the WISC-III: What they don't measure. *Journal of Psychoeducational Assessment, 15*(1), 27–39.

Rourke, B. P. (1998). Significance of verbal-performance discrepancies for subtypes of children with learning disabilities: Opportunities for the WISC-III. In A. Prifitera & D. Saklofske (Eds.), WISC-III *clinical use and interpretation.* San Diego, CA: Academic Press.

Saklofske, D., Hildebrand, D. K., Reynolds, C. R., & Willson, V. L. (1998). Substituting Symbol

Search for Coding on the WISC-III: Canadian normative tables for Performance and Full Scale IQ scores. *Canadian Journal of Behavioural Science*, 30(2), 57–68.

Sattler, J. M. (1992). *Assessment of children: Revised and updated third edition.* San Diego, CA: Author.

Schwean, V. L., Saklofske, D., Yackulic, R. A., & Quinn, D. (1993). WISC-III performance of ADHD children. *Journal of Psychoeducational Assessment monograph series, Advances in psychological assessment: Wechsler Intelligence Scale for Children—Third Edition*, 56–79.

Scoring Assistant for the Wechsler Scales. [Computer software.] (1992). San Antonio, TX: The Psychological Corporation.

Semrud-Clikeman, M., & Lorys-Vernon, A. (1988, July). *Discriminate validity of neurocognitive measures in diagnosing children with attention deficit disorder/hyperactivity.* Paper presented at the Annual European Meeting of the International Neuropsychological Society, Finland.

Spruill, J. (1998). Assessment of mental retardation with the WISC-III. In A. Prifitera & D. Saklofske (Eds.), *WISC-III clinical use and interpretation.* San Diego, CA: Academic Press.

Squire, L. R. (1987). *Memory and brain.* New York: Oxford Univ. Press.

Wechsler, D. (1939). *Wechsler-Bellevue Intelligence Scale.* New York: The Psychological Corporation.

Wechsler, D. (1949). *Wechsler Intelligence Scale for Children.* New York: The Psychological Corporation.

Wechsler, D. (1974). *Wechsler Intelligence Scale for Children—Revised.* San Antonio, TX: The Psychological Corporation.

Wechsler, D. (1991). *Wechsler Intelligence Scale for Children—Third Edition.* San Antonio, TX: The Psychological Corporation.

Wechsler, D. (1996). *Wechsler Intelligence Scale for Children—Third Edition, Canadian Supplement.* Toronto: Harcourt Brace and Company Canada, Ltd., and The Psychological Corporation, U.S.A.

Weiss, L. G., Saklofske, D., Prifitera, A., Chen, H. Y., & Hildebrand, D. (1999). The calculation of the WISC-III General Ability Index using Canadian norms. *Canadian Journal of School Psychology*, 14(2), 1–10.

WISC-III Writer: The Interpretive Software System. (1994). [Computer software.] San Antonio, TX: The Psychological Corporation.

CHAPTER 2

The Das–Naglieri Cognitive Assessment System in Theory and Practice

J. P. DAS
University of Alberta

JACK A. NAGLIERI
George Mason University

It is almost a truism that a test has to have a theory that makes it intelligible and guides its interpretation. The Das–Naglieri Cognitive Assessment System (CAS; Naglieri & Das, 1997a) not only is a relatively new measure of intellectual ability, but also heralds the beginning of a new way of looking at intelligence. The reconceptualization of intelligence rides, as it were, on the coattails of information processing theory that ushered in the cognitive revolution. Essentially, the theoretical base of the CAS is cognitive psychology and neuropsychology as integrated in PASS theory; PASS is an acronym for the four major cognitive functions, which are Planning, Attention, Simultaneous, and Successive processing (Das, Naglieri, & Kirby, 1994).

Consistent with cognitive psychological research, PASS theory aims at unraveling the cognitive processes that determine performance on the CAS. In line with neuropsychological research, the processes are multidimensional, reflecting the interdependent workings of functional regions of the brain. We do not believe that a unidimensional undifferentiated mass of "general ability" (the so-called g) is very useful for understanding the variety of intellectual abilities that characterize individuals. Neither is the concept of g informative in establishing a profile of children's cognitive processing for diagnosis of learning and attentional difficulties, for example. Additionally, a global unitary IQ score cannot guide instruction or suggest remediation. The advantages of PASS theory and its operationalization in the CAS will become apparent throughout this chapter.

We shall begin our presentation with a short introduction to PASS theory, delineating its neuropsychological basis (mainly influenced by Luria) and describing the four cognitive functions. This will be followed by a practical presentation of the CAS, including a discussion of its structure and administration as well as interpretation of the test scores. Finally, we will discuss the prediction of school achievement vis-à-vis other contemporary tests. Because assessment alone—without an implication for what to do next with the child who was assessed—is no longer enough, we briefly discuss the value of PASS theory and the CAS in guiding intervention that can ameliorate the cognitive difficulties identified by the CAS. The focus of the whole chapter is to provide a basic theoretical understanding of cognitive processes, detailed information about assessment procedures, and discussion of some possibilities for intervention, all as they apply to the individual child.

PASS PROCESSES AND THE FOUR FUNCTIONAL REGIONS OF THE BRAIN

Function is the core concept of Luria's functional organization of cognitive processes in the brain. Luria (1973) distinguishes a functional system from a static notion of abilities as follows: "The presence of a constant task, performed by variable (variative) mechanisms, bringing the process to a consistent (invariant) result is one of the basic features distinguishing the work of every functional system" (p. 28). Functional systems, according to Luria, have both *depth* and *spread*. Processing of information in simultaneous quasi-spatial arrays, for example, is spread over a large area of the occipital and parietal lobes. Successive information processing—that is, ordering information temporally—likewise is broadly localized in the temporal and fronto-temporal areas of the brain. Planning and making decisions may inhere in the whole of the frontal lobes.

Any kind of information that is received through the senses must go through a coding process, such as coding of visual information, and passes through three hierarchical levels of the brain. The first level may be described simply as the projection area, where the modality characteristic of the information is intact. The second level, above the projection area, is referred to as the projection-association area. As information reaches this area, it loses part of its modality tag; visual and auditory experiences (e.g., the sights and sounds of a car accident) become fused together so that it becomes difficult to say with certainty if a specific piece of "eyewitness" information was seen rather than heard. Above the projection-association area is the third (tertiary) level, which consists of overlapping zones, where information is typically amalgamated and the modality tags are absent. This grand amalgamation is necessary because it allows information to be integrated from different sensory organs without any separation due to modality of input; this subsequently makes it easier to act on the information.

Luria (1966, 1980, 1982) described human cognitive processes within a framework of three functional blocks or units. The first unit regulates cortical arousal and attention; the second unit codes information using simultaneous and successive processes; and the third unit provides for planning, self-monitoring, and structuring of cognitive activities. Luria's work on the functional aspects of brain structures formed the basis of the PASS theory, and it was used as a blueprint for defining the important components of human intellectual competence that could then be assessed by the CAS. The four PASS processes and their essential features are summarized in the following section, which also provides a rationale for the construction of the CAS tests.

PASS AND THE ASSESSMENT OF COGNITIVE PROCESSES BY CAS

The CAS (Naglieri & Das, 1997a) is based on the PASS theory and is designed to integrate contemporary cognitive psychological and neuropsychological theory with psychometrics, because "psychological measurement, no matter how direct, has little meaning unless it is theory based" (Crocker & Algina, 1986). PASS theory, and its application in the CAS, recognizes that human cognitive functioning includes four components situated within the knowledge base of the individual. These components are: (1) planning—the control processes of cognition, executive functions, strategy, and intentionality; (2) attention—focused cognitive activity and resistance to distraction; and (3) simultaneous and (4) successive processing—the two forms of operating on information.

Planning is the mental process by which a person determines, selects, and uses efficient solutions to problems. It involves problem solving, formation of mental representations, impulse control, control of processing, and retrieval of knowledge.

Attention is the process that allows us to selectively attend to some stimuli while ignoring others. It involves focused cognitive activity, and its key elements are selective attention, resistance to distraction, orienting response, vigilance, and reticular formation as substrate.

Simultaneous processing integrates stimuli into groups. Stimuli are seen as whole, or gestalt, each piece being related to the others. Simultaneous processing is associated with the integrity of the parieto-occipital-temporal regions and can involve verbal or nonverbal stimuli.

Successive processing integrates stimuli in a specific serial order, forming a chain-like progression of stimuli. Successive processing can involve verbal or nonverbal stimuli and is associated with the fronto-temporal regions.

PASS

- Cognition is information processing
- Supports functional segmentation of brain
- Cognitive processes define intelligence
- Four processes: Planning, Attention, Simultaneous, and Successive

Knowledge Base

- <u>Tacit</u>, and <u>Experiential</u> and <u>Spontaneous</u> OR <u>Explicit</u> and <u>Instructed</u>
- Both types reside in long-term memory
- Working memory is actively used in PASS

Input

<u>External</u>: visual, auditory, etc., presented all at once or one after another

<u>Internal</u>: images and thoughts accessed from knowledge base

Output

In three modes:

<u>Movement</u>—gross and fine

<u>Mimetic</u>—gestures, dance, music

<u>Language</u>—oral and written, graphics, sign

FIGURE 2.1
PASS theory of cognition.

A schematic presentation of PASS theory is shown in Figure 2.1. The figure begins by emphasizing that PASS processes provide a theoretical view of ability considerably different from the traditional approach of general intelligence. Next, the importance of knowledge and skills is noted, along with the types of input and output.

CAS DESCRIPTION

The CAS is an individually administered test designed for children and adolescents aged 5 through 17 years. The test consists of 12 regularly administered subtests, which are organized into four PASS Scales. There is also a to-

TABLE 2.1
Organization of the CAS Scales and Subtests (Standard Battery)

Full Scale

  Planning

    Matching Numbers[a]

    Planned Codes[a]

    Planned Connections

  Simultaneous

    Nonverbal Matrices[a]

    Verbal-Spatial Relations[a]

    Figure Memory

  Attention

    Expressive Attention[a]

    Number Detection[a]

    Receptive Attention

  Successive

    Word Series[a]

    Sentence Repetition[a]

    Speech Rate (ages 5–7 years) or Sentence Questions (ages 8–17 years)

[a]Subtests in each PASS Scale that are included in the CAS Basic Battery.

tal score, called a Full Scale. The PASS Scales and Full Scale standard scores can be obtained using two combinations of subtests. One combination is called the Basic Battery and the other is called the Standard Battery. The Basic Battery includes 8 subtests (two per PASS Scale); the Standard Battery includes all 12 subtests, as shown in Table 2.1.

Full Scale

The Full Scale (FS) score is an overall measure of cognitive functioning, with a mean (M) set at 100 and a standard deviation (SD) set at 15. The score yields a measure of the child's overall level of cognitive functioning based on the four PASS Scales.

PASS Scales

The PASS Scale scores (each with an M of 100 and an SD of 15) are composed of the sum of subtest scaled scores included in each respective scale. These scores represent a child's cognitive functioning in specific areas and are used to identify specific strengths and weaknesses in cognitive processing. The PASS Scales, not the PASS subtests, are the focus of CAS interpretation.

Subtests

The subtests (each set at an M of 10 and an SD of 3) are measures of the specific PASS process corresponding to the scale on which they are found. They are not considered to represent their own set of specific abilities, but rather are measures of one of the four types of processes. They do vary in content (some are verbal, some are not; some involve memory, others do not; etc.), but the most important point is that each is an effective measure of a specific PASS process.

Standardization

The CAS was standardized for children aged 5–17 years, using a stratified random sampling plan that resulted in a sample that closely matches the U.S. population. Children from both regular education and special education settings were included. During the standardization and validity study data-collection program, the CAS was administered to a total of 3072 children. Of that sample, 2200 children made up the normative sample and an additional 872 children participated in reliability and validity studies. A group of achievement tests was also administered to a 1600-person subsample of the 2200-person standardization group.

The CAS standardization sample was stratified on the basis of Age (5 years 0 months through 17 years 11 months); Gender (Female, Male); Race (Black, White, Asian, Native American, Other); Hispanic origin (Hispanic, Non–Hispanic); Region (Midwest, Northeast, South, West); Community Setting (Urban/Suburban, Rural); Classroom Placement (Full-Time Regular Classroom, Part-Time Special Education Resource, Full-Time Self-Contained Special Education); Educational Classification (Learning Disability, Speech/Language Impairment, Social-Emotional Disability, Mental Retardation, Giftedness, and Non–Special Education); and Parental Educational Attainment Level (less than high school degree, high school graduate or equivalent, some college or technical school, four or more years of college). The methods used to collect the data were designed to yield high-quality data on a sample that closely represents the U.S. population; for details on the representativeness of the sample, see the CAS Interpretive Handbook (Naglieri & Das, 1997b).

Administration

The CAS, like other tests of its kind, must be administered and scored as prescribed in the test's Administration and Scoring Manual (Naglieri & Das, 1997c). It is, of course, the obligation of the user to ensure that administration is consistent with applicable professional standards and that an appropriate environment is maintained. For example, developing and maintaining rapport, as well as following directions precisely, are important. Only a few important points regarding administration of the CAS will be discussed in this chapter.

Administration Directions

The instructions to the child include both spoken statements and nonverbal actions by the examiner. Examiners need to carefully follow the instructions for gestures (indicated in parenthetical statements following or preceding the text) corresponding to the oral directions. The combination of oral and nonverbal communication is designed to ensure that the child understands the task.

Subtest Administration Order

It is important to administer the CAS subtests in the prescribed order, to retain the integrity of the test and reduce the influence of extraneous variables on the child's performance. For example, the Planning subtests are administered first, because they give the child flexibility to solve the items in any manner. In contrast, the Attention subtests must be completed in the prescribed order (i.e., left to right and top to bottom). By administering the Planning subtests before the Attention subtests, the amount of constraint increases over time. If the Attention subtests were administered before the Planning ones, the rigid instructions for the Attention subtests might inhibit the child's performance on subsequent Planning subtests.

Strategy Assessment Phase of the Planning Subtests

All the CAS Planning subtests include a phase called Strategy Assessment, during which the examiner observes whether the child uses strategies to complete the items. Strategy Assessment was developed to gather information about *how* the child completes the items. In addition, it is used to help describe the standard scores that are obtained (see sections on Scoring and Interpretation, later in this chapter). Strategy Assessment information allows the examiner to describe the standard score in relation to the percentage of children within the standardization sample who used that particular strategy. This description can help explain a particularly high or low Planning score and can be integrated into the entire evaluation.

Strategy Assessment is conducted for each Planning subtest in two ways. Observed Strategies are those seen by the examiner through careful observation at the time the child completes the items. Reported Strategies are obtained following completion of the item(s); the examiner elicits this information by saying, "Tell me how you did these," or "How did you find what you were looking for?" or some similar statement. The child can communicate the strategies by either verbal or nonverbal (gesturing) means. Information is recorded in the "Observed" and "Reported" sections of the Strategy Assessment Checklist included in the Record Form.

"Provide Help" Guidelines

Several methods, including presentation of samples and demonstration items as well as opportunities for the examiner to clarify the requirements of the task, have been used to ensure that the child understands what is being requested. If, however, the child does not seem ready or appears in any way confused or uncertain, the examiner is instructed to "provide a brief explanation if necessary" (Naglieri & Das, 1997c, p. 8). This instruction gives the examiner freedom to provide explanation by any appropriate means, to ensure that the child understands the task. The explanation can be in any form, including gestures, verbal statements, or other communication in any language. The intent is to give the examiner full decision-making authority to clarify the demands of the subtest, and to enable the examiner to be certain that the child understands what to do. The freedom to "provide help," however, is not to be construed to mean the examiner can teach the child how to do the test.

Administration of the CAS to Bilingual or Hearing-Impaired Children

Instructions for administration of the CAS were designed so that a child with an adequate working knowledge of English can benefit from the samples and demonstrations provided. In those cases where additional help is needed, examiners may augment the English instructions when the "provide additional help when needed" prompt is given. During these introductory points where the subtest goals are being communicated, examiners who know the child's native language or who can use sign language may, when instructed, provide necessary assistance. In such cases, the examiner must decide when it is appropriate to use the alternative method of communication.

Age Partition

Children aged 5–7 and 8–17 years are given different instructions, and in some cases different sets of items, to allow testing to be tailored to particular age groups. For example, two of the Attention subtests have different types of stimuli so that the content of the test can be made more appropriate for children in either age group. Specialized content was selected to ensure that 5- to 7-year-olds would easily understand the items and that older children would not view subtests as too infantile. For example, Expressive Attention contains pictures of animals for 5- to 7-year-olds but is composed of words for 8- to 17-year-olds. Similarly, Speech Rate is administered only to children aged 5–7 years and Sentence Questions only to children aged 8–17 years, so that the task given to each group is age-appropriate. In addition, children aged 8–17 typically begin with more advanced items on some of the subtests.

Discontinue Rule

Administration of some subtests is discontinued after failure on four consecutively numbered items. This applies to all Simultaneous subtests and to all but one of the Successive subtests (i.e., Speech Rate).

Time Limits

The time limits for various items vary, as shown in the Administration Directions manual and the Record Form. These limits are provided in total seconds (e.g., 150) as well as in minutes and seconds (e.g., 2:30), to accommodate professionals who use a digital stopwatch and those who use an analog stopwatch. The point at which to begin timing is indicted within the directions found in the Administration and Scoring Manual. Following these instructions carefully will ensure accurate evaluation of the time a child takes to complete the items. Where time limits are not provided (e.g., Nonverbal Matrices), examiners should exercise good judgment about when to encourage the child to attempt the next item.

Rates of Presentation of Stimuli

Six subtests require stimuli to be presented at a specific rate or for an exact period of time. Word Series requires administration at the rate of 1 word per second, and Sentence Repetition and Sentence Questions are presented at the rate of 2 words per second. Figure Memory involves stimuli that are presented for exactly 5 seconds. There is also a 30-second exposure time limit for each item in the Verbal-Spatial Relations subtest. These time limits must be followed exactly.

Spoiled Subtests

If one of the three regularly administered subtests in the Standard Battery is spoiled, examiners should use the remaining two subtests and compute the PASS Scale using the Basic Battery norms. Because the Full Scale may be based on either 8 or 12 subtests, the calculation of the Full Scale would then be computed using the Basic, not the Standard, Battery. Alternatively, examiners may prorate the sum of three subtests in the PASS scale using the table provided by Naglieri (1999).

Scoring the CAS

The CAS is scored using procedures that are typical in the field of intellectual assessment.

1. Subtest raw scores are obtained.
2. Raw scores are converted to subtest scaled scores.
3. PASS Scale and CAS Full Scale standard scores are obtained from the sum of the respective subtest scaled scores.

Subtest Raw Scores

The CAS subtest raw scores are calculated using one or more of the following methods: (a) number correct, (b) time to completion, and (c) number of false detections. These measurements are used either in isolation or in combination, depending on the goals of the subtest. Some subtest raw scores are based on number correct; others are based on total time; and some are the combination of number correct and total time, or number correct, total time, and number of false detections. Each of the raw score methods is more fully described below.

Number Correct.   Nonverbal Matrices, Verbal-Spatial Relations, Figure Memory, Word Series, Sentence Repetition, and Sentence Questions subtests are scored using the number of items correct. This is obtained by summing the number of correct items and assigning credit for those items not administered below any starting point.

Time in Seconds.   The raw score for Planned Connections and Speech Rate is the sum of the time (in seconds) taken to complete all items. To compute the raw score, simply add the time scores for the items administered.

Time and Number Correct.   The raw scores for the Matching Numbers, Planned Codes, and Expressive Attention subtests are based on the combination of time and number correct. The number correct and time are combined into a ratio score using a Ratio Score Conversion Table included in the Record Form. This table has a heading called "Accuracy Score" at the top, and the leftmost column contains time scores in 3-second intervals. To combine the number correct and time into a ratio score, find the row that contains the item time in seconds; then find the column for the Accuracy Score earned by the child. The number at the juncture of the row and column is the ratio score for that item. For example, if a child earned a total time score of 43 seconds with an accuracy score of 38, then the ratio score is 54. The ratio scores for each item are summed, as indicated on the Record Form, to obtain a raw score for the subtest.

Time, Number Correct, and Number of False Detections.   The raw scores for Number Detection and Receptive Attention are obtained using ratio scores. In these subtests, however, the Accuracy Score is the number of correct responses minus the number of false detections (the number of times the child underlined a stimulus that is not a target).

Converting Raw Scores to Subtest Scaled Scores

The CAS subtest scaled scores (M = 10, SD = 3) are obtained using age-based tables included in the Administration and Scoring Manual. The norms tables are divided according to the child's chronological age in years, months, and days.

PASS Scale Standard Scores from the Sum of Subtest Scaled Scores

Each PASS Scale score (M = 100, SD = 15) is derived from the sum of the appropriate subtest scaled scores. The Standard Battery score is calculated from the sum of all three subtest scaled scores within each PASS Scale; the Basic Battery score is calculated from the sum of scores of the first two subtests within each PASS Scale. The Full Scale score (M = 100, SD = 15) is obtained from the sum of the subtest scaled scores from either the Standard or the Basic Battery. All these scores are obtained from the appropriate norms table, which also includes percentile ranks and confidence intervals (90 and 95%).

CAS INTERPRETATION

This section contains a brief review of methods that can be used as guides to interpreting the CAS. A complete discussion of the methods for interpreting the CAS can be found in Naglieri (1999). These interpretative steps should be applied within the context of all available information about the child so that a comprehensive view of the child is achieved and a thorough plan for treatment, if appropriate, can be developed, implemented, and evaluated. The section includes the essential steps for interpreting results and is followed by an illustration of how CAS results can be used to identify a cognitive problem and a subsequent intervention.

Steps for Interpreting CAS Results

Interpretation of CAS scores can involve any or all of the steps, depending on the specific purposes of the assessment. Analysis may include an examination of the PASS Scales and subtests, comparison of CAS results with tests of achievement, or comparisons of CAS scores obtained over time.

Step 1. Examine the child's performance on the Full Scale and PASS Scale standard scores in relation to the performances of peers.

Step 2. Compare the four PASS standard scores for meaningful discrepancies within the child.

Step 3. Compare subtest scores within each PASS Scale for meaningful discrepancies, if appropriate.

Step 4. Compare the child's Full Scale and PASS standard scores with achievement scores.

Step 1

Evaluate the child's overall levels of performance by describing the PASS and Full Scale standard scores using the descriptive categories, confidence intervals, and percentile ranks. This information should be recorded on the front of the CAS Record Form, as shown in Figure 2.2.

The Full Scale score is intended to be an overall estimate of processing based on the combination of the four PASS areas. That is, it is intended to be a convenient summary of performance. It will be a good overall description of a child's cognitive processing when the four PASS Scale scores are similar. However, when there is significant variability among the PASS Scale standard scores, the Full Scale will not show important relative strengths and weaknesses (as discussed in the section that follows). When this happens, the Full Scale score should be described as a midpoint between extreme scores and should be deemphasized.

Step 2

One of the main goals of the CAS is to examine differences in the four PASS Scale scores for an individual child, so that cognitive strengths or weaknesses may be found. This is accomplished by examining the statistical significance of the variation in PASS scores, that is, interpreting the profile using an intraindividual (i.e., ipsative; see Kaufman, 1994) method. Such an approach gives the professional a way to determine when the variation in PASS scores is meaningful. When the variation is not significant, any differences are assumed to reflect measurement error. Meaningful, or reliable, variation can be interpreted within the context of the theory, related to strategy use, and evaluated in relation to achievement tests.

When a PASS score is significantly above the child's mean score, a cognitive processing strength is found. When a PASS score is significantly lower than the child's mean score, a weakness is detected. Note that the strengths and weaknesses are determined relative to the child's own average level of performance. This approach has been used in intelligence testing (see Kaufman, 1994; Naglieri, 1993; Sattler, 1988) for some time. The steps needed to determine if a child's PASS profile is significant are enumerated below.

1. Calculate the average of the four PASS standard scores.
2. Subtract the mean from each of the PASS standard scores to obtain the intraindividual difference scores.

DAS · NAGLIERI

Cognitive Assessment System

Record Form

Jack A. Naglieri   J.P. Das

CAS Subtests	Raw Scores	Scaled Scores (Appendix A)			
Matching Numbers	4	6			
Planned Codes	25	8			
Planned Connections	416	6			
Nonverbal Matrices	13		10		
Verbal Spatial Relations	14		9		
Figure Memory	9		10		
Expressive Attention	28			9	
Number Detection	34			10	
Receptive Attention	37			12	
Word Series	10				10
Sentence Repetition	8				11
Speech Rate/ Sentence Questions	9				10
Sum of Subtest Scaled Scores	20	29	31	31	111
	PLAN	SIM	ATT	SUC	FS
PASS Scale Standard Scores (Appendix B)	79	98	102	102	93
Percentile Rank (Appendix B)	8	45	55	55	32
___% Confidence Intervals (Appendix B) Lower	74	92	94	95	88
Upper	89	105	109	108	98

FIGURE 2.2

Completed CAS record form.

3. Compare the intraindividual difference scores (ignore the sign) to the values in Table 4.3 presented by Naglieri (1999) or to the more detailed tables in the CAS Administration and Scoring Manual (Naglieri & Das, 1997c). When the difference score is equal to or greater than the tabled values, the score differs significantly from the child's average PASS Scale standard score.

4. Label any significant score that is above the mean as a strength, and those below the mean as a weakness. Any variation from the mean that is not significant should be considered chance fluctuation.

"The Case of Leslie," presented later in this chapter, uses the PASS scores presented in Table 2.2 to illustrate the interpretive process. The values needed for determination of significance for the Standard and Basic Batteries are provided by Naglieri (1999) and Naglieri and Das (1997b).

Illustration of the Method.   The PASS scores provided in Table 2.2 vary from a low of 81 in Planning to a high of 98 in the Attention and Successive scales. The child's mean score for the four PASS scales is 91.5. When compared to this mean, and using the values needed for significance for the Standard Battery, the Planning score is significantly lower than the child's mean. This indicates that the child's Planning score is significantly weak relative to the overall level of performance.

Relative and Cognitive Strengths and Weaknesses.   When there is a significant strength or weakness in the PASS Scale profile, the level of performance in relation to the standardization sample should also be considered. If a child has a significant intraindividual difference score that also falls below 90 (i.e., in the Low Average range or lower), then this difference should be labeled a *cognitive weakness*. This is true for the case of Leslie; her Planning scale stan-

TABLE 2.2
Leslie's CAS Scores

	Standard score	Percentile	90% confidence interval range	Difference from mean	Difference needed	SIG/NS
Planning	81	10	76–91	−10.5	9.7	SIG
Simultaneous	89	23	83–96	−2.5	8.6	NS
Attention	98	45	91–106	6.5	9.9	NS
Successive	98	45	92–105	6.5	8.6	NS
PASS Mean	91.5					
Full Scale	88	21	84–93			

Note: Differences needed are at the .05 level. SIG, statistically significant; NS, not statistically significant.

dard score is significantly lower than her mean PASS scores *and* it falls below the Average category. Alternatively, when a child has a statistically significant weakness that falls within the Average range (90–110), this should be viewed as a *relative weakness*, because it is low in relation to the child's mean but still in the average range of normative expectations. In such an instance, the finding may be important for a variety of reasons. For example, it could explain uneven academic performance for a child who typically performs very well. A cognitive weakness is a more serious finding, because it represents poor performance relative to peers as well as in comparison to the child's own level.

Base Rates of Occurrence. The frequency of occurrence of intraindividual PASS scale differences can also be examined. This is determined through use of the actuarial tables provided in Appendix D of the CAS Administration and Scoring Manual (Naglieri & Das, 1997b). These tables list the frequency of occurrence of all possible intraindividual difference scores in the standardization sample, and they can help determine how typical the PASS profile is. For example, using the data provided for Leslie (see Table 2.2), the difference of 10.5 found for the Planning Scale occurred in about 25% of the CAS standardization sample. The importance of this finding is therefore augmented by the fact that a weakness of this size is uncommon among those included in the normative group.

Step 3

Variation in CAS subtests is examined with the same method used for studying the PASS profile. The subtest scaled scores are compared to the child's mean subtest score, and the significance of the differences is evaluated. In addition, the frequency of occurrence of subtest differences is compared to that found for the normal standardization sample. These variations should also be interpreted within the context of the PASS theory, consideration of strategy use, and other relevant variables. It is important to note, however, that the approach described so far in this chapter is based on the assumption that the four theoretically derived PASS Scales will provide the most important interpretive information. When the professional chooses to go further and examine the variation of the CAS subtests, the method discussed by Naglieri (1999) should be followed. Although this level of analysis gives a more specific examination of the child's performance, it has the disadvantage of involving scores with lower reliability than the PASS Scales. Subtest-level analysis is considered only when there is specific reason to do so. For example, the significance of the differences among the child's subtest scaled scores can be important in determining if a weakness in Planning is the result of poor performance on a single subtest, or if it is due to consistently poor performances across subtests. The weakness may reflect the child's failure to use a strategy on one of the Planning subtests, in contrast to the other two subtests for which the child was able to devise a strategy.

Step 4

The scores a child obtains on the CAS can be compared to those obtained from achievement tests, to help determine if achievement is, in fact, below reasonable expectations. This sort of comparison can be helpful when interventions are being planned as well as when eligibility for special education services is being considered. There are two methods for comparing the CAS scores to achievement: simple- and predicted-difference methods. Both of these approaches fit within a theoretical framework designed to discover if the child has a PASS cognitive weakness and an associated academic weakness. First, the simple-difference method for comparing CAS with achievement will be presented, and then a theoretical system for interpretation of these differences will be discussed. For information about the predicted-difference method, see Naglieri and Das (1997b).

Ability/Achievement Discrepancy

The CAS scores can be compared to achievement test scores using the simple-difference method and the values necessary for significance at the .01 and .05 levels, for both the Standard and Basic Batteries, as provided by Naglieri and Das (1997b) and Naglieri (1999). (See Naglieri, 1999, for details about how these values were computed.) These values are used in the following manner. First, compare the difference between the two scores to the tabled values (ignore the sign). Any difference that is equal to or greater than the tabled value is significant. For example, Leslie earned a CAS Full Scale standard score of 88 on the Standard Battery and a K-TEA Computation score of 72. The 16-point difference between the two scores is significant (a 10-point difference is needed).

THE CAS AND ABILITY/ACHIEVEMENT DISCREPANCY OR CONSISTENCY: A NEW METHOD

The significance of the difference between PASS scores and achievement can be used to determine if an ability/achievement discrepancy is present, in much the same way as has been done with traditional IQ tests. In many places such a determination contributes to the conclusion that the child may be eligible for special services, because the discrepancy has provided information indicating that the child's actual level of achievement is not consistent with the level predicted by the IQ score. This method, however, only demonstrates that there is an unexplained difference between ability and academic achievement; it yields little information about why the discrepancy exists. Assuming that the academic weakness is not due to poor instruction, sensory limitations, emotional problems, and so forth, we have identified a child as disabled partially on the basis of not finding an intellectual reason.

The CAS often detects if there is a cognitive explanation for an academic problem, as well as detecting ability/achievement discrepancy. When a child's Full Scale or separate PASS Scale standard scores are significantly higher than achievement, a "traditional" discrepancy is found. In addition, the CAS can help determine whether there is a weakness in a specific area of achievement (e.g., reading decoding) that is related to a specific weakness in a PASS area (e.g., successive processing). Thus, it is possible to find a *consistency* between two scores (reading decoding and Successive) as well as a *discrepancy* between other CAS scales and achievement. The consistency between reading decoding and successive processing is indicated by a nonsignificant difference between these scores. This finding allows the practitioner to suggest that reading decoding and successive processing are related, as suggested by Kirby and Williams (1991), and such a suggestion has intervention implications (see sections on intervention, later in this chapter).

To apply the discrepancy/consistency method, compare each of the PASS and Full Scale scores to achievement. In the example of Leslie, her Math Calculation score is significantly lower than her Full Scale, Simultaneous, Attention, and Successive scales. Her Planning score, however, is not significantly different from her achievement in math. The lack of a significant difference between Planning and Math Calculation scores (a relationship anticipated from previous research summarized by Das et al., 1994) provides an explanation for the academic problem. Considering the strong relationships found between math calculation skills and planning processing (Das et al., 1994; Kirby & Williams, 1991), this connection is warranted.

The discrepancy/consistency relationship is illustrated in Figure 2.3. The figure shows the triangular relationship among the variables. At the base of the triangle are the two weaknesses, one in achievement (K-TEA Math Calculation) and one in cognitive processing (Planning). At the top of the triangle are the child's high scores. When this relationship is found, the practitioner has detected a cognitive weakness and an associated academic weakness, both of which warrant intervention. Should an academic weakness be found without an associated PASS processing difficulty, it would be appropriate to consider variables in the environment that may be responsible for the academic failure, such as quantity and quality of instruction, motivation of the child, and so on. In such an instance, direct instruction in the academic area should be considered.

A CASE ILLUSTRATION: INTERPRETING AND COMMUNICATING CAS RESULTS AND SUGGESTING INTERVENTION

The practitioner needs a good understanding of the PASS theory and the nature of the four types of processing to adequately use the CAS and communicate the results in oral and written form. Readers of this chapter might want to refer to other sources, such as Naglieri (1999), Naglieri and Das (1997b), or

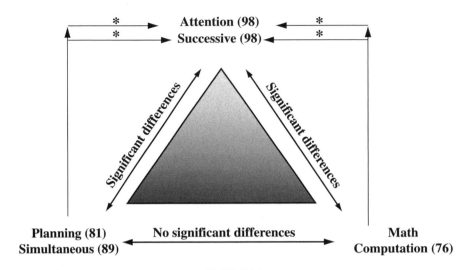

FIGURE 2.3
Using PASS scores and achievement scores for the
discrepancy / consistency method. Note: * = significant
difference (p = .05), from Naglieri (1999) Table 4.10.

Das et al. (1994), for more information on PASS or its foundation. In this section we provide a case example to illustrate how the information about the test results can be communicated.

The Case of Leslie

Leslie is a young girl who attends a school for children with learning disabilities. This child, whose name has been changed, is one of the subjects who participated in a math intervention study reported by Naglieri and Gottling (1997). Both CAS interpretation and results of the classroom intervention will be provided in this example; Leslie's CAS scores have already been reported in Table 2.2. The following text describes Leslie's performance on the CAS and the K-TEA Mathematics Computation achievement test, but without additional test results that might normally be included in a full report. Thus, this example is not intended to provide a complete case study with all other test data that typically would accompany a full evaluation. The aim is to show how the PASS and Full Scale results might be used to identify an appropriate instructional approach.

Test Results and Interpretation

Leslie earned a CAS Full Scale standard score of 88, which falls within the Low Average classification and is ranked at the 21st percentile. This means that her overall score is equal to or greater than 21% of the scores obtained by the children her age who were included in the standardization group. There is a 90% probability that Leslie's true Full Scale score falls within the range of 84–90. There was, however, significant variation among her scores on the four separate PASS Scales that constitute the CAS, which means that the Full Scale scores will be higher and lower than those of the separate scales included in the test. For example, her scores ranged from 81 in Planning to 98 in both the Attention and Successive scales. In this case, the Full Scale score does not accurately represent all of the separate scores from which it is made, and it therefore should not be reported. The range of scores does indicate, however, important variation within Leslie's PASS Scales that warrants consideration. The Planning scale score, in particular, is significantly lower than the mean of the four PASS Scales. This indicates that an important cognitive weakness has been found.

Leslie earned a significantly low score on the CAS Planning scale. This cognitive weakness reflects the difficulty she had using efficient and effective strategies for problem solving, self-monitoring, and revising her plans of action. She had difficulty making decisions about how to complete many of the questions and failed to monitor the quality of her work. For example, when required to record a specific code that corresponded to one of four different letters, she did so in a way that showed no apparent plan or method. This is in contrast to about 90% of children her age who have an effective plan to solve these questions.

Leslie's poor performance in Planning is particularly important because it is a weakness both in relation to her average PASS score and relative to the scores of her peers. The cognitive weakness in Planning suggests that Leslie will have difficulty with tasks that demand development and/or use of strategies to solve problems, make decisions about how to do things, generally control behavior, self-monitor, and self-correct. These activities are especially important, for example, in academic areas such as mathematics computation.

Leslie's poor performance on the K-TEA Mathematics Computation (76; 5th percentile) is consistent with her Planning score of 81 (there is no significant difference between these scores). These two low scores both are significantly lower than her Simultaneous, Attention, and Successive scores, thus providing evidence of an ability/achievement discrepancy. Her low scores in mathematics computation and Planning processing are likely related, and this consistency has implications for intervention (see later section of this report).

Leslie's Attention was assessed by subtests that required her to focus on specific features of test questions and to resist reacting to distracting parts of the tests. She was able to focus concentration well enough to earn a score of 98 on the CAS Attention Scale, which ranks at the 45th percentile and falls within the Average classification (90% range is 91–106). Attention was measured by subtests that required her to respond only to specific stimuli (for example, the number 1 when it appeared in an outline typeface) and not to respond to distracting stimuli (when the number 1 appeared in a regular typeface). Leslie's Attention score indicates that she demonstrated typical performance in both identifying targets and avoiding responses to distracting stimuli.

Leslie earned a score of 89 on the Simultaneous processing scale (90% confidence interval = 83–96). This score ranks her at the 23rd percentile and falls at the juncture of Average and Low Average classifications. These tests required that she relate parts into a group or whole, understand relationships among words and diagrams, and work with spatial relationships. Leslie's score on the Simultaneous scale illustrates that she can integrate information into groups at a level that is just below average.

Leslie also earned an Average score of 98 on the Successive processing scale, which is ranked at the 45th percentile (90% confidence interval = 92–105). Her successive processing was assessed by tests that required her to work with information in a specific linear order (e.g., repeating words in order as spoken by the examiner or comprehending information that is based on word order).

In conclusion, Leslie earned CAS scores that ranged from 81 to 98 and showed evidence of a cognitive weakness in Planning. This cognitive weakness in Planning is accompanied by a comparable score on the K-TEA Math Computation subtest because both measures demand careful control of thinking and acting, selection of appropriate strategies to complete the math or nonacademic problems, and checking of her work (self-monitoring). These results indicate that interventions that address both the mathematical and Planning processing demands of these tasks should be considered.

Design of an Intervention for Leslie

In order to improve Leslie's use of planning processes in doing math computation, the intervention described by Naglieri and Gottling (1995, 1997) was applied. Consultation between the school psychologist and the teacher resulted in an intervention plan to assist Leslie within the context of an instruction given to the entire class. The teacher taught in half-hour sessions, following the format of 10 minutes of math worksheet activity, 10 minutes of discussion, and 10 minutes of math worksheets. The math worksheets included problems covered in the class during the previous weeks. During the 10-minute discussion period, the teacher facilitated an interaction that encouraged all the children to reflect on how they completed the work and how they would go about completing the pages in the future. The teacher did not attempt to reinforce or otherwise encourage the children to complete the math in any special way. Instead, the children were encouraged to think about how they did the work, what methods were effective, why some methods work better than others, and so on. The goal was to teach the children to be self-reflective and self-evaluative when they think about what they are doing. (See Naglieri, 1999, for a planning facilitation handout.)

Response to Intervention

Leslie reported that she used several strategies for completing the math pages. First, she found it difficult to concentrate because she was sitting next to someone who was disruptive. Her solution was to move to a quieter part of the room. Second, she noticed that she often did not keep the columns of numbers straight, so she drew light lines to make columns. Third, Leslie realized that she did the mathematics problems quickly and with little checking, which caused errors. Fourth, she realized it was better to solve the problems correctly rather than just get as many finished as she could in the time allotted. These new insights were applied to the math pages she completed during the intervention phase.

The results of intervention were positive. Leslie got more math problems correct per page over the course of the intervention sessions. These results show that, by improving Leslie's use of planning processes, her performance in math calculation improved considerably over her initial level. For more information on this and other interventions, see Naglieri (1999).

INTERVENTION FOR READING DISABLED CHILDREN: PASS READING ENHANCEMENT PROGRAM (PREP)

The PREP (Das, 1999a) is based on the PASS theory of intelligence. Is it an advantage that a remedial program be heavily grounded in a reasonable theory? Yes! The program is understood in the framework given by the PASS theory; hence, it provides us with a program that is prescribed for improving reading.

The training tasks in PREP are recommended for those with generally poor reading skills and for those with specific reading deficits, such as dyslexia, in order to promote the same processes that are basic to reading, spelling, and comprehension. The pathway starts with the cognitive and learning difficulties that lead to reading disability; with the application of PREP, the cognitive difficulties are reduced along with the learning problems, and, consequently, reading is improved. Understanding the program's underlying theory is an important aspect of its use. The PASS profiles of dyslexics and generally poor readers are different; therefore, remediation can be focused according to the cognitive difficulties revealed by the CAS.

A typical dyslexic has very poor ability for decoding words, that is, a difficulty in phonological coding but not in comprehension. The dyslexic's profile shows a significant weakness in the Successive processing scale. This is especially true among beginning readers. The generally poor reader often shows a pervasive difficulty in more than one of the PASS processes. Poor reading as well as poor comprehension may be present. Both successive and simultaneous processing may be weak. Ideally, it is recommended that the PREP tasks be selected for emphasizing the weak processes as assessed by CAS.

What Is PREP? What Does It Do?

PREP aims at improving the information processing strategies—namely, *simultaneous* and *successive* processing—that underlie reading, while at the same time avoiding the direct teaching of word-reading skills. PREP is also founded on the belief that the transfer of principles can be made easier through experiencing the tasks and guided discovery rather than by direct teaching and learning of rules. Accordingly, the program is structured so that strategies are learned tacitly rather than through direct teaching. Thus, those who have been given PREP are likely to use these self-learned strategies in appropriate ways. *Attention* and *planning* are also involved in each task. Specifically, attention is required and used in performing each task, and planning is challenged by encouraging the children to come up with their own strategies as they engage in discussions, both during and following their performance.

What Are the Structure and Content of PREP?

The PREP program consists of 8 to 10 tasks that vary considerably in content and the requirements of the student. Each task involves both a global training component and a curriculum-related bridging component (see Figure 2.4). The global component includes structured, nonreading tasks that require the application of simultaneous or successive strategies. These tasks also provide children with the opportunity to internalize strategies in their own way, thus facilitating transfer (Das, Mishra, & Pool, 1995). The bridging component involves the same cognitive demands as its global component and provides training in simultaneous and successive processing strategies, which have been closely linked to reading and spelling (Das et al., 1994). PREP encourages participants to develop their own strategies, focus on what is relevant, and move away from irrelevant items or events.

The global tasks begin with content that is familiar and nonthreatening, so that strategy acquisition occurs in small stages (Das et al., 1994). Complexity is introduced gradually, and only after a return to easier content. Through verbal mediation (i.e., through specific discussions of strategies used), the global and bridging components of PREP encourage children to apply their strategies to academic tasks such as word decoding. The global and bridging components are further divided into three levels of difficulty; this allows the

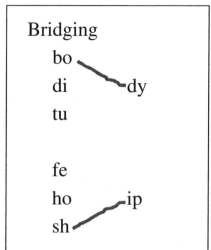

FIGURE 2.4
Illustration of a PREP training task, joining shapes (successive).

child to progress in strategy development and, for those who already have some successful processing strategies in place, to begin at an appropriate level.

A system of prompts is integrated into each global and bridging component. The series of prompts creates a scaffolding network that supports and guides the child, to ensure that tasks are completed with a minimal amount of assistance and a maximal amount of success. A record of these prompts provides a monitoring system that helps teachers determine when material is too difficult for a child or when a child is able to successfully progress to a more difficult level. A criterion of 80% correct responses is required before a child can proceed to the next level of difficulty. If this criterion is not met, an alternate set of tasks, at the same difficulty level, is used to provide the additional training required.

Efficacy of PREP

Children model the adults in their family and later in their community; this modeling facilitates internalization of the language, which reflects thoughts. The adults act as "middlepersons" and help to pass on a literate culture, and children's zone of potential learning expands. Every child has some room to develop, as advocated by Vygotsky (1962) in his seminal work, *Thought and Language*. Disadvantaged children have a much broader zone than children who are advantaged and who get exposure to language and thinking that adequately prepares them for participation in a literate society. The Carlson and

Das study tested PREP's success with culturally disadvantaged children whose disadvantage centered around the absence of a literacy environment, that is, absence of a reading atmosphere at home, and absence of the opportunity to hear and use long and thoughtful sentences in American English. The children did not have the advantage of learning in a literate culture.

The PREP program was used by Carlson and Das (1997) for disadvantaged, underachieving students in Chapter 1 programs in Hemet, California. Chapter 1 is an official category for children who need special educational assistance, but who are not identified as learning disabled or mentally retarded. Their major problem lies in reading, spelling, and comprehension.

In this study, students were instructed during two 50-minute sessions per week for 3 months. Both the PREP (22 students) and control (15 students) groups continued to participate in the regular Chapter 1 program. Word Attack, Letter Identification, and Word Identification subtests of the Woodcock Reading Mastery Tests—Revised (WRMT-R) were administered at the beginning and end of the study. The results showed word reading improvement in pre- to posttest performance following training in PREP, as well as significant "interaction" effects; that is, the students who received PREP remediation gained significantly more than children in the control group in word identification and word attack. This study provides strong support for the utility of PREP in improving word reading by teaching students to use appropriate processing strategies. The investigation by Carlson and Das (1997) is one of several studies that have demonstrated the efficacy of PREP (Das, 1999b).

SUPPORT FOR PASS THEORY AND THE CAS

In this final section we briefly summarize some of the research evidence regarding PASS theory and the CAS. Both PASS theory and the CAS are well-researched alternatives to other perspectives on ability. The most important dimensions of validity evidence for the CAS include: (a) sensitivity to the problems of exceptional children, (b) strong prediction of achievement, (c) relevance to intervention, and (d) test fairness for minority children. (For more information on research in these areas, see Naglieri, 1999, in press.)

Sensitivity to Children's Cognitive Variation

Traditional measures of general intelligence (e.g., the Wechsler Intelligence Scale for Children—Third Edition [WISC-III]) have not been shown to detect many of the problems exceptional children experience (Siegel, 1988). For example, the difficulty in using the WISC-III to accurately identify learning-disabled children is well documented, despite the widespread use of the WISC-III and attempts to identify specific types of children using scale or subtest profiles (McDermott, Fantuzzo, & Glutting, 1990; Kavale & Forness,

1984). Importantly, Kaufman and Lichtenberger (2000) stated, "although some patterns on the WISC-III are reported fairly consistently for children with learning disabilities, these patterns do not have adequate power on which to base differential diagnosis. The ACID and SCAD profiles may provide useful information about a child's cognitive abilities on a case-by-case basis, but the presence or absence of these profiles cannot justify making a diagnosis of LD [Learning Disabled]" (p. 205). Schwean and Saklofske (1998) state the issue even more clearly: "There is little support for the use of the WISC-III as a reliable diagnostic indicator of ADHD, nor is it clinically useful in discriminating between various subtypes of this population" (p. 113). Naglieri (in press) argued that the Wechsler Scales do not show sensitivity to the problems that many exceptional children have, because the concept of general intelligence that is used is both ill-defined and incomplete. Hence, repeated attempts to validate Wechsler profile analysis have met with lack of support. It is important to note that past and new approaches to scale and subtest analysis (e.g., using the cross-battery approach advocated by Mc-Grew and Flanagan, 1998) lack adequate empirical support. In fact, the results of research presented by Woodcock (1998) on the Gf-Gc approach are consistent with the paucity of discriminant validity evidence on Gf-Gc, which is discussed by McGrew, Flanagan, Keith, and Vanderwood (1997) and Horn and Noll (1997). Moreover, Kaufman (2000) stated: "there is no evidence that [Carroll and Horn's approaches] yield profiles for exceptional children, are directly relevant to diagnosis, or have relevance to eligibility decisions, intervention, or instructional planning—all of which are pertinent for school psychologists" (p. 27).

Naglieri (1999) provides a review of research on cognitive profiles from the WISC-III (Wechsler, 1991), the Woodcock-Johnson Tests of Cognitive Ability—Revised (WJ-R; Woodcock & Johnson, 1989), and the CAS (Naglieri & Das, 1997a) for children with attention-deficit/hyperactivity disorder (ADHD) and learning disabilities, based upon information taken from the test manuals and a recent publication by Woodcock (1998). Wechsler (1991) reported studies involving children with learning disabilities (LD) and ADHD, which showed that the profiles of WISC-III Index scores for the LD and ADHD children were essentially the same. Woodcock (1998) reported profiles for the seven Gf-Gc clusters for children with learning disabilities and attention deficit disorders, and his results also showed similar profiles for the groups. These data illustrate that these tests do not yield distinctive profiles of scores for the LD and ADHD samples used. In contrast, Naglieri and Das (1997b) reported results for the CAS for children with reading disorders and attention deficit disorders who earned PASS scores that show a different pattern. Children with ADHD were poor in planning, while those with reading disabilities were poor in successive processing.

The performance of ADHD children was more fully examined by Paolitto (1999), who found that the CAS "is a useful tool in the assessment and

identification of children with ADHD. The CAS was able to successfully identify about three of every four children having ADHD" (p. 4). He also reported
that the CAS showed a total classification accuracy of about 70%. These findings also support the view of Barkley (1997, 1998) that ADHD involves problems with behavioral inhibition and self-control, which are associated with
poor executive functioning (from PASS, Planning processing). It appears that
the failure of traditional IQ tests to show sensitivity to the cognitive problems
of children with ADHD and LD supports suggestions by Naglieri (1999) and
Sternberg (1999) that traditional intelligence tests are based upon insufficient and incomplete models of intelligence.

Relationship to Achievement

Some researchers have suggested that prediction of achievement is a very
important dimension of validity for a test of cognitive ability (Brody, 1992;
Cohen, Swerdlik, & Smith, 1992). Naglieri (1999) studied this question for a
variety of IQ tests and found that the correlation between the Full Scale
scores obtained from various tests of ability and those of tests of achievement varies considerably. Naglieri summarized several large-scale correlation studies between intelligence test composite scores and achievement
test scores reported by the test authors. He found that the median correlation between the WISC-III (Wechsler, 1991) Full Scale IQ (FSIQ) and Wechsler
Individual Achievement Test (WIAT) scores (Wechsler, 1992) was .59 for a national sample of 1284 children aged 5–19. A similar median correlation of .60
was found between the Differential Ability Scales (DAS; Elliott, 1990) General
Conceptual Ability score and achievement for 2400 children included in the
standardization sample. The median correlation between the Woodcock-
Johnson Revised Broad Cognitive Ability Extended Battery (Woodcock &
Johnson, 1989) score and the Woodcock-Johnson Revised Achievement Test
Batteries (data reported by McGrew, Werder, & Woodcock, 1991) was .63 (N
= 888) for children aged 6, 9, and 13 years. This value was very similar to the
median correlation between the Kaufman Assessment Battery for Children
(K-ABC; Kaufman & Kaufman, 1983) Mental Processing composite and
achievement, which was .63 for 2636 children aged 2½ through 12½ years.
Importantly, the K-ABC only has two scales and does not include verbal/
achievement content such as that found in the first three tests. The median
correlation between the CAS Full Scale and the WJ-R Test of Achievement
(Naglieri and Das, 1997b) was .70 for a representative sample of 1600 children
aged 5–17 years who closely match the U.S. population.

The examination of the correlations between achievement and intelligence suggests that the Wechsler scales predicted achievement adequately,
accounting for about 35% of the variance, but not as much as the CAS, which
accounted for nearly 50% of the variance in achievement. This is a substan-

tial increase in the amount of variance accounted for. Moreover, when intelligence is viewed as a multidimensional construct, it may (as in the case of the CAS) or it may not (as in the case of the WJ-R) improve the prediction of achievement, in comparison to the Wechsler scales. Interestingly, the WJ-R has the largest number of factors, yet it did not predict achievement better because of that. In fact, the two-factor K-ABC did about as well as the seven-factor Gf-Gc model of Woodcock. In addition, the two cognitively based tests of intelligence (the K-ABC and the CAS) showed the best prediction of achievement. This is even more important when one recalls that neither the CAS nor the K-ABC includes subtests that can easily be considered measures of achievement (e.g., Information, Arithmetic, and Vocabulary) and which overlap in content with the achievement test scores being predicted.

Relevance of PASS to Intervention

One of the most important practical uses of an IQ test is making the connection between assessment results and intervention. Although this has been illustrated in an earlier section, we will revisit the issue briefly, because the concept of using intelligence test scores for the purpose of instructional decision making has had considerable intuitive appeal for some time. Researchers have found, however, that tests of general intelligence have not been useful for "providing effective aptitude-treatment interactions (ATIs) for evaluating how children best learn, or for determining how a particular child's style of learning is different from the styles manifested by other children" (Glutting & McDermott, 1990, p. 296). Although this research is difficult to conduct and replicate (Peterson, 1988), it can be concluded that students low in ability generally respond poorly to instruction and those high in ability generally respond well.

The research summarized by Naglieri and Johnson (in press) and described earlier in this paper has shown a connection between planning and intervention (Cormier, Carlson, & Das, 1990; Kar, Dash, Das, & Carlson; 1992; Hald, 2000; Naglieri & Gottling, 1995, 1997; Naglieri & Johnson). The results of this research are in direct contrast to those of ATI research that suggest that children with low ability improve minimally but those with high ability improve the most (Snow, 1976). As a group, these studies suggest that a cognitive strategy instruction that teaches children to better use planning processes is especially useful for those who need it the most. These intervention findings support Naglieri and Gottling's (1997) suggestion that the PASS addresses calls for a theoretical model of cognitive processing that is related to children's academic performance (Geary, 1989). These results also support the view that PASS may meet the need for a "theory of the initial properties of the learner which interact with learning . . . [and] accounts for an individual's end state after a particular educational treatment" (Snow, 1989, p. 51).

By changing the way aptitude was conceptualized (e.g., from the general-intelligence construct used in past research to current PASS theory), evidence was found for an interaction between process and instruction.

Test Fairness—Reducing Mean Score Differences

Fair assessment of children who come from minority groups or low socio-economic backgrounds is a problem of considerable importance (Ford-Harris, 1998). Naglieri (1999) has argued that all of traditional intelligence tests are problematic for children with limited English language or academic skills (especially arithmetic and verbal concepts) because the verbal and quantitative tests are better viewed as tests of achievement than of ability (Naglieri, 1999). The inclusion of subtests such as Vocabulary, Information, Arithmetic, and Similarities has led many to consider the Verbal IQ scale to be a measure of achievement. In fact, Kaufman and Lichtenberger (2000) state that "the Verbal Scale does measure achievement" (p. 133). This raises considerable questions about interpretation of the Verbal IQ score, especially if it is conceptualized as a measure of verbal intelligence.

Researchers have found that intelligence tests that do not have verbal achievement subtests (e.g., the K-ABC and the CAS) yield smaller race differences than traditional IQ tests (Naglieri & Ronning, 2000; Wasserman & Becker, 1999). Wasserman and Becker summarized research that examined mean score differences between African-American and White children on several tests of intelligence. They reported that the standard score difference between the groups was 11.0 on the WISC-III, 12.7 on the Stanford-Binet IV, and 4.9 on the CAS. A difference between African-American and White children on the K-ABC of 6.0 standard score points was reported by Naglieri (1986). Recently, Naglieri and Rojahn (in press) found that minority children were more likely to be identified as mentally retarded according to their WISC-III scores (especially because of low Verbal Scale IQs) than when assessed with the CAS. These data strongly suggest that tests that do not include verbal and achievement items yield smaller differences between African-American and White children. Thus, the effect of removing verbal achievement from the measurement of ability, with a focus on cognitive processing, has led to an increase in fairness to minority populations.

SUMMARY

The essentials of CAS have been discussed briefly in the present chapter. We began with a discussion of PASS theory within the contexts of neuropsychology and cognitive psychology, and presented the rationale for tests in the CAS. Next, the operationalization of PASS theory was discussed in some detail, in the explanation of practical aspects of the CAS. Intervention procedures to improve cognitive processes that specifically relate to arithmetic and reading were suggested. Finally, a brief review of some relevant research on test fairness was provided. Our research on cognitive processes that led to PASS theory began in the 1970s, and the first significant account of the theory appeared in 1975 (Das, Kirby, & Jarman, 1975). Several articles and books (Das, Kirby, & Jarman, 1979; Das et al., 1994; Das, Kar, & Parrila, 1996; Naglieri & Das, 1997b; Naglieri, 1999) followed these publications. As we begin a new century, it is reasonable to look at intelligence from a new perspective of cognitive processes and find a theoretically guided tool to measure it. In a small way, we have responded to such expectations by providing both a theory and a tool for assessment of intelligence.

References

Barkley, R. A. (1997). ADHD and the nature of self-control. New York: Guilford.

Barkley, R. A. (1998). Attention-deficit hyperactivity disorder: A handbook for diagnosis and treatment (2nd ed.). New York: Guilford.

Brody, N. (1992). Intelligence. San Diego, CA: Academic Press.

Carlson, J. S., & Das, J. P. (1997). A process approach to remediating word-decoding deficiencies in Chapter 1 children. Learning Disability Quarterly, 20, 93–125.

Cohen, R. J., Swerdlik, M. E., & Smith, D. K. (1992). Psychological testing and assessment (2nd ed.). Mountain View, CA: Mayfield.

Cormier, P., Carlson, J. S., & Das, J. P. (1990). Planning ability and cognitive performance: The compensatory effects of a dynamic assessment approach. Learning and Individual Differences, 2, 437–449.

Crocker, L., & Algina, J. (1986). Introduction to classical and modern test theory. Toronto: Holt, Rinehart and Winston.

Das, J. P. (1999a). PASS Reading Enhancement Program. Deal, NJ: Sarka Educational Resources.

Das, J. P. (1999b). Dyslexia and reading difficulties. Edmonton: University of Alberta Developmental Disabilities Centre.

Das, J. P., Kar, B. C., & Parrila, R. K. (1996). Cognitive planning: The psychological basis of intelligent behavior. New Delhi: Sage.

Das, J. P., Kirby, J. R., & Jarman, R. F. (1975). Simultaneous and successive syntheses: An alternative model for cognitive abilities. Psychological Bulletin, 82, 87–103.

Das, J. P., Kirby, J. R., & Jarman, R. F. (1979). Simultaneous and successive cognitive processes. New York: Academic Press.

Das, J. P., Mishra, R. K., & Pool, J. E. (1995). An experiment on cognitive remediation of word-reading difficulty. Journal of Learning Disabilities, 28(2), 66–79.

Das, J. P., Naglieri, J. A., & Kirby, J. R. (1994). Assessment of Cognitive Processes. Needham Heights, MA: Allyn & Bacon.

Elliott, C. D. (1990). Differential Ability Scales (DAS) introductory and technical handbook. San Antonio, TX: The Psychological Corporation.

Ford-Harris, D. Y. (1998). The underrepresentation of minority students in gifted education: Problems and promises in recruitment and retention. Journal of Special Education, 32, 4–14.

Geary, D. C. (1989). A model for representing gender differences in the pattern of cognitive abilities. American Psychologist, 44, 1155–1156.

Glutting, J. J., & McDermott, P. A. (1990). Principles and problems in learning potential. In C. R. Reynolds & R. W. Kamphaus (Eds.), Handbook of psychological and educational assessment of children: Intelligence & achievement (p. 296–347). New York: Guilford.

Hald, M. E. (2000). A PASS cognitive processes intervention study: Comparing the Planning Facilitation *method to planning facilitation with direct instruction in mathematics calculation error patterns.* Unpublished doctoral dissertation, University of Northern Colorado, Greeley.

Horn, J. L., & Noll, J. (1997). Human cognitive capabilities: Gf-Gc theory. In D. P. Flanagan, J. L. Genshaft, & P. L. Harrison (Eds.), *Contemporary intellectual assessment: Theories, tests and issues* (pp. 53–92). New York: Guilford.

Kar, B. C., Dash, U. N., Das, J. P., & Carlson, J. S. (1992). Two experiments on the dynamic assessment of planning. *Learning and Individual Differences,* 5, 13–29.

Kaufman, A. S. (1994). *Intelligent testing with the WISC-III.* New York: Wiley.

Kaufman, A. S. (2000). Seven questions about the WAIS-III regarding differences in abilities across the 16 to 89 year life span. *School Psychology Quarterly,* 15, 3–29.

Kaufman, A. S., & Kaufman, N. L. (1983). *Kaufman Assessment Battery for Children.* Circle Pines, MN: American Guidance Service.

Kaufman, A. S., & Lichtenberger, E. O. (2000). *Essentials of WAIS-III assessment.* New York: Wiley.

Kavale, K. A., & Forness, S. R. (1984). A meta-analysis of the validity of the Wechsler scale profiles and recategorizations: Patterns or parodies? *Learning Disability Quarterly,* 7, 136–151.

Kirby, J. R., & Williams, N. H. (1991). *Learning problems: A cognitive approach.* Toronto: Kagan and Woo.

Luria, A. R. (1966). *Human brain and psychological processes.* New York: Harper & Row.

Luria, A. R. (1973). *The working brain: An introduction to neuropsychology.* New York: Basic Books.

Luria, A. R. (1980). *Higher cortical functions in man (2nd ed., rev. & expanded).* New York: Basic Books.

Luria, A. R. (1982). *Language and cognition.* New York: Wiley.

McDermott, P. A., Fantuzzo, J. W., & Glutting, J. J. (1990). Just say no to subtest analysis: A critique of Wechsler theory and practice. *Journal of Psychoeducational Assessment,* 8, 290–302.

McGrew, K. S., & Flanagan, D. (1998). *The intelligence test desk reference.* New York: Allyn & Bacon.

McGrew, K. S., Flanagan, D. P., Keith, T. Z., & Vanderwood, M. (1997). Beyond *g*: The impact of Gf-Gc specific cognitive abilities research on the future use and interpretation of intelligence tests in the schools. *School Psychology Review,* 26, 189–210.

McGrew, K. S., Werder, J. K., & Woodcock, R. W. (1991). *Woodcock-Johnson technical manual.* Itasca, IL: Riverside.

Naglieri, J. A. (1993). Pairwise and ipsative WISC-III IQ and Index Score Comparisons. *Psychological Assessment,* 5, 133–116.

Naglieri, J. A. (1999). *Essentials of Das-Naglieri CAS assessment.* New York: Wiley.

Naglieri, J. A. (in press). Can profile analysis of ability test scores work? An illustration using the PASS theory and CAS with an unselected cohort. *School Psychology Quarterly.*

Naglieri, J. A., & Das, J. P. (1997a). *Cognitive Assessment System.* Itasca, IL: Riverside.

Naglieri, J. A., & Das, J. P. (1997b). *Cognitive Assessment System interpretive handbook.* Itasca, IL: Riverside.

Naglieri, J. A., & Das, J. P. (1997c). *Cognitive Assessment System administration and scoring manual.* Itasca, IL: Riverside.

Naglieri, J. A., & Gottling, S. H. (1995). A cognitive education approach to math instruction for the learning disabled: An individual study. *Psychological Reports,* 76, 1343–1354.

Naglieri, J. A., & Gottling, S. H. (1997). Mathematics instruction and PASS cognitive processes: An intervention study. *Journal of Learning Disabilities,* 30, 513–520.

Naglieri, J. A., & Johnson, D. (in press). Effectiveness of a cognitive strategy intervention to improve math calculation based on the PASS theory. *Journal of Learning Disabilities.*

Naglieri, J. A., & Rojahn, J. (in press). Evaluation of African-American and White children in Special Education programs for children with mental retardation using the WISC-III and Cognitive Assessment System. *American Journal of Mental Retardation.*

Naglieri, J. A., & Ronning, M. E. (2000). Comparison of White, African-American, Hispanic, and Asian children on the Naglieri Nonverbal Ability Test. *Psychological Assessment,* 12, 328–334.

Paolitto, A. W. (1999). Clinical validation of the Cognitive Assessment System with children with ADHD. *ADHD Report,* 7, 1–5.

Peterson, P. L. (1988). Selecting students and services for compensatory education: Lessons from aptitude-treatment interaction research. *Educational Psychologist, 23*, 313–352.

Sattler, J. M. (1988). *Assessment of children*. San Diego, CA: Author.

Schwean, V. L., & Saklofske, D. H. (1998). WISC-III assessment of children with attention deficit/hyperactivity disorder. In A. Prifitera & D. Saklofske (Eds.), WISC-III *clinical use and interpretation* (pp. 91–118). New York: Academic Press.

Siegel, L. S. (1988). IQ is irrelevant to the definition of learning disabilities. *Journal of Learning Disabilities, 22*, 469–479.

Snow, R. E. (1976). Research on aptitude for learning: A progress report. In L. S. Shulman (Ed.), *Review of research in education* (pp. 50–105). Itasca, IL: Peacock.

Snow, R. E. (1989). Aptitude-treatment interaction as a framework for research on individual differences in learning. In P. L. Ackerman, R. J. Sternberg, & R. Glasser (Eds.), *Learning and individual differences: Advances in theory and research* (pp. 13–60). New York: Freeman.

Sternberg, R. J. (1999). A triarchic approach to the understanding and assessment of intelligence in multicultural populations. *Journal of School Psychology, 37*, 145–160.

Vygotsky, L. S. (1962). *Thought and language*. Cambridge, MA: M.I.T. Press.

Wasserman, J. D., & Becker, K. A. (1999). *Recent Advances in intellectual assessment of children and adolescents: New research on the Cognitive Assessment System* (CAS). Itasca, IL: Riverside Publishing Research Report.

Wechsler, D. (1991). *Manual for the Wechsler Intelligence Scale for Children—Third Edition*. San Antonio, TX: The Psychological Corporation.

Wechsler, D. (1992). *Manual for the Wechsler Individual Achievement Test*. San Antonio, TX: The Psychological Corporation.

Woodcock, R. W. (1998). *WJ-R and Bateria-R in neuropsychological assessment* (*Research Report No 1*). Itasca, IL: Riverside.

Woodcock, R. W., & Johnson, M. B. (1989). *Woodcock-Johnson Tests of Cognitive Ability—Revised*. Itasca, IL: Riverside.

Assessment with the Differential Ability Scales

BRUCE GORDON

Royal University Hospital

COLIN D. ELLIOTT

University of California, Santa Barbara

INTRODUCTION AND OVERVIEW

A decade has passed since the Differential Ability Scales (DAS; Elliott, 1990a) was introduced to the stable of tests for assessing cognitive abilities in children. For many clinicians, weaned on a diet of Wechsler and Stanford-Binet scales, the DAS remains unfamiliar ground. However, with its strong psychometric properties, emphasis on profiling distinct cognitive abilities, and high appeal to young children, the DAS has much to offer. In this chapter, we wish to argue that the DAS is an extremely valuable addition to a clinician's set of tools, both for assessing the learning and developmental problems with which children frequently present and for translating those assessment results into practical recommendations.

Theoretical Perspectives

The DAS was developed based on an eclectic blend of theories about cognitive development ranging from those of Spearman (1923) to those of J. P. Das (Das, Kirby, & Jarman, 1979). There are several distinguishing theoretical characteristics about the test.

It is no accident the DAS is named the Differential *Ability* Scales and not the "Differential Intelligence Scales." Elliott (1990b) rejects the possibility that any test can measure "intelligence," saying that the term has been so vaguely and variously defined as to have become practically meaningless. He quotes Spearman (1927), who described intelligence as "a word with so many meanings that finally it has none" (p. 14). Instead, Elliott sets the goal of the DAS so as to measure a range of "cognitive abilities." *Cognitive ability* refers to a more specific and narrower domain of human cognition than the term intelligence. For all age levels from 3 years, 6 months and upward, six subtests, measuring a number of cognitive abilities, form an overall composite score reflecting Spearman's *g*. Psychometric *g* is defined by Elliott (1990c) as "the general ability of an individual to perform mental processing that involves conceptualization and transformation of information" (p. 20). From this definition comes the term used to describe the most general DAS composite score: General Conceptual Ability (GCA).

However, the raison d'être of the DAS is not just to be another measure of children's overall cognitive ability or intelligence. Instead, Elliott (1990c) intends it to be an assessment tool that creates a profile of a child's strengths and weaknesses across a range of distinct cognitive abilities. To accomplish this, a major focus in the development of the DAS was to create a battery of subtests with sufficiently high specificity and reliability as to allow the clinician to interpret each as measuring something unique and distinct from the others. While the DAS provides meaningful information about more general factors, the intended focus for the clinician's interpretive efforts is at the subtest or lower-order composite level. This shift, to analysis at the subtest level and away from focusing on general ability, reflects the theoretical tradition of Thurstone (1938) and his concept of a number of specific "primary mental abilities." This tradition has been continued in the more recent work of Cattell and Horn (e.g., Cattell, 1971; Horn & Cattell, 1966; Horn, 1985; Horn & Noll, 1997) and Carroll (1993, 1997). The hope is that the creation of a reliable profile of a child's cognitive strengths and weaknesses will lead to a better understanding of his or her learning difficulties, and ultimately to practical recommendations to classroom teachers about remediation (Elliott, 1990c).

The structure of the DAS assumes a hierarchical organization of cognitive ability (Elliott, 1990b). Subtests, or specific measures of distinct abilities, make up the base of this structure. However, since all ability measures are intercorrelated, these subtests will tend to group together at a second, higher, level in what are referred to as *clusters*. These clusters, in turn, are interrelated, which yields an estimate of psychometric *g* that is at the apex of this hierarchical structure. Factor analyses of DAS data show that this hierarchy becomes more differentiated as a child develops (Elliott, 1990c).

While the development and structure of the DAS is not formally linked to the Horn-Cattell model, the ability clusters proposed in the DAS are interpretable in terms of the Horn-Cattell factors. For preschool-age children, abilities are seen as clustering into verbal and nonverbal factors, which are similar to Gc and Gv in the Horn-Cattell theory. For school-age children, a third cluster of cognitive abilities becomes differentiated, which reflects fluid reasoning (Gf); at its heart is the ability to integrate complex verbal and spatial information. The function of this third cluster is very similar to that of "planning" in the Luria and J. P. Das tradition (Das et al., 1979).

Finally, the DAS is influenced by research from cognitive psychology and neuropsychology (McCarthy & Warrington, 1990) in its approach to memory abilities. This research suggests that visual and verbal short-term memory are quite distinct and doubly dissociated. Because of this, the DAS does not represent short-term memory as a separate and unitary cluster such as is attempted by the Short-term Memory Area Composite on the Stanford-Binet Intelligence Scale—Fourth Edition (Thorndike, Hagen, & Sattler, 1986). Instead, auditory and visual short-term memory subtests on the DAS are partitioned as separate measures that do not cluster together.

NATURE OF THE TEST

The DAS is an individually administered measure of cognitive abilities, standardized for children between 2 years, 6 months and 17 years, 11 months. It is based on the British Ability Scales (BAS; Elliott, Murray, & Pearson, 1979, Elliott, 1997a). The DAS is essentially two test batteries. The first is geared to preschoolers from age 2 years, 6 months to 5 years, 11 months. The second is designed for school-age children from age 6 years, 0 months to 17 years, 11 months. Although these are the nominal age ranges of the two batteries, they were completely co-normed across the age range 5 years, 0 months through 7 years, 11 months, and may be used equivalently in that age range. Thus, the school-age battery may be used appropriately to assess relatively gifted 5-year-olds. Most important, for the majority of clinicians, the preschool battery may be used to assess average and lower functioning 6- and 7-year-olds for whom the school-age materials are developmentally less appropriate.

The preschool and school-age batteries are similar in structure. Both feature a set of core subtests designed to measure general cognitive ability. The six core subtests in each battery were selected because of their relatively high correlation with g; they thus measure more complex mental processing. Both the preschool and school-age batteries also contain a set of diagnostic subtests. These are intended to measure more specific or distinct skills such as short-term memory or speed of information processing. They have a lower correlation with g, and measure less complex mental processing.

The preschool battery of the DAS is further divided into an upper and lower preschool level. The lower level is specifically designed for children from 2 years, 6 months to 3 years, 5 months. The upper preschool level is used for assessing children from 3 years, 6 months to 7 years, 11 months. Table 3.1 provides information on the core subtests for the preschool battery while Table 3.2 provides information on the diagnostic subtests that can be used with preschoolers and early school-age children.

The core subtests of the upper preschool level consist of all of the subtests listed in Table 3.1, with the exception of Block Building. These six core subtests combine to provide an estimate of overall cognitive ability (GCA). They are also divided into verbal and nonverbal clusters or factors as illustrated in Table 3.1. The Verbal Ability cluster is designed to measure acquired verbal concepts and knowledge. The Nonverbal Ability cluster is designed to measure complex nonverbal (primarily spatial) reasoning abilities. The sixth core subtest, Early Number Concepts, is not grouped with either cluster. Originally hypothesized as a part of the Verbal Ability cluster, factor analyses revealed Early Number Concepts loading significantly on both the verbal and nonverbal factors (Elliott, 1990c). Because of the subtest's high correlation with g and the important clinical content it covers, it was decided to retain Early Number Concepts as part of the core subtests measuring overall cognitive ability. All of the diagnostic subtests can be used with children at the

TABLE 3.1
Preschool Subtests of the Differential Ability Scales

Subtest	What the child does	Cluster	Usual age range	Extended/ Out-of-level age range
Block Building	Uses wooden blocks to copy designs from a model.	None	2:6–3:5	3:6–4:11
Verbal Comprehension	1. Points out body parts on a picture of a teddy bear. 2. Follows verbal directions with toys.	Verbal	2:6–5:11	6:0–6:11
Picture Similarities	Matches a target picture to the most similar of four options.	Nonverbal	2:6–5:11	6:0–7:11
Naming Vocabulary	Names pictures.	Verbal	2:6–5:11	6:0–8:11
Pattern Construction	Builds designs from pictures or models using squares or cubes with colored patterns.	Nonverbal	3:6–17:11	3:0–3:5
Early Number Concepts	1. Counts objects. 2. Answers questions about numerical and mathematical concepts.	None	3:6–5:11	2:6–3:5 6:0–7:11
Copying	Copies line drawings with a pencil.	Nonverbal	3:6–5:11	6:0–7:11

TABLE 3.2
Diagnostic Subtests of the Differential Ability Scales

Subtest	What the child does	Usual age range	Out-of-level age range
Recall of Objects—Immediate	Looks at a card with 20 pictured objects for 60 or 20 seconds. The card is then taken away and the child names as many objects as he or she can remember. This is repeated over 3 trials.	4:0–17:11	None
Recall of Objects—Delayed	Between 10 and 30 minutes after the Recall of Objects—Immediate subtest, the child is asked to name as many of the pictured objects as he or she can still remember.	4:0–17:11	None
Matching Letter-Like Forms	Finds an exact match to an abstract drawing from six pictured options. The five incorrect options are reversals or rotations of the target.	4:6–5:11	4:0–4:5 6:0–7:11
Recall of Digits	Repeats back a sequence of numbers.	3:0–17:11	2:6–2:11
Recognition of Pictures	Looks at a picture of one or several objects for 5 or 10 seconds. Then picks out those objects from a second picture that includes additional distractors.	3:0–7:11	2:6–2:11 8:0–17:11
Speed of Information Processing	1. Looks at a row of circles, each with a different number of boxes in it. Child marks the circle with the most boxes. 2. Looks at a row of numbers. Child marks the highest number.	6:0–17:11	5:0–5:11

upper preschool level, primarily to provide more specific information on visual and verbal short-term memory abilities. The Matching Letter-Like Forms subtest provides information on a child's visual discrimination skills and may be relevant to the child's readiness to acquire reading and writing skills (Elliott, 1990c). The Speed of Information Processing subtest can be used to assess this skill only with 5-year-olds showing average and above abilities in this area.

The lower preschool level of the DAS consists of four core subtests: Block Building, Verbal Comprehension, Picture Similarities, and Naming Vocabulary. These subtests combine to produce an overall composite, or GCA, score. The lower preschool level is not differentiated into clusters, but it does yield a Special Nonverbal Composite based on the child's performance on the

Block Building and Picture Similarities subtests. The Recall of Digits and Recognition of Pictures diagnostic subtests can be used to explore the short-term memory abilities of most 2-year-olds and all 3-year-olds at the lower preschool level.

The school-age battery of the DAS consists of the core subtests outlined in Table 3.3 and the diagnostic subtests described in Table 3.2. The six core subtests combine to provide an estimate of overall cognitive ability (GCA) and are further divided into three clusters, as outlined in Table 3.3. The Verbal Ability cluster is designed to measure complex verbal mental processing. The Spatial Ability cluster measures complex visual-spatial processing. The Nonverbal Ability cluster consists of reasoning subtests that involve minimal verbal instructions and minimal verbal responses from the child. However, verbal mediation strategies are generally essential for solving these problems. Thus the Nonverbal Reasoning subtests require an integration of ver-

TABLE 3.3
School-Age Subtests of the Differential Ability Scales

Subtest	What the child does	Cluster	Usual age range	Extended/ Out-of-level age range
Recall of Designs	Looks at an abstract line drawing for 5 seconds. Drawing is removed and the child draws it from memory with a pencil.	Spatial	6:0–17:11	5:0–5:11
Word Definitions	Provides a verbal definition of a word.	Verbal	6:0–17:11	5:0–5:11
Pattern Construction	Builds designs from pictures or models using squares or cubes with colored patterns.	Spatial	3:6–17:11	3:0–3:5
Matrices	Selects from four or six options the one that would best complete an abstract visual pattern.	Nonverbal	6:0–17:11	5:0–5:11
Similarities	Describes verbally how three related words are similar.	Verbal	6:0–17:11	5:0–5:11
Sequential & Quantitative Reasoning	1. Completes a series of abstract figures by drawing in the missing figure. 2. Determines the relationship shared between two pairs of numbers and then uses it to provide the missing number of an incomplete pair.	Nonverbal	6:0–17:11	5:0–5:11

TABLE 3.4
Achievement Tests of the Differential Ability Scales

Subtest	What the child does	Usual age range	Out-of-level age range
Basic Number Skills	Solves math problems on a worksheet.	6:0–17:11	None
Spelling	Spells words dictated by the clinician.	6:0–17:11	None
Word Reading	Pronounces words presented on a card.	6:0–17:11	5:0–5:11

bal and visual information. Elliott (1997b) considers that the three DAS clusters measure the following factors in the Horn-Cattell tradition: Verbal cluster (Crystallized, Gc); Spatial cluster (Visual Processing, Gv); and Nonverbal Reasoning cluster (Fluid, Gf).

The school-age battery also features three measures of academic achievement, as outlined in Table 3.4. The achievement subtests were co-normed with the cognitive subtests, thus allowing for analyses of ability/achievement discrepancies. The DAS manual (Elliott, 1990a) provides support for use of both simple-difference and regression models to explore whether assessment results suggest the possibility of a learning disability.

TECHNICAL INFORMATION

Standardization Sample

The DAS was standardized between 1987 and 1989 on a sample of 3475 children selected to match the 1988 U.S. Census on the stratification variables of age, gender, ethnicity, geographic location, and parent education level. The preschool sample was further stratified to match the census data according to the proportion of children who had attended a preschool educational program. Detailed census records were used in order that, at each age level of the test, the standardization sample matched the population at that particular age level in terms of the *joint distributions* of ethnicity, geographic location, and parent education level.

This is an unusually stringent constraint in sampling, and it is far more difficult to achieve than representative distributions on each stratification variable taken singly. This, and other procedural refinements in sampling, makes the DAS unique in its sampling accuracy (Elliott, 1997b). A sample of 175 children was used for each 6-month age interval at the preschool range, while a sample of 200 children was used at each age level of the school-age range (Elliott, 1990c).

Reliability

Internal consistency reliability is high at the level of the GCA and cluster scores (Elliott, 1990c). GCA score reliability ranges from an average of .90 at the lower preschool level to .94 at the upper preschool level, to .95 for the school-age battery. Cluster score reliability ranges from .88 to .92. Internal consistency at the subtest level is relatively strong, with some exceptions, with reliability coefficients ranging from .70 to .92. Of the 26 possible internal reliability coefficients at the subtest level, 17 were greater than .8 and 4 were greater than .9.

Test-retest reliability data suggest GCA and cluster scores are very stable (Elliott, 1990c). GCA test-retest scores correlate between .89 and .93 across the three age groups sampled, while the range is from .79 to .90 for cluster scores. At the subtest level, test-retest reliabilities range from .38 to .93 for preschoolers and from .47 to .97 for school-age children. The mean subtest reliability coefficient is .78 (Kamphaus, 1993). The practice effect on the GCA is roughly 3 points for preschoolers and 6 points for school-age children. Four DAS subtests, which require a significant amount of clinician judgment to score, were examined for interrater reliability. Coefficients were found to be .9 or above.

DAS scores were also evaluated in terms of specificity, or how much of the score variance is reliable and unique to that measure. The higher the specificity of a measure, the more confident the clinician can be about interpreting the score as measuring something unique in comparison to what is measured by the other tests in the battery. McGrew and Murphy (1995) argue that specificity is high when it accounts for 25% or more of the test's total variance and when it is greater than the error variance. Each DAS subtest meets these criteria for high specificity, with values ranging from .30 to .82 (Elliott, 1990c). Elliott (1997b) presents data showing that the DAS has significantly greater specificity than other popular measures of cognitive ability for children.

Validity

Construct validity for the DAS is supported by confirmatory and exploratory factor analyses supporting a 1-factor model at the lower preschool level, a 2-factor (verbal/nonverbal) model at the upper preschool level, and a 3-factor (verbal/nonverbal/spatial) model for school-age children (Elliott, 1990c). Keith's (1990) independent hierarchical confirmatory factor analyses reported consistent results that Elliott (1997b) found were essentially in agreement with the DAS data analyses given in the test handbook (Elliott, 1990c). Elliott (1997b) also reports joint factor analysis of the DAS and the WISC-R (Wechsler, 1974) that support a verbal/nonverbal/spatial-factor model for school-age children.

Elliott (1990c) also provides evidence supporting the convergent and discriminant validity of the DAS cluster scores. The Verbal Ability cluster score consistently correlates much higher with the verbal composite score than it does with the nonverbal composite score of other cognitive ability tests for children. Similarly, the Nonverbal Reasoning and Spatial Ability cluster scores correlate significantly lower with the verbal composite score of other tests than does the DAS Verbal Ability cluster score.

Evidence for the concurrent validity of the DAS is provided by studies (Wechsler, 1991; Elliott, 1990c) showing consistently high correlations between the GCA and the composite scores of other cognitive batteries such as the Wechsler Intelligence Scale for Children—Third Edition (WISC-III; Wechsler, 1991), the Wechsler Preschool and Primary Scale of Intelligence—Revised (WPPSI-R; Wechsler, 1989), and the Stanford-Binet Intelligence Scale—Fourth Edition (Thorndike et al., 1986). High correlations were also found between the DAS achievement tests and other group or individual achievement tests as well as with actual student grades (Elliott, 1990c).

Bias

Extensive effort was put into ensuring the fairness of the DAS across cultures. Test items were first reviewed for possible bias by a panel representing women and several ethnic groups, and, based on its recommendations, a number of items were changed or dropped from the test. To aid statistical analyses of bias, an additional 600 Hispanic and African-American children were tested along with the standardization sample in order that each test item could be analyzed for differential item difficulty across cultures. The children in this bias oversample also assisted in ensuring that test scoring rules reflected possible culture-specific responses from minority children. Finally, the analyses showed that there was no unfair bias against minority children in the ability of the DAS GCA score to predict school achievement (Elliott, 1990c).

Further analyses of these data have examined construct bias in the DAS (Keith, Quirk, Schartzer, & Elliott, 1999). This was accomplished by conducting hierarchical, multisample confirmatory factor analysis of the DAS standardization data, including data from the bias oversample. Results showed that the DAS measured the same constructs for all three ethnic groups (Black, White, and Hispanic) across the entire age range of 2½ through 17 years. Thus it was concluded that the DAS shows no construct bias across groups.

Administration

There are several notable differences in administering the DAS compared to most other cognitive batteries for children. The vast majority of DAS subtests reject the traditional model of establishing basal and ceiling levels, which presumes that the child would have passed all items before the basal and failed all items after the ceiling. Instead, most DAS subtests are administered using an adaptive or tailored testing model. The goal is to have the child work primarily on items that are of moderate difficulty and reduce the number of items administered that are either too hard or too easy for that child. To do this, most DAS subtests designate a set of items that are typically appropriate for most children at a given age level. The child completes all of the items in that set, reaching a decision point. If the child experiences a reasonable combination of success and failure within the item set (which is defined specifically for each subtest), the clinician can now proceed to the next subtest. If the child experiences very little success on the initial item set, the clinician follows up by dropping back and administering the items from the next-easiest item set. If the child reaches the initial decision point and experiences almost complete success, the clinician continues on with more difficult items until reaching a decision point where the child has begun to experience some degree of difficulty, usually defined as failing three items overall. Each subtest also has a "mercy rule," or alternative stopping point, so that administration of a subtest can be stopped partway through an item set if a child has failed so many items in succession that it is clear that further items will be too hard for the child.

In order to ensure that the child understands the nature of the task, several subtests feature "teaching items." Teaching, using explicit instructions provided in the manual, is provided to a child who fails the first items of the subtest. Since feedback is provided to the child about failures, the manual encourages the examiner to provide positive feedback when a child passes a teaching item.

The average administration time for the school-age battery of the DAS is estimated to be 45 minutes for the core subtests, another 20 minutes for the achievement battery, and up to 20 additional minutes if all of the diagnostic subtests are used. At the upper preschool level, the core subtests are estimated to take about 40 minutes, and administration takes an additional 25 minutes if all of the diagnostic subtests are used. At the lower preschool level, the core subtests take about 25 minutes, and administration takes an additional 10 minutes if the examiner chooses to use both of the diagnostic subtests.

Scoring

Test Scores

The DAS requires one more step in the process of calculating test scores by hand than most other cognitive batteries for children, because of its use of item sets. Raw scores from each subtest must first be converted into an "ability score." This conversion is accomplished directly on the Record Form through a Rasch scaling procedure (Elliott, 1990c), and it essentially provides a measure of the child's ability based on both the number of items passed and the relative difficulty of those items. A child will obtain a higher ability score for passing 5 difficult items than for passing 5 very easy items. The ability score itself is usually not clinically interpreted but from it a normative score for the subtest can be obtained from the tables in the manual.

The GCA, cluster scores, Special Nonverbal Composite, and achievement test scores are all provided in the form of standard scores with a mean of 100 and a standard deviation (SD) of 15. Core and diagnostic subtests produce T scores with a mean of 50 and an SD of 10. Grade-based percentile scores are also provided for the achievement battery.

An appealing feature of the DAS is the flexibility given to the clinician in subtest selection by the provision of extended norms for subtests outside their usual age range. All of the upper preschool core subtests were standardized on 6- and 7-year-olds, while all of the school-age core subtests were standardized on 5-year-olds. Some of the preschool subtests are too easy for higher functioning 6-year-olds, while some of the school-age subtests are too hard for lower functioning 5-year-olds. However, it is possible to use the upper preschool core subtests with average and lower functioning 6- and 7-year-olds and obtain a T score value. Similarly, it is also possible to use the school-age subtests with average and higher functioning 5-year-olds.

In addition, a number of subtests were standardized over an even wider age range than the overlapping preschool and school-age ranges. For example, Recognition of Pictures, a preschool diagnostic subtest, was normed across the entire DAS age range of 2 years, 6 months through 17 years, 11 months. Although its usual age range is 3 years, 6 months through 7 years, 11 months, it can be administered out-of-level with 2½- to 3½-year-olds of average to high ability and to 8- to 17-year-olds of average to low ability. This makes the subtest a valuable additional measure of visual short-term memory for school-age children.

Extended GCA norms are also provided to calculate an estimate of overall cognitive ability for extremely low functioning children. Thus, it is possible to use the Lower Preschool level core subtests to obtain an extended GCA score for children up to 7 years old. The Upper Preschool level core subtests can be used to calculate an extended GCA score for children up to 14 years old. As will be elaborated, these extended norms are extremely helpful in accurate assessment of children with severe intellectual disabilities.

Interpretation

The DAS uses a classification system for GCA and cluster scores which is descriptive of the child's functioning rather than utilizing diagnostic-sounding terminology. Table 3.5 outlines this system.

TABLE 3.5
Descriptive Classification Labels for GCA and Cluster Scores

GCA & Cluster Score	Descriptive Category
130 and above	Very high
120–129	High
110–119	Above average
90–109	Average
80–89	Below average
70–79	Low
69 and below	Very low

Another particularly strong feature of the DAS is the excellent support provided to the clinician in the process of interpreting test results by the test handbook (Elliott, 1990c). The clinician is guided through a systematic plan of attack for interpreting DAS test scores as well as given a clear rationale for this approach. Encouragement is given to first checking for significant differences between the cluster scores themselves and also between the cluster scores and the GCA. Detailed ipsative analyses of subtest relative strengths and weaknesses is not encouraged unless a significant difference is found between subtest scores within a cluster. This approach should significantly reduce the risk of Type I error during subtest analyses. A further section of the test handbook provides guidance on clinical interpretation of subtest profiles, with tables outlining underlying processes involved in each subtest.

CLINICAL SIGNIFICANCE

Psychometric Considerations

The DAS is an extremely valuable addition to the group of tests available for assessing cognitive ability in children. A number of features stand out that make the DAS more than just another battery. Reviewers are very pleased with the test's very strong psychometric characteristics, including the high reliability of the various DAS scales and the careful attention paid to ensuring a representative standardization sample as well the fairness of the test (Aylward, 1992; Braden, 1992; Kamphaus, 1993; Flanagan & Alfonso, 1995; Anastasi & Urbina, 1997).

Two important features of the DAS design, co-norming and high specificity, make it particularly useful for clinicians:

- *Co-norming*: For children with learning disabilities, the co-normed achievement battery allows for reliable analyses of ability/achievement discrepancies using the regression model preferred by many clinicians (Reynolds, 1990; Braden, 1992). The co-norming of the achievement battery means the percentage of children showing a particular discrepancy between GCA and an achievement subtest is known rather than estimated.

- Specificity: The assessment of children with possible learning disabilities forms a major portion of the work of school psychological services. Therefore, it is critical for a test battery to be able to detect significant strengths and weaknesses in scores, thereby aiding the clinician in understanding the specific learning processes with which the child is struggling. The DAS has the highest level of specificity in subtests and lower-order composites (Verbal, Nonverbal Reasoning, and Spatial) of any published battery (Elliott, 1997b). Such high levels of specificity will lead not only to greater accuracy but also to a higher incidence in the detection of specific, significantly high and low scores in subtests and clusters. Common cognitive profile patterns in learning disabled children are discussed more fully in the next section.

Special Populations

The DAS places less emphasis on verbal responses than most cognitive batteries for children. That, combined with its special composite score made up of only nonverbal subtests, offers advantages in the assessment of children with hearing impairments or speech dyspraxias, or those for whom English is a second language.

From our clinical experience, one of the greatest advantages of the DAS is its high appeal for preschoolers. For a test to provide a reliable and valid assessment when used with young children, it must not only have good psychometric characteristics but also look interesting enough so that they want to participate in the assessment and keep going when the work starts becoming difficult. The DAS does this much better than any of its current competitors because the test includes many items that involve little toys and activities that children do with their hands. Many of us who work with preschoolers lamented the changes made to the Stanford-Binet when the Fourth Edition was released (Thorndike et al., 1986); gone were most of the great little toys and activities from the Stanford-Binet L-M (Terman & Merrill, 1960), replaced in the new version by a much greater requirement for the child to focus on looking at pictures. The DAS restores the Stanford-Binet L-M approach to working with preschoolers.

Another important advantage of the DAS for preschoolers is that administration time for the core subtests is significantly shorter than that typically needed for competitors like the Stanford-Binet or WPPSI-R. An experienced examiner can complete the core subtests of the DAS and obtain a reliable and valid estimate of overall cognitive ability in about 30 to 40 minutes. Our experience is that the Stanford-Binet Fourth Edition or WPPSI-R takes about 15 to 30 minutes longer than the DAS to obtain a similar estimate. This is a critical advantage in working with a population not known for having lengthy attention spans for intense diagnostic work.

Also, our clinical experience convinces us that the DAS is the test of choice for the intellectual assessment of children with developmental delays and mental retardation. The DAS offers great flexibility in choosing an individually tailored assessment battery for children with developmental disabilities. As well, it offers much greater sensitivity to the differential diagnosis of severe and profound mental retardation.

On first glance one might think, from evidence presented in the DAS *Handbook* (Elliott, 1990c), that the DAS may not be sensitive to identifying intellectually gifted children. A sample of 62 students previously identified as gifted, chosen from the standardization sample, showed a mean GCA of only 118.1. Braden (1992) speculates that this may be due to regression to the mean, a "Flynn effect" from using updated norms to evaluate these children, or variation in the definition of "giftedness" used to designate the students. It is certainly always the case that when children are selected according to certain criteria (say, Wechsler IQ plus achievement test scores), there will be regression to the mean when other criteria are applied (such as DAS GCA scores). The more extreme the scores, the greater the phenomenon. This seems the most likely explanation of the effect that Braden observed. There is no evidence that ceiling effects in subtests result in any lack of sensitivity in identifying intellectually gifted children. Even for the oldest DAS age group (17 years, 6 months through 17 years, 11 months), maximum scores on all core subtests yield a GCA of 156, indicating ample score range for assessing older gifted students. A further advantage of the DAS in assessing intellectually gifted children is the nature of the composites. Only those subtests that are the best measures of "g" are used to estimate composite scores (clusters and GCA). The exclusion of subtests that have low g saturations is unique to the DAS, making the GCA a particularly well-focused measure of g.

COMMON PATTERNS AND
INTERPRETATION HYPOTHESES

Profile Analyses

As previously discussed, the DAS was created with the intention of providing a profile of a child's cognitive strengths and weaknesses, with the hope that this profile would lead to a better understanding and more effective remediation of possible learning difficulties. A major strength of the DAS is the comprehensive and lucid description of a method for the systematic interpretation of the DAS profile (Elliott, 1990c). This intent follows in the traditional wisdom passed on to most student clinicians in the first days of their cognitive assessment courses. Most of us were taught that, in interpreting intelligence tests with children, it is important to look beyond the overall composite scores to the unique information about the child that can be garnered from careful examination of the patterns of performance on the various subtests of the measure. Major texts on assessment with children emphasize this approach (Sattler, 1992; Kamphaus, 1993; Kaufman, 1994). Kaufman states that the composite scores tell us about the "what" of a child's abilities while the subtests bring to light the "how." It will be argued that the DAS lower-order composites (Verbal, Nonverbal Reasoning, and Spatial) are also particularly important in illuminating the "how."

The analysis of subtest profile patterns to better understand a child's learning strengths and weaknesses is controversial, and McDermott, Glutting, and colleagues (e.g., McDermott & Glutting, 1997; Glutting, McDermott, Konold, Snelbaker, & Watkins, 1998; Glutting, McDermott, Watkins, Kush, & Konold, 1997) have been very active in questioning such procedures. At the beginning of the last decade, McDermott, Fantuzzo and Glutting (1990) made a general statement advising "that psychologists just say 'no' to subtest analysis." This was on the basis of a critique of practice using the WISC-R, but the recommendation came to be perceived as generalized to all cognitive tests. One of McDermott, Fantuzzo, and Glutting's concerns centers on the relatively lower reliability and stability of subtest scores in comparison with composites. McDermott et al. argue that, because subtests typically have lower reliability and stability than composites, it is likely that the pattern of strengths and weaknesses among subtests that appears one day might not be there the next. Another concern relates to the use of ipsative scores in profile interpretation. Ipsative scores are produced by subtracting the child's average normative score across various subtests from each individual subtest score, thereby removing the mean elevation of scores (i.e., variance associated with g). We emphasize that although they have applied these critiques to the DAS, the critiques do not constitute a major threat to DAS profile interpretations for the following reasons:

1. Interpretation of high and low subtest and composite scores is only recommended when differences between scores are statistically significant. This takes account of the reliability of the measures being compared. Relatively lower reliability results in larger differences being required for significance. Moreover, the DAS method adjusts significant differences for multiple comparisons. Because several comparisons are being made, differences required for significance are greater than for a simple comparison of two scores. This conservative approach is designed to ensure that only reliable differences, not attributable to measurement error, are reported.

2. McDermott and Glutting's negative conclusions about the value of profile analysis using ipsative scores do not apply to the DAS, which uses direct comparisons of normative subtest and composite scores. The only time scores are "ipsatized" is when the mean standardized T-score for the core subtests is subtracted from individual subtest scores for the purpose of evaluating whether that subtest score is, overall, significantly high or low. The ipsatized score (or the difference score, to put it another way) is never reported: Once a subtest score is identified as significantly high or low, the unadjusted T-score itself is reported. Also note that the composite scores are never ipsatized in the DAS procedure.

Glutting et al. (1997) also make the point that the interpretation of a profile should be done with reference to *base rate* information. Base rate refers to the frequency with which a particular profile is found in the population. Glutting et al. correctly assert that statistically significant differences (those that are reliable, i.e., unlikely to have arisen because of measurement error) can be quite common and ordinary, even though very "significant." To address this problem, Holland and McDermott (1996), using hierarchical multistage cluster analyses of the DAS standardization sample, identified seven core profile types in this sample that are representative of the child population. Five of these profiles, shown by a total of 71 percent of the sample, were flat in terms of their scores on the DAS core subtests (although there is some variation among the diagnostic subtests). The differences between the groups were defined mainly by variation in general ability. In other words, the profiles varied in the altitude rather than in the pattern of their scores. The remaining two core profile types were defined by (a) 16 percent of students who have relatively high Verbal versus low Spatial subtest scores, and (b) 13 percent of students who have relatively high Spatial versus low Verbal subtest scores. The Verbal and Spatial cluster scores were 10 points different in both cases. These two profile types will be discussed more fully, later in this section.

Attempts to show the utility of profile analyses with the DAS have concentrated mostly on children with learning disabilities, and in particular with children with reading disabilities. Elliott (1990c) examined DAS profiles for children from the standardization sample with previously identified learning disabilities. He reported that children with learning disabilities tend to score lower on the diagnostic subtests relative to their performance on the core subtests. The greatest differences are shown on the Recall of Objects, Recognition of Pictures, and Speed of Information Processing subtests. Similarly, Kercher and Sandoval (1991) reported finding a characteristic DAS subtest profile in children with reading disabilities. Their study found children with reading disabilities scoring significantly lower than typical children on the Recall of Digits and Recall of Objects diagnostic subtests. They argue that this likely reflects a particular difficulty for these children with auditory and sequential processing and perhaps with verbal labeling as well. By way of contrast, a study by Shapiro, Buckhalt, and Herod (1995) reported a relatively flat profile of core and diagnostic subtests in a sample of 83 children with learning disabilities. Of course, studies such as these, examining mean profiles for such groups as "Learning Disabled" (LD), which are likely to be heterogeneous in profiles and causal factors, hide any possible major profile differences among subgroups.

To address this problem, cluster analyses have often been used to place individuals in subgroups according to their profile similarities. Using this method, Elliott (1990c) examined the profiles of 136 children from the standardization sample identified with reading disabilities because of the significant discrepancy between GCA and their performance on the Word Reading subtest. Four distinct profile types were identified among these children. Elliott argues that this supports the possibility of using subtest profile analyses to make clinically helpful distinctions between children with different types of learning disabilities.

McIntosh and Gridley (1993) examined DAS subtest profiles of 83 children with various learning disabilities. Cluster analyses indicated six distinct profile patterns, four of which showed little variation among subtest scores and were dominated primarily by their overall cognitive ability. The other two clusters showed more variation in subtest performance. Students in one cluster were characterized by difficulties with processing visual-spatial information, together with low scores on three diagnostic subtests: Recall of Objects, Recognition of Pictures, and Speed of Information Processing. The key characteristic of children in the other cluster was a relative weakness in the Nonverbal Reasoning cluster. This suggests that a major difficulty for these children may be with fluid reasoning or with the integration of visual and verbal information, important in successful performance of many complex tasks.

In another study with preschool children, McIntosh (1999) explored the ability of the DAS to discriminate between typical preschoolers and those identified as being "at-risk" for developmental or behavioral problems. The children in the at-risk group showed their greatest differences in performance compared to the typical children on the Picture Similarities core subtest and the Recall of Digits diagnostic subtest. McIntosh argued that poor performance on these two subtests is a particularly good screener for children at-risk for developmental problems.

Combined, these studies suggest that DAS profile analyses are useful in better understanding the unique difficulties experienced by children with particular learning disabilities. These results demonstrate that the diagnostic subtests and the cluster scores, as opposed to the overall GCA, provide the key information about these unique difficulties. In these studies, a variety of DAS cluster and subtest profiles are reported. It seems common, both in studies of a normal population and in studies of children with disabilities, to find some groups with flat cluster and/or subtest profiles. Looking only at cluster scores, some studies find groups with relatively high Verbal versus Spatial scores, relatively high Spatial versus Verbal scores, and relatively low Nonverbal Reasoning versus Verbal and Spatial scores. In most studies, there is considerable variability among the diagnostic subtests.

Profiles of Samples of Dyslexic and Learning Disabled Children

Introduction

The following study addresses most of the issues raised by critics of profile interpretation, and also aims to identify a number of distinct profiles of DAS cluster scores among groups of normal and exceptional children. This study is principally based on an examination of patterns of cluster scores, measuring Verbal, Nonverbal Reasoning, and Spatial abilities.

Method

Subjects.   Three major sources of data were used:

1. DAS *Standardization Sample*. This consists of 2400 children aged 6 years, 0 months through 17 years, 11 months. A total of 353 poor readers were identified in this total sample. Poor readers are defined as those with DAS Word Reading standard scores below 85. These poor readers were further subdivided into two subsamples:

   - Poor Readers with No Significant Discrepancy: 86 poor readers whose observed Word Reading score was not significantly lower than that predicted from their GCA
   - Poor Readers with Significant Discrepancy: 267 poor readers whose observed Word Reading score was significantly lower than that predicted from their GCA

   This sample provides data constituting a baseline against which results from the other two samples may be evaluated.
2. *Dyslexic Sample*.[1] This sample consists of 160 children identified as dyslexic by psychologists of the Dyslexia Institute in Great Britain. From a research perspective, this sample has the major advantage that the DAS had *not* been used in the original diagnostic process to identify these individuals as dyslexic. No information is available as to how much time elapsed between their initial identification and the subsequent DAS assessment. It seems likely that many would have received a considerable period of intervention for their reading difficul-

---

[1] The data for this sample are used by kind permission of Dr. Martin Turner, Head of Psychology, Dyslexia Institute, Staines, England.

ties before their DAS assessment. The sample was divided into two subsamples, as follows:

- Dyslexics with DAS Word Reading standard scores below 85
- Dyslexics with DAS Word Reading scores between 85 and 100

3. *Learning Disabled* (LD) *Sample*.[2] This sample consists of 53 children identified as learning disabled, with the WISC-III used as the initial assessment battery. Once again, this sample has the major advantage that the DAS had *not* been used in the original diagnostic process to identify these individuals as learning disabled. The sample was reevaluated on the DAS three years after their initial assessment. Dumont, Cruse, Price, and Whelley (1996) report full details of the sample, the procedure, and the initial findings.

Definition of Subgroups.   The subgroups were defined according to the possible combinations of high and low scores that may be found among the three DAS clusters, and also including subgroups with flat cluster profiles. Children in all three samples were placed into subgroups based upon the presence or absence of significant discrepancies between cluster scores that were significant at the 95% confidence level, adjusted for multiple comparisons. The differences were obtained from Tables B.4 and B.5 in the DAS *Introductory and technical handbook* (Elliott, 1990c), and are similar to the differences indicated on the DAS Record Form.

Even among poor readers with a significant discrepancy between GCA and Word Reading (or, more properly, between observed Word Reading and Word Reading predicted from the GCA), it would be expected that there would be a proportion of children with flat cognitive test profiles. Poor reading has many causes, and there is no reason to believe that children who have difficulty with reading because of lack of exposure to teaching through absences from school, poor teaching, or poor motivation, should have anything other than normal (i.e., flat) cognitive profiles. Other poor readers may have verbal or spatial disabilities, both of which are amply reported in the literature (Snow, Burns, & Griffin, 1998; Rourke, Del Dotto, Rourke, & Casey, 1990). Finally, we may find some individuals whose Nonverbal Reasoning ability is lower than both their Verbal and Spatial abilities. Such a group had been identified by McIntosh and Gridley (1993). The second author has also received many questions and comments during the past several years from psychologists who have observed LD children showing this profile pattern. Finally, there may be some individuals who show the reverse pattern, with Nonverbal Reasoning (NVR) ability higher than both Verbal and Spatial, although no research studies have identified such a subgroup. The subgroups are, therefore, as follows:

[2] The data for this sample are used by kind permission of Dr. Ron Dumont, Director, M.A. and Psy.D. Programs in School Psychology, Fairleigh Dickinson University, Teaneck, NJ.

- *Flat Cluster Profile.* No significant differences among the three DAS cluster scores.
- *Low Spatial, High Verbal.* Verbal cluster significantly higher than Spatial cluster. Possible nonverbal learning disability.
- *Low Verbal, High Spatial.* Verbal cluster significantly lower than Spatial cluster. Pattern typically reported for poor readers. (See, e.g., Snow et al., 1998; British Psychological Society, 1999).
- *High NVR.* Nonverbal Reasoning cluster higher than both the Verbal and Spatial scores, and significantly higher than at least one of them. Interpreted as signifying good ability to process complex auditory-visual information.
- *Low NVR.* Nonverbal Reasoning cluster lower than both the Verbal and Spatial scores, and significantly lower than at least one of them. Interpreted as indicating difficulty in processing complex auditory-visual information.

Results

Table 3.6 shows the frequency and percentages of children in the standardization sample who had each profile. Because the DAS standardization sample was chosen to stringently match U.S. census data, we can assume that these percentages provide a good estimate of the rates of each profile in the U.S. school-age population. Fifty percent of the total standardization sample had a flat cluster profile. However, 66.3% of the poor readers who had

TABLE 3.6
Number and Percentage of Students Drawn from the
DAS Standardization Sample with Various Profile Types

Type of profile	Poor readers with no discrepancy	Poor readers with discrepancy	Total DAS standardization sample
Flat Cluster Profile	57	121	1203
	66.3%	45.3%	50.1%
Low Spatial, High Verbal	6	16	257
	7.0%	6.0%	10.7%
Low Verbal, High Spatial	8	63	239
	9.3%	23.6%	10.0%
High NVR	8	28	355
	9.3%	10.5%	14.8%
Low NVR	7	39	346
	8.1%	14.6%	14.4%
Column Totals	86	267	2400

Note: The subsamples in the first two columns form 14.7% of the total standardization sample.

no discrepancy between observed and predicted Word Reading scores had a flat cluster profile. The range of GCA scores in this particular group is quite restricted, ranging from 54 to 84. The group likely contains many children functioning in the mild to moderate range of mental retardation who would be expected to be more likely to show a flat cluster profile.

The larger group of poor readers who had a significant discrepancy between observed and predicted Word Reading scores showed a larger variance in GCA scores, ranging from 46 to 118. Compared with the total standardization sample, a slightly smaller percentage (45.3%) of these poor readers showed flat profiles. Also, about a quarter (23.6%) of this subgroup, as might be expected, had significantly lower Verbal than Spatial ability. In the total sample, 10% of children had Low Spatial and High Spatial scores, and 14% to 15% showed Low and High NVR profiles.

Table 3.7 shows the results for the dyslexic and learning disabled samples. They are remarkably similar for the two samples, despite the data being gathered in different countries and in different settings. Chi-square tests showed that there is no significant difference between the two dyslexic groups (Word Reading below 85 and Word Reading 85–100; $\chi^2 = 5.13$; $df = 4$; N.S.), nor is there any significant difference between the combined dyslexic groups and Dumont et al.'s (1996) LD sample ($\chi^2 = 1.337$; $df = 4$; N.S.). About one third of these samples had *flat cluster profiles*, fewer than in the standardization sample but still a substantial proportion. Both the dyslexics with Word Reading below 85 group and the Dumont sample had 11% to 12% in the *Low Verbal*, *High Spatial* subgroup. This is about half the frequency of Low Verbal children in the comparable subgroup from the standardization sample who were poor

TABLE 3.7
Number and Percentage of Dyslexic and LD Students with Various DAS Profiles

Type of profile	Dyslexic with WORD READING below 85	Dyslexic with WORD READING 85–100	Dumont et al. (1996) LD sample
Flat Cluster Profile	28	28	20
	34.5%	35.5%	37.7%
Low Spatial, High Verbal	4	12	5
	4.9%	15.2%	9.4%
Low Verbal, High Spatial	10	7	6
	12.3%	8.9%	11.3%
High NVR	5	4	1
	6.2%	5.1%	1.9%
Low NVR	34	28	21
	42.0%	35.4%	39.6%
Column Totals	81	79	53

readers with ability-achievement discrepancies. One wonders if Low Verbal children tend not to be identified as dyslexic or learning disabled. It seems possible that many such children may be found in inner-city and poor socio-economic environments. They may thereby get special education services from other sources or designations (e.g., Title 1 funding in the United States). Such children may often be considered to be "garden-variety" poor readers, to use Stanovich's (1988) term, rather than dyslexic or LD. Further research is needed to clarify these issues. Turning to the *Low Spatial, High Verbal* subgroup, both samples showed a similar proportion, compared to the total DAS standardization sample, of students with this profile. Dumont et al.'s sample had 9.4% and the combined dyslexic sample had 10% with this profile. It is possible that a number of children with this profile have a Nonverbal learning disability (Rourke et. al., 1990).

There is a highly significant difference between the frequencies for each profile for the combined dyslexic and LD samples, on the one hand, and the standardization sample, on the other. Comparison of the frequencies for each profile for the combined dyslexic/LD sample and the Poor Readers with Discrepancy, taken from the standardization sample, yields a chi-square of 48.48 ($df = 4$; $p < .001$). Similarly, comparison of the combined dyslexic/LD sample and total standardization sample yields a chi-square of 94.71 ($df = 4$; $p < .001$). The differences that account for the highest chi-square values are for children with the Low NVR profile.

Very few dyslexic or LD children had a *High* NVR profile—considerably fewer than the proportion in the total DAS sample. However, more than one third of the dyslexic and LD samples fell into the *Low* NVR subgroup. The results from the Dumont et al. (1996) LD sample and the dyslexic sample are remarkably similar, providing mutual cross-validation of these findings. The mean profile for the combined dyslexic and LD children who are in this subgroup (N = 83) is shown in Figure 3.1. The differences between the mean scores are dramatic; the Nonverbal Reasoning mean is lower than both Verbal and Spatial means by more than one standard deviation.

Discussion

Why should children with reading disabilities score poorly on the two DAS subtests measuring Nonverbal Reasoning? The answer seems most plausibly to lie in the nature of the tasks of reading and "nonverbal" reasoning. Reading requires a high level of visual/verbal integration in order to convert visual printed codes into sounds and words. For fluent reading, and for recognition of common words or letter strings, an individual needs information in the auditory/verbal and visual processing systems to be effectively integrated. Similarly, to perform well on the DAS Nonverbal Reasoning tasks (or, indeed, on any good measures of fluid reasoning) one needs good integration of the visual and verbal processing systems. These tasks are presented visually, hence the term "nonverbal" that describes them. But to solve the problems effec-

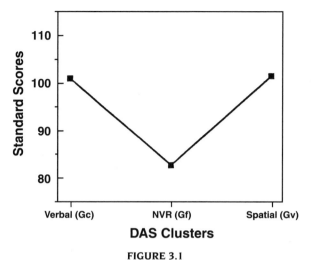

FIGURE 3.1
Mean score on DAS clusters for dyslexic and
LD children in the low NVR subgroup.

tively, the use of internal language to label and to mediate the solution of the problems is generally essential. Even if an individual has excellent verbal and spatial abilities, if the two brain processing systems specialized for those abilities do not "talk" to each other effectively, this may have an adverse effect on performance both in reasoning and in reading acquisition.

Readers may wonder why these striking findings, on two independent samples, have not been reported previously for other test batteries. The short and simple answer (since there is insufficient space to elaborate on it) is that all other psychometric batteries used with children, with one exception, do not have separate measures of Verbal ability (Gc), Spatial ability (Gv), and Nonverbal Reasoning ability (Gf).[3]

Case Example

The case of Mike (age 7 years, 11 months) is typical of a dyslexic or reading-disabled student with a low NVR profile. Mike was referred for assessment

[3]The one exception is the Woodcock-Johnson Tests of Cognitive Ability—Revised (WJ-R; Woodcock & Johnson, 1989). A lack of research evidence on such difficulties with fluid reasoning tasks for dyslexic and learning disabled children may be due to one of two possible reasons: (a) a lack of research with substantial samples, or (b) a problem with the subtests that purport to measure Gv and Gf. For example, the correlation between the two WJ-R subtests measuring Gv (Visual Closure and Picture Recognition) is very low: 0.22 at age 6 years, 0.30 at age 9 years, and 0.29 at age 13 years. Such low correlations beg the question of whether the composite formed from such a weak pairing measures anything meaningful. In comparison, the correlations between the two DAS measures of Gv (Recall of Designs and Pattern Construction) are 0.56, 0.54, and 0.61 for the same age groups.

TABLE 3.8
DAS Subtest, Cluster, and Achievement Scores for Mike

DAS subtest or cluster	Score
Core Subtests	(T-Score)
Word Definitions	53
Similarities	49
Matrices	40
Sequential & Quantitative Reasoning	47
Recall of Designs	59
Pattern Construction	61
Diagnostic Subtests	
Recall of Digits	40 (L)
Recall of Objects (Immediate)	50
Speed of Information Processing	61 (H)
Clusters	(Standard Score)
Verbal	101
Nonverbal Reasoning	88 (L)
Spatial	116 (H)
GCA	102
Achievement Tests	(Standard Score)
Word Reading	79 (L)
Spelling	87 (L)
Basic Number Skills	91 (L)

Note: In the Score column, "L" denotes a statistically significant low score and "H" a statistically significant high score. These are explained more fully in the text.

because, despite being self-evidently bright verbally and very capable in visual-motor tasks, he had had persistent problems since starting school in learning to read fluently and to spell accurately. His scores on the DAS are shown in Table 3.8. There are no significant differences between the two Verbal, the two Nonverbal Reasoning, or the two Spatial subtests. However, his Nonverbal Reasoning (NVR) cluster score is significantly lower than his Spatial cluster score, and his NVR score is lower than his Verbal score (this difference falling just short of statistical significance). Nevertheless, his NVR score is well below both the Verbal and Spatial scores, making his profile fit the low NVR subgroup. His NVR and Spatial scores are also significantly different from his GCA score, and are consequently marked "L" and "H," respectively. As discussed earlier, it seems probable that while Mike is fluent verbally and has good Spatial skills, he has problems in auditory-visual integration that arguably have influenced his acquisition of reading skills.

Turning to the diagnostic subtests, Mike's score on Recall of Digits is significantly low, in comparison with his mean T-score, derived from the six core subtests. His score on Speed of Information Processing is significantly high. He therefore appears to have a significant weakness in auditory short-term memory, in addition to his relative weakness in auditory-visual integration. His parents and teacher also commented that Mike often quickly forgets verbally given instructions. They put this down to inattention, but an alternative hypothesis is a relative weakness in verbal short-term processing. On the other hand, his speed of visual information processing is relatively high, supporting his good Spatial ability.

On the three DAS achievement tests, Mike's obtained scores on Word Reading, Spelling, and Basic Number Skills are all significantly lower than the scores predicted from his GCA score (Word Reading and Spelling have predicted scores of 101; Basic Number Skills has a predicted score of 102). The difference of 22 points between Mike's observed and predicted scores on Word Reading is found in fewer than 5% of children.

So, what would appropriate intervention recommendations be for a boy like Mike? Previous research (e.g., Bryant, 1968) had suggested that poor auditory-visual integration was not a cause of poor reading acquisition. In spite of this, for many years, teachers of dyslexic children have actively advocated multisensory teaching methods. Teachers appear to have long held to the view that dyslexic children have difficulty integrating visual and verbal information. The reader will recall that it is hypothesized that a relative weakness in this ability underlies the Low NVR profile found in the samples of dyslexic and LD children, reported earlier. Thus, it was recommended that a multisensory teaching method should be used with Mike. His poor auditory short-term memory should also be taken into account by (a) minimizing the length of verbal instructions; (b) using repetition where necessary; and (c) using his strengths with visual short-term memory to compensate for his relatively poor auditory short-term memory, perhaps by keeping a notebook of things to remember. Useful references to multisensory teaching approaches are given by Thomson and Watkins (1998), Augur and Briggs (1992), and Walker and Brooks (1993). The 40% of children in this study who were found to be reading disabled may well benefit from such an approach.

ADVANTAGES AND DISADVANTAGES

Use with Children with Developmental Disabilities

The clinical experience of the first author leads us to argue that the DAS is the test of choice for the intellectual assessment of children with developmental delays or mental retardation. One of the reasons for this assertion is the flexibility the DAS offers to tailor a battery of test activities to fit the child's developmental level. For example, the extended GCA norms allow the clinician to use the upper preschool level core subtests with children up to 13 years,

11 months. For school-age children with severe or profound mental retardation, this provides an invaluable alternative to the WISC-III. It permits a valid estimate of overall cognitive ability while using a set of test activities that are most appropriate for the child's developmental level. The upper preschool core subtests offer the clinician the chance to see children with severe disabilities working on activities in which they will experience a fair degree of success balanced with their failures. Similarly, it is a real advantage that the upper preschool subtests are fully normed through 7 years, enabling them to be used in assessing the vast majority of 6- and 7-year-olds likely to be referred for developmental delays. This allows these appealing and developmentally appropriate test activities to be used to obtain comprehensive, accurately normed assessment results with these children.

Another excellent feature for working with children with developmental difficulties is the provision of an alternative method of administration of the Pattern Construction subtest, using nontimed norms. Normative comparison can be made for children based only on their ability to complete the designs rather than their speed in doing so. For many children with milder forms of cerebral palsy, our experience is that they are capable of copying the patterns but somewhat awkward and slower in doing so. The nontimed norms allow a way of teasing out the problem-solving skills from the fine motor difficulties.

A critical feature for the clinician working with children with mental retardation is that the DAS is superior to other intellectual batteries in its ability to differentiate moderate, severe, and profound intellectual disabilities. As Table 3.9 shows, the DAS provides a lower floor in terms of overall test score than the WPPSI-R or Stanford-Binet across the entire preschool age range if the clinician uses the extended norms options available. For school-age children, the extended norms option allows for estimates of intellectual disability down to 5 standard deviations below the mean, to the border of the severe to profound intellectual disability range. The Stanford-Binet and WISC-III permit estimates down to only 4 standard deviations below the mean, or just

TABLE 3.9
Minimum Possible Composite Test Scores on the DAS, WPPSI-R,
and Stanford-Binet across Preschool Age Levels

Age Level → Test Score ↓	2–0	2–6	3–0	3–6	4–0	4–6	5–0	5–6	6–0
DAS GCA[1]	—	54	49	35	26	< 25	< 25	< 25	< 25
WPPSI-R Full Scale IQ	—	—	62	57	48	45	43	42	41
Stanford-Binet Test Composite[2]	80	76	65	60	50	45	42	37	36

[1] DAS and WPPSI-R scores are based on raw scores of zero for each subtest.
[2] Stanford-Binet minimum possible test composite score based on analyses of lowest possible score, assuming a raw score of 1 on at least one subtest.

to the border of the moderate to severe intellectually disabled range. Discussion of the low floor of the DAS may strike some like the scene in the movie *This Is Spinal Tap* where the band boasts about being the only group with "amplifiers that go up to 11"; however, there are definite real-world advantages. Being able to distinguish between moderate and severe mental retardation is of significant help in providing practical educational programming recommendations to maximize a student's learning potential. Also, many preschool services demand documentation of a developmental delay of at least 3 standard deviations below the mean, and for many age ranges in the preschool years the DAS is the only test that can do this.

While GCA and cluster scores boast low floor levels for preschoolers, Flanagan and Alfonso (1995) caution that several of the subtests have inadequate floors. They define a floor as inadequate if a raw score of 1 does not produce a standard score more than 2 standard deviations below the mean. By this definition, all four core subtests at the lower preschool level, which starts at 2 years, 6 months, have adequate floors for age 3 years, 3 months and older. Inadequate floors are shown by Block Building up to 3 years, 2 months; Picture Similarities up to 2 years, 11 months; and Naming Vocabulary up to 2 years, 8 months. Verbal Comprehension has an adequate floor at all ages. Flanagan and Alfonso point out that the low floor on the DAS for children from 2 years, 6 months to 3 years, 6 months would come from an assessment where the child had actually succeeded at doing very little. Given this, the Bayley Scales of Infant Development—Second Edition (Bayley, 1993) would likely be the better assessment tool for children in this age range with very significant delays, to obtain a more comprehensive assessment of their developmental skills.

The three new subtests added to make up the upper preschool level (Pattern Construction, Early Number Concepts, and Copying) have inadequate floors from 3 years, 6 months through 3 years, 11 months. However, in practice this is not a major problem; if a clinician were to find that a child below 4 years had raw scores of 0 or 1 on these three subtests, then Block Building should always be administered and the child assessed using the four core subtests, which have good floors at the lower preschool level for 3½- to 4-year-olds.

Use with School-Age Children

So far we have argued for the advantages of the DAS in the assessment of preschoolers and children with developmental disabilities. Clinicians often wonder, however, what would recommend the DAS over the WISC-III or Stanford-Binet for more typical school-age children. The correlation between the GCA and the Full Scale IQ of the WISC-III is .92 (Wechsler, 1991). Further, Dumont et. al. (1996) found with a sample of children with learning disabilities that the DAS GCA produced, for the vast majority of the children, the same intelligence level classification as that provided by the WISC-III 3 years earlier, when confidence intervals were taken into account. This evidence supports the notion that the DAS and WISC-III estimate overall cognitive ability equally well in school-age children. However, the DAS has two major advantages. First, it can provide this estimate in significantly less time than the WISC-III. In our experience, it takes about 45 to 60 minutes to complete the six core school-age subtests on the DAS with a school-age child as compared to about 60 to 90 minutes to complete the 10 to 13 WISC-III subtests. The potential time saving can be very valuable to the clinician who is using the intellectual battery primarily to obtain a good estimate of overall cognitive ability but who also needs time to assess other important areas about the child, such as emotional functioning. The second major advantage for the DAS is the Nonverbal Reasoning composite. It was demonstrated earlier that this is a critical element in the assessment of school-age children with learning disabilities. The NVR element is absent from the WISC-III and all other test batteries except the Woocock-Johnson—Revised (WJ-R), in which it can be argued that both the Gf and Gv factors are measured less effectively than in the DAS.

Limited Sampling of Verbal Skills

For some assessment situations, a disadvantage of the DAS is that it provides a more limited sampling of expressive language than most other assessment batteries. At the preschool level, the child only has to speak to provide single-word answers to the Naming Vocabulary subtest and to count out loud the number of squares on Early Number Concepts. Especially with 3-year-olds and up, it is vital for the clinician to get some idea of how well the children can express themselves in phrases and sentences to complete a thorough developmental assessment. In the first author's clinic, he often supplements the DAS with the Verbal Reasoning subtests from the Stanford-Binet Fourth Edition. In many settings, if the clinician suspects that the child has a specific language disorder, further in-depth language assessment by a speech and language pathologist would be appropriate.

The school-age battery is somewhat better with the verbal core subtests requiring the child to give a verbal definition of a word and describe how three words are similar. Still, there is no equivalent of the WISC-III's Comprehension subtest, which often allows a sensitive clinician insight into a child's social skills and common sense knowledge. For most of us, our training as clinicians emphasizes that administering an intellectual assessment battery to a child is about more than just obtaining an estimate of overall cognitive ability; it is also a structured clinical interview with the potential for insight into the child's personality. The more limited opportunity for verbal expression on the DAS may detract from this purpose somewhat.

This more limited sampling of verbal content was quite deliberate (Elliott, 1997b), and, as we have previously discussed, it does offer advantages in the assessment of children with hearing impairments, oral-motor difficulties, or those who are from different cultures. However, this advantage does come with a price: a more limited developmental assessment of language for many other children.

Difficulties in Mastering Administration and Scoring

Many have commented (Aylward, 1992; Braden, 1992) that the DAS is a difficult test for the clinician to learn to administer and score. The use of item sets requires a mental shift for many examiners who have been indoctrinated to follow simple basal and ceiling rules. To complicate matters further, most tests require the examiner to keep in mind two possible situations for discontinuing the subtest, either at the decision point or if enough consecutive failures occur. A good example of this complexity comes on the Pattern Construction subtest with 4-year-olds. Novice DAS clinicians must learn the rules so that, for most 4-year-olds, they will administer items 1 to 7 to reach the decision point. There, they will stop if the child has failed to obtain the maximum time bonuses on more than two items. However, if the child is experiencing great difficulties, the clinician must also stop if the child has obtained four first trial failures on five consecutive items. So the clinician must simultaneously keep in mind two complicated stopping rules.

There is a definite reward for the clinician able to master these rules. Many of us have suffered along with the preschoolers struggling on the WPPSI-R's Block Design subtest. Its discontinuance requirement is that the child fail both trials of three consecutive items. This process, of needing to fail six times in a row, can often lead a child to feel quite discouraged and less eager to try anything else. The option to stop Pattern Construction on the DAS at item 7, while many 4-year-olds are still experiencing a good deal of success, is a real boon to rapport. In general, while the DAS stopping rules are more complex than other tests, once they are mastered, they typically result in more efficient administration and a more pleasant experience for the child.

Another issue with respect to the complexity of learning to score the DAS by hand is the double transformation of raw scores required to obtain a subtest T score. First, the raw score must be matched to the appropriate item set and converted to an ability score. Next, the ability score is then taken to the norms tables for transformation into a T score. We are all aware of the literature indicating the surprising number of clerical errors made in calculating test scores (Alfonso & Pratt, 1997). This double transformation may make the possibility of clerical error twice as likely in hand-scoring the DAS, and extra caution is required by the clinician to prevent these types of errors. Fortunately, the recent availability of scoring software for the DAS (Elliott, Dumont, Whelley, & Bradley, 1998) will no doubt help to alleviate the problem. With the software, the clinician just enters the subtest ability scores, with no further need to look up information in tables.

Comprehensiveness of the Achievement Battery

One disadvantage of the DAS achievement battery is the lack of a measure of reading comprehension. The Word Reading subtest looks at basic word recognition skills, but does not really assess the critical function of how well children are able to understand written information in the manner they are likely to encounter it in the real world. There is no compelling reason for the DAS to replicate the comprehensiveness of academic content coverage provided by the Wechsler Individual Achievement Test (WIAT; The Psychological Corporation, 1992), but the addition of a measure of reading comprehension would have been welcomed by many clinicians.

RECOMMENDATIONS

To be effective, assessment must be about more than generating a set of test scores. Assessment must lead to a better understanding of our clients and offer insight into how to solve the problems with which they present. As the following case study illustrates, the DAS can be very useful for the clinician who strives to determine a child's relative cognitive strengths and weaknesses and then to translate this profile into an effective treatment plan.

The Case of Jean-Guy: Background Information

Jean-Guy is a 6-year-old boy with Williams Syndrome seen for a review psychological assessment at the request of his school. On three earlier assessments, when he was 14, 23, and 38 months old respectively, the Bayley Scales of Infant Development—Second Edition had been used. Each time, Jean-Guy had shown a very significant delay in his overall cognitive development with his composite score on the Bayley each time falling below the minimum of 50. Thus, while the results suggested that Jean-Guy had an overall intellectual disability (or mental retardation), it was not possible to determine from the Bayley results whether his intellectual disability was in the moderate or severe range.

Jean-Guy was now in his second year of kindergarten. His work with a speech and language pathologist had led to many gains in his expressive language skills. His parents were quite heartened by these gains, and had asked his teachers when they expected that Jean-Guy might catch up to the other children. His teachers referred Jean-Guy to the school psychologist to try to determine his long-term prognosis and learning needs. The school psychologist attempted unsuccessfully to assess Jean-Guy using the WISC-III. Jean-Guy found the WISC items extremely difficult, and after a few attempts at the first three subtests began to refuse to try. The school psychologist felt that the results suggested that Jean-Guy had a very significant intellectual disability, but his parents found it hard to believe that opinion, since they felt that Jean-Guy had been bored by the WISC items and had not shown what he was truly capable of doing. The school psychologist suggested a referral to a clinic specializing in children with intellectual disabilities.

Tests Used

The clinic psychologist elected to assess Jean-Guy's cognitive abilities with the DAS. She chose to work with him using the upper preschool level subtests, since she felt that the preschool activities would give Jean-Guy a better balance of success and failure than the School Age Battery.

Along with the DAS, the clinic psychologist administered the Vineland Adaptive Behavior Scales (Sparrow, Balla, & Cicchetti, 1984) by interviewing Jean-Guy's parents. The Vineland is a structured interview that gathers information on adaptive behavior skills in areas such as communication, self-help, and social skills.

Assessment Results and Interpretation

Jean-Guy was very cooperative with trying all of the DAS preschool subtests. He was able to stay focused on his work and genuinely seemed to be enjoying himself. His parents observed the DAS being administered and commented when it was over that they felt this time that Jean-Guy had been able to show both what he was good at and what was difficult for him.

Table 3.10 shows Jean-Guy's scores on the DAS and the Vineland. Jean-Guy's GCA score of 51 suggested that he was currently functioning in the moderate range of mental retardation. However, there was a very significant difference between his Verbal cluster score (70) and his Nonverbal cluster score (43). This pattern of relative strengths with verbal reasoning accompanied by very significant difficulty with visual or nonverbal problem solving is seen frequently in children with Williams Syndrome (Jarrold, Baddely, & Hewes, 1998).

Jean-Guy's performance on the Naming Vocabulary subtest was significantly higher than his average overall subtest performance. He was able to name many of the pictures shown to him. However, on the pictures that he did not name, Jean-Guy tended to echo back the psychologist's prompt rather than making an attempt or saying that he didn't know the answer. Jean-Guy had much more difficulty with the Verbal Comprehension subtest. His T score of 24 was significantly below his Naming Vocabulary score, and was very similar to his performance on the Nonverbal subtests. Jean-Guy had been able to follow directions when they involved picking out the right toy in a group, but he began making mistakes as soon as the verbal directions involved two steps or positional concepts such as "on" or "under." Similarly, his

TABLE 3.10
Assessment Results for Jean-Guy

DAS	
Subtest	T score (mean = 50, SD = 10)
Verbal Comprehension	24
Picture Similarities	20
Naming Vocabulary	40
Pattern Construction	20
Early Number Concepts	20
Copying	20
Composite score (mean = 100, SD = 15)	
Verbal Cluster	70
Nonverbal Cluster	43
General Conceptual Ability (GCA)	51
GCA (Extended norms)	44
Vineland Adaptive Behavior Scales: Interview Edition	
Domain	Standard score (mean = 100, SD = 15)
Communication	53
Daily Living Skills	46
Socialization	57
Adaptive Behavior Composite	48

low performance on the Early Number Concepts subtest seemed primarily due to his difficulty understanding all of what he was being asked to do from the verbal instructions.

The clinic psychologist wondered if Jean-Guy's Verbal cluster score (70) might be underestimating his degree of difficulty with expressive and receptive language skills. The Verbal cluster score is pulled up by Jean-Guy's strong performance on Naming Vocabulary, which involves only providing a one-word answer to name a picture. Some children with Williams Syndrome can initially seem quite verbally adept, with good vocabularies. However, on careful listening to their speech, it is sometimes noted that their conversations tend to be quite superficial and feature stereotyped phrases. This is sometimes referred to as "cocktail party speech" (Udwin & Yule, 1990). Indeed, Jean-Guy's score on the communication section of the Vineland suggested that he was showing a very significant deficit in his practical communication skills. Information from the Vineland indicated that Jean-Guy had difficulty with describing events that had happened to him as well as with asking questions to seek out more information from another person. The Verbal cluster score did not seem sensitive to the full degree of difficulty Jean-Guy was experiencing. However, the relatively lower scores on Verbal Comprehension and Early Number Concepts had served to "red-flag" the problem. It should be noted that because Jean-Guy's scores on the two verbal subtests were significantly different, the Verbal cluster score should be interpreted with caution, if at all.

There were no differences between Jean-Guy's T scores on the Nonverbal cluster subtests. He was unable to copy even a straight line on the Copying subtest, and his only success on Pattern Construction seemed almost by accident. While his T score on Picture Similarities was also very low, Jean-Guy was able to successfully match a number of the items. He also obviously enjoyed the task and seemed happy to persist even when the items became difficult.

Since four of the six subtests had T scores of 20, the minimum possible T score, the clinic psychologist elected to use the extended norms option. Elliott (1990c) recommends this when several T scores are at floor level, in order to provide a more accurate estimate of the degree of cognitive delay. The GCA score from the extended norms option was 44. While somewhat lower than Jean-Guy's original GCA, the extended norms option did provide evidence that Jean-Guy's intellectual disability was in the moderate instead of the severe range. This was consistent with the adaptive behavior data from the Vineland.

Recommendations from the Assessment

The first goal of this assessment was to provide Jean-Guy's parents and teachers with information about his prognosis. His parents had been encouraged by their hard-won gains with his expressive language. They had been reluctant to see his developmental problems as a permanent disability, as suggested by the school psychologist, because they did not feel his assessment was valid. From their point of view, Jean-Guy had simply not participated enough with the WISC-III subtests for them to believe that the psychologist could conclude something so major from the data. However, Jean-Guy did participate and focus more on the DAS upper preschool subtests. He experienced a number of successes along with his failures. His parents agreed, before hearing the test results, that they felt he had given a good showing of what he was capable of doing. They were still grief-stricken when the diagnosis of moderate mental retardation was discussed, but a major source of their resistance to the news was removed. Effective assessment and treatment planning for children with mental retardation involves much more than merely a test of cognitive ability. It requires a weaving together of information from multiple sources to form a comprehensive picture of the child's strengths and needs (see Gordon, Saklofske, & Hildebrand [1998] for more information). However, the DAS results were an important step in helping Jean-Guy's family better appreciate the degree of his disability and begin to work together with his teachers on a more effective treatment plan. Three key practical recommendations came out of the assessment.

- Jean-Guy's educational program should focus on practical or functional skills. The best environment for the development of Jean-Guy's social skills was his neighborhood school with age-level peers. However, simply having him work with the same academic content at a much slower pace than the other children seemed a plan doomed to much frustration. Instead, an ecological inventory was completed with Jean-Guy's parents and teachers to identify and prioritize the practical skills he needed to increase his independence. Wolery and Wilbers (1994) provide excellent practical resources on how to design an inclusive functional program for children with mental retardation.
- It was recommended that Jean-Guy continue to receive services from the school speech and language pathologist. While his Verbal cluster score was a relative strength, the assessment revealed a number of quite significant difficulties with Jean-Guy's receptive and expressive language skills. The focus of the next phase of Jean-Guy's treatment was to build the gains he had made with expressive vocabulary into better conversation skills as well as to increase his ability to understand verbal directions. Concurrently, Jean-Guy's teachers were encouraged to keep their verbal directions short in length and also to consider pairing them with visual prompts and cues (e.g., gesturing to what they wanted Jean-Guy to pick up, along with telling him).
- Jean-Guy showed very significant difficulties with visual-spatial activities, like many children with Williams Syndrome. An occupational therapist was invited to join the team. She recommended placing an emphasis on functional fine-motor activities such as dressing skills. She suggested adaptations such as Velcro fasteners for Jean-Guy's shoes, to compensate for his extreme difficulties in learning to tie laces. She also encouraged patience with academic content such as printing and letter recognition skills, explaining that both drew on visual-spatial skills where Jean-Guy showed his greatest weakness. She recommended using an inked stamp with Jean-Guy's name on it in order to allow him to "print" his name with the other children.

INSIGHTS FROM EXPERIENCE

From our clinical work, we are convinced that the DAS is a very welcome and indeed necessary addition to the roster of tests currently available to assess cognitive abilities in children. Its strong psychometric characteristics, including its overlapping preschool and school-age batteries, the range of skills measured by the DAS clusters and subtests, and its high cluster and subtest specificity, allow the clinician to feel confident that one is obtaining a valid estimate of the client's cognitive abilities. The DAS offers unique advantages to the clinician in the assessment of a number of special populations frequently encountered in our work. We have argued in this chapter that the DAS is the test of choice in working with children with intellectual disabilities. Moreover, the DAS offers unique insights into the assessment of learning disabilities. Finally, the user-friendliness of the DAS preschool subtests offers major advantages to the clinician working with younger children.

References

Alfonso, V. C., & Pratt, S. I. (1997). Issues and suggestions for training professionals in assessing intelligence. In D. P. Flanagan, J. L. Genshaft, & P. L. Harrison (Eds.), *Contemporary intellectual assessment: Theories, tests, and issues* (pp. 326–344). New York: Guilford.

Anastasi, A., & Urbina, S. (1997). *Psychological testing* (7th ed., pp. 226–232). Upper Saddle River, NJ: Prentice Hall.

Augur, J., & Briggs, S. (Eds.). (1992). *The Hickey multisensory language course* (2nd ed.). London: Whurr.

Aylward, G. P. (1992). Review of the Differential Ability Scales. In J. J. Kramer & J. C. Conoley (Eds.), *Eleventh Mental Measurements Yearbook* (pp. 281–282). Lincoln, NE: Buros Institute of Mental Measurements.

Bayley, N. (1993). *Bayley Scales of Infant Development—Second Edition*. San Antonio, TX: The Psychological Corporation.

Braden, J. P. (1992). The Differential Ability Scales and special education. *Journal of Psychoeducational Assessment, 10,* 92–98.

British Psychological Society (1999). *Dyslexia, literacy and psychological assessment. Report by a working party of the Division of Educational and Child Psychology.* Leicester, England: British Psychological Society.

Bryant, P. E (1968). Comments on the design of developmental studies of cross-modal matching and cross-modal transfer. *Cortex, 4,* 127–137.

Carroll, J. B. (1993). *Human cognitive abilities: A survey of factor analytic studies.* New York: Cambridge Univ. Press.

Carroll, J. B. (1997). The three-stratum theory of cognitive abilities. In D. P. Flanagan, J. L. Genshaft, & P. L. Harrison (Eds.), *Contemporary intellectual assessment: Theories, tests, and issues* (pp. 122–130). New York: Guilford.

Cattell, R. B. (1971). *Abilities: Their structure, growth and action.* Boston: Houghton-Mifflin.

Das, J. P., Kirby, J. R., & Jarman, R. F. (1979). *Simultaneous and successive cognitive processes.* New York: Academic Press.

Dumont, R., Cruse, C. L., Price, L., & Whelley, P. (1996). The relationship between the Differential Ability Scales (DAS) and the Wechsler Intelligence Scale for Children—Third Edition (WISC-III) for students with learning disabilities. *Psychology in the Schools, 33,* 203–209.

Elliott, C. D. (1990a). *Differential Ability Scales.* San Antonio, TX: The Psychological Corporation

Elliott, C. D. (1990b). The nature and structure of children's abilities: Evidence from the Differential Ability Scales. *Journal of Psychoeducational Assessment, 8,* 376–390.

Elliott, C. D. (1990c). *Differential Ability Scales: Introductory and technical handbook.* San Antonio, TX: The Psychological Corporation.

Elliott, C. D. (1997a). *British Ability Scales—Second Edition*. Windsor, England: NFER-NELSON.

Elliott, C. D. (1997b). The Differential Ability Scales. In D. P. Flanagan, J. L. Genshaft, & P. L. Harrison (Eds.), *Contemporary intellectual assessment: Theories, tests, and issues* (pp. 183–208). New York: Guilford.

Elliott, C. D., Dumont, R., Whelley, P., & Bradley, J. (1998). *Scoring assistant for the Differential Ability Scales*. San Antonio, TX: The Psychological Corporation.

Elliott, C. D., Murray, D. J., & Pearson, L. S. (1979). *British Ability Scales*. Windsor, England: National Foundation for Educational Research.

Flanagan, D. P., & Alfonso, V. C. (1995). A critical review of the technical characteristics of new and recently revised intelligence tests for children. *Journal of Psychoeducational Assessment*, 13, 66–90.

Glutting, J. J., McDermott, P. A., Konold, T. R., Snelbaker, A. J., & Watkins, M. W. (1998). More ups and downs of subtest analysis: Criterion validity of the DAS with an unselected cohort. *School Psychology Review*, 27, 599–612.

Glutting, J. J., McDermott, P. A., Watkins, M. W., Kush, J. C., & Konold, T. R. (1997). The base rate problem and its consequences for interpreting children's ability profiles. *School Psychology Review*, 26, 176–188.

Gordon, B., Saklofske, D. H., & Hildebrand, D. K. (1998). Assessing children with mental retardation. In H. B. Vance (Ed.), *Psychological assessment of children* (2nd ed., pp. 454–481). New York: Wiley. Holland, A. M., & McDermott, P. A. (1996). Discovering core profile types in the school-age standardization sample of the Differential Ability Scales. *Journal of Psychoeducational Assessment*, 14, 131–146.

Horn, J. L. (1985). Remodeling old models of intelligence: Gf-Gc theory. In B. B. Wolman (Ed.), *Handbook of intelligence* (pp. 267–300). New York: Wiley.

Horn, J. L., & Cattell, R. B. (1966). Refinement and test of the theory of fluid and crystallized intelligence. *Journal of Educational Psychology*, 57, 253–270.

Horn, J. L., & Noll, J. (1997). Human cognitive capabilities. In D. P. Flanagan, J. L. Genshaft, & P. L. Harrison (Eds.), *Contemporary intellectual assessment: Theories, tests, and issues* (pp. 53–91). New York: Guilford.

Jarrold, C., Baddeley, A. D., & Hewes, A. K. (1998). Verbal and nonverbal abilities in the Williams Syndrome phenotype: Evidence for diverging developmental trajectories. *Journal of Child Psychology, Psychiatry, & Allied Disciplines*, 39, 511–523.

Kamphaus, R. W. (1993). *Clinical assessment of children's intelligence*. Boston: Allyn & Bacon.

Kaufman, A. S. (1994). *Intelligent Testing with the WISC-III*. New York: Wiley.

Keith, T. Z. (1990). Confirmatory and hierarchical confirmatory analysis of the Differential Ability Scales. *Journal of Psychoeducational Assessment*, 8, 391–405.

Keith, T. Z., Quirk, K. I., Schartzer, C., & Elliott, C. D. (1999). Construct bias in the Differential Ability Scales? Confirmatory and hierarchical factor structure across three ethnic groups. *Journal of Psychoeducational Assessment*, 17, 249–268.

Kercher, A. C., & Sandoval, J. (1991). Reading disability and the Differential Ability Scales. *Journal of School Psychology*, 29, 293–307.

McCarthy, R. A., & Warrington, E. K. (1990). *Cognitive neuropsychology: An introduction*. San Diego, CA: Academic Press.

McDermott, P. A., Fantuzzo, J. W., & Glutting, J. J. (1990). Just say no to subtest analysis: A critique of Wechsler theory and practice. *Journal of Psychoeducational Assessment*, 8, 290–302.

McDermott, P. A., & Glutting. J. J. (1997). Informing stylistic learning behavior, disposition, and achievement through ability subtests—Or, more illusions of meaning? *School Psychology Review*, 26, 163–175.

McGrew, K. S., & Murphy, S. (1995). Uniqueness and general factor characteristics of the Woodcock-Johnson Tests of Cognitive Ability—Revised. *Journal of School Psychology*, 33, 235–245.

McIntosh, D. E. (1999). Identifying at-risk preschoolers: The discriminant validity of the Differential Ability Scales. *Psychology in the Schools*, 36, 1–10.

McIntosh, D. E., & Gridley, B. E. (1993). Differential Ability Scales: Profiles of learning-disabled subtypes. *Psychology in the Schools, 30,* 11–24.

The Psychological Corporation. (1992). *Wechsler Individual Achievement Test.* San Antonio, TX: Author.

Reynolds, C. R. (1990). Conceptual and technical problems in learning disability diagnoses. In C. R. Reynolds & R. W. Kamphaus (Eds.), *Handbook of psychological and educational assessment of children: Intelligence and achievement* (pp. 571–592). New York: Guilford.

Rourke, B. P., Del Dotto, J. E., Rourke, S. B., & Casey, J. E. (1990). Nonverbal learning disabilities: The syndrome and a case study. *Journal of School Psychology, 28,* 361–385.

Sattler, J. M. (1992). *Assessment of children* (3rd ed., rev.). San Diego, CA: Author.

Shapiro, S. K., Buckhalt, J. A., & Herod, L. A. (1995). Evaluation of learning disabled students with the Differential Ability Scales (DAS). *Journal of School Psychology, 33,* 247–263.

Snow, C. E., Burns, M. S., & Griffin, P. (Eds.). (1998). *Preventing reading difficulties in young children.* Washington, DC: National Academy Press.

Sparrow, S. S., Balla, D. A., & Cicchetti, D. A. (1984). *Vineland Adaptive Behavior Scales.* Circle Pines, MN: American Guidance Service.

Spearman, C. (1923). *The nature of "intelligence" and the principles of cognition.* London: Macmillan.

Spearman, C. (1927). *The abilities of man.* London: Macmillan.

Stanovich, K. (1988). Explaining the differences between the dyslexic and the garden-variety poor reader: The phonological-core variable-difference model. *Journal of Learning Disabilities, 21,* 590–612.

Terman, L. M., & Merrill, M. A. (1960). *Stanford-Binet Intelligence Scale.* Boston: Houghton Mifflin.

Thomson, M. E., & Watkins, E. J. (1998). *Dyslexia: A teaching handbook* (2nd ed.). London: Whurr.

Thorndike, R. L., Hagen, E. P., & Sattler, J. M. (1986). *Technical manual for the Stanford-Binet Intelligence Scale, Fourth Edition.* Chicago: Riverside.

Thurstone, L. L. (1938). *Primary mental abilities.* Chicago: University of Chicago Press.

Udwin, O., & Yule, W. (1990). Expressive language in children with Williams Syndrome. *American Journal of Medical Genetics, S6,* 108–114.

Walker, J., & Brooks, L. (1993) *Dyslexia Institute literacy programme.* London: James and James.

Wechsler, D. (1974). *Wechsler Intelligence Scale for Children—Revised.* San Antonio, TX: The Psychological Corporation.

Wechsler, D. (1989). *Wechsler Preschool and Primary Scale of Intelligence Scale—Revised.* San Antonio, TX: The Psychological Corporation.

Wechsler, D. (1991). *Wechsler Intelligence Scale for Children—Third Edition.* San Antonio, TX: The Psychological Corporation.

Wolery, M., & Wilbers, J. S. (1994). *Including children with special needs in early childhood programs.* Washington, DC: National Association for the Education of Young Children.

Woodcock, R. W., & Johnson, M. B. (1989). *Woodcock-Johnson Psycho-Educational Battery—Revised.* Chicago: Riverside.

CHAPTER

4

Brief Cognitive Assessment of Children: Review of Instruments and Recommendations for Best Practice

REX B. KLINE

Concordia University, Montreal

SCOPE

The literature about brief cognitive assessment is very large, and it is not possible in a single chapter to comprehensively consider all aspects of this area. This chapter deals mainly with issues about and specific tests for the group probably seen most often by psychologists for brief intelligence testing: school-age children about 5–16 years of age. Considered first are various contexts for brief cognitive testing in school or clinic settings. Desirable characteristics and limitations of brief cognitive tests are discussed next, followed by reviews of some individually administered tests for brief intelligence testing. The occasionally overlooked, but often valuable, role of parent-informant data in screening for child cognitive dysfunction is also addressed. After review of the aforementioned issues and measures, general

Communication about this work can be directed to Dr. Rex B. Kline, Department of Psychology (PY 151-6), 7141 Sherbrooke St. West, Montreal, Quebec, H4B 1R6, Canada; or *rbkline@vax2 .concordia.ca*; or via *http://www-psychology.concordia.ca./department/faculty/rexbkline.html*.

recommendations for the best practice of brief cognitive assessment are offered. This chapter concludes with note of issues pertinent to this topic but
that cannot here be covered in great detail. These issues include the evaluation of children who are members of minority groups or who do not speak English as a first language.

INTRODUCTION

The time required to administer a full-battery, individually administered cognitive ability test such as those discussed in this book—for example, the
Wechsler Intelligence Scale for Children—Third Edition (WISC-III; Wechsler,
1991), the Differential Ability Scales (DAS; Elliot, 1990), the Cognitive Assessment System (CAS; Das & Naglieri, 1997), and the Woodcock-Johnson—
III (WJ III; Woodcock, McGrew, & Mather, 2001)—can be significant. Although
it is often possible to test younger children (e.g., <8 years old) in about
an hour or so, older children may require two or more hours of testing time.
While various interpretive software programs are available for some full-
battery tests, the time required to initially score the results and enter raw test
scores and then edit a computer-generated report is still quite substantial.[1]

Although there are instances when there is really no substitute for a full-
battery evaluation (more about this point, later), psychologists who work in
school or clinic settings often get more requests for testing than they can
manage within a reasonable time frame. For instance, school psychologists
often receive numerous referrals at the very end of the school year. Pediatric
psychologists who consult on medical units in hospitals are sometimes
asked just before the discharge date to test a child inpatient and make a report. The use of brief cognitive assessment tests is one way to help reduce the
length of a waiting list for testing or to determine priorities for a more extensive evaluation. By "brief" it is meant that the administration time is about
30 minutes or less. For very young children, the time saved by using a brief
cognitive measure may be relatively little compared to use of a full-battery
test, but the absolute time economy for older children will typically be more
substantial.

[1] Most of the newer intelligence tests are accompanied by supportive software that minimally
calculates standard scores and that may provide some tables and figures. Programs such as the
WISC-III and WAIS-III Writer are intended to support report writing by generating interpretive
statements about test results but also enabling the psychologist to enter other important information about the client (e.g., behavior, family, language). Readers who routinely give full-battery
WISC-IIIs can consult Kline (1998b) for a review of the Kaufman WISC-III Integrated Interpretive
System (K-WIIS; Kaufman, Kaufman, Doughterty, & Tuttle, 1996). This computer program accepts as input background information, examiner observations about child test behavior, and
WISC-III standard scores, and then produces the text of a whole report. Although this program
has limitations that are discussed in Kline (1998b), it nevertheless can significantly reduce the
time needed to produce a report.

Considered next are some common contexts for which the use of brief measures of intelligence may be potentially valuable.

CONTEXTS FOR BRIEF COGNITIVE TESTING

In general, there are three contexts in which the use of brief cognitive ability tests may be especially pragmatic. The first is in mandatory reevaluations of children in public schools who are receiving special education services. That is, provincial, state, or federal guidelines about the definition or funding of specific special education categories may require reevaluations of students who receive such services at regular intervals, say, every 2 or 3 years (e.g., U.S. Department of Education, 1992). For children administered a full-battery intelligence test at their previous assessment, there may be little point in re-administering the whole battery, especially if it is clear, based on grades, teacher reports, or achievement test scores, that the child is not ready to be placed solely in a regular classroom. For such situations, the advice given by Ross-Reynolds (1990) seems very sensible: The time spent giving and scoring a full-battery test in reevaluations may be better spent by using a brief intelligence measure. The time saved can then be devoted to evaluation of the effectiveness of the child's special education program.

A second context for the use of brief intelligence tests is when children are referred for other types of assessments but when it is nevertheless important to screen for overall cognitive status. That is, sometimes referral questions mainly concern issues about personality characteristics or general psychological adjustment. These types of referrals are probably more common in clinic than in school settings, but there are times when examiners decide it is important to use a brief intelligence test even if the referral question did not specifically mention cognitive status. For example, in one instance the author was asked to assess a 5-year-old girl seen in a hospital-based child guidance clinic about her appropriateness for psychotherapy, specifically play therapy. The child was referred by a social worker who was seeing the child's low-income family to help them deal with recent multiple stressors. After interviewing the child, it seemed apparent to the author that her language skills and overall vocabulary breadth were very limited for her age. It is important to note that this child spoke English as a first (and only) language. Screening for cognitive status is much more difficult with multilingual children; see the discussion at the end of this chapter. The child was administered the Slossen Intelligence Test (SIT; Slossen, 1982), a brief measure of verbal skills described later in this chapter. The child's overall SIT IQ score was less than 70, which fell below the 1st percentile for her age. This result helped to quantify the author's impression of limited verbal facility, which was also of concern for the planning of psychotherapy with this child.

Another potential application of brief cognitive ability tests is in the screening of relatively large numbers of children. For example, some school districts offer so-called "developmental kindergartens" that offer preschool experience for at-risk children. These children may be referred to such programs by general medical practitioners, pediatricians, or social workers. Referred children may shows signs of developmental delay. The purpose of a special pre-kindergarten program is to prepare at-risk children for later entry into regular classrooms or to determine the need for special services. The availability of quickly administered tests of general cognitive status would facilitate planning within these kinds of programs.

A final context for brief intelligence tests was mentioned earlier: when a psychologist has a waiting list of referrals for cognitive assessment. Use of brief intelligence tests may help psychologists have initial contact with more children and set priorities for later, more extensive testing. For example, referred children who are floundering in regular classrooms and who obtain very low scores on a cognitive screening test may have higher priority for follow-up testing than children with more normal-range scores. Also, ability/achievement discrepancies suggestive of a learning disability or other significant difficulties signal the need for a prompt and comprehensive assessment. Discussed later in the chapter is the incorporation of parent-informant data in screening for the need for special education services. Parent-informant data may also be helpful in the context of brief intelligence testing described above, the evaluation of large numbers of children.

However time-economical brief intelligence tests may be, there are at least two situations when their use is inappropriate. The first is for the formal diagnosis of mental retardation. Diagnostic criteria for mental retardation, such as those outlined in the fourth edition of the *Diagnostic and Statistical Manual* (DSM-IV; American Psychiatric Association, 1994), typically involve IQ-score cutoffs, such as a requirement that the child's overall IQ score is less than 70. (The other DSM-IV criterion for a diagnosis of retardation is impairment of adaptive behavior skills; see Sattler, 1988, and Kamphaus, 1993, for reviews of measures for adaptive behavior assessment.) There are profound implications for a diagnosis of retardation, some of which are potentially beneficial, such as eligibility for special education services for cognitively impaired children. Other implications, though, such as labeling effects or stigma associated with this disorder, may not be so benevolent. Obviously, in such instances one needs the most accurate estimate of overall cognitive status possible. For reasons discussed later, brief intelligence tests are simply not precise enough for this purpose; only a full-battery, individually administered measure will suffice. (See Spruill, 1998, for discussion about the use of the WISC-III and other IQ tests in the assessment of mental retardation.)

A second context in which brief intelligence tests are inadequate is when test results may influence determination of the eligibility of referred children for special education services. This is especially true when eligibility for learning disability services is considered. Provincial, state, or federal definitions of a learning disability are often based on discrepancies between IQ and achievement scores—either absolute discrepancies or regression-based ones (e.g., Frankenberger & Fronzaglio, 1991; Gridley & Roid, 1998)—and it is thus crucial to accurately measure both domains, that of overall cognitive ability as well as that of specific scholastic achievement. Brief measures of intelligence are again inadequate for a placement decision with important implications for a child's educational career.

ESSENTIAL CHARACTERISTICS OF A BRIEF COGNITIVE ABILITY TEST

Necessary attributes of a brief intelligence test, as outlined in this section, are a combination of basic requirements from measurement theory and specific requirements for the assessment of cognitive status. Properties of the first type include all the attributes necessary for any kind of psychological test, including reliability, validity, a normative sample that is large and representative, and accuracy and clarity of test manuals (e.g., see *Standards for educational and psychological testing*; American Psychological Association, 1985). The requirement for reliability—which generally involves the consistency, stability, and precision of test scores—is critical, due to the inherent brevity of screening tests. In general, reliability is affected by characteristics of both the sample and the test. Specifically, the reliabilities of test scores are generally lower in samples with limited amounts of individual differences (i.e., range restriction) or when they are derived from tests that have relatively few items, are subjectively scored without clear criteria, are made up of items that vary a great deal in content, or measure phenomena very susceptible to rapid temporal variation, such as current mood states (Nunnally & Bernstein, 1994).

An obvious way to make a test more reliable is to make it longer. The *Spearman-Brown prophecy formula* estimates the effect of changing the length of a test (e.g., see Nunnally & Bernstein, 1994, pp. 262–264). Suppose that the reliability coefficient for a 10-item measure is only .50, an inadequate value for a useful test. (Recommendations for evaluating whether a test's reliability is satisfactory will be discussed momentarily.) If the test's length were to be tripled to 30 items, then the predicted reliability of the longer version generated by the Spearman-Brown prophecy formula is .75. This still is not exceptionally high, but it is better than the original value, .50.[2] Note that this prophecy formula generates only an estimate; the actual reliability of a test

---

[2] The Spearman-Brown prophecy formula is $r_{xx\,est} = (k\,r_{xx\,est})/(1 + (k - 1)\,r_{xx})$, where r_{xx} is the reliability of the original test, k is the factor by which its length is changed, and $r_{xx\,est}$ is the estimated (prophesied) reliability of the length-altered test. For the example in text, $r_{xx} = .50$, $k = 3$, and $r_{xx\,est} = 3(.50)/(1 + (3 - 1).50) = .75$.

with new items must still be evaluated. Also, the Spearman-Brown formula assumes that the psychometric properties of new items are comparable to those already in the test. Adding poor items to a test can actually reduce its reliability.

It is the general rule that longer tests are more reliable than shorter ones that, in large part, accounts for the superior reliability of full-battery intelligence tests over their brief counterparts. Thus, one crucial consideration in the selection of a brief cognitive ability test is its reliability. Specifically, if the reliability of a brief test is too low, then the administration time it saves may not be worth the cost in terms of low stability of its scores. Now, what is an acceptable level of reliability? Although there is no "gold standard" for reliability, some general guidelines can be offered. Reliability coefficients greater than .90 can be considered "good" and can be used as a minimal standard when test scores affect important decisions about individuals, such as ones discussed earlier about special education eligibility. Reliabilities of IQ or summary scores from modern, well-constructed, full-battery IQ tests are typically .90 or greater (e.g., Kamphaus, 1993; Sattler, 1988). Only some brief intelligence tests (described later) have reliabilities so high. Lower reliabilities, such as values about .70–.80, may be adequate either in earlier stages of test construction and validation or for research concerned mainly with the comparison of groups, such as when the study of group mean differences is of main interest. Reliabilities much lower than .70 are probably inadequate for just about any purpose, much less for individual assessment.

Scores from a brief intelligence test should also be valid, which, broadly speaking, concerns their interpretation. Perhaps the most critical aspect of validity in the realm of brief cognitive testing is the concurrent validity of scores from brief cognitive tests against those derived from full-battery IQ tests, such as Full Scale IQ scores from the WISC-III. Not only should IQ scores from brief tests be highly correlated with full-battery IQ scores—correlations that exceed .80 could be viewed as acceptable—but the absolute levels of scores should be comparable, too. For example, a child who obtains a WISC-III Full Scale IQ score of 90 should ideally obtain a similar score on a brief intelligence test. Note that a high correlation between two sets of scores indicates only similar rank orders, *not* whether their absolute levels are comparable. For example, suppose that we have a set of IQ scores for a group of children. Let us add 20 points to each child's score and then correlate the original scores with the "enhanced" ones (i.e., the ones with 20 points added). Because the rank order of the two sets of scores is identical, the correlation between them is 1.00 even though (a) the mean scores differ by 20 points and (b) no individual child has scores across the two sets (original and "enhanced") within 20 points of the each other.

Test reliability affects the interpretation of a score as an indicator of the level of some construct. That is, scores from tests with less-than-perfect reliability (which describes all applied tests) should be viewed as a "guess" around which some band of error exists. The notion of confidence intervals constructed around observed test scores directly expresses this view (see Nunnally & Bernstein, 1994, pp. 258–260). For example, psychologists often report IQ scores with associated confidence intervals as a way to communicate a degree of uncertainty (unreliability) about the scores; the use of 95% confidence intervals, in particular, seems common (e.g., Kaufman, 1994), although interval sizes from 68 to 99% are also used. For example, a child's Full Scale IQ of 110 from the WISC-III may be presented in a test report along with the confidence interval 103–118, which says that a more reasonable estimate of the child's "true" IQ score is the range 103–118 instead of the specific score of 110.

As the reliability of a test goes down, the size of confidence intervals around its observed scores gets ever wider, which conveys increasing error. For IQ scores from full-battery intelligence tests with good reliabilities, the sizes of 95% confidence intervals are about a full standard deviation, which is about ±7 points for scores reported in a metric where the mean is 100 and the standard deviation is 15. For example, the confidence interval 103–118 for a WISC-III Full Scale IQ says that a child's "true" IQ score could reasonably vary within a whole standard deviation, 15 points. Of course, a confidence interval of any size does not guarantee that a child's "true" IQ score falls within that range; in fact, it may not. For this example, the child's "true" IQ score could be, say, 120, which falls outside the interval 103–118. Although such an outcome is statistically unlikely, it can still happen, which is a good reason why the upper and lower bounds of a confidence interval should not be seen as absolute limits.

It is suggested later in this chapter that scores from even the best brief intelligence tests should be seen as reasonably varying within a range of *at least* 10 points on either side of the obtained score. (Again, this is for standard scores where the standard deviation is 15.) This general recommendation seems to suit one of the most psychometrically sound measures described later, the Kaufman Brief Intelligence Test (K-BIT; Kaufman & Kaufman, 1990). Tests not as reliable as the K-BIT will have even greater bands of error around their scores. Greater error is the main reason why brief intelligence tests (even the K-BIT) are not suitable for classification or diagnostic testing of individual children.

Other requirements for brief intelligence tests concern norms derived from a test's standardization sample. Specifically, (1) the norms should be relatively modern and (2) based on a standardization sample that is representative in terms of relevant stratification variables such as gender, race/ethnicity, geographic region, socioeconomic status, and, for children's tests, regular versus special education status. The necessity for a modern set of norms—say, no older than 20 years—is due to a phenomenon sometimes called the "Flynn effect" after J. R. Flynn (1994), who reported that average IQ scores (in a metric where the standard deviation is 15) tend to increase by about 3–4 points (and sometimes more, depending upon the country) every 10 years. These increases may reflect genuine improvements in crystallized knowledge and/or abstract problem-solving ability in the general population. Such gains could be due to factors like improved educational opportunities, wider or easier access to information (e.g., the Internet), or more widespread experience dealing with abstract stimuli (e.g., through the use of computers). Whatever the sources of the improvements, norms from cognitive ability tests tend to go out of date. For example, suppose that in 1960 the average IQ score in the general population on some test was 100. By the year 2000, the average IQ score on the same test using its 1960 norms may be about 110, due to the Flynn effect. If this same test were re-normed with a contemporary standardization sample, average IQ scores would drop back to about 100. Thus, IQ scores based on older norms may not be directly comparable with IQ scores based on more modern norms; specifically, the former scores tend to be too high, due to the Flynn effect.

There is another problem with the norms of older tests. Standardization samples of older tests tend not to be representative in terms of race/ethnicity. For instance, members of minority groups were not specifically represented in the standardization sample of the Stanford-Binet Intelligence Scale until the 1970s (Thorndike, 1973). This situation violated what is today considered a basic tenet of responsible test use: The interpretation of standard scores is limited to the reference group on which they are based, and the use of a test with groups not represented in its normative sample is problematic. In contrast, the standardization samples of contemporary cognitive ability tests are typically stratified to match multiple aspects of the general population according to current census data. The availability of Canadian norms for the WISC-III (Wechsler, 1996) is an example of this principle.

A final requirement concerns breadth of test content. Ideally, a brief intelligence test should tap more than a single cognitive domain. However, some tests widely used by psychologists as brief ability measures have only one kind of item content. Some of these single-domain tests (among others described later) include the Peabody Picture Vocabulary Test—III (PPVT-III; Dunn & Dunn, 1997), which assesses receptive vocabulary through pictures of familiar objects, and the Raven's Progressive Matrices (RPM; Raven, Court, & Raven, 1986), which taps nonverbal reasoning through pictures of geometric patterns. Although some single-domain measures have psychometric properties comparable to those of brief intelligence tests with more than one kind of item content (e.g., the K-BIT), it is probably better not to place all of one's measurement eggs in a single content basket. Considerations and cautions in the use of single-domain tests as brief intelligence tests are discussed later.

LIMITATIONS OF ALL BRIEF INTELLIGENCE TESTS

The two main limitations of brief intelligence tests were noted in the previous section: Brief tests tend not to be as reliable as or provide information about as many ability areas as full-battery tests. Both limitations are probably features of the inevitable trade-off between saving time and getting comprehensive information. Both can also be handled by using brief measures for the screening purposes for which they are intended and *never* using them for classification or diagnosis, points also discussed earlier.

There is another objection to brief intelligence tests, but this one may have relatively little merit, at least in one regard. The objection is that unlike full-battery scales with their dozen or so subtests, brief intelligence tests do not yield a cognitive ability profile that can be interpreted with scatter analysis. A profile is a graphical summary constructed by drawing lines that connect subtest scores on a record form of a full-battery test, such as the one for many Wechsler scales. Scatter analysis is the interpretation of "peaks and valleys" in a cognitive ability profile. In this approach, relatively high scores are taken to indicate cognitive strengths; by the same token, relatively low scores are believed to show relative cognitive weaknesses. The description of specific cognitive strengths or weaknesses is typically based on rational analyses. For instance, if a child has a relatively low score on the Picture Arrangement subtest of a Wechsler scale, then hypotheses about poor social reasoning skills might be entertained in a scatter analysis. These hypotheses are not based on empirical results; instead, they are ones that seem plausible given the item content of the Picture Arrangement subtest, and must then be "tested" to determine their utility in describing the child's needs and effecting "positive" changes.

Although the practice of scatter analysis of subtest scores dates back to the first intelligence tests, there is actually little empirical evidence that supports the practice. For instance, scores on the Picture Arrangement subtest of the Wechsler scales do not seem to covary with social reasoning skills (see, e.g., Kamphaus, 1998; Lipsitz, Dworkin, & Erlenmeyer-Kimling, 1993). There is similar dearth of evidence for many other subtest-based interpretations (see, e.g., Kline, Snyder, & Castellanos, 1996; McDermott, Fantuzzo, Glutting, Watkins, & Baggaley, 1992). The evidence for the validity of interpretations based on more broad-band, summary scores is much more substantial. For example, differences between Verbal and Performance IQs of Wechsler scales are associated with specific patterns of achievement and psychological adjustment among children with learning disabilities (see, e.g., Rourke, 1998). The inability to interpret a profile of subtest scores on a brief intelligence test may not be such a hindrance after all.

TYPES AND DESCRIPTIONS OF
BRIEF INTELLIGENCE TESTS

Three categories of brief cognitive measures and specific examples from each are described in this section. The first category includes tests constructed specifically as brief intelligence tests. Tests described from this category include the K-BIT (Kaufman & Kaufman, 1990) and the Slossen Intelligence Test—Revised (SIT-R; Slossen, 1991). Three other, recently published brief tests are also described: the Wide Range Intelligence Test (WRIT; Glutting, Adams, & Sheslow, 1999) and the Slossen Intelligence Test—Primary (SIT-P; Erford, Vitali, & Slossen, 1999), and the Wechsler Abbreviated Scale of Intelligence (WASI; Wechsler, 1999).

The second category of brief intelligence measures represents short forms of full-battery IQ tests. Short forms of full-battery tests are usually made up of two or more subtests selected from the whole battery of about a dozen or more subtests. This method of creating a brief intelligence measure may be the most common one in applied settings. It is also a topic for which the literature is quite large. There are some distinct advantages and disadvantages associated with this method, both of which are discussed later along with recommendations for using short forms.

The third category includes single-domain tests used by some practitioners for brief cognitive assessment. Tests of this type include the PPVT-III (Dunn & Dunn, 1997), the RPM (Raven et al., 1986), and the Matrix Analogies Test (MAT; Naglieri, 1985), among others. Some potential limitations of single-domain tests as brief intelligence measures were described earlier. These limitations are reiterated later, when specific single-domain tests are considered.

Tests Specifically Constructed as Brief Intelligence Measures

Kaufman Brief Intelligence Test (K-BIT)

The K-BIT by Kaufman and Kaufman (1990) is a brief measure of cognitive status that can be administered in about 15–30 minutes. Its relatively large normative sample (N = 2022), stratified by gender, geographic region, socioeconomic status, and race/ethnicity according to 1990 census data for the United States, spans ages 4–90 years. Standardization sample age groups from 4–10 years of age each have about 100 cases, age groups from 10 to 20 years may have fewer subjects for each year, and older subjects were combined into much broader age groups (ages 20–34 years, N = 200; 34–54 years, N = 150; and ages 55–90 years, N = 100). Although the test spans a wide age range, it seems that the norms are more adequate for persons younger than 20 years old than for older individuals. For school-age children, though, the K-BIT's norms seem acceptable.

The K-BIT has two subtests, Vocabulary and Matrices, both of which are presented to subjects via an easel placed on the table that shows associated pictorial stimuli. Two tasks, Expressive Vocabulary (45 items) and Definitions (37 items), make up the Vocabulary subtest. Expressive Vocabulary items are given to subjects of all ages and require naming of pictured objects. The

Definitions part of the Vocabulary subtest requires subjects aged 8 years or older to guess a word that fits two clues, one a partial spelling of the word and the other an oral description of the word. The Definitions task is the only one on the K-BIT to have a maximum time limit (30 minutes). The clue-based format of this task is similar to the Riddles subtest of the Kaufman Assessment Battery for Children (K-ABC; Kaufman & Kaufman, 1983) and to the Definitions subtest of the Kaufman Adolescent and Adult Intelligence Test (KAIT; Kaufman & Kaufman, 1993). All items are dichotomously scored (1/0) according to criteria listed in the K-BIT manual. The number of correct items on the Expressive Vocabulary and Definitions tasks are summed to form the overall score for the K-BIT Vocabulary subtest. Altogether, the K-BIT Vocabulary subtest may measure vocabulary breadth, verbal knowledge through pictures, and word definitions, all of which could also be described as crystallized intelligence.

The second K-BIT subtest, Matrices, is administered to all subjects. This subtest has 48 dichotomously scored items and uses a multiple-choice format. Examinees are required either to select one of five choices that best goes with a stimulus picture or one of six to eight choices that solves a pattern in a 2×2 or 3×3 matrix. Early items involve pictures of familiar objects, but stimuli for later items become more abstract. The latter format is very similar to ones used in other matrix reasoning–type tasks, such as the RPM test. Note that the Matrices subtest of the K-BIT does not require a spoken response, as examinees can simply point to their choice. All task stimuli are also pictorial, so there is no manipulation of objects by examinees. The Matrices subtest may measure visual-spatial reasoning or the ability to solve visual analogies, both of which may also reflect fluid intelligence more than crystallized intelligence.

Raw scores on K-BIT Vocabulary and Matrices subtests are converted to standard scores with a mean of 100 and a standard deviation of 15. The two subtest scores are also combined to form the K-BIT Composite, which is the test's overall estimate of cognitive ability. Standard K-BIT Composite scores have the same mean and standard deviation as for the Vocabulary and Matrices subtests.

Reliabilities of K-BIT subtest and composite scores are generally good. For example, the average split-half reliability for ages 4–19 years for the Vocabulary subtest is .91 (range = .89–.93), for the Matrices subtest it is .85 (range = .74–.92), and for the K-BIT Composite it is .92 (range = .88–.95; these values are somewhat higher for adults aged 20–90 years. Average test-retest reliabilities for a sample of 232 subjects aged 5–89 years evaluated over intervals of 12–145 days (mean = 21 days) were also generally high (Vocabulary, .94; Matrices, .85; Composite, .94).

A test's reliability coefficients are used to estimate values of the standard error of measurement, which in turn influence the size of confidence intervals around examinees' scores. Although values of the standard error of

measurement for the K-BIT Composite vary by age, a conservative overall figure would be 5. Multiplying this value by 2 yields a value that approximates
the width of a 95% confidence interval. That is, the interval 10 points (i.e.,
20 points wide) around a K-BIT Composite standard score reflects the anticipated amount of error at a confidence level often used by psychologists. This
derivation is also one of the reasons why it was suggested earlier that scores
from even reliable brief intelligence tests, like the K-BIT, should be seen as
having a band of uncertainty of about 10 points on either side.

The K-BIT manual (Kaufman & Kaufman, 1990) also provides tables for
the comparison of Vocabulary and Matrices standard scores for the same
child. These tables are (1) based on information about standard errors of
measurement for each subtest, and (2) indicate absolute magnitudes of
differences between Vocabulary and Matrices scores required for statistical significance at the .05 and .01 levels. However, K-BIT examiners are advised to use these tables with caution in the interpretation of "significant"
Vocabulary-Matrices score differences. Here's why: First, experience with full-
battery IQ tests suggests that statistically significant differences in scale
scores, even at the .01 level, are very common in the general population (i.e.,
the base rate is high). For instance, a WISC-III Verbal-Performance IQ discrepancy of 11 points is statistically significant at the .05 level, but between
25–50% of cases in the test's normative sample obtain a discrepancy this
large or even greater (Kaufman, 1994; Sattler, 1992); these base rates are even
higher for some minority groups (e.g., Prifitera, Weiss, & Saklofske, 1998).
Finding a statistically significant scale score difference does not imply that it
is rare or atypical. Second, results of K-BIT research summarized below suggest that differences between Vocabulary and Matrices subtest scores do not
generally relate to external criteria. Finally, the K-BIT manual itself cautions
against overinterpretation of Vocabulary-Matrices differences.

Results of about 20 studies described in the test's manual indicate that
correlations between K-BIT Composite scores and IQ scores from full-
battery intelligence tests, such as the Wechsler Intelligence Scale for Children—Revised (WISC-R) and the Wechsler Adult Intelligence Scale—Revised (WAIS-R), are about .60–.80 (Kaufman & Kaufman, 1990). These results
are generally consistent with those reported in subsequent published studies about the K-BIT, including ones conducted with nonreferred Kindergarten
or Grade 1 students (Lassiter & Bardos, 1995), referred children and adolescents (Prewett, 1992b, Prewett & McCaffery, 1993; Slate, Graham, & Bower,
1996), and adjudicated delinquents (Hayes, 1999; Prewett, 1992a).

Several other studies with the K-BIT concerned differences between
scores on its Vocabulary and Matrices subtests as predictors of external criteria. For example, within a sample of referred adults, Naugle, Chelune,
and Tucker (1993) found high correlations between K-BIT and WAIS-R scale
scores (rs of about .70–.90). Correlations between difference scores across
the two tests (K-BIT Vocabulary-Matrices, WAIS-R Verbal-Performance), how-

ever, were much lower (*r*s of about .20–.60). Magnitudes of correlations reported by Canivez (1996) for learning disabled children for similar sets of difference scores from the K-BIT and the WISC-III are comparable.[3] Within a large sample of psychiatric inpatients, Klinge and Dorsey (1993) found that K-BIT Vocabulary-Matrices differences were unrelated to level of reading skill.

Findings that differences between K-BIT Vocabulary and Matrices scores may have limited external validity are not surprising. Because difference scores reflect the measurement errors of both of their constituent scores, their reliability may not be high, which in turn limits the absolute magnitudes of the correlations of difference scores with other variables (Nunnally & Bernstein, 1994). This is a general problem of difference scores, whether they are from the K-BIT or any other test. There is also some evidence that the K-BIT Vocabulary-Matrices distinction does not correspond directly to the Verbal-Performance distinction of Wechsler scales. For example, Burton, Naugle, and Schuster (1995) conducted confirmatory analyses (Kline, 1998a) of theoretical models of the factor structure of the K-BIT and WAIS-R within a sample of referred adults. The best-fitting model was one with two separate (albeit correlated) verbal factors, one defined by Verbal scale subtests of the WAIS-R and the other consisting of the Expressive Vocabulary and Definitions tasks of the K-BIT. Differences in item format across the verbal tasks of the two batteries may in part account for this finding. That is, K-BIT verbal items can typically be answered with a single word. In contrast, some items from the Verbal scales of Wechsler tests, such as those from the Comprehension task, require longer, more elaborate responses. Another format difference concerns the K-BIT Matrices subtest, which requires no essential motor involvement, and Wechsler Performance scale subtests that require the manipulation of materials, such as the Block Design task. For all the reasons cited here, (1) the K-BIT Vocabulary-Matrices model should not be viewed as a "mini" or proxy Wechsler Verbal-Performance model, and (2) most of the interpretive efforts for the K-BIT should concern its Composite score.

With the exception of criticism about the limited sizes of normative samples for individuals older than 20 years of age, reviews of the K-BIT have generally been positive (Miller, 1995; Parker, 1993; Young, 1995). Overall, the K-BIT seems to offer sound psychometric characteristics for a screening test that can typically be administered in under 30 minutes. That the K-BIT taps both verbal and visual-spatial abilities (i.e., it is not a single-domain test) is also a plus. Used within the limits of the "±10 rule" for scores from brief intelligence tests, discussed earlier, the K-BIT can be recommended.

---

[3] The study by Canivez (1996) is a good example of how to study differences in classifications based on a full-battery IQ test and on a brief measure. Specifically, Canivez used the sensitivity-specificity-predictive values, which provides detailed information about correct classification rates of a screening measure classification given estimates of the base rates of some diagnostic entity (e.g., Glaros & Kline, 1988).

Slossen Intelligence Test—Revised (SIT-R)

The original version of the SIT (Slossen, 1963) was a brief intelligence test for ages 6 months to 27 years. SIT items were grouped by age, and the test's total score yielded a ratio IQ. For school-age children or adolescents, the SIT was essentially a single-domain measure of crystallized verbal intelligence because all its item were verbal. The second edition of the SIT (Slossen, 1982) was little changed except for an expanded normative sample. The next major version is the revised 1991 edition (SIT-R; Slossen, 1991) for ages 4 years and older. Although the SIT-R yields a deviation IQ in the form of its Total Standard Score (TSS) and its normative sample is reasonably large (N = 1854), minority groups are underrepresented in the latter. Also, SIT-R items are still primarily verbal and tap mainly language-oriented crystallized intelligence.

Evidence for the reliability and validity of the SIT-R seems generally satisfactory. For instance, internal consistency and test-retest reliabilities reported in the SIT-R manual are all about .80–.90 (Slossen, 1991). Also reported in the manual are correlations between the TSS of the SIT-R and scale scores from full-battery IQ tests; again, these values are typically .70–.90 (Slossen, 1991).

Although reviewers of the 1991 SIT-R generally note improvements over earlier editions, they also mention some important limitations of the SIT-R. Because scores on the SIT-R depend a great deal on English-language fluency, the SIT-R may be inappropriate for use with children who do not speak English as a first language or for screening situations when it is also important to assess nonverbal abilities (Kamphaus, 1995). Watson (1995) noted that analyses summarized in the SIT-R's manual that purport to demonstrate an absence of test bias may not be technically correct. Both Kamphaus and Watson also criticized the SIT-R manual for not doing more to prevent users from over- or misinterpreting the test's summary score, the TSS.

To summarize, the SIT-R has a relatively long history but has not generally kept pace with modern methods and standards of test construction. The recent publication of 1998 norms (N = 1800, ages 4–65 years) based more directly on current United States census data represents another in a series of incremental improvements in the test (Slossen, 1998), but it seems difficult to recommend the SIT-R over a psychometrically superior screening measure such as the K-BIT or others described below. The main drawback of the SIT-R is that it is basically a single-domain test of crystallized verbal intelligence, which also limits the usefulness of the test with children who are not fluent in English. The only way to get data about other ability areas would be to supplement use of the SIT-R with other measures, which offsets the advantage of its short administration time.

New Tests for Brief Intelligence Testing

Several new tests for brief cognitive assessment were published very recently. Consequently, it was not possible for the author to carefully review the technical merits of these tests; readers should consider the descriptions presented here as more informational than critical. The SIT-P (Erford et al., 1999) is for children ages 2–8 years and requires about 10–30 minutes to administer. Unlike the SIT-R, the SIT-P has verbal and performance items. Included among the latter are a symbol search–type task, a paper-and-pencil drawing task, and a block design–type task. The SIT-P yields three standard scores, Verbal, Performance, and a composite Total Standard Score; all three scores have a mean of 100 and a standard deviation of 15. The specific estimation of visual-spatial skills distinguishes the SIT-P from the SIT-R and makes the SIT-P more similar to the K-BIT in this sense. Unlike the K-BIT, the SIT-P has tasks that require the manipulation of objects, such as paper and pencil or blocks, which may convey useful informational about fine-motor coordination. The absence of norms for children older than 8 years may limit the usefulness of the SIT-P in school settings, though.

The WRIT (Glutting et al., 1999) is another new brief cognitive ability measure for persons 4–80 years of age that requires about 20–30 minutes to administer. The WRIT's standardization sample is relatively large (N = 2285) and the test was co-normed with the Wide Range Achievement Test—3 (WRAT-3; Wilkinson, 1993). Four subtests (Vocabulary, Verbal Analogies, Matrices, and Diamonds) yield scores that contribute to three standard scale scores, a Verbal-Crystallized IQ (the first two subtests), a Visual-Fluid IQ (the last two subtests), and a General IQ for the whole test. Part of the Diamonds subtest requires the manipulation of objects, so both the WRIT and the SIT-P (but not the K-BIT) have a motor component. Also, the wide age range of the WRIT (4–80 years) relative to the much narrower one of the SIT-P (2–8 years) may favor use of the WRIT in school settings.

Of these two new measures, the WRIT seems to be more adequate as a screening measure than the SIT-P. Both are probably better than the SIT-R, and the WRIT seems psychometrically comparable to the K-BIT, at least based on the author's initial impressions. Both the SIT-P and WRIT need more critical review before well-founded recommendations about their use can be made.

The WASI (Wechsler, 1999) was developed in the tradition of the Wechsler scales. The test was carefully standardized on a representative American sample (N = 2245) and may be used with individuals in the 6–89 age range. The test includes four familiar subtests: Vocabulary, Similarities, Block Design, and Matrix Reasoning, which may be combined to yield Verbal, Performance, and Full Scale (2- and 4-subtest) IQ scores. The psychometric properties are most impressive, with average reliabilities for the FSIQ-4 of .96 for children and .98 for adults; stability coefficients are .93 and .92, respectively. FSIQ-2 and FSIQ-4 correlations with other Wechsler scales such as the WISC-III (.82, .87, respectively) and WAIS-III (.82, .92) are reported, and they have been replicated in independent studies (Saklofske, Caravan, & Schwartz, 2000). Clinical validity data are also presented in the manual. A significant advantage of the WASI is the links to other Wechsler scales thereby providing some greater robustness to the use of this test as either a screening instrument, preceding the administration of the longer Wechsler scales, or for purposes of quick and efficient retesting and follow-up.

Short Forms of Full-Battery IQ Tests

The literature about the development of short forms from full-battery, individually administered IQ tests has a long history and is quite large. In fact, there are numerous citations about this topic for literally every major full-battery IQ test, including the 1911 Binet-Simon (e.g., Doll, 1917), the 1939 Wechsler-Bellevue, Form I (e.g., Robin, 1943), the 1955 WAIS and 1981 WAIS-R, (e.g., Jones, 1962; Kaufman, Ishikuma, & Kaufman-Packer, 1991), the 1974 WISC-R (e.g., Silverstein, 1982), and all contemporary tests for children and adults (e.g., WAIS-III, Ryan & Ward, 1999; WISC-III, Campbell, 1998; Fourth Edition Stanford-Binet, Volker, Guarnaccia, & Scardapane, 1999; K-ABC, Kaufman & Applegate, 1988). Indeed, the manuals of some full-battery intelligence tests include information about short forms. For instance, the manual for the Fourth Edition Stanford-Binet (Thorndike, Hagen, & Sattler, 1986) presents a "quick" four-subtest short form (Vocabulary, Pattern Analysis, Quantitative, Bead Memory) and an "abbreviated" six-subtest short form that adds the Memory for Sentences and the Memory for Digits subtests to the four of the "quick" form.

There are clear practical advantages to short forms of full-battery tests: Not only are many examiners already familiar with the full-battery version, the psychometric characteristics of the subtests are known (i.e., they are summarized in the test's manual). There are two major ways to construct a short form of a full-battery IQ test: (1) select a relatively smaller number of subtests from the whole battery and administer them in their original form, or (2) administer a "split" version of either the whole test or a subset of its tasks. An example of the former is Silverstein's two-subtest short form of the WISC-R that includes the Vocabulary and Block Design subtests, each administered in its entirety and scored using the standard norms tables. A child's total standard score across these two subtests can be converted to an estimated IQ score. An example of a "split" short form is one by Satz and Mogel (1962) for the WAIS: Examiners administered the Digit Span and Digit Symbol subtests in their original form while giving only every third item on Information, Picture Completion, and Vocabulary and every second item on the rest of the subtests. Total raw scores on "split" subtests were then multiplied by a constant before the regular norms tables were used to generate standard scores. Hobby (1980) developed a similar split short form for the WISC-R, in which only the odd items of most subtests were administered.

Of the two methods for making short forms described above, the "split" method has generally fallen out of favor. Some reviewers of short forms, such as Kaufman (1990) and Silverstein (1990), doubted whether the norms for a full-version subtest applied when only half (or fewer) of its items were administered. For instance, eliminating items not only violates the standard administration of the subtest but also steepens the increase in difficulty across the remaining items due to the reduction in the number of easier ones. The latter condition may also reduce subjects' opportunities for practice with easier items before they encounter more difficult ones.

The tactic of making short forms of full-battery tests by administering a small number of subtests in their entirety (e.g., a dyad, triad, or tetrad of tasks) may be superior to the "split" method, but is also not without potential problems. For example, using the standard norms tables of a full-battery test when only a few subtests were administered assumes that are no context effects, which means the same scores would presumably be obtained if the whole battery were given. For instance, when the full battery is given, the subtests are given in a specific order, and if changing this order has an effect on subjects' scores, then there is a context effect (here due to order). Subjects' motivation levels may also be different if they know that the total testing time will be, say, two hours instead of only 20 minutes. There is indeed evidence for order effects for at least some Wechsler subtests (e.g., Thompson, Howard, & Anderson, 1986); there may very well be order effects for subtests of other IQ tests, too. Also, the reliability and relevance of subtest combinations can vary considerably. For example, the combination of Block Design and Vocabulary from the WISC-III is a much more powerful predictor of achievement than is the combination of Object Assembly and Coding. Another problem concerns how the concurrent validity of short form tests is evaluated. The most common practice is to give a full-battery IQ test and then correlate scores from the whole scale with those from short forms, such as the Vocabulary–Block Design dyad. Because scores from Vocabulary and Block Design contribute substantially to the Full Scale IQ, correlations between the short-form dyad and the full-battery IQ may be spuriously high (e.g., Kaufman, 1990; Silverstein, 1990).

There is no magical solution to the two problems just described—they seem to be inherent limitations of using a dyad, triad, etc., of subtests as a short form in lieu of the whole test. Perhaps the best way for examiners to deal with these issues is not to overinterpret scores from short forms of full-battery tests; that is, not to use short-form scores for diagnostic or classification purposes, and to view such scores as having wider bands of error around them than scores based on whole tests

A final problem is more a practical one, but it is not an easy one to solve: Which short form to use? For a specific test like one of the Wechsler scales, there may be numerous possible short forms. For an IQ test with 12 subtests, for example, there are 66 different two-subtest short forms, 220 possible three-subtest short forms, and 495 different four-subtest short forms of the whole test. (These values are the numbers of combinations of 12 objects taken two, three, or four at a time, respectively.) Allowing the inclusion of short forms with at least five subtests increases the total number of candidate short forms even more. There are, typically, numerous different short forms described in the literature for a given full-battery IQ test. In his review of selected short forms of the WAIS-R, for instance, Kaufman (1990) describes at least a dozen different dyad, triad, or tetrad short forms.

Some recommendations are offered to help readers sift through what can be a confusing array of choices about short forms of full-battery intelligence tests. First, one stream of work in the literature that seems to be abating is the search for the "best" short form for specific clinical groups, such as geriatric populations or psychiatric inpatients (Kaufman, 1990). Due to problems like the unreliability of some diagnostic labels used to form special groups and poor generalization of tests developed for specific groups to other clinical populations, it seems more fruitful to focus on making short forms that have good psychometrics and the potential for general application.

Second, a short form of a full-battery IQ test should be made up of at least two subtests, one that taps verbal abilities and another that measures visual-spatial skills. Perhaps the most widely used two-subtest short form of Wechsler scales has been the dyad of Vocabulary from the Verbal scale and Block Design from the Performance scale. Both of these subtests are "g-rich" (g refers to a general ability factor), in that they seem to measure complex reasoning and also tend to be the best predictors of overall IQ scores from their respective scales. Sattler (1992) reports that the estimated reliability of this dyad for the WISC-III is about .90 and that the estimated correlation with Full Scale IQ scores is about .80. Using tables presented in sources like Sattler (1992), it is also possible to convert the sum of two subtest scores into IQ-type summary scores with a mean of 100 and a standard deviation of 15. Although this dyad may arguably be the "best" two-subtest short form, administration times for the Vocabulary and Block Design subtests can be relatively long. The scoring of the Vocabulary subtest also requires the differentiation between 1-point and 2-point responses. Another dyad with psychometric properties almost as good as those for Vocabulary–Block Design but with simpler scoring (0/1) and quicker administration times is Information–Picture Completion. This dyad would not reflect verbal fluency as well as the Vocabulary–Block Design dyad (many Information items can be answered with one word), nor does it involve the manipulation of materials.

Of course, there are other two-subtest short forms of the WISC-III (and other Wechsler scales; e.g., see tables H-6 and L-12 of Sattler, 1992). In general, readers are advised to (1) use dyads with one Verbal scale subtest and one Performance scale subtest, (2) pick a single dyad as a "standard" battery for screening purposes, and (3) avoid using the Digit Span, Symbol Search, and Object Assembly subtests in dyads. Scores from the first two subtests are not used in the derivation of WISC-III IQ scores in the standard norms tables, and the last subtest has less adequate psychometric properties (Kaufman, 1994). Also, readers should (4) "see" a band of error of *at least* 10 points around IQ-type scores derived from two-subtest short forms and, as with any brief intelligence test method, should not use such scores for classification or diagnosis.

The next level of short forms for Wechsler tests with equal numbers of Verbal scale and Performance scale tasks are four-subtest short forms (tetrads). Of course, tetrads require greater administration time, but they provide more stable estimates of general cognitive level. Nevertheless, readers should "see" a band of error of *at least* 8 points on either side of a tetrad-based IQ-type score. A combination of the two dyads described above into a Vocabulary-Information–Picture Completion–Block Design short form yields scores that are quite reliable (> .90) and correlate highly (about .90) with Full Scale IQ scores (Sattler, 1992). Another widely used tetrad is Vocabulary-Arithmetic–Picture Arrangement–Block Design, but the inclusion of the Arithmetic task is not ideal because (1) it may be more of an achievement task than a reasoning task, and (2) it is affected by distractibility or attentional problems. Indeed, the Arithmetic subtest does not, in factor analyses, usually load on the same factor with other Verbal scale subtests (see, e.g., Kaufman, 1994). Selection from among other possible tetrads for Wechsler tests should follow the same general principles given above for dyads.

Also described in the literature for Wechsler scales are numerous short forms made up of five or more subtests, but administration times rise accordingly. Noteworthy among these shorter forms of the WISC-III is an eight-subtest form described by Prifitera et al. (1998; see also Weiss, Saklofske, Prifitera, Chen, & Hildebrand, 1999) that yields a composite score called the General Ability Index (GAI). The GAI is the sum of the four subtest scores that contribute to the WISC-III's Verbal Comprehension Index (VCI) and the four subtests that contribute to the Perceptual Organization Index (POI). Prifitera et al. note that the GAI may better estimate the general reasoning ability of children who obtain very low scores on WISC-III subtests especially susceptible to distractibility or learning problems, specifically the Arithmetic subtest (which contributes to the Verbal IQ but not to the VCI) and the Coding subtest (which contributes to the Performance IQ but not to the POI.)

Single-Domain Tests as Brief Intelligence Measures

There are numerous quick, single-domain tests that psychologists working in various settings have used as brief intelligence tests. Some of the most popular quick tests are discussed here, but their limitations as a group are outlined first. For the reasons discussed earlier, such as the inability to assess more than one kind of cognitive skill and outdated or nonrepresentative normative samples for some quick tests, the use a single-domain test as the sole instrument in brief cognitive testing is not the best practice. Using two single-domain tests, such as a verbal task and a visual-spatial one, is better than using just one, but there may be no straightforward way to combine scores from two different tests into a single summary score. This is especially true if the normative samples of two tests are not similar. Also, if a psychologist is going to administer two single-domain tests, then one may as well use brief tests like the K-BIT, WRIT, and WASI, which have two subtests each (two or four for the WASI), or a two-subtest short form of a full-battery IQ test. Either of these alternatives may at least yield meaningful composite scores. With these limitations in mind, individual single-domain measures are considered next.

Perhaps the single-domain test used most often as a brief measure of intelligence is the Peabody Picture Vocabulary Test (PPVT), now in its third edition (PPVT-III; Dunn & Dunn, 1997) and normed for persons 2½ to 90 years old. The test was first published in 1959 (Dunn, 1959) and was revised in 1981 (PPVT-R; Dunn & Dunn, 1981). Although the PPVT has certainly been much improved over time regarding its standardization, normative sample, and manuals, it has retained the same basic format as a multiple-choice test of receptive vocabulary. Briefly, the PPVT-III requires the child to choose the one picture from a group of four that best corresponds to a word spoken by the examiner. Because no verbal response is required from the child and only one correct picture is associated with each stimulus word, the PPVT-III taps a relatively narrow aspect of children's general vocabulary knowledge. For instance, the one word−one correct picture format of the PPVT-III does not allow observation of the child's ability to associate multiple meanings with a word or to choose appropriately among them. The PPVT-III's format also provides no information about the child's ability to combine words for meaningful communication, such as the conveyance of intentions to other people (Sattler, 1988).

As with its predecessors the PPVT and the PPVT-R, correlations between PPVT-III summary scores with IQs from full-battery cognitive ability tests are generally about .70−.90. Not surprisingly, correlations with Verbal IQ scores from the Wechsler scales are among the highest (Dunn & Dunn, 1997). The overall magnitudes of these correlations with full-battery IQ scores are about the same as for the K-BIT, WRIT, SIT-P, and short forms of full-battery tests, so the PPVT-III predicts IQ scores just as well as these other measures. The assessment of a relatively narrow range of ability (i.e., hearing vocabulary) is a drawback relative to tests like the K-BIT, WRIT, or SIT-P, though. To offset this limitation, the PPVT-III could be used in combination with one of tests described below.

Other single-domain tests include the RPM (Raven et al., 1986) and the MAT (Naglieri, 1985). As mentioned, the Matrices subtests of the K-BIT, WRIT, and WASI have essentially the same format as the RPM and MAT: multiple choice, where the child picks the best solution to a visual-geometric analogy. Figural reasoning tests with matrices, like the RPM and MAT, have a long history in the cognitive test literature, and their applications include the study of cultural differences (e.g., Raven & Summers, 1986) and generational changes in intelligence (e.g., Flynn, 1994), among others. Matrices tests have very good internal consistency and test-retest correlations, and do tend to correlate very highly with each other (e.g., Saklofske, Yackulic, Murray, & Naglieri, 1992). There is also abundant evidence that summary scores from tests like the RPM and MAT correlate with IQ scores from full-battery intelligence tests in the range of about .50–.80 (e.g., Kamphaus, 1993; Sattler, 1988).

Like the PPVT-III, the RPM and MAT predict overall IQ scores just about as well as brief tests like the K-BIT, WRIT, and SIT-P. Also, figural reasoning tests like the RPM and MAT provide useful information about abstract visual-spatial reasoning skills, especially for children with poor motor coordination or with a language or hearing deficit. The RPM in particular has a companion vocabulary test (Raven et al., 1986), which means that verbal ability can be assessed along with visual-spatial skills. This feature of the RPM offsets the potential limitation of assessing a single cognitive domain (i.e., visual-spatial). The MAT (or the RPM without its vocabulary test) could be used together with the PPVT-III, but there may be no straightforward way to combine scores based on different normative samples into a single composite score.

Paper-and-pencil drawing tests are a third major category of single-domain tasks considered here. These tests include the Bender Visual Motor Gestalt Test (or more simply, the Bender-Gestalt [B-G]; Bender, 1938) and the Developmental Test of Visual-Motor Integration (VMI; Beery, 1982), both of which require the child to draw copies of geometric figures of generally increasing complexity. Other tasks involve the drawing of a human figure. There are several variations here, including the Goodenough-Harris Drawing Test (Goodenough, 1926; Harris, 1963) and Draw-a-Person: A Quantitative System (Naglieri, 1988), among others. Drawing tasks are also included in some full-battery IQ tests, such as the Copying subtest of the Fourth Edition Stanford-Binet.

Scoring systems for all the drawing tasks mentioned above are based either on the number of errors in reproducing geometric figures, such as in the Koppitz (1975) system for the B-G, or on the number of details (eyes, ears, nose, etc.) included in human figure drawings.[4] In general, there is a wide-enough range of individual differences among children about 5–10 years of age to reasonably discriminate among them with drawing tasks. Scores on drawing tasks outside this age range are too uniform, either because the tasks are too hard for younger children or too easy for older ones. For example, the average number of errors on the B-G for children older than 12 years of age is about one or two. Drawing tasks like the B-G or VMI may be useful in the screening of adolescents or adults for brain damage because the tasks should be easy for these groups, but, in general, such tasks' usefulness with older children is limited.

[4]There are also systems to identify so-called "emotional indicators" in children's human figure or B-G drawings (e.g., Koppitz, 1975; Machover, 1949). However, there is essentially no evidence for the external validity of such "indicators," and readers are urged not to make personality interpretations of children's drawings.

The absolute values of correlations of drawing tasks scores with full-battery IQ scores are typically lower than for the PPVT-III or figural reasoning–type tasks, about .20–.60 (Kamphaus, 1993; Sattler, 1988, but see also Saklofske & Braun, 1992). The use of drawing tasks as brief intelligence measures is also limited by potential confounding explanations of low scores. For example, although low-functioning children tend to perform relatively poorly on drawing tasks, the same results can be caused by deficient fine-motor coordination in children of normal overall cognitive ability. For both of these reasons, use of a drawing task as the only brief intelligence measure is not satisfactory. It is much better to use drawing tasks together with other kinds of quick measures. This would be especially advantageous for screening measures that do not require the child to manipulate materials, such as the K-BIT.

There are other, less widely used single-domain tests used for cognitive screening reviewed in Kamphaus (1993) and Sattler (1988) as well as in the Buros Mental Measurement Yearbooks, but it is beyond the scope of this chapter to review them in detail. The next section concerns a type of information that is sometimes overlooked but that nevertheless can be very useful for brief intellectual testing of children.

PARENT-INFORMANT DATA
FOR COGNITIVE SCREENING

Federal law in the United States requires parental input when children are considered for special education placement (e.g., Federal Register, 1977). Although this demand can be met through relatively unstructured interviews, a more systematic way to gather parental observations (usually from mothers) is with an objective questionnaire. There are now several parent-informant questionnaires that are normed by child age and gender and provide information about child adjustment in several different domains. Examples of parent-informant measures include the Parent Rating Scale (PRS) of the Behavior Assessment System for Children (BASC; Reynolds & Kamphaus, 1992), the Child Behavior Checklist (CBCL; Achenbach, 1991), and the Conners' Parent Rating Scale—Revised (CPRS-R; Conners, 1997), among others.

Although each of the parent-informant measures listed above is psychometrically sound and supported by a wealth of empirical studies about its external validity, all of them are oriented much more toward the identification of emotional or behavioral problems than toward screening for cognitive or academic dysfunction. For instance, the CBCL and the PRS of the BASC have scales that assess adjustment problems like internalizing, externalizing, poor social skills, atypical behavior, or attentional problems, but they lack scales about child cognitive status. The CPRS-R does have a Cognitive Problems scale, but this type of scale is relatively rare among parent-informant inventories (e.g., Kline, 1994). Parent observations about child psychopathology can be invaluable when the goal is to screen for adjustment problems or when evaluations concern eligibility for classroom placements or services for emotionally impaired children. However, the general absence of scales about child cognitive status on parent-informant measures limits their usefulness for screening in this area. This is unfortunate, because the use of a parent-informant questionnaire can be very time economical. For example, parents can typically complete such questionnaires with little examiner supervision, and some parent questionnaires can be administered with a computer, which afterward can score the responses and generate a profile.

An exception to the general rule that parent-informant questionnaires provide little information about cognitive status is the Personality Inventory for Children (PIC; Lachar, 1992; Wirt, Lachar, Klinedinst, & Seat, 1984). In addition to scales that assess child emotional and behavioral problems, the PIC has three scales about child cognitive status, including Achievement, Intellectual Screening, and Development. There is ample evidence that parent ratings on these and other PIC scales have validity against external criteria about child intellectual and scholastic functioning. For example, correlations between scores on PIC cognitive scales and IQ scores from individually administered tests are about .50–70 (Kline, Lachar, & Sprague, 1985). The PIC also predicts the placement of children in regular or special education classrooms (Kline, Lachar, Gruber, & Boersma, 1994; Lachar, Kline, & Boersma, 1986). For example, Kline, Lachar, and Boersma (1993) developed within geographically heterogeneous samples of regular and special education students a series of classification rules based on PIC scales that may be useful in screening for cognitive or academic problems. Specifically, the decision rule

IF $(3 \times$ ACH $+$ IS $+ 4 \times$ DVL $+ 3 \times$ D $+ 2 \times$ FAM $+ 2 \times$ HPR $- 2 \times$ PSY$)$ ≥ 700
    Classify as SPECIAL EDUCATION
ELSE
    Classify as REGULAR EDUCATION,

where ACH, IS, DVL, D, FAM, HPR, and PSY refer to standard scores on (respectively) the Achievement, Intellectual Screening, Development, Depression, Family Relations, Hyperactivity, and Psychosis scales of the PIC, is about 90% accurate in the classification of regular and special education students. Although other decision rules presented by Kline et al. (1993) concern more specific discriminations among special education categories (e.g., emotionally impaired versus learning disabled or cognitively impaired), there is potential value in classification rules like the one presented above for more general screening.[5]

---

[5]The revised second edition of the PIC should be available about the time this work is published.

A parent-informant questionnaire with scales about child cognitive or scholastic status could be incorporated into a screening battery that also includes an individually administered brief intelligence test, without a great increase in examiner time. This type of approach also more closely approximates the ideal of multi-informant assessment of children, in this case a parent, who provides observations via an objective questionnaire; the examiner, who interacts directly with the child; and the test itself (considered the third "informant"), which provides a standardized and norm-based estimate.

Considered next is another important problem in brief intelligence testing.

ASSESSMENT OF MINORITY OR IMMIGRANT CHILDREN

Cognitive assessment of minority children requires special consideration. Even when minority children speak English as a first language, examiners who are not also members of the same minority group need to be aware of subtle differences in language use or subcultural traditions or attitudes that can affect the child's behavior in the testing situation and his or her resulting test scores. Some cultural minorities may view mental health professionals with less trust than others, for instance, or prefer to resolve problems in a family context instead of in individual counseling with an outsider. This challenge is not diminished for brief intelligence testing. Accordingly, psychologists should approach the cognitive screening of minority children with the same preparation as for more extensive cognitive evaluations. Selecting a modern test—one with a contemporary normative sample that includes minority groups and has good psychometric properties—certainly aids in this preparation. Readers can find more information about testing minority children in Jones (1988), Puente and Salazar (1998), and Sattler (1988).

The issues mentioned above are just as pressing in the evaluation of children who do not speak English as a first language, such as the children of immigrants or of groups that have long resided in North America but speak other languages (e.g., French Canadians in Quebec, Hispanic-American children in the United States). Although it is well beyond the scope of this section to deal with the many technical issues involved, there are very few cognitive ability tests in languages other than English that have appropriate normative samples. Such tests, if generally available, would also require examiners who are fluent in the same language. Also, non-English tests would be most useful in places like Quebec, where the majority language is French, but they would have less value in places where English is the main instructional language at school, such as the United States. As readers may know, direct translation of English-language tests to other languages is also very problematic. For example, vocabulary words in English may be, once translated, more or less common in other languages, which makes the item relatively more easy or difficult in the other language. The use of the original norms tables for translated tests may also be inappropriate.

When children who speak other first languages are tested in English, their scores on brief tests should not be viewed as estimates of their general intelligence. This is especially true for brief tests with predominantly verbal tasks, which may reflect more facility with English rather than verbal reasoning ability or general intelligence per se. Tests with language-based tasks, such as the K-BIT with its Vocabulary subtest or a Wechsler short form with a Verbal scale subtest, should not be avoided; indeed, scores on such tests may provide valuable information about the child's English language skills. Examiners should also not view nonverbal tests, such as the RPM, as somehow providing more "pure" estimates of general intelligence. Readers should remember that scores on nonverbal measures are often highly correlated with scores from verbal tasks. Also, children's performances on nonverbal tasks with relatively complicated instructions may also be affected by limited language skills. Thus, basically the same sets of brief tests can be used with children who do not speak English as a first language, but examiners need to exercise even more caution about test score interpretation.

SUMMARY: RECOMMENDATIONS
FOR BEST PRACTICE

This chapter reviewed issues about and specific instruments for brief intelligence testing of school-age children. Recommendations for best practice in this area are summarized as follows: Modern tests constructed specifically as brief cognitive measures that assess more than one type of ability are probably the best overall choice. The Kaufman Brief Intelligence Test (K-BIT) and Wechsler Abbreviated Scale of Intelligence (WASI) can be recommended with confidence; new tests like the Wide Range Intelligence Test (WRIT) and the Slossen Intelligence Test—Primary (SIT-P) require more study but seem promising. Because the older Slossen Intelligence Test—Revised (SIT-R) measures essentially just one domain (crystallized verbal intelligence) and is based on an obsolete model of test organization, it cannot be recommended as a brief intelligence measure.

A second-best, but still acceptable, choice is a short form of a full-battery IQ test. Short-form IQ tests typically consist of dyads or, at most, tetrads of subtests. Subtests selected for a short form should, as a set, measure more than one kind of ability; for instance, it would be reasonable to create dyads from Wechsler tests by pairing one subtest from the Verbal scale and one from the Performance scale. A two-or-more-subtest short form should also have good estimated reliability and correlation with IQ scores from the whole version of the test. It is also recommended that examiners select and use the same short form for all children, which at least standardizes this aspect of cognitive screening.

The use of single-domain tests, such as the Peabody Picture Vocabulary Test—III, the Matrix Analogies Test, or the Raven's Progressive Matrices, as brief intelligence measures is less optimal than the two alternative discussed above. Although these tests have adequate psychometric properties and correlate relatively highly with IQ scores from full-battery tests, the use of one type of item content limits the range of information about a child's cognitive skills, and these tests are, therefore, of less clinical value in differential diagnosis and program creation. These tests are best used in combinations that complement what each individual test measures, such as when a figural reasoning task is used with a verbal task.

Composite scores from any brief measure should *never* be used for purposes of classification, such as for the determination of eligibility for special education services or for the assignment of a specific diagnosis like mental retardation. It was suggested that an error band of at least ±10 points be "seen" around a composite score from a brief intelligence test. Only a full-battery cognitive ability test administered and interpreted by a skilled psychologist can provide more precise estimates or be used for classification or diagnostic purposes.

Examiners need to be especially cautious when testing children who are members of minority groups or who do not speak English as a first language. Especially for the latter group, it is strongly recommended that scores from brief cognitive measures generally *not* be interpreted as estimates of general intelligence. Instead, scores for such children are probably best seen as rough estimates of English language proficiency (for verbal tasks) or of visual-spatial ability (for nonverbal tasks), with some language component required for understanding task instructions.

With these recommendations in mind, it is hoped that the time saved by using brief intelligence tests can benefit both examiners and the children they serve.

References

Achenbach, T. M. (1991). *Manual for the Child Behavior Checklist/4-18 and 1991 Profile*. Burlington, VT: Univ. of Vermont Department of Psychiatry.

American Psychiatric Association. (1994). *Diagnostic and statistical manual of mental disorders* (4th ed.). Washington, DC: Author.

American Psychological Association. (1985). *Standards for educational and psychological testing*. Washington, DC: Author.

Beery, K. E. (1982). *Revised administration, scoring, and teaching manual for the Developmental Test of Visual-Motor Integration*. Cleveland, OH: Modern Curriculum Press.

Bender, L. (1938). A Visual Motor Gestalt Test and its clinical use. *American Orthopsychiatric Association Research Monograph*, No. 3.

Burton, D. B., Naugle, R. I., & Schuster, J. M. (1995). A structural equation analysis of the Kaufman Brief Intelligence Test and the Wechsler Adult Intelligence Scale—Revised. *Psychological Assessment, 7*, 538–540.

Campbell, J. W. (1998). Internal and external validity of seven Wechsler Intelligence Scale for Children—Third Edition short forms in a sample of psychiatric inpatients. *Psychological Assessment*, 10, 43.

Canivez, G. L. (1996). Validity and diagnostic efficiency of the Kaufman Brief Intelligence Test in reevaluating students with learning disability. *Journal of Psychoeducational Assessment*, 14, 4–19.

Conners, C. K. (1997). *Conners' Rating Scales—Revised technical manual*. North Tonawanda, NY: Multi-Health Systems.

Das, J. P., & Naglieri, J. A. (1997). *Das-Naglieri Cognitive Assessment System—standardization test battery*. Chicago: Riverside.

Doll, E. A. (1917). A brief Binet-Simon scale. *Psychology Clinic*, 11, 254–261.

Dunn, L. M. (1959). *Peabody Picture Vocabulary Test*. Circle Pines, MN: American Guidance Service.

Dunn, L. M., & Dunn, L. (1981). *Peabody Picture Vocabulary Test—Revised*. Circle Pines, MN: American Guidance Service.

Dunn, L. M., & Dunn, L. M. (1997). *Peabody Picture Vocabulary Test—III examiners manual*. Circle Pines, MN: American Guidance Service.

Elliot, C. D. (1990). *Differential Ability Scales: Introductory and technical handbook*. San Antonio, TX: The Psychological Corporation.

Erford, B. T., Vitali, G. J., & Slossen, S. W. (1999). *Slossen Intelligence Test—Primary manual*. East Aurora, NY: Slossen Educational Publications.

Federal Register. (1977, Aug. 23). *Regulations implementing Education for All Handicapped Children Act of 1975*, 42, 42474–42518.

Flynn, J. R. (1994). IQ gains over time. In R. J. Sternberg (Ed.), *Encyclopedia of human intelligence* (pp. 617–623). New York: Macmillan.

Frankenberger, W., & Fronzaglio, K. (1991). A review of states' criteria for identifying children with learning disabilities. *Journal of Learning Disabilities*, 24, 495–500.

Glaros, A. G., & Kline, R. B. (1988). Understanding the accuracy of tests with cutting scores: The sensitivity, specificity, and predictive value model. *Journal of Clinical Psychology*, 44, 1013–1023.

Glutting, J., Adams, W., & Sheslow, D. (1999). *Wide Range Intelligence Test administration manual*. Wilmington, DE: Wide Range.

Goodenough, F. L. (1926). *Measurement of children's intelligence by drawings*. New York: Harcourt Brace Janovich.

Gridley, B. E., & Roid, G. H. (1998). The use of the WISC-III with achievement tests. In A. Prifitera & D. Saklofske (Eds.), *WISC-III clinical use and interpretation* (pp. 249–288). New York: Academic Press.

Harris, D. B. (1963). *Children's drawings as measures of intellectual maturity: A revision and extension of the Goodenough Draw-a-Man Test*. New York: Harcourt, Brace, and World.

Hayes, S. C. (1999). Comparison of the Kaufman Brief Intelligence Test and the Matrix Analogies Test—Short Form in an adolescent forensic population. *Psychological Assessment*, 11, 98–101.

Hobby, K. L. (1980). *WISC-R split-half short form manual*. Los Angeles: Western Psychological Services.

Jones, R. L. (1962). Analytically developed forms of the WAIS. *Journal of Consulting Psychology*, 26, 289.

Jones, R. L. (Ed.). (1988). *Psychoeducational assessment of minority group children*. Berkeley, CA: Cobb & Henry.

Kamphaus, R. W. (1993). *Clinical assessment of children's intelligence*. Boston: Allyn & Bacon.

Kamphaus, R. W. (1995). Review of the Slossen Intelligence Test [1991 Edition]. In J. C. Conoley & J. C. Impara (Eds.), *Twelfth Mental Measurements Yearbook* (pp. 954–956). Lincoln, NE: Buros Institute of Mental Measurements.

Kamphaus, R. W. (1998). Intelligence tests interpretation: Acting in the evidence of evidence. In A. Prifitera & D. Saklofske (Eds.), *WISC-III clinical use and interpretation* (pp. 40–58). New York: Academic Press.

Kaufman, A. S. (1990). *Assessing adult and adolescent intelligence*. Boston: Allyn & Bacon.

Kaufman, A. S. (1994). *Intelligent testing with the WISC-III*. New York: Wiley.

Kaufman, A. S., & Applegate, B. (1988). Short forms of the K-ABC Mental Processing and Achievement scales at ages 4 to 12½ years for clinical and screening purposes. *Journal of Clinical Child Psychology*, 17, 359–369.

Kaufman, A. S., Ishikuma, T., & Kaufman-Packer, J. L. (1991). Amazingly short forms of the WAIS-R. *Journal of Psychoeducational Assessment*, 9, 4–15.

Kaufman, A. S., & Kaufman, N. L. (1983). K-ABC *administration and scoring manual*. Circle Pines, MN: American Guidance Service.

Kaufman, A. S., & Kaufman, N. L. (1990). *Manual for the Kaufman Brief Intelligence Test* (K-BIT). Circle Pines, MN: American Guidance Service.

Kaufman, A. S., & Kaufman, N. L. (1993). *Manual for the Kaufman Adolescent and Adult Intelligence Test* (KAIT). Circle Pines, MN: American Guidance Service.

Kaufman, A. S., Kaufman, N. L., Doughterty, E. H., & Tuttle, K. S. C. (1996). *Kaufman WISC-III Integrated Interpretive System* (K-WIIS). Odessa, FL: Psychological Assessment Resources.

Kline, R. B. (1994). New objective rating scales for child assessment, I. Parent- and teacher-informant inventories: The Behavior Assessment System for Children, the Child Behavior Checklist, and the Teacher Report Form. *Journal of Psychoeducational Assessment*, 12, 289–306.

Kline, R. B. (1998a). *Principles and practice of structural equation modeling*. New York: Guilford.

Kline, R. B. (1998b). Review of the Kaufman WISC-III Integrated Interpretive System (K-WIIS, Version 1.00). *Journal of Psychoeducational Assessment*, 16, 365–384.

Kline, R. B., Lachar, D., & Boersma, D. C. (1993). Identification of special education needs with the Personality Inventory for Children (PIC): A hierarchical classification model. *Psychological Assessment*, 5, 307–316.

Kline, R. B., Lachar, D., Gruber, C. P., & Boersma, D. C. (1994). Identification of special education needs with the Personality Inventory for Children (PIC): A profile-matching strategy. *Assessment*, 1, 301–314.

Kline, R. B., Lachar, D., & Sprague, D. (1985). The Personality Inventory for Children (PIC): An unbiased predictor of cognitive and academic status. *Journal of Pediatric Psychology*, 10, 461–477.

Kline, R. B., Snyder, J., & Castellanos, M. (1996). Lessons from the Kaufman Assessment Battery for Children (K-ABC): Toward a new assessment model. *Psychological Assessment*, 8, 7–17.

Klinge, V., & Dorsey, J. (1993). Correlates of the Woodcock-Johnson Reading Comprehension and Kaufman Brief Intelligence Test in a forensic psychiatric population. *Journal of Clinical Psychology*, 49, 593–598.

Koppitz, E. M. (1975). *The Bender-Gestalt Test for young children* (Vol. 2): *Research and application*. New York: Grune & Stratton.

Lachar, D. (1992). *Personality Inventory for Children (PIC) revised format manual supplement*. Los Angeles: Western Psychological Services.

Lachar, D., Kline, R. B., & Boersma, D. (1986). The Personality Inventory for Children (PIC): Approaches to actuarial interpretation in clinic and school settings. In H. M. Knoff (Ed.), *The psychological assessment of child and adolescent personality* (pp. 273–308). New York: Guilford.

Lassiter, K. S., & Bardos, A. N. (1995). The relationship between young children's academic achievement and measures of intelligence. *Psychology in the Schools*, 32, 170–177.

Lipsitz, J. D., Dworkin, R. H., & Erlenmeyer-Kimling, L. (1993). Wechsler Comprehension and Picture Arrangement subtests and social adjustment. *Psychological Assessment*, 5, 430–437.

Machover, K. A. (1949). *Personality projection in the drawing of the human figure*. Springfield, IL: Charles C. Thomas.

McDermott, P. A., Fantuzzo, J. W., & Glutting, J. J., Watkins, M. W., & Baggaley, A. R. (1992). Illusions of meaning in the ipsative assessment of children's ability. *Journal of Special Education*, 25, 504–526.

Miller, M. D. (1995). Review of the Kaufman Brief Intelligence Test. In J. C. Conoley and J. C. Impara (Eds.), *Twelfth Mental Measurements Yearbook* (pp. 533–534). Lincoln, NE: Buros Institute of Mental Measurements.

Naglieri, J. A. (1985). *Matrix Analogies Test—short form*. San Antonio, TX: The Psychological Corporation.

Naglieri, J. A. (1988). *Draw-a-Person*: A *Quantitative System*. San Antonio, TX: The Psychological Corporation.

Naugle, R. I., Chelune, G. J., & Tucker, G. D. (1993). Validity of the Kaufman Brief Intelligence Test. *Psychological Assessment*, 5, 182–186.

Nunnally, J. C., & Bernstein, I. H. (1994). *Psychometric theory* (3rd ed.). New York: McGraw-Hill.

Parker, L. D. (1993). The Kaufman Brief Intelligence Test: An introduction and review. *Measurement and Evaluation in Counseling and Development*, 26, 152–156.

Prewett, P. N. (1992a). The relationship between the Kaufman Brief Intelligence Test (K-BIT) and the WISC-R with incarcerated juvenile delinquents. *Educational and Psychological Measurement*, 52, 977–982.

Prewett, P. N. (1992b). The relationship between the Kaufman Brief Intelligence Test (K-BIT) and the WISC-R with referred students. *Psychology in the Schools*, 29, 25–27.

Prewett, P. N., & McCaffery, L. N. (1993). A comparison of the Kaufman Brief Intelligence Test (K-BIT) with the Stanford-Binet, a two-subtest short form, and the Kaufman Test of Educational Achievement (K-TEA) Brief Form. *Psychology in the Schools*, 30, 299–304.

Prifitera, A., Weiss, L. G., & Saklofske, D. H. (1998). The WISC-III in context. In A. Prifitera & D. Saklofske (Eds.), WISC-III *clinical use and interpretation* (pp. 1–39). New York: Academic Press.

Puente, A. E., & Salazar, G. D. (1998). Assessment of minority and culturally diverse children. In A. Prifitera & D. Saklofske (Eds.), WISC-III *clinical use and interpretation* (pp. 227–288). New York: Academic Press.

Raven, J. C., Court, J. H., & Raven, J. (1986). *Manual for the Raven's Progressive Matrices and Vocabulary Scales (Section 2)—Coloured Progressive Matrices* (1986 edition, with U.S. norms). London: Lewis.

Raven, J. C., & Summers, B. (1986). *Manual for the Raven's Progressive Matrices and Vocabulary Scales— research supplement no. 3*. London: Lewis.

Reynolds, C. R., & Kamphaus, R. W. (1992). *Behavior Assessment System for Children*. Circle Pines, MN: American Guidance Service.

Robin, A. I. (1943). A short form of the Wechsler-Bellevue test. *Journal of Applied Psychology*, 27, 320–324.

Ross-Reynolds, J. (1990). Best practices in conducting reevaluations. In A. Thomas & J. Grimes (Eds.), *Best practices in school psychology*—II (pp. 195–206). Washington, DC: National Association of School Psychologists.

Rourke, B. P. (1998). Significance of verbal-performance discrepancies for subtypes of children with learning disabilities: Opportunities for the WISC-III. In A. Prifitera & D. Saklofske (Eds.), WISC-III *clinical use and interpretation* (pp. 139–156). New York: Academic Press.

Ryan, J. J., & Ward, L. C. (1999). Validity, reliability, and standard error of measurement for two seven-subtest short forms of the Wechsler Adult Intelligence Scale—III. *Psychological Assessment*, 11, 207–211.

Saklofske, D. H., & Braun, S. M. (1992). A psychometric study of the Draw-A-Person: A Quantitative Scoring System. *Canadian Journal of School Psychology*, 8, 111–115.

Saklofske, D. H., Caravan, G., & Schwartz, C. (2000). Concurrent validity of the Wechsler Abbreviated Scale of Intelligence (WASI) with a sample of Canadian children. *Canadian Journal of Social Psychology*, 16, 87–94.

Saklofske, D. H., Yackulic, R. A., Murray, W. M., & Naglieri, J. A. (1992). Performance of Canadian children on the Matrix Analogies Test—Short Form. *Canadian Journal of School Psychology*, 8, 52–57.

Sattler, J. M. (1988). *Assessment of children* (3rd ed.). San Diego, CA: Author.

Sattler, J. M. (1992). *Assessment of children* WISC-III *and* WPPSI-R *supplement*. San Diego, CA: Author.

Satz, P., & Mogel, S. (1962). Abbreviation of the WAIS for clinical use. *Journal of Clinical Psychology*, 18, 77–79.

Silverstein, A. B. (1982). Two- and four-subtest short forms of the WISC-R. *Journal of Consulting and Clinical Psychology*, 51, 415–418.

Silverstein, A. B. (1990). Short forms of individual intelligence tests. *Psychological Assessment*, 2, 3–11.

Slate, J. R., Graham, L. S., & Bower, J. (1996). Relationships of the WISC-R and K-BIT for an adolescent clinical sample. *Adolescence, 31*, 777–782.

Slossen, R. L. (1963). *Slossen Intelligence Test (SIT) for children and adults*. New York: Slossen Educational Publications.

Slossen, R. L. (1982). *Slossen Intelligence Test (SIT) for children and adults* (2nd ed.). East Aurora, NY: Slossen Educational Publications.

Slossen, R. L. (1991). *Slossen Intelligence Test—Revised (SIT-R) for children and adults*. East Aurora, NY: Slossen Educational Publications. (1991 revision by C. L. Nicholson & T. H. Hibpshman.)

Slossen, R. L. (1998). *Slossen Intelligence Test—Revised (SIT-R) for children and adults technical manual calibrated norms tables*. East Aurora, NY: Slossen Educational Publications. (1998 revision by C. L. Nicholson & T. H. Hibpshman.)

Spruill, J. (1998). Assessment of mental retardation with the WISC-III. In A. Prifitera & D. Saklofske (Eds.), *WISC-III clinical use and interpretation* (pp. 73–90). New York: Academic Press.

Thompson, A. P., Howard, D., & Anderson, J. (1986). Two- and four-subtest short forms of the WAIS-R: Validity in a psychiatric sample. *Canadian Journal of Behavioural Science, 178*, 287–293.

Thorndike, R. L. (1973). *Stanford-Binet Intelligence Scale, Form L-M, 1972 norms tables*. Boston: Houghton Mifflin.

Thorndike, R. L., Hagen, E. P., & Sattler, J. M. (1986). *Stanford-Binet Intelligence Scale: Guide for administering and scoring the Fourth Edition*. Chicago: Riverside.

U.S. Department of Education. (1992). Assistance to states for the education of children with disabilities programs and preschool grants for children with disabilities. *Federal Register, 57*, 44794–44852.

Volker, M. A., Guarnaccia, V., & Scardapane, J. R. (1999). Short forms of the Stanford-Binet Intelligence Scale: Fourth Edition for screening potentially gifted preschoolers. *Journal of Psychoeducational Assessment, 17*, 226–235.

Watson, T. S. (1995). Review of the Slossen Intelligence Test [1991 Edition]. In J. C. Conoley & J. C. Impara (Eds.), *Twelfth Mental Measurements Yearbook* (pp. 956–958). Lincoln, NE: Buros Institute of Mental Measurements.

Wechsler, D. (1991). *Wechsler Intelligence Scale for Children-Third Edition* (WISC-III). San Antonio, TX: The Psychological Corporation.

Wechsler, D. (1996). *Manual: Canadian supplement to the Wechsler Intelligence Scale for Children—Third Edition*. Toronto: The Psychological Corporation.

Wechsler, D. (1999). Wechsler Abbreviated Scale of Intelligence. San Antonio, TX: The Psychological Corporation.

Weiss, L. G., Saklofske, D. H., Prifitera, A., Chen, H. Y., & Hildebrand, D. K. (1999). The calculation of the WISC-III General Ability Index using Canadian norms. *Canadian Journal of School Psychology, 14*, 1–11.

Wilkinson, G. S. (1993). *Wide Range Achievement Test—3 administration manual*. Wilmington, DE: Wide Range.

Wirt, R. D., Lachar, D., Klinedinst, J. K., & Seat, P. D. (1984). *Multidimensional description of child personality: A manual for the Personality Inventory for Children*. Los Angeles: Western Psychological Services.

Woodcock, R. W., McGrew, K. S., & Mather, N. (2001). *Woodcock-Johnson III examiner's manual*. Itasca, IL: Riverside.

Young, J. W. (1995). Review of the Kaufman Brief Intelligence Test. In J. C. Conoley & J. C. Impara (Eds.), *Twelfth Mental Measurements Yearbook* (pp. 534–536). Lincoln, NE: Buros Institute of Mental Measurements.

CHAPTER

5

Assessment with the
Woodcock-Johnson III

NANCY MATHER
University of Arizona

NOEL GREGG
University of Georgia

ASSESSMENT WITH THE WOODCOCK-JOHNSON III

The Woodcock-Johnson Tests of Cognitive Abilities (WJ III COG) and the Woodcock-Johnson Tests of Achievement (WJ III ACH; Woodcock, McGrew, & Mather, 2001) are revised versions of the WJ-R Tests of Cognitive Abilities and Achievement (Woodcock & Johnson, 1989). These two co-normed instruments form the Woodcock-Johnson III (WJ III), a comprehensive battery of individually administered tests designed to measure various intellectual and academic abilities. The WJ III covers a wide age range (preschool through mature adulthood). Depending on the purpose of the assessment, the WJ III COG and WJ III ACH may be used independently or in conjunction with each other.

Historical Foundation

The original Woodcock-Johnson Psycho-Educational Battery (WJ) provided the first comprehensive, co-normed battery of cognitive abilities, achievement, and interest (Woodcock & Johnson, 1977). The *Tests of Cognitive Ability* presented a multifactor approach to test interpretation by providing four interpretive factors: Comprehension-Knowledge (G*c*), Fluid Reasoning (G*f*), Short-Term Memory (G*sm*), and Processing Speed (G*s*). The *Tests of Achievement* consisted of 10 tests organized into four curricular areas: reading, mathematics, written language, and knowledge.

The Woodcock-Johnson—Revised (WJ-R; Woodcock & Johnson, 1989) was designed to expand and increase the diagnostic capabilities of the WJ. Similar to the organization of the WJ, the tests were divided into two main batteries: the *Tests of Cognitive Ability* (WJ-R COG) and the *Tests of Achievement* (WJ-R ACH). Both the WJ-R COG and WJ-R ACH have two easel test books: the Standard Battery and the Supplemental Battery.

For the 1989 WJ-R COG, interpretation was enhanced by the measurement of seven factors that represent major components of human intellectual abilities (McGrew, 1994; Reschly, 1990; Ysseldyke, 1990). Two additional factors (*Grw*, a reading/writing factor, and *Gq*, a quantitative ability factor) were measured by the WJ-R ACH. Thus, nine *Gf-Gc* abilities were measured across the WJ-R COG and WJ-R ACH.

The WJ-R Tests of Achievement consisted of 14 tests organized into four curricular areas: reading, mathematics, written language, and knowledge. Several new tests were added to the reading and written language areas. To facilitate pre- and posttesting, parallel alternate forms of the Tests of Achievement, Forms A and B, were available. In addition, both the WJ-R COG and WJ-R ACH have direct Spanish-language counterparts, the Batería-R COG and the Batería-R ACH (Woodcock & Munoz-Sandoval, 1996a, 1996b), that contain all of the same tests and interpretive features. Although the basic features of the WJ-R have been retained in the third edition, the extensive re-norming and the new tests, clusters, and interpretive procedures improve and increase the diagnostic power. In addition, two empirically derived theories guided development of the WJ III.

Theoretical Model

The WJ III COG is based on the Cattell-Horn-Carroll (CHC) theory of cognitive abilities, a merging of two theories of intellectual abilities: *Gf-Gc* theory and Carroll's three-stratum theory. *Gf-Gc* theory is a model that has been developed and refined over the last 60 years. Carroll's (1993) three-stratum theory is based upon his extensive investigation of the structure of human cognitive abilities. Interpretation of these theories is enhanced by the Cognitive Performance Model (CPM; Woodcock, 1993, 1998).

Gf–Gc Theory

The first theory that guided the development of the WJ III stems primarily from the factor analytic students of Raymond Cattell and John Horn. At an American Psychological Association conference, Cattell (1941) proposed that human abilities consisted of two types: Fluid intelligence (*Gf*) and crystallized intelligence (Gc). As a result of this early conceptualization, the framework for this evolving theory is often referred to as Gf-Gc theory (Cattell, 1941; Horn, 1965, 1991; Horn & Noll, 1997). Based on the research conducted in the last 40 years, as well as the work of Cattell, Horn, and Carroll, this theory has been expanded to include 9 or 10 broad factors. McGrew (1997) provided a Gf-Gc taxonomy that integrated research from Carroll (1993; 1998) as well as from Horn and Noll (1997). This taxonomy included three additional broad abilities: quantitative knowledge (Gq), decision/reaction time or speed (CDS), and a reading/writing factor (Grw). This purpose of this framework was to provide a bridge between the theoretical and empirical research on the factors of intelligence and the interpretation of assessment batteries (McGrew, 1997).

Three-Stratum Theory

The second theory that guided test development was three-stratum theory (Carroll, 1993). Using the results from exploratory factor analysis, Carroll developed a similar theory describing the content and structure of cognitive abilities. Within this theory, Stratum III represents a general factor (g); Stratum II represents the broad abilities; and Stratum I encompasses the many narrow abilities (Carroll, 1993, 1998). In the WJ III, the General Intellectual Ability score represents Stratum III; the broad abilities of Gf-Gc theory represent Stratum II; and the tests within the battery represent Stratum I.

The combination of these two similar theories into CHC theory provides a comprehensive and empirically supported psychometric framework for understanding the structure of human cognitive abilities (McGrew & Flanagan, 1998). CHC theory is viewed as dynamic, rather than static, and in the future will most likely include more factors (Woodcock, 1990). Although the WJ III is based upon this theory, Flanagan and McGrew (1997) remind us that no current measurement instrument taps all of the broad and narrow abilities identified by Carroll (1993, 1998). Carroll (1993) also noted that although Gf-Gc theory covers the major domains of intellectual functioning, numerous details about human cognitive abilities need to be filled in through future research.

Cognitive Performance Model

The application of CHC theory, as the basis for interpreting the meaning and implications of test scores, is enhanced by a simple dynamic model called the Cognitive Performance Model (CPM; Woodcock, 1993, 1998). The CPM, shown in Figure 5.1, implies that the various Gf-Gc abilities are not autonomous, but fall into several functional categories. The level and quality of an individual's cognitive performance result from the interaction among three

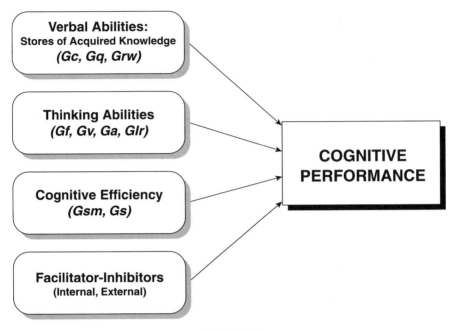

FIGURE 5.1
Cognitive performance model.

types of cognitive factors: (a) stores of acquired knowledge, (b) thinking abilities, and (c) cognitive efficiency. Noncognitive factors, described as facilitator-inhibitors, represent personality attributes such as motivation, as well as extrinsic factors, such as family support.

The acquired knowledge factor represents domains of specific information, as well as recall of procedures used to perform certain tasks. The thinking abilities factor draws upon information that cannot be processed automatically and must be processed with some level of intent. The cognitive efficiency factor includes speed of processing and short-term memory. These abilities are important prerequisites for smooth, automatic, cognitive processing. Facilitator-inhibitors represent the noncognitive factors that impact cognitive performance for better or for worse, often overriding or mediating strengths and weaknesses among cognitive abilities. Facilitator-inhibitors include internal factors (e.g., health, emotional status, or persistence), as well as external factors (e.g., distractions in the environment or type of instruction).

Experienced clinicians know that scores obtained from cognitive tests must be interpreted with caution because the observed performance may be affected by environmental and test situation variables. The CPM emphasizes the concept that both cognitive and noncognitive variables interact to produce performance. In other words, cognitive performance is rarely the result of a single influence.

DESCRIPTION OF THE WJ III

The WJ III COG has two separate easel books that contain the tests of the Standard and Extended batteries. Table 5.1 depicts the organizational format and the clusters and tests included in the WJ III COG. The notations indicate which tests are timed (T) and which are recorded (R). Table 5.2 provides a brief description of the WJ III COG tests grouped under the CPM model. Supplemental tests are described at the end of the section.

Like the WJ III COG, the WJ III ACH has two easel books that contain the tests of the Standard and Extended batteries. Table 5.3 depicts the organization and tests of the WJ III ACH. Table 5.4 provides a brief description of the

TABLE 5.1
WJ III COG Organization

Test	Standard Battery	Extended Battery
Verbal Ability:		
Verbal Comprehension-Knowledge (Gc)	1. Verbal Comprehension (Picture Vocabulary, Synonyms, Antonyms, and Verbal Analogies)	11. General Information
Thinking Abilities:		
Long-Term Retrieval (Glr)	2. Visual-Auditory Learning	12. Retrieval Fluency (T)
Visual-Spatial Thinking (Gv)	3. Spatial Relations	13. Picture Recognition
Auditory Processing (Ga)	4. Sound Blending (R)	14. Auditory Attention (R)
Fluid Reasoning (Gf)	5. Concept Formation	15. Analysis-Synthesis
Cognitive Efficiency:		
Processing Speed (Gs)	6. Visual Matching (T)	16. Decision Speed (T)
Short-Term Memory (Gsm)	7. Numbers Reversed (R)	17. Memory for Words (R)
Supplemental (Ga, Gsm, Glr, Gs, Gf)	8. Incomplete Words (R) (Ga)	18. Rapid Picture Naming (T) (Gs)
	9. Auditory Working Memory (R) (Gsm)	19. Planning (Gf)
	10. Visual-Auditory Learning—Delayed (Glr)	20. Pair Cancellation (T) (Gs)

(T) = Timed, (R) = Recorded

TABLE 5.2
Description of WJ III COG Tests

Verbal Ability (G*c*)

Test 1: Verbal Comprehension measures word knowledge through four tasks. The first task requires naming pictured objects, the second requires providing antonyms, the third requires providing synonyms for orally presented words, and the fourth requires providing analogies.

Test 10: General Information measures aspects of acquired knowledge. The task measures the ability to identify common or typical characteristics of certain objects.

Thinking Abilities/Processes (G*lr*, G*v*, G*a*, G*f*)

Long-Term Retrieval (G*lr*)

Test 2: Visual-Auditory Learning measures an aspect of associative and meaningful memory. The task requires pairing novel visual symbols (rebuses) with familiar words and then translating the symbols into verbal phrases and sentences (visual-auditory association task).

Test 12: Retrieval Fluency measures an aspect of ideational fluency. The task measures the ability to list orally as many items as possible in several categories (things to eat or drink, first names of people, and animals) in 1 minute.

Visual-Spatial Thinking (G*v*)

Test 3: Spatial Relations measures an aspect of visualization. The task measures the ability to select the component parts from a series of visual shapes that are needed to form a whole shape

Test 13: Picture Recognition measures an aspect of recognition memory. The task requires the identification of a subset of previously presented pictures within a larger set of pictures.

Auditory Processing (G*a*)

Test 4: Sound Blending measures an aspect of phonemic processing. The task measures the ability to synthesize sounds to make a whole word (auditory blending).

Test 14: Auditory Attention measures an aspect of speech discrimination and selective attention. The task measures the ability to differentiate among similar sounding words with increasing levels of background noise.

Fluid Reasoning (G*f*)

Test 5: Concept Formation measures an aspect of inductive reasoning. The task measures the ability to examine a set of geometric figures and identify the rules when shown instances and noninstances of the concept.

Test 15: Analysis-Synthesis primarily measures general sequential reasoning (deductive logic). The task measures the ability to analyze the presented components of an incomplete logic puzzle and then determine the missing components.

Cognitive Efficiency

Short-Term Memory (G*sm*)

Test 7: Numbers Reversed measures aspects of short-term auditory memory span and working memory. The task requires rearranging a series of numbers presented orally in reverse order.

Test 17: Memory for Words measures short-term auditory memory span. The task measures the ability to repeat lists of unrelated words in the correct sequences.

Processing Speed (G*s*)

Test 6: Visual Matching measures an aspect of visual perceptual speed. The task has an early development component that requires pointing to the two identical pictures in a row of

Table 5.2 — *Continued*

assorted colored shapes. The next component requires locating quickly and circling two identical numbers ranging from one to three digits, in a row of six numbers.

Test 16: Decision Speed measures an aspect of conceptual reasoning speed. The task measures the ability to rapidly scan a row of pictures and then circle the two drawings that are most related.

Supplemental (*Glr, Gf, Gs*)

Test 8: Visual-Auditory Learning—Delayed (*Glr*) measures an aspect of associative and meaningful memory using previously presented symbols. The task requires the subject to recall and relearn, after 30 minutes to 8 hours or 1 to 8 days, the visual-auditory associations from the Visual-Auditory Learning test.

Test 9: Auditory Working Memory (*Gsm*) measures aspects of short-term auditory memory span and working memory. The task involves retaining two types of information (words and numbers) that are presented orally in a specified random order and then reordering that information sequentially.

Test 10: Incomplete Words (*Ga*) measures one aspect of phonemic processing. The task requires the subject to identify words with missing phonemes (auditory analysis).

Test 18: Rapid Picture Naming (*Glr/Gs*) measures aspects of lexical retrieval and fluency. The task requires the subject to name common objects rapidly.

Test 19: Planning (*Gv*) measures an aspect of spatial scanning and planning. The task requires the subject to use forward thinking by planning a tracing route that covers as many segments of a visual pattern as possible without retracing or lifting the pencil.

Test 20: Pair Cancellation (*Gs*) measures an aspect of sustained attention. The task measures the ability to rapidly scan and circle a repeated pattern in a row of pictures.

WJ III ACH tests that are grouped under related achievement areas. Supplemental tests are described at the end of the section. To increase the reliability of decisions, cluster scores, rather than single test scores, form the basis for interpretation of the WJ III.

Norms

To date, the WJ III has the largest standardization sample of any individually administered ability or achievement test. The total normative sample included 8818 individuals living in more than 100 geographically and economically diverse communities in the United States. The examinees were randomly selected within a stratified sampling design that controlled for 10 specific variables, including socioeconomic status. The preschool sample includes 1143 children from 2 to 5 years of age (not enrolled in kindergarten). The kindergarten to 12th grade sample is composed of 4784 students, the college/university sample is based on 1165 students, and the adult sample includes 1843 individuals.

TABLE 5.3
Organization of WJ III ACH

Test	Standard Battery	Extended Battery
Reading (*Grw*)		
Basic Reading Skills	1. Letter-Word Identification	13. Word Attack
Reading Fluency	2. Reading Fluency (T)	
Reading Comprehension	9. Passage Comprehension	17. Reading Vocabulary
Oral Language (*Gc*)		
Oral Expression	3. Story Recall (R)	14. Picture Vocabulary
Listening Comprehension	4. Understanding Directions (R)	15. Oral Comprehension (R)
Mathematics (*Gq*)		
Math Calculation Skills	5. Calculation	
Math Fluency	6. Math Fluency (T)	
Math Reasoning	10. Applied Problems	18. Quantitative Concepts
Written Language (*Grw*)		
Basic Writing Skills	7. Spelling	16. Editing
Writing Fluency	8. Writing Fluency (T)	
Written Expression	11. Writing Samples	
Knowledge (*Gc*)		19. Academic Knowledge
Supplemental (*Glr, Grw, Ga*)	12. Story Recall—Delayed (*Glr*)	20. Spelling of Sounds (R) (*Ga*)
	H Handwriting Legibility Scale	21. Sound Awareness (R) (*Ga*)
		22. Punctuation & Capitalization (*Grw*)

(T) = Timed, (R) = Recorded

Brief Overview of the Psychometric Properties of the Test

For the tests, the number of items and average item density was set so that all tests have a reliability of .80 or higher. Most cluster score reliabilities are at .90 or higher. The WJ III Technical Manual (McGrew & Woodcock, 2001) contains extensive information on the reliability and validity of the WJ III. The precision of each test and cluster score is reported in terms of the Standard Error of Measurement. The reliability of the various WJ III ability/achievement discrepancy scores is reported, along with the intra-ability discrepancy scores (intra-cognitive, intra-achievement, and intra-individual). Odd-even correlations, corrected by the Spearman-Brown formula, were used to estimate reliability for each untimed test.

The Rasch single-parameter logistic test model was used to guide test

TABLE 5.4
Description of the WJ III ACH Tests

Reading

Test 1: Letter-Word Identification measures an aspect of reading decoding. The task requires identifying and pronouncing isolated letters and words.

Test 2: Reading Fluency measures reading speed. The task requires reading and comprehending simple sentences rapidly.

Test 9: Passage Comprehension measures an aspect of reading comprehension. The task requires reading a short passage and then supplying a key missing word.

Test 13: Word Attack measures aspects of phonological and orthographic coding. The task requires applying phonic and structural analysis skills to the pronunciation of phonically regular nonsense words.

Test 17: Reading Vocabulary measures reading vocabulary through three tasks: reading words, providing synonyms and antonyms, and completing analogies.

Mathematics

Test 5: Calculation measures the ability to perform mathematical computations, from simple addition facts to calculus.

Test 6: Math Fluency measures aspects of number facility and math achievement. The task requires rapid calculation of simple, single-digit addition, subtraction, and multiplication facts.

Test 10: Applied Problems measures the ability to analyze and solve practical mathematical problems.

Test 18: Quantitative Concepts measures aspects of quantitative reasoning and math knowledge. The task requires applying mathematical concepts and analyzing numerical relationships.

Written Language

Test 7: Spelling measures the ability to write the correct spellings of words presented orally.

Test 8: Writing Fluency measures aspects of writing ability and expressive fluency. The task requires formulating and writing simple sentences quickly.

Test 11: Writing Samples measures the ability to write sentences in response to a variety of demands that are then evaluated based on the quality of expression.

Test 16: Editing measures the ability to identify and correct mistakes in spelling, punctuation, capitalization, or word usage in short typewritten passages.

Test 20: Spelling of Sounds measures aspects of phonological and orthographic coding. The task requires spelling nonsense words that conform to conventional phonics and spelling rules.

Test 22: Punctuation and Capitalization measures the ability to apply punctuation/capitalization rules.

Handwriting (H) provides a rating of writing legibility. The samples of writing evaluated may come from the Writing Samples test or another source.

Oral Language

Test 3: Story Recall measures aspects of language development, listening ability, and meaningful memory. The task requires listening to passages of gradually increasing length and complexity and then recalling the story elements.

Test 4: Understanding Directions measures aspects of language development and listening ability. The task requires pointing to objects in a picture after listening to instructions that increase in linguistic complexity.

(continues)

Table 5.4—*Continued*

Test 12: Story Recall—Delayed measures an aspect of meaningful memory using previously presented stories. The task requires the subject to recall, after 1 to 8 hours or 1 to 8 days, the story elements presented in the Oral Recall test.

Test 14: Picture Vocabulary measures word knowledge. The task requires naming common to less familiar pictured objects.

Test 15: Oral Comprehension measures aspects of listening ability and language development. The task requires listening to short passages and then supplying the missing final word. (Taped)

Test 21: Sound Awareness measures various aspects of phonological awareness, including rhyming and phonemic manipulation tasks.

Academic Knowledge

Test 19: Academic Knowledge measures aspects of general information and acquired content or curricular knowledge in various areas of the biological and physical sciences, history, geography, government, economics, art, music, and literature.

development, item calibration, scaling, and cluster composition. The technical criteria for item selection were stringent; all selected items had to fit the Rasch measurement model as well as other criteria, including bias and sensitivity reviews. The evidence of concurrent validity comes from studies using a broad age range of individuals. For the WJ III COG, scores were compared with performances on other intellectual measures appropriate for individuals at the ages tested, such as the *Wechsler Intelligence Scale for Children—Third Edition* (WISC-III), the *Differential Ability Scale* (DAS), the *Universal Nonverbal Intelligence Test* (UNIT), and the *Leiter-R*. The correlations between the WJ III General Intellectual Ability (GIA) score and the WISC-III Full Scale IQ range from .69 to .73. Because these correlations are based on a sample of restricted range, they most likely underestimate the relationship. For the WJ III ACH, scores were compared with other appropriate achievement measures, including the *Wechsler Individual Achievement Tests*, the *Kaufman Tests of Educational Achievement*, and the *Wide Range Achievement Test*—3. The magnitude of the correlations suggests that the WJ III ACH is measuring skills similar to those measured by other achievement tests.

Supported by factor-analytic research, the WJ III provides valid scores for general intellectual ability (g), seven Gf-Gc factors of cognitive ability, and several areas of academic performance. Factor loadings are all high, and the relationships between the tests and the factors are supported by good fit statistics. Further construct validity evidence is apparent by examining the intercorrelations among the tests within each battery. As is to be expected, tests assessing the same broad cognitive ability or achievement area are more highly correlated with each other than with tests that assess different abilities.

Administration

Each test requires about 5 to 10 minutes to administer. The WJ III COG Standard Battery takes about 40 minutes to administer, whereas the WJ III ACH Standard Battery takes about 1 hour. As with the WJ-R, a guiding principle of the WJ III is selective testing. Depending upon the purpose of the referral, an examiner can conduct a comprehensive or focused assessment. For example, for a student referred for a reading evaluation, an evaluator may wish to administer only the cognitive/linguistic tests related to reading performance, as well as the specific academic measures of reading performance. It would rarely be necessary to administer all of the tests of the WJ III to one person.

The batteries require a trained examiner for administration. In contrast to the administration procedures, interpretation of the WJ III requires a higher level of knowledge and skill. Because of the relative complexity in administration and interpretation of the WJ III COG, this battery requires more advanced training in clinical assessment than does the WJ III ACH.

Test Session Observation Checklist

The WJ III also includes a new procedure for gathering qualitative information that can be used to help interpret behavior during testing. A seven-category, criterion-referenced Test Session Observation Checklist is included on each Test Record that was field-tested on the normative sample from the WJ III standardization. The checklist provides a method to help categorize and describe the individual's behavior under the standardized test administration conditions. Each of the seven items uses a wide range of descriptors to help identify typical and atypical behaviors during testing. The seven areas include: the individual's levels of conversational proficiency, cooperation, activity, attention and concentration, self-confidence, care in responding, and response to difficult tasks.

Scoring

With the exception of the estimated age and grade equivalents that are provided on the Test Record, the WJ III, unlike the WJ and the WJ-R, is scored only by computer. The computer scoring requires the examiner to calculate the number correct for each subtest or test and then enter these scores into the WJ III *Compuscore and Profiles Program* (Schrank & Woodcock, 2001). Tables 5.5 and 5.6 illustrate sample test reports from the scoring program.[1]

---

[1] The results in these tables were generated from the pilot version of the Compuscore and Profiles program.

TABLE 5.5
Case One: Jovita, WJ III COG—Score Summary

COMPUSCORE VERSION 1.1
SCORE REPORT

Name: School Age, Jovita   School: Little Rock
Date of Birth: 02/25/1992
Age: 8 years, 8 months   Grade: 3.2
Sex: Female
Dates of Testing: 10/30/2000 (COG)   Examiner: Nancy Mather
                   11/02/2000 (ACH)

TABLE OF SCORES: *Woodcock-Johnson* III *Tests of Cognitive Abilities* and *Tests of Achievement*
Norms based on grade 3.2

CLUSTER/Test	RAW	GE	EASY	to DIFF	RPI	PR	SS (68% BAND)
GIA (Ext)	—	2.5	1.3	4.6	85/90	35	94 (92–96)
Verbal Ability (Ext)	—	4.3	2.9	6.0	95/90	74	110 (105–114)
Thinking Ability (Ext)	—	3.2	1.4	7.7	90/90	50	100 (97–103)
Cognitive Efficiency (Ext)	—	1.8	1.2	2.6	60/90	13	83 (80–87)
Comprehension-Knowledge (Gc)	—	4.3	2.9	6.0	95/90	74	110 (105–114)
Long-Term Retrieval (Glr)	—	1.9	K.3	8.0	85/90	21	88 (83–93)
Visual-Spatial Thinking (Gv)	—	9.8	3.7	>18.0	97/90	92	121 (116–127)
Auditory Processing (Ga)	—	1.0	K.1	3.2	75/90	12	83 (77–88)
Fluid Reasoning (Gf)	—	3.7	2.4	6.0	93/90	60	104 (99–109)
Processing Speed (Gs)	—	2.1	1.5	2.8	64/90	17	86 (82–89)
Short-Term Memory (Gsm)	—	1.4	K.7	2.3	56/90	16	85 (80–90)
Phonemic Awareness	—	K.4	<K.0	2.1	67/90	7	78 (72–83)
Phonemic Awareness III	—	K.5	<K.0	1.4	49/90	2	69 (65–73)
Working Memory	—	1.3	K.5	2.1	47/90	10	81 (77–85)
Broad Attention	—	1.8	K.9	2.9	71/90	16	85 (81–88)
Cognitive Fluency	—	2.1	1.0	3.6	80/90	27	91 (88–93)
Executive Processes	—	3.2	1.8	5.5	90/90	51	100 (96–105)
Knowledge	—	3.2	2.1	4.6	90/90	51	100 (96–105)
Oral Language (Ext)	—	3.3	1.7	5.8	91/90	53	101 (97–105)
Oral Expression	—	4.0	1.7	7.2	93/90	62	105 (99–110)
Listening Comprehension	—	3.0	1.7	4.7	88/90	45	98 (94–103)
Total Achievement	—	1.5	1.1	1.9	19/90	2	70 (68–72)
Broad Reading	—	1.1	K.9	1.3	1/90	0.2	58 (56–60)
Broad Mathematics	—	3.1	2.3	4.0	88/90	46	98 (95–101)
Broad Written Language	—	1.1	K.7	1.5	18/90	1	64 (59–68)
Basic Reading Skills	—	1.1	K.9	1.3	0/90	<0.1	54 (50–57)
Reading Comprehension	—	1.2	K.9	1.5	7/90	2	68 (65–71)
Math Calculation Skills	—	3.0	2.1	4.1	88/90	44	98 (94–101)
Math Reasoning	—	3.2	2.6	4.0	90/90	51	101 (96–105)
Basic Writing Skills	—	1.2	K.9	1.6	11/90	2	68 (63–72)
Written Expression	—	1.3	K.8	1.8	38/90	2	68 (61–74)

Table 5.5— *Continued*

CLUSTER/Test	RAW	GE	EASY to	DIFF	RPI	PR	SS (68% BAND)
Academic Skills	—	1.4	1.1	1.7	4/90	0.2	58 (55–61)
Academic Fluency	—	1.6	1.0	2.2	43/90	4	75 (72–77)
Academic Applications	—	1.5	1.2	1.9	29/90	5	75 (72–79)
Academic Knowledge	—	3.2	2.0	4.6	90/90	50	100 (94–106)
Phoneme/Grapheme Knowledge	—	1.3	1.0	1.6	14/90	3	71 (67–76)
Verbal Comprehension	—	5.6	3.9	7.7	98/90	87	117 (112–122)
Visual-Auditory Learning	18-E	2.7	1.2	10.3	88/90	43	97 (93–102)
Spatial Relations	52-C	>18.0	9.5	>18.0	99/90	98	131 (124–138)
Sound Blending	12	K.4	<K.0	1.5	58/90	8	79 (72–85)
Concept Formation	18-C	3.6	2.5	5.5	93/90	57	103 (97–108)
Visual Matching	24-2	1.7	1.2	2.2	29/90	6	77 (73–81)
Numbers Reversed	7	1.5	K.9	2.2	46/90	17	85 (80–91)
Incomplete Words	14	K.3	<K.0	3.4	76/90	19	87 (81–93)
Auditory Work Memory	7	K.9	<K.0	1.9	47/90	11	82 (77–87)
General Information	—	3.3	2.1	4.6	90/90	51	101 (94–107)
Retrieval Fluency	29	K.7	<K.0	5.7	81/90	5	75 (68–82)
Picture Recognition	38-D	3.7	1.2	10.2	91/90	55	102 (97–107)
Auditory Attention	33	2.1	K.6	9.6	87/90	41	96 (91–101)
Analysis-Synthesis	21-D	3.8	2.3	6.5	93/90	59	103 (98–109)
Decision Speed	23	3.0	2.1	4.2	88/90	46	99 (94–103)
Memory for Words	14	1.3	K.3	2.6	65/90	24	89 (83–96)
Rapid Picture Naming	82	1.7	K.9	2.7	65/90	28	91 (89–93)
Planning	—	2.8	<K.0	>18.0	90/90	47	99 (91–107)
Pair Cancellation	43	3.0	1.9	4.2	88/90	45	98 (95–100)

Form A of the following achievement tests was administered:

CLUSTER/Test	RAW	GE	EASY to	DIFF	RPI	PR	SS (68% BAND)
Letter-Word Identification	17	K.9	K.7	1.1	0/90	<0.1	52 (49–55)
Reading Fluency	7	1.5	1.2	1.9	11/90	8	79 (76–81)
Story Recall	—	3.2	K.2	>18.0	90/90	49	100 (90–110)
Understanding Directions	—	1.8	K.7	3.5	78/90	26	90 (85–96)
Calculation	14	3.5	2.8	4.4	93/90	63	105 (98–113)
Math Fluency	22	1.7	<K.0	3.6	79/90	9	80 (76–84)
Spelling	15	K.9	K.6	1.2	3/90	1	64 (59–69)
Writing Fluency	4	1.6	1.0	2.3	47/90	9	80 (74–85)
Passage Comprehension	10	1.0	K.8	1.3	2/90	1	65 (61–69)
Applied Problems	29	3.1	2.5	3.9	89/90	49	99 (95–104)
Writing Samples	4-A	1.1	K.7	1.5	29/90	<0.1	54 (41–66)
Word Attack	4	1.4	1.2	1.6	5/90	4	75 (69–80)
Picture Vocabulary	24	4.3	2.6	6.2	95/90	65	106 (100–111)
Oral Comprehension	18	3.9	2.7	5.9	94/90	63	105 (100–110)
Editing	2	1.7	1.3	2.2	31/90	11	81 (76–87)
Reading Vocabulary	—	1.4	1.1	1.7	24/90	7	78 (75–82)
Quantitative Concepts	—	3.4	2.6	4.3	92/90	56	102 (96–109)
Academic Knowledge	—	3.2	2.0	4.6	90/90	50	100 (94–106)

(*continues*)

Table 5.5— *Continued*

CLUSTER/Test	RAW	GE	EASY to DIFF		RPI	PR	SS (68% BAND)
Spelling of Sounds	9	1.1	K.6	1.4	32/90	3	71 (65–76)
Sound Awareness	12	K.5	K.1	1.1	17/90	1	67 (63–70)

DISCREPANCIES	STANDARD SCORES			DISCREPANCY		Significant at + or −1.50 SD (SEE)
	Actual	Predicted	Differ-ence	PR	SD	

Intra-Individual

DISCREPANCIES	Actual	Predicted	Difference	PR	SD	Significant
Comprehension-Knowledge (Gc)	110	86	+24	99	+2.40	Yes
Long-Term Retrieval (Glr)	88	89	−1	46	−0.10	No
Visual-Spatial Thinking (Gv)	121	93	+28	98	+2.00	Yes
Auditory Processing (Ga)	83	93	−10	23	−0.72	No
Fluid Reasoning (Gf)	104	89	+15	88	+1.18	No
Processing Speed (Gs)	86	93	−7	31	−0.49	No
Short-Term Memory (Gsm)	85	92	−7	31	−0.49	No
Phonemic Awareness	78	92	−14	14	−1.06	No
Working Memory	81	91	−10	21	−0.82	No
Basic Reading Skills	54	91	−37	<0.1	−4.00	Yes
Reading Comprehension	68	91	−23	1	−2.24	Yes
Math Calculation Skills	98	91	+7	70	+0.53	No
Math Reasoning	101	88	+13	90	+1.27	No
Basic Writing Skills	68	92	−24	1	−2.20	Yes
Written Expression	68	92	−24	2	−2.13	Yes
Oral Expression	105	89	+16	90	+1.29	No
Listening Comprehension	98	88	+10	79	+0.82	No
Academic Knowledge	100	90	+10	82	+0.93	No

DISCREPANCIES	STANDARD SCORES			DISCREPANCY		Significant at + or −1.50 SD (SEE)
	Actual	Predicted	Differ-ence	PR	SD	

Intellectual Ability/Achievement Discrepancies*

DISCREPANCIES	Actual	Predicted	Difference	PR	SD	Significant
Broad Reading	58	96	−38	<0.1	−3.37	Yes
Basic Reading Skills	54	97	−43	<0.1	−3.77	Yes
Reading Comprehension	68	96	−28	0.4	−2.62	Yes
Broad Mathematics	98	97	+1	55	+0.12	No
Math Calculation Skills	98	98	0	50	0.00	No
Math Reasoning	101	97	+4	64	+0.35	No
Broad Written Language	64	97	−33	0.1	−3.01	Yes
Basic Writing Skills	68	97	−29	1	−2.51	Yes
Written Expression	68	97	−29	1	−2.52	Yes
Oral Language (Ext)	101	96	+5	66	+0.41	No
Oral Expression	105	97	+8	74	+0.66	No
Listening Comprehension	98	97	+1	55	+0.11	No
Academic Knowledge	100	96	+4	63	+0.34	No

*These discrepancies based on GIA (Ext) with ACH Broad, Basic, and Applied clusters.

TABLE 5.6
Case Two: Tom, WJ III COG—Score Summary

COMPUSCORE VERSION 1.1
SCORE REPORT

Name: College, Tom
Date of Birth: 10/02/1979
Age: 21 years, 1 month
Sex: Male
Dates of Testing: 10/25/2000 (COG)
10/30/2000 (ACH)

Organization: University of Georgia
Department: LDC
Grade: 13.2

Examiner: Noel Gregg

TABLE OF SCORES: *Woodcock-Johnson* III *Tests of Cognitive Abilities* and *Tests of Achievement*
Norms based on grade 13.2 (4-year college/university)

CLUSTER/Test	RAW	GE	EASY to DIFF		RPI	PR	SS (68% BAND)
GIA (Ext)	—	11.9	7.5	17.3	81/90	28	91 (89–93)
Verbal Ability (Ext)	—	>18.0	>18.0	>18.0	99/90	98	130 (124–135)
Thinking Ability (Ext)	—	6.9	2.9	13.1	75/90	10	81 (78–83)
Cognitive Efficiency (Ext)	—	6.7	5.0	8.9	35/90	9	80 (77–82)
Comprehension-Knowledge (*Gc*)	—	>18.0	>18.0	>18.0	99/90	98	130 (124–135)
Long-Term Retrieval (*Glr*)	—	6.1	1.6	>18.0	84/90	18	86 (82–90)
Visual-Spatial Thinking (*Gv*)	—	1.2	<K.0	4.0	45/90	1	63 (59–67)
Auditory Processing (*Ga*)	—	11.1	4.5	14.3	77/90	16	85 (79–91)
Fluid Reasoning (*Gf*)	—	10.8	6.9	>18.0	84/90	37	95 (91–99)
Processing Speed (*Gs*)	—	4.1	3.2	5.1	3/90	1	64 (61–66)
Short-Term Memory (*Gsm*)	—	13.0	10.7	>18.0	90/90	50	100 (95–105)
Phonemic Awareness	—	7.3	2.5	13.0	72/90	17	86 (81–90)
Phonemic Awareness III	—	6.2	2.7	12.9	70/90	11	81 (77–86)
Working Memory	—	9.8	6.9	13.0	70/90	26	90 (87–94)
Broad Attention	—	9.4	6.3	13.0	71/90	10	81 (77–85)
Cognitive Fluency	—	3.9	2.4	5.9	16/90	2	68 (67–70)
Executive Processes	—	8.1	4.8	13.0	74/90	11	82 (79–85)
Knowledge	—	>18.0	17.5	>18.0	99/90	94	124 (119–128)
Oral Language (Ext)	—	>18.0	13.3	>18.0	96/90	88	118 (113–123)
Oral Expression	—	>18.0	>18.0	>18.0	98/90	96	125 (120–131)
Listening Comprehension	—	14.5	11.1	>18.0	92/90	60	104 (98–109)
Total Achievement	—	10.6	8.1	13.0	72/90	20	87 (86–89)
Broad Reading	—	6.9	5.5	8.4	11/90	5	75 (73–77)
Broad Math	—	13.0	10.0	>18.0	89/90	47	99 (97–101)
Broad Written Language	—	>18.0	12.9	>18.0	95/90	80	113 (107–119)
Basic Reading Skills	—	9.0	6.8	12.8	72/90	25	90 (87–93)
Reading Comprehension	—	16.4	12.3	>18.0	94/90	68	107 (102–112)
Math Calculation Skills	—	13.4	10.3	>18.0	90/90	51	100 (96–104)
Math Reasoning	—	13.5	10.1	>18.0	91/90	53	101 (97–105)
Basic Writing Skills	—	13.0	10.6	16.6	88/90	46	99 (95–102)
Written Expression	—	>18.0	12.9	>18.0	96/90	83	115 (108–121)

(continues)

Table 5.6— *Continued*

CLUSTER/Test	RAW	GE	EASY	to DIFF	RPI	PR	SS (68% BAND)
Academic Skills	—	17.4	13.0	>18.0	95/90	73	109 (105−113)
Academic Fluency	—	6.4	5.1	7.9	9/90	3	73 (71−74)
Academic Applications	—	13.1	9.6	>18.0	90/90	49	100 (96−103)
Academic Knowledge	—	>18.0	16.5	>18.0	98/90	86	116 (111−122)
Phoneme/Grapheme Knowledge	—	3.9	2.5	6.2	34/90	2	70 (67−74)
Verbal Comprehension	—	>18.0	17.7	>18.0	99/90	97	128 (121−135)
Visual-Auditory Learning	17-E	2.9	1.3	11.6	73/90	10	81 (76−86)
Spatial Relations	24-D	<K.0	<K.0	K.3	15/90	<0.1	50 (46−54)
Sound Blending	20	6.8	2.7	11.9	59/90	15	85 (80−90)
Concept Formation	32-E	8.9	5.5	13.1	74/90	32	93 (90−96)
Visual Matching	36-2	4.1	3.4	4.9	1/90	0.4	60 (56−63)
Numbers Reversed	15	10.4	7.4	13.0	66/90	27	91 (86−96)
Incomplete Words	23	8.2	2.2	>18.0	82/90	27	91 (85−97)
Auditory Work Memory	25	9.2	6.4	13.1	74/90	26	90 (86−95)
Visual-Auditory Learning— Delayed	25	—	—	—	—	—	—
General Information	—	>18.0	>18.0	>18.0	99/90	97	129 (122−136)
Retrieval Fluency	94	>18.0	2.8	>18.0	91/90	62	105 (98−111)
Picture Recognition	42-D	6.4	2.3	>18.0	79/90	28	91 (87−95)
Auditory Attention	44	13.0	8.9	>18.0	89/90	45	98 (88−108)
Analysis-Synthesis	28-E	13.4	8.5	>18.0	90/90	52	101 (89−113)
Decision Speed	26	4.1	3.0	5.5	11/90	3	72 (69−76)
Memory for Words	20	>18.0	>18.0	>18.0	98/90	74	109 (103−116)
Rapid Picture Naming	90	2.8	1.8	4.0	1/90	2	71 (69−72)
Planning	—	>18.0	K.9	>18.0	92/90	74	109 (103−116)
Pair Cancellation	68	6.9	5.1	9.1	43/90	11	82 (80−84)

Form A of the following achievement tests was administered:

CLUSTER/Test	RAW	GE	EASY	to DIFF	RPI	PR	SS (68% BAND)
Letter-Word Identification	70	15.4	11.6	>18.0	95/90	66	106 (101−111)
Reading Fluency	32	3.4	2.8	4.0	0/90	1	64 (62−65)
Story Recall	—	>18.0	10.0	>18.0	95/90	87	117 (110−124)
Understanding Directions	—	11.9	6.2	>18.0	83/90	34	94 (88−99)
Calculation	35	>18.0	>18.0	>18.0	97/90	83	114 (108−120)
Math Fluency	93	8.0	5.3	12.5	70/90	8	79 (76−81)
Spelling	50	13.9	12.9	>18.0	92/90	56	102 (98−107)
Writing Fluency	30	>18.0	12.9	>18.0	94/90	64	105 (100−111)
Passage Comprehension	37	11.3	7.5	>18.0	80/90	31	93 (87−98)
Applied Problems	49	13.0	9.7	14.6	85/90	42	97 (93−101)
Writing Samples	15-E	>18.0	13.9	>18.0	97/90	97	129 (117−141)
Story Recall—Delayed	—	—	—	—	—	—	—
Word Attack	20	4.3	3.0	6.1	26/90	4	73 (69−77)
Picture Vocabulary	40	>18.0	>18.0	>18.0	99/90	94	124 (118−130)
Oral Comprehension	30	>18.0	13.7	>18.0	97/90	80	112 (105−120)
Editing	22	11.7	8.9	15.0	83/90	37	95 (90−100)
Reading Vocabulary	—	>18.0	15.4	>18.0	98/90	87	117 (113−121)
Quantitative Concepts	—	>18.0	10.6	>18.0	95/90	63	105 (100−110)
Academic Knowledge	—	>18.0	16.5	>18.0	98/90	86	116 (111−122)

Table 5.6— *Continued*

CLUSTER/Test	RAW	GE	EASY to DIFF		RPI	PR	SS (68% BAND)
Spelling of Sounds	22	3.3	1.8	6.4	44/90	7	78 (74–82)
Sound Awareness	38	4.7	2.8	10.3	64/90	17	86 (81–90)
Punctuation & Capitals	29	12.9	9.2	>18.0	86/90	37	95 (87–103)

DISCREPANCIES	STANDARD SCORES			DISCREPANCY		Significant at + or −1.50 SD (SEE)
	Actual	Predicted	Differ-ence	PR	SD	

Intra-Individual

DISCREPANCIES	Actual	Predicted	Difference	PR	SD	Significant
Comprehension-Knowledge (Gc)	130	96	+34	>99.9	+4.01	Yes
Long-Term Retrieval (Glr)	86	100	−14	11	−1.23	No
Visual-Spatial Thinking (Gv)	63	101	−38	0.3	−2.80	Yes
Auditory Processing (Ga)	85	100	−15	13	−1.13	No
Fluid Reasoning (Gf)	95	99	−4	35	−0.39	No
Process Speed (Gs)	64	101	−37	0.3	−2.71	Yes
Short-Term Memory (Gsm)	100	99	+1	53	+0.09	No
Phonemic Awareness	86	100	−14	13	−1.15	No
Working Memory	90	99	−9	24	−0.72	No
Basic Reading Skills	90	99	−9	16	−0.99	No
Reading Comprehension	107	98	+9	83	+0.97	No
Math Calculation Skills	100	99	+1	53	+0.07	No
Math Reasoning	101	99	+2	58	+0.21	No
Basic Writing Skills	99	99	0	49	−0.03	No
Written Expression	115	98	+17	93	+1.49	No
Oral Expression	125	97	+28	99.6	+2.69	Yes
Listening Comprehension	104	98	+6	68	+0.46	No
Academic Knowledge	116	98	+18	97	+1.83	Yes

DISCREPANCIES	STANDARD SCORES			DISCREPANCY		Significant at + or −1.50 SD (SEE)
	Actual	Predicted	Differ-ence	PR	SD	

*Intellectual Ability/Achievement Discrepancies**

DISCREPANCIES	Actual	Predicted	Difference	PR	SD	Significant
Broad Reading	75	94	−19	3	−1.94	Yes
Basic Reading Skills	90	94	−4	36	−0.36	No
Reading Comprehension	107	94	+13	88	+1.19	No
Broad Mathematics	99	97	+2	57	+0.17	No
Math Calculation Skills	100	98	+2	57	+0.18	No
Math Reasoning	101	96	+5	66	+0.42	No
Broad Written Language	113	94	+19	96	+1.79	Yes
Basic Writing Skills	99	96	+3	58	+0.20	No
Written Expression	115	95	+20	97	+1.84	Yes
Oral Language (Ext)	118	93	+25	99	+2.54	Yes
Oral Expression	125	95	+30	99.5	+2.59	Yes
Listening Comprehension	104	94	+10	81	+0.88	No
Academic Knowledge	116	95	+21	96	+1.81	Yes

*These discrepancies based on GIA (Ext) with ACH Broad, Basic, and Applied clusters.

Derived Scores

A variety of derived scores are reported on the scoring program's Table of Scores. In addition to age norms (age 2 to 90+), grade norms are also provided (from kindergarten through first year graduate school). The age- and grade-equivalent scores used in the WJ III do not possess the limitations associated with age- or grade-equivalents from many other tests; group-administered instruments are particularly limited, because they represent the median performance of individuals at the defined age- or grade-equivalent. Because the WJ III grade norms are continuous (rather than extrapolated), a third-grade individual who obtains a grade equivalent of 8.0 obtained the same score, using the same items, that was obtained by the median norming student in grade 8.0.

A criterion-referenced Relative Proficiency Index (RPI) is reported that describes the relative ease or difficulty with which the individual will find similar grade- (or age-) level tasks. This RPI is then represented as a developmental or instructional zone that has implications in regard to the difficulty level of school assignments. For example, a student in the first month of sixth grade has an easy level of reading at beginning first grade and a difficult level of reading at the end of second grade. Clearly, sixth-grade reading materials would be too difficult for this student to read independently.

For the percentile ranks and standard scores, examiners may select to report a 68%, 90%, or 95% confidence band around the standard score. Additional scores are provided for interpretation of the discrepancy procedures. The two most useful scores for interpreting the presence and severity of any discrepancy are the *discrepancy percentile rank* (DISCREPANCY PR) and the *discrepancy standard deviation* (DISCREPANCY SD). The DISCREPANCY PR displays the percentage of the population with a similar positive or negative discrepancy (such as 95% or 5%). The DISCREPANCY SD is a standardized z score that transforms the same discrepancy into standard deviation units, such as using a criterion of + or −1.5 standard deviations.

CLINICAL SIGNIFICANCE

Due to the recent publication of the WJ III, our clinical experiences, as well as the number of studies in the published literature, are limited. Therefore, we will discuss several of the new features of the test and explain how these features will be useful to those engaged in clinical practice. In addition, we will present case studies of two individuals who were administered the normative version of the WJ III. Because the final norm tables were not yet available when this chapter was prepared, a pilot version of the WJ III Compuscore and Profiles program was used.

Discrepancy Procedures

The WJ III provides several diagnostic procedures for helping an evaluator describe a person's abilities. The main options for analyzing within-individual variability are the intra-ability discrepancies. The WJ III has three intra-ability discrepancy procedures: (a) intra-individual, (b) intra-cognitive, and (c) intra-achievement. The purpose of the intra-ability discrepancy procedure is diagnosis, or to help determine an individual's strengths and weaknesses (Mather & Schrank, 2001). One notable feature of the WJ III is the provision of a new intra-individual discrepancy procedure. This intra-individual discrepancy procedure allows examiners to analyze an individual's cognitive and academic performance across the cluster scores of the WJ III COG and WJ III ACH.

The WJ III also provides procedures for evaluating three types of ability/achievement discrepancies. The purpose of the ability/achievement discrepancies is to predict achievement (Mather & Schrank, 2001). In addition to use of the GIA-Standard or GIA-Extended scores and the Predicted Achievement scores in the WJ III COG, the WJ III ACH contains an ability/achievement discrepancy procedure. For this procedure, the Oral Language cluster may be used as the measure of ability to predict academic achievement. The Oral Language ability/achievement procedure has particular relevance for helping clinicians distinguish between individuals with adequate oral language capabilities, but poor reading and writing abilities (i.e., specific reading disabilities), and individuals whose oral language abilities are commensurate with their reading and writing performance. In the first case, intervention would focus on reading and writing development; in the second case, intervention would be directed to all aspects of language.

Special Clinical Clusters

The WJ III contains several special clinical clusters that will help evaluators to make informed decisions regarding instructional programming and the need for accommodations. Although additional research is needed on the clinical efficacy of these clusters, a substantial body of research documents the importance of these abilities to scholastic and vocational success. The WJ III clinical clusters provide a psychometrically sound score based upon extensive exploratory and confirmatory factor analyses (McGrew & Woodcock, 2001). It is important to keep in mind the multidimensional nature of any task or factor when attempting to measure a cognitive processing area (e.g., working memory, attention). For instance, a cancellation task, like the Pair Cancellation test of the WJ III, involves sustained attention, processing speed, and motoric speed, as well as executive functioning. Careful consideration of an individual's performance across the WJ III (COG as well as ACH) and behavioral observations will provide evidence of whether good or poor performance can be attributed to the cognitive factor under investigation or to something else.

Broad Attention

The WJ III Broad Attention cluster measures four different cognitive aspects of attention: The Numbers Reversed Test measures attentional capacity; The Auditory Working Memory test measures the ability to divide information in short-term memory; The Auditory Attention test measures the ability to attend to speech sounds; and the Pair Cancellation test measures the ability to sustain attention. This broad sampling of tasks may assist evaluators in the identification of individuals with attentional difficulties, particularly when accompanied with systematic behavioral observations, both within the test setting and the natural environment. Attention is a superordinate construct with multifactorial attributes. Barkley (1996) suggests that individuals with learning disabilities have trouble sustaining attention, whereas individuals with attention-deficit/hyperactivity disorder (ADHD) appear deficient in response inhibition and the capacity to delay response. Furthermore, internal factors, such as motivation, may influence attentional performance as much as the format of a task (Barkley, 1996). Therefore, practitioners are cautioned to consider multiple factors when interpreting the results of this cluster.

Phonological Awareness and
Phoneme/Grapheme Knowledge

A powerful feature of the WJ III is inclusion of new measures of phonological awareness, as well as measures of phoneme/grapheme knowledge. Phonological awareness measures on the WJ III include a variety of tasks, such as rhyming, deletion, closure, and speech discrimination. Phoneme/grapheme knowledge is measured through the abilities to read and spell nonwords with regular English spelling patterns. A substantial body of research has documented the relationship between poor phonological awareness and delayed literacy development. Deficits in phonological skill have been identified as a major cause of severe reading problems (Ehri, 1994; Morris et al., 1998; Wagner, Torgesen, Laughon, Simmons, & Rashotte, 1993). These clusters will be useful as early intervention measures to identify children at risk for reading failure, as well as to document the cause of reading failure in older students. In addition, a comparison of performance on phonological awareness tasks to performance on tasks involving knowledge of sound-symbol relationships will help evaluators determine appropriate treatment plans. For example, a child with poor phonological awareness may initially need attention directed toward the development of these oral language abilities. A child with good phonological awareness, but poor reading, will require direct instruction in phoneme/grapheme relationships.

Cognitive and Academic Fluency

The WJ III contains several measures of fluency, or speed of processing. Automaticity refers to the ability to perform tasks rapidly with ease. The ability to work easily and efficiently is an important factor for both scholastic and vocational success. The fluency tests should help evaluators document weaknesses in the speed of performance that will be particularly relevant to a need for accommodations, such as extended time. The Cognitive Fluency Cluster consists of the following tests: Retrieval Fluency, Decision Speed, and Rapid Picture Naming. The Academic Fluency Cluster consists of Reading Fluency, Math Fluency, and Writing Fluency.

Recent research has confirmed the importance of cognitive processing speed to the process of reading, particularly decoding (Denckla & Cutting, 1999; Wolf, 1999; Wolf & Segal, 1999). While debate is ongoing as to which associated cognitive abilities impact most on the automatic processing of reading and spelling words, the importance of fluency and speed to the acquisition of literacy is well supported. As Ehri (1998) noted, the key to skilled reading is processing words in text quickly without having to pay conscious attention to the words.

The relationship between the Cognitive and Academic Fluency Clusters and reading comprehension and written expression is unclear, particularly with the adolescent and adult populations. Considerable controversy exists regarding the nature of the relationship between reading rate and comprehension and production of text (Carver, 1997; Kintsch, 1998; Perfetti, 1985). Reading rate may reflect the strength of retrieval from long-term memory (Kintsch, 1998) or the efficiency in which an individual is able to code information (Perfetti, 1985). Reading rate and reading comprehension appear to be dissociable factors (Palmer, MacLeod, Hunt, & Davidson, 1985; Rupley, Willson, & Nichols, 1998). The Cognitive and Academic Fluency Clusters of the WJ III will provide a strong psychometric tool for exploring this relationship across the life span.

Working Memory

The construct of working memory and its relationship to academic performance has been a topic of recent investigation. Generally, the conceptualization of working memory is described as a "mental workspace consisting of activated memory representations that are available in a temporary buffer for manipulation during cognitive processing" (Stoltzfus, Hasher, & Zacks, 1996, p. 66). Although researchers appear to adhere to the same definition, controversy exists about the best way to measure the components. Therefore, many different types of measures have been designed to investigate the construct of working memory (Baddeley & Hitch, 1974; Daneman & Carpenter, 1980; Wagner, Torgesen, & Rashotte, 1999).

The Working Memory Cluster is composed of two tests: Numbers Reversed and Auditory Working Memory. This cluster will provide researchers and practitioners a psychometrically strong tool to investigate the relationships among an individual's working memory and achievement (e.g., reading decoding, reading comprehension, calculation, spelling). Clinically, it will be interesting to observe a student's performance on this cluster in comparison to the Wechsler Memory Scale—III (WMS-III; Wechsler, 1997) Working Memory Index and/or the Phonological Memory Comprehensive Composite Score on the *Comprehensive Test of Phonological Processing* (CTOPP; Wagner et al., 1999). Each of the working memory composite scores across these different measures (WJ III, WMS-III, and the CTOPP) are composed of different types of tasks. Therefore, a student might show varied performance across these different composite scores of working memory due to the difference in the type of tasks. For instance, on the WJ III Auditory Working Memory test, the individual is required to recall real words, not just letters or numbers. For students with specific word recall problems, such a task might present significant problems that would not be observed on the Letter-Numbers Subtest (WMS-III) or on a numbers reversed task. On the CTOPP, the Phonological Memory Cluster contains a test that requires repetition of nonwords, as well as a digit-reversed task. The recall of nonwords could prove more difficult for students with significant phonological processing deficits as compared to tasks involving letters, numbers, or real words. Practitioners should, therefore, look at the performance of an individual across different types of working memory tests, because significant discrepancies may provide an important piece of diagnostic information.

Executive Processing

The Executive Processing Cluster consists of the following tests: Concept Formation, Planning, and Pair Cancellation. As with the constructs of processing speed, working memory, and attention, definition and measurement problems have surrounded the construct of executive functioning. The Executive Processing Cluster attempts to provide professionals with a broad measure of cognitive processes (planning, self-regulation, and reasoning) that have been identified in the literature as components of executive functioning. Recent research investigating the academic performance (reading, written expression, and mathematics) of individuals with learning disabilities has identified a strong relationship between difficulties with academic tasks and executive functioning (Meltzer, 1994). The Executive Processing Cluster will provide a means for researchers and practitioners to add to the body of literature investigating the relationships between executive functioning and school performance.

Academic Skills, Fluency, and Application

The WJ III ACH provides clusters of three different facets of academic performance: basic skills, fluency and rate, and problem solving. A comparison among these three areas will help evaluators describe an individual's academic strengths and weaknesses, as well as make recommendations for an effective treatment plan. For example, one individual may perform poorly on tasks that are of a lower order, such as those involved in decoding, encoding, and calculating, but then do well on tasks that involve the application of information, logical thinking, and problem solving. Another individual may demonstrate the opposite pattern and may have mastered the coding aspects of the symbol system, but then struggles with higher-order tasks involving language and reasoning. Still another individual may have strengths in both the coding and symbolic aspects of language, but may comprehend and complete tasks at a very slow rate. Clearly, the implications differ.

ADVANTAGES AND DISADVANTAGES

The WJ III is based upon a comprehensive theory of intellectual functioning. The combination of Carroll's three-stratum theory with *Gf-Gc* theory provides a comprehensive and empirically supported framework for understanding the structure of human cognitive abilities. The instrument is a valuable tool for helping an examiner develop diagnostic and clinical hypotheses. The WJ III is unique in that it provides a wide age range, comprehensive system for measuring: (a) general intellectual ability, (b) specific cognitive abilities, (c) predicted achievement, (d) oral language, and (e) achievement. The co-normed batteries facilitate comparisons among these areas.

Discrepancy Procedures

A major advantage of this instrument is the variety of discrepancy procedures. Because all norms for the WJ III COG and the WJ III ACH are based on data from the same sample of subjects, examiners can report discrepancies between and among an individual's WJ III scores without applying a correction for the statistical phenomenon of regression to the mean. This correction procedure would require use of a regression equation or a table based upon a regression equation. The WJ III discrepancy scores do not contain error from any unknown differences that would exist when using two tests based on different norming samples.

The intra-ability discrepancies allow the examiner to analyze patterns of variability and generate hypotheses regarding an individual's learning abilities. On the intra-ability discrepancies, identification of specific cognitive and academic strengths, as well as any cognitive inefficiencies and academic weaknesses, can help the examiner formulate ideas for intervention, leading to appropriate treatment interventions. For example, test results may indicate that an individual is low in both phonological awareness and phoneme/grapheme knowledge. The examiner may hypothesize that poor phonological awareness has affected the development of word identification and spelling skill. Therefore, the treatment recommendation would be to develop phono-logical awareness, coupled with direct instruction in word identification and spelling.

The intra-individual discrepancy procedure is in line with current thinking about the identification of specific learning disabilities. Identification of patterns of strengths and weaknesses among these abilities may help professionals more accurately identify a specific reading, mathematics, or writing disability. Many individuals with these types of disabilities do not demonstrate a significant discrepancy between traditional IQ and achievement measures because their various cognitive processing weaknesses are reflected in the intelligence test score. Fletcher and colleagues (1998) recommended that a more appropriate procedure than aptitude-achievement discrepancy would be to evaluate "domain-specific achievement skills and abilities correlated with those skills" (p. 186). In the intra-individual discrepancy procedure, co-varying cognitive and achievement weaknesses can be viewed as observable symptoms of the same underlying disability.

Interpretation of the Predicted Achievement Clusters

Some users may not understand the purpose of the WJ III COG Predicted Achievement clusters and equate this procedure as the sole method for documenting the existence of a learning disability. On the WJ III COG, the Predicted Achievement clusters are used to predict academic performance in each curricular area using a mix of the cognitive tasks statistically associated with performance in the particular area, that is, they include the cognitive tests most relevant to the specific achievement domain.

In the field of learning disabilities, the main criterion used for identification of a learning disability is a discrepancy between aptitude (equated with potential for school success) and achievement. In other words, a specific learning disability is characterized as "unexpected" poor performance based upon a person's other capabilities. The WJ III Predicted Achievement clusters were not designed to predict future performance, to document unexpected poor performance, or to estimate one's "potential" for school success (Mather & Schrank, 2001). They merely reflect the relationship between the cognitive variables most related to an area of academic performance and the actual present level of achievement.

In some cases, students with specific learning disabilities may not exhibit Predicted Achievement/Achievement discrepancies, because a weak ability or weak abilities are included in the predictive score. For example, the tests of Sound Blending and Visual Matching are part of the Reading Aptitude cluster. A student with poor basic reading skills will often obtain low scores on measures of phonological awareness as well as on measures of processing speed. Thus, the Predicted Achievement cluster for reading will be lowered, and the individual will not evidence an Predicted Achievement/Achievement discrepancy. The cluster predicts that the student will struggle with reading, and he or she does. This lack of discrepancy does not rule out the existence of a specific reading disability. It shows that the person's cognitive abilities related to reading, as well as his or her reading skills, are weak.

In many cases, the most sensitive procedures for substantiating the existence of specific learning disabilities on the WJ III are the intra-ability discrepancies, as well as the GIA/Achievement and Oral Language Ability/Achievement Discrepancies. The student with the profile described above would most likely evidence weaknesses in Auditory Processing and Processing Speed, as well as in Basic Reading and Writing Skills. This joint evaluation of an individual's cognitive and achievement abilities is a promising avenue for helping professionals to identify domain-specific learning disabilities.

Interpretation of Gf-Gc Abilities

Another advantage of the WJ III is the application of Gf-Gc theory to the interpretation of cognitive abilities. Each of the factors measures a broad intellectual ability and each test measures a narrow aspect of the broad ability. By analyzing the varied patterns of strengths and weaknesses exhibited by an individual, an evaluator can deduce the types of tasks that will be easy and the types of tasks that will be difficult for the person within an educational or vocational setting. Table 5.7 provides a few examples of possible performance implications.

Wide Range of Measurement

Another major advantage of the WJ III is that it is designed to provide a range of measurement from the age of 2 years through mature adulthood. Separate college norms (two-year college, four-year college, and first-year graduate levels) are provided. This comprehensive age range allows an examiner to follow an individual's performance at different periods of development.

Complexity of the Instrument

The WJ III is a complex, multifaceted instrument. The complexity of this instrument may be viewed as both an advantage and a disadvantage. Although computer scoring simplifies the scoring process, learning to administer and then interpret this instrument require extensive study and clinical experience. Although an examiner may use selective testing and just administer certain portions of the instrument, mastery of the entire scope of interpretive options may seem overwhelming to beginning and less experienced examiners.

TABLE 5.7
Sample Performance Implications of the *Gf-Gc* Broad Abilities in the WJ III COG

Gf-Gc Ability	Sample Implications
Short-Term Memory (*Gsm*)	Ease in remembering just-imparted instructions or information and following complex or multistep verbal directions.
Processing Speed (*Gs*)	Efficiency in executing easy cognitive tasks; amount of time needed for responding to well-practiced tasks.
Comprehension-Knowledge (*Gc*)	Ease in using and comprehending general information and vocabulary; knowledge of procedures.
Visual Processing (*Gv*)	Facility on tasks involving spatial orientation, object-space relationships, awareness of visual detail, and visual imagery.
Auditory Processing (*Ga*)	Facility on tasks involving speech discrimination, phonological awareness, and sound manipulation. Ability to apply this knowledge to the interpretation of phoneme-grapheme relationships.
Long-Term Retrieval (*Glr*)	Ease in recalling relevant information and in learning and retrieving names; amount of practice and repetition needed to learn information; ability to remember previously learned material.
Fluid Reasoning (*Gf*)	Ease in grasping abstract concepts, generalizing rules, and seeing implications; ability to change strategies if first approach does not work.

Clinical Clusters

Although the clinical clusters will assist skilled evaluators in diagnosis, caution must be exercised in interpreting the results. As noted, the abilities subsumed under "executive functioning" or "attention" are broad and multifaceted and do not represent factorially pure constructs. One would not want to assume that because an individual has a low score on Broad Attention that he or she has attention-deficit/hyperactivity disorder. This type of diagnosis must be coupled with qualitative information. Future validity research will help clarify the application and interpretation of the clinical clusters.

Interpretation of Cluster Scores

Cluster scores form the basis for interpretation of the WJ III. On occasion, a cluster score may mask individual differences in test performance that have clinical implications. Each test within a cluster is composed of two qualitatively different narrow abilities. In some instances, the tests within a cluster will differ significantly from each other. For example, in the WJ III ACH, the Broad Reading cluster includes one measure of word reading ability (Letter-Word Identification), one measure of reading rate (Reading Fluency), and one measure of reading comprehension (Passage Comprehension). An individual may have mastered the decoding aspects of reading, but have trouble understanding what he or she reads. When the test scores within a cluster differ significantly, the meaning of the cluster score must be interpreted with caution. Additional testing may be needed to document a specific difficulty.

CASE STUDIES

Two brief case studies are presented to illustrate how the WJ III can provide diagnostic information to substantiate an individual's strengths and weaknesses, as well as to help an evaluator derive information for intervention and accommodation purposes. For these examples, the scores are described using the WJ III verbal classification for standard scores and percentile ranks. More in-depth case reports would include additional qualitative and quantitative information. One example represents an elementary-level student and the other represents a postsecondary/college student.

Jovita

Jovita, an 8-year-old third grader, was referred due to difficulties with reading and written expression. Her first-grade teacher reported that Jovita had a very difficult time with phonological awareness and letter-identification activities. She was referred at the end of first grade for special education placement but did not have a large enough score discrepancy between ability and achievement measures to qualify for services. Jovita's third-grade teacher observed that she tried to read very fast, but did not recognize many words. The teacher noted that on occasion Jovita would refuse to write and put her head down on her desk during writing times. In contrast, Jovita was successful on classroom tasks involving listening and speaking. Because Jovita continued to be frustrated on all tasks involving any type of reading or writing, her third-grade teacher initiated another referral to try and discover the nature of her difficulties. The WJ III was administered as a means to identify whether or not Jovita had specific processing deficits that were affecting reading and writing performance as well as her present levels of academic functioning.

Background Information

Jovita lives with her mother and two older brothers. Her mother works full-time at a local convenience store. Jovita's mother had an uneventful pregnancy and delivery. All developmental milestones were met with normal limits. Jovita did experience recurring ear infections, which were initially treated with antibiotics, and then a myringotomy was performed to insert tubes. Since the myringotomy, Jovita has been free of ear infections and has been an otherwise healthy child.

Jovita's mother reported reading to her children every night. She reported that Jovita has always enjoyed being read to since she was an infant. Because of Jovita's early reading experiences, her mother was surprised when Jovita had difficulty learning to read in school.

Summary—Cognitive WJ III

Jovita's verbal ability (acquired knowledge and language comprehension) and thinking ability (intentional cognitive processing) were in the average range. However, her cognitive efficiency (automatic cognitive processing) was in the low-average range. (See Table 5.5 for an overview of Jovita's scores.)

When compared with others at her grade level, Jovita's performance was superior in visual-spatial thinking; average in comprehension-knowledge and fluid reasoning; and low-average in long-term retrieval, auditory processing, processing speed, and short-term memory. Jovita's cognitive performance may be further influenced by her cognitive fluency, executive processes, and knowledge (average), her working memory capacity and attentional resources (low-average), and her phonemic awareness (low to very low).

Summary—Achievement WJ III

When compared to others at her grade level, Jovita's overall level of achievement was low. Her math calculation skills, math reasoning, and academic knowledge all were within the average range. Her oral expression and listening comprehension were also average. In contrast, her scores on basic reading, reading comprehension, written language, basic writing skills, and written expression were very low. Additionally, her academic skills, academic applications, and academic fluency and knowledge of phoneme-grapheme relationships were all significantly low.

Jovita attempted to pronounce words, but she appeared to rely mainly on initial and final consonant sounds. Consequently, she mispronounced many medial vowel sounds. Even though many of her responses were close approximations, her use of partial alphabetic cues resulted in a very low score in letter/word identification. Similar error patterns were apparent in spelling. When asked to write short responses and simple sentences, Jovita said that her hand was too tired from the other writing test. When asked later to write a few more answers, she replied that her hand was always tired. Therefore, her obtained score on the Writing Samples test is likely an underestimate of writing performance and more a reflection of her frustration with writing.

Discrepancy Analysis

When her abilities across the WJ III COG and ACH were compared, Jovita demonstrated significant strengths in comprehension-knowledge and visual-spatial thinking. She had significant weaknesses in basic reading and writing skills, reading comprehension, and written expression. When her General Intellectual Ability—Extended (GIA-EXT) was compared to her academic performance, Jovita's performance was significantly lower than predicted in all measured areas of reading and writing.

Recommendations

Assessment results suggest that Jovita should be eligible for learning disability services. Treatment recommendations would focus on provision of age-appropriate oral language activities, an adaptation of reading and writing materials to her present instructional levels (approximately beginning first grade), and direct instruction in phonological awareness and phoneme/grapheme relationships. In addition, efforts must be made to address her negative feelings toward reading and writing and her occasional refusals to engage in these activities.

Tom (Postsecondary/College)

Tom, a 21-year-old right-handed college student was selected due to his unusual profile. He requested an evaluation to support a request for appropriate accommodations. Tom reported that it takes him an extraordinary amount of time to read and write. He reports that he sees words in mirror images and finds it easier to write backward than forward. Because a complete reversal of letters is very unusual in the adult population, the WJ III was chosen to help identify any specific cognitive processes that might be impacting his academic performance.

Background Information

Tom reached developmental milestones within normal age ranges. All visual and auditory acuity screening was within normal limits. He received speech therapy for articulation in second grade. He remembers his second-grade teacher rubbing his hand with sandpaper because she thought he was a smart aleck for writing backward. After his mother contacted school officials about the matter, he was referred to special education. At the beginning of the third grade, he was diagnosed with dyslexia and attended resource classes for 1 year.

Tom reported that he did not like classes in special education because they moved too slowly for him and he wanted to take more challenging courses. By high school, Tom was taking advanced placement classes. He noted that he often missed questions on exams, particularly when required to use "bubble" sheets that included "b's" and "d's." Tom is now attending a

4-year college and believes that, to be successful, he needs accommodations in the academic setting.

Summary—Cognitive WJ III

Tom's verbal ability (acquired knowledge and language comprehension) was in the superior range when compared to others in his grade group. His thinking ability (intentional cognitive processing) was in the low-average range. It is important to note the impact of Tom's low score on the Spatial Relations test on his Thinking Ability cluster score. This score should not be interpreted as an inability to reason, but rather as reflecting his difficulty with visual-spatial thinking. Tom's cognitive efficiency (automatic cognitive processing) was low-average. (See Table 5.6 for a summary of Tom's results.)

When compared to others in his grade group, Tom's performance was superior in comprehension-knowledge; average in fluid reasoning and short-term memory; low-average in long-term retrieval and auditory processing; and very low in visual-spatial thinking and processing speed. His knowledge was in the superior range; his working memory in the average range; his phonemic awareness, broad attention, and executive processes in the low-average range; and his cognitive fluency in the very low range.

Summary—Achievement WJ III

When compared to others at his grade level, Tom's overall level of achievement was in the low-average range. He demonstrated a significant strength in oral expression and oral language. His written expression and academic knowledge were within the high-average range. Tom was not penalized for "backward writing" on any of the writing tests. His reading, writing, and math performance fell within the average range. His academic skills and academic applications were both within the average range, but his academic fluency was significantly low. Tom's phoneme/grapheme knowledge was also low.

Discrepancy Analysis

When his abilities across the WJ III COG and ACH clusters are compared, Tom demonstrated a significant strength in comprehension-knowledge, knowledge, and oral expression. He demonstrated significant weaknesses in visual-spatial thinking and processing speed. These findings suggest that Tom has good verbal abilities, including a rich vocabulary and considerable knowledge. In contrast, he has severe weaknesses in visual-spatial thinking and speed of processing.

Recommendations for Accommodations

Based upon his history of difficulties, his slow processing speed and his unusual writing style, Tom was deemed eligible for an accommodation of extended time on all examinations. In addition, he received copies of all of his textbooks on tape. He was further allowed to tape-record any lectures that required extensive note-taking. Additionally, results supported the use of a proofreader, scribe, and note taker. Tom was also encouraged to seek a substitution for any foreign language requirement that would be part of his program of study. Application of these accommodations will increase the chances of Tom's success in a postsecondary setting.

CONCLUSION

Cognition, thinking, intelligence, and ability are all terms used throughout the literature to refer to an individual's abilities to process information and solve problems. The term "problem solving" provides an accurate description of the dynamic nature of cognitive and academic development (Hoy & Gregg, 1994). Cognitive and academic abilities are dynamic processes, rather than the end products of development. As Rogoff (1990) clearly stated: "The thinking organism is active in participating in an event, exploring a situation, directing attention, attempting solution" (p. 31).

The WJ III provides a unique means by which to observe the interactive and dynamic patterns produced during cognitive and academic problem solving, in tasks requiring lower-level and/or higher-level processing. New tests have been added to the WJ III that measure important clinical factors, such as working memory, planning, cognitive fluency, and attention. The procedures for investigating ability/achievement and intra-ability discrepancies have been expanded. While the WJ and the WJ-R provided a means to observe the dynamic interaction between intra-cognitive and intra-achievement abilities, the WJ III provides a new intra-individual discrepancy procedure that allows for a more in-depth examination of the multidimensional interaction among cognitive and achievement abilities, allowing evaluators to examine an individual's abilities across cognitive and achievement clusters.

The WJ III provides a sophisticated and comprehensive tool by which to observe the cognitive and academic abilities of individuals across the life span and to explore the dynamic nature of intellectual and academic development. As noted by Woodcock (1997), the primary purpose of an assessment instrument such as the WJ III is not to determine an IQ score, but to find out more about the problem. We feel certain that this instrument will prove to be a valuable diagnostic tool for many practitioners, because it will help them accomplish the primary goal of many assessments: to identify, address, and attempt to remedy the problems experienced by an individual.

References

Baddeley, A. D., & Hitch, G. (1974). Working memory. In G. H. Bower (Ed.), *The psychology of learning and motivation: Advances in research and theory* (Vol. 8, pp. 47–89). New York: Academic Press.

Barkley, R. A. (1996). Critical issues in research on attention. In G. R. Lyon & N. A. Krasnegor (Eds.), *Attention, memory and executive function* (pp. 45–96). Baltimore, MD: Brookes.

Carroll, J. B. (1993). *Human cognitive abilities: A survey of factor-analytic studies.* Cambridge, England: Cambridge Univ. Press.

Carroll, J. B. (1998). Human cognitive abilities: A critique. In J. J. McArdle & R. W. Woodcock (Eds.), *Human cognitive abilities in theory and practice* (pp. 5–23). Mahwah, NJ: Erlbaum.

Carver, R. P. (1997). Reading for one second, one minute, or one year from the perspective of rauding theory. *Scientific Studies of Reading, 1,* 453–471.

Cattell, R. B. (1941). Some theoretical issues in adult intelligence testing. *Psychological Bulletin, 38,* 592.

Daneman, M., & Carpenter, P. A. (1980). Individual differences in working memory and reading. *Journal of Verbal Learning and Verbal Behavior, 19,* 450–466.

Denckla, M. B., & Cutting, L. E. (1999). History and significance of rapid automatized naming. *Annals of Dyslexia, XLIX,* 29–44.

Ehri, L. C. (1994). Development of the ability to read words: Update. In R. Ruddell, M. Ruddell, & H. Singer (Eds.), *Theoretical models and processes of reading* (pp. 323–358). Newark, DE: International Reading Association.

Ehri, L. C. (1998). Grapheme-phoneme knowledge is essential for learning to read words in English. In J. L. Metsala & L. C. Ehri (Eds.), *Word recognition in beginning literacy* (pp. 3–40). Mahwah, NJ: LEA.

Flanagan, D. P., & McGrew, K. S. (1997). A cross-battery approach to assessing and interpreting cognitive abilities: Narrowing the gap between practice and cognitive science. In D. P. Flanagan, J. L. Genshaft, & P. L. Harrison (Eds.), *Contemporary intellectual assessment: Theories, tests, and issues* (pp. 314–325). New York: Guilford.

Fletcher, J. M., Francis, D. J., Shaywitz, S. E., Lyon, G. R., Foorman, B. R., Stuebing, K. K., & Shaywitz, B. A. (1998). Intelligent testing and the discrepancy model for children with learning disabilities. *Learning Disabilities Research & Practice, 13(4),* 186–203.

Horn, J. L. (1965). *Fluid and crystallized intelligence.* Unpublished doctoral dissertation, University of Illinois, Urbana-Champaign.

Horn, J. L. (1991). Measurement of intellectual capabilities: A review of theory. In K. S. McGrew, J. K. Werder, & R. W. Woodcock, *WJ-R Technical Manual* (pp. 267–300). Itasca, IL: Riverside.

Horn, J. L., & Noll, J. (1997). Human cognitive capabilities: Gf-Gc theory. In D. P. Flanagan, J. L. Genshaft, & P. L. Harrison (Eds.), *Contemporary intellectual assessment: Theories, tests, and issues* (pp. 53–91). New York: Guilford.

Hoy, C., & Gregg, N. (1994). *Assessment: The special educator's role.* Pacific Grove, CA: Brooks/Cole.

Kintsch, W. (1998). *Comprehension: A paradigm for cognition.* Cambridge, England: Cambridge Univ. Press.

Mather, N., & Schrank, F. A. (2001). *Use of the WJ III discrepancy procedures for learning disabilities identification and diagnosis* (Assessment Service Bulletin No. 3). Itasca, IL: Riverside.

McGrew, K. S. (1994). *Clinical interpretation of the Woodcock-Johnson Tests of Cognitive Ability—Revised.* Boston: Allyn & Bacon.

McGrew, K. S. (1997). Analysis of the major intelligence batteries according to a proposed comprehensive Gf-Gc framework. In D. P. Flanagan, J. L. Genshaft, & P. L. Harrison (Eds.), *Contemporary intellectual assessment: Theories, tests and issues.* New York: Guilford.

McGrew, K. S., & Flanagan, D. P. (1998). *The intelligence test desk reference* (ITDR): Gf-Gc Cross-Battery Assessment. Boston: Allyn & Bacon.

McGrew, K. S., & Woodcock, R. W. (2001). *WJ III technical manual.* Itasca, IL: Riverside.

Meltzer, L. (Ed.). (1994). *Strategy assessment and instruction for students with learning disabilities: From theory to practice.* Austin, TX: PRO-ED.

Morris, R. D., Stuebing, K. K., Fletcher, J. M., Shaywitz, S., Lyon, G. R., Shankweiler, D. P., Katz, L., Francis, D. J., & Shaywitz, B. A. (1998). Subtypes of reading disability: Variability around a phonological core. *Journal of Educational Psychology, 90,* 347–373.

Palmer, J., MacLeod, C. M., Hunt, E., & Davidson, J. E. (1985). Information processing correlates of reading. *Journal of Memory and Language, 24,* 59–88.

Perfetti, C. A. (1985). *Reading ability*. London: Oxford Univ. Press.

Reschly, D. J. (1990). Found: Our intelligences: What do they mean? *Journal of Psychoeducational Assessment, 8*, 259–267.

Rogoff, B. (1990). *Apprenticeship in thinking: Cognitive development in social context*. New York: Oxford Univ. Press.

Rupley, W. H., Willson, V. L., & Nichols, W. D. (1998). Exploration of the developmental components contributing to elementary school children's reading comprehension. *Scientific Studies in Reading, 2*, 143–158.

Schrank, F. A., & Woodcock, R. W. (2001). WJ III *Compuscore and Profiles Program* [Computer software]. Itasca, IL: Riverside.

Stoltzfus, E. R., Hasher, L., & Zacks, R. T. (1996). Working memory and aging: Current status of the inhibitory view. In J. T. E. Richardson, R. W. Engle, L. Hasher, R. H. Logie, E. R. Stoltzfus, & R. T. Zacks (Eds.), *Working memory and human cognition* (pp. 66–88). New York: Oxford Univ. Press.

Wagner, R. K., Torgesen, J. K., Laughon, P., Simmons, K., & Rashotte, C. A. (1993). The development of young readers' phonological processing abilities. *Journal of Educational Psychology, 85*, 1–20.

Wagner, R. K., Torgesen, J. K., & Rashotte, C. A. (1999). *Comprehensive Test of Phonological Processing*. Austin, TX: PRO-ED.

Wechsler, D. (1997). *Wechsler Memory Scale—Third Edition*. San Antonio, TX: The Psychological Corporation.

Wolf, M. (1999). What time may tell: Towards a new conceptualization of developmental dyslexia. *Annals of Dyslexia, XLIX*, 2–28.

Wolf, M., & Segal, D. (1999). Retrieval-rate, accuracy and vocabulary elaboration (RAVE) in reading-impaired children: A pilot intervention program. *Dyslexia: An International Journal of Theory and Practice, 5*, 1–27.

Woodcock, R. W. (1990). Theoretical foundations of the WJ-R measures of cognitive ability. *Journal of Psychoeducational Assessment, 8*, 231–258.

Woodcock, R. W. (1993). An informational processing view of Gf-Gc theory. *Journal of Psychoeducational Assessment* [Monograph Series: WJ-R Monograph], 80–102.

Woodcock, R. W. (1997). The Woodcock-Johnson Test of Cognitive Ability—Revised. In D. P. Flanagan, J. L. Genshaft, & P. L. Harrison (Eds.), *Contemporary intellectual assessment: Theories, tests and issues* (pp. 230–246). New York: Guilford.

Woodcock, R. W. (1998). Extending Gf-Gc theory into practice. In J. J. McArdle & R. W. Woodcock (Eds.), *Human cognitive abilities in theory and practice* (pp. 137–156). Mahwah, NJ: Erlbaum.

Woodcock, R. W., & Johnson, M. B. (1977). *Woodcock-Johnson Psycho-Educational Battery*. Allen, TX: DLM.

Woodcock, R. W., & Johnson, M. B. (1989). *Woodcock-Johnson Psycho-Educational Battery—Revised*. Itasca, IL: Riverside.

Woodcock, R. W., McGrew, K. S., & Mather, N. (2001). *Woodcock-Johnson III*. Itasca, IL: Riverside.

Woodcock, R. W., & Muñoz-Sandoval, A. F. (1996a). *Batería Woodcock-Muñoz: Pruebas de aprovechamiento—Revisada*. Itasca, IL: Riverside.

Woodcock, R. W., & Muñoz-Sandoval, A. F. (1996b). *Batería Woodcock-Muñoz: Pruebas de habilidad cognitiva—Revisada*. Itasca, IL: Riverside.

Ysseldyke, J. (1990). Goodness of fit of the Woodcock-Johnson Psycho-Educational Battery-Revised to the Horn-Cattell Gf-Gc theory. *Journal of Psychoeducational Assessment, 8*, 268–275.

PART

II

Achievement Assessment

CHAPTER

6

Wechsler Individual Achievement Test

DONNA RURY SMITH

The Psychological Corporation

INTRODUCTION

The measurement of academic achievement using standardized test instruments is a routine activity in today's schools. In fact, with renewed interest in student performance and increased emphasis on teacher and school accountability, the time spent testing school children is actually increasing. This phenomenon is true not only for large-scale, high-stakes group assessment, but also for the use of individually administered achievement instruments. For school psychologists, the passage of the Education for All Handicapped Children Act (1975) became the driving force behind their assessment practices (Fagan & Wise, 1994), and numerous achievement instruments have been published in the last two decades.

Student achievement is typically evaluated for four possible reasons using an individually administered tool:

- To determine where the student falls along a continuum of skill acquisition
- To identify those students who score at the lower and upper ends of the continuum for purposes of intervention (e.g., remediation or acceleration/enrichment)
- To determine eligibility for special programs
- To measure effectiveness of instruction or intervention

Handbook of Psychoeducational Assessment
Copyright © 2001 by Academic Press. All rights of reproduction in any form reserved.

In practice, however, an individual achievement test is most often administered with an intelligence or ability test to determine if there is a significant discrepancy between the two scores. For some time, this discrepancy model has been the cornerstone for the process of determining whether a referred student has a learning disability. In recent years, there has been considerable discussion about this model; some researchers are promoting models that do not rely on an ability test score as part of the decision-making process. Others redefine a learning disability as a failure to respond to intervention/treatment regardless of ability level (Abbott, Reed, Abbott, & Berninger, 1997). However, the controversy surrounding the continued use of ability testing in the ability-achievement paradigm does not negate the use of achievement testing. In fact, most researchers as well as educators continue to rely heavily on individually administered achievement batteries to evaluate student progress and to guide instruction.

WECHSLER INDIVIDUAL ACHIEVEMENT TEST (WIAT)

The WIAT, introduced in 1992 by The Psychological Corporation, is a comprehensive norm-referenced battery designed to assess the achievement of academic skills in students in kindergarten through grade 12 (ages 5.0 to 19.11).

Its use is recommended (a) to evaluate individual performance in relationship to grade- or agemates, (b) to identify individual strengths and weaknesses across a broad range of academic skills, (c) to compare a student's general ability level with his or her level of achievement using two different methods of discrepancy analysis—the simple-difference method and the predicted-achievement method, and (d) to guide instructional intervention planning. The WIAT is currently in revision and differences between the two editions will be discussed later in this chapter.

Unique Features

Two unique features have been the hallmark of the WIAT. First, although a few other achievement tests are co-normed with ability tests (e.g., the Woodcock-Johnson Psycho-Educational Battery—Revised (WJPB-R); Woodcock & Johnson, 1989), the WIAT is the only individual achievement battery directly linked with the Wechsler scales. Measurement experts (Reynolds, 1990) stress the value of using tests normed on the same standardization sample when employing a discrepancy model to determine eligibility for a specific learning disability. Second, the WIAT is distinct for its comprehensive coverage in assessing all areas of learning disability as specified in U.S. federal law (Education for All Handicapped Children Act, 1975; Individuals with Disabilities Education Act, 1997).

Subtest Content

WIAT items encompass a wide range of curriculum objectives. Item development began with a review of educational research, a search through representative curriculum guides, and consultation with curriculum specialists; it produced the scope and sequence of curriculum objectives outlined in the manual (see p. 123, Wechsler Individual Achievement Test Manual; The Psychological Corporation, 1992). Final test items were selected after extensive field testing and item analysis using both item response theory (Lord, 1980) and conventional methods. The record forms delineate specific skills as they are evaluated. Scores from each of the eight subtests contribute to one of the four composite scores.

Reading Composite Subtests

Basic Reading is designed to assess the student's ability to identify beginning or ending sounds by letter name, to match a written word with the appropriate picture, and to read words orally from a word list. Students in grade 3 or above begin with the word list. Items are scored dichotomously and the examiner is able to record the student's behavior when presented with unfamiliar words. It is recommended that only those students with Basic Reading raw scores of 8 or higher be given Reading Comprehension.

Reading Comprehension is composed of short passages (carefully constructed and analyzed for appropriate grade-level readability) that the student must read and orally presented comprehension questions that must be answered verbally. Standardization procedure requires the continued presentation of the passage as the student responds to the questions. Early items offer visual cues to assist the beginning reader, but standard scores are not available for 5-year-olds or students in kindergarten.

Mathematics Composite Subtests

Mathematics Reasoning was developed to measure problem solving when a student is presented with word problems that require determination and application of the appropriate processes necessary for solution (e.g., addition and subtraction), comparison and ordering of fractions and decimals, interpretation of graphs and statistics, and computation of practical problems related to money, time, and measurement. Many items are presented visually, and text is provided for most items so that the student can read the question along with the examiner.

Unlike other subtests, **Numerical Operations** contains item sets, and each item must be given within the specific item set. The first set measures the ability to write dictated numerals; the following sets ask the student to write answers to increasingly difficult computational problems that require an understanding of whole numbers, fractions, decimals, and the solution of basic algebraic equations.

Language Composite Subtests

Two developmental levels of listening comprehension are represented in the **Listening Comprehension** subtest: (a) nine receptive vocabulary items and (b) 26 items similar to Reading Comprehension in that the student listens to a short passage, then responds verbally to questions about it.

Oral Expression measures various language skills. The beginning items parallel the receptive vocabulary tasks on Listening Comprehension with expressive vocabulary items that require a verbal response rather than a pointing one. The balance of the subtest items measure the child's ability to communicate effectively by requiring him or her to provide detailed descriptions, accurate directions, and logical sequences of information in response to visual cues, with responses evaluated using a scoring rubric.

Writing Composite Subtests

The final two subtests, **Spelling** and **Written Expression,** contribute to the Writing Composite score. Spelling is a dictation test in which a word is pronounced, used in a sentence, then repeated for the student to write. About 10% of the words are homonyms, requiring that the word be spelled in context; the balance was selected from seven different basal spelling series.

Written Expression consists of a single (with an alternate) verbal prompt to which the student (only grades 3–12) must respond by composing a descriptive or narrative discourse. Scoring methods include holistic scoring and analytic scoring—the latter focusing on specific elements of writing such as ideas and development, organization, vocabulary, sentence structure, and mechanics. Because it provides a profile of strengths and weaknesses, only the analytic scoring method is used to derive standard scores.

TECHNICAL EVALUATION

Standardization Sample

The WIAT norms were derived from a standardization sample of 4252 children in 13 age groups ranging from 5.0 to 19.11 years and enrolled in grades K–12. The sample was representative of the U.S. population in 1988 based on stratification of age, grade, gender, race/ethnicity, geographic region, and parent education level. A small degree of case weighting, described on page 131 in the WIAT manual, was used to adjust the race/ethnicity proportions.

Further, the sample was drawn from both public and private school settings, and students receiving mainstream special services were not excluded. As a result, 6% of the standardization sample consisted of students with learning disabilities, speech/language disabilities, emotional disturbance, or physical impairments. In a 1999 review of four widely used achievement test batteries (Alfonso & Tarnofsky, 1999), the WIAT standardization sample was rated as *adequate* based on the number of variables representing U.S. population, and *good* based on size of normative sample and recency of data.

Reliability

WIAT internal consistency has been rated from adequate to very good by reviewers Nicholson (1992), Thompson (1993), and Alfonso and Tarnofsky (1999). Split-half reliability coefficients, corrected by the Spearman-Brown formula, range from .83 to .92 for all subtests across ages and from .77 to .92 for subtests across grades. Reliability coefficients for the composite scores, computed using a formula suggested by Nunnally (1978), range from .90 to .97 across ages and from .88 to .97 across grades. Test-retest stability for five grade groups ($n = 367$) with a median retest interval of 17 days produced corrected r coefficients ranging from .61 to .95 on subtests and from .65 to .97 on composites. The majority of the reported composite coefficients were .90 or higher. Standard error of measurement (SEM) was calculated for each standard score at each grade and age and is reported for both the fall and spring standardization samples. For composite scores the average SEMs for the fall ranged from 4.35 (Reading) to 5.19 (Language); for the spring they ranged from 3.87 (Reading) to 4.91 (Writing). Interscorer reliability is reported for Reading Comprehension and Listening Comprehension as an average correlation of .98; for Oral Expression as an average coefficient of .93; and as average coefficients of .89 for Written Expression (prompt 1) and .79 (prompt 2).

Validity

Evidence of three traditional types of validity—content, construct, and criterion evidence—were evaluated in order to demonstrate that the WIAT measures what it is intended to measure. Even though the content validity was assessed by a panel of national curriculum experts and deemed representative, school curricula vary. Users should review achievement test items to determine how closely the items match what is taught in their school.

Evidence of construct validity includes the expected intercorrelations among subtests reported by age, intercorrelations with the Wechsler scales (see Table D.6 of the WIAT manual), studies of group differences between the standardization sample and various clinical groups as well as differences between the various age/grade groups, and a multitrait-multimethod study of the WIAT and other achievement tests (Roid, Twing, O'Brien, & Williams, 1992). In summary, there was a striking consistency in the correlations among scores on the reading, mathematics, and spelling subtests of the WIAT and those of the corresponding subtests on the other achievement measures.

Since the majority of school psychologists' assessment time is spent with students with learning disabilities (Smith, Clifford, Hesley, & Leifgren, 1992), WIAT scores were correlated with school grades, group-administered achievement tests, and clinical study groups. Flanagan (1997) notes that a strength of the WIAT is the demonstrated treatment validity because "data are reported that indicate that the WIAT effectively aids in diagnosis of educational/clinical concerns" (p. 84). Special study groups included children classified as gifted and children with mental retardation, emotional disturbance, learning disabilities, attention-deficit/hyperactivity disorder (ADHD), or hearing impairment. Mean composite scores ranged from 112.1 (SD = 9.9) to 117.8 (SD = 9.5) for gifted children, from 58.0 (SD = 10.2) to 66.3 (SD = 10.3) for children with mental retardation, and from 74.6 (SD = 12.0) to 92.8 (SD = 12.6) for children with learning disabilities. These results confirmed predicted expectations for achievement scores in each group.

Independent studies (Slate, 1994; Martelle & Smith, 1994; Saklofske, Schwean, & O'Donnell, 1996; Michalko & Saklofske, 1996) have provided additional evidence of WIAT validity. Saklofske, Schwean, and O'Donnell (1996) studied a sample of 21 children on Ritalin and diagnosed with ADHD and obtained subtest and composite means quite similar to those reported in the WIAT manual. Gentry, Sapp, and Daw (1995) compared subtest scores on the WIAT and the Kaufman Test of Educational Achievement (K-TEA) for 27 emotionally conflicted adolescents and found higher correlations between pairs of subtests (range of .79 to .91) than those reported in the WIAT manual. Because comparisons are often made between the WIAT and the WJPB-R, Martelle and Smith (1994) compared composite and cluster scores for the two tests in a sample of 48 students referred for evaluation of learning disabilities. WIAT composite score means were reported as 83.38 (SD = 10.31) on Reading, 89.32 (SD = 10.60) on Mathematics, 99.24 (SD = 11.84) on Language, and 80.32 on Writing. WJPB-R cluster score means were 87.67 (SD = 11.80) on Broad Reading, 92.09 (SD = 11.62) on Broad Mathematics, and 83.88 (SD = 8.24) on Broad Written Language. Although global scales of the WIAT and WJPB-R relate strongly to each other, mean WIAT composites were 3 to 6 points lower than mean scores on the WJPB-R clusters. Subtest analysis indicated some differences in the way skills are measured; for example, the two reading comprehension subtests (WIAT Reading Comprehension and WJPB-R Passage Comprehension) are essentially unrelated (r = .06). Study authors suggest that "for students with learning disabilities, the two subtests measure reading comprehension in different ways, resulting in scores that may vary greatly from test to test" (p. 7). In addition to a strong relationship between the WIAT Mathematics Composite and the WJPB-R Broad Mathematics cluster, WIAT Numerical Operations correlated equally well with Applied Problems ($r = .63$) and with Calculation ($r = .57$) on the WJPB-R, suggesting that WIAT Numerical Operations incorporates into one subtest those skills measured by the two WJPB-R subtests. At the same time, the WJPB-R Quantitative Concepts subtest does not have a counterpart on the WIAT. The Language Composite of the WIAT, however, is a unique feature of that test.

ADMINISTRATION AND SCORING

WIAT is administered in both school and clinical settings. School-based examiners (generally school psychologists, educational diagnosticians, reading specialists, or special education teachers), like their more clinically-based colleagues (psychologists, neuropsychologists, and psychometricians), typically use the WIAT as part of a comprehensive psychoeducational evaluation. Examiners must have graduate-level training in the use of individually administered assessment instruments to be eligible to administer and interpret WIAT results. Administration time is approximately 30–50 minutes for children in kindergarten through grade 2 and about 55–60 minutes, excluding the time for Written Expression, for grades 3–12. It can take as long as 15 additional minutes to administer Written Expression. Although a student's start point should be determined by current grade placement, beginning at a start point for an earlier grade is permissible if the student is low-functioning. Likewise, starting at the next-higher grade level is acceptable when a student is known to function above grade placement. All subtests except Written Expression are untimed. Testing materials include two stimulus booklets (on easel frames) which contain all administration directions, a record form, and a response booklet.

Types of WIAT Scores

Raw scores are computed for each subtest, but cannot be compared accurately to each other because each subtest has a different number of items and a different range of possible total scores. Comparisons across subtests or comparison of an individual student's performance to age- or grade-peers is best made by using the derived scores (e.g., standard scores or percentile ranks) included in the test manual appendix.

Standard Scores

The distribution of WIAT standard scores forms a normal curve ($M = 100$; $SD = 15$). Approximately 68% of students in the standardization sample scored between 85 and 115 (within 1 standard deviation of the mean), and 95% scored between 70 and 130 (within 2 standard deviations of the mean). WIAT standard scores can also be transformed into stanines, normal curve equivalents, and percentile ranks. The WIAT manual cautions against inappropriate use of grade- and age-equivalent scores as they are easily misunderstood by parents and teachers.

Score Limitations

WIAT scores cannot be interpreted by reporting standard scores if the student's age or grade falls outside the WIAT age/grade range. Some examiners have used the WIAT with older students and adults in spite of the fact that no age or grade norms are currently available, but results from such administration must be used cautiously and out-of-range testing should be reported. Because of ceiling effects, caution should also be used when testing gifted adolescents.

INTERPRETATION

Qualitative Analysis

The IDEA Amendments of 1997 emphasize that a major purpose of evaluating a student is to "determine the educational needs of such child." Experienced examiners have learned that test results (e.g., scores) provide only a piece of the puzzle and that valuable information is available to the astute examiner who knows how to supplement subtest and composite standard scores with qualitative analysis of the student's performance while being tested. Error analysis, behavioral observation, and testing the limits provide abundant information about a student's strengths and weaknesses and how to optimize the learning experience. Nonetheless, an examiner may wish to administer criterion-referenced assessment tools such as the *Stanford Diagnostic Reading Test, Fourth Edition* (Karlsen & Gardner, 1995) and the *Stanford Diagnostic Mathematics Test, Fourth Edition* (The Psychological Corporation, 1995) for additional diagnostic assessment of specific skills. The new *Process Assessment of the Learner* (PAL) *Test Battery for Reading and Writing* (Berninger, in press), a diagnostic reading/writing assessment, provides a focused evaluation of the underlying processes that contribute to the acquisition of reading and writing skills. Using the Wechsler Individual Achievement Test—Second Edition (WIAT II; The Psychological Corporation, in press) and the PAL Test Battery together yields powerful information that can lead to educational decision making based on empirical evidence. The relationship between the two tests will be more closely examined later in this chapter.

USE WITH OTHER POPULATIONS

Research investigating the psychometric properties of the WIAT has in large part been limited to U.S. samples, although a 1996 study by Michalko and Saklofske considered its use with Canadian children. They found preliminary evidence supporting the reliability and validity of the instrument with their Saskatchewan sample ($n = 90$). Correlations in the expected moderate range resulted between subtests of similar content. Correlations between WIAT reading and math composites and the group-administered Canadian Achievement Test/2 (CAT/2; Canadian Test Centre, 1992)—considered to be one of the most psychometrically sound and widely used English measures of academic achievement in Canada (Bachor & Summers, 1985)—range from .65 (grade 4) to .81 (grade 6) in reading, and from .49 (grade 6) to .61 (grade 4) in math. Each of the three grade levels studied (grades 4, 5, and 6) scored significantly higher on several of the WIAT subtests and composite scores in comparison to the U.S. standardization sample. This could be the result of the small Canadian sample size or of a sample that was not representative of the Canadian student population. Study authors concluded that larger, more nationally representative studies should be conducted to determine if the development of Canadian norms is warranted.

USING THE WIAT WITH THE WECHSLER INTELLIGENCE SCALES

Although there is considerable variability among professionals regarding the procedures necessary to establish that a referred student has a learning disability, the most common practice is the inclusion of a statistically significant ability-achievement discrepancy. For this reason the WIAT was linked to the *Wechsler Intelligence Scale for Children—Third Edition* (WISC-III; Wechsler, 1991) through a sample of 1118 children aged 5–19; to the *Wechsler Preschool and Primary Scale of Intelligence—Revised* (WPPSI-R; Wechsler, 1989) through a sample of 84 5-year-olds; and to the *Wechsler Adult Intelligence Scale—Revised* (WAIS-R; Wechsler, 1981) with a sample of 82 adolescents aged 17–19 who were administered both tests during WIAT standardization. The demographic characteristics of the linking samples are reported in the WIAT manual (p. 130). This linking feature is especially important to the many clinical and school psychologists who continue to favor WISC-III as their ability measure of choice (Hegstrom, 1999).

Two controversial issues related to the use of the ability-achievement paradigm warrant further discussion. The first issue concerns the examiner's decision to use either the simple-difference or the predicted-achievement method. Braden and Weiss (1988) caution that using the simple-difference method can be problematic because the relationship between achievement and ability scores is ignored. Further, error of measurement is omitted if the simple difference is not further tested for statistical significance. They recommend that when the simple-difference method is employed the user should (a) determine if the difference is statistically significant and (b) establish how frequently the statistically significant difference occurred in the standardization sample. WIAT Table C.8 (Wechsler, 1992, p. 355) presents the subtest and composite score differences required between the WIAT and the Wechsler Full Scale IQ (FSIQ) for statistical significance. Tables C.9, C.10, and C.11 (Wechsler, p. 356) report the percentage of children in the respective standardization samples whose achievement standard score was below FSIQ by a specified amount.

To illustrate, if a 9-year-old youngster scored an FSIQ 102 on WISC-III with standard scores of 89 (simple difference of 13) on the WIAT reading composite and 73 (simple difference of 29) on the math composite, both scores would meet the required difference for significance, which would be 8.82 ($p = .05$) for reading and 9.75 ($p = .05$) for math. Further, while 10% of the standardization sample had a similar difference in reading, less than 1% had such a large difference in math.

However, Thorndike (1963) argued that underachievement should be defined as the discrepancy of actual achievement from the *predicted* value based on a regression equation between aptitude and achievement. WIAT Table C.4 (Wechsler, 1992, p. 352) provides differences required for statistical significance using the predicted-achievement method and Tables C.5 and C.6 (Wechsler, p. 353) chart the differences obtained by children in the WISC-III and WPPSI-R standardization linking samples.

In comparison, the same 9-year-old student with an FSIQ of 102 has a predicted reading composite score of 101 (predicted difference is 12) and a predicted math composite score of 101 (predicted difference is 28). The difference required for statistical significance at $p = .05$ is 17.04 for reading and 12.46 for math. In the WISC-III linking study, 10–15% of students had a similar difference in reading, and again, less than 1% had such a significant score in math.

The second controversial issue concerns which Wechsler IQ score should be employed to calculate the differences. The WIAT manual reports predicted subtest and composite standard scores only from the Full Scale IQ. Flanagan and Alfonso (1993a, 1993b) provide additional tables reporting the differences using Wechsler Verbal IQ (VIQ) or Performance IQ (PIQ), which they computed using the predicted-achievement formula in the WIAT manual (see pp. 188–189 of the manual). They employed the predicted-achievement method because it takes into account regression to the mean and measurement error, but note that the FSIQ may be misleading. In cases where VIQ and PIQ scores differ significantly from each other, using one of those scores may represent a more accurate estimate of ability than using the Full Scale IQ score.

Conversely, Glutting, Youngstrom, Ward, Ward, and Hale (1997) proposed that using FSIQ is preferable to using WISC-III VIQ, PIQ, or Index scores. They concluded that FSIQ is the "most parsimonious and powerful predictor of academic achievement obtainable from the WISC-III," and that using VIQ, PIQ, or Index scores as predictors leads to more "laborious calculations with meager dividends" (p. 300).

Another important issue surrounding the use of WISC-III and WIAT in the ability-achievement paradigm has been to evaluate the fairness of using WISC-III IQ scores to predict WIAT scores across groups. In a 1995 study, Weiss and Prifitera analyzed 1000 cases of students aged 6–16 ($Mdn = 10.5$) from the WIAT standardization data that were considered representative of the 1988 U.S. population. They examined differential prediction of the four WIAT composite standard scores across ethnic groups and genders using regression equations developed with the WISC-III Full Scale IQ. Differential prediction was observed in 4 of the 12 comparisons, but in each case the magnitude of the effect size was small. Results suggested that there is no compelling reason to not use the WISC-III/WIAT regression equations. In fact, the study provides considerable evidence in support of the hypothesis that WISC-III FSIQ adequately predicts achievement scores on the WIAT across racial/ethnic groups and genders using a common regression equation calculated from the total sample.

Although some examiners assume that the same process can be used by plugging in the numbers from a non-Wechsler ability test, the WIAT manual clearly warns that "alternative ability measures should be used with extreme caution" when applying the formula (p. 189).

REVIEWS OF WIAT

The WIAT is an achievement battery that has been widely used by both school psychologists and special educators. Reviewers have noted both positive and negative attributes of the instrument.

Cohen (1993), Nicholson (1992), Thompson (1993), and Treloar (1994) consider the following to be advantages of the WIAT:

1. The overall standardization sample, reliability, and validity
2. Ease of administration
3. The link between the WIAT and the Wechsler IQ scales
4. The ability-achievement discrepancy analysis with both simple-difference and predicated-difference data

5. Coverage of all areas mandated by federal legislation to assess for learning disabilities
6. The close association to educational curricula

At the same time, Thompson (1993) voiced concern related to complexity of task and/or directions when testing very young or low-functioning children. Sharp (1992), Riccio (1992), Woitaszewski and Gridley (1995) and Alfonso and Tarnofsky (1999) noted problems with inadequate floor items (or, the number of appropriate items for kindergarten or older low-functioning students). Woitaszewski and Gridley, along with Hishinuma and Tadaki (1997), noted lower reliability with very young children.

These issues have been addressed in the WIAT manual with a precaution about testing very young children. The new WIAT II should alleviate these concerns with the downward extension of the age range, the inclusion of a large number of at-risk 4-year-olds in the standardization sample, the addition of several new pre-reading, pre-writing and early-math concept tasks, and the inclusion of age-appropriate directions.

Reviewers have also noted problems related to the scoring procedures for Oral Expression and Written Expression. Specifically, the scoring is too subjective and verbatim responses are difficult to record (Thompson, 1993), scores for low-scoring students appear to be inflated (Sharp, 1992; Woitaszewski & Gridley, 1995), and there is an overemphasis on spelling on the Written Expression composite score (Sharp). On the WIAT II, the scoring rubrics for both Oral Language and Written Expression were reworked in consultation with leading researchers in the field of writing instruction and assessment, and spelling carries less weight when calculating the Written Language composite score.

Sharp (1992) and Woitaszewski and Gridley (1995) have observed depressed reliability coefficients for Listening Comprehension, Oral Expression, and Written Expression. When revising these subtests for the WIAT II, additional items with higher reliabilities were included and problematic items were either dropped or reworked.

Riccio (1992) noted a lack of evidence of construct validity for Oral Expression with no correlational data presented with other measures of language. He also noted that Written Expression correlational studies were limited only to other spelling tests rather than writing sample measures. WIAT II standardization added validity studies with the Peabody Picture Vocabulary Test—III (PPVT-III; Dunn & Dunn, 1997) and the Oral and Written Language Scales (OWLS; Carrow-Woolfolk, 1995). Riccio also mentions the problem of limited content of subtests. Specifically, Written Expression contained only a single writing prompt and Listening Comprehension had items that were limited because they did not require an oral response. WIAT II focuses on the writing process rather than just the product by assessing writing skills at the word, sentence, and discourse levels. A new scoring rubric is in place for both Written Expression and Oral Expression tasks. Listening Comprehension as well as Oral Expression items require the student to respond in both verbal and non-verbal ways. One Oral Expression task, for example, asks the student to generate a story based on sequential pictorial cues.

Finally, Cohen (1993) believes there is a lack of evidence that the WIAT is useful in program planning, program evaluation, or placement decision making. WIAT II development required input from curriculum specialists, classroom teachers, and researchers in both the U.S. and Canada to ensure appropriate item selection. The new WIAT II scoring software helps the classroom teacher use the qualitative and quantitative information from the test to develop a focused intervention plan. One of the primary goals of the WIAT revision was to more closely link assessment to intervention. This is evident with the inclusion of an entire chapter in the WIAT II manual dedicated to intervention.

WIAT II: A STRONGER LINK BETWEEN ASSESSMENT AND INTERVENTION

Although the WIAT II retains the basic features of the original, it incorporates several changes and additions that enhance the diagnostic utility of the instrument, addresses the criticisms leveled at the WIAT, and extends its use to new populations. In addition, a primary goal of the test development team was to form a closer link between the WIAT II and intervention planning and implementation. Discussion of the most noteworthy differences between the two versions of the instrument follows.

An Expanded Age Range

The age range of WIAT II extends down to 4 years and stretches to include adults enrolled in higher education (e.g., 2- or 4-year degree-seeking programs) as well as non-student adults. Student norms continue to be reported by age and grade, whereas adult norms are reported by age bands similar to those in the Wechsler Adult Intelligence Scale—Third Edition (WAIS-III; Wechsler, 1997). This age extension has necessitated the addition of more floor and ceiling items (the former of which also addresses the need for easier items for low-functioning students). As a result, there are more items that can be categorized as measuring pre-reading or beginning math concepts. A greater number of difficult items lets administrators adequately assess college students and adults with learning disabilities for the purposes of remediation, modification, and accommodation.

Testing All Levels of Language Skills in Reading

Three reading subtests contribute to the Reading Composite score on the new instrument. They include Word Reading (Basic Reading renamed), Reading Comprehension, and a new subtest—Pseudoword Decoding. Based on the research of Berninger (1998), the WIAT II measures reading skills at all levels of language—namely, the subword, word, and text levels—for both diagnostic and intervention-planning purposes.

Subword Level

Because a measure of phonological awareness is the best single predictor of reading achievement in young children (Stanovich, Cunningham, & Cramer, 1984; Berninger, 1998), **Word Reading** includes pre-reading items such as letter naming and requires both application of the alphabet principle with sound-symbol relationships and identification of beginning or ending sounds and of rhyming words. **Pseudoword Decoding** measures the student's ability to identify the appropriate sounds of letters or groups of letters and blend them into a new word by applying acquired phonetic and structural analysis skills. Nonsense words are best suited for this task so that it mimics the act of reading a new, unfamiliar word and taps word-attack skills instead of stored reading vocabulary. It was therefore essential that WIAT II pseudowords be linguistically correct and phonemically representative of the developmental sequence of grapheme-phoneme relationships. According to Joshi (1995), many tests utilizing nonsense words have been developed without knowledge of these requirements.

Word Level

School psychologists and diagnosticians may relate to the experience of being confronted by a classroom teacher who disagrees with the results of a word-reading test with the comment, "That is not how the student reads in my class!" This discrepancy is often based on the teacher's expectation of automaticity (the ability to recognize and say a word quickly). Most word-reading tests do not penalize the student who laboriously decodes a new word. By introducing a measure of automaticity to Word Reading, the WIAT II user is able to compare reading accuracy to reading automaticity, providing a more functional measure of non-contextual word reading.

Text Level

The end result of reading, however, is not the pronunciation of familiar or new words, but the application of that skill to comprehension of text. One of the major goals in WIAT II **Reading Comprehension** was to develop a subtest that is more representative of reading as it occurs in the classroom or in the "real world." To this end, passages were lengthened and varied to include narrative, descriptive, and functional messages. Colorful illustrations and more

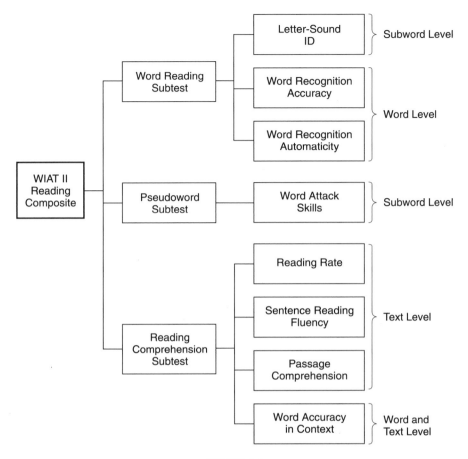

FIGURE 6.1
WIAT II Reading subtests measure at the subword, word, and text levels.

culturally diverse passages were designed to engage readers across a wide age span. Examiners have voiced concern about the practice of allowing the student to continue to view the WIAT passage while answering comprehension questions. The WIAT II addresses this concern by providing items that tap more higher-order comprehension skills such as identifying or summarizing the main idea, drawing conclusions, making inferences or generalizations, and defining unfamiliar words by using context cues. Two additional goals of WIAT II development were to create a measure of reading rate and a means to assess word reading in context.

Figure 6.1 shows how WIAT II reading subtests measure all levels of language.

Evaluating All Levels of Written Language

The WIAT II **Written Language** subtests measure writing at the subword, word, and text level in order to have a better understanding of the writing process as it relates to the writing product.

Subword and Word Levels

Spelling performance is a good indicator of phonological skills, and spelling acquisition, like grapheme-phoneme conversion skill, progresses through distinct stages. The new **Spelling** subtest is familiar, as it retains the dictation format, but additional error analysis based on developmental trends and word morphology is introduced. New spelling items include letter production and more high-frequency words. Some homonyms have been replaced by more discriminating, frequently-used homonyms (e.g., they're, their, and there).

Timed Alphabet Writing is a new task based on current research (Berninger et al., 1992; Berninger, Cartwright, Yates, Swanson, & Abbott, 1994) indicating that this activity is a strong predictor of reading, spelling, and writing skill acquisition for primary-grade students. Word fluency on the new **Written Expression** subtest is tapped by asking the student to write the name of as many things as he/she can in a specific category within a given time frame. Written Expression word fluency can also be compared to Oral Expression word fluency.

Text Level

Rather than offering a single writing prompt, the WIAT II provides multiple opportunities for a student to demonstrate writing skills at the sentence as well as the discourse level. Further, the new writing prompts, which replace the current descriptive/narrative essay requirement, ask the student to produce a persuasive essay stating and supporting a position. Because persuasive writing is more demanding than descriptive/narrative writing, the examiner can more readily identify problems with higher-order writing skills such as organizing ideas, presenting both sides of an argument, and defending a position. Essays are evaluated using a new rubric that allows both holistic and analytical scoring.

Figure 6.2 shows how the WIAT II writing subtests measure all levels of language.

A New Oral Expression Subtest

Significant revisions are also evident in the new **Oral Language** subtests that include Listening Comprehension and Oral Expression. These subtests are

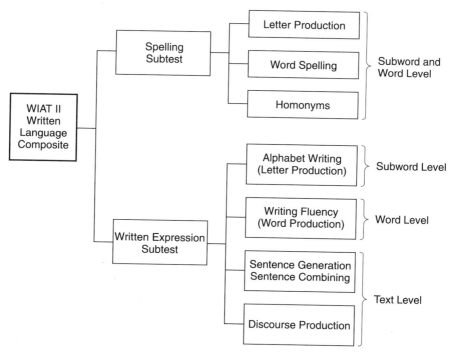

FIGURE 6.2

WIAT II Written Language subtests measure at the subword, word, and text levels. Copyright 1999 by The Psychological Corporation. All rights reserved. Adapted with permission of the author.

intended to help the examiner identify students who would benefit from a more comprehensive language evaluation by assessing samples of expressive and receptive language skills similar to those required in the classroom. The student is provided multiple opportunities to demonstrate language facility at the word and text levels when he/she is asked to generate words or discourse in response to visual cues, match verbal and visual information, repeat sentences, give detailed directions, and explain the steps in a familiar process.

Math Subtest Changes

The major changes in **Math Reasoning** on the WIAT II are the addition of floor and ceiling items; an increase in the number of more demanding, multi-step problems; and more items related to time, money, measurement, and the interpretation of graphically represented data. **Numerical Operations** begins with number identification items and ends with algebraic equations and is presented in a more traditional format rather than in item sets.

Table 6.1 summarizes the changes from the WIAT to the WIAT II subtest by subtest.

TABLE 6.1
A Comparison of WIAT and WIAT II Subtests

WIAT Subtest	Measures	WIAT II Subtest	Measures
Basic Reading	• Accuracy of word recognition	Word Reading	• Letter identification • Phonological awareness • Alphabet principle (letter-sound awareness) • Accuracy of word recognition • Automaticity of word recognition
		Pseudoword Decoding	• Phonological decoding • Accuracy of word attack
Reading Comprehension	• Literal comprehension • Inferential comprehension	Reading Comprehension	• Literal comprehension • Inferential comprehension • Lexical comprehension • Reading rate • Oral-reading accuracy • Oral-reading fluency • Oral-reading comprehension • Word recognition in context
Spelling	• Alphabet principle (sound-letter awareness) • Written spelling of regular and irregular words • Written spelling of homonyms (integration of spelling and lexical comprehension)	Spelling	• Alphabet principle (sound-letter awareness) • Written spelling of regular and irregular words • Written spelling of homonyms (integration of spelling and lexical comprehension)
Written Expression	• Descriptive writing (evaluated on extension and elaboration, grammar and usage, ideas and development, organization, unity and coherence, and	Written Expression	• Timed alphabet writing • Word fluency (written) • Sentence combining • Sentence generation • Written responses to verbal and visual cues • Descriptive writing (evaluated on organization, vocabulary, and mechanics) • Persuasive writing (evaluated on organization, vocabulary, theme

Table 6.1 — *Continued*

	sentence structure and variety) • Narrative writing (evaluated on the same criteria as descriptive)		development, and mechanics) • Writing fluency (based on word count)
Numerical Operations	• Numeral writing • Calculation (addition, subtraction, multiplication, and division) • Fractions, decimals, and algebra	Numerical Operations	• Counting • One-to-one correspondence • Numeral identification and writing • Calculation (addition, subtraction, multiplication, and division) • Fractions, decimals, and algebra
Mathematics Reasoning	• Quantitative concepts • Problem solving • Money, time, and measurement • Geometry • Reading and interpreting charts and graphs • Statistics	Mathematics Reasoning	• Quantitative concepts • Multistep problem solving • Money, time, and measurement • Geometry • Reading and interpreting charts and graphs • Statistics and probability • Estimation • Identifying patterns
Listening Comprehension	• Receptive vocabulary • Listening—literal • Listening—inferential comprehension	Listening Comprehension	• Receptive vocabulary • Expressive vocabulary • Listening—inferential comprehension
Oral Expression	• Expressive vocabulary • Giving directions • Explaining steps in sequential tasks	Oral Expression	• Word fluency (oral) • Auditory short-term recall for contextual information • Story generation • Giving directions • Explaining steps in sequential tasks

Canadian Standardization

The WIAT II has simultaneously gone through the entire development process in the U.S. and Canada. For the Canadian standardization, expert curriculum reviews were conducted by representatives of each province, p-values for each item were compared to those achieved by U.S. examinees, and about a dozen unique Canadian items (e.g., money and measurement) were developed. Analysis of standardization data will determine if differences between the two samples necessitate separate norms. WIAT and WIAT II equating studies are also being conducted in Australia, where items have undergone a similar review.

A WIAT–WIAT II CASE STUDY

One way to illustrate the changes from the WIAT to the WIAT II is to investigate how one student performs on each. Abby is an African-American, 11-year-old (11.9), sixth-grade student at a small rural school in the southern United States. Both of her parents are high school graduates, and her teacher is concerned about her inconsistent classroom performance, especially in reading. Her IQ scores, as measured on the WISC-III, are at the lower end of the average range. Abby's reading standard scores on the WIAT (given 2 weeks after the WISC-III) are provided below along with the predicted scores in parentheses, which are based on her WISC-III performance as reported in Table C.1 in the WIAT manual (p. 346):

Basic Reading 90 (87)
Reading Composite 89 (85)
Reading Comprehension 93 (85)

Abby's reading achievement scores are slightly higher than predicted and within the same range as her ability scores. Her teacher's concerns do not appear warranted based on these scores, and it is unlikely that Abby would qualify for special education services as a student with a reading disability.

Since WIAT II norms are still under development, comparisons can only be made at the item level. WIAT II was administered between the WISC-III and the WIAT. Abby makes similar errors on the WIAT Basic Reading and the WIAT II Word Reading, but overall, her responses to the two word lists are only slightly below the mean for her grade/age. On the WIAT II, Abby demonstrates good automaticity, with no self-corrections, but tends to read unfamiliar words based on beginning letter(s) and word configuration on both lists. She does not attend to visual detail nor take time to sound out the words she does not immediately recognize, thereby making an error on both subtests when she misreads "phonograph" as "photograph." On WIAT II Pseudoword Decoding, she makes numerous errors on both vowel sounds and consonant blends. When presented with an unfamiliar nonsense word she quickly reads a "real" word that resembles the configuration of the unknown word and matches its beginning and/or ending sound. As a result, a word she should decode easily like "dreep" is read as "drip," and "clurt" becomes "shirt."

Abby's performance on the more demanding WIAT II Reading Comprehension tasks reveal several significant problem areas even though she reads the passages quickly. When asked to read a sentence or short passage aloud, she makes several word-reading errors and fails to use context cues to self-correct. As a result, Abby misses many comprehension questions dealing with specific details, main idea, drawing conclusions, or making predictions. Her ability to read grade-level text is suspect, as she relies heavily on pictorial clues to respond. Since she subvocalizes as she reads, her errors are also detected and reported by the examiner. This performance matches Abby's teacher's report of her inconsistent ability to understand what she has just read in spite of the fact that she appears to be actively engaged in the reading process.

Abby's performance on the WIAT II reading tasks may not be significantly discrepant from her IQ-based predicted performance, but considerable information has been gleaned about her reading strengths (e.g., reliance on visual cues) and weaknesses (e.g., poor attention to visual detail, poor phonological coding, and underdeveloped comprehension strategies), and she could definitely benefit from intervention in the classroom. Certain recommendations can assist the teacher in meeting Abby's educational needs. These include spending a few minutes daily improving her phonemic awareness (Pseudoword Decoding provides a list of unmastered letter-sounds), giving her opportunities to read aloud and discuss comprehension questions with a partner, and teaching her specific reading strategies such as using context cues to improve understanding. In addition, assessment with the PAL Test Battery for Reading and Writing can identify which specific underlying processes are deficient, and results from this instrument can direct remediation efforts.

THE WIAT II AND THE PAL TEST BATTERY
FOR READING AND WRITING

A single test cannot measure all things for all people. The primary focus of the WIAT II will continue to be related to eligibility issues and the identification of student strengths and weaknesses; however, its contribution to intervention planning and the evaluation of program effectiveness should not be overlooked. This role has been significantly enhanced by linking WIAT II to the PAL Test Battery for Reading and Writing (Berninger, in press). For students who demonstrate deficits or unexplained performance on any of the WIAT II reading or writing subtests, the PAL Test Battery is the diagnostic tool that helps the examiner establish the developmental level of the underlying processes that are necessary to acquire reading and writing skills. In addition, using the WIAT II with the PAL Test Battery for Reading and Writing yields an enhanced means of establishing learning disability eligibility—namely, the identification of specific processing deficits.

Reading

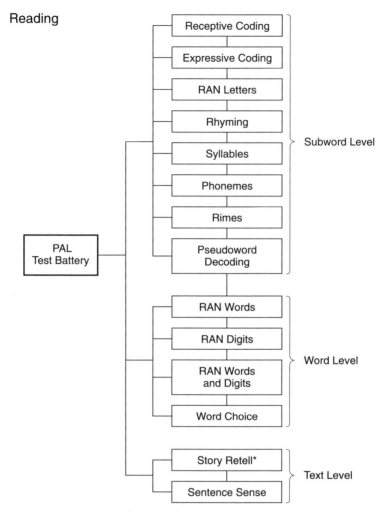

FIGURE 6.3
PAL Reading subtests measure at the subword, word, and text levels.

For example, when a student's WIAT II Reading Composite score is significantly lower than predicted based on his/her IQ (or is statistically significantly below the IQ score), the next step would be to look at performance on the Word Reading, Pseudoword Decoding, and Reading Comprehension subtests to pinpoint problem areas. By following up with the PAL Test Battery for Reading and Writing, the exact process (e.g., phonemic awareness, phoneme discrimination, orthographic coding, and rapid automatized naming) is evaluated and the student's performance can be placed on the developmental continuum.

Figure 6.3 describes the PAL Test Battery for Reading and Writing subtests that measure processes at the subword, word, and text levels.

Once this diagnostic information is obtained, specific intervention planning can occur. The Individual Education Plan (IEP) team can move beyond the referral question, "Does this student qualify for services because of a specific learning disability?" to "What specifically needs to occur in this student's instructional program so that identified skill gaps can be closed?" With this approach, assessment drives intervention; likewise, intervention directs ongoing assessment because a target instructional plan has been outlined (a true IEP), along with a timeline and course of action to evaluate intervention effectiveness and response to treatment of the student.

Even though we have been measuring student achievement for close to a hundred years, the primary goal of the next generation of test instruments, like the WIAT II, should be to evaluate student performance in a fair manner and to be able to produce both quantitative and qualitative test results to guide instruction, thereby enhancing student success. Only by shifting emphasis from "the numbers" (e.g., the student's test scores) to the student's specific instructional needs will the value of achievement assessment be fully appreciated.

References

Abbott, S., Reed, L., Abbott, R., & Berninger, V. W. (1997). Year-long balanced reading/writing tutorial: A design experiment used for dynamic assessment. *Learning Disability Quarterly, 20,* 249–263.

Alfonso, V. C., & Tarnofsky, M. (1999). Review of the psychometric properties of the reading components of four achievement batteries. Poster session presented at the meeting of the American Psychological Association, Boston.

Bachor, D. G., & Summers, G. (1985). The Canadian Achievement Test and the Canadian Test of Basic Skills: A critical review. BC *Journal of Special Education, 9,* 175–179.

Berninger, V. W. (1994). *Reading and writing acquisition: A developmental neuropsychological perspective.* Madison, WI: Brown & Benchmark. Reprinted by Westview Press, 1996.

Berninger, V. W. (1998). *Process Assessment of the Learner* (PAL): *Guides for intervention manual.* San Antonio, TX: The Psychological Corporation.

Berninger, V. W. (in press). *Process Assessment of the Learner* (PAL): *Test Battery for Reading and Writing.* San Antonio, TX: The Psychological Corporation.

Berninger, V. W., Cartwright, A., Yates, C., Swanson, H. L., & Abbott, R. (1994). Developmental skills related to writing and reading acquisition in the intermediate grades: Shared and unique variance. *Reading and Writing: An Interdisciplinary Journal, 6,* 161–196.

Berninger, V. W., Yates, C., Cartwright, A., Rutberg, J., Remy, E., & Abbott, R. (1992). Lower-level developmental skills in beginning writing. *Reading and Writing: An Interdisciplinary Journal, 4,* 257–280.

Braden, J. P., & Weiss, L. (1988). Effects of simple-difference versus regression discrepancy methods: An empirical study. *Journal of School Psychology, 26,* 133–142.

Carrow-Woolfolk, E. (1995). *Oral and Written Language Scales.* Circle Pines, MN: American Guidance Service.

Cohen, L. G. (1993). Test review: Wechsler Individual Achievement Test. *Diagnostique*, 18(3), 255–268.

Dunn, L. M., & Dunn, L. M. (1997). *Peabody Picture Vocabulary Test—Third Edition*. Circle Pines, MN: American Guidance Services.

Education for All Handicapped Children Act of 1975, Pub. L. No. 94-142.

Fagan, T. K., & Wise, P. S. (1994). *School psychology: Past, present, and future*. White Plains, NY: Longman.

Flanagan, D. P., & Alfonso, V. C. (1993a). Differences required for significance between Wechsler verbal and performance IQs and WIAT subtests and composites: The predicted-achievement method. *Psychology in the Schools*, 30, 125–132.

Flanagan, D. P., & Alfonso, V. C. (1993b). WIAT subtest and composite predicted-achievement values based on WISC-III verbal and performance IQs. *Psychology in the Schools*, 30, 310–320.

Flanagan, R. (1997). Wechsler Individual Achievement Test: Test review. *Journal of Psychoeducational Assessment*, 15(1), 83–84.

Gentry, N., Sapp, G. L., & Daw, J. L. (1995). Scores on the Wechsler Individual Achievement Test and the Kaufman Test of Educational Achievement—Comprehensive Form for emotionally conflicted adolescents. *Psychological Reports*, 76, 607–610.

Glutting, J. J., Youngstrom, E. A., Ward, T., Ward, S., & Hale, R. L. (1997). Incremental efficacy of WISC-III factor scores in predicting achievement: What do they tell us? *Psychological Assessment*, 9(3), 295–301.

Hegstrom, K., Zaske, K., & Smith, D. (1999). *Survey of test usage among clinical psychology and school psychology*. Paper presented at the meeting of the American Psychological Association, Boston.

Hishinuma, E. S., & Tadaki, S. (1997). The problem with grade and age equivalents: WIAT as a case in point. *Journal of Psychoeducational Assessment*, 15, 214–225.

Hutton, J. B., Dubes, R., & Muir, S. (1992). Assessment practices of school psychologists: Ten years later. *School Psychology Review*, 21, 271–284.

Individuals with Disabilities Education Act Amendments of 1997, H.R. 5, 105th Cong., 1st Sess. (1997).

Joshi, R. M. (1995). Assessing reading and spelling skills. *School Psychology Review*, 24(3), 361–375.

Karlsen, B., & Gardner, E. F. (1995). *Stanford Diagnostic Reading Test, Fourth Edition*. San Antonio, TX: The Psychological Corporation.

Lord, F. M. (1980). *Applications of item response theory to practical testing problems*. Hillsdale, NJ: Erlbaum.

Martelle, Y., & Smith, D. K. (1994, March). *Relationship of the WIAT and WJ-R Tests of Achievement in a sample of students referred for learning disabilities*. Paper presented at the meeting of the National Association of School Psychologists, Seattle, WA.

Michalko, K. T., & Saklofske, D. H. (1996). A psychometric investigation of the Wechsler Individual Achievement Test with a sample of Saskatchewan schoolchildren. *Canadian Journal of School Psychology*, 12(1).

Nicholson, C. L. (1992, Fall). New tests: Wechsler Individual Achievement Test. CEDS, *Communique*, 20(1), 3–4.

Nunnally, J. (1978). *Psychometric theory* (2nd ed.). New York: McGraw-Hill.

The Psychological Corporation. (1992). *Wechsler Individual Achievement Test*. San Antonio, TX: Author.

The Psychological Corporation. (1995). *Stanford Diagnostic Mathematics Test, Fourth Edition*. San Antonio, TX: Author.

The Psychological Corporation. (in press). *Wechsler Individual Achievement Test, Second Edition*. San Antonio, TX: Author.

Reynolds, C. R. (1990). Critical measurement issues in learning disabilities. *Journal of Special Education*, 18, 451–476.

Riccio, C. A. (1992). The WIAT: A critical review. *Child Assessment News*, 2(5), 10–12.

Roid, G. H., Twing, J. S., O'Brien, M. S., & Williams, K. T. (1992, March). *Construct validity of the Wechsler Individual Achievement Test: A multitrait-multimethod approach*. Paper presented at the meeting of the National Association of School Psychologists, Nashville, TN.

Saklofske, D. H., Schwean, V. L., & O'Donnell, L. (1996). WIAT performance of children with ADHD. *Canadian Journal of School Psychology*, 12(1), 55–59.

Sharp, A. (1992). The WIAT: Evaluation of assessment for provision of services under the Individuals with Disabilities Education Act (IDEA). *Child Assessment News*, 2(5), 8–10.

Slate, J. R. (1994). WISC-III correlations with the WIAT. *Psychology in the Schools*, 31, 278–285.

Smith, D., Clifford, E., Hesley, J., & Leifgren, M. (1992). *The school psychologists of 1991: A survey of practitioners*. Paper presented at the meeting of the National Association of School Psychologists, Seattle, WA.

Stanovich, K. E., Cunningham, A. E., & Cramer, B. (1984). Assessing phonological awareness in kindergarten children: Issues of task compatibility. *Journal of Experimental Child Psychology*, 38, 175–190.

Thompson, S. S. (1993). Review of Wechsler Individual Achievement Test. *Journal of Psychoeducational Assessment*, 11, 292–297.

Thorndike, R. L. (1963). *The concepts of over- and under-achievement*. New York: Bureau of Publication, Teachers College, Columbia University.

Treloar, J. M. (1994). New products: Wechsler Individual Achievement Test (WIAT). *Intervention in School and Clinic*, 29(4), 242–246.

Wechsler, D. (1981). *Wechsler Adult Intelligence Scale—Revised*. San Antonio, TX: The Psychological Corporation.

Wechsler, D. (1989). *Wechsler Preschool and Primary Scale of Intelligence—Revised*. San Antonio, TX: The Psychological Corporation.

Wechsler, D. (1991). *Wechsler Intelligence Scale for Children—Third Edition*. San Antonio, TX: The Psychological Corporation.

Wechsler, D. (1992). *Wechsler Individual Achievement Test manual*. San Antonio, TX: The Psychological Corporation.

Wechsler, D. (1997). *Wechsler Adult Intelligence Scale—Third Edition*. San Antonio, TX: The Psychological Corporation.

Weiss, L. G., & Prifitera, A. (1995). An evaluation of differential prediction of WIAT achievement scores from WISC-III FSIQ across ethnic and gender groups. *Journal of School Psychology*, 33(4), 297–305.

Woitaszewski, S., & Gridley, B. E. (1995, October). A closer look at the Wechsler Individual Achievement Test: A second opinion. *Communique*, 20–21.

Wolf, M., Bally, H., & Morris, R. (1986). Automaticity, retrieval processes, and reading: A longitudinal study in average and impaired reading. *Child Development*, 57, 988–1000.

Woodcock, R. W., & Johnson, M. B. (1989). *Woodcock-Johnson Psycho-Educational Battery—Revised*. Chicago: Riverside.

CHAPTER

7

Assessment for Reading and Writing Intervention: A Three-Tier Model for Prevention and Remediation

VIRGINIA W. BERNINGER AND SCOTT A. STAGE
University of Washington

DONNA RURY SMITH AND DENISE HILDEBRAND
The Psychological Corporation

In this chapter we describe an "assessment for intervention" model and its scientific support. The model is designed to translate research on prevention and treatment of reading and writing disabilities into practice. In the *first tier* (also called *tier* 1) of assessment for intervention—*screening for early intervention*, all K–2 students in a school are screened to identify those who are at-risk for reading and writing problems. The screening measures are brief, but research-based. Children who are identified as being at-risk receive early intervention. Intervention should be science-based, which means that a theory-driven experiment in which competing hypotheses are tested provides empirical evidence that an intervention is effective in improving student learning outcome.

In the *second tier* (also called *tier* 2) of assessment for intervention—*modifying the regular instructional program and monitoring the progress of students*—the classroom program is modified for students who fail to respond or who respond very slowly to tier 1 early intervention. The modification may consist of adding necessary curriculum components, changing pedagogical practices, revising instructional materials, or providing additional practice of skills. The goal of tier 2 is to assess whether all the essential curriculum components are in place, add them if needed, and modify how they are delivered if necessary. Curriculum-based measurement can be used to monitor progress. A multidisciplinary collaborative team uses a problem-solving approach in which further curriculum modifications are made and monitored if the student does not make progress after the initial modification.

In the *third tier* (also called *tier 3*) of assessment for intervention—*diagnosis and treatment of referred children*—students who have failed to respond or who responded very slowly to early intervention (first tier) and/or curriculum modification, as indicated by progress monitoring (second tier), are given a thorough assessment. The purpose of this assessment is not merely to make a placement decision about whether the student qualifies for special education services. Rather, the assessment should serve two additional purposes: (a) to diagnose, based on current scientific knowledge, why the student is having difficulty learning to read or write and (b) to design and implement a systematic and coordinated treatment plan and evaluate student response to it. Tier 3 intervention is usually more intensive than Tier 1 or Tier 2 intervention.

There are three noteworthy features of the assessment for intervention model. First, systematic application of the three-tier model can reduce the amount of time school psychologists spend doing comprehensive evaluations for special education placement. Because at-risk children are identified and given intervention early in their schooling, many severe problems are prevented and there are fewer students in the upper grades who require time-consuming assessment or pull-out special education services. Consequently, school psychologists have more time for their balanced role of assessment, consultation, and intervention specialist for mental health and behavioral as well as academic problems. Second, assessment and intervention are linked bidirectionally. In all tiers, assessment (of the student—tiers 1 and 3, or of the curriculum—tier 2) precedes intervention, but response to intervention is also assessed routinely and intervention is modified depending on the student's response to it. Third, in all tiers assessment and intervention should be science-based.

As we make the transition to the 21st century, education is evolving from a philosophical enterprise based on the latest fad and frequent pendulum swings to a scientific enterprise based on assessment and instructional practices that have been validated in research. For example, in the United States two recent developments are promoting science-based educational practice. The first development is the Workforce Investment Act of 1998, which established the National Institute for Literacy to provide a national resource for literacy programs. This institute offers the most up-to-date research information available—for example, from the National Institute of Child Health and Human Development (NICHD) and other sources—on phonemic awareness, systematic phonics, fluency, and reading comprehension. All schools that receive federal funding for reading (e.g., from Titles I and VII of the Elementary and Secondary Education Act of 1965, the Head Start Act, and the Individuals with Disabilities Education Act) are required to consult the available information. The Workforce Investment Act also supports the creation of new ways to offer services of proven effectiveness. The second development—the National Reading Excellence Act—empowers the National Institute for Literacy to provide competitive grants to states that implement science-based reading programs for the purpose of increasing the odds that all children will be readers by the end of third grade.

In this chapter we provide a brief overview of the scientific support for each of the three tiers of the assessment for intervention model and introduce an assessment instrument—*Process Assessment of the Learner Test Battery for Reading and Writing* (PAL-RW) (Berninger, 2001). The PAL-RW is a science-based instrument that can be used for assessment at each tier of the model, as we explain. The Learning Triangle in Figure 7.1 captures the complexities of the assessment for intervention process and we will reference it throughout the chapter to assist our readers in integrating the dynamic interrelationships among individual differences in learners' processing abilities (what the PAL-RW is designed to assess), pedagogical approaches for intervention (what teachers do), and curriculum/materials (what teachers use). We will also refer to the *Process Assessment of the Learner* (PAL): *Guides for Reading and Writing Intervention* (PAL Intervention Guides; Berninger, 1998a), which is an instructional resource for pedagogical approaches and curriculum/instructional materials linked to the PAL-RW.

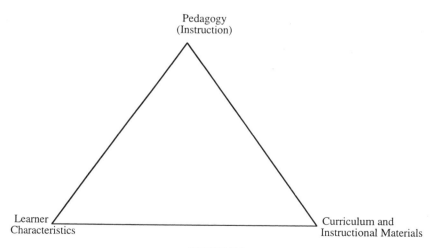

FIGURE 7.1
The Learning Triangle.

FIRST TIER: SCREENING FOR EARLY INTERVENTION

Research-Validation of Screening Measures

Reading

Numerous studies have documented the critical role of phonological skills in learning to read (e.g., Adams, 1990; Ball & Blachman, 1991; Bradley & Bryant, 1983; Liberman, Shankweiler, Fischer, & Carter, 1974; Wagner & Torgesen, 1987). The research evidence for the important role of orthographic skills (e.g., Adams, 1990; Barker, Torgesen, & Wagner, 1992; Berninger & Abbott, 1994; Berninger, Yates, & Lester, 1991; Cunningham & Stanovich, 1990; Olsen, Forsberg, & Wise, 1994) and rapid naming skills (e.g., Denckla & Rudel, 1976; Felton, Wood, Brown, Campbell, & Harter, 1987; Wolf, 1984, 1986, 1991; Wolf, Bally, & Morris, 1986) in learning to read is also growing.

In our earlier assessment studies with unreferred primary-grade children (first through third grade), both orthographic and phonological measures contributed unique variance over and beyond their shared covariance to the prediction of real word reading and pseudoword reading (e.g., Berninger & Abbott, 1994). In our more recent assessment studies with a referred sample of elementary students (first through sixth grade) who qualified as probands in our family genetics study for reading and writing disability (Berninger, Abbott, Thomson, & Raskind, 2001), four language factors—Verbal IQ, phonological, orthographic, and rapid naming—were used in structural models for predicting three reading factors: reading accuracy, reading rate, and reading comprehension. For reading accuracy, only the direct paths from the orthographic factor and the phonological factor were significant, indicating that each contributed unique variance. For reading rate, only the direct paths from the orthographic factor and the rapid naming factor were significant, indicating that each contributed unique variance. For reading comprehension, only the direct paths from Verbal IQ and the phonological factor were significant, indicating that each contributed unique variance. Thus, all four predictor factors are valid for screening for reading problems but each factor predicts different components of the functional reading system in school-aged children with reading problems. The orthographic factor predicts reading accuracy and reading rate. The phonological factor predicts reading accuracy and reading comprehension. Rapid naming predicts reading rate. Verbal IQ predicts reading comprehension.

Reading real words and reading pseudowords tap different mechanisms that may not develop at the same rate (see Berninger, 1998a). Reading real words taps the word-specific mechanism that activates orthographic, phonological, and semantic codes for words in the mental dictionary, whereas reading pseudowords taps the phonological decoding mechanism that activates orthographic and phonological but not semantic codes. Reading real words may also activate phonological decoding in addition to the word-specific mechanism. Children who grow significantly in both mechanisms achieve at a higher level in reading than children who grow in only one mechanism, and children who grow in only one mechanism achieve at a higher rate than children who grow in neither mechanism (Berninger, 1994; Berninger, Abbott, & Stage, 1999).

Writing

Our research over the past decade has shown that orthographic, fine motor, oral language (especially phonological), and reading skills are important for learning to write (for a review, see Berninger, 1994, 1998a). Orthographic coding is the rapid representation and analysis of written words in short-term memory, whereas phonological coding is the representation and analysis of spoken words in short-term memory. Our earlier assessment studies with unreferred primary-grade students showed that orthographic coding, fine-motor skills, and orthographic-motor integration contributed uniquely to handwriting and compositional fluency (Berninger, Yates, Cartwright, Rutberg, Remy, & Abbott, 1992); orthographic and phonological coding contributed uniquely to spelling (Berninger & Abbott, 1994); and Verbal IQ contributed uniquely to compositional quality along with the skills that also contributed to compositional fluency (Berninger et al.). More recently we studied the phenotype for writing disability from a systems perspective (see PAL Intervention Guides for discussion of the functional reading and writing systems) with a referred sample (Berninger, Abbott, Thomson et al., 2001). The specific language factors that were the best predictors depended on the component writing skill in the structural model. For example, in children with reading and writing disabilities, the orthographic factor contributed uniquely to handwriting, but the orthographic *and* phonological factors contributed uniquely to spelling and composition.

Screening Battery

Based on these studies with unreferred and referred students, we propose the screening battery for beginning reading in Table 7.1 and for beginning writing in Table 7.2. The PAL-RW in Tables 7.1 and 7.2 has the advantage that all measures are normed on the same sample, which is representative of the U.S. population. Some of the measures in these two tables are group-administered, but some are individually administered. In most cases the screening should require 20 minutes or less.

Research-Validated Early Intervention

The purpose of the screening is to identify students who would benefit from early intervention. The exact criterion used for identifying students for early

TABLE 7.1
Screening Battery for First Tier Early Intervention for Reading

Grade/Skill	Subskill	Tests[a]
Kindergarten		
Orthographic	Naming alphabet letters	
	Accuracy	WIAT II
	Rate	PAL-RW
Phonological	Nonword memory	CTOPP
	Rhyming	PAL-RW
	Syllable Segmentation	PAL-RW
Rapid Naming	Colors and/or Objects	NEPSY, CTOPP
First grade		
Orthographic[b]	Alphabet Task	PAL-RW, WIAT II
Phonological[b]	Phoneme Segmentation	PAL, CTOPP
Rapid Naming[b]	Letters	PAL, CTOPP
	Letters and Numbers	CTOPP
Verbal Intelligence (estimated)	Expressive Vocabulary vocabulary	WISC- III
Word-Specific Reading		
Accuracy	Single-Word Reading	WRMT-R, WIAT II
Rate	Real-Word Efficiency	TOWRE
Pseudoword Reading		
Accuracy	Single-Word Decoding	WRMT-R, WIAT II, PAL-RW
Rate	Pseudoword Efficiency	TOWRE

[a]CTOPP = Comprehensive Test of Phonological Processing (Wagner, Torgesen, & Rashotte, 1999)

NEPSY (Korkman, Kirk, & Kemp, 1998)

PAL-RW = Process Assessment of the Learner Test Battery for Reading and Writing (Berninger, 2001)

TOWRE = Test of Word Reading Efficiency (Torgesen, Wagner, & Rashotte, 1999)

WIAT II = Wechsler Individual Achievement Test—Second Edition (The Psychological Corporation, in press)

WRMT-R = Woodcock Reading Mastery Test—Revised (Woodcock, 1987)

[b]For any child who does not score above the at-risk range on the first-grade screen, also administer the kindergarten screen.

intervention can be established based on the population a particular school serves. If all the students tend to be below the national mean, the early intervention might be done with the whole class. In schools with average performance above the national mean, only those children scoring at or below a locally-defined criterion (e.g., one-third standard deviation or more below the national mean) might be flagged for early intervention. In schools

TABLE 7.2
Screening Battery for First Tier Early Intervention for Writing

Grade/Skill	Subskill	Tests[a]
Kindergarten		
Handwriting		
Accuracy	Copy Task	PAL-RW
Automaticity	Alphabet Task	PAL-RW, WIAT II
First Grade		
Orthographic	Alphabet Task	PAL-RW, WIAT II
Phonological	Phoneme Segmentation	PAL, CTOPP
Verbal Intelligence (estimated)	Expressive Vocabulary	WISC III vocabulary
Pseudoword Reading	Decoding	WRMT-R, WIAT II, PAL-RW
Spelling	Dictation	WIAT II, WRAT-3

[a] CTOPP = Comprehensive Test of Phonological Processing (Wagner, Torgesen, & Rashotte 1999)

PAL-RW = Process Assessment of the Learner Test Battery for Reading and Writing (Berninger, 2001)

WIAT II = Wechsler Individual Achievement Test—Second Edition (The Psychological Corporation, in press)

WRMT-R = Woodcock Reading Mastery Test—Revised (Woodcock, 1987)

WRAT-3 = Wide Range Achievement Test—Third Edition (Wilkinson, 1993)

with average performance at the national mean, those children at or below one standard deviation might be flagged. Regardless of the exact criterion used, it is based on performance on language skills related to reading and writing acquisition and also on reading or writing skills rather than on IQ-achievement discrepancy, which is not a valid predictor of which children will benefit from early intervention for reading (Stage, Abbott, Jenkins, & Berninger, 2000).

Phonological Awareness

Students at or below the criterion on phonological measures may benefit from the 24-lesson phonological awareness training program on pages 196 to 219 of the PAL Intervention Guides. The "sound games" described there include listening to target sounds in words, detecting a deleted sound, deleting a target sound, and substituting a target sound for the deleted sound. First graders who played these sound games, which take about 10 minutes, improved significantly in their standard scores for age in word recognition (Berninger, Abbott, & Stage, 1999). Second graders who played these sound games improved significantly in their standard scores for age in spelling (Berninger, Vaughan, et al., 1998) or word recognition (Berninger & Traweek, 1991).

Orthographic Awareness

Students at or below the criterion on orthographic measures may benefit from the "looking games" on pages 191 to 193 of the PAL Intervention Guides. These looking games include spelling back a whole word, a target letter, or letter group in a word; or retrieving the letters that come before or after a target letter in the alphabet. First graders who played some of these games, which take about 10 minutes, improved significantly in their standard scores for age in word recognition (Berninger, Abbott, & Stage, 1999). Second graders who played some of these games improved significantly in their standard scores in spelling (Berninger et al., 1998) or word recognition (Berninger & Traweek, 1991).

Talking Letters

Students who struggle with beginning reading (Berninger, Abbott, et al., 2000) or with beginning spelling (Berninger et al., 1998; Berninger, Vaughan, et al., 2000) benefit from explicit instruction in the alphabet principle. The PAL Intervention Kit contains the PAL Intervention Guides and the *Talking Letters Teacher Guide and Student Desk Cards* (Berninger, 1998b) used in our research to teach the alphabet principle to beginning readers and spellers. The Talking Letters Teacher's Guide explains the theoretical concepts underlying this approach, which draws on work in linguistics and cognitive neuroscience, to teach spelling-phoneme correspondence. It also has blackline masters for overheads for group instruction, which can be used in conjunction with student cards in the PAL Intervention Kit for children to use at their desk while reading and composing.

Rapid Automatic Naming

Few research studies have investigated how to remediate a deficit in rapid automatic naming, which is the most prevalent deficit in children and adults with reading and writing disabilities (Berninger, Abbott, et al., 2001). Training studies by Levy, Abello, and Lysynchuk (1997) suggest that pretraining in speed of naming words before they are encountered in text and repeated reading of text may improve ability to access name codes for printed words quickly and automatically.

Vocabulary Knowledge

Although it is unlikely that reading instruction will substantially alter verbal reasoning ability for age, it is likely that instruction that promotes a schema for learning word meanings (Nagy & Scott, 1990) may improve reading comprehension and word-level expression in written composition. For instructional strategies for promoting word learning, see Bear, Invernizzi, Templeton, and Johnston (1996).

Handwriting Automaticity

Students at or below the criterion on the alphabet task or the finger function tasks may benefit from the Handwriting Lessons program (Berninger, 1998c) in the PAL Intervention Kit. This program is based on research in which first graders who received training that combined numbered arrow cues and writing letters from memory with frequent letter naming improved in handwriting automaticity and in composition (Berninger, Vaughan, et al., 1997). The Handwriting Lessons manual contains detailed information on the theoretical rationale, derived from cognitive neuroscience, and the scientifically validated approach to teaching handwriting automaticity. The manual also includes blackline masters for the 24 lessons used by Berninger, Vaughan, et al. with first graders at-risk for handwriting problems. Each teacher-directed lesson provides practice for each of the 26 letters as well as a composition starter to promote transfer from handwriting automaticity training to authentic written communication.

Instructional Protocols Aimed at All Levels of Language

Design experiments (Brown, 1992) integrate components needed to achieve desired outcomes. The reading tutorial on pages 233 to 256 of the PAL Intervention Guides integrates orthographic and phonological awareness, alphabet principle, whole word and word-family strategies, oral reading and rereading for fluency, and comprehension monitoring within the same instructional session. For other similar tutorials based on the principle of design experiments, see Abbott, Reed, Abbott, and Berninger (1997). Likewise, for writing tutorials aimed at all levels of language in the same instructional session, see pages 257 to 261 of the PAL Intervention Guides and Berninger, Abbott, Whitaker, Sylvester, and Nolen (1995).

SECOND TIER: ASSESSING CURRICULUM, MODIFYING THE REGULAR PROGRAM, PROGRESS MONITORING, AND PREREFERRAL COLLABORATIVE PROBLEM SOLVING

Most psychoeducational assessment focuses on the student—that is, learner variables rather than pedagogical methods, curriculum components, or instructional materials (see Figure 7.1). In contrast, most teachers focus on pedagogy, curriculum, and instructional materials with little consideration of how individual differences in students affect their responses to instruction. From the lay public's perspective, inadequate student learning outcome is attributed primarily to the teacher. However, all angles of The Learning Triangle in Figure 7.1 influence student learning outcome, and all angles and intersecting sides of The Learning Triangle need to be taken into account in the assessment and intervention process. Berninger (1998a) discusses the importance of assessing the curriculum before assuming that a poor student learning outcome is due to learner characteristics. Based on existing research, she outlines what necessary components of curriculum should be in place for a student to develop a functional reading system and a functional writing system. She argues that before a student is referred for comprehensive assessment to determine eligibility for special education services, the collaborative team should assess the curriculum, add missing but necessary components, and empirically monitor student progress in response to the modified general education program. In some cases students respond favorably to modifications in the curriculum and assessment for special education is not needed. In this section we review empirical research that supports an approach in which, following an assessment of curriculum, curriculum-based materials are used to monitor student progress in response to curriculum modifications.

Over the past decade, a growing number of states (e.g., Florida, Illinois, Iowa, Kansas, Minnesota, and Washington) have engaged in initiatives that utilize collaborative problem-solving prereferral interventions with general education students who experience academic difficulties (Browning, Davidson, & Stage, 1998; Ysseldyke & Marston, 1998). Initially, teachers work directly with the student and the student's parent(s). If the teacher is unable to change the student's academic progress, the student is discussed by a collaborative problem-solving team that may include the following professionals: the school psychologist, the special educator, the speech and language pathologist, the social worker, the nurse, the principal, the Title I teacher, and the general education teacher. The team uses consultation methodology in which problems are identified, possible solutions are brainstormed, a potential solution is implemented and evaluated, another potential solution is implemented and evaluated if the first approach is not effective, and so on until an effective solution is found (e.g., Cole & Siegel, 1990; Ikeda, Tilly, Stumme, Volmer, & Allison, 1996; Reschly & Ysseldyke, 1995).

The team uses curriculum-based measures (CBM) both to identify problems and to monitor student progress (Fuchs & Fuchs, 1986; Shapiro, 1996; Shinn, 1995). In the area of reading, the number of correctly read words per minute from the student's reading curriculum is often used as the CBM tool. Oral reading fluency or the number of correctly read words per minute yields adequate concurrent validity with various standardized measures in the elementary grade levels (Marston, 1989). Reading readiness CBMs include letter-naming fluency (Kaminski & Good, 1996) and letter-sound fluency (Daly, Wright, Kelly, & Martens, 1997). In order to identify the extent of a student's academic problem compared to the average student at that grade level, normative data are collected three or four times throughout the school year (e.g., fall, winter, and spring; see Habedank, 1995, for a description of this procedure). The distribution of scores on the various CBM tools allows the collaborative problem-solving team to determine where a given student falls on the continuum of scores by grade level and classroom. With the school normative data, aim lines are graphed for the expected progress that a student needs to make in order maintain pace with classmates. Weekly progress is monitored so that the collaborative problem-solving team can determine (a) if the student is making progress toward attaining a minimal level of competency, which is usually set at the 25th percentile and (b) if there is need for further academic intervention. In summary, the collaborative problem-solving teams use prereferral reading interventions that are monitored with letter-naming fluency, letter-sound fluency, and oral reading fluency to determine whether the student is making sufficient academic gains in the general education setting.

The Student Responsive Delivery System (Browning, Davidson, & Stage, 1999), a state-wide pilot project in Washington using collaborative problem-solving teams,[1] is described as a Tier 2 model other states could adopt, especially for schools serving a high percentage of minority and low-income students who may score poorly on standardized tests. For use of CBM to make nondiscriminatory educational programming decisions without relying solely on special education programs, see Baker, Plasencia-Peinado, and Lezcano-Lytle (1998), Canter and Marston (1994), and Shinn, Collins, and Gallagher (1998).

The second author of this chapter is a member of the team that conducted the following three studies.

Kindergarten to First Grade CBM Study

In the first study, the participants were 59 kindergarten students from a school serving ethnically diverse and low-income students in rural Washington (i.e., 62% Native American, 24% Hispanic, 12% European American, and 1% Asian, with 81% of the student population qualifying for free or reduced lunch) (Stage, Sheppard, Davidson, & Browning, 1999). Two measures were individually administered at the end of their kindergarten year—letter-sound fluency and letter-naming fluency. These same students received four oral-reading fluency CBMs during their first-grade year. Research has shown that (a) students who cannot form letter-sound associations are at-risk for learning the alphabet principle, which is crucial for beginning reading (e.g., Adams, 1990; Berninger, 1998a; Bradley & Bryant, 1983; Ehri & Robbins, 1992;

---

[1]The Student Responsive Delivery System in Washington State is sponsored by the State Office of Public Instruction, the Washington State Association of School Psychologists, the Washington State Speech and Hearing Association.

Foorman, 1995; Share & Stanovich, 1995), (b) students who cannot name letters rapidly and automatically are at-risk for automatic access to name codes for written symbols during lexical access to the mental dictionary (e.g., Perfetti, 1985; Wagner & Torgesen, 1987), which is also crucial for beginning reading (e.g., Wolf, 1984, 1991; Wolf, Bally, & Morris, 1986), and (c) oral-reading fluency is an index of the degree to which students can automatically recognize words and coordinate the word recognition and sentence-level comprehension processes temporally in working memory (see Berninger, 1999, 2001).

Three different letter-naming forms were used. Each form had 104 lowercase and uppercase letters randomly arranged across 11 rows with 10 letters on each row, with the exception of the last row, which had only 4 letters. Likewise, three different letter-sound forms were used that were arranged similarly to the letter-naming forms. Correct letter-sounds were coded in association with the Open Court Reading Series (1995) Guide to Letter-Sounds. Alternate forms of the letter-sounds and letter-naming tasks yielded high correlations and interrater reliability (rs = .90s). During first grade, four oral-reading fluency measurements were administered in October, January, March, and May (the University of Oregon CBM Reading Probes available from the School Psychology Program). A growth-curve analysis using Hierarchical Linear Modeling (HLM) (Bryk, Raudenbush, & Congdon, 1996) was used to evaluate whether kindergarten letter-sound and letter-naming fluency measures predicted the students' initial first-grade oral-reading fluency and growth in oral-reading fluency over the course of first grade.

The average letter-sound fluency score was 9.39 (SD = 9.17) correct letter-sounds per minute with a range of 0 to 40 letter-sounds per minute. The average letter-naming fluency score was 20.44 (SD = 14.41) correct letter-names per minute with a range of 1 to 63. The two measures were correlated (r = .79). The results of the growth-curve analysis for the group showed that kindergarten letter-sound fluency performance predicted initial first-grade oral-reading fluency performance (p = .001), but kindergarten letter-naming fluency performance did not (p = .464). However, kindergarten letter naming did predict slope in first-grade oral-reading fluency (p = .035), whereas kindergarten letter-sound fluency did not (p = .08). These results suggest that a certain level of letter-sound knowledge is needed initially for oral-reading skill to develop, but that rate of lexical access to name codes will predict response to reading instruction in first grade. Further evidence of the importance of rate of lexical access was that letter-naming fluency predicted word recognition performance better than the phonological awareness and phonological coding in working memory tasks when all measures were entered into regression equations simultaneously, replicating work by Torgesen et al. (1999).

However, when these group analyses were supplemented with the calculation of HLM growth curves for individual children, interesting relationships

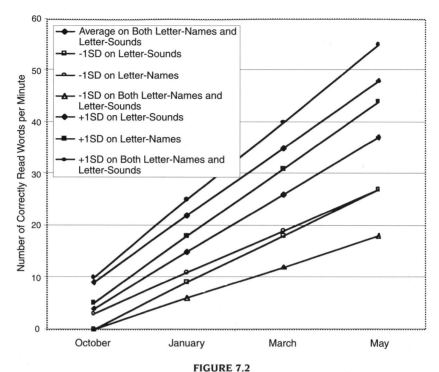

FIGURE 7.2

Students' first-grade oral-reading fluency growth curves by kindergarten letter-naming and letter-sound fluency.

between growth in letter-name fluency and letter-sound fluency became evident. These relationships demonstrated that children need to master both skills for fluent oral reading (see Figure 7.2). The middle curve in Figure 7.2 shows the performance of the students (44%, 26/59) who performed in the average range on the letter-naming and the letter-sound fluency tasks (i.e., between +1 SD and −1 SD). The growth curves above this line show the growth made by students (10%, 6/59) who were 1 standard deviation above average on letter-naming fluency only, growth made by students (8%, 5/59) who were 1 standard deviation above average on letter-sound fluency only, and growth by students (12%, 7/59) who were 1 standard deviation above average on both measures. The growth curves below this line show the growth made by students (13%, 8/59) who were 1 standard deviation below average on letter-naming fluency only, growth by students (5%, 3/59) who were 1 standard deviation below average on letter-sound fluency only, and growth made by students (7%, 4/59) who were 1 standard deviation below average on both measures. Clearly, those who were most fluent in oral reading were best in both letter-sound fluency and letter-naming fluency and those who were least fluent in oral reading were the worst in letter-sound and letter-naming fluency.

The collaborative problem-solving team used the data generated in the first year of the project to monitor the progress of individual students in the next cohort of kindergartners in the same school. Aim lines based on the first-year data were used to evaluate progress of the new cohort in the second year of the project so that those who needed a modification of the regular curriculum could be identified. In this study the modification of the curriculum consisted of additional instruction in the alphabet code with an attempt to make the code as explicit as possible. Thus, local schools can generate building-based norms for identifying children who need Tier 2 intervention and for evaluating their responses to modification of the regular curriculum.

First- to Second-Grade CBM Study

In the second study, conducted at the same school, 99 first-grade students' end-of-the-year oral-reading fluency was used to predict their initial second-grade oral-reading fluency (Stage, in press). A previous study had indicated that students' reading progress is influenced by their classmates' ability level (Share, Jorm, Maclean, & Matthews, 1984). Therefore, slopes for the classroom in which students are instructed may be a more sensitive index for aim lines than slope for grade in a local school (Fuchs, 1998).

The growth-curve analysis showed that students' first-grade oral-reading fluency significantly predicted their initial second-grade oral-reading fluency ($p < .001$), but that the classroom effect did not reliably distinguish growth in oral-reading fluency over the course of the year ($p = .35$). The average growth in the students' second-grade oral-reading fluency was divided into quartiles so that students who were performing in the lower 25th percentile could be monitored. Figure 7.3 shows the growth curves in oral-reading fluency of the second-grade students by quartile. The difference in the spacing between the three quartile slopes indicates that the students' oral-reading fluency was not normally distributed. The distribution was positively skewed, with the majority of students performing between the first and second quartiles. Therefore, the growth-curve analysis was also conducted after transforming the first-grade reading-fluency variable by taking the square root of each score (see Tabachnick & Fidell, 1989, for a discussion on the transformation of non-normal distribution scores). The results yielded similar findings. Because the statistical results were not altered, the results of the initial analysis are considered adequate for interpretation and graphic representation.

At the end of the school year, 28 students who continued to score in the lower 25th percentile were invited to attend summer school that provided individualized reading instruction using the Open Court Reading Series (1995), which research has shown is an effective program for at-risk beginning read-

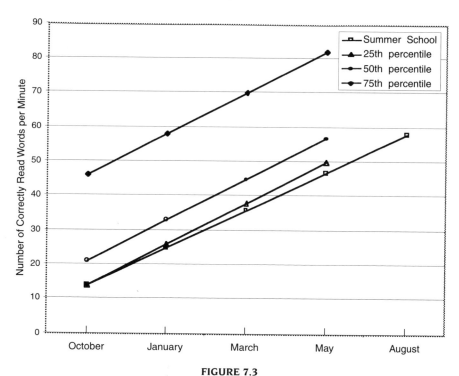

FIGURE 7.3

Second-grade reading growth by first-grade quartiles and summer-school student growth.

ers (Foorman, Francis, Fletcher, Schatschneider, & Mehta, 1998). On average, students attended 25.5 summer-school days with a standard deviation of 4.4 days. The range was from 29 to 16 days. Growth-curve analysis showed that, on average, students had significant growth ($p < .0001$) during summer school, but there was individual variability in the summer-school students' growth over the course of the year ($p < .0001$). To investigate the number of students who had significant reading growth, the student's slope was divided by twice the standard error. The results indicated that all the students had significant growth at $p < .05$. A comparison of the summer-school students' August oral-reading fluency with the general education students' May oral-reading fluency showed that 71% (20 out of 28 students) of the summer-school students read at least 50 or more words per minute, which was above the 25th percentile rank as determined by the second-grade May distribution. However, it is possible that if the general education students' oral-reading fluency had been measured in August, they might have shown the same increase, negating the appearance that the summer-school students had actually improved compared to the regular education students (see Cook & Campbell, 1979).

The eight students who did not make sufficient progress were targeted for collaborative problem-solving intervention for the following academic year in order to determine whether they required specialized educational services. That is, students who did not respond to initial early intervention during the regular school year (Tier 1) or additional curriculum modification (more instruction during summer school—Tier 2) became candidates for Tier 3.

Evaluating Prereferral Intervention across Sites

Pilot-site buildings included 14 elementary schools, 2 middle schools, 2 high schools, and 1 middle/high school combination. Program evaluation data collected during the 1998–99 school year indicated that 215 students participated in the collaborative problem-solving process, with 138 students (i.e., 64%) needing no further intervention because their academic and/or behavioral difficulty was resolved (Browning et al., 1999). Of the 215 students, 58 (27%) were further considered for special education services, 28 (13%) were found eligible for special education services, and 19 (9%) were determined to be in need of monitoring by the problem-solving team the following academic year.

Four findings are emphasized. First, the number of students requiring full assessment for special education was reduced by 73%. Second, only 13% of the students needing academic and behavioral assistance were found to require special education services. A service delivery model is needed that includes a range of services from early intervention to modified regular program to pull-out services. Such a model will reduce the number of assessments and pull-out placements that are necessary. Third, CBM can be used to identify and monitor the progress of children who do not respond or respond slowly to Tier 1 early intervention and thus need additional intervention in the form of greater intensity (additional instruction) or modification of the regular program. Fourth, CBM is most likely to be effective if implemented within a collaborative, problem-solving framework in which the multidisciplinary team plans and evaluates curriculum modifications.

Commercially Available CBM Tools

The *Academic Competence Scales* (ACES) (Di Perna & Elliott, in press) provide an empirically validated approach to using teacher ratings in collaborative problem solving for students referred for academic problems. The *Academic Intervention Monitoring System* (AIMS) (Di Perna & Elliott) provides an empirically validated approach to using teacher ratings in monitoring progress. Another tool for monitoring progress is the *Standard Reading Passages* (Children's Educational Services, 1987). The PAL-RW could also be used to monitor student response to curriculum modifications for prereferral intervention.

Orthographic, phonological, and rapid automatic naming (RAN) tasks,

like the ones on the PAL-RW, predict growth curves for prereferral interventions for reading (e.g., Berninger, Abbott, et al., 2000; Berninger, Abbott,
Zook, et al., 1999); and orthographic and phonological tasks, like the ones on
the PAL-RW, predict growth curves for prereferral interventions for spelling
(Berninger et al., 1998). For examples of prereferral intervention protocols for
reading and use of standardized tests in evaluating response to intervention,
see Abbott et al. (1997), Berninger, Abbott, et al. (1997), and Berninger and
Traweek (1991). For examples of prereferral intervention protocols for writing
and use of standardized tests in evaluating response to intervention, see
Berninger et al. (1995), Berninger, Abbott, et al. (1997), Berninger et al. (1998),
and Berninger (1998a, pp. 257–261). Berninger, Abbott, and Stage (1999)
found that following a moderately intensive intervention for first graders at-
risk for reading problems (24 twenty-minute lessons over a four-month period that aimed instruction at all components of a functional reading system), half of the 128 children reached grade level or above and maintained
their relative gains at the beginning and end of second grade. The other half,
who had improved, as a group, but were still not at grade level, received continuous tutoring in second grade and made additional relative gains, demonstrating that some students will need more-intensive intervention over a
longer period of time. Only a few children failed to respond to early intervention by the end of second grade. We turn now to Tier 3 in the model, for those
cases in which Tier 1 and Tier 2 are not sufficient.

THIRD TIER: DIAGNOSIS AND TREATMENT PLANS

Tier 1 assessment for intervention can prevent many reading and writing disabilities and/or reduce the severity of these disabilities, but it does not elim-
inate all disabilities (Berninger, Abbott, & Stage, 1999; Berninger, Abbott,
Zook, et al., 1999). When children do not respond to Tier 1 early intervention
or Tier 2 modification of the regular curriculum, or continue to struggle to
keep up with the regular curriculum, then Tier 3—in-depth assessment—is
called for. The purpose of this assessment is not just to decide whether the
student qualifies for special education services and, if so, under which category—that is, to make an eligibility and placement decision. The purpose of
the Tier 3 assessment is also to diagnose why the student is having so much
difficulty; that is, if there is a discrepancy between ability and achievement,
why there is a discrepancy. Simply demonstrating that a discrepancy exists is
not sufficient to diagnose a learning disability, which is only one cause of underachievement. This process also helps to identify those students who may
not demonstrate an ability-achievement discrepancy, but who have significant deficits in the underlying processes essential to the acquisition of reading and writing skills such that intensive instructional intervention is warranted. Further, it is necessary to demonstrate that science-validated marker

variables for reading or writing disability are also present. The PAL-RW is designed to assess such research-validated marker variables. Although education professionals are often reluctant to "label" students, many parents seek diagnostic explanations and acknowledgment of learner differences (see lower left corner of Figure 7.1 and Berninger, 1998a). A small percentage of students continue to struggle despite appropriate instruction and sometimes considerable extra help; in such severe cases the diagnosis of dyslexia or dysgraphia may be warranted. Failure to go beyond eligibility and placement decisions in assessment to diagnoses and acknowledgment of learning differences can fuel adversarial relationships between the family and school (Berninger, 1998a).

The approach to diagnosis that we recommend utilizes clinical hypothesis testing. For an example of branching diagnosis applied to clinical hypothesis testing for writing disability, see Berninger and Whitaker (1993). To test clinical hypotheses, we use multimodal assessment (e.g., Shapiro, 1996), including interviewing parents and reviewing records for developmental, educational, and family history; observing the student in and out of the classroom; interviewing the student; analyzing parent and teacher rating scales; administering standardized, normed tests and criterion-referenced tests; and reviewing portfolios or work products. Results are used for differential diagnosis involving five axes (see Berninger, 1998a): Axis 1, Development Across Multiple Domains; Axis 2, Comorbid Medical Conditions; Axis 3, Brain Functions; Axis 4, Academic Functioning in School; and Axis 5, Community, Family, School, and Classroom Factors. Students with mental retardation or with a specific reading or writing disability will be classified differently on Axis 1 and possibly Axis 2, but may have some similar problems on Axis 4 (e.g., poor reading relative to age peers). A student with a neurologically based learning disorder due to brain damage will have an Axis 2 diagnosis, whereas a student with dyslexia and/or dysgraphia will not because, although these disorders are brain-based, they are not related to brain damage or a medical condition (Berninger, 1994).

We begin the process of differential diagnosis by ruling mental retardation in or out (see Table 7.3), because this Axis 1 diagnosis is relevant to establishing reasonable expectations for rate of learning and levels of learning outcomes. If mental retardation is ruled out, we continue the differential diagnosis process by considering whether a primary language disability exists (see Table 7.3). Although children with a primary language disability will probably have reading problems, not all students with reading problems have a primary language disability. If a student has both a language disability on Axis 1 and reading problems on Axis 4, he or she may need treatment and accommodation throughout the school years because so much instruction in school involves oral language. If a primary language disability is ruled out, we proceed to determine whether a reading disability exists, with or without comorbid writing disability (see Table 7.3). When the specific reading

TABLE 7.3
Differential Diagnosis among Mental Retardation, Primary Language Disability,
and Specific Reading and/or Writing Disability

1. Does the student meet criteria for mental retardation?

    A. Significant delays over time in cognitive, language, motor, and social development not attributable to cultural difference or lack of stimulation?

    D. Significant delays over time in adaptive functioning?

    E. Comorbid developmental disabilities and/or medical conditions?

2. Does the student meet criteria for primary language disability?

    A. Expressive language disorder?

    B. Mixed receptive and expressive language disorder?

    C. Comorbid developmental disabilities and/or medical conditions?

3. Does the student meet criteria for specific reading disorder (including dyslexia, i.e., severe reading disorder)?

    A. Developmental history

        1. Did the student have preschool language difficulties?

        2. Did the student struggle in learning to name letters?

        3. Did the student struggle in learning letter-sound correspondence?

        4. Did the student struggle in recognizing single words out of context?

        5. Is the student's oral reading of text slow and dysfluent?

        6. Does the student persist in making spelling errors beyond grade 3 that resemble the invented spelling of younger children?

        7. Is there a family history of reading and/or writing problems?

    B. Educational history

        1. Was the student given *explicit instruction* in orthographic and phonological awareness, the alphabet principle for word recognition and spelling, reading comprehension, and the planning, translating, and reviewing/revising components of writing?

        2. Was the student given daily experience in reading specific words in reading material at his or her instructional or independent reading level and in writing for varied purposes?

        3. Was the student taught by a *certificated teacher* with *supervised experience in teaching reading and writing to at-risk students* and with appropriate *training in the structure of language*?

        4. Was the student a *slow responder or nonresponder* to appropriate reading and writing instruction over a 2-year period?

    C. Are there comorbid attention, math, and/or writing problems? Can mental retardation, primary language disorder, other developmental disorder (e.g., autism and pervasive developmental disorder), or neurological condition (e.g., cerebral palsy and neurofibromatosis) be ruled out?

    D. Is there significant, unexpected achievement relative to verbal reasoning ability in the following measures[a,b]?

        1. Single word reading—accuracy

            a. Word specific mechanism (WRMT-R Word Identification, WIAT II Word Reading, WRAT-3 Reading)

(continues)

Table 7.3— *Continued*

      b. Phonological decoding (WRMT-R Word Attack, WIAT II or PAL-RW Pseudoword Decoding)

    2. Automaticity of single-word recognition

      a. Real word (TOWRE real-word efficiency)

      b. Pseudoword (TOWRE pseudoword efficiency)

    3. Fluency of oral reading of text (GORT-3 rate)

    4. Comprehension/Memory

      a. Text-based

        1) Cloze (WRMT-R Passage Comprehension)

        2) Story retell (QRI, PAL-RW Test Battery)

      b. Integration of text and background knowledge

        1) Factual and inferential questions—multiple choice (GORT-3 comprehension)

        2) Factual and inferential questions—open-ended (QRI, WIAT II)

    5. Marker variables[c]

      a. Orthographic coding and/or representation in memory

      b. Phonological coding and/or representation in memory

      c. Rapid automatic naming

E. Is there significant, unexpected achievement in writing relative to verbal reasoning ability in the following measures?[a,b]

    1. Handwriting automaticity (PAL-RW, WIAT II alphabet task)

    2. Spelling (WIAT II, WRAT-3 Spelling)

    3. Compositional fluency and quality (WIAT II, WJ-R)

    4. Marker variables[c]

      a. Alphabet task

      b. Orthographic coding

      c. Finger function tasks

      d. Phonological nonword memory

      e. Phonological deletion

      f. Orthographic word-specific representation

      g. Pseudoword reading

      h. Verbal working memory

[a]CTOPP = Comprehensive Test of Phonological Processing (Wagner, Torgesen, & Rashotte 1999)

GORT-3 = Gray Oral Reading Test—Third Edition (Wiederholt & Bryant, 1992)

NEPSY (Korkman, Kirk, & Kemp, 1998)

PAL-RW = Process Assessment of the Learner Test Battery for Reading and Writing (Berninger, 2001)

QRI = Qualitative Reading Inventory (Leslie & Caldwell, 1990)

WJ-R = Woodcock Johnson Psychoeducational Battery—Revised (Woodcock & Johnson, 1990)

Table 7.3— *Continued*

WIAT II = Wechsler Individual Achievement Test, Second Edition (The Psychological Corporation, in press)

WRMT-R = Woodcock Reading Mastery Test—Revised (Woodcock, 1987)

[b]Verbal IQ may be a more realistic gauge of expected level of achievement of functional reading or writing systems than Performance IQ (see Berninger, 1998a). Reading disability is more likely to have a genetic or constitutional basis when reading ability is discrepant from IQ than when both reading and IQ are low (Olson, Datta, Gayan, & DeFries, in press).

[c]The Process Assessment of the Learner Test Battery for Reading and Writing has subtests for each of these marker variables, which also lead to instructionally relevant recommendations for students whose achievement is not below the level expected based on Verbal IQ

disability involves severe difficulty in learning to read and spell words, it is often referred to as dyslexia. See Berninger (2000) for a description of how the phenotype for dyslexia may express itself in different ways at different stages of development. When the specific writing disability involves severe difficulty in handwriting and/or spelling, it is often referred to as dysgraphia. Students may overcome their reading problems (become compensated dyslexics) only to face persistent spelling and written-expression problems. However, other students may have no difficulty learning to read but have severe difficulty with handwriting, spelling, and/or written composition. The diagnosis of dyslexia or dysgraphia should be reserved, however, for those students who do not have general developmental delays (Axis 1), primary language disability (Axis 1), or brain damage (Axis 2), and continue to struggle despite considerable and appropriate instructional intervention. See Berninger (1998d) for further discussion of subtypes of learning disabilities involving written language. The case study we discuss next illustrates the process of differential diagnosis, summarized in Table 7.3, for a student referred for reading problems.

Case Study

Benjamin, who had just completed fifth grade in another state, was referred for evaluation because of increasing frustration with reading since third grade. Mental retardation was ruled out because (a) based on developmental history his motor and language milestones were early, (b) in third grade his Full Scale IQ on the Wechsler Intelligence Scale for Children—Third Edition (WISC-III; The Psychological Corporation, 1991) was 100 (Verbal IQ 105, Performance IQ 95), and (c) his overall behavioral adaptation appeared to be age-appropriate when evaluated in third grade. In third grade the psychologist who assessed him described the boy as having "an even, usually happy disposition" and as a child who "resists becoming discouraged by difficulties or minor setbacks." He did not have any comorbid Axis 2 medical conditions.

Likewise, primary language disabilities were ruled out on the basis of reported early language milestones and good listening and verbal expression skills. However, despite a recent hearing exam confirming that his hearing was normal, Benjy often told his mother that he cannot hear the sounds she is talking about in words. Thus, the examiner formulated a clinical hypothesis that the boy had phonological processing problems. This hypothesis was tested during the formal testing with a task in which Benjy was asked to repeat polysyllabic pseudowords without a designated syllable, phoneme, or rime unit (the part of a syllable in which the initial phoneme in the onset position is deleted) (Berninger, Cartwright, Yates, Swanson, & Abbott, 1994).

The following information gleaned from the parent interview is relevant to the differential diagnosis for dyslexia. Benjy lived with both biological parents, a younger brother who was learning to read very easily, and a sister who was a toddler. There was a family history of problems in learning to read. His mother had spent a great deal of time helping him with reading over the years, though as a preadolescent he was beginning to be reluctant to accept her help. The problems with reading were obvious to Benjy's teachers and parents from first grade on, but he did not receive any special help with reading at school. Finally, in third grade, the school psychologist evaluated him and documented a severe discrepancy between IQ and achievement in reading and written expression. His math achievement was grade appropriate. Thus, his problems were specific to reading and writing. Although he qualified for special education, the school did not develop an Individual Education Plan (IEP) and instead chose to provide pull-out support services for the regular program. To his mother's knowledge, Benjy never had any systematic phonics instruction at school. Beginning in fourth grade his parents paid for him to get phonics instruction at a private tutoring center.

In the fourth and fifth grades Benjy received all A's and B's on his report card, even though it seemed to his parents that he was having problems in reading (with word recognition, not comprehension), handwriting, spelling, and composition, and was overtly angry and aggressive every day when his mother picked him up from school. On the state's Assessment of Academic Skills, given in fifth grade, Benjy met most of the standards, which all stressed higher-level thinking skills in reading and math. Basic skills in word recognition and spelling were not considered in the standards. Benjy described a typical day in fifth grade in this way: The teacher gave the class ten worksheets and told them they had 1 hour to complete them. The teacher sat at her desk and told the class to do the work and not bother her. According to his mother, these worksheets were in preparation for taking the state's Assessment of Academic Skills. Benjy could not recall a regular spelling program in fifth grade. He thought he took maybe 10 or 12 spelling tests, but there would be a bunch in a row and then none for a long time. Benjy's attention was excellent throughout the formal testing and his mother's rating of his attentional behaviors fell in the normal range.

Formal testing included many of the recommended measures in Table 7.3. Benjy's age-corrected standard scores for word recognition had decreased about 0.5 standard deviation unit since third grade and ranged from 74 (4th percentile) on the Basic Reading subtest of the Wechsler Individual Achievement Test (WIAT; The Psychological Corporation, 1992) to 72 (3rd percentile) on the Word Identification and 74 (4th percentile) on the Word Attack subtests of the Woodcock Reading Mastery Test—Revised (WRMT-R; Woodcock, 1987). He did somewhat better when words were in context, achieving the equivalent of a standard score for age of 80 (9th percentile) on the Gray Oral Reading Test—Third Edition (GORT-3; Wiederholt & Bryant, 1992), and an instructional level in the third- to fifth-grade range on the criterion-referenced Qualitative Reading Assessment (QRI; Leslie & Caldwell, 1990). However, his reading rate was slow—a standard score of 70 (2nd percentile) on GORT-3 rate. His reading comprehension varied depending on whether responses were open-ended (WIAT standard score 82, 12th percentile) or multiple choice (GORT-3 standard score 110, 75th percentile).

To determine if Benjy also had a comorbid writing disability, measures of handwriting, spelling, and composition were given. Residual problems in handwriting automaticity were evident when writing the alphabet in lowercase manuscript from memory. Benjy wrote *g* for *j*, could not remember how to make a lowercase *k*, and transposed the order of *m* and *n*. His standard score for age was 80 (9th percentile) on the Wide Range Achievement Test—Third Edition (WRAT-3; Wilkinson, 1993) Spelling subtest and 69 (2nd percentile) on the WIAT Spelling subtest. Written composition was a relative strength on the Woodcock-Johnson—Revised (WJ-R); Benjy's standard score for age was 86 (18th percentile) on Writing Samples, which scores content independent of spelling, and 91 (28th percentile) on Writing Fluency. His spelling errors resembled the invented spellings of younger children.

Benjy had significant difficulty with phonological processing of phonemes in polysyllabic words. His speed of naming familiar letters or digits or alternating letters and digits (Wolf et al., 1986; Wolf, 1986) was significantly delayed. Although he did reasonably well on the orthographic measures out of sentence context, when he had to integrate letter information with sentence meaning on a comprehension test that required close attention to letter information, his errors reflected a tendency to reverse letters in word context. He showed strength in verbal working memory, which was grade-appropriate.

Assessment of social-emotional status showed that Benjy had signs of depression, anxiety, aggression, and low self-esteem. These emotional problems appeared to be secondary to his chronic problems with written language, as emotional problems were not evident in third grade and had appeared and escalated as the task demands at school had increased for both reading and writing. The examiner concluded that Benjy had both dyslexia and dysgraphia. Had he gotten appropriate Tier 1 and Tier 2 assessment for intervention during the first two grades, his problems would likely have been much less severe. Although he did not appear to have received appropriate educational programming at school for his learning disability during the third through fifth grades, he had received explicit code instruction outside of school, some support services at school, and considerable help from his mom. Although he had met most of his state's standards on the Assessment of Academic Skills and received A's and B's on his report card in fifth grade, he had a significant discrepancy in both reading and writing relative to his intellectual ability and low achievement in reading and spelling single words. His reading rate was slow compared to age peers. This result serves as a reminder that some students who are meeting standards on state assessments for accountability of student learning outcome and who receive good grades may have undiagnosed reading and writing disabilities. Moreover, Benjy had shown deficits on the marker language variables that research has shown are related to specific reading and writing disability (e.g., Berninger, 1994; Berninger, Abbott, et al., 2001). Benjy returned to his home state for sixth grade, where he finally received specialized instruction for his reading and writing disabilities. We recommended instruction aimed at all the necessary instructional components for the functional reading and writing systems (see PAL Intervention Guides for a list of commercially available instructional resources, organized by these instructional components, including but not restricted to phonological awareness and the alphabet principle).

CONCLUDING REMARKS

Many reading and writing disabilities could be prevented or reduced in severity if a three-tier model of assessment for intervention were implemented in the schools. This model would require a restructuring of how special education is funded, to provide schools with financial resources for all three tiers. In the first tier, students are screened for marker language variables and those at-risk are given early intervention. In the second tier, the regular curriculum is modified and student progress in response to the modified curriculum is monitored. Finally, in the third tier, those students who continue to struggle despite early intervention and curriculum modification are given a thorough assessment for diagnosis and treatment planning. Although not all students with reading or writing problems early in school have learning disabilities, some do. Dyslexia and dysgraphia, which, respectively, are the most severe forms of specific reading and writing disability, do exist (see Berninger, 1998d, 2000), but the learning outcome for students with dyslexia and/or dysgraphia will be much better if schools do not wait until students fail for several years before beginning the process of assessment for intervention. Although biologically based (Olson, Datta, Gayan, & DeFries, in press), dyslexia and dysgraphia are treatable disorders (Abbott & Berninger, 1999; Berninger, 2000; Richards et al., 1999).

Acknowledgments

The research supporting the three-tier model was funded by the National Institute of Child Health and Human Development Grants HD 25858-10 and P5033812-04.

This chapter was based on presentations at (a) the Fall Conference for the Washington State Association of School Psychologists and the British Columbia Association of School Psychologists, British Columbia, November 1998, (b) the annual meeting of the National Association of School Psychologists, Las Vegas, March 1999, and (c) the Summer Workshop for the Washington Association of School Administrators/Directors of Special Education, Wenatchee, Washington, August 1999.

Although the PAL-RW is based on the research of the first author of this chapter, who is also author of the test battery, the last two authors have contributed substantially to its development and standardization.

References

Abbott, S., & Berninger, V. W. (1999). It's never too late to remediate: Teaching word recognition to fourth through seventh grade students. *Annals of Dyslexia, 49*, 223–250.

Abbott, S., Reed, E., Abbott, R., & Berninger, V. W. (1997). Year-long balanced reading/writing tutorial: A design experiment used for dynamic assessment. *Learning Disabilities Quarterly, 20,* 249–263.

Adams, M. J. (1990). *Beginning to read: Thinking and learning about print.* Cambridge, MA: MIT Press.

Baker, S. K., Plasencia-Peinado, J., & Lezcano-Lytle, V. (1998). The use of curriculum-based measurement with language-minority students. In M. R. Shinn (Ed.), *Advanced applications of curriculum-based measurement* (pp. 175–213). New York: Guilford.

Ball, E. W., & Blachman, B. A. (1991). Does phoneme awareness training in kindergarten make a difference in early word recognition and developmental spelling? *Reading Research Quarterly, 26,* 49–66.

Barker, T., Torgesen, J., & Wagner, R. (1992). The role of orthographic processing skills on five different reading tasks. *Reading Research Quarterly, 27,* 335–345.

Bear, D., Invernizzi, M., Templeton, S., & Johnston, F. (1996). *Words their way: Word study for phonics, vocabulary, and spelling instruction.* Columbus, OH: Merrill.

Berninger, V. W. (1994). *Reading and writing acquisition: A developmental neuropsychological perspective.* Madison, WI: Brown & Benchmark. Reprinted by Westview Press (now Perseus Books), 1996.

Berninger, V. W. (1998a). *Process Assessment of the Learner* (PAL): *Guides for reading and writing intervention.* San Antonio, TX: The Psychological Corporation.

Berninger, V. W. (1998b). *Talking letters. Teacher guide and student desk cards in* PAL Intervention Kit. San Antonio, TX: The Psychological Corporation.

Berninger, V. W. (1998c). *Talking letters handwriting lessons in* PAL Intervention Kit. San Antonio, TX: The Psychological Corporation.

Berninger, V. W. (1998d). Assessment, prevention, and intervention for specific reading and writing disabilities in young children. In B. Wong (Ed.), *Learning Disabilities* (2nd ed., pp. 529–555). New York: Academic Press.

Berninger, V. W. (1999). Coordinating transcription and text generation in working memory during composing: Automatized and constructive processes. *Learning Disability Quarterly, 22,* 99–112.

Berninger, V. W. (2000). Dyslexia, the invisible, treatable disorder: The story of Einstein's Ninja Turtles. *Learning Disabilities Quarterly, 23,* 175–195.

Berninger, V. W. (2001). *Process Assessment of the Learner Test Battery for Reading and Writing* (PAL-RW). San Antonio, TX: The Psychological Corporation.

Berninger, V. W., & Abbott, R. (1994). Multiple orthographic and phonological codes in literacy acquisition: An evolving research program. In V. W. Berninger (Ed.), *The varieties of orthographic knowledge I: Theoretical and developmental issues* (pp. 277–317). Dordrecht: Kluwer Academic.

Berninger, V. W., Abbott, R., Brooksher, R., Lemos, Z., Ogier, S., Zook, D., & Mostafapour, E. (2000). A connectionist approach to making predictability of English orthography explicit to at-risk beginning readers: Evidence for alternative, effective strategies. *Developmental Neuropsychology, 17,* 241–271.

Berninger, V. W., Abbott, R., & Stage, S. (1999, April). *Educational and biological factors in preventing and treating dyslexia.* Society for Research in Child Development, Albuquerque, NM.

Berninger, V. W., Abbott, R., Thomson, J., & Raskind, W. (2001). Language phenotype for reading and writing disability: A family approach. *Scientific Studies of Reading* 5(1), 59–105.

Berninger, V. W., Abbott, R., Whitaker, D., Sylvester, L., & Nolen, S. (1995). Integrating low-level skills and high-level skills in treatment protocols for writing disabilities. *Learning Disabilities Quarterly, 18,* 293–309.

Berninger, V. W., Abbott, R., Zook, D., Ogier, S., Lemos, Z., & Brooksher, R. (1999). Early intervention for reading disabilities: Teaching the alphabet principle in a connectionist framework. *Journal of Learning Disabilities, 32,* 491–503.

Berninger, V. W., Abbott, S., Reed, L., Greep, K., Hooven, C., Sylvester, L., Taylor, J., Clinton, A., & Abbott, R. (1997). Directed reading and writing activities: Aiming intervention to working brain systems. In S. Dollinger & L. DiLalla (Eds.), *Prevention and intervention issues across the life span* (pp. 123–158). Hillsdale, NJ: Erlbaum.

Berninger, V. W., Cartwright, A., Yates, C., Swanson, H. L., & Abbott, R. (1994). Developmental skills related to writing and reading acquisition in the intermediate grades: Shared and unique variance. *Reading and Writing: An Interdisciplinary Journal, 6,* 161–196.

Berninger, V. W., & Traweek, D. (1991). Effects of two-phase reading intervention on three orthographic-phonological code connections. *Learning and Individual Differences, 3,* 323–338.

Berninger, V. W., Vaughan, K., Abbott, R., Abbott, S., Brooks, A., Rogan, L., Reed, E., & Graham, S. (1997). Treatment of handwriting fluency problems in beginning writing: Transfer from handwriting to composition. *Journal of Educational Psychology, 89,* 652–666.

Berninger, V. W., Vaughan, K., Abbott, R., Brooks, A., Abbott, S., Rogan, L., Reed, E., & Graham, S. (1998). Early intervention for spelling problems: Teaching spelling units of varying size within a multiple connections framework. *Journal of Educational Psychology, 90,* 587–605.

Berninger, V. W., Vaughan, K., Abbott, R., Brooks, A., Begay, K., Curtin, G., Byrd, K., & Graham, S. (2000). Language-based spelling instruction: Teaching children to make multiple connections between spoken and written words. *Learning Disability Quarterly, 23,* 117–135.

Berninger, V. W., & Whitaker, D. (1993). Theory-based, branching diagnosis of writing disabilities. *School Psychology Review, 22,* 623–642.

Berninger, V. W., Yates, C., Cartwright, A., Rutberg, J., Remy, E., & Abbott, R. (1992). Lower-level developmental skills in beginning writing. *Reading and Writing: An Interdisciplinary Journal, 4,* 257–280.

Berninger, V. W., Yates, C., & Lester, K. (1991). Multiple orthographic codes in acquisition of reading and writing skills. *Reading and Writing: An Interdisciplinary Journal, 3,* 115–149.

Bradley, L., & Bryant, P. E. (1983). Categorizing sounds and learning to read—a causal connection. *Nature*, 310, 21–43.

Brown, A. (1992). Design experiments: Theoretical and methodological challenges in creating complex interventions in classroom settings. *The Journal of the Learning Sciences*, 2, 141–178.

Browning, M., Davidson, M., & Stage, S. A. (1998). *Student Responsive Service Delivery: Project Evaluation Report*. Olympia, WA: Office of Public Instruction, Department of Special Education.

Browning, M., Davidson, M., & Stage, S. A. (1999). *Student Responsive Service Delivery: Project Evaluation Report*. Olympia, WA: Office of Public Instruction, Department of Special Education.

Bryk, A. S., Raudenbush, S. W., & Congdon, R. T. (1996). *Hierarchical linear and nonlinear modeling with the* HLM/2L *and* HLM/3L *programs*. Lincolnwood, IL: Scientific Software.

Canter, A., & Marston, D. (1994). From CBM to discrepancy formulae to problem solving: One step in the evolution of noncategorical special education services. *Communiqué*, 22, 14–17.

Children's Educational Services. (1987). *Standard Reading Passages*. Minneapolis, MN: Author. (16525 W. 78th St., Suite 162, Eden Prairie, MN 55346-4358)

Cole, E., & Siegel, J. (Eds.). (1990). *Effective consultation in school psychology*. Toronto: Hogrege & Huber.

Cook, T. D., & Campbell, D. T. (1979). *Quasi-experimentation: Design and analysis issues for field settings*. Boston: Houghton Mifflin.

Cunningham, A., & Stanovich, K. (1990). Assessing print exposure and orthographic processing skill in children: A quick measure of reading experience. *Journal of Educational Psychology*, 82, 733–740.

Daly, E. J., III, Wright, J. A., Kelly, S. Q., & Martens, B. K. (1997). Measures of early academic skills: Reliability and validity with a first grade sample. *School Psychology Quarterly*, 12, 268–280.

Denckla, M., & Rudel, R. (1976). Rapid 'automatized' naming (R.A.N.): Dyslexia differentiated from other learning disabilities. *Neuropsychologia*, 14, 471–479.

Di Perna, J., & Elliott, S. (in press). *Academic Competence Scales* (ACES) and *Academic Intervention Monitoring System* (AIMS). San Antonio, TX: The Psychological Corporation.

Ehri, L. C., & Robbins, C. (1992). Beginners need some decoding skill to read words by analogy. *Reading Research Quarterly*, 27, 12–26.

Felton, B., Wood, F., Brown, I., Campbell, S., & Harter, M. (1987). Separate verbal memory and naming deficits in attention deficit disorder and reading disability. *Brain and Language*, 31, 171–184.

Foorman, B. R. (1995). Research on "the great debate": Code-oriented versus whole language approaches to reading instruction. *School Psychology Review*, 24, 376–392.

Foorman, B. R., Francis, D., Fletcher, J., Schatschneider, C., & Mehta, P. (1998). The role of instruction in learning to read: Preventing reading failure in at-risk children. *Journal of Educational Psychology*, 90, 37–55.

Fuchs, L. S. (1998). Computer applications to address implementation difficulties associated with curriculum-based measurement. In M. R. Shinn (Ed.), *Advanced applications of curriculum-based measurement* (pp. 89–112). New York: Guilford.

Fuchs, L. S., & Fuchs, D. (1986). Effects of systematic formative evaluation: A meta-analysis. *Exceptional Children*, 53, 199–208.

Habedank, L. (1995). Best practices in developing local norms for problem solving in the schools. In A. Thomas & J. Grimes (Eds.), *Best practices in school psychology—III* (pp. 701–715). Washington DC: The National Association of School Psychologists.

Ikeda, M. J., Tilly, D., III, Stumme, J., Volmer, L., & Allison, R. (1996). Agency-wide implementation of problem solving consultation: Foundations, current implementation, and future directions. *School Psychology Quarterly*, 11, 228–243.

Kaminski, R. A., & Good, R. H., III. (1996). Toward a technology for assessing basic early literacy skills. *School Psychology Review*, 25, 215–227.

Korkman, M., Kirk, U., & Kemp, S. (1998). NEPSY. San Antonio, TX: The Psychological Corporation.

Leslie, L., & Caldwell, J. (1990). *Qualitative Reading Inventory* (QRI). Glenview, IL: Scott, Foresman/Little Brown.

Levy, B. A., Abello, B., & Lysynchuk, L. (1997). Transfer from word training to reading in context: Gains in reading fluency and comprehension. *Learning Disability Quarterly*, 20, 173–188.

Liberman, I., Shankweiler, D., Fischer, F., & Carter, B. (1974). Explicit syllable and phoneme segmentation in the young child. *Journal of Experimental Child Psychology*, 18, 201–212.

Marston, D. B. (1989). A curriculum-based measurement approach to assessing academic performance: What it is and why do it. In M. R. Shinn (Ed.), *Curriculum-based measurement: Assessing special children* (pp. 18–78). New York: Guilford.

Nagy, W., & Scott, J. (1990). Word schemas: Expectations about the form and meaning of new words. *Cognition and Instruction*, 1, 105–127.

Olson, R., Datta, H., Gayan, H., & DeFries, J. (in press). A behavioral-genetic analysis of reading disabilities and component processes. In R. Klein & P. McMullen (Eds.), *Converging methods for understanding reading and dyslexia.* Cambridge, MA: MIT Press.

Olson, R., Forsberg, H., & Wise, B. (1994). Genes, environment, and the development of orthographic skills. In V. W. Berninger (Ed.), *The varieties of orthographic knowledge I: Theoretical and developmental issues* (pp. 27–71). Dordrecht: Kluwer Academic.

Open Court Reading. (1995). *Collections for young scholars.* Chicago and Peru, IL: SRA/McGraw-Hill.

Perfetti, C. A. (1985). *Reading ability.* New York: Oxford Univ. Press.

The Psychological Corporation. (1991). *Wechsler Intelligence Scale for Children—Third Edition.* San Antonio, TX: Author.

The Psychological Corporation. (1992). *Wechsler Individual Achievement Test.* San Antonio, TX: Author.

The Psychological Corporation. (in press). *Wechsler Individual Achievement Test—Second Edition.* San Antonio, TX: Author.

Reschly, D. J., & Ysseldyke, J. E. (1995). School psychology paradigm shift. In A. Thomas & J. Grimes (Eds.), *Best practices in school psychology* (3rd ed., pp. 17–31). Washington, DC: The National Association of School Psychologists.

Richards, T., Corina, D., Serafini, S., Steury, K., Dager, S., Marro, K., Abbott, R., Maravilla, K., & Berninger, V. W. (2000). Effects of phonologically-driven treatment for dyslexia on lactate levels as measured by proton MRSI. *American Journal of Radiology*, 21, 916–922.

Shapiro, E. (1996). *Academic skills problems: Direct assessment and intervention* (2nd ed.). New York: Guilford.

Share, D. L., Jorm, A. F., Maclean, R., & Matthews, R. (1984). Sources of individual differences in reading acquisition. *Journal of Educational Psychology*, 76, 1309–1324.

Share, D. L., & Stanovich, K. E. (1995). Cognitive processes in early reading development: Accommodating individual difference into a model of acquisition. *Issues in Education*, 1, 1–57.

Shinn, M. R. (1995). Curriculum-based measurement and its use in a problem-solving model. In A. Thomas & J. Grimes (Eds.), *Best practices in school psychology—III* (pp. 547–567). Washington DC: The National Association of School Psychologists.

Shinn, M. R., Collins, V. L., & Gallagher, S. (1998). Curriculum-based measurement and its use in a problem-solving model with students from minority backgrounds. In M. R. Shinn (Ed.), *Advanced applications of curriculum-based measurement* (pp. 143–174). New York: Guilford.

Stage, S. A. (in press). *Program evaluation using hierarchical linear modeling with curriculum-based measurement reading probes. School Psychology Quarterly.*

Stage, S., Abbott, R., Jenkins, J., & Berninger, V. W. (2000). Predicting response to early reading intervention using Verbal IQ, reading-related language abilities, attention ratings, and Verbal IQ–word reading discrepancy. To appear in special issue of *Journal of Learning Disabilities.*

Stage, S. A., Sheppard, J., Davidson, M., & Browning, M. (1999). *Prediction of first grader's growth in oral reading using their kindergarten letter-sound and letter-naming fluency.* Unpublished manuscript.

Tabachnick, B. G., & Fidell, L. S. (1989). *Using multivariate statistics* (2nd ed.). New York: Harper & Row.

Torgesen, J. K., Wagner, R. K., & Rashotte, C. A. (1999). *Test of Word Reading Efficiency* (TOWRE). Austin, TX: PRO-ED.

Torgesen, J. K., Wagner, R. K., Rashotte, C. A., Rose, E., Lindamood, P., Conway, T., & Garvan, C. (1999). *Preventing reading failure in young children with phonological processing disabilities: Group and individual responses to instruction.* Unpublished manuscript.

Wagner, R. K., & Torgesen, J. K. (1987). The nature of phonological processing and its causal role in the acquisition of reading skills. *Psychological Bulletin, 101,* 192–212.

Wagner, R. K., Torgesen, J. K., & Rashotte, C. A. (1999). *Comprehensive Test of Phonological Processing* (CTOPP). Austin, TX: PRO-ED.

Wiederholt, J., & Bryant, B. (1992). *Gray Oral Reading Test—Third Edition* (GORT-3). Odessa, FL: Psychological Assessment Resources.

Wilkinson, G. (1993). *Wide Range Achievement Test—Third Edition* (WRAT-3). Wilmington, DE: Wide Range.

Wolf, M. (1984). Naming, reading, and the dyslexias: A longitudinal overview. *Annals of Dyslexia, 34,* 87–115.

Wolf, M. (1986). Rapid alternating stimulus naming in the developmental dyslexias. *Brain and Language, 27,* 360–379.

Wolf, M. (1991). Naming speed and reading: The contribution of the cognitive neurosciences. *Reading Research Quarterly, 26,* 123–141.

Wolf, M., Bally, H., & Morris, R. (1986). Automaticity, retrieval processes, and reading: A longitudinal study in average and impaired reading. *Child Development, 57,* 988–1000.

Woodcock, R. (1987). *Woodcock Reading Mastery Test—Revised* (WRMT-R). Circle Pines, MN: American Guidance Service.

Woodcock, R., & Johnson, B. (1990). *Woodcock-Johnson Psychoeducational Battery—Revised Tests of Achievement* (WJ-R). Chicago: Riverside.

Ysseldyke, J., & Marston, D. (1998). Origins of categorical special education services and a rationale for changing them. In D. J. Reschly, W. D. Tilly III, & J. P. Grimes (Eds.), *Functional and noncategorical identification and intervention in special education* (pp. 1–14). Des Moines, IA: Iowa Department of Education.

CHAPTER

8

Assessment for Math Talent and Disability: A Developmental Model

JULIE BUSSE AND VIRGINIA W. BERNINGER
University of Washington

DONNA RURY SMITH AND DENISE HILDEBRAND
The Psychological Corporation

INTRODUCTION AND OVERVIEW

The last several decades have produced valuable research on identification and treatment of reading disabilities. In contrast, assessment and intervention of math disabilities has received much less research attention. Disabilities in math, which may or may not co-occur with reading disabilities, often go undiagnosed and untreated in the schools. The publication of standards for the teaching of mathematics by the National Council of Teachers of Mathematics (NCTM; 1989) has helped focus national attention on the importance of math education and excellence in the United States and has spurred reform efforts and research. In the wake of the NCTM standards, psychologists are being challenged to have a greater understanding of how students learn mathematics, and how to recognize math talent or underachievement for purposes of intervention.

This chapter discusses how to screen, to monitor progress in response to educational interventions, and to make in-depth assessments and educational recommendations for students with math talent or disability, and in some cases those with both math talent and disability. As we have recommended for reading (Berninger, 1998, and the chapter by Berninger, Stage, Smith, & Hildebrand, in this volume), we recommend a 3-tier developmental model in which screening for early intervention takes place early in development, curriculum and instruction are modified as necessary throughout schooling, and comprehensive assessment is conducted for those who respond poorly to curricular modifications. We begin with a description of a functional math system—that is, the basic components necessary to solve mathematical problems. This system has both domain-specific components unique to mathematics and domain-general components that are shared with other domains such as reading and writing. By understanding the different components that contribute to mathematical problem solving, psychologists are better prepared to troubleshoot which components are underdeveloped and interfering with the functioning of the system or are already developed and require little or no intervention or further practice. We then describe application of our developmental approach for maximizing Math Talent and preventing Math Disability. Next, we discuss the use of standardized assessment instruments for screening, monitoring progress, and diagnosing math talent and math disability in reference to each component of the functional math system. In addition, we discuss process assessment of math skills, in which the aim is not to identify the level of achievement, but to understand the processes needed to achieve the desired learning outcome and to explain why a student may be underachieving in some aspect of the functional math system. Assessment-intervention links are also discussed for students with math talent and math disabilities. Finally, two cases are presented to illustrate application of our "assessment for intervention" approach to the math domain.

FUNCTIONAL MATH SYSTEM

The functional math system is the set of component processes that must be coordinated for an individual student to engage in optimal, developmentally appropriate mathematical thinking and problem solving. Figure 8.1 graphically portrays the theoretical model of the *domain-specific functional math system* guiding the development of the *Process Assessment of the Learner* (PAL) *Test Battery for Math* (Berninger, in press). The functional math system is organized around the central problem-solving space, which has connections from modules for (a) reasoning, (b) arithmetic computation, and (c) conceptual knowledge. These modules may also have connections with each other. Three kinds of reasoning ability may contribute to mathematical problem solving: verbal reasoning, quantitative reasoning, and visual-spatial reasoning (see Robinson, Abbott, Berninger, & Busse, 1996, for evidence that these three kinds of reasoning are unique and not redundant). At least seven kinds of conceptual

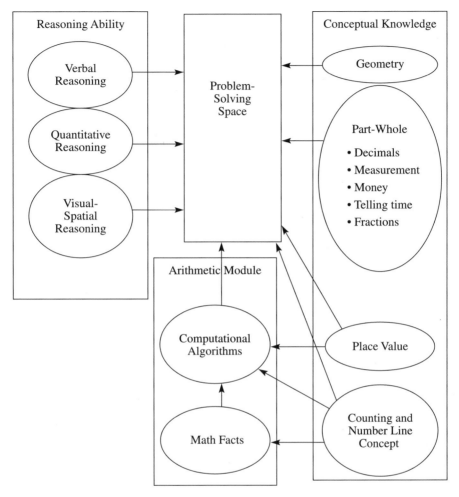

FIGURE 8.1
Functional math system.

knowledge may contribute to mathematical problem-solving ability in elementary and middle school students (concepts in Figure 8.1 are representative, not exhaustive). Counting, which is initially rote and then reflects one-to-one correspondence with objects counted and understanding of the number line, emerges first and may also contribute to learning math facts in the arithmetic module. The place value concept emerges next and contributes to computational algorithms as well as problem solving. Part-whole relationship knowledge then emerges and contributes to conceptual knowledge of fractions, time, measurement, money, decimals, and probability, all of which may contribute to mathematical problem solving. The arithmetic module is organized hierarchically, with math facts feeding into computational algorithms that feed into problem solving. Math facts are the "data" that are entered into the four basic calculating operations—addition, subtraction, multiplication, and division. Not represented in Figure 8.1, but important for the functional math system, is knowledge of the terms used in math problem solving (e.g., *first, more than*, and so on) and knowledge of how to use math tools such as graphs and charts with data or calculators.

Figure 8.2 graphically portrays the theoretical model of *domain-general processes* that affect the domain-specific components of the functional math system. These domain-general processes also guided the development of the PAL Test Battery for Math. When skills are first learned or novel problems are encountered, students often approach them strategically. However, with practice and experience, most students automatize certain component math skills, such as retrieval of math facts and application of calculation algorithms, and begin to apply strategies to higher-level tasks in the problem-solving space. Strategies also undergo development, with simple strategies evolving into more-complex ones, and managed by a metacognitive system that controls a variety of executive functions such as self-monitoring and self-regulating. In some cases, students with learning disabilities use strategies effectively to compensate for problems in automaticity, but sometimes they use strategies ineffectively.

Three memory mechanisms play a critical role in math problem solving. Short-term memory encodes orally or visually presented numbers in transient stores. Long-term memory contains math facts, procedures for computational algorithms, and conceptual knowledge in long-term stores. Working memory (e.g., Case, 1985; Swanson, 1996) is a processing space where incoming stimulus information is held and where representations from long-term memory are retrieved and stored until processing is completed— that is, the math problem is solved. Short-term and long-term memory are storage mechanisms that differ in duration of the store, whereas working memory is a mechanism that has both storage and processing components. Yates's (1996) multiple-regression analyses showed that for 60 first and second graders, a short-term auditory memory task and a short-term visual memory task uniquely predicted calculation, whereas measures of working memory and rapid automatic naming of switching stimuli (letters, numbers, and colors) were the best predictors of math problem solving. Thus, short-term and working memory are especially important in learning math. The incoming data and retrieved information from long-term memory is often declarative knowledge (factual *knowledge that*), whereas the processing that occurs in working memory is often procedural knowledge (*knowledge how*).

Both temporal processing (e.g., ordering steps of a multistep procedure) and spatial processing (e.g., moving in vertical, horizontal, or diagonal coor-

Dimension 1	Strategies (Metacognitive and Executive Functions)	vs.	Automaticity
Dimension 2	Short Term Memory STM vs.	Working Memory WM vs.	Long-Term Memory LTM
Dimension 3	Declarative Knowledge	vs.	Procedural Knowledge
Dimension 4	Temporal Processing	vs.	Visual/Spatial Processing
Dimension 5	Input-Output Combinations		Listening-Speaking Reading-Speaking Listening-Writing Reading-Writing
Dimension 6	Finger Skills (Fine Motor Planning and Sensori-Symbol Integration		
Dimension 7	Concrete Operational Representations	vs.	Formal Operational Representations

FIGURE 8.2

Domain-general system dimensions that interact with the domain-specific functional math system.

dinates in space) are needed to carry out multistep calculations. Students' listening or reading skills can affect their ability to represent a problem accurately, while their speaking and/or writing abilities can affect their ability to communicate their approach to solving a problem or to the final solution. Also, finger function skills (i.e., planning sequential fine-motor acts and sensori-symbol integration), can affect paper-and-pencil calculation. Finally, level of cognitive development affects the functional math system. When students are still in the concrete operational stage, manipulatives are useful in representing and solving problems. However, when students have developed formal operational thought, they may solve problems more efficiently by mentally manipulating abstract symbols represented in their minds.

To date, little research has examined how the domain-general processes affect the functioning of the domain-specific math system. The research that does exist has primarily focused on the transition from strategies to automaticity. For example, a major task of beginning mathematics is acquiring basic number facts in the arithmetic module. Initially, children rely primarily on procedural strategies, such as counting in the conceptual knowledge base, to obtain these math facts (Goldman, Pellegrino, & Mertz, 1988; Groen & Parkman, 1972; Nesher, 1986). With practice, children become more accurate and efficient in their strategy use. To illustrate, initially, students often use a "count-all" strategy—to compute 2 + 3, the student counts "1, 2, [pause] 3, 4, 5," using 2 fingers to represent the quantity 2 and 3 fingers to represent the quantity 3—but later progresses to using the "count-on" or "min" strategy that involves starting to count with the larger addend ("3") and only using the smaller addend ("4, 5") to count higher. Eventually, after much successful practice, students make the transition to direct, automatic retrieval of math facts from memory and no longer need to count (Cooney, Swanson, & Ladd, 1988; Siegler, 1988). Automaticity refers to the ability to make the transition from using effortful strategies when performing low-level basic skills to quick, efficient performance. Resnick and Ford (1981) suggested that automaticity, or the ability to get skills on "automatic pilot," may function in the learning of mathematics in a way similar to reading. This transition from procedural strategies to automatic retrieval is conceptually analogous to the transition in reading from phonological decoding to automatic word recognition. In both reading and arithmetic, automatizing a low-level process, such as word recognition, math fact retrieval, or computational algorithms, frees up limited capacity in working memory for the higher-level cognitive processes of reading comprehension (e.g., LaBerge & Samuels, 1974) or math problem solving. Rapid automatic naming of digits (e.g., Wolf, 1986; Wolf, Bally, & Morris, 1986) may index the degree to which access to numerals is automatized. In some cases, faulty strategies may be automatized, rendering it difficult to unlearn them. Thus, automaticity may have advantages as well as disadvantages.

Clearly, the interactions of the domain-specific functional math system and the domain-general systems are complex and require further research. Fortunately, however, standardized tests are now or will soon be available that permit psychologists to assess the level to which each of the components of these systems is developed relative to age or grade peers. Table 8.1 lists test instruments that might be used to assess each of the components in Figures 8.1 and 8.2. These tests are described more fully later in this chapter.

The tests in Table 8.1 can be used to screen primary grade children for early intervention for math talent or math disability. Such tests might also be

TABLE 8.1
Assessing Domain-Specific and Domain-General Features of the Functional Math System*

Reasoning Ability	Test Instrument
Verbal reasoning	WISC-III[g] Verbal Comprehension Factor
	SB-IV[d] Verbal Reasoning
	CogAT[a] Verbal
Quantitative reasoning	SB-IV Quantitative Reasoning
	CogAT Quantitative
Visual-spatial reasoning	WISC-III Performance IQ
	SB-IV Visual-Spatial Reasoning
Arithmetic Module	
Fact retrieval ($+, -, \times, \div$)	PAL[c] Fact Retrieval
	(accuracy and automaticity for 4 input-output combinations: oral-spoken, oral-written, written-oral, written-written)
Computational algorithms	WIAT[e] and WIAT II[f] Numerical Operations
	WRAT-3[i] Arithmetic
	WJ-R[h] Calculation
	KM-R[b] Operations
	(separate subtests for written addition, subtraction, multiplication, division, and mental computation)
	PAL Written Computations
	(verbal think aloud—analyze steps in process and not just final product)
Conceptual Knowledge	
Counting and number line	Selected items on KM-R Numeration
	Selected items on WIAT or WIAT II Mathematical Reasoning
	Selected items of WRAT-3 Arithmetic (depending on student's age)
	PAL Counting (automaticity)
Place value	Selected items on KM-R Numeration
	PAL Place Value
Part-whole relationships	KM-R Rational Numbers
	Selected items on WIAT or WIAT II
	Selected items on WJ-R Quantitative Concepts
Time	KM-R Time and Money
	Selected items on WIAT or WIAT II
	Selected Items on WJ-R Quantitative Concepts

(*continues*)

Table 8.1— *Continued*

Measurement	KM-R Measurement
	Selected items on WIAT or WIAT II
	Selected items on WJ-R Quantitative Concepts
Money	KM-R Time and Money
	Selected items on WIAT or WIAT II
	Selected items on WJ-R Quantitative Concepts
Geometry	KM-R Geometry
	Selected items on WIAT or WIAT II
	Selected items on WJ-R Quantitative Concepts
Problem-solving space	KM-R Estimation and Interpreting Data and Problem Solving
	WIAT or WIAT II Math Reasoning
	WJ-R Applied Problems
	WISC III Arithmetic subtest
	SB-IV Number Series and Matrices subtest
	PAL Processes Related to Solving Multi-Step Word Problems
Strategies	Think-alouds while student solves any domain-specific type problem
	Student interviews
Automaticity	PAL Counting Automaticity
	PAL Calculations
	PAL RAN for single-digit and double-digit numbers
Short-Term Memory	WISC-III Digit Span (Digits Forward)
Working Memory	PAL Quantitative Working Memory
	PAL Visual-Spatial Working Memory
	PAL Verbal Working Memory
	WISC-III Digit Span (Digits Backwards)
Long-term memory	PAL Math Facts
Declarative knowledge versus procedural knowledge	Verbalization of knowledge versus application of knowledge
Temporal versus visual-spatial processing	Observe student performing written calculations to evaluate whether steps of calculation are out of order or errors are made in moving right to left, left to right, up to down, down to up, or diagonally during computational algorithms
Input-output combinations	PAL Calculations

Table 8.1 — *Continued*

| Concrete versus formal operations | Testing the limits with concrete manipulatives like cuisenaire rods |
| | Piagetian tasks (see Berninger & Yates, 1993) |

* This table is meant to be a suggestive rather than exhaustive listing of tests for assessing the functional math system.

[a] CogAt = Cognitive Abilities Test (Thorndike & Hagen, 1993)

[b] KM-R = Key Math—Revised (Connolly, 1988)

[c] PAL = Process Assessment of the Learner (PAL) Test Battery for Math (Berninger, in press)

[d] SB-IV = Stanford Binet Intelligence Scale, 4th Ed. (Thorndike, Hagen, & Sattler, 1986)

[e] WIAT = Wechsler Individual Achievement Test (The Psychological Corporation, 1992)

[f] WIAT II = Wechsler Individual Achievement Test—Second Edition (The Psychological Corporation, in press)

[g] WISC-III = Wechsler Intelligence Scale for Children—Third Edition (The Psychological Corporation, 1991)

[h] WJ-R = Woodcock-Johnson Psycho-Educational Battery—Revised (Woodcock & Johnson, 1990)

[i] WRAT-3 = Wide Range Achievement Test—Third Edition (Wilkinson, 1993)

used to monitor progress during early intervention or in response to curriculum modifications. More-comprehensive, in-depth assessment of all components may be warranted at a later time, if the student does not respond to intervention and is suspected to have a math disability.

GIFTEDNESS AND TALENT

Early Identification

Early identification of talent is a crucial step in developing Math Talent, which is highly valued in an increasingly technical, scientific society. In order to nurture the excitement and curiosity of math talented children and foster their math achievement, they need to be identified at an early age, but little research has focused on young children with math talent. Pletan, Robinson, Berninger, and Abbott (1995) were among the first to study math talent early in development and found that parents can reliably identify advanced mathematical ability in their preschool and kindergarten children. Four- to six-year-olds nominated by their parents as being advanced in math scored at the 95th percentile or better on the *Wechsler Preschool and Primary Scale of Intelligence—Revised* (WPPSI-R; The Psychological Corporation, 1989) or the *Wechsler Intelligence Scale for Children—Revised* (WISC-R; The Psychological Corporation, 1975) Arithmetic subtests and at the 92nd percentile or better on the *Kaufman Assessment Battery for Children* (K-ABC; Kaufman & Kaufman, 1983) Arithmetic subtest. The study also found that parents' responses to a questionnaire about their children's math-advanced activities correlated significantly with scores on the standardized tests. Parents responded to items in this questionnaire that asked about their child's mathematical behavior (e.g., "Can tell whether a nickel or a dime is more money," "Counts to one thousand by hundreds," and "Can play a complicated game like Monopoly (no help)"). Based on the parent responses that correlated most with test performance, the investigators constructed a 20-item parent questionnaire that psychologists could give when young children are referred for math talent. Those identified by this screening as likely, based on the psychologists' judgment, to have early math talent could then be given appropriate subtests of the Wechsler scales or the K-ABC to evaluate how advanced they may be in math reasoning. In addition, the math precocity exhibited by these preschoolers and kindergartners was not just a "flash in the pan." Robinson, Abbott, Berninger, Busse, and Mukhopadhyay (1997) followed these children for two years and found that they maintained or even increased their high level of math performance relative to their peers, thereby demonstrating the reliability and validity of early identification and its benefits in developing math talent.

Early identification and intervention in math are not always possible in the preschool years, but should be possible in all first- and second-grade classrooms. We recommend that all first- and second-grade students be screened. Although by second-grade, students may have scores from school-wide, group-administered math achievement tests, if the tests do not have an adequate ceiling they may underestimate gifted children's math abilities. One exception is the *Cognitive Abilities Test* (CogAT; Thorndike & Hagen, 1993), which provides out-of-level testing that can be administered to groups and has been found effective as a screener for math talent in the early grades (Yates, 1996). Parent nomination and/or selection by way of a short teacher questionnaire should also be included to increase screening validity by providing data from multiple sources.

Yates (1996) developed a two-level screening for both math talent and math disability in the first and second grades. In the first level, the Verbal and Quantitative scales of the CogAT—a multiple-choice test read by the examiner—are administered. At these grade levels, the test assesses relational concepts (e.g., largest) and quantitative concepts (e.g., one-half) and children do not have to be able to read or write numerals to answer items. In the second level, children who achieve high or low scores on the quantitative CogAT are then individually tested to obtain a more complete picture of their math abilities. The *Key Math—Revised* (KM-R; Connolly, 1988), a diagnostic achievement test that evaluates conceptual knowledge, calculation skills, and problem solving ability, is especially recommended for complete assessment of the functional math system of mathematically precocious children. In addition, two subtests of the *Stanford-Binet Intelligence Scale—Fourth Edition* (SB-IV; Thorndike, Hagen, & Sattler, 1986), Number Series and Matrices, or other tests in Table 8.1, may provide unique and useful information about the mathematical reasoning and visual-spatial abilities of children who scored high on the CogAT. Appropriate assessment should include measures of both calculation and math reasoning, because many gifted children may not know their math facts even though they excel at math reasoning (N. M. Robinson, personal communication, September 15, 1998). Detailed descriptions of such measures and their use in assessing the functional math system are provided later in this chapter.

After grade 2, screening of children for math talent should be performed on the basis of parent and teacher referral and of high performance on standardized tests. The KM-R can be used to evaluate more precisely whether the student is advanced in math and, if so, in what areas. The Center for the Advancement of Academically Talented Youth at Johns Hopkins University offers high-achieving seventh and eighth graders across the country the opportunity to take the SAT, and high-achieving second through sixth graders the opportunity to take similar out-of-level tests.[1] Students who score well are given letters of recognition and provided with information on educational planning and the opportunity to meet other talented students in their area.

Modifying Curriculum and Monitoring Progress

Many schools do not have gifted programs for children in primary grades, and for those that do, students typically must have high verbal scores to qualify, even though math talent may develop independently of verbal ability (Keating, 1991). Thus, many mathematically talented children may not be identified or provided with appropriate math instruction in the early grades. However, many math-talented students in the early grades can benefit from modification of the regular program. The most common intervention for math-talented students from pre-kindergarten to 12th grade is acceleration (Sowell, 1993), which comes in many forms and includes service-delivery and curriculum-delivery options (Schiever & Maker, 1991). Acceleration through altered service delivery provides the standard curriculum to students at a younger than usual age or grade. Examples of service-delivery acceleration are early entrance to kindergarten and grade skipping. Acceleration through altered curriculum delivery involves speeding up the pace at which material is presented (e.g., telescoping, in which students complete 2 years of work in 1 year, and self-paced study). Acceleration can be offered in the regular classroom or through special classes. Another common intervention for gifted students is enrichment, the goal of which is to offer students a curriculum

[1] Detailed information about participation in the searches for mathematical talent, which now extend down to second grade, can be found by contacting the Institute for Academic Advancement of Youth, Johns Hopkins University, 3400 N. Charles St., Baltimore, MD 21218; 410-516-0337; or www.jhu.edu/gifted.

that is greater in depth or breadth than the standard curriculum. An enriched curriculum generally refers to a more varied educational experience—a curriculum that has been modified either in content or in teaching strategies. Enrichment can be offered as additions to the general classroom program or as special classes after school or on weekends through clubs that target specific interests (e.g., Robinson et al., 1997).

Sowell (1993) reviewed empirical research mostly from the 1970s and 1980s on programs for mathematically gifted students. These programs primarily used acceleration or enrichment, or a combination of the two. Consistent acceleration for math-gifted students resulted in faster learning. Several of the studies showed dramatic changes in rates of achievement when students were allowed to learn at a faster pace. Studies on enrichment programs were not conclusive, with some studies demonstrating improvement on cognitive and affective measures relative to a control group and others failing to show a difference. In addition, this line of research is plagued by ill-defined and inconsistent operationalization of "enrichment." It is therefore difficult to draw conclusions about the efficacy of enrichment programs.

Acceleration is not as easy to implement in the elementary grades; students are not typically grouped by ability in math the way they often are for reading instruction to accommodate children with varied reading levels. Most elementary school teachers are not well trained in math and may be uncomfortable teaching it (Ginsburg, 1997), which may make them less willing to attempt individualized instruction for math-talented students in their general education classrooms. Elementary schools also do not have the flexibility of secondary school organization where independent, sequential, mixed-grade math courses provide a ready-made acceleration option for high-ability students. However, in schools that have a mathematics block, primary-grade children can be sent to a higher grade just for math instruction. Providing teacher support, such as an older peer tutor or a parent volunteer, can make acceleration more feasible in the regular classroom.

For older students there are myriad options for acceleration in math. Allowing gifted students to move at a faster than normal pace in order to facilitate their math development can be accomplished through independent study; taking college courses while in high school; completing two or more years of math in a single year; skipping a grade; taking intensive summer courses, honors or AP classes, or correspondence or on-line courses offered through universities; or participating in math clubs, "bowls," individual tutoring, or mentoring. Kolitch and Brody (1992) found that some students have difficulty finding appropriately challenging classes after exhausting the standard high-school curriculum. Psychologists should help students plan ahead in order to ensure a continuous math curriculum at the appropriate level. They should also monitor student progress to make sure that modification of the curriculum results in greater depth and breadth of learning or faster learning.

MATH DISABILITY

Nature of Math Disability

The burgeoning research on the development of mathematical cognition in young children has provided a theoretical basis for studying school-age children with Math Disability (MD). Although deficits in math skills are common among children (Badian, 1983; Kosc, 1974), it is only recently that considerable research attention has been paid to explicating the nature of MD. Russell and Ginsburg (1984) found that elementary school children with MD demonstrated qualitatively similar performance to somewhat younger children in a variety of informal math concepts and skills. However, they exhibited severe deficiencies in the rapid retrieval of number facts and the ability to solve complex story problems. Geary and his colleagues have conducted a series of investigations on young children with MD, which showed that second-grade MD children used strategies similar to typical first graders (e.g., relying on counting). In contrast, nonimpaired children had shifted to a greater use of automatic retrieval, suggesting that a characteristic of MD may be a developmental lag in automatic retrieval (Geary, 1990; Geary, Brown, & Samaranayake, 1991). However, the term "lag" implies potential for catch-up, and in some cases the problem in automatic retrieval may persist throughout development. The MD children were also less accurate in their use of strategies. Follow-up work by Geary, Bow-Thomas, and Yao (1992) suggests that the difficulties MD children show in using computational strategies is tied to delays in learning basic counting principles. This body of work implies that MD is characterized by deficits in rapid, automatic fact retrieval and/or strategy use. Further research is needed on whether students with MD have delays only in *developing* automaticity and/or effective strategies or whether these deficits are persistent and lifelong.

Geary's MD group, however, was delayed in reading as well as mathematics, suggesting a more general form of learning disability. Jordan and Montani (1997) found in their comparison of math and reading disabilities that children with only a math disability have deficits specifically associated with math fact retrieval. These deficits may be due to a disability in automatic processing (Garnett & Fleischner, 1983; Roditi, 1988; Yates, 1996). Recent research showed that children with reading disabilities only and those with dual disability in math and reading differed only in rapid automatic naming and not in Verbal IQ or phonological awareness processing (Busse, Thomson, Abbott, & Berninger, 1999). More research is needed on math disability that does and does not co-occur with reading disabilities.

Math disability, like reading disability, is likely to be heterogeneous. Geary (1993) identified three subtypes of MD, in which children showed deficits in (a) retrieval of math facts, (b) application of algorithms, and (c) visual-spatial understanding of the number system. Shurtleff, Fay, Abbott, and Berninger

(1988) found that in a sample of students referred for assessment of learning disorders, fingertip number writing (in a neuropsychological battery) was correlated with paper–and–pencil math calculation, suggesting that sensory (kinesthetic)-symbol integration may also play a role in learning math. Likewise, Berninger and Colwell (1985) found a relationship between neurodevelopmental measures of finger function and paper-and-pencil calculation. Problems with both verbal short-term memory and long-term memory retrieval have also been postulated to explain dual disability in reading and math (Ackerman, Anhalt, & Dykman, 1986; Brandys & Rourke, 1991; Siegel & Linder, 1984). We propose that any component in Figures 8.1 and 8.2 could be underdeveloped and contribute to less than optimal math functioning.

Screening for Early Intervention

Children with deficits in math ability need intervention as early as possible. The screening approach developed by Yates (1996) to identify math talent can also be used to screen for math learning disabilities. The CogAT is administered to all first- and second-grade students. Children who obtain low scores on the Quantitative CogAT or whose Quantitative CogAT scores are significantly lower than their Verbal CogAT scores are selected for further assessment and prereferral intervention (i.e., modification of teaching methods, curricula content or organization, or instructional materials). Further assessment includes both standardized achievement measures and process measures, found in Table 8.1, to determine why the student is having difficulty in math. Students may also be selected for more comprehensive assessment and intervention based on teacher and parent referral. Measures in Table 8.1 may be used not only for screening and process-oriented assessment but also for progress monitoring once intervention is implemented.

Definition and Diagnostic Assessment

In our view, Math Disability is characterized by unexpected difficulty in the arithmetic module, conceptual knowledge base, or problem-solving space of the domain-specific functional math system (see Figure 8.1), given the student's verbal, quantitative, and/or visual-spatial reasoning ability. Processes in the domain-general systems may explain the unexpected underachievement (see Figure 8.2). This definition implies a discrepancy between reasoning ability and achievement in component math skills, but psychologists should be flexible in how the discrepancy is defined—there is not one and only one way to define discrepancy meaningfully. What is more important is a thorough, comprehensive assessment of all the components in Figures 8.1 and 8.2 (see Table 8.1), so that there is a full picture of strengths and weaknesses for generating instructional interventions. Both Verbal and Performance IQs should be taken into account in determining if math achievement is unexpectedly low, because both verbal and nonverbal/visual-spatial reasoning contribute to math problem solving (Robinson et al., 1996; Robinson et al., 1997).

Fleischner and Manheimer (1997) advocated two methods psychologists can use to supplement standardized tests in math assessment: error analysis and interviews. It is important to ask students to show their work on assessment measures and to observe the process they go through in generating the work provided. Error analysis of these work samples provides a vital link between ongoing assessment and intervention. For example, by examining several incorrect answers to the same or similar types of items, the psychologist may be able to determine if the student failed the item because he or she lacked knowledge of basic math facts, made a systematic procedural error, or lacked basic concepts. Common error patterns have been published to help with this process (e.g., Enright, 1990). It is sometimes impossible, however, to determine by looking at a student's written work why an item was failed. A further step in revealing a student's problem-solving strategies is interviewing. Often interviewers simply ask the student to explain the way he or she solved a problem. This technique is sometimes referred to as a "think-aloud." If the student has difficulty providing an after-the-fact explanation, use of a think-aloud while solving a new, similar problem may be helpful.

Assessment and evaluation of math learning problems have traditionally only involved accuracy in computation, but true mastery of mathematics skills involves more than rote computation—students also need to be able to perform math computations fluently. For example, if a student is trying to learn the steps to solve a multi-digit subtraction problem, but has not yet automatized 1-digit subtraction facts and relies on counting instead, much more time and energy must be devoted to the prerequisite skill of single-digit subtraction and less attention is available for learning the steps to solve the new type of problem. Fluency/automaticity may be assessed on an individual or group basis using timed problem sets based on the curriculum or via subtests of the PAL Test Battery for Math (Berninger, in press; see Table 8.1). Fluency goals should be incorporated into objectives for MD students, but progress toward meeting them should be monitored. In some cases (see the second case at the end of this chapter) fluency may be so impaired that bypass strategies are needed.

Interventions for Math Disability

Explicit Instruction and Instructional Strategies

In response to the NCTM standards and the math reform movement in general, researchers in the field of math disabilities are emphasizing the need for explicit instruction for MD students (Fleischner & Manheimer, 1997), because it results in "more predictable, more generalizable, and more functional achievement" (Jones, Wilson, & Bhojwani, 1997, p. 154). A basic tenet of constructivism, which currently is the dominant pedagogical approach in mathematics education, is that teachers do not transmit knowledge directly to students; rather, students construct knowledge through active engagement. However, research suggests that it is unlikely that MD students will learn certain knowledge and skills in mathematics if they are not given explicit instruction (Engelmann, 1993; Jitendra, Kameenui, & Carnine, 1994). In addition to specific concepts and skills, Carnine (1997) emphasizes the need to explicitly teach strategies to MD students.

Students with MD often have difficulty making inferences from abstract examples. They also often have trouble translating what they understand based on concrete examples into symbolic, abstract form. Due to these difficulties, Fleischner & Manheimer (1997) advocated using the following principles when teaching math explicitly to students of all ages with MD: (a) present new topics in sequence, beginning with concrete representations using manipulatives, even with older students;[2] (b) ask students to use pictures to demonstrate their understanding of the topic and have them explain their understanding to their peers; (c) give explicit instruction in how symbols represent mathematical operations and check that students can use symbols in written work; and (d) check for abstract understanding by asking students to find alternate solutions for problems or explain their reasoning so others understand their method.

Teaching to All Components of the Functional Math System Including Problem Solving

Due to their deficits in performing basic calculation skills, students with MD often receive instruction that focuses on repetitive computation practice while complex problem solving is given short shrift. Baroody and Hume (1991) propose that such children are "curriculum disabled." Although MD children may need more opportunity than their typically developing peers to master basic math facts and algorithms, their instructional program should not be based on extensive drilling and endless worksheets of written computations. The NCTM standards (1989, 1991) emphasize that the goal for all children is to become competent problem solvers and mathematical reasoners. Examples of the kinds of problems children should solve, consistent with NCTM standards, are visual representation of number, equivalence, symmetry, reversibility of operations, patterns, zero and negative numbers, infinity, bases other than ten, probability, and estimation. Just as reading and writing

---

[2]On the basis of clinical experience, we recommend taking cues for the utility of concrete manipulatives in older students from the students themselves. One study (unpublished data) showed that middle-school students may no longer need manipulatives and use them as projectiles!

instruction should be aimed at all components of a functional reading and writing system (Berninger, 1998), so should math instruction be aimed at all components of the functional math system in Figure 8.1.

Young mathematically talented children benefit from a math curriculum that challenges them to (a) solve everyday mathematical problems, (b) find multiple solutions, and (c) engage in constructivist problem solving (e.g., Kamii, 1985, 1994) in which the group collaboratively works together to solve open-ended problems (e.g., Hiebert et al., 1996) that reflect the NCTM (1989) standards (see Robinson et al., 1997). Students with MD are likely to benefit from such a curriculum as well (see Cawley & Miller, 1989; Thornton, Langrall, & Jones, 1997). Successfully teaching MD students to solve complex problems (e.g., Bottge & Hasselbring, 1993) demonstrates that these children can perform beyond typical expectations. Students with MD often have average or above average math reasoning skills, despite their poor performance on written calculation tasks. Thornton et al. argue for a curriculum that is broad and balanced to allow MD students to use their strengths in their mathematical development instead of focusing exclusively on their weakest areas. They recommend a greater emphasis on math problems that utilize number sense and estimation, data analysis, spatial reasoning, and pattern analysis. See Waxman, Robinson, and Mukhopadhyay (1997) and the catalogues for Critical Thinking Books & Software and Free Spirit Publishing Self-Help for Kids (addresses in the reference list) for instructional activities and materials for developing math problem-solving skills.

Jones et al. (1997) caution, however, that MD students need explicit instruction and many opportunities to practice these types of problems independently if they are to generalize problem-solving skills. Cawley, Fitzmaurice, Shaw, Kahn, and Bates (1978) argue that students are more likely to generalize the math skills they learn to problem solving if they have experience with problems presented in various ways and have opportunities to vary their mode of response. Teachers can present problems to students by using objects, manipulatives, pictures, or other visual prompts, presenting them in oral or written form. Likewise, students should choose from these methods to respond to problems that the teacher presents. In addition to choosing various ways to respond to problems, students with MD learn better when they have the opportunity to describe and justify their problem-solving strategies and solutions (Fleischner & Manheimer, 1997; Thornton et al., 1997). Sharing strategies and justifying solutions can be performed as part of dyadic, small-group, or large-group discussions.

Cooperative Learning and Peer Tutoring

Schools are increasingly using students to help each other learn, in both regular and special education classrooms. Two forms of this peer assistance that are validated as effective in the research literature are cooperative learning and peer tutoring. Cooperative learning is when students spend time in small heterogeneous groups where they are expected to help each other learn. Fleischner and Manheimer (1997) recommended the use of cooperative learning groups for students with math disabilities in regular education classrooms. Slavin (1983) analyzed studies of cooperative learning and found that it increased achievement when two conditions were present. First, it was necessary for students to be held individually accountable for their performance. Second, the group reward needed to account for individual performance.

Peer tutoring can take the form of two classmates helping each other practice skills they have learned. Alternately, a higher-achieving or older student can assist a lower-achieving or younger student. Peer tutoring has been found effective with mainstreamed learning disabled students (Maheady, Sacca, & Harper, 1987) and effective in learning math facts (Greenwood, 1991) and computational algorithms (Fantuzzo, King, & Heller, 1992). However, for students with learning disabilities, peer tutoring on math operations resulted in greater improvement in calculation than transfer to concepts and applications (e.g., numeration, geometry, measurement, charts and graphs, money, and word problems; Fuchs, Fuchs, Phillips, Hamlett, & Karns, 1995). One possibility, which requires research, is that peer tutoring is most effective in improving skills in the arithmetic module but that a combination of teacher-directed instruction and constructivist problem solving involving the whole class may be more effective in developing math concepts and problem solving (see Figure 8.1).

Practice

Homework or independent practice is an important part of an instructional program for students with MD (Carnine, 1997). They will typically need more practice than their typically developing peers to achieve fluency and retention (Jones et al., 1997). Carnine (1989) has developed guidelines for designing effective practice exercises, including the following: (a) assign manageable quantities of work as skills are learned; (b) provide review 1 or 2 days after initial learning; (c) supervise initial practice to prevent students from practicing incorrect procedures; (d) provide initial practice that separates concepts and their applications; (e) relate the practice of subskills to the whole task; (f) preteach component skills of algorithms and strategies; (g) ensure that exercises allow for independent practice of skills with high levels of success; and (h) require fluency as part of practice by timing performance. However, practice in retrieving math facts should be balanced with opportunity to solve math problems, and in some cases when students cannot automatize math fact retrieval, they should be taught compensatory strategies.

Progress Monitoring

Either the tests or subtests in Table 8.1 or curriculum-based measures can be used to monitor the progress of students who were identified through screening for early intervention, of students referred by teachers to child-study teams that recommend curriculum modifications, and of students with diagnosed MD. In addition, the Academic Intervention Monitoring System (AIMS; Di Perna & Elliott, in press), which has been empirically validated for monitoring intervention effectiveness, can be used for this purpose.

ACHIEVEMENT AND PROCESS MEASURES FOR MATH ASSESSMENT

We now describe the measures in Table 8.1 that are relevant for screening, progress monitoring, or comprehensively assessing mathematical talent or disability. We also discuss their reliability and validity.

The KM-R

This instrument is a diagnostic inventory of mathematics achievement divided into three main areas (Basic Concepts, Basic Operations, and Applications) and consisting of thirteen subtests. Most items in the KM-R are presented in easel format and require a verbal response.

The Basic Concepts area is made up of three subtests: Numeration, Rational Numbers, and Geometry. Numeration items include counting, ordination, place value, and rounding. For example, one item requires the student to read aloud and order a series of two-digit numbers, another to provide the next two numbers in a sequence of three-digit numbers that is increasing by tens, and a third to indicate the total number of blocks in a picture where the blocks are grouped into hundreds, tens, and ones. The Rational Numbers conceptual subtest assesses understanding of part-whole relationships. One item asks students to identify what fraction of a group of items is red, and another requires a fraction to be expressed as a decimal. The Geometry subtest covers ideas related to shape, angles, geometric vocabulary, and perspective. In one item, the student is asked to tell how many blocks are in a stack when not every block can be seen in the figure. In another item, the student is presented with a two-dimensional figure that includes dotted lines. The student is asked what the figure would be if it were folded along the lines to form a three-dimensional object.

The Basic Operations area consists of five subtests: Addition, Subtraction, Multiplication, Division, and Mental Computation. Each of the four operations subtests consists of pictures of common objects as well as written arithmetic problems. For example, a subtraction item shows a picture of two children and asks how many more cookies one child has than the other. Multiplication calculation includes multiplying a two-place number by a one-place number, presented vertically. The mental computation test does not allow the use of paper and pencil, and the student must answer within 15 seconds to receive credit. Items range in difficulty from simple math facts to complex, multistep problems and are presented orally or in written form.

The Applications area has five subtests: Measurement, Time and Money, Estimation, Interpreting Data, and Problem Solving. Measurement covers areas of temperature, length, weight, volume, and area. Items require estimation, reading common measurement devices, and calculating and converting from one unit to another using both metric and standard U.S. measurement systems. One example is an item that shows a pitcher of water, gives the capacity in quarts, and asks the student how many cups that is. Items on the Time and Money subtest ask students to determine the value of coins, make change, update the balance of a checkbook, figure out time zones or days of the week, and read a calendar. The Estimation subtest covers a wide range of topics, such as asking the student how many playing cards it would take to cover the surface of a book. Other items require rounding, such as asking the student to estimate the total cost of several items added together. The Interpreting Data subtest asks students to interpret data presented in various forms, such as bar graphs, pie charts, bus schedules, tax tables, or athletic scores. The Problem Solving subtest presents items that require application of problem-solving concepts and procedures in story-problem format. For some items, students are not asked to solve problems but rather to state how they would solve the problem or what additional information they would need to solve it.

Reliability coefficients were calculated using alternate form, split-half, and item response theory methods. For total test scores, estimates ranged in the .90s, depending on the method used and the grade level. For the three broad test areas and the individual subtests, internal reliability ranged from the .50s to the .80s. The KM-R was constructed to correspond to essential mathematics content and trends in mathematics education. The separate domains were developed to enhance the use of the test in evaluating a student's specific mathematical skills and deficits in addition to performance relative to age peers. To evaluate construct validity, subtests were correlated with area scores. In all cases correlations were higher for subtests and their associated area scores than for the other area scores, supporting the organization of the three broad areas. The total test score on the KM-R correlated .76 with total mathematics scores on the Iowa Test of Basic Skills (ITBS) and .66 with the Comprehensive Test of Basic Skills (CTBS).

The SB-IV

Although not an achievement test, the SB-IV (Thorndike et al., 1986) contains two subtests—Number Series and Matrices—relevant to assessment of components of the functional math system. The tests are presented in easel format and the student responds orally. Number Series is designed to assess quantitative reasoning. Each item presents a series of numbers and the child is asked to provide the next number in the series. Matrices is designed to measure visual-spatial reasoning. Each item consists of a square matrix; earlier items are 2 × 2 with four boxes, but more difficult items use a 3 × 3 matrix with nine boxes. Each of the boxes in the matrix contains a picture, symbol, or geometric pattern. The designs in the boxes are related to each other in some way to form a pattern. One box is empty and the child must choose from an array the design that belongs in the box. Kuder-Richardson—20 (KR-20) reliability coefficients (averaged across ages 7–17) were .90 for Number Series and .90 for Matrices. Test-retest coefficients (averaged across elementary ages) were .61 for Number Series and .63 for Matrices. Validity information provided in the SB-IV is only calculated for the Composite and Area Scores and not for individual subtests.

The Wechsler Individual Achievement Test (WIAT)

The WIAT (The Psychological Corporation, 1992) and the forthcoming second edition of the WIAT (WIAT II; The Psychological Corporation, in press) contain two subtests for assessing math achievement: Numerical Operations and Mathematical Reasoning. The Numerical Operations subtest, in both editions of the WIAT, consists of written calculation items covering the four basic operations as well as fractions, decimals and percentages, negative numbers, exponents, and algebra. Mathematical Reasoning items are presented orally in easel format, and the child is provided with scrap paper. Domains of mathematical knowledge in both editions of this subtest are wide-ranging and include, but are not restricted to, measurement, money, time, reading graphs and charts, multistep problems using the four operations, and averaging. The WIAT II has items yoked to the NCTM (1989, 1991) standards and includes a guide to error analysis. Spearman-Brown split-half reliability coefficients (averaged across ages 5–17) for the WIAT were .92 for the Math Composite, .85 for Numerical Operations, and .89 for Math Reasoning. Test-retest reliability coefficients for the WIAT (averaged across grades 1–10) were .91 for the Math Composite, .86 for Numerical Operations, and .89 for Mathematical Reasoning. Reliability and validity information are not yet available for the forthcoming WIAT II (see chapter on this test in this volume).

Woodcock-Johnson Psycho-Educational Battery—Revised (WJ-R)

The WJ-R (Woodcock & Johnson, 1990) contains three subtests useful for assessing students' math skills: Calculation, Applied Problems, and Quantitative Concepts. The Calculation subtest consists of 58 items that measure written calculation skills in the four basic operations as well as fractions, decimals, algebra, and trigonometry. The Applied Problems subtest is designed to measure practical problem solving. Items are presented in easel format and read aloud, and the student is provided with scrap paper. Except for the KM-R, the WJ-R is unique among the achievement batteries profiled here in that it includes a subtest specifically designed to assess conceptual knowledge in mathematics separate from math reasoning. The Quantitative Concepts subtest covers naming numbers, identifying shapes and arithmetic symbols, identifying the first and last object in an array, and providing the missing number in a series. Internal consistency, split-half reliability estimates for school-aged children were in the high .80s to low .90s for Calculation and Applied Problems and in the high .70s to high .80s for Quantitative Concepts.

The Wide Range Achievement Test—
Third Edition (WRAT-3)

The WRAT-3 (Wilkinson, 1993) includes only one subtest for assessing math achievement. The Arithmetic subtest is divided into oral and written sections. The oral section is composed of the first 15 items of the test, which are administered to children 7 and younger. Children age 8 and above begin with the written arithmetic problems. The WRAT-3 should not be used alone to assess math ability because it does not contain a subtest measuring math reasoning or problem-solving ability. It needs to be supplemented with other measures in Table 8.1. Another possible limitation of the test is that it has a time limit, which the WJ-R and the WIAT do not. However, if a student has a rate (automaticity) problem rather than an accuracy problem with math calculation, the WRAT-3 might be used to document that by comparing performance on the WRAT-3 with the WJ-R or the WIAT. Alternatively, the KM-R Mental Computation subtest, which has a 15-second time limit, could be used for this purpose. Reliability coefficients calculated by several methods (alternate forms, Rasch person separation, and test-retest) were reported for school-aged children for the WRAT-3 Arithmetic subtest to be in the high .80s to high .90s.

PAL Test Battery for Math

The PAL Test Battery for Math (Berninger, in press) may have subtests for automaticity of counting and fact retrieval; concept of place value; processes of written computation; verbal, quantitative, and visual-spatial working memory; processes relevant to word-problem solving; and rapid automatic naming of 1- and 2-place numbers. The manual will report reliability and validity information and provide suggestions for qualitative assessment. These subtests can be used for screening, progress monitoring, and in-depth diagnostic assessment.

ILLUSTRATIVE CASES

Fourth-Grade Girl

AB had no difficulty learning to read, memorize math facts, or learn computational algorithms for addition and subtraction. However, she had inordinate difficulty in learning the concept of part-whole relationships, especially as this concept relates to fractions and telling time, and in solving problems requiring visual-spatial concepts. She had some difficulty in learning multiplication involving multi-place multipliers and in learning long division. In-depth assessment following her failure to respond to special help by the Chapter 1 teacher revealed that her Verbal IQ (110) was significantly higher than her Performance IQ (85). Error analysis showed that her errors in multi-step multiplication and long division were due to her difficulty in dealing with the frequent changes in spatial directions (top-down, diagonal, bottom-up, left-right) rather than any difficulty with retrieval of math facts or verbalization of the steps of the computational algorithm. Her math disability appeared to be specific to visual-spatial reasoning and the concepts of part-whole relationships, fractions, time, and geometry shown in Figure 8.1. Instructional recommendations included use of a digital watch rather than a watch with a clock face, visual representations of part-whole relationships needed to grasp the concept of fractions, use of grid paper for multiplication and division computations, and strategies for representing word problems both visually and verbally.

Sixth-Grade Boy

Unlike AB, CD had been qualified for special education since first grade on the basis of a severe discrepancy between his superior IQ and low achievement in reading, math, and written expression. However, he had been served under an inclusion model and had never really received any specialized instruction aimed specifically at his problems in math, let alone reading or writing. There was a history of learning problems on both sides of his family, with his father reporting a great deal of difficulty with paper-and-pencil calculation when he was in school. CD had extreme difficulty with "minute math," a typical instructional activity designed to develop automaticity of math fact retrieval in which children are asked to write as many answers to randomly presented math facts as they can in 1 minute. Progress monitoring showed that his performance on this written task deteriorated over the course of the year, although his mother noted progress in math fact retrieval at home when he was allowed to answer orally. CD lamented that he had been denied participation in the interesting math program his friends were in (an advanced math curriculum that emphasized constructivist problem solving) and was instead drilled in boring computation. Progress monitoring also showed that he remained significantly delayed in math computation (fourth-grade level), reading (third-to-fourth-grade level), and written expression (third-to-fourth-grade level).

However, formal assessment showed that his Arithmetic subtest scaled score on the *Wechsler Intelligence Scale for Children—Third Edition* (WISC-III; The Psychological Corporation, 1991) was in the superior range, indicating talent in quantitative reasoning that did not involve paper-and-pencil calculation. Process assessment revealed phonological processing in the average range, but severe deficits in rapid automatic naming (Wolf, 1986; Wolf et al., 1986), orthographic coding, and finger function (fine-motor planning). Consistent with the findings of Busse et al. (1999), CD had dual disability in reading and math, associated with a deficit in automaticity, and disabilities across the academic curriculum in low-level word recognition, calculation, handwriting, and spelling skills. Intervention included use of a tutor 4 days a week after school. The tutor was trained in teaching both gifted and learning disabled students and had taught the advanced math curriculum oriented to problem solving. The tutor integrated reading and math through use of word problems to develop both reading and math skills. Instructional activities focused on development of math problem-solving skills using mental computation, with support from a calculator as needed. Paper-and-pencil calculation was permitted if CD chose to use it. All minute math was eliminated; this task may be appropriate for developing automaticity in some children but not in a student with a diagnosed problem in automaticity and finger function. The goal, based on CD's wish, was to integrate him eventually into the advanced math track, which stressed mathematical reasoning.

DEVELOPMENTAL MODEL OF ASSESSMENT FOR INTERVENTION FOR MATH TALENT AND MATH DISABILITY

As in this volume's chapter on assessing reading and writing, we propose a 3-tier model (summarized in Table 8.2) for assessing math talent and disability. At each tier, the focus is on both math talent and math disability. Early in schooling, the purpose of assessment is to identify students with mathematical talent or specific disabilities in the functional math system. Identified students receive early intervention to stimulate their math talent or to overcome specific weaknesses in their functional math system. In some cases, a certain student will exhibit both mathematical talent—for example,

TABLE 8.2
Developmental, 3-Tier Model for Identifying Math Talent and Math Disability and Providing Appropriate Instructional Intervention

Developmental Level	Math Talent	Math Disability
Tier 1: Early screening and intervention		
Pre-K and K	Parent questionnaire (see Pletan et al., 1995)	
	K-ABC Math subtest or WPSSI-R Math subtest	
1st and 2nd	CogAT Verbal (group)	CogAT AT Verbal (group)
	CogAT Quantitative (group)	CogAT Quantitative (group)
	Key Math-R (individual)	Math PAL (individual)
	(see Yates, 1996)	(see Yates, 1996, and text)
Tier 2: Prereferral intervention and modification of the regular program	Acceleration or enrichment with progress monitoring (see text)	Instructional interventions aimed at automaticity of math fact retrieval and calculation, algorithms, concepts of number line, place value, and part-whole; progress monitoring with PAL for Math, other tests in Table 8.1, or AIMS.
Tier 3: In-depth diagnostic	Group tests with sufficient ceiling (see text)	Complete assessment of domain-specific and domain-general components (see Table 8.1)

in reasoning—and specific disabilities—for example, in automatic retrieval of math facts. In such cases early intervention should be directed to both the ability and the disability. Later in schooling, at any grade level, students may first require modification of the regular program for either math talent or disability and then progress monitoring to evaluate the effectiveness of the curriculum modification. In some cases, students' exceptionalities—either strengths or weaknesses—may be so pronounced that formal assessment may be required. In the case of math talent, instruments with sufficient ceiling are needed to evaluate whether the student requires acceleration through the curriculum. In the case of math disability, in-depth assessment of all components of the functional math system are needed to pinpoint specific areas for instructional intervention. The goal in both cases is to optimize math achievement in an increasingly technological society.

Acknowledgments

Preparation of this chapter was supported by the National Institute of Child Health and Human Development Grant P5033812-04.

This paper was based on a presentation at the annual meeting of the American Psychological Association, Boston, August 1999.

The last two authors of this chapter have contributed substantially to the development and validation of the PAL Test Battery for Math based on the research of the second author and her students (the first author, Cheryl Yates, and Hillary Shurtleff) and colleagues (Nancy Robinson and Robert Abbott) and other researchers.

References

Ackerman, P. T., Anhalt, J. M., & Dykman, R. A. (1986). Arithmetic automatization failure in children with attention and reading disorders: Associations and sequela. *Journal of Learning Disabilities*, 19, 222–232.

Badian, N. A. (1983). Dyscalculia and nonverbal disorders of learning. *Progress in Learning Disabilities*, 5, 222–232.

Baroody, A., & Hume, J. (1991). Meaningful mathematics instruction: The case of fractions. *Remedial and Special Education*, 12(3), 54–68.

Berninger, V. W. (1998). *Process Assessment of the Learner: Guides for intervention*. San Antonio, TX: The Psychological Corporation.

Berninger, V. W. (in press). *Process Assessment of the Learner (PAL) Test Battery for Math*. San Antonio, TX: The Psychological Corporation.

Berninger, V. W., & Colwell, S. (1985). Relationships between neurodevelopmental and educational findings. *Pediatrics*, 75, 697–702.

Berninger, V. W., & Yates, C. (1993). Formal operational thought in the gifted: A post-Piagetian perspective. *Roeper Review. A Journal on Gifted Education*, 15, 220–224.

Bottge, B. A., & Hasselbring, T. S. (1993). A comparison of two approaches for teaching complex, authentic mathematical problems to adolescents in remedial math classes. *Exceptional Children*, 59, 556–566.

Brandys, C. F., & Rourke, B. F. (1991). Differential memory abilities in reading and arithmetic disabled children. In B. F. Rourke (Ed.), *Neuropsychological validation of learning disability subtypes* (pp. 73–96). New York: Guilford.

Busse, J., Thomson, J., Abbott, R., & Berninger, V. W., (1999, August). *Cognitive processes related to dual disability in reading and calculation*. Boston: American Psychological Association.

Carnine, D. (1989). Designing practice activities. *Journal of Learning Disabilities*, 22, 603–607.

Carnine, D. (1997). Instructional design in mathematics for students with learning disabilities. *Journal of Learning Disabilities*, 30(2), 130–141.

Case, R. (1985). *Intellectual development: Birth to adulthood*. New York: Academic Press.

Cawley, J. F., Fitzmaurice, A. M., Shaw, R., Kahn, H., & Bates, H. (1978). Mathematics and learning disabled youth: The upper grade levels. *Learning Disability Quarterly*, 2(1), 29–44.

Cawley, J. F., & Miller, J. (1989). Cross-sectional comparisons of the mathematical performance of children with learning disabilities: Are we on the right track toward comprehensive programming? *Journal of Learning Disabilities*, 22, 250–259.

Connolly, A. (1988). *Key Math—Revised* (KM-R). Circle Pines, MN: American Guidance.

Cooney, J. B., Swanson, H. L., & Ladd, S. F. (1988). Acquisition of mental multiplication skill: Evidence for the transition between counting and retrieval strategies. *Cognition and Instruction, 5,* 323–345.

Critical Thinking Books & Software. Catalogue. P.P. Box 448, Pacific Grove, CA 93950. 800-458-4849. Website: www.criticalthinking.com.

Di Perna, J., & Elliott, S. (in press). *Academic Competence Scales (ACES) and Academic Intervention Monitoring System* (AIMS). San Antonio, TX: The Psychological Corporation.

Engelmann, S. (1993). Priorities and efficiency. LD *Forum,* 18(2), 5–8.

Enright, B. E. (1990). Mathematics assessment tips: A checklist of common errors. *Diagnostique,* 16(1), 45–48.

Fantuzzo, J., King, J., & Heller, L. (1992). Effects of reciprocal peer tutoring on mathematics and school adjustment: A component analysis. *Journal of Educational Psychology,* 84, 331–339.

Fleischner, J., & Manheimer, M. (1997). Math interventions for students with learning disabilities: Myths and realities. *School Psychology Review,* 26, 397–413.

Free Spirit Publishing Self-Help for Kids. Catalogue. 400 First Avenue North, Suite 616–714. Minneapolis, MN 55401-1724. 800-735-7323.

Fuchs, L., Fuchs, D., Phillips, N., Hamlett, C., & Karns, K. (1995). Acquisition and transfer effects of classwide peer-assisted learning strategies in mathematics for students with varying learning histories. *School Psychology Review,* 24, 604–620.

Garnett, K., & Fleischner, J. E. (1983). Automatization and basic fact performance of learning disabled children. *Learning Disability Quarterly,* 6, 223–230.

Geary, D. C. (1990). A componential analysis of an early learning deficit in mathematics. *Journal of Experimental Child Psychology,* 49, 363–383.

Geary, D. C. (1993). Mathematical disabilities: Cognitive, neuropsychological, and genetic components. *Psychological Bulletin,* 114, 345–362.

Geary, D. C., Bow-Thomas, C. C., & Yao, Y. (1992). Counting knowledge and skill in cognitive addition: A comparison of normal and mathematically-disabled children. *Journal of Experimental Child Psychology,* 54, 372–391.

Geary, D. C., Brown, S. C., & Samaranayake, V. A. (1991). Cognitive addition: A short longitudinal study of strategy choice and speed of processing differences in normal and mathematically disabled children. *Developmental Psychology,* 27, 787–797.

Ginsburg, H. P. (1997). Mathematics learning disabilities: A view from developmental psychology. *Journal of Learning Disabilities,* 30(1), 20–33.

Goldman, S. R., Pellegrino, J. W., & Mertz, D. L. (1988). Extended practice of basic addition facts: Strategy changes in learning disabled students. *Cognition and Instruction,* 5, 223–265.

Greenwood, C. (1991). Longitudinal analysis of time, engagement, and achievement in at-risk versus non-risk students. *Exceptional Children,* 57, 521–535.

Groen, G. J., & Parkman, J. M. (1972). A chronometric analysis of simple addition. *Psychological Review,* 79, 329–343.

Hiebert, F., Carpenter, T., Fennema, E., Fuson, K., Human, P., Murray, H., Oliver, A., & Wearne, D. (1996). Problem solving as a basis for reform in curriculum and instruction: The case of mathematics. *Educational Researcher,* 25, 12–21.

Jitendra, A. K., Kameenui, E., & Carnine, D. (1994). An exploratory evaluation of dynamic assessment of the role of basals on comprehension of mathematical operations. *Education and Treatment of Children,* 17, 139–162.

Jones, E., Wilson, R., & Bhojwani, S. (1997). Mathematics instruction for secondary students with learning disabilities. *Journal of Learning Disabilities,* 30(2), 151–163.

Jordan, N. C., & Montani, T. O. (1997). Cognitive arithmetic and problem solving: A comparison of children with specific and general mathematics difficulties. *Journal of Learning Disabilities,* 30(6), 624–634, 684.

Kamii, C. (1985). *Young children re-invent arithmetic.* New York: Teachers College Press.

Kamii, C. (1994). *Young children continue to reinvent arithmetic, third grade. Implications of* Piaget's *theory.* New York: Teachers College Press.

Kaufman, A., & Kaufman, N. (1983). *Kaufman Assessment Battery for Children* (K-ABC). Circle Pines, MN: American Guidance Service.

Keating, D. (1991). Curriculum options for the developmentally advanced: A developmental alternative to gifted education. *Exceptionality Education Canada,* 1, 53–83.

Kolitch, E. R., & Brody, L. E. (1992). Mathematics acceleration of highly talented students: An evaluation. *Gifted Child Quarterly,* 36(2), 78–86.

Kosc, L. (1974). Developmental dyscalculia. *Journal of Learning Disabilities,* 7, 164–177.

LaBerge, D., & Samuels, S. J. (1974). Toward a theory of automatics information processing in reading. *Cognitive Psychology,* 6, 293–323.

Maheady, L., Sacca, M. K., & Harper, G. F. (1987). Classwide student tutoring teams: The effects of peer-mediated instruction on the academic performance of secondary mainstreamed students. *The Journal of Special Education,* 21, 107–121.

National Council of Teachers of Mathematics. (1989). *Curriculum and evaluation standards for school mathematics.* Reston, VA: Author.

National Council of Teachers of Mathematics. (1991). *Professional standards for teaching mathematics.* Reston, VA: Author.

Nesher, P. (1986). Learning mathematics: A cognitive perspective. *American Psychologist,* 41, 1114–1122.

Pletan, M., Robinson, N., Berninger, V. W., & Abbott, R. (1995). Parents' observations of kindergartners who are advanced in mathematical reasoning. *Journal for the Education of the Gifted,* 19(1), 31–44.

The Psychological Corporation. (1975). *Wechsler Intelligence Scale for Children—Revised* (WISC-R). San Antonio, TX: Author.

The Psychological Corporation. (1989). *Wechsler Preschool and Primary Scale of Intelligence—Revised* (WPPSI-R). San Antonio: TX: Author.

The Psychological Corporation. (1991). *Wechsler Intelligence Scale for Children—Third Edition* (WISC-III). San Antonio, TX: Author.

The Psychological Corporation. (1992). *Wechsler Individual Achievement Test* (WIAT). San Antonio, TX: Author.

The Psychological Corporation. (in press). *Wechsler Individual Achievement Test—Second Edition* (WIAT II). San Antonio, TX: Author.

Resnick, L., & Ford, W. (1981). *The psychology of mathematics for instruction.* Hillsdale, N.J.: Erlbaum.

Robinson, N., Abbott, R., Berninger, V. W., & Busse, J. (1996). The structure of abilities in math-precocious young children: Gender similarities and differences. *Journal of Educational Psychology,* 88(2), 341–352.

Robinson, N., Abbott, R., Berninger, V. W., Busse, J., & Mukhopadhyay, S. (1997). Developmental changes in mathematically precious young children: Longitudinal and gender effects. *Gifted Child Quarterly,* 41, 145–158.

Roditi, B. N. (1988). Automaticity, cognitive flexibility, and mathematics: A longitudinal study of children with and without learning disabilities (Doctoral Dissertation, Tufts University). *Dissertation Abstracts International,* 49(6-B), 2396.

Russell, R. L., & Ginsburg, H. P. (1984). Cognitive analysis of children's mathematics difficulties. *Cognition and Instruction,* 1, 217–244.

Schiever, S. W., & Maker, C. J. (1991). Enrichment and acceleration: An overview and new directions. In N. Colangelo & G. A. Davis (Eds.), *Handbook of Gifted Education* (pp. 99–110). Boston: Allyn & Bacon.

Shurtleff, H., Fay, G., Abbott, R., & Berninger, V. W. (1988). Cognitive and neuropsychological correlates of academic achievement: A levels of analysis assessment model. *Journal of Psychoeducational Assessment,* 6, 298–308.

Siegel, L. S., & Linder, B. (1984). Short-term memory processes in children with reading and arithmetic learning disabilities. *Developmental Psychology,* 20, 200–207.

Siegler, R. S. (1988). Strategy choice procedures and the development of multiplication skill. *Journal of Experimental Psychology: General, 117,* 258–275.

Slavin, R. E. (1983). When does cooperative learning increase student achievement? *Psychological Bulletin, 94,* 429–445.

Sowell, E. J. (1993). Programs for mathematically gifted students: A review of empirical research. *Gifted Child Quarterly, 37*(3), 124–129.

Swanson, H. L. (1996). Individual age-related differences in children's working memory. *Memory & Cognition, 24,* 70–82.

Thorndike, R., & Hagen, E. (1993). *Cognitive Abilities Test (CogAT).* Chicago: Riverside.

Thorndike, R., Hagen, E., & Sattler, J. (1986). *The Stanford-Binet Intelligence Scale, 4th Ed.* Chicago: Riverside.

Thornton, C., Langrall, C., & Jones, G. (1997). Mathematics instruction for elementary students with learning disabilities. *Journal of Learning Disabilities, 30*(2), 142–150.

Waxman, B., Robinson, N., & Mukhopadhyay, S. (1997). *Teachers nurturing young, math-talented children,* RM 96228. Storrs, CT: National Research Center on Gifted and Talented.

Wilkinson, G. (1993). *Wide Range Achievement Tests—Revised* (WRAT-R). Wilmington, DE: Wide Range.

Wolf, M. (1986). Rapid alternating stimulus naming in the developmental dyslexias. *Brain and Language, 27,* 360–379.

Wolf, M., Bally, H., & Morris, R. (1986). Automaticity, retrieval processes, and reading: A longitudinal study in average and impaired reading. *Child Development, 57,* 988–1000.

Woodcock, R., & Johnson, B. (1990). *Woodcock-Johnson Psycho-Educational Battery—Revised Tests of Achievement* (WJ-R). Chicago: Riverside.

Yates, C. (1996). Screening for mathematical abilities and disabilities in 1st and 2nd grade children. (Doctoral Dissertation, University of Washington, 1996). *Dissertation Abstracts International, 57*(7A), 2864.

PART

III

Behavior Assessment

CHAPTER

9

Behavior Assessment System for Children (BASC): Toward Accurate Diagnosis and Effective Treatment

GAIL S. MATAZOW
University of Alberta

R. W. KAMPHAUS
University of Georgia

INTRODUCTION

Behavior rating scales provide information on the range and degree of psychopathology (Erhardt & Conners, 1996) as well as normal behavior and adaptive behavior functioning. There is emerging consensus that in order to understand the full range of child psychopathology and adaptive behavior deficits, normal behavioral development must be fully conceptualized (Jensen, Koretz, et al., 1993; Kamphaus & Frick, 1996; Kazdin, 1995). Researchers have defined and studied child psychopathology largely through diagnostic syndromes that use a categorical model (Kamphaus, Huberty, DiStefano, & Petoskey, 1997), generally as conceptualized through the *Diagnostic and Statistical Manual of Mental Disorders, Fourth Edition* (DSM-IV; American Psychiatric Association, 1994). One of the major limitations of this method is that children who do not meet diagnostic criteria (i.e., subsyndromal conditions) but have significant functional impairment are not identified (Cantwell, 1996).

Handbook of Psychoeducational Assessment
257

A DIMENSIONAL APPROACH

An alternate method to the study of child psychopathology and adaptive behavior functioning is a dimensional approach that allows for the study of behaviors through grouping of constructs or dimensions. In this method, children are studied on a particular dimension or several dimensions of behavior (Meehl, 1995). Because a dimensional approach includes all children, even those that are not diagnosed through a categorical method, it results in a greater understanding of the full range of child behavior (Kamphaus, Petoskey, et al., 1999).

Behavior rating scales are the foundation of dimensional approaches (Erhardt & Conners, 1996). Such rating scales are useful in a number of contexts, including identifying children with behavior problems, predicting future socioemotional and behavioral adjustment, and distinguishing adjusted individuals from those with clinical disorders and/or from those amongst clinical subtypes (Edelbrock & Costello, 1988; Harris, Wilkinson, Trovato, & Pryor, 1992; Hodge & McKay, 1986). Additional advantages associated with rating scales, as identified by Erhardt and Conners, include their "brevity, low cost, ease of administration and scoring, aggregation of an informant's experience with a child across time and settings, potential for assessing low frequency behaviors, and capacity to measure both broadly and narrowly defined areas of disturbance" (p. 115).

NATURE OF THE ASSESSMENT SYSTEM

This chapter describes the BASC (Reynolds & Kamphaus, 1992), which is a rating scale that includes assessment of clinical constructs, adaptive behavior functioning, and self-perceptions of children from ages 2½ to 18 years. The BASC was developed using a blend of rational/theoretical and empirical approaches to test development (Martin, 1988). This method is in contrast to factor analytic methods as used in other rating scales, which do not incorporate the rational/theoretical underpinnings of the construct being measured (e.g., anxiety, hyperactivity, and so on). Thus, the BASC allows the user to form an understanding of the child's behavior and socio-emotional functioning by examining the scale profile.

A new addition to the original BASC scales is the BASC Attention-Deficit/Hyperactivity Disorder (ADHD) Monitor (Kamphaus & Reynolds, 1998), which is designed to comprehensively assess the primary symptoms of ADHD. The original BASC teacher, parent, and self-report forms highlight co-occurring behavior and/or emotional problems across a variety of domains (Kamphaus & Frick, 1996). If there is indication of problems on the Attention Problems and/or Hyperactivity scales, the diagnosis of ADHD becomes a possibility. At this point, the BASC ADHD Monitor may be administered to enhance treatment planning and evaluation by providing a more thorough assessment of the primary symptoms of ADHD during the course of somatic and/or behavioral treatment.

VERSIONS

The original BASC is *multimethod* in that it has four components, which may be used individually or in any combination:

1. Parent and teacher rating scales that contain descriptions of children's observable behavior, including clinical and adaptive behavior functioning
2. Self-report rating scale in which children describe their emotions and self-perceptions
3. Structured developmental history
4. Classroom observation system that has components for recording and classifying behavior

The BASC ADHD Monitor is a second step toward comprehensive evaluation, diagnosis, and treatment of children with features of ADHD.

The BASC is *multidimensional* in that it measures aspects of behavior and personality from a clinical and adaptive functioning perspective. In addition, a broad-range assessment of child behavior functioning is permitted as this measure does not classify, and thereby diagnose, children based on a categorical approach but provides a level of functioning that is compared to the normative sample.

TEACHER AND PARENT RATING SCALES

Teacher Rating Scale (TRS)

The TRS is a comprehensive measure of a student's behavior (both normal and problematic) and adaptive functioning in the school setting. It has a form for each of 3 age levels: preschool (ages 2½–5), child (ages 6–11), and adolescent (ages 12–18). The TRS has descriptors of behavior that are rated by the teacher on a 4-point response scale of frequency, ranging from "Never" to "Almost Always." The TRS requires about 10 to 20 minutes for completion.

The TRS provides assessment of clinical problems in the domains of externalizing problems, internalizing problems, and school problems; adaptive skills; and the behavior symptoms index. The behavior symptoms index provides an analysis of the child's overall level of problematic behavior.

TABLE 9.1
Composites and Scales in the TRS and PRS

Composite scale	Teacher Rating Scale			Parent Rating Scale		
	Preschool	Child	Adoles-cent	Preschool	Child	Adoles-cent
Externalizing Problems	*	*	*	*	*	*
Aggression	*	*	*	*	*	*
Hyperactivity	*	*	*	*	*	*
Conduct Problems		*	*		*	*
Internalizing Problems	*	*	*	*	*	*
Anxiety	*	*	*	*	*	*
Depression	*	*	*	*	*	*
Somatization	*	*	*	*	*	*
School Problems		*	*			
Attention Problems	*	*	*	*	*	*
Learning Problems		*	*			
(Other Problems)						
Atypicality	*	*	*	*	*	*
Withdrawal	*	*	*	*	*	*
Adaptive Skills	*	*	*	*	*	*
Adaptability	*	*		*	*	
Leadership		*	*	*	*	*
Social Skills	*	*	*	*	*	*
Study Skills		*	*			
Behavioral Symptoms Index	*	*	*	*	*	*

Note: Italicized scales compose the Behavioral Symptoms Index.
Source: From *Behavior Assessment System for Children: Manual* (p. 3), by C. R. Reynolds and R. W. Kamphaus, 1992, Circle Pines, MN: American Guidance Service. Copyright 1992 by American Guidance Service, Inc. Reprinted and adapted with permission.

Table 9.1 shows the scales for all levels of the TRS and PRS. Due to developmental changes in the behavioral and adaptive functioning of children, there are slight differences between levels of the areas assessed. Items on scales and composites with the same name (e.g., aggression, depression, and so on) between teacher and parent rating scale contain essentially the same content at all age levels. In addition to normative information, individual critical items may be noted in the event of highly problematic behavior (i.e., indices of suicidal behavior) and/or medical conditions (i.e., medication usage). The TRS includes a validity scale in the form of an "F" index (i.e., "fake bad") designed to detect a negative response set from the teacher. The BASC computer-scoring software provides two additional validity indices: consistency and response pattern. The consistency index measures agreement between highly similar items (e.g., "inattentive" and "distractible") and the response pattern index detects unusual patterns of responses (e.g., alternating "sometimes" and "almost always" ratings for successive items).

Parent Rating Scale (PRS)

The PRS is a comprehensive measure of child behavior (both normal and problematic) and adaptive behavior functioning in the home and community settings. The PRS has descriptors of behavior that are rated by the parent in the same 4-choice response format as the TRS and takes about 10 to 20 minutes to complete. Like the TRS, the PRS has a form for each of 3 age levels: preschool, child, and adolescent. The scales in varying age levels of the PRS are generally similar in content and structure. The PRS assesses highly similar areas of clinical problems and adaptive behavior domains as the TRS. However, the TRS includes the School Problems composite, which includes Learning Problems and Study Skills—areas best observed and rated by teachers. The PRS offers the same normative sample as the TRS: national age norms (general, female, and male) and clinical norms. Like the TRS, the PRS includes the validity scales of an F index—patterning and consistency—and has critical items that may be noted. Table 9.2 provides a description of all the scales on the PRS and TRS.

TABLE 9.2
BASC Teacher and Parent Rating Scales and Descriptions

Scale	Description
Aggression	The tendency to act in a hostile manner (either verbally or physically) that is threatening to others.
Conduct Problems	The tendency to engage in antisocial and rule-breaking behavior, including destroying property.
Hyperactivity	The tendency to be overly active, rush through work or activities, and act without thinking.
Anxiety	The tendency to be nervous, fearful, or worried about real or imagined problems.
Depression	Feelings of unhappiness, sadness, and stress that may result in an inability to carry out everyday activities (neurovegetative symptoms) or may bring on thoughts of suicide.
Somatization	The tendency to be overly sensitive to and complain about relatively minor physical problems and discomforts.
Attention Problems	The tendency to be easily distracted and unable to concentrate more than momentarily.
Learning Problems	The presence of academic difficulties, particularly in understanding or completing schoolwork.
Atypicality	The tendency to behave in ways that are immature, considered "odd," or commonly associated with psychosis (such as experiencing visual or auditory hallucinations).
Withdrawal	The tendency to evade others to avoid social contact.
Adaptability	The ability to adapt readily to changes in the environment

(continues)

Table 9.2—*Continued*

Scale	Description
Leadership	The skills associated with accomplishing academic, social, or community goals, including, in particular, the ability to work well with others.
Social Skills	The skills necessary for interacting successfully with peers and adults in home, school, and community settings.
Study Skills	The skills that are conducive to strong academic performance, including organizational skills and good study habits.

Note: The PRS does not include TRS composite scales of Learning Problems, Study Skills, or School Problems.

Source: From *Behavior Assessment System for Children*, by C. R. Reynolds and R. W. Kamphaus, 1992, Circle Pines, MN: American Guidance Service. Copyright 1992 by American Guidance Service, Inc. Reprinted with permission.

SELF-REPORT OF PERSONALITY FORMS

Self-Report of Personality (SRP)

The SRP is an inventory of statements designed to evaluate the behavioral, personality, and emotional functioning of children via self-perceptions. The SRP has a form for each of 2 age levels: child (ages 8–11) and adolescent (ages 12–18). The SRP has statements of behavior that are rated as "True" or "False" and takes about 30 minutes to complete.

The forms for the 2 age levels overlap considerably in scale, structure, and individual items. The SRP provides assessment of Clinical Maladjustment, School Maladjustment, and Personal Adjustment. In addition, there is an overall composite score, the Emotional Symptoms Index (ESI), which provides an analysis of the individual's overall level of problematic emotional functioning. Table 9.3 shows the scales for all levels of the SRP. Like the PRS and TRS, there are slight differences between levels in the areas assessed due to developmental changes. Also like the PRS and TRS, the SRP includes individual critical items that may be noted to highlight medical conditions and/or behaviors of particular concern. The SRP includes three validity scales: an F index designed to detect a negative response set, an "L" index that assesses social desirability or a positive response set, and a "V" index designed to detect invalid responses due to poor reading comprehension, failure to follow instructions, or failure to cooperate with the testing process. The L index is not included on the child SRP as raw scores on such scales are often found to be negatively correlated with age (Reynolds & Richmond, 1985). Consistency and patterning indexes are included for the SRP as well.

Like the TRS and PRS, the SRP may be interpreted with reference to national age norms (general, female, and male) or to clinical norms. Table 9.4 includes scale definitions.

TABLE 9.3
Composites and Scales in the SRP

Composite/Scale	Child	Adolescent
Clinical Maladjustment	*	*
Anxiety	*	*
Atypicality	*	*
Locus of Control	*	*
Social Stress	*	*
Somatization	*	*
School Maladjustment	*	*
Attitude to School	*	*
Attitude to Teachers	*	*
Sensation Seeking		*
(Other Problems)		
Depression	*	*
Sense of Inadequacy	*	*
Personal Adjustment	*	*
Relations with Parents	*	*
Interpersonal Relations	*	*
Self-Esteem	*	*
Self-Reliance	*	*
Emotional Symptoms Index	*	*

Note: Italicized scales compose the Emotional Symptoms Index.
Source: From *Behavior Assessment System for Children: Manual* (p. 3),
by C. R. Reynolds and R. W. Kamphaus, 1992, Circle Pines, MN:
American Guidance Service. Copyright 1992 by American Guidance Service, Inc. Reprinted with permission.

Structured Developmental History (SDH)

The SDH is a compilation of historical and background information about the referred child and his or her family. It is completed as an interview or questionnaire format. Data provided includes information on referral, primary caregiver (including educational and occupational information), child care, siblings, personal health (i.e., pregnancy, birth, development, medical history and issues), family health, friendships, recreation/interests, behavior/temperament, adaptive skills, and educational history. This instrument requires about 15 to 25 minutes for completion. There are no structured scoring criteria. Population norms and ethnicity information are not available. Information about reliability, validity, or internal consistency are also not available. Interpretation and analysis of the SDH are completed by examiner review.

This instrument was developed as a result of the compilation of over 20 similar interview formats (Reynolds & Kamphaus, 1992). The SDH is recommended as a means of documenting developmental events and medical or

TABLE 9.4
Student Self-Report of Personality Scale Definitions

Scale	Definition
Anxiety	Feelings of nervousness, worry, and fear; the tendency to be overwhelmed by problems
Attitude to School	Feelings of alienation, hostility, and dissatisfaction regarding school
Attitude to Teachers	Feelings of resentment and dislike of teachers; beliefs that teachers are unfair, uncaring, or overly demanding
Atypicality	The tendency toward gross mood swings, bizarre thoughts, subjective experiences, or obsessive-compulsive thoughts and behaviors often considered "odd"
Depression	Feelings of unhappiness, sadness, and dejection; a belief that nothing goes right
Interpersonal Relations	The perception of having good social relationships and friendships with peers
Locus of Control	The belief that rewards and punishments are controlled by external events or other people
Relations with Parents	A positive regard toward parents and a feeling of being esteemed by them
Self-Esteem	Feelings of self-esteem, self-respect, and self-acceptance
Self-Reliance	Confidence in one's ability to solve problems; a belief in one's personal dependability and decisiveness
Sensation Seeking	The tendency to take risks, to like noise, and to seek excitement
Sense of Inadequacy	Perceptions of being unsuccessful in school, unable to achieve one's goals, and generally inadequate
Social Stress	Feelings of stress and tension in personal relationships; a feeling of being excluded from social activities
Somatization	The tendency to be overly sensitive to, experience, or complain about relatively minor physical problems and discomforts

Source: From *Behavior Assessment System for Children: Manual* (p. 58), by C. R. Reynolds and R. W. Kamphaus, 1992, Circle Pines, MN: American Guidance Service. Copyright 1992 by American Guidance Service, Inc. Reprinted with permission.

related problems in the family that may have significant impact on a child's current behavior. The SDH provides a structural basis for gathering the child and family history. Due to the comprehensiveness of this form, the SDH is an asset to the evaluation of a child, regardless of whether the other BASC components are used.

Student Observation System (SOS)

The SOS allows for direct observation and evaluation of everyday classroom behavior ranging from preschool to high-school levels. The SOS is unique in that it is the only structured assessment instrument that may be used directly by the clinician. This scale is designed to assess a broad spectrum of behaviors, including adaptive and maladaptive behavior. The SOS has two methods of identifying children's behaviors in the classroom: (a) behavior key and checklist—the clinician observes the child for 15 minutes and, at the end of this time period, notes the frequency of each of 65 specific behaviors (grouped into 13 categories) for the *entire* period, and (b) momentary time sampling (i.e., systematic coding during 3-second intervals, spaced 30 seconds apart, over a 15-minute period) to record the range of the child's behavior, including positive (e.g., teacher-student interaction) and negative (e.g., inappropriate movement or inattention) behaviors.

The SOS may be appropriately used in regular and special education classes. It can be used in the initial assessment as part of the diagnostic system or for repetitive evaluations on the effectiveness of educational, behavioral, psychopharmacological, or other treatments. The SOS can contribute to a functional assessment by denoting frequency, duration, intensity, antecedent events, consequences, and ecological analysis of settings as related to behavior functioning.

BASC ADHD Monitor

The BASC ADHD Monitor was specifically developed to provide a second step toward comprehensive evaluation and treatment planning for individuals considered for diagnosis of ADHD. These rating scales allow for differentiation of the three subtypes of ADHD: ADHD Predominantly Inattentive Type, ADHD Predominantly Hyperactive-Impulsive Type, and ADHD Combined Type. (This differentiation approximates the categorization as in DSM-IV.) With this differentiation, the clinician is afforded the opportunity to design a comprehensive, specific treatment program that is aimed at reducing behavioral problems. The Monitor also includes the Internalizing and Adaptive Skills scales, which encourage further comprehensive treatment planning and evaluation of treatment effectiveness to include these important constructs in the treatment plan. Given the increasing awareness that children diagnosed with ADHD often have comorbid diagnoses (including aggressive and conduct problems as well as depression and anxiety), comprehensive evaluation of a multitude of childhood behaviors is necessary.

The BASC, and newly developed BASC ADHD Monitor, represent "a coordinated multi-step assessment system that allows the clinician to proceed from referral for ADHD to diagnosis, treatment design, and treatment evaluation with greater ease and precision" (Kamphaus, Reynolds, & Hatcher, 1999, p. 571). As with other versions of the BASC, the Monitor utilizes information provided by parents, teachers, and a classroom observer to assess a variety of constructs (Table 9.5). The Monitor was developed particularly to evaluate treatment of children diagnosed with ADHD with greater efficiency. This is

TABLE 9.5
BASC ADHD Monitor Constructs

Component	Scales
Parent Monitor	Attention Problems Hyperactivity Internalizing Problems Adaptive Skills
Teacher Monitor	Attention Problems Hyperactivity Internalizing Problems Adaptive Skills
BASC SOS	Response to Teacher/Lesson Peer Interaction Work on School Subjects Transition Movement Inappropriate Movement Inattention Inappropriate Vocalization Somatization Repetitive Motor Movements Aggression Self-Injurious Behavior Inappropriate Sexual Behavior Bowel/Bladder Problems
ADHD Monitoring Plan	All monitor components and scales
ADHD Monitor ASSIST	All monitor components and scales

Source: From *Behavior Assessment System for Children* (BASC) ADHD *Monitor,* by R. W. Kamphaus and C. R. Reynolds, 1998, Circle Pines, MN: American Guidance Service. Copyright 1998 by AGS. Reprinted with permission.

possible due to the Monitor's efficient evaluation of problematic behaviors through repeated assessment and dissemination of information about the referred child.

Current epidemiological estimates of ADHD in the U.S. population are 3% to 5% (Rapoport & Castellanos, 1996), with approximately 2% to 6% of elementary-aged schoolchildren receiving psychostimulant medication treatment at any given time (Bender, 1997). The comorbidity of additional psychiatric disorders, including learning disabilities, anxiety disorders, aggression, and so on, are well known (Frick et al., 1991; Last, 1993). The magnitude of children diagnosed with ADHD, as well as the high comorbidity rate, suggests that children with these problems are likely to receive a variety of medical and behavioral treatments from health care and related professionals in psychology, medicine, and education. Given that this disorder is pervasive across settings, assessment and treatment strategies require frequent and accurate communication among all treatment providers, including parents, physicians, teachers, clinicians, and the child.

The BASC ADHD Monitor was designed to enhance the work of all individuals who provide services to children with ADHD. To this end, it has the following purposes: to provide accurate and frequent feedback regarding behavioral conduct, internalizing problems, and adaptive skills to the prescribing physician; to ensure ongoing assessment of ADHD problems in an efficient, timely, and cost-effective manner; to incorporate input from multiple informants for assessment of behavior across settings; to allow for assessment of specific behavioral outcomes to demonstrate accountability of services; to link assessment to treatment; and to allow teachers to use a single form for evaluating treatment effectiveness.

BASC Monitor interpretation can vary depending on the instrument(s) used, theoretical orientation of the clinician, the nature of the referral question(s) posed, and other factors. In evaluating monitor results, aside from diagnostic issues the clinician often asks whether or not significant change has occurred in response to treatment. For the parent and teacher monitors, four questions are typically posed: (a) is treatment affecting symptoms of inattention; (b) is treatment affecting symptoms of hyperactivity; (c) is treatment affecting internalizing symptoms; and (d) is treatment affecting adaptive skills? The questions related to change are manifold and are parallel with the SOS, with which clinicians may be assessing changes at the item or scale level.

The Monitor attempts to assess treatment effects by measuring multiple dimensions of behavior, as opposed to producing a single score. Interpretation based on differences between single scores is fraught with problems. For example, if a child's T score on the Hyperactivity scale decreases from 80 to 67 in response to treatment, is this a statistically significant improvement? Is this reduction in frequency and magnitude of symptoms clinically significant (i.e., meaningfully or functionally significant) as assessed by parents, teachers, and others who interact with the child on a daily basis? Would this interpretation of improvement be modified if the pre- and posttreatment scores were 90 and 77, respectively? Quantification of change by a single score tends to be limited, so it is often more meaningful to incorporate multiple dimensions of behavior. These dimensions include hyperactivity, attention problems, internalizing behavior, and adaptive skills.

The BASC ADHD Monitor allows the establishment of a T score baseline so that subsequent behavior may be accurately measured and evaluated. The SOS is designed specifically for classroom-based interventions, and should not be considered when evaluating home-based interventions unless home- and school-based interventions are linked. The SOS allows the clinician to prioritize behaviors for classroom-based interventions.

TECHNICAL INFORMATION

Development and Standardization of the BASC

The BASC was developed over a period of nearly six years. Emphasis was placed on constructing self-report and behavior-rating measures with strong content and construct validity, as research in personality and behavioral assessment suggests that such an approach produces scales that are more stable and provide more replicable results than do purely empirically derived scales (Martin, 1988). For the TRS, PRS, and SRP, an initial set of constructs was chosen based on a variety of reasons: the authors found these conceptualized constructs of behavior to be the most useful in their clinical practice and consultation, they had the potential to provide information about both positive behavioral traits and pathological behaviors or emotional functioning, and they were supported by historical precedent (Reynolds & Kamphaus, 1992). It was decided that each item was allowed to contribute to only one scale, to "preserve the distinctiveness of the scales" (Reynolds & Kamphaus, p. 69) and to aid profile interpretation. It was further decided that, when possible, each item would be placed on the same scale at the different age levels of each instrument and on the parent and teacher forms. The authors felt that such "consistency of scale composition has important benefits for consistent interpretation of scales and for across-source and across-time score comparisons" (Reynolds & Kamphaus, p. 69).

After the items were formulated and subjected to data-based debate, two item tryouts were conducted and the forms were analyzed using traditional item analysis and exploratory factor analysis. Final item selection and scale definition was based on the item content as it pertained to the construct underlying its scale and statistical interpretation (i.e., covariance structural analysis and reliability analyses). The structure of the composite scales for each level of the TRS, PRS, and SRP was determined through factor analysis of the scale intercorrelations.

The BASC normative data were collected from 1988 to 1991 at 116 sites representing various regions of the United States and Canada. The sites represented a diverse sampling of the population by geographic region, parental educational attainment (SES), ethnicity, and child exceptionality. The PRS, TRS, and SRP samples were formally stratified to approximate 1986–1988 U.S. Census Bureau statistics. Stratification variables included grade level, gender, and ethnicity. Schools were solicited for participation based on their demographic characteristics, and replacement schools in the same geographic region were available for possible participation. Clinical norm samples consisted of children being served in school or clinical settings for emotional or behavioral problems. Both T score and percentile norms were developed for each scale.

The BASC norms are based on a large normative sample that is representative of the general population of U.S. children with regard to sex, race/ethnicity, clinical or special education classification, and, for the PRS, parent education. These norms are subdivided by age. The total normative sample for varying ages is as follows for each of the three scales: TRS—4–5 = 888, 6–11 = 1259, and 12–18 = 809; PRS—4–5 = 309, 6–11 = 2084, and 12–18 = 1090; and SRP—8–11 = 5413 and 12–18 = 4448. Four sets of norm tables were developed (i.e., General, Female, Male, and Clinical) for all teacher, parent, and self-report scales based on a linear transformation of raw scores to T scores (M = 50, SD = 10). For most applications the general norms (which combine female and male norms) are the recommended basis of comparison. The general norms answer the question, "How commonly does this level of rated or self-reported behavior occur in the general population at this age?" These norms are used if the clinician wishes to note differences between males and females on various behavioral characteristics. Gender-specific norms are used if the clinician wishes to assess a behavior that is known to be more common in males or females. For example, if the clinician is attempting to discern whether the level of anxiety in a girl is elevated, female norms may be the appropriate choice as females, in general, tend to have higher anxiety levels than males. Conversely, if the clinician is attempting to understand the level of aggression in a boy, male norms may be the appropriate choice as males, in general, tend to exhibit higher aggression levels. Thus, the clinician has latitude in choosing the appropriate norms for the question at hand.

The BASC forms come in two formats: hand scoring or computer entry. The hand-scoring forms are self-scored, which allows for rapid scoring without use of templates or keys. Each form includes a profile of scale and composite scores. The computer-entry forms are entered via key-item responses into a microcomputer so scoring takes 5 minutes or less.

Reliability of the BASC

The BASC manual (Reynolds & Kamphaus, 1992) provides three types of reliability evidence: internal consistency, test-retest reliability, and interrater reliability. The TRS reliability evidence, as noted in the manual, is as follows: internal consistencies of the scales averaged above .80 for all three age levels; test-retest correlations had median values of .89, .91, and .82, respectively, for the scales at the three age levels; and interrater reliability correlations revealed values of .83 for four pairs of teachers and .63 and .71 for mixed groups of teachers. The PRS reliability evidence, as noted in the manual, is as follows: internal consistencies of the scales were in the middle .80s to low .90s at all three age levels; test-retest correlations had median values of .85, .88, and .70, respectively, for the scales at the three age levels; and interparent reliability correlations revealed values of .46, .57, and .67 at the three age levels. The SRP reliability evidence, as presented in the manual, is as follows: internal consistencies averaged about .80 for each gender at both age levels and test-retest correlations had median values of .76 at each age level. The manual provides documentation of correlations with other instruments of behavioral functioning.

Validity of the BASC

The manual presents extensive evidence of factor analytic support for the construct validity of the scales using both principal axis and covariance structure analysis methods.

Concurrent validity studies reported in the BASC manual as well as independent studies (Kline, 1994; Vaughn, Riccio, Hynd, & Hall, 1997) reflect relatively high correlations between the BASC TRS and the CBCL TRF (Achenbach Child Behavior Checklist, Teacher Rating Form) scales of similarly named factors (rs ranged from high .60 to low .90s on teacher forms and from .50 to .81 on parent forms). Moderately high correlations were also found between the Externalizing, Internalizing, and Total test scores of these instruments (rs ranged from .73 to .92).

The results of predictive discriminant analysis studies using the subscales of the PRS demonstrated that 78.08% of cases that in fact had ADHD were correctly classified as such (Vaughn et al., 1997). Furthermore, children who were diagnosed with ADHD Predominantly Inattentive Type and ADHD Combined Type were correctly classified via use of the PRS in 81.3% and 81.6% of the cases, respectively (Vaughn et al., 1997).

In comparable predictive discriminant analysis studies using the subscales of the TRS, 67.16% of cases with ADHD were correctly classified (Vaughn et al., 1997).

INTERPRETATIVE GUIDELINES FOR THE BASC

The BASC manual (Reynolds & Kamphaus, 1992) provides considerable detail about interpretation. Additional interpretative guidelines are provided next, to supplement those found in the BASC manual.

Specify Treatment Objectives and Target Behaviors

Given the frequency with which comorbid conditions occur in childhood psychopathology, it is necessary to specify treatment objectives and target behaviors. For example, comorbid conditions are often noted in children with ADHD and aggression. If the child is receiving psychostimulant medication, but not engaged in cognitive-behavior therapy to decrease aggression, it follows that change should not be expected on the aggression scale. Conversely, if a child has indications of ADHD and depression, and cognitive-behavior therapy is offered for depressive symptoms, a mild decrease in inattention may occur that is secondary to treatment but it is likely that symptoms of ADHD will continue to occur. Thus, treatment objectives should always be linked to actual treatments so that parents, teachers, and mental health practitioners have realistic expectations of response to treatment. Any of the BASC components (i.e., the PRS, TRS, SRP, and SOS) may be used to identify target behaviors for intervention.

Record Treatment Data

Accurate treatment records are necessary to draw inferences about treatment and outcomes. The BASC ADHD Monitor forms include space for documentation of the nature of various treatments along with their onset, cessation, and adherence. The collection of treatment information allows the clinician to be confident in the assessment of change.

Collection of Data Points

The BASC was designed for collection of three or more data points (i.e., parent report, teacher report, self-report, and observation system), so that accurate assessment is ensured. To this end, multiple reporters across multiple settings enable the collection of multiple data points. For example, assessment of disruptive behavior disorders such as ADHD requires that such behavior be evident in two or more settings (e.g., home and school). The BASC allows for such data collection, with the added advantage of a standardization sample that also incorporated multiple reporters across multiple settings. Clinical experience suggests that at the very least, parent and teacher reports be obtained for children and adolescents who have been referred for disruptive behavior disorders. Conversely, parent reports and self-reports should be obtained for children and adolescents who have been referred for mood and anxiety-related disorders. At times, it is possible to obtain varying information from multiple reporters. Clinical experience along with additional sources of information such as individual and structured interviewing provide the necessary information to formulate diagnostic impressions. For example, if a parent does not endorse items that result in moderate to clinically significant elevation on the Depression scale, but the child provides moderate elevation on the Depression scale, further interviewing is required to determine whether a depressive disorder exists. As always, diagnostic impressions are based on the preponderance of findings across multiple raters in multiple settings.

Clinical Significance of the BASC

Clinical significance should be considered of primary importance in the assessment of change. Research efforts on the outcomes of children with various disorders will eventually provide diagnostic guidelines for determining clinical significance. Jacobson and Traux (1991) noted three potential indicators of clinical significance, as it relates to change subsequent to psychotherapy: (a) the level of behavioral/emotional functioning subsequent to therapy should fall outside the range of the dysfunctional population, where the range is defined as more than 2 standard deviations below the mean of that population in the direction of functionality; (b) the level of functioning subsequent to therapy should fall within the range of the normal population, where the range is defined as within 2 standard deviations of the mean of that population; and (c) the level of functioning subsequent to therapy places the client closer to the mean of the normal population than it does to the mean of the dysfunctional population. Additional considerations include whether the response to treatment makes a real difference in the day-to-day life of the individual and whether the goals of treatment are realistic for the syndrome. With regard to real changes from response to treatment, in a severe case of ADHD with a response to psychopharmacotherapy that reduces the score on an inattention scale from 90 to 75, the individual is still more overactive than 99% of children his or her age. Conversely, if a child's social skills score reduces from 73 to 58 due to response to a behavior disorders class, the child would be able to attend a regular class with peers who have good social skills. In the first example, there is no meaningful difference in the child's actual ability to function effectively in the normal setting. However, one must consider whether normal functioning is an appropriate goal for a child with an inattention scale score of 90, which is 4 standard deviations above the mean. In effect, a reduction of 15 standard score points represents a moderate, and perhaps realistic, expectation for change.

Prior to establishment of treatment outcomes, the clinician must demarcate a measure of clinical significance that is appropriate for each child and the syndrome. Children with mental retardation or autism may require establishment of very modest treatment outcomes, whereas children with depression or oppositional behavior may allow for enhanced treatment expectations based on expected change due to increased cognitive abilities that allow for greater profit from intervention. Setting appropriate goals for change is likely an important topic for discussion among parents and other health service providers prior to the implementation of treatment. After initial diagnosis, which includes any comorbid conditions and all relevant factors related to diagnosis (e.g., depression and sense of inadequacy or hopelessness; or ADHD and depression), the establishment of treatment goals is the primary step that is achieved from BASC interpretation.

Other Methodological Issues

Francis, Fletcher, Stuebing, Davidson, and Thompson (1991) have provided statistical procedures and formulae for assessing individual growth models of change. They have discussed some of the measurement prerequisites necessary for the accurate assessment of change, such as including interval scales of measurement, being relatively free of ceiling or floor effects, encouraging collection of three or more observations in order to assess an individual growth trajectory, and refraining from use of age-based standard scores for measuring change. The BASC uses an interval scale of measurement (i.e., T scores), which allows for precise computation of change indices.

The question has been raised about the appropriateness of considering ceiling and floor effects for assessing behavior change. On clinical scales, individuals who do not have any problematic behaviors, thereby obtaining a "0" score, are viewed as functioning within normal limits on individual items. Ceiling and floor effects, on a behavior rating scale, would detract from the usefulness of the scale for assessing behavior change. The BASC T score range is not artificially restricted to a prespecified range, as would be the case if ceiling and floor effects were incorporated into the standardization procedures. The T score scales were based on the distributional properties of the construct as samples from the population (Reynolds & Kamphaus, 1992). The occurrence of ceiling and floor effects on the BASC is unlikely.

The BASC uses age-based standard scores (T scores) as the standard for measuring change. For many children, the effects of age-based standard scores on the interpretation of change will be nonexistent because raw scores are not significantly different across age groups. For example, the raw scores for ages 8 to 11 on the BASC PRS do not differ significantly, allowing for the use of 1 norm table for this age group. When normative tables change, the clinician is well-advised to consider raw scores in addition to T scores when assessing change over the given time period.

Another methodological issue to consider is the reliability of long-term difference scores. The long-term stability of the BASC scales is currently known only for a 7-month period (Reynolds & Kamphaus, 1992), but additional research may provide information about malleability as detected by the scales. As stated earlier, expected change can be assessed, to some degree, by considering specific syndromes and well-documented effects of particular treatment(s).

Communication between Providers

Due to the complexity of the presentation of symptoms commonly associated with children's disorders, as well as the multitude of settings that are directly affected by such symptoms, children often receive multimodal therapy including somatic, behavior, social, and educational interventions. Communication between providers is crucial for establishment and maintenance of effective treatment paradigms. BASC results are designed, through simple graphical output, to foster communication between parents, physicians, teachers, psychologists, and other clinicians. The T scores and percentile ranks are provided to enhance quantitative interpretation, to provide a means for precise indication of comparison of normal and dysfunctional behavior, and to allow for change indices. It is essential that, as part of the sharing of information of all individuals involved in a case, competent interpretation of test scores be appropriately provided.

PATTERNS AND INTERPRETATIONS FROM THE BASC

During the standardization process, TRS and PRS data were collected for children who have been diagnosed with conduct disorder, behavior disorder, depression, emotional disturbance, ADHD, learning disability, mild mental retardation, and autism. SRP data was also collected on children who were diagnosed with the above-mentioned disorders, except from children who had autism. The BASC manual provides data on the mean T scores of these clinical groups. For purposes of brevity, only a portion of the diagnostic categories provided in the BASC manual will be presented in this chapter, but common diagnostic syndromes or particularly unique diagnostic syndromes will be included.

Children in the conduct disorder sample included individuals who were diagnosed with variants of conduct disorder and oppositional defiant disorder, or individuals who were adjudicated delinquents but were assigned a code. These children score highest on the Conduct Problems scale of the TRS, but also have high scores on the Aggression and Hyperactivity scales. (Similar results were obtained on the PRS.) In addition, they had moderately high scores on all of the other clinical scales and moderately low scores on all of the adaptive scales. (On the PRS, moderately high scores were noted on the Depression and Attention Problems scales.) The elevations on the additional scales may be hypothesized to show an indication of the teacher's or parent's difficulty and stress in managing these children.

The depression sample included children who were diagnosed with major depression, dysthymia, and depressive disorder NOS (not otherwise specified). On the TRS, the combined child and adolescent sample had high means scores on the scales of Conduct Problems and Depression and a low score on the Adaptability scale. The high Depression score supports the construct validity of that scale. (On the PRS, the combined child and adolescent sample had high scores on the Conduct Problems, Depression, and Aggression scales and an extremely low score on the Adaptability Scales. The Atypicality, Hyperactivity, and Attention Problems scores were also high, but the Social

Skills score was low.) The high Conduct Problems scores on the TRS and PRS may reflect the existence of depression in children with conduct disorder or it may reflect that children with depression and conduct problems are more apt to be referred for services than children suffering only from depression. On the SRP, the combined child and adolescent group scored highest on the Depression scale. Relatively high scores on the SRP occur in scales including Locus of Control, Attitude to School, Attitude to Teachers, Sense of Inadequacy, and Social Stress. The group scored extremely low on the scales of Relations with Parents and Interpersonal Relations.

Children in the ADHD sample were collected as part of a research study on ADHD. On the TRS, high scores were noted on scales of Attention Problems, Hyperactivity, and Learning Problems, with a low score on Study Skills. On the PRS, high scores were noted on scales of Attention Problems, Hyperactivity, Aggression, Conduct Problems, and Depression, with a low score on the Adaptability scale. The PRS profile was more differentiated than the TRS profile, suggesting that parents are capable of identifying ADHD symptoms. On the SRP, the profile is flat and close to the mean of 50. It appears that the problems experienced by ADHD children are not particularly reflected by the SRP.

Children in the autism sample included those diagnosed with autistic disorder or pervasive developmental disorder NOS. On the TRS, the combined child and adolescent sample had extremely high scores on the Withdrawal and Atypicality scales and very low scores on the Leadership, Social Skills, and Study Skills scales. These results are consistent with the socially avoidant and uncommunicative character of autistic children. The group also had high scores on the Attention Problems and Learning Problems scales, which is consistent with their frequent lack of response to instruction.

Much of the recent BASC research has focused on the assessment and diagnosis of ADHD in clinical populations. Researchers (Doyle, Ostrander, Skare, Crosby, & August, 1997; Vaughn et al., 1997) concluded that the BASC PRS and the ASEBA Child Behavior Checklist were generally equivalent for the diagnosis of ADHD Combined Type. Doyle et al. (1997) stated a preference for the BASC due to the rational derivation of its scales. Vaughn et al. (1997) found the BASC PRS and TRS, and the ASEBA CBCL and TRF results to differ significantly for cases of ADHD Predominantly Inattentive Type, and they asserted that the "BASC scales are more accurate" (p. 356).

The BASC and Interview Formats

Behavior rating scales, such as the BASC, are norm-referenced tests that are essential for clinical and psychoeducational assessment. Norm-referenced tests are standardized on a clearly defined group (such as children with behavior difficulties), termed the *norm group*, and are scaled so that each individual score reflects a rank within the norm group. Norm-referenced tests provide guidelines for further investigation toward identification and diagnosis of clinical psychopathology. Additional benefits include quickness of administration, ease of administration, and an index for evaluating change in many different aspects of the child's behavioral and social worlds, including developmental changes and the effects of remediation (Sattler, 1988). Such instruments are useful as screening tools, but do not provide sufficient information to generate specific psychiatric diagnoses (Schaughency & Rothlind, 1991).

A common method for enhancing the diagnostic process is use of interview techniques. The interview format allows information to be obtained from the mother, father, teacher, child, or a combination of these informants. Most often, several informants are interviewed.

Interviews can be unstructured, semistructured, and/or structured diagnostic formats that include specific criteria for psychiatric disorders and, depending on the method, standardized procedures for obtaining information. Interviews frequently use a branching format whereby additional items are asked only if screening symptom(s) or problem behavior(s) are present (Schaughency & Rothlind, 1991). Interview formats, whether unstructured, semistructured, or structured, allow the interviewee to convey information in their own words.

Examples of structured interviews include the *Diagnostic Interview for Children and Adolescents* (DICA; Reich, 2000) and the *Schedule for Affective Disorders and Schizophrenia for School-Age Children* (K-SADS; Ambrosini, 2000). A structured interview format that included DSM-IV diagnostic criteria was found to be an improvement over an informal interview, as the latter format reduced the criterion variance (i.e., the application of different rules to make a diagnosis) by using specific criteria for psychiatric disorders and by providing standard guidelines for obtaining information about diagnostic criteria of individual clinical syndromes (Biederman, Keenan, & Faraone, 1990). In addition, structured interviews elicit more consistent symptom reporting by reducing information variability due to decreased use of different data collection methods (Biederman et al., 1990; Chen, Faraone, Biederman, & Tsuang, 1994; Hart, Lahey, Loeber, & Hanson, 1994).

There has been little research on the relationship between behavior rating scales and interview formats (Jensen, Salzberg, Richters, & Watanabe, 1993). However, it has been our experience clinically that the combination of norm-referenced tests such as the BASC and structured interview formats has provided an excellent basis from which to derive diagnostic formulation(s).

Intervention Planning

Based on clinically significant (i.e., 70+ T score on most clinical scales, 30− T score on adaptive scales) and moderately significant (i.e., 60 to 69 T score on most clinical scales, 31 to 39 T score on adaptive scales) indices on the

BASC across multiple raters (i.e., parent and teacher, parent and child), the clinician can identify areas of problematic behaviors. Further evaluation, usually in the form of structured and/or individual interviews, provides supplementary information toward diagnosis. This information is the groundwork for effective intervention planning, as salient and unique features of a child are incorporated to compose an individualized treatment program. Such programs vary depending on the diagnoses, individuals involved in the treatment paradigm (i.e., parents, teacher, clinicians, and child), and treatment goals. It is useful to include multiple aspects of a child's environment in intervention planning, as such programs tend to provide a comprehensive basis for building effective functioning.

ADVANTAGES OF THE BASC

The BASC is a multimethod measure that includes multiple raters across multiple settings. This ability to glean information from rating scales that use similar items, and were developed and standardized across multiple raters simultaneously, is particularly advantageous for the clinician. It is possible to access children's functioning in a variety of contexts that are directly comparable. This feature is unique to rating scales in that the BASC standardization process obtained information from a number of raters (i.e., parent, teacher, and self) within the same family group at a similar point in time, whereas other rating scales obtained such information at different times from varying standardization samples (i.e., different parent, teacher, and child samples).

The BASC is multidimensional in that it has included the clearly important procedure of studying adaptive behavior simultaneously with psychopathology. Adaptive behavior functioning, and variants of such behavior, are critical in understanding models of child psychopathology. Adaptive behavior has been found to be related to the social-emotional behavior of children with pediatric herpes encephalitis virus (Wolters, Brouwers, Moss, & Pizzo, 1994), predictive of academic achievement (diSibio, 1993), a core deficit for children with ADHD (Stein, Szumowski, Blondis, & Roizen, 1995), and a protective factor against the development of internalizing problems for children with sickle-cell disease (Brown, Eckman, Baldwin, & Buchanan, 1995).

It must be remembered that the original BASC was developed for comprehensive evaluation of problematic behaviors in children. It was not intended as a diagnostic tool for DSM-IV diagnoses. The BASC ADHD Monitor provides delineation of behaviors of ADHD. However, the prudent clinician uses the BASC as well as the entire structured interview in determining diagnostic impressions. In this way, common problematic symptoms that are evident in disruptive behavior and internalizing dimensions are explored. This is particularly important to ensure that bias is not introduced by assessing for one primary disorder. For example, if the clinician asks only diagnostic criteria related to ADHD, there is the risk that a child is actually depressed but is exhibiting behavior that is reflective of ADHD. It is for this very reason that the BASC explores varying problematic behaviors. Even if elevations are apparent only on the Externalizing Problems composite, a follow-up structured interview or individual interview that explores these behaviors as well as internalizing behaviors, school problems, and adaptive skills is essential. This approach ensures that accurate diagnosis is made and that comorbid conditions are identified.

There are a number of features about the BASC that make it particularly salient for assessing child and adolescent psychopathology.

Relevance to Target Group

The item content of the BASC scales was selected from research findings, other measures, and clinical experience. The items were constructed with assistance from professionals and students, then carefully evaluated for readability, acceptability, and comprehensiveness. It has been stated that the BASC has been carefully developed and "represents a synthesis of what is known about developmental psychopathology and personality development" (Sandoval & Echandia, 1994, p. 420).

Compatibility with Clinical Theories and Practice

The BASC normative sample was selected to be representative of the 1990 U.S. population aged 2½ to 18 years, including exceptional children and taking into account race and ethnicity. In addition, there was overlap of the samples across the PRS, TRS, and SRP, to ensure comparability between norms. Clinical samples were drawn from self-contained classrooms, community mental health centers, residential schools, juvenile detention centers, and university and hospital outpatient mental health clinics (Flanagan, 1995). Moreover, a sample of about 1000 children was collected in Canada. This diversity of sampling procedures enhances comparability with clinical theories and current psychology practice.

Simple and Teachable Methods

The record forms for the TRS, PRS, and SRP are clear, efficient to complete, easily understandable, and readily scored. Minimal training, aside from careful review as amply stated in the BASC manual, is necessary for accurate administration and scoring of the BASC. The single record form for the PRS, TRS, and SRP is conveniently designed for efficient scoring (Flanagan, 1995; Kline, 1994). Hoza noted that "minimal self-instructional training is required in order to use the SOS appropriately, and hence it can be used by a wide variety of clinicians and educational professionals with varied training backgrounds" (1994, p. 9).

Use of Multiple Respondents

The BASC is multimethod in that it collects data from teachers, parents, and children. Thus, information about clinical and adaptive behavior functioning is available from school and home settings.

Ease of Understanding by Nonprofessionals

Clinicians as well as researchers have noted the ease with which parents are able to understand and readily complete the rating forms. The clinical and adaptive profiles are easily interpreted and available for presentation to parents and school personnel (Flanagan, 1995; Sandoval & Echandia, 1994). In addition, printouts from computer scoring are readily understandable and offer graphical representation of results as well as a brief narrative (Davis, 1995).

Usefulness in Provision of Clinical Services

Clinicians as well as researchers have noted that the BASC provides comprehensive integration of information about a child. The BASC has proven useful in describing behavioral and emotional variables that assist in diagnosis from an educational and clinical standpoint (Flanagan, 1995). In addition, the BASC is helpful with assessment needs, as it includes a description of adaptive and maladaptive behavior, which is not evaluated in other behavior rating scales. The BASC is also useful in assisting with decisions for educational classification, evaluation of behavior treatment, and research regarding childhood emotional and behavior disorders (Adams & Drabman, 1994).

Diagnostic Considerations

The BASC provides an estimation of dimensions of behavior and emotions to DSM-IV criteria, treatment programming, and educational classifications that suggest areas of additional evaluation in discerning childhood psychopathology (Adams & Drabman, 1994). Researchers have noted that the BASC is particularly useful for identifying subtypes of ADHD, as compared to the ASEBA Child Behavior Checklist (Vaughn et al., 1997).

Gender Differences

The BASC normative samples of the TRS, PRS, and SRP reveal gender differences. Specifically, results from the TRS and PRS reveal higher raw scores for males compared to females on the scales of Aggression, Conduct Problems, Hyperactivity, Attention, and Learning Problems. Results from the SRP demonstrate increased raw scores for males compared to females on scales of Sensation Seeking, Attitude to School, Attitude to Teachers, and Self-

Esteem. Conversely, results from the TRS and PRS reveal higher raw scores for females on scales of Social Skills, Study Skills, Leadership, and Depression. On the SRP, results reveal higher raw scores for females on scales of Anxiety and Interpersonal Relations. These differences in scores reflect real differences between males and females in the incidence of behavioral and emotional problems.

INSIGHTS FROM EXPERIENCE

Low correlations have typically been found between parent and teacher ratings across specific symptoms (Barkley, Fischer, Edelelock, & Smallisch, 1991). However, combined parent and teacher reports have consistently resulted in stronger correlations with diagnoses than by parent or teacher report only (Landau, Milich, & Widiger, 1991; Biederman et al., 1990).

Clinical experience supports a strategy in which the child and parent are interviewed and complete rating scales if the child is exhibiting behavior reflective of an internalizing (i.e., mood-related, anxiety, withdrawal, and learning problems) disorder. Clinical acumen supports the contention that children, in particular, are the best reporters of internalizing states. Parents can provide valuable conjunction information in children with such disorders. Teachers, however, may not be exposed to subtle aspects of behavior, as evident in mild and moderate depression, and in fact may observe the child exhibiting more disruptive behaviors. Thus, child and parent data are particularly useful for children suspected of having an internalizing dimension to their misbehavior.

Alternatively, the parent and teacher are interviewed for children who are exhibiting disruptive behavior disorders (i.e., attention, impulsivity, and hyperactivity problems; and oppositional behavior, conduct problems, and aggressive behavior). The standardization sample, as well as clinical experience, provides strong evidence for parent and teacher reports for such disorders.

On self-report measures, a profile of particular concern includes moderate to significant elevations on scales assessing depression, sense of inadequacy, and self-reliance. Clinical experience has revealed that individuals with such a pattern often have feelings of dysphoria and anhedonia, with concomitant symptoms associated with major depressive disorder or dysthymia. However, the combination of a significant sense of inadequacy and lack of self-reliance lends toward an interpretation of helplessness and hopelessness. When such patterns are observed, the careful clinician should consider inquiring about suicidal ideation and intent.

Clinical experience supports the practice of using the BASC in conjunction with a structured interview, with information obtained from at least two raters across four measures (i.e., two BASC rating scales and two structured interview formats). This practice lends itself to careful, comprehensive diagnostic impressions with considerable information that is particularly useful in treatment planning.

The BASC has also proven to be highly effective in that identical items are not included on multiple scales. On measures that do use such an approach, the clinician often needs to examine item content on clinically significant scales, as multiple interpretations can be offered for the elevation. Clinical experience has proven that such perusal is usually unnecessary with the BASC.

The BASC validity scale(s) offer an opportunity to assess whether the rater is marking infrequently endorsed items or, for self-report, is presenting an impression that is more favorable than may be the case. Such information allows the clinician to hypothesize about the accuracy of the ratings as well as other factors that may be affecting the individual's analysis of the behavior. Clinical experience has revealed that PRS and TRS validity scores that are within the caution or extreme range are often reflective of adults that are particularly stressed in managing the child's behavior. It is often useful to discuss the apparent difficulties and consider additional sources of information.

Overall, the BASC is a highly useful measure for behavior evaluation and intervention. The scales were rationally derived, and clinical experience reveals that elevations on specific BASC scales are generally in keeping with referral concerns.

CASE STUDIES

Jessica

Jessica is an eighth-grade student referred for determination of ADHD and learning disabilities. Previous diagnoses included major depression and generalized anxiety (childhood type), for which she is on medication. Concentration problems have been particularly evident since grade 7. Reportedly, Jessica requires absolute quiet to complete assignments and she has difficulty remaining on task. Jessica's mother denied complaints of inattention and concentration problems when Jessica was in elementary school. Jessica has had academic difficulties since grade 2. The school apparently switched from a whole language to a phonics approach when she was in grade 4, which was beneficial and her reading grades improved to grade level. In grade 6, her grades in language arts were in the B to D range. In the past 1½ years her marks have noticeably decreased. Jessica's mother indicated that Jessica exhibits considerable oppositional defiant behavior with temper outbursts when denied a request, and that she is quite emotional, with frequent crying outbursts. Her medical history includes mononucleosis at 10 years of age. Jessica's current medications consists of Prozac and Respiradol for depression and Zantac for stomach pain. She is also participating in psychotherapy.

Jessica presently has academic difficulties in language arts. Comments on report cards note that at the end of grade 2, she was achieving at mid–grade 2 level in reading and writing. Time management and work habits were indicated as areas where Jennifer needed improvement. At the end of grade 5, Jessica achieved C's in reading and B's in writing, mathematics, French, music, and computer education. In March of grade 8, she obtained D's in reading, social studies, technology lab, and physical education. She attained a C in French, a B in health, and an A– in home education. She obtained failing grades in mathematics. Comments revealed that Jessica was absent for most of the term in language arts and work incompletion was common across subjects.

Intellectual functioning (assessed with the Wechsler Intelligence Scale for Children—Revised [WISC-III]) revealed average to high average functioning (Full Scale IQ [FSIQ] = 75th percentile), with perceptual-performance abilities (Performance IQ [PIQ] = 91st percentile) significantly better developed than verbal-expressive skills (Verbal IQ [VIQ] = 50th percentile). Academic assessment (evaluated with the Wechsler Individual Achievement Test [WIAT]) was variable depending on the area assessed. Jessica's reading fell within average limits, with scores at the 39th percentile on sight reading and the 73rd percentile on reading comprehension. Mathematical computation and reasoning both fell within average limits, with computation at the 50th percentile and reasoning at the 42nd percentile. Spelling fell within low average limits, at the 21st percentile.

Behavior functioning indices (i.e., the BASC PRS and SRP, and the K-SADS: Parent and Self-Report) were variable depending on the rater and the rating scale. Results from the PRS and SRP revealed that the number of infrequently endorsed items fell within the acceptable range, indicating that neither rater attempted to portray an overly negative picture of behavior functioning. Jessica's mother endorsed items on the BASC that resulted in clinically significant elevations on scales that assess conduct problems, depressive symptoms, somatization or complaints of bodily functioning, withdrawal, and attention problems. Moderate elevations were noted on the PRS on scales assessing decreased social skills and decreased leadership. Jessica's behavior rating scale resulted in elevations that fell within the clinically significant range on scales assessing negative attitude toward school and teachers, feeling that events are externally mediated and she has little control over consequences, negative relations with parents, depression, sense of inadequacy, and decreased self-esteem. Moderate elevations were noted on the self-report on scales assessing somatization, social stress, anxiety, and decreased self-reliance. The T scores are shown in Table 9.6.

On the K-SADS, both Jessica and her mother endorsed items related to major depression, including dysphoria, anhedonia, numerous vegetative and cognitive symptoms, and previous suicidal thought and intent. Jessica denied having a suicide plan at the present. With regard to attention functioning, both Jessica and her mother endorsed almost all the inattention items, with no hyperactivity or impulsivity items. They stated that the onset of attention problems was grade 7. In addition, both Jessica and her mother endorsed almost all the items related to oppositional defiant disorder and generalized anxiety disorder.

The results of this evaluation resulted in diagnoses of major depression, generalized anxiety (childhood type), and oppositional defiant disorder. (ADHD was not diagnosed due to the late onset of the attention problems, which was after age 7.) Recommendations included monitoring of medication management for depression and anxiety, continuation of psychotherapy, and close monitoring for future suicidal ideation and plan.

Jerry

Jerry is a 5-year-old male who is currently being served in a preschool special education program for children with developmental disabilities. He has a history of developmental delays in both cognition and language that qualified

TABLE 9.6
BASC Parent Rating and Self-Report Profile
for Case Study 1: Jessica

Scale	Parent rating T score	Self-report T score
Hyperactivity	52	
Aggression	57	
Conduct Problems	70	
Anxiety	45	61
Depression	100	80
Sense of Inadequacy	—	72
Somatization	70	65
Social Stress	—	63
Atypicality	68	55
Locus of Control	—	73
Withdrawal	84	
Attention Problems	79	
Social Skills	38	
Leadership	34	
Attitude to School	—	71
Attitude to Teachers	—	74
Sensation Seeking	—	60
Relations with Parents	—	30
Interpersonal Relations	—	54
Self-Esteem	—	26
Self-Reliance	—	32

Source: From *Behavior Assessment System for Children: Manual*, by C. R. Reynolds and R. W. Kamphaus, 1992, Circle Pines, MN: American Guidance Service. Copyright 1992 by American Guidance Service, Inc. Reprinted with permission.

TABLE 9.7
Parent and Teacher BASC ADHD Monitor T Scores
for Jerry at Intake at Health Service

Scale	Mother	Preschool teacher
Hyperactivity	94	68
Attention Problems	68	67
Internalizing	70	53
Adaptive Skills	40	45

Source: From *Behavior Assessment System for Children* (BASC)
ADHD *Monitor*, by R. W. Kamphaus and C. R. Reynolds, 1998,
Circle Pines, MN: American Guidance Service. Copyright
1998 by AGS. Reprinted with permission.

him for this service. Simultaneously, he is being seen at a community health center for treatment of ADHD. There is a positive family history of ADHD, with diagnosis having been documented for both his father and older sister.

Jerry's initial diagnosis and referral to the health service were made by school personnel. His treating physician, a pediatric neurologist, prescribed Ritalin, 10 milligrams bid, as beginning dosage for symptoms of hyperactivity and attention problems.

BASC ADHD Monitor parent and teacher ratings were obtained at the time of initial visit. The T scores are shown in Table 9.7.

Jerry returned to the clinic 1 month later for a medication check. His T scores at follow-up showed substantial improvement in hyperactivity symptomatology across settings (see Table 9.8). In addition, maternal ratings suggested substantially improved attention and fewer internalizing problems. The treating physician, while uncertain whether or not maternal ratings were in part a product of placebo effects, noted that the reduced hyperactivity across settings alone warranted maintenance of the current dosage for at least 1 more month.

TABLE 9.8
Parent and Teacher BASC ADHD Monitor T Scores for
Jerry at 1-Month Medication Check at Health Service

Scale	Mother	Preschool teacher
Hyperactivity	59	55
Attention Problems	55	64
Internalizing	50	52
Adaptive Skills	45	44

Source: From *Behavior Assessment System for Children* (BASC)
ADHD *Monitor*, by R. W. Kamphaus and C. R. Reynolds, 1998,
Circle Pines, MN: American Guidance Service. Copyright 1998
by AGS. Reprinted with permission.

CONCLUSIONS

The BASC is a multimethod and multidimensional behavior rating scale that is useful for identifying children with behavior problems, determining the range and magnitude of psychopathology, and assessing behavior change over time. The BASC is unique in that it includes clinical scales that are reflective of childhood psychopathology, and adaptive behavior functioning. The BASC is based on a dimensional approach in which behaviors are studied through the grouping of constructs or dimensions. To supplement the original BASC, the BASC ADHD Monitor was developed to aid in comprehensive evaluation, diagnosis, and treatment of children with features of ADHD.

The BASC has a number of features that render its use particularly advantageous for childhood assessment. The multimethod approach allows information to be gathered from parents, teachers, and a self-report. In addition, a structured developmental history format ensures that relevant background information is obtained from the parent or guardian. Finally, the classroom observation system is useful for assessing the target child's behavior at a given time (i.e., momentary time sample method) and for generally observing the target child's behavior within the classroom (i.e., rating scale method). The multimethod approach is particularly powerful due to the comprehensiveness of information obtained from a number of raters and methods. In addition, the well-developed and extensive normative basis of the BASC, including scaled scores, ensures that accurate analysis of behavior is achieved.

The multidimensional approach is an added advantage of the BASC, as it measures aspects of behavior and personality from a clinical and adaptive behavior functioning viewpoint. Thus, the clinician is well able to develop an understanding of the child's behavior in relation to common childhood clinical syndromes and daily living skills/socialization. Many, if not most, children with psychopathology have areas in which they are functioning entirely within normal limits. For example, a child with features of ADHD may have normal social skills and self-esteem. The BASC allows for identification of problematic behavior as well as areas of normalcy and/or strengths.

The BASC does not classify, and thereby diagnose, children on a categorical basis, but provides a level of functioning compared to the normative sample. Thus, one is well able to monitor progress and/or deterioration in behavior functioning. In a diagnostic method, an if-then format exists in that one qualifies for the syndrome based on identification of a minimal number of items endorsed or one does not qualify for the diagnosis. Thus, gradients of psychopathology, and change over time, are not revealed. While the normative and diagnostic methods each are useful for certain contexts, the BASC has extensive application in school and clinical settings as a means of determining whether there is indication of behavioral disorder and, subsequently, as a means of assessing change.

As reviewed in this chapter, the BASC is useful for interpretation in the following contexts: identification of treatment objectives and target behaviors for intervention, assistance in drawing inferences between treatment and outcomes, collection of multiple data points, assessment of change, and assistance in communication between treatment providers and caregivers.

The BASC is appropriately used as an integral part of the evaluation process in identification of problematic behaviors and adaptive behavior functioning. When used in conjunction with a structured interview format, ensuring that information is obtained from a number of raters, the clinician is equipped to render diagnostic formulations. The BASC is a landmark system for obtaining childhood psychopathology diagnosis and intervention planning due to its comprehensive collection of data points based on a normative sample composed of parents, teachers, and target children. In addition, the theoretical derivation of the BASC, as well as the standardization process, ensures that scaled scores are reliable and valid. Clinical experience with the BASC has left the impression that the scores obtained are functionally similar to a teacher's or parent's observation of problematic behavior in the target child. In other words, it has been the experience of these authors that a teacher's or parent's report is similar to scores obtained on the BASC, including the magnitude of problematic behavior. When scores on a parent or teacher form are elevated compared to information from other sources, a number of interpretations are possible: an elevated validity scale, a certain behavior is evident in only one setting (e.g., oppositional behavior only in the home or school setting), or the rater does not readily observe such behavior in that setting (e.g., depression in the school setting). Overall, however, the BASC provides an excellent basis for identification of problematic behavior and monitoring of intervention planning.

References

Adams, C. D., & Drabman, R. S. (1994). BASC: A critical review. *Child Assessment News*, 4, 1–5.

Ambrosini, P. J. (2000). Historical development and present status of the Schedule for Affective Disorders and Schizophrenia for School-Age Children (K-SADS). *Journal of the American Academy of Child and Adolescent Psychiatry*, 39, 49–58.

American Psychiatric Association. *Diagnostic and Statistical Manual of Mental Disorders* (4th ed.). Washington, DC: American Psychiatric Association.

Barkley, R. A., Fischer, M., Edelelock, C., & Smallisch, L. (1991). Hyperactive children diagnosed by research criteria: III. Mother-child interactions, family conflicts, and maternal psychopathology. *Journal of Child Psychiatry*, 32, 233–255.

Bender, W. N. (1997). Medical interventions and school monitoring. In W. N. Bender (Ed.), *Understanding ADHD: A practical guide for teachers and parents* (pp. 107–122). Upper Saddle River, NJ: Merrill.

Biederman, J., Keenan, K., & Faraone, S. V. (1990). *Journal of the American Academy of Child and Adolescent Psychiatry*, 29(5), 698–701.

Brown, R. T., Eckman, J., Baldwin, I. K., & Buchanan, I. (1995). Protective aspects of adaptive behavior in children with sickle cell syndromes. *Children's Health Care*, 24, 204–222.

Cantwell, D. P. (1996). Classification of child and adolescent psychopathology. *Journal of Child Psychology and Psychiatry*, 37, 3–12.

Chen, W. F., Faraone, S. V., Biederman, J., & Tsuang, M. T. (1994). Diagnostic accuracy of the child behavior rating scales for attention-deficit hyperactivity disorder: A receiver-operating characteristic analysis. *Journal of Consulting and Clinical Psychology*, 62(5), 1017–1025.

Davis, H. (1995). Behavior assessment system for children. *Protocol: Maryland School Psychologists' Association*, 15, 21–23.

diSibio, M. (1993). Conjoint effects of intelligence and adaptive behavior on achievement in a nonreferred sample. *Journal of Psychoeducational Assessment*, 11, 304–313.

Doyle, A., Ostrander, R., Skare, S., Crosby, R. D., & August, G. J. (1997). Convergent and criterion-related validity of the behavior assessment system for children—parent rating scale. *Journal of Clinical Child Psychology*, 26, 276–284.

Edelbrock, C., & Costello, A. J. (1988). Convergence between statistically derived behavior problem syndromes and child psychiatric diagnoses. *Journal of Abnormal Psychology*, 16, 219–231.

Erhardt, D., & Conners, C. K. (1996). Methodological and assessment issues in pediatric psychopharmacology. In J. M. Weiner (Ed.), *Diagnosis and psychopharmacology of childhood and adolescent disorders* (2nd ed.). New York: Wiley.

Flanagan, R. (1995). A review of the behavior assessment system for children (BASC): Assessment consistent with the requirements of the Individuals with Disabilities Education Act (IDEA). *Journal of School Psychology*, 33, 177–186.

Francis, D. J., Fletcher, J. M., Stuebing, K. K., Davidson, K. C., & Thompson, N. M. (1991). Analysis of change: Modeling individual growth. *Journal of Consulting and Clinical Psychology*, 59, 27–37.

Frick, P. J., Kamphaus, R. W., Lahey, B. B., Loeber, R., Christ, M. A. G., Hart, E. L., & Tannenbaum, L. E. (1991). Academic underachievement and the disruptive behavior disorders. *Journal of Consulting and Clinical Psychology*, 59, 289–295.

Harris, J., Wilkinson, S. C., Trovato, J., & Pryor, C. (1992). Teacher-completed child behavior checklist ratings as a function of classroom-based interventions: A pilot study. *Psychology in the Schools*, 29, 42–52.

Hart, E. L., Lahey, B. B., Loeber, R., & Hanson, K. S. (1994). Criterion validity of informants in the diagnosis of disruptive behavior disorders in children. *Journal of Consulting and Clinical Psychology*, 62(2), 410–414.

Hodge, R. D., & McKay, V. (1986). Criterion-related validity data for the Child Behavior Checklist—Teacher Report Form. *Journal of School Psychology*, 24, 387–393.

Hoza, B. (1994). Review of the behavior assessment system for children. *Child Assessment News*, 4, 5–10.

Jacobson, N. S., & Traux, P. (1991). Clinical significance: A statistical approach to defining meaningful change in psychotherapy research. *Journal of Consulting and Clinical Psychology*, 59, 12–19.

Jensen, P. S., Koretz, D., Locke, B. Z., Schneider, S., Radke-Yarrow, M., Richters, J. E., & Rumsey, J. M. (1993). Child and adolescent psychopathology research: Problems and prospects for the 1990s. *Journal of Abnormal Child Psychology*, 21, 551–580.

Jensen, P. S., Salzberg, A. D., Richters, J. E., & Watanabe, H. K. (1993). Scales, diagnoses and child psychopathology: CBCL and DISC relationships. *Journal of American Academy of Child Adolescence and Psychiatry*, 32(2), 397–405.

Kamphaus, R. W., & Frick, P. J. (1996). *Clinical assessment of child and adolescent personality and behavior.* Needham Heights, MA: Allyn & Bacon.

Kamphaus, R. W., Huberty, C. J., DiStefano, C., & Petoskey, M. D. (1997). A typology of teacher rated child behavior for a national U.S. sample. *Journal of Abnormal Child Psychology*, 25, 253–263.

Kamphaus, R. W., Petoskey, M. D., Cody, H., Rowe, E. W., Huberty, C. J., & Reynolds, C. R. (1999). A typology of parent rated child behavior for a national U.S. sample. *Journal of Child Psychology and Psychiatry*, 40, 607–616.

Kamphaus, R. W., & Reynolds, C. R. (1998). *Behavior Assessment System for Children* (BASC) ADHD *Monitor.* Circle Pines, MN: American Guidance Service.

Kamphaus, R. W., Reynolds, C. R., & Hatcher, N. M. (1999). Treatment planning and evaluation with the BASC: The Behavior Assessment System for Children. In M. Maruish (Ed.), *The use of psychological testing for treatment planning and outcome assessment* (2nd ed., pp. 563–497). Mahwah, NJ: Erlbaum.

Kazdin, A. E. (1995). *Conduct disorders in childhood and adolescence.* Thousand Oaks, CA: Sage.

Kline, R. B. (1994). New objective rating scales for child assessment: Parent- and teacher-informant inventories of the Behavior Assessment System for Children: The Child Behavior Checklist and the Teacher Report Form. *Journal of Psychoeducational Assessment, 12,* 289–306.

Landau, S., Milich, R., & Widiger, T. A. (1991). Conditional probabilities of child interview symptoms in the diagnosis of attention deficit disorder. *The Journal of Child Psychology and Psychiatry and Allied Disciplines, 32*(3), 501–513.

Last, C. G. (1993). Introduction. In C. G. Last (Ed.), *Anxiety across the lifespan: A developmental perspective* (pp. 1–6). New York: Springer-Verlag.

Martin, R. P. (1988). *Assessment of personality and behavior problems: Infancy through adolescence.* New York: Guilford.

Meehl, P. E. (1995). Bootstrap taxometrics: Solving the classification problem in psychopathology. *American Psychologist, 50,* 266–275.

Rapoport, J. L., & Castellanos, F. X. (1996). Attention-deficit hyperactivity disorder. In J. M. Wiener (Ed.), *Diagnosis and psychopharmacology of childhood and adolescent disorders* (2nd ed., pp. 265–292). New York: Wiley.

Reich, W. (2000). Diagnostic Interview for Children and Adolescents (DICA). *Journal of the American Academy of Child and Adolescent Psychiatry, 39,* 59–66.

Reynolds, C. R., & Kamphaus, R. W. (1992). *Behavior Assessment System for Children: Manual.* Circle Pines, MN: American Guidance Service.

Reynolds, C. R., & Richmond, B. O. (1985). *Revised Children's Manifest Anxiety Scale: Manual.* Los Angeles: Western Psychological Services.

Sandoval, J., & Echandia, A. (1994). Behavior assessment system for children. *Journal of School Psychology, 32,* 419–425.

Sattler, J. (1988). *Assessment of Children* (3rd ed.). San Diego, CA: Author.

Schaughency, E. A., & Rothlind, J. (1991). Assessment and classification of attention deficit hyperactivity disorders. *School Psychology Review, 20*(2), 187–202.

Stein, M. A., Szumowski, E., Blondis, T. A., & Roizen, N. J. (1995). Adaptive skills dysfunction in ADD and ADHD children. *Journal of Child Psychology and Psychiatry, 36,* 663–670.

Vaughn, M. L., Riccio, C. A., Hynd, G. W., & Hall, J. (1997). Diagnosing ADHD (Predominantly Inattentive and Combined Type subtypes): Discriminant validity of the Behavior Assessment System for Children and the Achenbach Parent and Teacher Rating Scales. *Journal of Clinical Child Psychology, 26*(4), 349–357.

Wolters, P. L., Brouwers, P., Moss, H. A., & Pizzo, P. A. (1994). Adaptive behavior of children with symptomatic HIV infection before and after zidovudine therapy. *Journal of Pediatric Psychology, 19,* 47–61.

CHAPTER

10

The Achenbach System of Empirically Based Assessment

STEPHANIE H. MCCONAUGHY

University of Vermont

INTRODUCTION AND OVERVIEW

The Achenbach System of Empirically Based Assessment (ASEBA) is designed to facilitate assessment, intervention planning, and outcome evaluation among school, mental health, medical, and social service practitioners who deal with maladaptive behavior in children, adolescents, and young adults. The ASEBA rating forms contain items for assessing an individual's competencies and problems as reported by different informants, including parents, parent surrogates, teachers, and day care providers. Forms are also available for rating direct observations in group settings, for rating problems observed and reported during clinical interviews, and for adolescents and young adults to report on their own behavior.

The ASEBA forms provide multiple perspectives on an individual's functioning for standardized assessment and communication between practitioners from various disciplines. The forms and profiles also provide standardized documentation for practitioners' decisions about interventions and referrals. ASEBA forms are fully compatible with other assessment and diagnostic procedures, while providing valuable information not available through other procedures.

THE EMPIRICALLY BASED APPROACH

The *empirically based* approach to scale development is a hallmark of the ASEBA. This approach can be characterized as working "from the bottom up." That is, it starts with data on numerous items that describe particular behavioral and emotional problems. Informants such as parents, teachers, or the individuals being assessed use standard forms to rate each item on a scale for how true it is over a specific period, such as the past 6 months. Multivariate statistical analyses (such as principal components or factor analyses) are then applied to item scores obtained for large samples of clinically referred individuals to identify sets of problems that tend to occur together. These co-occurring problems constitute *syndromes* in the literal sense of "things that go together." Scores on the items that compose each syndrome are summed to obtain a total score for the syndrome, which reflects the *degree to which* an individual manifests the features of the syndrome.

The syndromes are then normed by using data from large samples of non-referred individuals. Raw scores for each syndrome are converted to T scores and percentiles that indicate the individual's standing on each syndrome scale relative to the normative sample. On most of the instruments, separate norms are provided for each gender and for different age ranges. The T scores and percentiles enable users to judge the severity of problems embodied in each syndrome—that is, the degree to which the problem scores for an individual deviate from normal scores found for individuals of the same age and gender.

In addition to syndrome scores, ASEBA profiles provide raw scores, T scores, and percentiles for groupings of syndromes designated as Internalizing and Externalizing, as well as for Total Problems. Internalizing includes emotional problems such as withdrawal, anxiety, depression, and somatic complaints, while Externalizing includes aggressive and delinquent behavior. The Internalizing and Externalizing scales were derived through factor analyses of scores on the syndrome scales.

To facilitate comparisons of reports from different informants, ASEBA computer scoring programs provide cross-informant comparisons of problem scales scored from parents, teachers, and adolescents' self-ratings, as well as from young adults' self-ratings and ratings by young adults' significant others.

Top-Down versus Bottom-Up Assessment

The empirically based approach to assessment and scale development has the advantage of not being dependent on preconceived notions of psychopathology or clinical impressions that often vary across practitioners. This "bottom-up" approach differs from "top-down" approaches that depend on a priori categorical diagnoses or classifications of problem patterns. The American Psychiatric Association's *Diagnostic and Statistical Manual of Mental Disorders, Fourth Edition* (DSM-IV; 1994) and the World Health Organization's *International Classification of Diseases* (ICD-10; 1992) are examples of top-down approaches to assessment. The DSM-IV and ICD-10 diagnostic categories were developed through negotiations among panels of experts who selected the target disorders and defined their symptoms and other descriptive characteristics. The presence or absence of each disorder is usually determined by interviewing referred individuals and/or their significant others (e.g., parents). If the symptoms and conditions required for a disorder are reported, then the individual is said to have the disorder. If the required number of symptoms or conditions are not reported, then the individual is said not to have the disorder even if some symptoms are reported. The ten categories of disabilities defined in the U.S. special education law—the Individuals with Disabilities Education Act (IDEA; Public Law 101-476, 1990; Public Law 105-17, 1997)—are other examples of a top-down classification system.

The empirical identification of syndromes does not involve any assumptions about whether the syndromes reflect diagnostic categories, like the diagnoses of the DSM-IV and ICD-10, nor does it involve assumptions about causes or the developmental course of particular syndromes. Instead, the name of each empirically based syndrome is a descriptive label of the problems it represents, such as Withdrawn or Aggressive Behavior. Scores on the syndromes provide starting points for investigating problem patterns, as reported by various informants. The problem patterns manifested by individual children can then be compared to the patterns that were previously identified in large clinical samples.

In addition to the problem scales, various ASEBA forms provide competence and adaptive scales for scoring an individual's strengths and positive aspects of functioning. Competence scales for children and adolescents assess activities, social involvement, and school performance. The ASEBA profiles thus serve as focal points for assessing the problems and competencies of individual children, communicating with other people about them, targeting interventions, and evaluating outcomes. The next section describes details of each of the currently available ASEBA forms and scoring profiles.

NATURE OF THE TEST

For children and adolescents, the ASEBA provides rating forms that can be completed by parents or parent surrogates, youths aged 11 to 18, teachers and day care providers, clinicians conducting interviews, and observers of behavior in group settings (e.g., school classrooms). For young adults aged 18 to 30, the ASEBA provides rating forms for obtaining their own self-ratings

TABLE 10.1
Forms in the Achenbach System of Empirically Based Assessment

Name of form	Filled out by
Child Behavior Checklist for Ages 1½–5 (CBCL/1½–5)	Parents and surrogates
Caregiver-Teacher Report Form for Ages 1½–5 (C-TRF)	Daycare providers and preschool teachers
Child Behavior Checklist for Ages 4–18 (CBCL/4–18)	Parents and surrogates
Teacher's Report Form for Ages 5–18 (TRF)	Teachers
Youth Self-Report for Ages 11–18 (YSR)	Youths
Young Adult Behavior Checklist for Ages 18–30 (YABCL)	Parents, surrogates, and spouses
Young Adult Self-Report for Ages 18–30 (YASR)	Young adults
Semistructured Clinical Interview for Children and Adolescents (SCICA)	Interviewers
Direct Observation Form (DOF)	Observers

and ratings from people who know them well, such as parents, spouses, and close friends. ASEBA forms can be used for initial assessments as well as for reassessments to monitor change and evaluate outcomes. Table 10.1 summarizes key features of ASEBA forms and scoring profiles. Each of these is described in the next sections.

Parent and Parent Surrogate Forms

Because children seldom seek mental health services for themselves, mental health practitioners must obtain data about their functioning from others who know the children. It is a natural part of the intake process for practitioners to request information about child clients from the adults who are responsible for them. ASEBA forms filled out by parents can be routinely used to document parents' views of their children's functioning.

Child Behavior Checklist for Ages 1½–5 (CBCL/1½–5)

The CBCL/1½–5 (Achenbach & Rescorla, 2000) is a 4-page form to be completed by parents or parent surrogates for children ages 1½ to 5. The first two pages contain 99 specific problem items, plus one open-ended item. For each item, the respondent is asked to circle 0 if it is *not true* of the child, 1 if it is *somewhat or sometimes true*, and 2 if it is *very true or often true*, based on the child's functioning during the preceding 2 months. Respondents are also asked to describe any additional problems, illnesses, and disabilities that the child has; what concerns them most about the child; and the best things about the child. Pages 3 and 4 of the CBCL/1½–5 contain the Language Development Survey (LDS) to be completed for all children under age 3, as well as for children over age 3 who are suspected of having language delays. Page 3 asks questions about the child's birth history and ear infections, languages spoken in the home, and any family history of language problems. Page 3 also asks the respondent to report the child's best multiword phrases. On page 4, the respondent is asked to circle the child's spontaneous vocabulary words from a list of 310 words that are among the first learned by most children. The CBCL/1½–5 can be completed by most people in about 10 to 15 minutes.

Ratings of the CBCL/1½–5 problem items are scored on a standardized profile for boys and girls. The profile provides scores for Total Problems, Internalizing, Externalizing, and 7 syndrome scales: Emotionally Reactive, Anxious/Depressed, Somatic Complaints, Withdrawn, Sleep Problems, Attention Problems, and Aggressive Behavior. The syndromes were derived from factor analyses of forms completed for 922 boys and 806 girls aged 1½ to 5 who had been referred to clinical settings or who scored above the median for Total Problems in a 1999 U.S. national sample and five other general population samples (for details, see Achenbach & Rescorla, 2000). In addition to the syndrome and broad scores, the CBCL/1½–5 also provides scores for five DSM-oriented scales. These scales (Affective Problems, Anxiety Problems, Pervasive Developmental Problems, Attention Deficit Hyperactivity Problems, and Oppositional Defiant Problems) are composed of items judged by experienced psychiatrists and psychologists to be consistent with DSM-IV diagnostic categories. The DSM-oriented scales are a new feature of the ASEBA scoring profiles. The CBCL/1½–5 LDS provides raw scores and percentiles for average length of the child's multiword phrases and for number of spontaneous vocabulary words, based on norms for ages 18–35 months. The CBCL/1½–5 scales were normed on 700 children who had not been referred for mental health or special education services in the past 12 months.

Child Behavior Checklist for Ages 4–18 (CBCL/4–18)

The CBCL/4–18 (Achenbach, 1991b) is the original ASEBA instrument on which other forms have been modeled. It is a 4-page form to be completed by a parent or parent surrogate for children ages 4 to 18. On the first two pages, parents provide information for 20 social competence items, covering their child's sports participation, hobbies and activities, social organizations, jobs and chores, friendships, relationships with other people, ability to play and work alone, and school functioning. In addition, page 2 provides open-ended items for describing illnesses and disabilities, what concerns the parent most about the child, and the best things about the child. Parents' reports of their child's favorite activities, the degree and quality of the child's involvement in activities, friendships, and the best things about the child provide practitioners with details of the child's strengths for discussion in clinical interviews with the parents and child.

On pages 3 and 4 of the CBCL/4–18, parents rate their child on 118 specific problem items, such as *Acts too young for age, Cries a lot, Cruel to animals, Gets in many fights, Sets fires,* and *Unhappy, sad, or depressed.* Open-ended items are also provided for the respondent to add if the child has physical problems without known medical cause, and/or other problems that are not specifically described on the CBCL. Each item is rated on a 0-1-2-point scale similar to the CBCL/1½–5, based on the child's functioning during the preceding 6 months. The CBCL/4–18 can be completed by most parents in about 15 to 20 minutes.

The CBCL/4–18 is scored on separate profiles for boys and girls for ages 4 to 11 and 12 to 18. The profile provides scores for Total Competence, 3 competence scales (Activities, Social, and School), plus Total Problems, Internalizing, Externalizing, and 8 syndrome scales (Withdrawn, Somatic Complaints, Anxious/Depressed, Social Problems, Thought Problems, Attention Problems, Delinquent Behavior, and Aggressive Behavior). The syndrome scales were derived from principal components analyses of forms completed by parents for 4455 children referred for mental health services. The CBCL/4–18 profile was normed on a U.S. nationally representative sample of 2368 children ages 4 to 18.

Young Adult Behavior Checklist (YABCL)

The YABCL (Achenbach, 1997) is designed to assess young adults ages 18 to 30 on the basis of reports by parents, parent surrogates, spouses, and others who know them well. It contains 105 specific problem items, plus 13 socially desirable items. Each item is rated on a 0-1-2-point scale, based on the preceding 6 months. Many of the YABCL problem items are similar to items on the CBCL/4–18. The YABCL can be used to assess young adult parents of children who are receiving services, as well as young adults who are receiving services themselves. It can also be used to assess progress and outcomes for young adults who were previously assessed with the CBCL/4–18. The YABCL can be completed in about 10 minutes.

The YABCL is scored on separate profiles for males and females for ages 18–30. The profile provides scores for Total Problems, Internalizing, Externalizing, and 8 syndromes (Anxious/Depressed, Withdrawn, Somatic Complaints, Thought Problems, Attention Problems, Intrusive, Aggressive Behavior, and Delinquent Behavior). The YABCL syndromes were derived from principal components analyses of 1532 males and females who were either referred for mental health services or who received Total Problems scores at or above the median of a national sample. The profile was normed on 1064 young adults drawn from follow-up studies of the CBCL/4–18 national sample. Because the CBCL/4–18 and the YABCL both have norms for age 18, users can decide which is the more appropriate form for a particular 18-year-old. The CBCL/4–18 is usually more appropriate for 18-year-olds who live with parents and attend high school, while the YABCL is more appropriate for 18-year-olds who live apart from their parents or no longer attend high school.

Self-Report Forms

As children approach adolescence, they develop better cognitive ability to observe and reflect on their own behavior. To obtain individuals' own views of their competencies and problems, the ASEBA includes self-report forms for youths ages 11 to 18 and young adults ages 18 to 30.

Youth Self-Report (YSR)

The YSR (Achenbach, 1991d) is a self-rating form for youths ages 11 to 18. It requires a mental age of 10 years and fifth-grade-level reading skills. (If reading skills are below fifth-grade level, the YSR can be read aloud to the respondent.) The YSR has most of the same social competence and problem items as the CBCL/4–18, but the items are stated in the first person. Sixteen CBCL/4–18 problem items considered inappropriate to ask youths were deleted and replaced with 16 socially desirable items that enable respondents to say something favorable about themselves. The favorable items are omitted from the Total Problem score. The remaining 102 YSR specific problem items all have counterparts on the CBCL/4–18 and 90 have counterparts on the Teacher's Report Form (TRF) described later. The YSR takes about 15 to 20 minutes to complete.

The YSR is scored on separate profiles for boys and girls ages 11 to 18. The profile provides scores for Total Competence and 2 competence scales (Activities and Social), plus Total Problems, Internalizing, Externalizing, and 8 syndrome scales comparable to those scored on the CBCL/4–18. The YSR syndrome scales were derived from principal components analyses of forms completed by 1272 youths referred for mental health services. The YSR profile was normed on 1315 nonreferred youths drawn from the same U.S. nationally representative sample used to norm the CBCL/4–18.

Young Adult Self-Report (YASR)

The YASR (Achenbach, 1997) is a self-rating form for young adults ages 18 to 30. The YASR has 110 specific problem items and 14 socially desirable items. Most of the problem items are similar to those on the YABCL, except that they are stated in the first person. In addition, the YASR has substance use items and adaptive functioning items that are scored on separate scales. The adaptive functioning items tap relations with friends and family, functioning in educational and job situations, and relations with spouse or partner, if relevant. The YASR can be completed in about 15 to 20 minutes.

The YASR is scored on separate profiles for males and females ages 18 to 30. The profile provides scores for Total Problems, Internalizing, Externalizing, and 8 syndromes comparable to those on the YABCL. The YASR syndromes were derived from principal components analyses of 1455 males and females who were referred for mental health services or who received Total Problem scores at or above the median of a national sample. The profile was normed on 1059 young adults drawn from the same sample used to norm the YABCL.

Teacher or Caregiver Forms

Many children who are referred for mental health services also have problems in school or day care settings. When feasible, it is often helpful for mental health practitioners to request parents' permission to obtain information from teachers or day care providers. ASEBA forms for obtaining teacher and caregiver reports include many of the same items as forms for parents and parent surrogates, but also include items that are specific to school and day care settings. By obtaining data from teachers or day care providers, practitioners obtain perspectives on children's functioning that differ from those of parents. These different perspectives enable practitioners to identify both similarities and differences in how a child appears to adults who play different roles in the child's life and see the child in different contexts. Reports by teachers or caregivers can also reveal strengths, problems, and other aspects of children's functioning that may not be evident to parents or evident in clinical settings.

Caregiver-Teacher Report Form (C-TRF) for Ages 1½–5

The C-TRF (Achenbach & Rescorla, 2000) is a 2-page form to be completed by day care providers or preschool teachers for children ages 1½ to 5. The C-TRF has 99 specific problem items, most of which are the same as the CBCL/1½–5 items. However, some items unique to the C-TRF concern problems that are more apt to be observed in day care and preschool settings than at home. For each item, caregivers rate the child on a 0-1-2 scale for how true the item is now or within the past 2 months. The C-TRF takes about 10 minutes to complete.

The C-TRF is scored on separate profiles for boys and girls ages 1½ to 5. The profile provides scores for Total Problems, Internalizing, Externalizing, and 6 syndromes similar to those on the CBCL/1½–5 (Emotionally Reactive, Anxious/Depressed, Somatic Complaints, Withdrawn, Attention Problems, and Aggressive Behavior). The C-TRF syndromes were derived from factor analyses of 1113 children who were referred for mental health or special education services or who had Total Problem scores at or above the median for their gender in general population samples. The C-TRF profile also provides scores for the same 5 DSM-oriented scales as the CBCL/1½–5. The C-TRF profile was normed on 1192 boys and girls who had not been referred for services.

Teacher's Report Form (TRF)

The TRF (Achenbach, 1991c) is a 4-page form to be completed by teachers of children ages 5 to 18. On the first 2 pages, teachers provide information about the child's academic performance and school adaptive functioning. Teachers also rate the child's school performance using a 5-point scale ranging from 1 (far below grade level) to 5 (far above grade level) for each academic subject. For adaptive functioning, teachers rate the child on 7-point scales in four areas: how hard he/she is working, how appropriately he/she is behaving, how much he/she is learning, and how happy he/she is. Additional space is provided for optional reports of ability and achievement test scores and current services for the child. On pages 3 and 4 of the TRF, teachers rate the child on 118 specific problem items, of which 93 have counterparts on the CBCL/4–18. The remaining items concern school behaviors that parents would not observe, such as Difficulty following directions, Fails to carry out assigned tasks, and Disrupts class discipline. Teachers rate the child on a 0-1-2 scale for how true each item is now or within the past 2 months. The TRF can be completed by most teachers in about 15 to 20 minutes.

The TRF is scored on separate profiles for boys and girls ages 5 to 11 and 12 to 18. The profile provides scores for Adaptive Functioning, Academic Performance, Total Problems, Internalizing, Externalizing, and 8 syndrome scales comparable to those scored on the CBCL/4–18 and YSR. The TRF Attention Problems scale can also be scored on Inattention and Hyperactivity-Impulsivity subscales for evaluations of these particular types of problems (see Achenbach, 1996; Achenbach & McConaughy, 1996, 1997). The TRF syndrome scales were derived from principal components analyses of forms completed for 2815 children referred for mental health or special education services. The TRF profile was normed on 1391 children drawn from the same U.S. nationally representative sample used to norm the CBCL/4–18 and YSR.

Direct Observation Form (DOF)

The DOF (Achenbach, 1986) is designed for rating direct observations of school-aged children in group situations, such as in classrooms or at recess. During a 10-minute period, the observer writes a narrative description of the child's behavior in space provided on the DOF form. The observer also checks boxes to indicate whether the child is on-task at the end of each 1-minute interval within the 10-minute period. After completing the observation, the observer rates the child on 96 specific problem items, using a 0-1-2-3-point scale for whether the item was observed during the 10-minute period. The DOF has 86 items that overlap with those on the TRF and 73 that overlap with those on the CBCL.

DOF ratings are scored on a combined profile for boys and girls ages 5 to 14. The profile provides a mean on-task score, and scores for Total Problems, Internalizing, Externalizing, and 6 syndrome scales (Withdrawn-Inattentive, Nervous-Obsessive, Depressed, Hyperactive, Attention Demanding, and Aggressive). The DOF syndrome scales were derived from principal components analyses of forms completed for 212 children referred for mental health or special education services. The profile was normed on 287 nonreferred children.

Because children's behavior may vary considerably from one occasion to another, at least three 10-minute samples of behavior on different days should be obtained. The DOF computer program can average all item and scale scores for up to six observation sessions. It then prints a profile based on the averaged scores. To compare a child's observed problems with those of other children in the same setting, the program can also print a profile of scores from one or two comparison children averaged over multiple occasions. DOF observations can be done by paraprofessionals such as teacher aides and child-care workers. The DOF is especially useful for documenting specific behaviors in classrooms and in other contexts such as group activities in residential facilities. Using the DOF, direct observers may detect behaviors that are not readily assessable by other means.

Semistructured Clinical Interview for Children and Adolescents (SCICA)

The SCICA (McConaughy & Achenbach, 1994) is a semistructured interview protocol for use by experienced clinical interviewers. Because it covers the topics typically included in initial clinical interviews, it is particularly well-suited for intake evaluations. The SCICA is also appropriate for special education evaluations of emotional and behavioral disorders (McConaughy, 1996, 2000; McConaughy & Achenbach, 1996). The SCICA protocol form provides instructions, open-ended questions, activities (e.g., kinetic family drawing), and tasks for screening fine- and gross-motor functioning. Additional questions for ages 13 to 18 cover somatic complaints, substance use, and trouble with the law. In columns provided on the protocol form, the interviewer separately notes observations of the child's behavior and the child's self-reported problems and responses. The SCICA takes from 60 to 90 minutes to administer, depending on whether brief achievement tests are included to assess the child's academic functioning.

After the SCICA is completed, the interviewer scores a set of 120 specific observation items that describe the child's behavior during the interview and a second set of 114 items that describe the child's self-reported problems. For ages 13 to 18, the SCICA rating form contains 19 additional self-report items. Each item is scored on a 0-1-2-3-point scale for whether the problem was observed or reported by the child during the interview.

The SCICA ratings are scored on a combined profile for boys and girls ages 6 to 12. The profile provides scores for Total Observations, Total Self-Reports, Internalizing, Externalizing, and 8 syndromes (Anxious/Depressed, Anxious, Family Problems, Withdrawn, Aggressive Behavior, Attention Problems, Strange, and Resistant). Scores on the Anxious/Depressed, Family Problems, and Aggressive Behavior scales are based on ratings of the child's self-reported problems, while scores on the remaining 5 syndromes are based on the interviewer's observations. The SCICA profile differs from other ASEBA profiles by providing scores that compare the individual to other clinically referred children instead of comparing the individual to nonreferred children from a normative sample. A revision of the SCICA in 2001 will offer scoring profiles for ages 6 to 11 and 12 to 18.

TECHNICAL INFORMATION

All the ASEBA profiles are available in hand-scored and computer-scored versions. Hand-scoring instructions and templates enable clinicians or clerical staff to score the forms in 10 to 15 minutes. Computer-scoring takes less time and has the additional advantages of providing cross-informant comparisons for instruments with comparable scales, such as the CBCL/4–18, TRF, and YSR. Prior to 1999, computer-scoring software was available only in DOS versions, which are described in the various manuals for the ASEBA forms. In fall 1999, Windows 95/98/NT software was released for generating new versions of the ASEBA profiles, as described in the next section.

ASEBA Assessment Data Manager (ADM)

The ASEBA Windows software contains modules for entering and scoring each rating form, plus an optional program for comparing multisource data. The program, called the Assessment Data Manager (ADM), provides a new way to manage ASEBA data. It coordinates data from multiple forms completed for each child, while also enabling users to link other data to ASEBA data. In fall 2000, ADM version 2.0 was released for ages 1½ to 30, including modules for entering and scoring the CBCL/1½–5, CBCL/4–18, C-TRF, TRF, YSR, YABCL, and YASR. A SCICA module will be released in 2001. Scoring and interpretation of ASEBA profiles are similar for each ASEBA form. In addition, there is an ADM module for scoring machine-readable scan forms (scan module) and a module that enables parents, teachers, and youths to enter their own data (client-entry module). Interpretation of ASEBA profiles is described in a later section.

Reliability of ASEBA

The manuals for the various ASEBA forms report extensive research on the reliability of the ASEBA scales. Reliability data are summarized in this section for the 9 ASEBA instruments listed in Table 10.1.

Test-Retest Reliability

Test-retest reliability indicates the degree to which scale scores obtained from the same informants remain consistent over brief periods during which the subject's competencies or problems are not likely to change. The ASEBA forms for parents, teachers, and self-reports all showed strong test-retest reliabilities. For the CBCL/4–18, 1-week test-retest reliabilities were .87 for Total Competence, .93 for Total Problems, .89 for Internalizing, .93 for Externalizing, and .82 to .95 for the 8 syndrome scales, with an average r of .89 across all scales. For the TRF, 15-day test-retest reliabilities were .93 for Adaptive Functioning and Academic Performance, .95 for Total Problems, .91 for Internalizing, .92 for Externalizing, and .82 to .96 for the 8 syndrome scales, with an average r of .92 across all scales. For the YSR, 1-week test-retest reliabilities were .80 for Total Competence, .79 for Total Problems, .80 for Internalizing, .81 for Externalizing, and .47 to .81 for the 8 syndrome scales, with an average r of .72 across all scales. The CBCL/1½–5 and C-TRF showed comparable test-retest reliabilities, with average rs of .85 and .76, respectively, across all problem scales. The YABCL and YASR showed 1-week test-retest reliabilities of .87 and .84, respectively, averaged across all scales.

For the SCICA, test-retest reliabilities were obtained by McConaughy and Achenbach (1994) for a sample of 20 American children ages 6 to 12 and by Kasius (1997) for a sample of 35 Dutch children ages 6 to 16. In both samples, children were seen in counterbalanced order by two different interviewers over a mean interval of 12 days. Test-retest correlations were .81 to .89 for Total Observations, .73 to .84 for Total Self-Reports, .55 to .69 for Internalizing, .84 to .90 for Externalizing, and .54 to .87 for 7 of 8 SCICA syndromes. Only the Withdrawn syndrome showed a nonsignificant test-retest correlation ($r = .30$) in the American sample, suggesting that children varied from one time to the next on this dimension. This was not the case in the Dutch sample, where the reliability was $r = .87$. No significant differences in mean scores were found in either the American or Dutch sample from Time 1 to Time 2 on any SCICA scale. Although these samples were relatively small, the lack of time effects showed that the SCICA did not manifest the attenuation effects that have been found for structured diagnostic interviews (Jensen et al., 1995).

Interrater Reliability

Also important to know is the degree to which two comparable raters agree on scores on the same instrument. Evaluations of interrater agreement must take into account the relatively greater agreement that usually occurs between informants who have similar relationships with the subject (e.g., two teachers in the same classroom or two parents), in contrast to lesser agreement between informants who have different relationships with the subject or who see the subject in different situations (e.g., a parent versus a teacher). Accordingly, meta-analyses of 119 studies showed an average correlation of .60 for agreement between similar informants, in contrast to average correlations of .28 between different informants and .22 between different informants and children's self-ratings (Achenbach, McConaughy, & Howell, 1987). In keeping with the meta-analytic findings, interrater agreement for ASEBA scores was highest for informants who had similar relationships with the subjects. Interparent agreement on the CBCL/4–18 was .79 for Total Competence and .76 for Total Problems, .65 for CBCL/1½–5 Total Problems, and .63 for YABCL Total Problems. Interrater agreement between two teachers on the TRF was .55 for Adaptive Functioning and .60 for Total Problems. Interrater agreement between pairs of caregivers and teachers on the C-TRF was .72 for Total Problems.

Cross-informant agreement between different types of raters on the ASEBA forms was also consistent with meta-analytic findings. Using data reported by Achenbach (1991a) for different gender and age groups, McConaughy (1993a) computed the following average rs for cross-informant agreement across scales of the CBCL/4–18, TRF, and YSR: .37 between parents and teachers, .38 between parents and youths' self-ratings, and .27 between teachers and youths' self-ratings. For the YABCL and YASR, the average r was .42 across all scales for parent ratings versus young adults' self-ratings (Achenbach, 1997).

Several studies have shown strong DOF interrater reliabilities between two observers of children in the same classroom, with average rs ranging from .86 to .92 for Total Problems and .83 to .90 for on-task scores (Reed & Edelbrock, 1983; McConaughy, Achenbach, & Gent, 1988; McConaughy, Kay, & Fitzgerald, 1998). There were also low to moderate significant correlations between DOF scores and scores on comparable scales of the CBCL/4–18 and TRF (Reed & Edelbrock, 1983; McConaughy et al., 1988).

Interrater reliabilities were obtained for SCICA raw scores from interviewers and videotape observers for an American sample (McConaughy & Achenbach, 1994) and a Dutch sample (Kasius, 1997). Interrater reliabilities were .52 to .61 for Total Observations, .58 to .79 for Total Self-Reports, .64 to .66 for Internalizing, .72 to .74 for Externalizing, and .45 to .85 for the 8 syndromes. Mean scores for interviewers were significantly higher than mean scores for videotape observers, suggesting that interviewer ratings may reflect more awareness of problems than ratings from those that viewed videotapes. Finally, moderate significant correlations have been found between comparable scales of the SCICA and CBCL/4–18, TRF, and DOF for the same subjects (Kasius, 1997; McConaughy & Achenbach, 1994). The moderate correlations indicated that data obtained from the SCICA did not completely overlap with data obtained from other sources.

Validity of the ASEBA

Validity concerns the accuracy with which procedures measure what they are supposed to measure. Because the ASEBA aims to provide standardized descriptions of the competencies and problems of subjects as reported by different informants as well as to discover useful patterns of co-occurring problems, validity must be judged from multiple perspectives.

Content Validity

The ASEBA problem items were chosen to describe behavioral and emotional problems that might be related to referral of subjects to mental health or other types of services. Content validity was demonstrated by significant differences between matched samples of clinically referred and nonreferred subjects for most problem items on each of the ASEBA forms. Referred children scored significantly higher than nonreferred children on 113 of 118 CBCL/4–18 problem items, 112 of 118 TRF items, 95 of 102 YSR items, 91 of 99 CBCL/1½–5 items, and 80 of 99 C-TRF items, as reported in the respective manuals. Because the items for allergies and asthma did not discriminate referred from nonreferred children, they are not included in the Total Problem scores for the CBCL/4–18 and YSR. All but 1 of the 105 YABCL and 110 YASR problem items discriminated clinically referred from nonreferred young adults.

Criterion-Related Validity

Criterion-related validity was tested by comparing matched samples of referred and nonreferred subjects on each of the CBCL/4–18, TRF, and YSR competence and problem scales (Achenbach, 1991b, 1991c, 1991d). Referred children scored significantly higher than nonreferred children on all CBCL/4–18 and YSR problem scales, and on all TRF problem scales except Somatic Complaints. Referred children scored significantly lower than nonreferred children on all CBCL/4–18 competence scales and all YSR competence scales except Activities. Referred children also scored lower than nonreferred children on the TRF academic performance and adaptive functioning scales. Referred preschool children scored significantly higher than nonreferred children on all CBCL/1½–5 and C-TRF problem scales (Achenbach & Rescorla,

2000). Referred young adults scored significantly higher than nonreferred young adults on all YABCL and YASR problem scales (Achenbach, 1997).

The criterion-related validity of the DOF was demonstrated in studies showing significant differences on DOF scales between children with behavioral disorders and matched controls in the same classroom (Reed & Edelbrock, 1983), between children with different behavior problem profile types (McConaughy et al., 1988), between teacher-identified children with attention-deficit/hyperactivity disorder (ADHD) and controls, and between ADHD Inattentive and Hyperactive/Impulsive subtypes (Skansgaard & Burns, 1998). The DOF also showed significant differences between children at-risk for behavioral or emotional problems whose parents and teachers participated in a primary prevention program and matched controls whose parents and teachers did not participate in the program (McConaughy, Kay, & Fitzgerald, 1999, 2000).

The criterion-related validity of the SCICA was tested by comparing demographically matched samples of referred and nonreferred children (McConaughy & Achenbach, 1994). Referred children scored significantly higher than nonreferred children on all SCICA scales except Anxious, for which $p = .09$. In addition, children classified as having emotional or behavioral disorders (EBD) requiring special education services scored significantly higher than matched nonreferred children on the SCICA Anxious/Depressed, Withdrawn, Attention Problems, Strange, and Resistant syndromes, as well as on Externalizing, Total Observations, and Total Self-Reports (McConaughy & Achenbach, 1996). Combinations of SCICA, CBCL/4–18, and TRF scales produced exceptionally high classification rates for children with EBD versus nonreferred children, with misclassifications of only 3 to 4% in discriminant analyses.

CLINICAL SIGNIFICANCE

Besides reliability and validity, it is important to consider the clinical utility of assessment procedures. ASEBA aims to document, sharpen, and standardize descriptions of children's functioning as seen by different informants. The quantification of descriptive data enables practitioners to determine the degree of deviance indicated by each informant's reports and to measure change from one occasion to another, such as from pre- to postintervention. Empirically based data can contribute directly to case formulations, the choice of interventions, and the evaluation of outcomes. A growing body of research has documented biological and psychological correlates of ASEBA syndromes (Achenbach & McConaughy, 1997). Numerous studies have also demonstrated the applicability of empirically based procedures to many kinds of behavioral, emotional, and medical conditions; types of interventions; and outcome evaluations. Berube and Achenbach (2000) list over 3500 publications that report use of ASEBA forms in 50 different countries. ASEBA forms have also been translated into 60 languages.

Empirically based assessment can help practitioners answer many kinds of questions that arise in contexts such as managed care, school settings, mental health services, residential treatment, child custody and placement decisions, evaluations of child abuse, and delinquency adjudications. Empirically based assessment is also applicable to behavioral and emotional functioning associated with illness, physical disabilities, and mild mental retardation. For example, a particular case may raise questions simultaneously about child custody, placement, abuse, and delinquency adjudication. Another case may involve a child who is ill, mentally retarded, and has a physical disability. Because it is seldom possible to understand a child's needs solely in terms of a single assessment question, ASEBA procedures can be integrated with other procedures to address multiple questions about children's functioning. Procedures, sequences of assessment, and integration of findings can then be tailored to specific questions that need to be answered, as discussed by Achenbach and McConaughy (1997).

Gender Differences

One important assessment-related question concerns possible differences in particular kinds of problems when they occur in males versus females. For several forms, ASEBA's gender-specific norms automatically take into account differences in problem and competence scores for males versus females. For example, males require higher raw scores than females to score in the borderline or clinically deviant ranges on the CBCL/4–18 Aggressive Behavior syndrome. This reflects the general tendency for males to show more aggressive behavior than females in normative samples. In contrast, the DSM-IV diagnosis of Conduct Disorder (CD) applies the same criteria equally to males and females, even though research has demonstrated significant gender differences for CD symptoms in nonreferred samples (Zoccolillo, 1993). On the CBCL/4–18, males also require higher raw scores than females to score in the borderline to clinical range on the Attention Problems syndrome. Females require higher raw scores than males to score in the borderline to clinical range on the Anxious/Depressed syndrome.

Long-Term versus Short-Term Problems

Another assessment-related question is whether a child's behavioral and emotional problems reflect chronic long-term patterns, or acute or transient short-term problems. Short-term problems may reflect developmental changes or situation-specific reactions. Distinguishing between long-term and short-term problems is often important for practitioners working in organizations that have long-term responsibilities to children, such as schools, health maintenance organizations (HMOs), or institutions. Such organizations need to tailor services depending on whether problems are acute or chronic. For example, research studies have suggested that adolescent-onset delinquent behavior may be specific to a particular developmental period and to particular environmental conditions (Moffitt, 1993). In contrast, aggressive behavior tends to be more stable and chronic across the life span (Achenbach, Howell, McConaughy, & Stanger, 1995a, 1995b; Stanger, Achenbach, & Verhulst, 1997).

Record reviews and parent interviews are often used to assess the duration of children's problems. In certain settings, ASEBA forms can also be administered over several intervals, such as every 2 months, 6 months, or 12 months, to assess whether problems are short-term or long-term. In mental health clinics and institutional settings, practitioners can administer ASEBA forms over regular intervals to monitor children's functioning during treatment. Similarly, ASEBA forms can be used to assess short- and long-term outcomes after termination of treatment or discharge from institutional placement. ASEBA forms can also be used to screen for behavioral and emotional problems at different intervals in settings such as schools and pediatric clinics.

Types of Interventions

Yet another assessment-related question is whether to implement interventions for identified problems on an individual basis (e.g., individual counseling), a small-group basis (e.g., small-group therapy for anxious children), or a large-group basis (e.g., social skills instruction). The ASEBA profiles can facilitate choices between individual and group interventions by helping practitioners identify children who all have similar problem patterns that can be addressed in group interventions. When children with similar profiles are identified in settings where group interventions are feasible, the profiles can guide the interventions. Following an intervention, the ASEBA forms can be readministered to evaluate outcomes by comparing the scale scores obtained by each child before and after the intervention. Settings that might utilize group interventions include schools, HMOs, residential treatment centers, psychiatric hospitals, and group homes.

When a child's adaptive functioning or home or school situation is very poor, questions arise about alternative placements. Along with information about the current environment, ASEBA profiles can be used to determine whether an individual's behavioral or emotional problems are severe enough to warrant alternative placements. Particular patterns of problems on the syndrome scale can also be examined to select placements that are best suited to a child's type of problems and treatment needs. This kind of information can be especially valuable in assessing needs for community mental health services, social services, and special education for emotional and behavioral problems.

Compatibility with Other Assessment Procedures

The ASEBA is compatible with other commonly used assessment procedures, including cognitive and achievement tests, family assessment, personality tests, developmental history interviews, medical examinations, and behavioral assessment. ASEBA forms can supplement other procedures with little cost or effort, while contributing data not likely to be obtained by other methods. Accordingly, Achenbach and McConaughy (1997) described a multiaxial model for assessment that includes parent reports, teacher reports, physical assessment, cognitive assessment, and direct assessment of the child. Various ASEBA forms are included in 3 of 5 assessment axes for different developmental age ranges.

COMMON PATTERNS AND INTERPRETATION

Syndrome Scales

Figure 10.1 shows the ADM-scored profile of syndrome scales for Sirena Johnson (not her real name) based on ratings by her mother on the CBCL/4–18. The profile displays each of the 8 CBCL/4–18 syndromes, with Internalizing syndromes on the left and Externalizing syndromes on the right side. Beneath the name for each syndrome is the total score (i.e., the raw sum of the "1" and "2" ratings for each item) followed by the T score and the percentile for the syndrome total score. Individual items that constitute the syndrome are listed below these three scores along with the rating for each item.

The profile also shows two broken lines that demarcate the borderline and clinical ranges for the syndrome scores. T scores from 67 (95th percentile) to 70 (98th percentile) are in the borderline clinical range, which indicates enough problems to be of concern, but not so many problems as to be clearly deviant from norms for the child's gender and age range. T scores above 70 are in the clinical range, which indicates clinical deviance from normative samples. To flag T scores that warrant attention, a "B" is printed to the right of scores in the borderline range and a "C" is printed to right of scores in the clinical range. Thus, according to the profile in Figure 10.1, Sirena scored in the borderline clinical range for Anxious/Depressed (T = 67) and Delinquent Behavior (T = 70), and in the clinical range for Aggressive Behavior (T = 82). This means that Sirena's mother was reporting more problems in these three areas than typically reported by parents of girls ages 12 to 18.

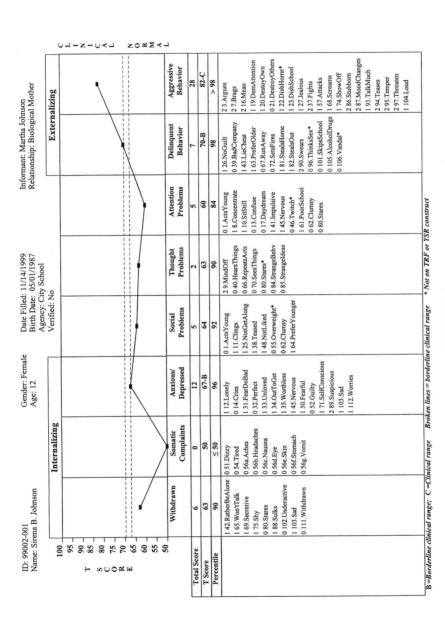

FIGURE 10.1

Windows-scored CBCL/4–18 syndrome profile for Sirena Johnson. From the CBCL/4–18-syndrome scale scores for girls aged 12–18. Copyright 1999 by T. M. Achenbach. Reprinted from permission of the author.

Total Problems, Internalizing, and Externalizing

In addition to the syndrome profile, the ADM produces a bar graph of the Total Problem, Internalizing, and Externalizing scores, as shown in Figure 10.2 for Sirena's CBCL/4–18. For these broad scales, T scores of 60 to 63 demarcate the borderline clinical range, while T scores above 63 demarcate the clinical range. As with the syndrome scales, broken lines on the profile show these cut points for the borderline and clinical ranges. These lower (less conservative) cut points are used for Total Problems, Internalizing, and Externalizing because these scales have more numerous and diverse items than do the syndrome scales. Figure 10.2 shows that Sirena scored in the borderline clinical range for Internalizing and in the clinical range for Externalizing and Total Problems compared to normative samples of girls ages 12 to 18. The right-hand side of the profile contains a list of other problems rated on the CBCL/4–18 that are not included in the syndrome scales. These other problems, except for Allergy and Asthma, are included in the Total Problems score.

Profile Types and Clinical T Scores

In the lower portion of the graphic display in Figure 10.2, scores for the CBCL/4–18 profile types are shown in boxes. The profile types are patterns that have been identified by cluster analyzing CBCL/4–18 profiles of syndrome scores obtained by children referred for mental health services (Achenbach, 1993). The left-hand box displays intraclass correlations (ICC) that indicate the degree to which an individual child's overall pattern of problems on the syndrome scales resembles profile types identified for the CBCL/4–18, TRF, and YSR. The right-hand box displays ICCs that indicate the degree to which a child's profile pattern resembles profile types that were identified only on the CBCL/4–18. An ICC above .444 indicates a significant association between an individual profile and a profile type. (An ICC of .444 is approximately equivalent to a Pearson r of .59.) With an ICC of .572, Sirena's CBCL/4–18 showed significant similarity to the Delinquent-Aggressive profile type.

Beneath the boxes that display the ICCs, the figure shows clinical T scores that indicate how Sirena's scores compare to large samples of *clinically referred* children of the same gender and age range. These scores, with a mean of 50 and standard deviation of 10, can be used to judge the similarity of a child's syndrome scale scores with scores from other clinically referred children. This is in contrast to the T scores in Figure 10.1 that compare the child's scores to normative samples. For Sirena, the clinical T scores indicated problems within 1 standard deviation of the means for clinical samples on 6 of 8 syndromes, but problems more than 1 standard deviation above the mean for Aggressive Behavior.

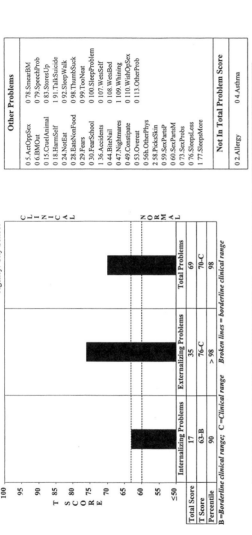

FIGURE 10.2

Windows-scored CBCL/4–18 Internalizing, Externalizing, and Total Problems profile for Sirena Johnson. From the CBCL/4–18-internalizing, externalizing, total problems, other problems, profile ICCs, & clinical T scores for girls aged 12–18. Copyright 1999 by T. M. Achenbach. Reprinted from permission of the author.

Other ASEBA Profiles

The ADM scoring system provides problem profiles similar to those shown in Figures 10.1 and 10.2 for each of the first 7 ASEBA forms listed in Table 10.1. In addition, profiles are provided for the CBCL/4–18 and YSR competence scales, the TRF academic performance and adaptive scales, and the YASR adaptive and substance use scales. Currently, computer-scored profiles for the DOF and SCICA are generated by separate DOS-based computer-scoring programs. An ADM module for the SCICA will be released in 2001.

ADVANTAGES AND DISADVANTAGES OF THE ASEBA

Advantages of ASEBA Forms and Profiles

The ASEBA offers several advantages for mental health providers, school psychologists, and other practitioners. First, the various rating forms provide quick and economical methods for obtaining information on children's competencies and problems. This efficiency in data gathering allows practitioners to devote more time to aspects of assessment that are not amenable to rating scales. For example, by having forms completed prior to interviews, practitioners can spend more time interviewing parents and teachers about aspects of their relationships and environments that may exacerbate or alleviate problems identified on the ASEBA forms. Second, the large pool of items on the ASEBA forms enables practitioners to assess a broad range of potential problems rather than focusing only on the most immediate or salient referral complaints. Third, the information obtained on the ASEBA forms is quantifiable and amenable to psychometric standards of reliability and validity, as discussed earlier. Fourth, the aggregation of individual items and scores into scales enables ASEBA users to organize diverse information into groupings of competencies and problem patterns. Fifth, the empirically based syndrome scales reflect patterns of co-occurring problems as reported by different types of informants. Sixth, the different but related ASEBA forms enable users to easily compare and integrate information reported by multiple informants across diverse situations.

Advantages of ASEBA ADM Software

The ADM modular software has several additional advantages for ASEBA users. First, the software provides improved, easy-to-read profiles, which can be output to a computer screen and to printers. Second, it produces narrative reports that can be imported to word processors and then integrated into user-generated documents. Importing the narrative reports can reduce the time required for writing psychological evaluation reports and clinical case notes. Computer-generated reports can also help guarantee accuracy in citing scores for the various ASEBA scales and interpreting levels of deviance. Third, the ADM software provides cross-informant comparisons for up to 8 ASEBA forms per person. The cross-informant comparisons are especially useful for integrating information from multiple perspectives, as discussed later in this article. Fourth, the software provides extra fields for adding the user's own variables and provides a database for automatically storing ASEBA data. Finally, in settings such as community mental health centers, hospitals, and large school districts, the ASEBA scan forms and client-entry program facilitate more efficient collection and storage of data.

Disadvantages of the ASEBA

Although the ASEBA offers many advantages to practitioners, it is also important to be aware of its limitations. One limitation is that the ASEBA is not designed to dictate specific forms of treatments or placement recommendations. This limitation applies to most other assessment procedures as well. ASEBA forms are designed to describe and quantify an individual's competencies and problems as reported by multiple informants. Practitioners must then integrate ASEBA data with other information to develop appropriate interventions.

A second limitation is that ASEBA syndrome or broad problem scores may not be as useful as direct observations for identifying specific target behaviors for individual behavioral intervention programs (BIP). For a BIP, direct observations and functional assessment are usually employed to identify and select a small number of specific behaviors that can be targeted in interventions (Kratochwill, Sheridan, & Lasecki, 1999; Nelson, Roberts, & Smith, 1998). However, high scores on certain ASEBA syndromes can pinpoint patterns of problems, such as attention problems or aggressive behavior, that warrant further behavioral assessment. Within these broad areas, practitioners can then focus direct observations and functional analysis on specific behaviors, such as failing to complete assignments or getting into fights. These specific behavior problems can then become targets for BIPs. To develop a BIP, baseline data are collected on each target behavior prior to an intervention. During and after interventions, additional data are obtained to measure changes in the target behaviors (for detailed discussions of observational techniques, functional analysis, and designing BIPs, see Kratochwill et al., 1999; McComas, Hoch, & Mace, 2000; Nelson et al., 1998).

Finally, as indicated earlier, ASEBA syndromes do not directly correspond to classification systems such as the DSM-IV, the ICD-10, or special education disability categories. While the lack of correspondence to categorical classifications might be considered a limitation, it also has the advantage of encouraging careful clinical thinking and integration of ASEBA data with other information for making diagnoses or disability determinations (see Achenbach & McConaughy, 1996; McConaughy, 1993b; McConaughy & Ritter, in press).

RECOMMENDATIONS AND CASE EXAMPLE

The case of 12-year-old Sirena Johnson, whose CBCL/4–18 profiles were shown earlier, illustrates the practical uses, interpretation, and integration of data from various ASEBA forms. Sirena was referred for a psychoeducational evaluation by her seventh-grade teachers who were concerned about her poor academic performance and possible emotional problems. When Sirena first arrived at Bailey Junior High School, she seemed shy and was hardly noticed. After her first month in school, however, her teachers began to worry about her appearance and attitude. Although she was an attractive girl, she often came to school in baggy, dirty clothes and seemed tired and "out of it." Sometimes she missed classes with no excuse from home. Other times she left classes complaining of headaches and stomachaches, for which the school nurse could find no medical causes. As time went on, Sirena became increasingly moody and defiant, especially when confronted about missing assignments. On some days, she exploded for no apparent reason, which led to detentions in the principal's office. Sirena seemed especially volatile in Mr. Marks's math class. She was more cooperative in Ms. Lee's English class, especially when she could choose her own reading materials and themes for writing assignments. When first-quarter grades were released, Sirena was failing or near-failing in 3 of her 5 courses. It was then that her teachers referred her to the school's multidisciplinary team (MDT) for a psychoeducational evaluation. After discussing the situation with the school psychologist, Sirena's mother, Martha Johnson, consented to the evaluation and agreed to complete the CBCL/4–18. Sirena's math and English teachers completed TRFs, and Sirena completed the YSR prior to an appointment with the school psychologist for a clinical interview and cognitive assessment. The special educator also administered individual achievement tests to assess her current academic performance.

Parent Report

Figures 10.1 and 10.2 showed the pattern of Sirena's problems, as reported by her mother on the CBCL/4–18. The profiles indicated severe internalizing and externalizing problems, with borderline clinical scores on the Anxious/Depressed and Delinquent Behavior syndromes and a clinical range score on the Aggressive Behavior syndrome. On the CBCL/4–18 competence scales (not shown in the figures), Sirena scored in the normal range on the Activities scale, in the clinical range on the Social scale, and in the borderline range on the School scale. Her Total Competence score was in the clinical range. On the competence scales, low scores indicate poor functioning, whereas on the problem scales, high scores indicate poor functioning. (For Total Competence, T scores from 37 to 40 [10th to 16th percentiles] are in the borderline range and T scores below 37 [below the 10th percentile] are in the clinical range. For the Activities, Social, and School scales, T scores of 30 to 33 [2nd to 5th percentiles] are in the borderline range and T scores below 30 are in the clinical range [below the 2nd percentile].) Ms. Johnson reported that although Sirena liked some sports and performed some chores at home, she had no hobbies, belonged to no social organizations, had only one close friend, and did things with friends outside of school less than once a week. Ms. Johnson's ratings of Sirena's school performance were also low, consistent with reports of poor grades from her teachers.

Teacher Reports

On their TRFs, Mr. Marks and Ms. Lee both scored Sirena in the clinical range for Adaptive Functioning (T < 37; < 10th percentile), reflecting low ratings of how hard she was working, how appropriately she was behaving, how much she was learning, and how happy she was compared to typical pupils in the same classes. On the TRF problem scales, Mr. Marks's ratings produced Total Problems, Internalizing, and Externalizing scores in the clinical range, while Ms. Lee's ratings produced a clinical range score for Internalizing and borderline clinical scores for Externalizing and Total Problems. On the TRF syndrome scales, both Mr. Marks and Ms. Lee scored Sirena in the borderline clinical range for Somatic Complaints and Anxious/Depressed, while Mr. Marks also scored her in the borderline clinical range for Delinquent Behavior and Aggressive Behavior. These results indicated that both teachers reported more internalizing problems than are typically reported by teachers of girls ages 12 to 18, but that Mr. Marks reported more severe externalizing problems than Ms. Lee. Both teachers scored Sirena below clinical cut points on the TRF Attention Problems syndrome and the Inattention and Hyperactive/Impulsive subscales, indicating that Sirena was not manifesting unusually high attention problems.

Sirena's Self-Ratings

On the YSR, Sirena's ratings of her competencies produced clinical range scores on the Total Competence and Social scales, but a normal range score on the Activities scale. These YSR scores were similar to the competence scores obtained from Ms. Johnson's CBCL/4–18. On the YSR problem scales, Sirena's self-ratings produced a clinical range score for Externalizing, but normal range scores for Internalizing and Total Problems. Sirena scored herself in the clinical range on the Delinquent Behavior scale and in the borderline clinical range on the Aggressive Behavior scale. These high scores indicated that Sirena acknowledged more delinquent and aggressive behavior than is typical for 11- to 18-year-old girls. Sirena's scores on all other YSR scales were in the normal range, although she did endorse several items on the Anxious/Depressed scale as "sometimes or somewhat true," including I *think about killing myself*. She also scored I *worry a lot* as "very true or often true."

Cross-Informant Comparisons

To provide a visual comparison of profile scores from multiple informants, the ADM computer program prints side-by-side scores for each of the 89 items that are similar across the CBCL/4–18, TRF, and YSR syndrome scales. Figure 10.3 shows the item comparisons for Ms. Johnson's CBCL/4–18, the TRFs completed by Sirena's teachers, and Sirena's YSR. By examining the cross-informant printout, the practitioner can quickly identify the items on which most informants agree and those on which reports vary. For Sirena, the school psychologist could see that all four informants, including Sirena, endorsed 6 items on the Aggressive Behavior scale (argues, demands attention, mood changes, talks too much, teases, and temper). However, Ms. Lee (TRF2) reported fewer problems on the Aggressive Behavior scale than the other informants. In addition, Ms. Johnson and both teachers endorsed 6 items on the Anxious/Depressed scale (lonely, feels worthless, nervous, fearful, self-conscious, and sad), while Sirena endorsed 4 of these same problems plus others on the same scale. Headaches, nausea, and stomachaches on the Somatic Complaints scale were reported by the two teachers and Sirena, but not Ms. Johnson.

In addition to the item-by-item comparisons, the ADM program computes and prints Q correlations between scores by pairs of informants on the 89 common items, as shown in Figure 10.4. The correlations obtained for each pair of informants are then compared to correlations obtained for large reference samples of the same types of informants—for example, pairs of parents and teachers. As shown in Figure 10.4, the printout indicates whether the correlations obtained for each informant pair were below average, average, or above average compared to the reference group. Using this information, the school psychologist could see that although the four informants did not always score each item the same way, their level of agreement was generally average to above average compared to reference samples of similar informant pairs.

Figure 10.5 shows the ADM printout of bar graph comparisons for Sirena's total scores on each of the 8 syndrome scales. This display makes it easy for practitioners to compare scale scores across informants. Figure 10.5 shows that Sirena's teachers were the only ones to score her in the borderline clinical range for Somatic Complaints, but that her teachers and her mother

ID: 99002   Name: Sirena B. Johnson   Gender: Female   Birth Date: 05/01/1987   Comparison Date: 10/15/1999

Form	Eval ID	Age	Informant	Relationship	Date
CBC1	001	12	Martha Johnson	Biological Mother	11/14/1999
TRF2	002	12	Marion Lee	Classroom Teacher (F)	11/16/1999
TRF3	003	12	Andrew Marks	Classroom Teacher (M)	11/15/1999
YSR4	004	12	Self	Self	11/14/1999

Form	Eval ID	Age	Informant	Relationship	Date

CBC TRF TRF YSR

I. Withdrawn

Item	1	2	3	4	5	6	7	8
42.RatherBeAlone	1	0	0	0				
65.Won'tTalk	1	0	0	0				
69.Secretive	1	0	0	2				
75.Shy	1	0	1	0				
102.NoEnergy	0	1	1	0				
103.Sad	0	1	2	0				
111.Withdrawn	0	0	0	1				

II. Somatic Complaints

Item	1	2	3	4	5	6	7	8
51.Dizzy	0	0	0	0				
54.Tired	0	0	0	0				
56a.Aches	0	0	0	0				
56b.Headaches	0	1	1	1				
56c.Nausea	0	0	0	0				
56d.Eye	0	0	0	0				
56e.Skin	0	0	0	0				
56f.Stomach	0	1	1	1				
56g.Vomit	0	0	0	0				

III. Anxious/Depressed

Item	1	2	3	4	5	6	7	8
12.Lonely	1	1	1	1				
14.Cries	0	0	0	1				
31.FearDoBad	1	0	0	1				
32.Perfect	0	0	0	1				
33.Unloved	1	0	1	0				
34.OutToGet	0	1	1	1				
35.Worthless	1	1	1	1				
45.Nervous	1	2	2	0				
50.Fearful	1	1	1	0				
52.Guilty	0	0	1	0				
71.SelfConscious	1	0	2	1				
89.Suspicious	2	0	1	0				
103.Sad	1	1	1	0				
112.Worries	1	1	0	0				

CBC TRF TRF YSR

IV. Social Problems

Item	1	2	3	4	5	6	7	8
1.ActsYoung	0	0	1	0				
11.Dependent	1	2	1	0				
25.NotGetAlong	1	1	1	0				
38.Teased	1	0	0	0				
48.NotLiked	0	0	0	0				
62.Clumsy	0	0	0	0				
64.PreferYounger	1	0	0	1				

V. Thought Problems

Item	1	2	3	4	5	6	7	8
9.MindOff	2	0	1	0				
40.HearsThings	0	0	0	0				
66.RepeatsActs	0	0	0	0				
70.SeesThings	0	1	0	0				
84.StrangeBehav	0	0	0	0				
85.StrangeIdeas	0	0	0	0				

VI. Attention Problems

Item	1	2	3	4	5	6	7	8
1.ActsYoung	0	0	0	0				
8.Concentrate	1	0	0	1				
10.SitStill	1	0	0	0				
13.Confuse	0	0	0	0				
17.Daydream	0	0	0	0				
41.Impulsive	1	0	0	1				
45.Nervous	1	2	2	0				
61.PoorSchool	1	2	0	0				
62.Clumsy	0	0	0	0				

VII. Delinquent Behavior

Item	1	2	3	4	5	6	7	8
26.NoGuilt	1	1	2	1				
39.BadCompany	0	1	1	1				
43.LieCheat	1	0	0	0				
63.PreferOlder	1	0	0	2				
82.StealsOther	1	0	0	0				
90.Swears	2	0	1	2				
101.SkipSchool	0	0	0	1				
105.AlcoholDrugs	0	0	0	0				

CBC TRF TRF YSR

VIII. Aggressive Behavior

Item	1	2	3	4	5	6	7	8
3.Argues	2	1	1	2				
7.Brags	2	0	1	0				
16.Mean	2	0	1	0				
19.DemAttention	1	0	2	1				
20.DestroyOwn	0	0	0	0				
21.DestroyOther	0	0	0	1				
23.DisobeySchool	0	1	0	1				
27.Jealous	1	0	1	0				
37.Fights	2	0	0	0				
57.Attacks	1	0	0	2				
68.Screams	1	0	0	2				
74.ShowOff	2	0	2	2				
86.Stubborn	2	1	2	1				
87.MoodChanges	2	1	2	1				
93.TalkMuch	1	1	1	1				
94.Teases	2	1	2	2				
95.Temper	2	1	2	2				
97.Threaten	2	1	1	1				
104.Loud	1	1	0	2				

Other Problems

Item	1	2	3	4	5	6	7	8
5.ActOppSex	0	0	0	0				
18.HarmSelf	0	0	0	0				
29.Fears	0	0	0	0				
30.FearSchool	1	0	0	0				
36.Accidents	1	0	0	0				
44.BiteNail	0	0	0	0				
46.Twitch	0	2	0	0				
55.Overweight	0	0	0	-				
58.PicksSkin	2	0	0	0				
79.SpeechProb	0	0	0	0				
83.StoresUp	0	0	0	0				
91.ThinksSuicide	0	0	0	1				
96.ThinksSex	0	0	0	0				
99.TooNeat	0	0	0	0				

{F}=Female {M}=Male

FIGURE 10.3

Windows-scored cross-informant comparisons of problem item scores for Sirena Johnson. From the cross-informant comparison-problem items common to the CBCL/TRF/YSR. Copyright 1999 by T. M. Achenbach, University of Vermont, 1 South Prospect St., Burlington, VT 05401-3456, http://Checklist.uvm.edu. Reprinted from permission of the author.

Q Correlations Between Item Scores							
		Cross-Informant	Q	Reference Group			
Forms	Informants	Agreement	Corr	25th %ile	Mean	75th %ile	
CBC1 x TRF2	Biological Mother x Classroom Teacher {F}	Average	0.13	0.07	0.19	0.30	
CBC1 x TRF3	Biological Mother x Classroom Teacher {M}	Above average	0.43	0.07	0.19	0.30	
CBC1 x YSR4	Biological Mother x Self	Average	0.34	0.22	0.33	0.43	
TRF2 x TRF3	Classroom Teacher {F} x Classroom Teacher {M}	Above average	0.65	0.29	0.43	0.58	
TRF2 x YSR4	Classroom Teacher {F} x Self	Average	0.10	0.08	0.17	0.26	
TRF3 x YSR4	Classroom Teacher {M} x Self	Above average	0.29	0.08	0.17	0.26	

FIGURE 10.4

Cross-informant correlations for Sirena Johnson. Copyright 1999 by T. M. Achenbach. Reprinted from permission of the author.

scored her in the borderline clinical range for Anxious/Depressed. Ratings by Sirena, Ms. Johnson, and Mr. Marks also produced high scores on Delinquent Behavior and Aggressive Behavior, whereas Ms. Lee's ratings were much lower on these scales. The ADM cross-informant program also prints a separate bar graph display for cross-informant comparisons of Internalizing, Externalizing, and Total Problems scores plus the ICCs for the cross-informant profile types (not shown). Along with the visual displays of syndrome profiles for each ASEBA form, the cross-informant bar graphs can be especially useful for presenting and summarizing evaluation results in MDT meetings.

Clinical Interview with Sirena

The school psychologist administered the SCICA to further assess Sirena's emotional and behavioral functioning and her own views of her problems, feelings, and life circumstances. Sirena was generally cooperative during the SCICA and answered most questions, though she was initially reluctant to discuss her feelings. As the interview progressed, she became more open, acknowledging feelings of worthlessness, worrying about her poor school performance, and feeling sad and lonely much of the time. She was candid about getting into trouble at school and sometimes in the community. She reported frequent arguments with her mother and with her math teacher, Mr. Marks, whom she felt did not like her. She also reported associating with kids in the neighborhood who shoplifted, but felt that she had no real close friends and seemed unsure of how to make friends. For much of the SCICA, Sirena appeared sad and apathetic, though her mood brightened when she discussed her interests in animals and natural science. She was occasionally restless and fidgeted with her clothing, but her conversation was generally logical and coherent.

On the SCICA profile, Sirena scored above the 80th percentile for self-reported problems on the Anxious/Depressed and Aggressive Behavior

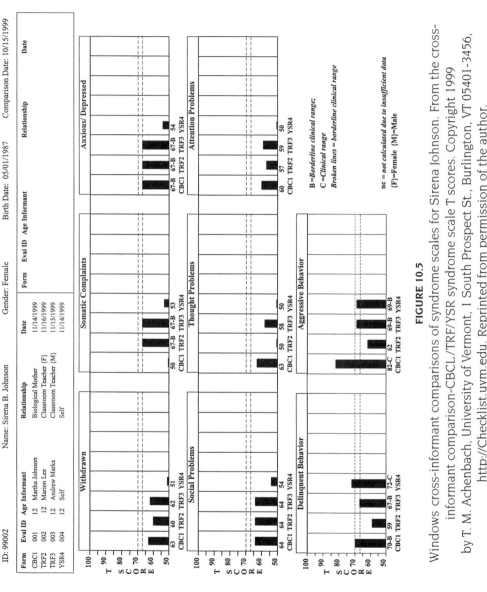

FIGURE 10.5

Windows cross-informant comparisons of syndrome scales for Sirena Johnson. From the cross-informant comparison-CBCL/TRF/YSR syndrome scale T scores. Copyright 1999 by T. M. Achenbach, University of Vermont, 1 South Prospect St., Burlington, VT 05401-3456, http://Checklist.uvm.edu. Reprinted from permission of the author.

syndromes. Since SCICA scores are based on a clinical sample rather than a normative sample, Sirena's high scores on these two scales indicated more problems than most other clinically referred 6- to 12-year-old children. Sirena scored near the 50th percentile on the SCICA Family Problems, Attention Problems, and Withdrawn syndromes, indicating problems typical of other clinically referred children. Much lower scores on the SCICA Anxious, Strange, and Resistant syndromes indicated fewer problems on these scales than most other clinically referred children.

Conclusions and Recommendations for Sirena

Cognitive testing indicated that Sirena had average overall intelligence, but high average verbal ability. Individual achievement testing indicated low average to average academic skills. The tests revealed no signs of specific learning disabilities that might account for Sirena's poor performance in school, although she lacked some basic math skills. In contrast, the combined results from the various ASEBA profiles indicated severe emotional and behavioral problems compared to normative and clinical samples. The ASEBA profiles were especially useful in demonstrating the severity of Sirena's internalizing problems, as well as her highly aggressive behavior.

Based on the results of the comprehensive evaluation, the MDT recommended that Sirena and Ms. Johnson seek individual and family counseling from the local community mental health agency. In addition, the MDT determined that Sirena qualified for special education services under the IDEA category of emotional disturbance (ED). A behavioral incentive plan was initiated at school, along with remedial services in math and accommodations in other classes to improve homework completion. A behavior modification program, coordinated between home and school, was also implemented to reduce aggressive behavior.

Sirena's low scores on the CBCL/4–18 and YSR Social scale suggested limited social involvement. Her teachers and mother all reported that she did not get along with other children. To address these problems, Sirena was enrolled in small-group sessions, led by the school psychologist, that focused on coping strategies and making friends with nondelinquent peers. The MDT also capitalized on Sirena's love for animals by arranging an after-school job at the local humane society. With the agreement of Ms. Johnson, the MDT planned to administer the CBCL/4–18, two TRFs, and the YSR again at the end of the school year to evaluate Sirena's progress.

INSIGHTS FROM EXPERIENCE

Special Education Evaluations of ED

The example of Sirena Johnson illustrated the use of ASEBA forms in a case that originated from teacher referrals for a psychoeducational evaluation. In school settings, the ASEBA forms can be used to evaluate emotional and behavioral problems as well as adaptive functioning and social competencies. The ASEBA forms are particularly useful for special education evaluations of ED, as defined in the IDEA (Achenbach & McConaughy, 1997; McConaughy, 1993a, 1993b; McConaughy & Achenbach, 1999; McConaughy & Ritter, in press). The IDEA specifies the following characteristics as indicative of ED: (a) an inability to learn that cannot be explained by intellectual, sensory, or other health factors; (b) an inability to build or maintain satisfactory interpersonal relationships with peers or teachers; (c) inappropriate types of behavior or feelings under normal circumstances; (d) a general pervasive mood of unhappiness or depression; or (e) a tendency to develop physical symptoms or fears associated with personal or school problems. To qualify as having ED, a child must show 1 or more of these 5 characteristics, and there must be evidence that the characteristic(s) has been exhibited over a long period of time and to a marked degree, and adversely affects educational performance.

Along with other data, scores on the ASEBA profiles can be used to assess whether a child's patterns of problems fits the IDEA definition of ED. For example, borderline to clinical range scores on the CBCL/4–18, TRF, and/or YSR Anxious/Depressed syndromes would show supporting evidence of the ED characteristic, a pervasive mood of unhappiness, especially if most informants endorsed items such as Unhappy, sad, or depressed and Feels worthless, as was true in Sirena's case. Similarly, borderline to clinical range scores on the Withdrawn and Social Problems syndromes would show supporting evidence of the ED characteristic, inability to build or maintain relationships, while borderline to clinical range scores on the Aggressive Behavior syndrome would show evidence of inappropriate behavior or feelings under normal circumstances.

After identifying particular patterns of problems that are characteristic of ED, the practitioner can use ASEBA norms and the borderline and clinical cut points to judge whether the problems meet the IDEA severity criterion of marked degree. Finally, low scores on the CBCL/4–18 School scale, TRF Adaptive Functioning, TRF Academic Performance, and low DOF on-task scores can be combined with findings from academic assessment to demonstrate whether the child's emotional and behavioral problems are having adverse effects on educational performance.

Assessment of ADHD

The ASEBA forms, along with other procedures such as structured diagnostic interviews, can be very useful in assessment of ADHD, as defined by the DSM-IV. The ASEBA Attention Problems scale contains many items similar to the symptoms of inattention and hyperactivity/impulsivity required for DSM-IV diagnoses of ADHD. In addition, the TRF Inattention and Hyperactivity-Impulsivity subscales provide scores that can be used in conjunction with other data to judge whether children exhibit the Inattentive,

Hyperactive-Impulsive, or Combined type of ADHD (Achenbach, 1996; Achenbach & McConaughy, 1997). As with evaluation of ED, the norms and cut points on the ASEBA syndromes facilitate judgments about the severity of attention problems, as reported by parents and teachers.

The ASEBA Attention Problems scores can be integrated with symptom reports from structured diagnostic interviews and other test data to formulate a diagnosis of ADHD and its subtypes. Thus, while the ASEBA Attention Problems syndrome is not synonymous with the DSM-IV diagnosis of ADHD, it can add important normative information, obtained efficiently and at low cost, for making such a diagnosis (for details of ADHD assessment, see Barkley, 1990 and DuPaul & Stoner, 1994). Likewise, scores on other ASEBA syndromes can facilitate DSM-IV diagnoses that are descriptively similar, such as ASEBA Anxious/Depressed scores for DSM-IV diagnoses of Dysthymia or Major Depression, and ASEBA Aggressive Behavior and Delinquent Behavior scores for diagnoses of conduct disorder or oppositional defiant disorder (Achenbach & McConaughy, 1996).

Screening for Problems and Communication among Professionals

The ASEBA forms can also be used to screen for emotional and behavioral problems even when such problems are not the stated reason for referral. For example, when a teacher refers a child for evaluation of learning disabilities, the TRF can be used to screen for other problems such as anxiety, attention problems, depression, social problems, or aggressive behavior. If some TRF problem scores fall in the borderline or clinical range, then the evaluation plan can be broadened to include the CBCL/4–18, YSR, DOF, and/or the SCICA, as deemed appropriate.

Because the ASEBA forms are widely used by mental health and medical practitioners as well as school practitioners, they can facilitate communication across these professions. The profiles scored from the ASEBA forms provide a common language among professional groups who use them. For example, in Sirena Johnson's case, the school psychologist who conducted her initial psychological evaluation could forward scored ASEBA profiles (with appropriate consent) to professionals in the community mental health center who were to provide individual and family interventions. Various professionals involved in a case can also use follow-up ASEBA profiles to communicate with each other about changes in an individual's functioning, as discussed below.

Evaluation of Progress and Outcomes

After appropriate periods of time, the ASEBA forms can be readministered to monitor progress and evaluate individual outcomes. By comparing broad scores and syndrome scores from Time 1 to Time 2, the practitioner can determine specific areas where problems have declined and other areas where they may have remained the same or increased. These comparisons can help determine where interventions need to be altered to produce desired results. Similar changes in competence or adaptive scores can be used to target areas of strength. After interventions have been completed, the ASEBA forms can be administered again in several months to assess outcomes. High problem scores on outcome evaluations may indicate need for further or different interventions.

Mental health and school professionals may also be involved in evaluating the effects of particular programs on groups of clients as well as on individual clients. The ASEBA forms can easily be incorporated into plans for group outcome evaluation, as has been done in some large mental health programs (e.g., Greenbaum et al., 1996). To conduct program evaluations, it is important to assess clients' preservice functioning as well as to examine scores for functioning after implementation of services. ASEBA forms can be used for both pre- and postassessment. To determine whether any improvements in scores can be attributed to the program itself, it is also important to assess a comparison group of clients who did not receive the program or who received a different program. Comparison of pre- and posttreatment scores on the ASEBA scales can then determine whether those who received Program A improved more than those who received Program B or no service. Because long-term effects of certain interventions may differ from immediate effects, it is desirable to repeat the ASEBA at longer intervals to determine if initial improvements continue. McConaughy, Kay, and Fitzgerald (1999, 2000) described this approach in their evaluation of 1- and 2-year outcomes of a school-based prevention program for elementary-aged children at-risk for emotional and behavioral problems.

CONCLUSION

The ASEBA is a family of standardized rating forms for evaluating an individual's problems and competencies, assessed from multiple perspectives. Because an individual's behavior is likely to vary from one situation to another, no one perspective can completely capture the full range of functioning. The ASEBA thus offers practitioners cost-effective forms for multi-perspective assessment, as well as empirically based scoring profiles for organizing assessment information. The ADM computer-scoring programs and modules offer additional methods for comparing information across informants and producing narrative reports that can be imported into evaluation reports. The well-demonstrated reliability and validity of the ASEBA warrants confidence in individual assessment findings. In addition, a vast ASEBA research base of over 3500 studies in 50 countries has enriched our understanding of the patterns and developmental course of psychopathology from early childhood through the transition to young adulthood.

References

Achenbach, T. M. (1986). *Direct Observation Form of the Child Behavior Checklist* (Rev. ed.). Burlington, VT: University of Vermont, Department of Psychiatry.

Achenbach, T. M. (1991a). *Integrative guide for the 1991 CBCL/4–18, YSR, and TRF profiles*. Burlington, VT: University of Vermont, Department of Psychiatry.

Achenbach, T. M. (1991b). *Manual for the Child Behavior Checklist/4–18 and 1991 Profile*. Burlington, VT: University of Vermont, Department of Psychiatry.

Achenbach, T. M. (1991c). *Manual for the Teacher's Report Form and 1991 Profile*. Burlington, VT: University of Vermont, Department of Psychiatry.

Achenbach, T. M. (1991d). *Manual for the Youth Self-Report Form and 1991 Profile*. Burlington, VT: University of Vermont Department of Psychiatry.

Achenbach, T. M. (1993). *Empirically based taxonomy: How to use the syndromes and profile types derived from the CBCL/4–18, TRF, and YSR*. Burlington, VT: University of Vermont, Department of Psychiatry.

Achenbach, T. M. (1996). Subtyping ADHD: A request for suggestions about relating empirically based assessment to DSM-IV. In R. Barkley (Ed.), ADHD *Report, 4*, 5–9.

Achenbach, T. M. (1997). *Manual for the Young Adult Self-Report and Young Adult Behavior Checklist*. Burlington, VT: University of Vermont, Department of Psychiatry.

Achenbach, T. M., Howell, C. T., McConaughy, S. H., & Stanger, C. (1995a). Six-year predictors of problems in a national sample: I. Cross-informant syndromes. *Journal of the American Academy of Child and Adolescent Psychiatry, 34*, 336–347.

Achenbach, T. M., Howell, C. T., McConaughy, S. H., & Stanger, C. (1995b). Six-year predictors of problems in a national sample: III. Transitions to young adult syndromes. *Journal of the American Academy of Child and Adolescent Psychiatry, 34*, 658–669.

Achenbach, T. M., & McConaughy, S. H. (1996). Relations between DSM-IV and empirically based assessment. *School Psychology Review, 25*, 330–342.

Achenbach, T. M., & McConaughy, S. H. (1997). *Empirically based assessment of child and adolescent psychopathology: Practical applications*. Thousand Oaks, CA: Sage.

Achenbach, T. M., McConaughy, S. H., & Howell, C. T. (1987). Child/adolescent behavioral and emotional problems: Implications of cross-informant correlations for situational specificity. *Psychological Bulletin, 101*, 213–232.

Achenbach, T. M., & Rescorla, L. A. (2000). *Manual for the ASEBA Preschool Forms and Profiles*. Burlington, VT: University of Vermont, Department of Psychiatry.

American Psychiatric Association. (1994). *Diagnostic and statistical manual for mental disorders* (4th ed.). Washington, DC: Author.

Barkley, R. A. (1990). *Attention Deficit Hyperactivity Disorder: A handbook for diagnosis and treatment*. New York: Guilford.

Berube, R., & Achenbach, T. M. (2000). *Bibliography of published studies using the Child Behavior Checklist and related materials: 2000 edition*. Burlington, VT: University of Vermont, Department of Psychiatry.

DuPaul, G. J., & Stoner, G. (1994). *ADHD in the schools: Assessment and intervention strategies*. New York: Guilford.

Greenbaum, P. E., Dedrick, R. F., Friedman, R. M., Kutash, K., Brown, E. C., Lardieri, S. P., & Pugh, A. M. (1996). National Adolescent and Child Treatment Study (NACTS): Outcomes for children with serious emotional and behavioral disturbance. *Journal of Emotional and Behavioral Disorders, 4*, 130–146.

Individuals with Disabilities Education Act. (1990). Pub. L. No. 101-476, 20 U.S.C. § 1401 *et seq.* (Reauthorized 1997, July). 20 U.S.C. § 1400 *et seq.*

Jensen, P., Roper, M., Fisher, P., Piacentini, J., Canino, G., Richters, J., Rubio-Stipec, M., Dulcan, M., Goodman, S., Davies, M., Rae, D., Shaffer, D., Bird, H., Lahey, B., & Schwab-Stone, M. (1995). Test-retest reliability of the Diagnostic Interview Schedule for Children (ver. 2.1): Parent, child, and combined algorithms. *Archives of General Psychiatry, 52*, 61–71.

Kasius, M. (1997). *Interviewing children: Development of the Dutch version of the Semistructured Clinical Interview for Children and Adolescents and testing of the psychometric properties.* Rotterdam, The Netherlands: Erasmus University.

Kratochwill, T., Sheridan, S. M., & Lasecki, K. L. (1999). Advances in behavioral assessment. In C. R. Reynolds & T. B. Gutkin (Eds.), *The handbook of school psychology* (3rd ed., pp. 350–382). New York: Wiley.

McComas, J. J., Hoch, H., & Mace, F. C. (2000). Functional analysis. In E. Shapiro & T. Kratochwill (Eds.), *Conducting school-based assessments of child and adolescent behavior* (pp. 78–120). New York: Guilford.

McConaughy, S. H. (1993a). Advances in empirically based assessment of children's behavioral and emotional problems. *School Psychology Review, 22*, 285–307.

McConaughy, S. H. (1993b). Evaluating behavioral and emotional disorders with the CBCL, TRF, and YSR cross-informant scales. *Journal of Emotional and Behavioral Disorders, 1*, 40–52.

McConaughy, S. H. (1996). The interview process. In M. Breen & C. Fiedler (Eds.), *Behavioral approach to the assessment of youth with emotional/behavioral disorders: A handbook for school-based practitioners* (pp. 181–223). Austin, TX: PRO-ED.

McConaughy, S. H. (2000). Self-report: Child clinical interviews. In E. Shapiro & T. Kratochwill (Eds.), *Conducting school-based assessments of child and adolescent behavior* (pp. 170–202). New York: Guilford.

McConaughy, S. H., & Achenbach, T. M. (1994). *Manual for the Semistructured Clinical Interview for Children and Adolescents.* Burlington, VT: University of Vermont Department of Psychiatry.

McConaughy, S. H., & Achenbach, T. M. (1996). Contributions of a child interview to multimethod assessment of children with EBD and LD. *School Psychology Review, 25*, 24–39.

McConaughy, S. H., & Achenbach, T. M. (1999). Contributions of developmental psychopathology to school psychology. In T. Gutkin & C. Reynolds (Eds.), *The handbook of school psychology* (3rd ed., pp. 247–270). New York: Wiley.

McConaughy, S. H., Achenbach, T. M., & Gent, C. L. (1988). Multiaxial empirically based assessment: Parent, teacher, observational, cognitive, and personality correlates of Child Behavior Profiles for 6–11-year-old boys. *Journal of Abnormal Child Psychology, 16*, 485–509.

McConaughy, S. H., Kay, P., & Fitzgerald, M. (1998). Preventing SED through Parent-Teacher Action Research and social skills instruction: First year outcomes. *Journal of Emotional and Behavioral Disorders, 6*, 81–93.

McConaughy, S. H., Kay, P., & Fitzgerald, M. (1999). The Achieving Behaving Caring Project for preventing ED: Two-year outcomes. *Journal of Emotional and Behavioral Disorders, 7*, 224–239.

McConaughy, S. H., Kay, P., & Fitzgerald, M. (2000). How long is long enough? Outcomes for a school-based prevention project. *Exceptional Children, 67*, 21–34.

McConaughy, S. H., & Ritter, D. (in press). Multidimensional assessment of emotional and behavioral disorders. In A. Thomas & J. Grimes (Eds.), *Best practices in school psychology—IV.* Washington, DC: National Association of School Psychologists.

Moffitt, T. E. (1993). "Life-course persistent" and "adolescence-limited" antisocial behavior: A developmental taxonomy. *Psychological Review, 100*, 674–701.

Nelson, J. R., Roberts, M. L., & Smith, D. J. (1998). *Conducting functional behavioral assessments.* Longmont, CO: Sopris West.

Reed, M. L., & Edelbrock, C. (1983). Reliability and validity of the Direct Observation Form of the Child Behavior Checklist. *Journal of Abnormal Child Psychology, 11*, 521–530.

Skansgaard, E. P., & Burns, G. L. (1998). Comparison of DSM-IV ADHD Combined and Predominantly Inattention Types: Correspondence between teacher ratings and direct observations of inattentive, hyperactivity/impulsivity, slow cognitive tempo, oppositional defiant, and overt conduct disorder symptoms. *Child and Family Behavior Therapy, 20*, 1–14.

Stanger, C., Achenbach, T. M., & Verhulst, F. C. (1997). Accelerated longitudinal comparisons of aggressive versus delinquent syndromes. *Developmental Psychopathology, 9*, 43–58.

World Health Organization. (1992). *Mental disorders: Glossary and guide to their classification in accordance with the Tenth Revision of the International Classification of Diseases* (10th ed.). Geneva: Author.

Zoccolillo, M. (1993). Gender and the development of conduct disorder. *Development and Psychopathology, 5*, 65–78.

CHAPTER

11

Assessment of Social Skills in Children and Adolescents

FRANK M. GRESHAM
University of California–Riverside

Few people would question the importance of social competence in the overall development and adjustment of children and adolescents. The ability to interact successfully with peers and significant adults is one of the most important aspects of a child's development. Moreover, the degree to which children and youth are able to establish and maintain satisfactory interpersonal relationships, gain peer acceptance, make friendships, and terminate negative or pernicious interpersonal relationships defines social competence and predicts adequate long-term psychological and social adjustment (Kupersmidt, Coie, & Dodge, 1990; Parker & Asher, 1987).

Social competence is also important because it is a component in the development of a variety of childhood disorders such as oppositional, defiant, and conduct disorders. For example, the development of oppositional, defiant, and antisocial behavior begins early in life and is stable over time (Kazdin, 1987). Oleweus (1979) found that aggressive antisocial behavior was as stable as measures of intelligence over 1-year ($r = .76$) and 5-year ($r = .69$) intervals for boys with antisocial behavior patterns. Developmentally, antisocial behavior begins early in life (2–3 years) and continues throughout the school years (Patterson, DeBaryshe, & Ramsey, 1989). School entry is a particularly critical period for children having early-onset difficulties in social behavior. Reid and Patterson (1991) suggested that many children exhibiting antisocial behavior patterns before school entry will continue coercive and aggressive behavior patterns with peers and teachers upon school entry and beyond. Without early identification and intervention, this behavior pattern will be maintained throughout their school careers and into adulthood. When children come to school with an oppositional, antisocial style of interacting, they fail to acquire and perform appropriate social skills in school and other settings.

Additionally, social competence is important for students demonstrating significant deficits or delays in cognitive, academic, and emotional/behavioral functioning. Such students may be classified into one of several so-called high-incidence disability groups specified in the Individuals with Disabilities Education Act (IDEA, 1997). These groups include students with specific learning disabilities, emotional disturbance, mild mental retardation, and attention-deficit/hyperactivity disorder (ADHD), all of whom are eligible for special education and related services as "Other Health Impaired" or under Section 504 of the Rehabilitation Act of 1973.

Psychologists, special educators, and other professionals who deal with children and youth on a consistent basis clearly require the knowledge and ability to conceptualize and assess social skills. This chapter presents readers with practical information and strategies for the conceptualization and assessment of social skills in children and youth. Before discussing specific assessment instruments and procedures, this chapter provides a brief discussion of the theoretical and empirical background on social competence. The theoretical work discussed has guided much of the development of assessment instrumentation. This chapter also includes some common patterns of social skills functioning and interpretative hypotheses of these patterns. Finally, a case study illustrates the assessment of social skills and gives intervention recommendations based on this assessment information.

THEORETICAL AND EMPIRICAL FOUNDATIONS

Definitional Issues

A recent comprehensive review of definitions of social skills by Merrell and Gimpel (1998) indicated that there were 15 definitions that have been used in the literature. Gresham (1986, 1998a) suggested that, although there are numerous social skill definitions, three general definitions or conceptualizations can be distilled from the literature on children's social skills.

One definition can be termed the *peer-acceptance definition*, which defines a person as socially skilled if peers accept him or her. This definition was featured in the work of many prominent researchers in the child development literature (Asher & Hymel, 1981; Gottman, 1977; Ladd, 1981; Oden & Asher, 1977). The major drawback of a peer-acceptance definition is that it does not identify what specific behaviors lead to peer acceptance.

Another definition—termed the *behavioral definition*—defines social skills as behaviors that increase the likelihood of being reinforced and decrease the likelihood of being punished or extinguished contingent upon one's social behavior. This definition has historically been endorsed by researchers operating from an applied behavior analytic or behavior therapy perspective (Bellack & Hersen, 1979; Foster & Ritchey, 1979; Strain, 1977; Strain, Cooke, & Apolloni, 1976). The major disadvantage of this definition is that it does not ensure that the behaviors identified are in fact socially significant behaviors that result in socially important outcomes. In other words, merely increasing the frequency of certain behaviors that are identified a priori as "social skills" does not establish the social validity of those behaviors (Wolf, 1978).

A third definition of social skills, based on the work of McFall (1982), has been termed the *social validity definition*. According to this definition, social skills are specific behaviors or behavior patterns that predict or otherwise result in important social outcomes for children and youth (Gresham, 1983, 1998b). Socially important outcomes represent outcomes that treatment consumers consider important, adaptive, and functional (Hawkins, 1991; Wolf, 1978). In short, socially important outcomes are those outcomes that make a difference in terms of an individual's functioning or adaptation to societal expectations. Socially important outcomes may include peer acceptance and friendships (McConnell & Odom, 1986; Newcomb, Bukowski, & Patee, 1993; Parker & Asher, 1987), teacher and parental acceptance (Gresham, 1992, 1998b; Gresham & Elliott, 1990; Merrell, 1993; Walker & McConnell, 1995a, 1995b), and school adjustment (Gresham & MacMillan, 1997; Hersh & Walker, 1983; Walker, Irvin, Noell, & Singer, 1992).

The social validity definition also distinguishes between the concepts of *social competence* and *social skills*. In this view, social skills are specific behaviors that an individual exhibits to perform competently on a social task. Social competence is an evaluative term based on judgments that a person has performed a social task competently. These judgments may be based on opinions of significant others (e.g., teachers, parents, and peers), comparisons to explicit criteria (e.g., number of social tasks correctly performed), and/or comparisons to a normative sample. In short, the social validity definition considers social skills to be *specific behaviors* that result in *judgments* about those behaviors (McFall, 1982).

Social Competence and Social-Behavioral Expectations in School

Schools are generally accessible to all children, their parents, and teachers, thereby making it an ideal place for teaching and refining students' social behavior. Schools are a microcosm of society and a place where students and adults work, play, eat, and live together for 6 hours per day, 5 days per week, and at least 180 days per year. By grade 5, children will have spent a minimum of 5400 hours in school (Gresham, 1997). During this time, children are exposed to literally hundreds of thousands of social interactions with peers and adults. As such, schools are a major socializing institution in society. For many children, school entry represents a particularly difficult period, putting them at-risk for problems in peer social interactions and relationships.

One way of understanding how children are considered at-risk for social competence difficulties is to examine the social behavior standards expected or set by significant others in the environments in which children function. For example, the standards, expectations, and tolerance levels that teachers hold for students' social behaviors influence teaching behaviors as well as peer interactions in classrooms (Hersh & Walker, 1983). Brophy and Good (1986) indicated that students perceived as being brighter or more competent receive more teacher attention, are given greater opportunities to respond, are praised more, and are given more verbal cues during teaching interactions than students perceived as being less competent.

Most teachers would consider a behavioral repertoire to be indicative of successful adjustment if: (a) academic performance (e.g., listening to teacher, completing tasks, and complying with teacher directions) is facilitated, and (b) disruptive or unusual behaviors challenging the teacher's authority and disturbing the classroom ecology (e.g., cheating, stealing, or defying the teacher) are absent (Gresham & Reschly, 1988; Hersh & Walker, 1983). Most students with high-incidence disabilities (e.g., specific learning disabilities, emotional disturbance, mild mental retardation, and ADHD) are considered problematic based on difficulties in their "teachability." *Teachability* represents a pattern of social behavior that Hersh and Walker (1983) call a *model behavior profile* expected by most teachers. Many, if not most, students with high-incidence disabilities probably were referred originally for assessment and placement into special education based on substantial deviations from this model behavioral profile.

Walker et al. (1992) presented a useful empirically based conceptual model of interpersonal social-behavioral competence for school settings (see Figure 11.1). This model describes both adaptive and maladaptive teacher and peer social-behavioral domains and outcomes. The adaptive teacher-related adjustment behaviors operationalize the model behavior profile described above and results in teacher acceptance and school success. The maladaptive domain is characterized by behaviors that disturb the classroom ecology and result in teacher rejection, school failure, and referral to special education.

The social behaviors in the adaptive peer-related adjustment domain are substantially different from those in the teacher-related adjustment domain. These behaviors are essential for the formation of friendships and peer acceptance (e.g., cooperation, support, and assistance of peers), but have little to do with classroom success and teacher acceptance. The maladaptive behaviors in this domain are likely to result in peer rejection or neglect (e.g., disruption, starting of fights, and bragging), but share many similarities with

Teacher-Related Adjustment Related-Behavioral Correlates		Peer-Related Adjustment Related-Behavioral Correlates	
Adaptive	Maladaptive	Adaptive	Maladaptive
• Complies promptly • Follows rules • Listens • Completes classwork • Follows directions • Cooperates	• Steals • Defies teacher • Tantrums • Disturbs others • Cheats • Swears • Aggressive • Ignores teacher	• Cooperates with peers • Supports peers • Defends self in arguments • Leads peers • Affiliates with peers • Assists peers	• Disrupts group • Acts snobbish • Aggresses indirectly • Starts fights • Short temper • Brags • Gets in trouble with teacher • Seeks help constantly
Outcome	*Outcome*	*Outcome*	*Outcome*
• Teacher acceptance • Academic success	• Teacher rejection • Referral to special education • School failure • School dropout • Low performance expectations	• Peer acceptance • Positive peer reactions • Friendships	• Social rejection • Loneliness • Weak social involvement

FIGURE 11.1

Model of interpersonal social-behavioral competence within school settings. Adapted from "A Construct Score Approach to the Assessment of Social Competence: Rationale, Technological Considerations, and Anticipated Outcomes," by H. Walker, L. Irvin, J. Noell, and G. Singer, 1992, *Behavior Modification*, 16, pp. 448–474.

the maladaptive behaviors in the teacher-related maladaptive domain. This model of social-behavioral functioning is essential for understanding the referral process and the goals and outcomes of social skills interventions, and predicting the outcomes of attempts to include all students with disabilities in general education classrooms.

Taxonomy of Social Skills

A great deal of empirical research has focused on developing a taxonomy or dimensional approach to classifying maladaptive behaviors. Achenbach has developed a reliable and valid classification system of externalizing and internalizing behavior patterns that are reflected in teacher, parent, and student rating scales (Achenbach, 1991a, 1991b, 1991c). McConaughy (see Chapter 10) discusses these instruments in greater detail. Quay and Peterson (1987) developed a similar taxonomy using the Behavior Problem Checklist.

More recently, Reynolds and Kamphaus (1992) developed the Behavioral Assessment System for Children (BASC), which uses a dimensional approach that emphasizes maladaptive behavior patterns in children and adolescents.

A recent synthesis by Caldarella and Merrell (1997) provided another taxonomy in a review of 21 investigations using 19 social skills rating scales or inventories. Studies in this synthesis of factor analytic research included 22,000 students ranging from 3–18 years of age with about equal gender representation across studies. Teacher rating scales were used in approximately three-quarters of the studies, with parent- and self-report measures being used in about 19 percent of the studies. Peer sociometrics were used in about 5 percent of the studies.

Table 11.1 presents Caldarella and Merrell's taxonomy, which includes five broad social skills domains: (a) peer relationships, (b) self-management, (c) academic, (d) compliance, and (e) assertion skills. This taxonomy provides useful directions for selecting target social skills for more in-depth assessment and intervention. A number of these social skill domains have been used in published social skills curricula and intervention programs (Elias & Clabby, 1992; Elliott & Gresham, 1992; Goldstein, 1988; Walker, McConnell, Holmes, Todis, Walker, & Golden, 1983). Candarella and Merrell point out that their taxonomy is useful because it: (a) provides a nomenclature to refer to typical social skill patterns, (b) identifies a profile of social skill dimen-

TABLE 11.1
Most Common Dimensions of Social Skills

Domain	Number of studies	Percentage of studies
Peer Relationships (social interaction, prosocial, peer-preferred, empathy, social participation)	11	52.38%
Self-Management (self-control, social convention, social independence, social responsibility, classroom compliance)	11	52.38%
Academic (school adjustment, respect for social rules at school, task orientation, academic responsibility, compliance)	10	47.62%
Compliance (social cooperation, competence, cooperation-compliance)	8	38.09%
Assertion (assertive social skills, social initiation, social activator)	7	33.33%

Source: Based on "Common Dimensions of Social Skills of Children and Adolescents: A Taxonomy of Positive Social Behaviors," by P. Caldarella and K. Merrell, 1997, *School Psychology Review*, 26, pp. 265–279.

sions on which students may have relative strengths and weaknesses, (c) can be used to design interventions to teach social skills, (d) can be used to measure the outcomes of social skills interventions, and (e) can facilitate theory development concerning the causes, prognosis, and responsiveness of students to social skill intervention procedures.

Classification of Social Skills Deficits

An important aspect of social skills assessment that has clear relevance for designing interventions is an accurate classification of the specific type(s) of social skill deficits a child may have. Gresham (1981a, 1981b) first distinguished between social skill *acquisition* and *performance* deficits. This distinction is important because it suggests different intervention approaches in remediating social skills deficits and may indicate different settings for carrying out social skills training (e.g., pullout groups versus contextually based interventions in naturalistic settings). A third type of social skill deficit may be called a *fluency* deficit, in which a child may know how to and wants to perform a given social skill, but executes an awkward or unpolished performance of that social skill. A fluency deficit in this sense is similar to readers who can accurately decode words, but render slow, dysfluent reading performances.

Social skill *acquisition deficits* refer to the absence of knowledge for executing a particular social skill even under optimal conditions. Social *performance deficits* represent the presence of social skills in an individual's behavioral repertoire, but the failure to perform these skills at an acceptable level in particular situations. Acquisition deficits can be thought of as "Can't do" or skill deficits whereas performance deficits are "Won't do" or motivational deficits. Fluency deficits stem from a lack of exposure to a number of competent models for particular social behaviors, from lack of practice, or from inadequate behavioral rehearsal of newly taught or infrequently used social skills.

Gresham and Elliott (1990) extended this social skills classification model to include the notion of *competing problem behaviors*. In this classification scheme, two dimensions of behavior—social skills and competing problem behaviors—are combined to classify social skills difficulties. Competing behaviors can include internalizing or overcontrolled behavior patterns (e.g., anxiety, depression, or social withdrawal) or externalizing behavior patterns (e.g., aggression, impulsivity, disruption). Figure 11.2 presents this social skills classification model.

The two-dimensional social skill deficit classification model depicted in Figure 11.2 is pivotal in linking assessment results to interventions for social skills deficits. It is inappropriate to teach a social skill to children who already have that skill in their repertoires (i.e., children with a performance deficit). Similarly, intervention procedures designed to increase the performance of a social skill (e.g., prompting or reinforcement) are not efficient in remediating acquisition deficits. Finally, children with fluency deficits do not require that

Competing behavior	Acquisition	Performance	Fluency
Present	Acquisition deficit	Performance deficit	Fluency deficit
Absent	Acquisition deficit	Performance deficit	Fluency deficit

FIGURE 11.2

Social skills classification model. Adapted from *Social Skills Rating System*, by F. M. Gresham and S. N. Elliot, 1990, Circle Pines, MN: American Guidance Center.

a skill be taught nor require antecedent/consequent procedures to increase the frequency of a behavioral performance. Instead, these children require more practice (i.e., opportunities to respond) and rehearsal (repetitions) of the skill for adequate and socially effective behavioral performances.

SOCIAL SKILLS ASSESSMENT METHODS

A variety of methods have been used to assess the social skills of children and youth, and many of these methods can provide useful information regarding the prosocial and competing problem behaviors. The tactic taken in this chapter is to focus on *behavioral assessment* procedures for assessing social skills. Although behavioral assessment shares many of the same methods with so-called traditional assessment, these two approaches differ dramatically in the assumptions they make about behavior, its "causes" or controlling variables, and the use of assessment information for treatment planning and evaluation.

Social skills assessment takes place in five major stages of the assessment/intervention sequence: (a) screening/selection, (b) classification, (c) target behavior selection, (d) functional assessment, and (e) evaluation of intervention. Gresham (1995) identified 12 major goals of social skills assessment, and these can be found in Table 11.2. Like all behavioral assessment methods, social skills assessment methods can be broadly classified as *indirect* and *direct* (Gresham, 1998a; Gresham & Lambros, 1998). Indirect behavioral assessment methods assess behavior that is removed in time and place from its actual occurrence. Examples of these methods include interviews, ratings by others, peer assessment methods, and analogue role-play measures. Direct measures assess behavior at the time and place of its actual occurrence and include naturalistic observations of social behavior (e.g., classroom and playground) and self-monitoring strategies.

Behavior rating scales are highlighted in this chapter because of their efficiency, economy, and validity in assessing key aspects of students' social behaviors. However, behavior rating scales cannot be used in isolation to ob-

TABLE 11.2
Goals of Social Skills Assessment

- Identify social skills strengths
- Identify social skills acquisition deficits
- Identify social skills performance deficits
- Identify social skills fluency deficits
- Identify competing problem behaviors
- Conduct functional assessment
- Determine the social validity of specific social skills for treatment consumers
- Select target behaviors for intervention
- Develop intervention strategies based on assessment information
- Select appropriate outcome measure(s)
- Evaluate effects of intervention
- Assess generalization of effects

tain a complete picture of a child or adolescent's social behavior. For this reason, I describe two additional social skill assessment methods: (a) functional assessment interviews, and (b) naturalistic observations of social behavior.

Functional Assessment Interviews

A functional assessment interview (FAI) has four primary goals: (a) to identify and define social skills difficulties, (b) to assist in the differentiation of social skill acquisition, performance, and fluency deficits, (c) to identify competing problem behaviors that interfere with acquisition, performance, and/or fluency, and (d) to obtain preliminary information regarding the possible functions of behavior. A *functional assessment* of behavior seeks to identify the functions or causes of behavior. This information is valuable because, once a behavioral function is identified, specific intervention strategies based on behavioral function can be prescribed.

Fundamentally, behavior may serve two functions: (a) to *obtain* something desirable (e.g., social attention, preferred activities, or material objects), and (b) to *avoid*, *escape*, or *delay* something undesirable or aversive (e.g., difficult tasks, social activities, or interruption of preferred activities). These two functions describe the processes of positive and negative reinforcement, respectively. For example, a child's social withdrawal behavior may serve to increase the frequency of adult and/or peer promptings to join an ongoing activity (i.e., the behavior may serve a social attention or positive reinforcement function). In contrast, social withdrawal may serve to allow a child to terminate social interactions with peers (i.e., it may serve an escape or negative reinforcement function).

Professionals conducting social skills assessments and interventions often work from a consultation framework in which they garner information about children's social behavior from third parties such as teachers and parents. During the initial stages of assessment, it is extremely important for interviewers to obtain as precise information as possible from these third parties to assist in a functional assessment. For example, a teacher might say, "Hank does not fit into the group very well," or "Don doesn't get along well with others." Although these statements may be true, they are not particularly informative regarding the exact nature of the social skill deficit, much less the functional assessment of behavior.

Persons conducting FAIs should engage in the following: (a) eliciting from the interviewee a specific, precise description of social skill deficits and competing problem behaviors, (b) formulating a tentative description of environmental conditions surrounding socially skilled and competing problem behaviors, and (c) evaluating the effects of social skills interventions in terms of measurable behavior change. The above steps also can be described as problem identification, problem analysis, and problem evaluation, respectively (Gresham, 1998a). Table 11.3 presents an example of a semistructured functional assessment interview that can be used to assess social skills for children and youth. For more specific and comprehensive information concerning FAIs, readers should consult the texts by Bergan and Kratochwill (1990) and O'Neill, Horner, Albin, Storey, Sprague, & Newton, (1997).

Naturalistic Observations of Social Behavior

Systematic behavioral observations represent one of the most important social skills assessment methods. Observational data are very sensitive to treatment effects and should be included in all social skills assessment and intervention activities. Although there are a variety of elaborate coding systems available for naturalistic observations of social behavior, I recommend that recording procedures be kept as simple as possible. Four factors should be considered in using systematic behavioral observations: (a) operational definitions of behavior, (b) dimension of behavior being measured, (c) number of behaviors assessed, and (d) number of observation sessions.

The first and most important step in collecting social skills observational data is to have an *operational definition* of the social behavior being measured. Operational definitions should describe the specific verbal, physical, temporal, and/or spatial parameters of behavior or environmental events (Gresham, Gansle, & Noell, 1993). Operational definitions should be clear, objective, and complete (Kazdin, 1984).

Walker and Severson (1992) provide a good example of an operational definition for the social skill of *participation*: "This is coded when the target child is participating in a game or activity (with two or more children) that has a clearly specified and agreed upon set of rules. Examples would be: kickball,

TABLE 11.3
Semistructured Functional Assessment Interview for Social Skills

A. PROBLEM IDENTIFICATION

1. What social skills are of most concern to you?

2. Please provide a clear, specific definition of the behaviors that concern you.

3. Do you see these behaviors as being primarily acquisition deficits ("Can't do"), performance deficits ("Won't do"), or fluency deficits ("Needs more practice")?

4. Approximately how often do you see these behaviors occurring? How often would you like them to occur?

5. What, if any, competing problem behaviors interfere with the acquisition, performance, or fluency of the desired social skills? Provide a definition of these behaviors.

6. About how often do these behaviors occur?

7. Are there activities or times of the day when these social skills are less likely? More likely?

8. Are there activities or times of the day when the competing problem behaviors are more likely? Less likely?

9. Is the desired social skill more likely to occur with some peers than others? Describe these typical social interactions.

10. How does the child's failure to perform the desired social skill affect other children? How does it affect you?

B. PROBLEM ANALYSIS

11. When the child performs the social skill, what happens? What do you do? What do peers do?

12. When the child performs the competing problem behavior, what happens? What do you do? What do peers do?

13. What purposes (functions) do you think the competing problem behavior serves for the child (social attention, task avoidance/escape, access to preferred activities)?

14. Does the child engage in competing problem behaviors that achieve the same results as the socially skilled behavior? Are the competing problem behaviors equally or more functional in obtaining reinforcement?

15. If competing problem behaviors are equally or more functional, are they more efficient and reliable in achieving that function? That is, do the competing problem behaviors achieve the same reinforcement more quickly and more consistently that the socially skilled alternative behavior?

16. Are the competing problem behaviors associated with the presence of a specific stimulus (e.g., person, place, thing, time of day) or are they associated with the presence of many stimuli and situations?

17. What are some situations or activities in which the desired social skill could be taught or facilitated using incidental teaching?

18. Describe how you might teach or facilitate the social skill in these situations or activities.

19. Are there peers in the classroom who might be recruited to assist in teaching or facilitating the desired social skill?

20. Do you think the desired social skill would be best taught in a small group outside of the classroom? Why or why not?

(continues)

Table 11.3—*Continued*

21. What types of strategies could you implement to decrease the competing problem behaviors? Describe how you might use these.

22. What aspects of the proposed intervention do you like the most? Why? Which do you like the least? Why?

23. Which aspects of the proposed intervention would be easiest to implement? Why? Which aspects of the proposed intervention would be the most difficult to implement? Why?

24. Here are some ways in which we could change the intervention. Do these changes make the intervention easier to implement? What additional changes would you recommend?

25. Do you think this intervention is likely to be effective? Why or why not?

C. PROBLEM EVALUATION

26. Describe how you think the intervention worked.

27. What behavior changes did you observe? Did these changes make a difference in the child's behavior in your classroom? How? In other settings? How?

28. Is the child's behavior now similar to that of average or typical peers? If not, do you think continued use of the intervention would accomplish this goal? Why or why not? How long do you think this might take if we continued the intervention?

29. How satisfied are you with the outcomes of this intervention ("Not Satisfied," "Somewhat Satisfied," "Satisfied," or "Very Satisfied")? If not satisfied or somewhat satisfied, what kinds of behavior changes would make you satisfied or very satisfied?

30. Would you recommend this intervention to others? Why or why not? What aspects of this intervention would you change before recommending this intervention to others?

four-square, dodgeball, soccer, basketball, tetherball, hopscotch, and so forth. Nonexamples include tag, jump rope, follow the leader, and other unstructured games" (pp. 23–24).

An efficient way of formulating an operational definition is though the functional assessment interview described in the previous section. Recall that the main purpose of an FAI is to obtain a clear and objective definition of target behaviors. Behavior rating scales (to be described in greater detail below) should be used to identify general areas of concern and normative levels of functioning in social skill and competing problem behavior domains. The FAI can be used to operationally define behaviors that most concern teachers and/or parents. Finally, direct observations of these behaviors in naturalistic settings (e.g., classroom or playground) are collected as *direct measures* of social behavior and to conduct descriptive functional assessment information.

Social behavior can be described and assessed along the behavioral dimensions of frequency, temporality, and quality. Frequency, or how often a social behavior occurs, is often used as an index of social competence. This, however, can be misleading: How often a person exhibits a social behavior may not predict important social outcomes such as peer acceptance (Gresham, 1983). Some social skills can be clearly defined as problems because they occur at low frequencies. Examples include saying "please," "thank you," and "excuse me," or asking permission to get out of one's seat in class or before leaving home.

Some social skills may be more appropriately measured using temporal dimensions of behavior such as duration, latency, or interresponse times. Examples of social skills that can be measured by duration are durations of social interactions with others, amount of time engaged in cooperative play, or the ratio of positive to negative social interactions. One easy way to assess the duration of social skills is to start a stopwatch when the child begins the behavior and stop it when the child is not engaged in the behavior. This process continues throughout the observation session. The duration is then calculated by dividing the elapsed time on the stopwatch by the total time observed and multiplying by 100, thereby yielding a percent duration.

Walker, Colvin, and Ramsey (1995) strongly recommend the use of duration recording of alone and negative social behavior on the playground for students demonstrating an antisocial behavior pattern. *Alone* means when a child is not within 10 feet of another child, is not engaged in any organized activity, and is not exchanging social signals (verbal or nonverbal) with any other children. *Negative social behavior* can be defined as when a child is displaying hostile behavior or body language toward peers; attempting to tease, bully, or otherwise intimidate others; reacting with anger or rejection to the social bids of peers; or displaying aggressive behavior with the intent to harm or force the submission of peers.

Antisocial children spend more time alone and are more negative in their social interactions than are non-antisocial students. Surprisingly, however, antisocial and non-antisocial students have not been found to differ in their durations of total positive social behaviors (Walker, Colvin, & Ramsey, 1995; Walker & Severson, 1992). Based on playground recording, if a student spends between 12% and 15% of the time in solitary activity ("alone") and engages in negative social interactions 10% or more of the time, he or she is at risk for antisocial behavior (Walker, Colvin, & Ramsey, 1995).

A particularly important aspect of social behavior is the *quality* of the behavior. In fact, it could be argued that the most important aspect of what makes a behavior "socially skilled" is its quality and not its frequency or temporal dimensions. Quality of social behavior, however, must be judged by others. This can be accomplished by exposing judges to videotaped or in vivo samples of a social behavior and having them rate its quality. This process is similar to what is being measured by behavior rating scales except that the measurement is direct rather than indirect and is based on a more limited sample of behavior.

Some children and adolescents have social skills deficits and competing problem behaviors limited to one or two behaviors. Other children exhibit multiple social skills deficits and competing problem behavior excesses, thereby presenting an unmanageable number of behaviors to assess.

An important decision assessors must make is how many behaviors to observe. This decision is influenced by the nature and severity of the child's social competence difficulties as well as by the degree of teacher and/or parent concern with each behavioral excess or deficit.

Some teachers and parents may list as many as 5 to 10 behaviors that they consider problematic. Although some children will display 10 or more problem behaviors and/or social skills deficits, not all of these behaviors are independent. Some behaviors are subsets of a larger class or category of behavior that share certain similarities. These larger categories, known as *response classes*, describe a class or category of behaviors that share similarities (topographical response class) or are controlled by the same environmental events (functional response class).

For example, a topographical response class of "social withdrawal" might include behaviors such as sulking, standing alone on the playground, walking away from peers, and ignoring social bids from peers to join in games or activities. Although these behaviors may appear different, they may belong to the same response class and the operational definition of social withdrawal would include all of the behaviors. In this example, social withdrawal could be measured using the duration recording procedure described earlier. Practitioners should determine which behaviors are and are not members of specific response classes for observational purposes and for conceptualizing social skills interventions.

Another consideration in using naturalistic observations is the number of times a child should be observed. The central issue here is the *representativeness* of observational data. That is, are the observations representative of the child's typical behavior in classroom, playground, or other settings? Based on observations of actual behavior, the observer infers that the observed behavior is representative of the child's typical behavior in that setting. Depending on the representativeness of the observational data, this inference may or may not be justified.

Observers cannot be present in classrooms or playgrounds every minute of every day. As such, observers must sample the behavior(s) of concern to obtain reasonable estimates of the baseline rates or durations of behavior. I recommend that observational data be collected for two to three sessions in the setting of concern (e.g., classroom or playground). These sessions should reflect the setting(s) of most concern to those referring the child for social skills assessment and intervention.

Additionally, social behaviors observed in naturalistic settings usually do not have a normative database against which to judge the severity of social skill deficits and competing behavioral excesses. To determine whether the observed behavior is a problem, one can compare the target child's behavior with another child's behavior that is not considered problematic. To accomplish this, choose a same-sex peer in the classroom and record the same behavior as the target child. This procedure allows the assessor to have a local "micro-norm," which can be used for comparison purposes.

Behavior Rating Scales

Ratings of social behavior by significant others such as teachers and parents represent a useful and efficient method of obtaining information in school and home settings. Behavior ratings can be used prior to FAIs to guide the direction and topics discussed in the interview. It should be noted that behavior ratings measure *typical performances* across a variety of situations over time rather than the actual frequencies of behavior at any given time (e.g., via direct observations of social behavior). Raters may also have their own idiosyncratic definitions of what constitutes a given social skill or problem behavior as well as their own notions of the relative frequency of behavior (e.g., "sometimes" versus "a lot").

Gresham and Elliott (1990) suggested that the following points be kept in mind when administering and interpreting data from behavior rating scales. First, ratings are summaries of observations of the relative frequency of specific behaviors. The precision of measurement with rating scales is relative, not exact, and needs to be supplemented with more direct methods of assessment.

Second, ratings of social behavior are evaluative judgments affected by the environment and a rater's standards for behavior. An individual's social behaviors may change depending on the situation and thus might be characterized as situationally specific rather than as traits or permanent characteristics of the individual (Achenbach, McConaughy, & Howell, 1987; Kazdin, 1979).

Third, the social validity of behaviors assessed and treated should be understood. The social validity of a behavior is reflected in the importance attributed to it by significant others in a child's environment.

Fourth, multiple raters of a child's social behavior may agree only moderately and, in some cases, very little. This reality is based on three factors: (a) many social behaviors are situationally specific, (b) all measures contain some degree of error, and (c) ratings scales use rather simple frequency response categories for quantifying behaviors that may range widely in their frequency, intensity, and duration.

Fifth, although many characteristics may influence social behavior, the child or adolescent's sex is particularly important (Gresham & Elliott, 1990). Sex is most consistently associated with differences in social behavior and therefore social skill ratings should be interpreted within a sex-relevant perspective.

REVIEW OF SELECTED SOCIAL SKILLS
RATING SCALES

Although there are a number of social skills rating scales available, four are distinguished by having large national standardization samples, displaying

adequate to excellent psychometric properties in terms of reliability and validity, and being easily obtained from reputable test publishing companies.
These rating scales are: (a) Walker-McConnell Scales of Social Competence
and School Adjustment, (b) School Social Behavior Scales, (c) Preschool and
Kindergarten Behavior Scales, and (d) Social Skills Rating System.

Walker-McConnell Scales of Social Competence and School Adjustment (SSCSA)

The SSCSA (Walker & McConnell, 1995a, 1995b) are social skills rating scales
designed to be completed by teachers and other school professionals. An
elementary version designed for children in grades K–6 and an adolescent version for students in grades 7 through 12 are commercially available.
Table 11.4 shows the subscales for the elementary and adolescent versions of
the SSCSA.

Both the elementary and adolescent versions of the SSCSA were standardized on a sample of over 2000 students representing the four geographic
regions of the United States. Each item of the scales is rated on a 5-point Likert scale reflecting the relative frequency of the behavior ("1—Never occurs"
to "5—Frequently occurs"). Each subscale shown in Table 11.4 is expressed
as a T score ($M = 10$, $SD = 3$) and a total score is expressed as a standard
score ($M = 100$, $SD = 15$). The manuals present extensive evidence for reliability and validity of the scales. Internal consistency reliabilities for the total scale range from .92 to .98 and test-retest reliabilities over a 3-week period range from .88 to .92. The manuals present a number of validity studies
showing that the scales differentiate behavior-disordered and normal groups,
antisocial and normal groups, and behaviorally at-risk and normal groups.
Criterion-related validity evidence shows that the scales significantly correlate with a variety of criterion measures, including sociometric status, academic achievement, other social skills rating scales, and arrest rates in antisocial and at-risk groups.

The elementary and adolescent versions of the SSCSA are a relatively brief
and user-friendly means of assessing social skills of students covering a wide
age range. A particularly impressive aspect of the scales is their broad and
rich research base, drawn from the authors' work at the University of Oregon.
Two drawbacks of the scales are that they do not include problem behavior
scales and they rely exclusively on teacher ratings.

School Social Behavior Scales (SSBS)

The SSBS (Merrell, 1993) is a 65-item teacher rating scale designed to measure two broad domains of social behavior: (a) social competence, and
(b) antisocial behavior. The SSBS was standardized on a sample of 1858 children and adolescents in grades K–12. Although the four geographic regions

TABLE 11.4
Scales and Subscales from Four Major Social Skills Assessment Instruments

I. Social Skills Rating System (Teacher, Parent, and Student Ratings) (Gresham & Elliott, 1990)

    A. Total Social Skills Scale (30 items—Teacher; 40 items—Parent; 40 items—Student)

        1. Cooperation (10 items—Teacher, Parent, and Student)

        2. Assertion (10 items—Teacher, Parent, and Student)

        3. Responsibility (10 items—Parent Only)

        4. Empathy (10 items—Student Only)

        5. Self-Control (10 items—Teacher, Parent, and Student)

    B. Total Problem Behavior Scale (18 items)

        1. Externalizing (6 items—Teacher; 6 items—Parent)

        2. Internalizing (6 items—Teacher; 6 items—Parent)

        3. Hyperactivity (6 items—Teacher; 6 items—Parent)

    C. Academic Competence Scale (9 items)

II. School Social Behavior Scales (Teacher Rating Only) (Merrell, 1993)

    A. Social Competence Scale (32 items)

        1. Interpersonal Skills (14 items)

        2. Self-Management Skills (10 items)

        3. Academic Skills (8 items)

    B. Antisocial Behavior Scale (33 items)

        1. Hostile-Irritable Behaviors (14 items)

        2. Antisocial-Aggressive Behaviors (10 items)

        3. Disruptive-Demanding Behaviors (9 items)

III. Walker-McConnell Scales of Social Competence and School Adjustment (Teacher Rating Only) (Walker & McConnell, 1995a, 1995b)

    A. Teacher-Preferred Social Behavior (16 items—Elementary Version)

    B. Peer-Preferred Social Behavior (17 items—Elementary Version)

    C. School Adjustment (10 items—Elementary Version; 15 items—Adolescent Version)

    D. Empathy (9 items—Adolescent Version)

    E. Self-Control (13 items—Adolescent Version)

    F. Peer Relations (16 items—-Adolescent Version)

IV. Preschool and Kindergarten Behavior Scales (Teacher Rating Only) (Merrell, 1994)

    A. Social Skills Scale (34 items)

        1. Social Cooperation (12 items)

        2. Social Interaction (11 items)

        3. Social Independence (11 items)

    B. Problem Behavior Scale (42 items)

        1. Externalizing Problems (27 items)

           a. Self-Centered/Explosive

(continues)

of the United States were included in the standardization sample, it was not geographically representative of the U.S. population, with about 40 percent of the sample coming from the states of Oregon and Washington. It is not clear how (if at all) this might affect social skills ratings of children and adolescents.

Each item of the SSBS is rated on a 5-point Likert scale reflecting the relative frequency of the social behavior ("1—Never" to "5—Frequently"). Table 11.4 shows that the Social Competence Scale has 32 items distributed across three subscales and the Antisocial Behavior Scale has 33 items distributed across three subscales. The Total Social Competence and Total Antisocial Behavior Scores on the SSBS are expressed as a standard score ($M = 100$, $SD = 15$) and as percentile ranks.

The SSBS has adequate psychometric properties with internal consistency reliabilities ranging from .91 to .98 and test-retest reliabilities (3 weeks) ranging from .72 to .83 for the Social Competence Scale and .53 to .71 for the Antisocial Behavior Scale. The manual also presents a large number of studies demonstrating the criterion-related and construct validity of the scale. As Demaray et al. (1995) point out, the SSBS has adequate to excellent reliability; has sufficient evidence for content, construct, and discriminant validity; and is user-friendly due to its detailed technical manual.

Preschool and Kindergarten Behavior Scales (PKBS)

The PKBS (Merrell, 1994) is a 76-item behavior rating scale that measures social skills and problem behaviors of children between the ages of 3–6 years old. The author indicates that the PKBS can be completed by teachers, parents, day care providers, or others who have sufficient exposure to a child's behavior to provide accurate ratings. The PKBS was standardized on a normative sample of 2855 children from 16 states distributed across the four geographic regions of the United States. According to the author, the PKBS was specifically developed for preschool children and was *not* a downward extension of existing social skills rating scales. The basis of this claim is unclear given that many of the items on the PKBS are virtually identical to items on the Social Skills Rating System—Preschool Version (Gresham & Elliott, 1990).

Each item on the PKBS is rated on a 4-point Likert scale reflecting the perceived frequency of the social behavior ("0—Never" to "3—Often"). As shown in Table 11.4, the PKBS has two major scales: (a) Social Skills (34 items), which has three subscales, and (b) Problem Behavior (42 items), which has two subscales. Total scale scores for Social Skills and Problem Behaviors are expressed as standard scores (M = 100, SD = 15).

The manual presents extensive data about the technical adequacy of the scale. Internal consistency reliability estimates are .96 for the Total Social Skills Scale and .97 for the Total Problem Behavior Scale. Three-month test-retest reliability estimates are .69 for the Total Social Behavior Scale and .78 for the Total Problem Behavior Scale. The manual also reports a number of studies attesting to the construct, criterion-related, and discriminant validity of the scale.

Social Skills Rating System (SSRS)

The SSRS (Gresham & Elliott, 1990) is a broad, multirater assessment of students' social behaviors that can affect teacher-student relations, peer acceptance, and academic performance. The SSRS consists of three separate ratings forms for teachers, parents, and students (grades 3–12), and has three forms: Preschool (ages 3–5 years), Elementary (grades K–6), and Secondary (grades 7–12). The SSRS uses the teacher, parent, and student rating forms to sample three domains: social skills, problem behaviors, and academic competence. Although the SSRS focuses on a comprehensive assessment of social skills, it also measures problem behaviors that compete or interfere with the acquisition and/or performance of socially skilled behaviors. Moreover, the SSRS examines academic competence because poor academic performance and social behavior problems frequently occur together.

The number of items on the SSRS varies, depending on the rating form and level used. In general, the SSRS forms should take a rater no longer than 15–20 minutes to complete, with many raters taking considerably less time. Each item on the SSRS is rated on a 3-point scale ("0—Never," "1—Sometimes," "2—Very Often") based on the rater's perceived frequency of a certain behavior. In addition, all SSRS forms (except the Student Elementary form) employ a 3-point Importance rating scale for the Social Skills Scale. Behaviors are rated as 0 if they are perceived to be "Not Important," 1 if they are perceived to be "Important," and 2 if they are perceived to be "Critical." The Importance rating scale documents the behavior standards and expectations of teachers, parents, and secondary students, and identifies behaviors for intervention programs based on a social validity criterion (Wolf, 1978).

The SSRS assesses the following social skills domains: Cooperation, Assertion, Responsibility (Parent Form only), Empathy (Student Form only), and Self-Control. These domains are captured by the acronym CARES. Three of these domains are consistent across the teacher, parent, and student

TABLE 11.5
SSRS Social Skills and Problem Behavior Domains

Domain	Description	Examples
Cooperation	Behaviors facilitating academic performance and success	Follows classroom rules; complies with teacher instructions
Assertion	Behaviors involving initiation of social interactions or expression of opinions	Introduces self; questions rules that may be unjust
Responsibility	Behaviors related to following rules in home and community settings	Asks others for assistance; refuses unreasonable requests
Empathy	Behaviors that express understanding of another person's feelings	Listens to others; feels sorry when bad things happen to others
Self-Control	Behaviors that involve inhibition of impulses or negative behavior	Controls temper in conflict situations; responds appropriately to teasing
Externalizing	Behaviors representing undercontrolled or acting-out behavior pattern	Fights; bullies; argues; gets angry
Internalizing	Behaviors representing overcontrolled or inhibited behavior pattern	Lonely; anxious; easily embarrassed; likes to be alone
Hyperactivity	Behaviors representing inattention, impulsivity, and overactivity	Easily distracted; interrupts others; moves excessively

forms: Cooperation, Assertion, and Self-Control. The SSRS also assesses three problem behavior domains: Externalizing Problems, Internalizing Problems, and Hyperactivity Problems. The Academic Competence Scale (Elementary and Secondary Teacher Forms) is composed of 9 items (e.g., reading, mathematics, motivation, general intelligence) reflecting academic performance. Social skills and problem behavior domains are shown in Table 11.5 along with examples.

The SSRS was standardized on a national sample of 4170 children and adolescents in grades 3 through 12, with equal numbers of boys and girls in the standardization sample. Preschool norms (ages 3–5 years) were constructed from a smaller tryout sample of children (N = 200). The standardization sample was stratified by race/ethnic groups and was slightly overrepresented by Blacks and Whites and underrepresented by Hispanics and other groups. The standardization sample was selected from the four geographic regions of the United States, with more children in the sample from the South and North Central regions and fewer children from the West and Northeast.

The SSRS provides extensive information about the psychometric properties of the scales. Internal consistency estimates for the Total Social Skills Scales range from .83 (Student Elementary/Secondary) to .94 (Teacher Preschool/Elementary), with subscale coefficient alphas ranging from .51 to .92 (M*dn* = .72). Coefficient alphas for the Total Problem Behavior Scale range from .73 (Parent/Preschool) to .88 (Teacher/Elementary), with subscale alphas ranging from .57 to .89 (M*dn* = .73). Coefficient alphas for the Academic Competence Scale were .95 for both the Elementary and Secondary teacher forms. Four-week test-retest reliabilities for the Total Social Skills Scale range from .68 (Student Form) to .87 (Parent Form). Social skill subscale stability estimates range from .52 to .88 (M*dn* = .70). Stability estimates for the Total Problem Behavior Scale range from .65 (Parent Form) to .84 (Teacher Form), with subscale stability estimates ranging from .48 to .84 (M*dn* = .66). The stability estimate for the Academic Competence Scale was .93.

The SSRS provides extensive evidence for content, criterion-related, and construct validity of the scales. The manual reports several methods by which the construct validity of the scales was established, including group differences, correlations with other tests, factor analysis, and convergent/discriminant validity evidence. The SSRS manual and research studies published over the past 10 years in refereed professional journals provide additional validity evidence for the SSRS.

Summary

The SSRS offers several unique features to facilitate more comprehensive assessment and intervention services for children experiencing social behavior problems. It is the first social skills rating scale to provide norms based on a large, national sample of boys and girls ages 3 through 18. Furthermore, it is the first multirater (teacher-parent-student) scale focusing on the social skills of children. Finally, the SSRS is the first rating scale specifically designed to advance intervention planning. The inclusion of importance ratings of social skills, combined with the theoretical and practical information provided in the *Assessment-Intervention Record*, provides professionals with useful information needed for intervention planning.

COMMON PATTERNS AND
INTERPRETATION HYPOTHESES

The SSRS potentially can yield a large number of social behavior patterns, given the number and type of raters completing the instrument, variability in scale and subscale patterns, and the age of the child being rated. For example, the Preschool SSRS has two scales (Social Skills and Problem Behavior), two raters (Teacher and Parent), and three levels (More, Average, and Fewer) yielding 12 possible profile combinations. At the subscale level, there are three Social Skill subscales (Cooperation, Assertion, and Self-Control) and two Problem Behavior subscales (Externalizing and Internalizing), which are consistent across Teacher and Parent raters. The Responsibility subscale is only present on the Parent form. Including the three levels (More, Average, and Fewer), there are 21 possible combinations for the SSRS Preschool form.

A similar logic can be used to derive the potential profile combinations for the SSRS Elementary and Secondary level forms. Note that Student SSRS ratings are included on the Elementary and Secondary forms and only teachers rate the student's Academic Competence. Some children who are rated as having deficient social skills by their teachers on the SSRS will not be rated deficient by their parents or by themselves. Alternatively, a junior high English teacher might rate a student as having poor social skills and excessive externalizing behavior whereas the student's other teachers will not see his or her social behavior as particularly problematic. Some teachers may view the child's social skills difficulties as being acquisition or skill deficits, whereas other teachers might view these behaviors as performance deficits. Some ratings may not be confirmed by direct observation of social behavior in naturalistic settings. For example, a teacher may rate a child as having poor social skills but this rating may not be corroborated by observation of the child in classroom and playground settings.

The point to keep in mind when interpreting ratings from multiple sources is that there are several reasons for discrepancies between raters' judgments of behavior. These discrepancies do not necessarily mean that either source is invalid or erroneous. Reasons for discrepancies between raters might include: (a) true differences in exhibition of the behavior in school versus home settings (situational specificity of behavior), (b) different standards of behavior at home versus school (situational tolerance of certain behaviors), and (c) different task demands at home versus school (situational requirements for social behavior and academic work). Professionals also should be aware of some common biases in ratings such as "halo effects" (i.e., the presence of a salient behavior affecting the ratings of other behaviors) and measurement errors (e.g., unreliability and regression effects). The job of the assessor is to use various methods to collect additional information that will serve to confirm or disconfirm hypotheses about the nature and presumed causes of social skills deficits.

RECOMMENDATIONS

The following case study illustrates a comprehensive assessment of a child's social behavior using the procedures and concepts described in this chapter. The SSRS is used instead of the other rating scales discussed in this chapter because of its multirater and comprehensive nature. Note that other assessment instruments and procedures are used in this case study to demonstrate what information might be needed in a case such as the one presented.

CASE STUDY

Name: Donald M.   **School:** Newport Coast Elementary   **Date:** 12/17/99
Date of Birth: 12/5/91   **Age:** 8-0   **Race:** White   **Teacher:** Janet Duffy

Reason for Referral

Don was referred by his third-grade teacher, Mrs. Duffy, because of what she described as extreme difficulties in social behavior, poor peer relationships (including peer rejection), aggressive and impulsive behavior, and poor academic performance. Up until the time of this referral, Don had not been referred for special education evaluation or been retained in any grade. However, Mrs. Duffy indicated that Don had been suspended from school twice during the current academic year for his aggressive and oppositional behavior. Mrs. Duffy and the school principal indicated on the referral form that they wanted to have Don evaluated for possible classification as Emotionally Disturbed.

Assessment Procedures

Social Skills Rating System—Teacher
Social Skills Rating System—Parent
Social Skills Rating System—Student
School Archival Records Search (SARS)
Teacher's Report Form
Classroom and Playground Observations
Child Behavior Checklist (Parent)
Critical Events Index (Teacher)
Functional Assessment Interviews
Critical Events Index (Parent)

Assessment Results

Background Information

Initial background information on Don was collected by conducting a systematic search of his cumulative records using the School Archival Records Search (SARS), which codes data that are readily available in students' school records. The SARS search indicated that Don has a history of school disciplinary contacts throughout his school career beginning in the first grade. Some examples of reasons in his file for these disciplinary contacts include fighting on the playground, swearing and talking back to the teacher and principal, fighting on the playground, and leaving class and wandering the halls. Additionally, there were a number of negative comments in his file such as "does not follow classroom rules," "is uncooperative in class," and "is oppositional and disrespectful."

Don's most recent group achievement test results on the Stanford Achievement Test (9th edition) showed the following percentile ranks: Total Reading, 26th percentile; Total Math, 30th percentile; Spelling, 10th percentile; and Total Language, 20th percentile. Don has only two school absences so far this year, does not receive Chapter I services, and has not been previously referred to the school study team for prereferral intervention or evaluation.

Behavior Ratings

Mrs. Duffy completed the Social Skills Rating System—Teacher (SSRS-T), the Teacher's Report Form (TRF), and the Critical Events Index (CEI) on Don in order to get an estimate on his social skills and competing problem behaviors. On the SSRS-T, Don obtained the following scores: Total Social Skills = 70 (2nd percentile); Total Problem Behavior = 133 (>98th percentile); and Academic Competence = 80 (9th percentile). Don's subscale scores on the Social Skills Scale were uniformly low across the Cooperation, Assertion, and Self-Control domains. Within the Problem Behavior Scale, Don showed particularly high scores on both the Externalizing and Hyperactivity subscales, but not the Internalizing subscale.

On the TRF, Don showed a high score on the Externalizing scale (>98th percentile) but not the Internalizing scale. Within the Externalizing scale, Don showed extremely high scores on the Aggressive Behavior (98th percentile) and Attention Problems (98th percentile) subscales. On the CEI, a checklist of low-frequency, high-intensity salient problem behaviors, the teacher noted the following: "has tantrums," "physically aggressive with other children," "ignores teacher warnings or reprimands," and "makes lewd or obscene gestures."

Mrs. MacMillan, Don's mother, completed the following rating scales: the Social Skills Rating System—Parent, the Child Behavior Checklist (CBCL), and the CEI. On the SSRS-P, Don obtained the following scores: Total Social Skills = 80 (9th percentile) and Total Problem Behavior = 117 (87th percentile). In the Social Skills Scale, Don showed particularly low scores on the Responsibility and Self-Control subscales. On the Total Problem Behavior Scale, Don had elevated scores on the Externalizing and Hyperactivity subscales. This pattern was corroborated by the results of the CBCL, which showed higher scores (>90th percentile) on the Aggressive Behavior and Attention Problems subscales. On the CEI, Mrs. MacMillan checked the following behaviors as being problematic at home: "steals," "has tantrums," "ignores parental warnings or reprimands," and "explosive temper outbursts."

Don completed the Social Skills Rating System—Student form and obtained a Total Social Skills Scale standard score of 98, which is in the 50th percentile. The only area in which Don noted some weaknesses was on the

Empathy subscale, noting low frequencies of feeling sorry for others, understanding how friends feel, and listening to friends' problems.

Classroom and Playground Observations

Systematic behavioral observations of Don's behavior in both classroom and playground settings were conducted on two separate days in the same week (Tuesday and Thursday). In the classroom, two behaviors were observed for two sessions for a total of 53 minutes (27 minutes or Tuesday and 26 minutes on Thursday): (a) *Academic Engaged Time* (AET), which was defined as attending to materials and tasks, making appropriate motor responses (e.g., writing), and asking for assistance properly, and (b) *Total Disruptive Behavior* (TDB), which was defined as being out of seat without permission; noncompliance; hitting, biting, or choking other students; and/or screaming, yelling, cursing, or criticizing others. For comparison purposes, Mrs. Duffy nominated a boy she considered average in these behaviors. Both AET and TDB were measured using duration recording, which reflected the percentage of time Don engaged in each behavior over the two sessions. Don's AET was calculated to be 14% and his TDB was 22%; the comparison boy's were 75% and 0%, respectively.

Two behaviors were then observed on the playground the Wednesday of the week following the classroom observations for a total of 20 minutes: (a) *Total Negative Social Interaction* (TN), which was defined as hitting, biting, choking, screaming, threatening, and/or other behaviors that disturb ongoing play activities, and (b) *Alone* (A), which was defined as behaviors in which Don was not within 10 feet of another student, was not socially engaged, and was not participating in any activity with other students. The behaviors of the same comparison boy used in the classroom observations were again observed. Don's TN duration was 15% and his A duration was 18%; the comparison boy's durations were 0% and 3%, respectively.

Functional Assessment Interviews

A semistructured FAI was conducted with Mrs. Duffy to clarify the social skills deficits and competing problem behaviors indicated on the SSRS-T and to obtain an idea of the functions served by the competing problem behaviors. Mrs. Duffy identified the following social skills deficits as the most important to target for intervention: (1) "Controls temper in conflict situations with peers and adults," (2) "Cooperates with peers," (3) "Follows teacher's directions," (4) "Makes transitions appropriately," and (5) "Finishes classroom assignments within time limits." Two of these social skills (controlling temper and cooperating with peers) were viewed as acquisition deficits; the remaining three skills (following directions, making transitions, and finishing assignments) were viewed as performance deficits.

With respect to competing problem behaviors, the following behaviors were seen as most problematic and disruptive to the classroom environment: (1) "Throws temper tantrums," (2) "Talks back," (3) "Acts impulsively," (4) "Argues," and (5) "Disturbs ongoing activities." Mrs. Duffy indicated that three of these behaviors (tantrums, arguing, and talking back) may serve a negative reinforcement function because they are most frequently exhibited in situations in which Don is required to perform academic tasks that he does not like (e.g., math calculation, language arts exercises requiring handwriting), thereby allowing him to escape task demands. The behavior of disturbing ongoing activities seemed to serve a social attention function in that Mrs. Duffy and Don's peers almost always responded in some way to this behavior. It is unclear from the FAI what particular function the impulsive behavior serves for Don.

A FAI was also conducted with Mrs. MacMillan via telephone to clarify her ratings on the SSRS-P, CBCL, and CEI in order to identify social skill acquisition and performance deficits and to determine possible functions that competing problem behaviors may be serving in the home for Don. Mrs. MacMillan identified the following behaviors as social skill or acquisition deficits: (a) "Controls temper," (b) "Ends disagreements calmly," (c) "Acknowledges praise," and (d) "Introduces self." The following behaviors were viewed as performance deficits: (a) "Requests permission to leave the house," (b) "Appropriately questions rules," (c) "Avoids trouble situations," and (d) "Cooperates with family."

Mrs. MacMillan viewed the following competing problem behaviors as the most problematic and disruptive in the home setting: (a) "Argues with others," (b) "Throws temper tantrums," (c) "Talks back to adults," (d) "Acts impulsively," (e) "Disturbs ongoing activities," and (f) "Disobeys rules." Mrs. MacMillan indicated that three of these behaviors (arguing, throwing temper tantrums, and talking back) seem to result in Don receiving a large amount of social attention from her, thereby serving a possible social attention (positive reinforcement) function. Two behaviors (disturbing activities and disobeying rules) seem to allow Don to avoid requests or demands his mother places on him (e.g., "Pick up your room," "Don't leave the house before completing your homework," "Leave your sister alone while she studies"). As in the teacher FAI, it was unclear what function impulsive behavior serves for Don.

SUMMARY AND INTERPRETATION

Donald MacMillan, an 8-year-old third-grade student, was referred for evaluation because of his difficulties in social behaviors and peer relationships, and his impulsive and aggressive behavior and poor academic performance.

Multimethod, multisource assessments showed that Don has extremely poor social skills functioning, based on both teacher and parent ratings on the SSRS, observations in the classroom and on the playground, school records, and a FAI with Don's teacher. Don, however, perceives his own social skills as being adequate, with the exception of empathy skills. The TRF and CBCL showed that Don has excessive amounts of Aggressive Behavior and Attention Problems, scoring at the 98th and 90th percentiles using teacher and parent ratings, respectively. Additionally, both teacher and parent CEI checklists show a number of serious and potentially harmful problem behaviors. This behavior pattern is consistent with what might be described as comorbidity of conduct disorder and attention-deficit/hyperactivity disorder.

Based on this pattern of behavior and the severity of his social skills deficits and behavioral excesses, Don is in need of intense intervention services. Recommendations for intervention services are found in the following section.

RECOMMENDATIONS FOR INTERVENTION SERVICES

1. An intensive behavioral intervention plan should be developed between the psychologist and Mrs. Duffy to address Don's social skills deficits and competing problem behaviors.
2. Specific intervention procedures for Don's escape-motivated behaviors (tantrums, arguments, and talking back) might be effectively addressed by reconsidering and revising the task demands for classroom academic assignments. For example, Mrs. Duffy indicated that Don dislikes tasks requiring handwriting and math calculation. As such, task requirements could be modified by having Don provide answers either verbally in a tape recorder or in a short-answer format. Math calculations could be reduced and supplemented with math word problem tasks. In addition, Mrs. Duffy might consider giving Don choices among activities and interspersing easier tasks with more difficult tasks.
3. Specific intervention procedures for Don's social attention–motivated behavior of disturbing ongoing activities might include differential reinforcement of incompatible behaviors (DRI) for staying in his seat and completing his assigned work, noncontingent attention of behavior delivered on a time-based schedule (e.g., every 5 minutes), and presentation of preferred activities in the classroom.
4. For the social skills acquisition deficits of controlling temper and cooperating with peers, it is recommended that Don be placed in a social skills training group designed to remediate acquisition deficits by using modeling, coaching, and behavioral rehearsal strategies.

Specific procedures for teaching these skills can be found in the *Social Skills Intervention Guide* (Elliott & Gresham, 1992), which teaches each social skill found on the SSRS.

5. For the performance deficits of following directions and making transitions, it is recommended that Mrs. Duffy use precorrection and incidental teaching strategies. For example, Mrs. Duffy could explain exactly what is required and what is going to happen *prior to* a given activity or transition. Also, when Don does not follow directions or appropriately make transitions, Mrs. Duffy could use these situations to prompt and reinforce correct performances of these skills.

6. To address Don's social skill acquisition and performance deficits and his competing problem behaviors, it is recommended that Mrs. MacMillan attend a parent training group that teaches fundamental knowledge and practical application of behavior change procedures.

7. Once the above intervention procedures are agreed upon, specific procedures for monitoring the integrity of the intervention plan and for evaluating the outcomes of these interventions should be developed by the psychologist and Mrs. Duffy.

8. If these intervention procedures are ineffective in bringing Don's behavior into acceptable levels, Don then should be considered for possible placement into a special education setting to receive more intensive intervention services.

References

Achenbach, T. (1991a). *Manual for the Child Behavior Checklist and 1991 Profile*. Burlington, VT: Univ. of Vermont Press.

Achenbach, T. (1991b). *Manual for the Teacher's Report Form and 1991 profile*. Burlington, VT: Univ. of Vermont Press.

Achenbach, T. (1991c). *Manual for the Youth Self-Report and 1991 Profile*. Burlington, VT: Univ. of Vermont Press.

Achenbach, T., McConaughy, S., & Howell, C. (1987). Child/adolescent behavioral and emotional problems: Implications of cross-informant correlations for situational specificity. *Psychological Bulletin, 101*, 213–232.

Asher, S., & Hymel, S. (1981). Children's social competence in peer relations: Sociometric and behavioral assessment. In J. Wine & M. Syme (Eds.), *Social competence* (pp. 125–157). New York: Guilford.

Bellack, A., & Hersen, A. (Eds.). (1979). *Research and practice in social skills training*. New York: Plenum.

Bergan. J., & Kratochwill, T. (1990). *Behavioral consultation and therapy*. New York: Plenum.

Brophy, J., & Good, T. (1986). Teacher behavior and student achievement. In M. Wittrock (Ed.), *Handbook of research on teaching* (3rd ed., pp. 328–375). New York: Macmillan.

Caldarella, P., & Merrell, K. (1997). Common dimensions of social skills of children and adolescents: A taxonomy of positive social behaviors. *School Psychology Review, 26*, 265–279.

Demaray, M., Ruffalo, S., Carlson, J., Busse, R., Olsori, A., McManus, S., & Leventhal, A. (1995).

Social skills assessment: A comparative evaluation of six published rating scales. *School Psychology Review*, 24, 648–671.

Elias, M., & Clabby, J. (1992). *Building social problem solving skills: Guidelines from a school-based program*. San Francisco: Jossey-Bass.

Elliott, S. N., & Gresham, F. M. (1992). *Social skills intervention guide*. Circle Pines, MN: American Guidance Service.

Foster, S., & Ritchey, W. (1979). Issues in the assessment of social competence in children. *Journal of Applied Behavior Analysis*, 12, 625–638.

Goldstein, A. (1988). *The Prepare Curriculum*. Champaign, IL: Research Press.

Gottman, J. (1977). Toward a definition of social isolation in children. *Child Development*, 48, 513–517.

Gresham, F. M. (1981a). Assessment of children's social skills. *Journal of School Psychology*, 19, 120–134.

Gresham, F. M. (1981b). Social skills training with handicapped children: A review. *Review of Educational Research*, 51, 139–176.

Gresham, F. M. (1983). Social validity in the assessment of children's social skills: Establishing standards for social competency. *Journal of Psychoeducational Assessment*, 1, 297–307.

Gresham, F. M. (1986). Conceptual issues in the assessment of social competence in children. In P. Strain, M. Guralnick, & H. Walker (Eds.), *Children's social behavior: Development, assessment, and modification* (pp. 143–179). New York: Academic Press.

Gresham, F. M. (1992). Social skills and learning disabilities: Causal, concomitant, or correlational? *School Psychology Review*, 21, 348–360.

Gresham, F. M. (1995). Best practices in social skills training. In A. Thomas & J. Grimes (Eds.), *Best practices in school psychology* (pp. 1021–1031). Washington, DC: National Association of School Psychologists.

Gresham, F. M. (1997). Social skills. In G. Bear, K. Minke, & A. Thomas (Eds.), *Children's needs: Psychological perspective* (2nd ed., pp. 515–526). Washington, DC: National Association of School Psychologists.

Gresham, F. M. (1998a). Social skills training with children: Social learning and applied behavior analytic approaches. In T. Watson & F. Gresham (Eds.), *Handbook of child behavior therapy* (pp. 475–498). New York: Plenum.

Gresham, F. M. (1998b). Social skills training: Should we raze, remodel, or rebuild? *Behavioral Disorders*, 24, 19–25.

Gresham, F. M., & Elliott, S. N. (1990). *Social skills rating system*. Circle Pines, MN: American Guidance Service.

Gresham, F. M., Gansle, K., & Noell, G. (1993). Treatment integrity in applied behavior analysis with children. *Journal of Applied Behavior Analysis*, 26, 257–263.

Gresham, F. M., & Lambros, K. M. (1998). Behavioral and functional assessment. In T. Watson & F. Gresham (Eds.). *Handbook of child behavior therapy* (pp. 3–22). New York: Plenum.

Gresham, F. M., & MacMillan, D. L. (1997). Social competence and affective characteristics of students with mild disabilities. *Review of Educational Research*, 67, 377–415.

Gresham, F. M., & Reschly, D. J. (1988). Issues in the conceptualization, classification, and assessment of social skills in the mildly handicapped. In T. Kratochwill (Ed.), *Advances in school psychology* (pp. 203–247). Hillsdale, NJ: Erlbaum.

Hawkins, R. (1991). Is social validity what we are interested in? Argument for a functional approach. *Journal of Applied Behavior Analysis*, 24, 205–213.

Hersh, R., & Walker, H. (1983). Great expectations: Making schools effective for all students. *Policy Studies Review*, 2, 147–188.

Individuals With Disabilities Education Act (IDEA). (1997). 20 U.S.C. Section 1400 (1990).

Kazdin, A. (1979). Situational specificity: The two-edged sword of behavioral assessment. *Behavioral Assessment*, 11, 57–75.

Kazdin, A. (1984). *Behavior modification in applied settings* (3rd ed.). Homewood, IL: Dorsey.

Kazdin, A. (1987). *Conduct disorders in childhood and adolescence.* London: Sage.

Kupersmidt, J., Coie, J., & Dodge, K. (1990). The role of peer relationships in the development of disorder. In S. Asher & J. Coie (Eds.), *Peer rejection in childhood* (pp. 274–308). New York: Cambridge Univ. Press.

Ladd, G. (1981). Effectiveness of a social learning method for enhancing children's social interaction and peer acceptance. *Child Development, 52,* 171–178.

McConnell, S., & Odom. S. (1986). Sociometrics: Peer-referenced measures and assessment of social competence. In P. Strain, M. Guralnick, & H. Walker (Eds.), *Children's social behavior: Development, assessment, and modification* (pp. 215–275). Orlando, FL: Academic Press.

McFall, R. (1982). A review and reformulation of the concept of social skills. *Behavioral Assessment, 4,* 1–35.

Merrell, K. W. (1993). *School social behavior scales.* Austin: Pro-ED.

Merrell, K. W. (1994). *Preschool and kindergarten behavior* scales. Austin: Pro-Ed.

Merrell, K. W., & Gimpel, G. (1998). *Social skills of children and adolescents: Conceptualization, assessment, treatment.* Mahwah, NJ: Erlbaum.

Newcomb, A., Bukowski, W., & Patee, L. (1993). Children's peer relations: A meta-analytic review of popular, rejected, neglected, controversial, and average sociometric status. *Psychological Bulletin, 113,* 306–347.

Oden, S., & Asher, S. (1977). Coaching children in social skills for friendship making. *Child Development, 48,* 496–506.

Oleweus, D. (1979). Stability of aggressive reaction patterns in males: A review. *Psychological Bulletin, 86,* 852–875.

O'Neill, R., Horner, R., Albin, R., Storey, K., Sprague, J., & Newton, J. (1997). *Functional analysis of problem behavior: A practical assessment guide* (2nd ed.). Pacific Grove, CA: Brooks/Cole.

Parker, J., & Asher, S. (1987). Peer relations and later personal adjustment: Are low-accepted children at risk? *Psychological Bulletin, 102,* 357–389.

Patterson, G., DeBaryshe, B., & Ramsey, E. (1989). A developmental perspective on antisocial behavior. *American Psychologist, 44,* 329–335.

Quay, H., & Peterson, D. (1987). *Manual for the Revised Behavior Problem Checklist.* Coral Gables, FL: Author.

Reid, J., & Patterson, G. (1991). Early prevention and intervention with conduct problems: A social interactional model for the integration of research and practice. In G. Stoner, M. Shinn, & H. Walker (Eds.), *Interventions for achievement and behavior problems* (pp. 715–740). Washington, DC: National Association of School Psychologists.

Reynolds, C., & Kamphaus, R. (1992). *Behavioral Assessment System for Children.* Circle Pines, MN: American Guidance Service.

Strain, P. (1977). An experimental analysis of peer social initiations on the behavior of withdrawn preschool children: Some training and generalization effects. *Journal of Abnormal Child Psychology, 5,* 445–455.

Strain, P., Cooke, R., and Apolloni, T. (1976). *Teaching exceptional children: Assessing and modifying social behavior.* New York: Academic Press.

Walker, H., Colvin, G., & Ramsey, E. (1995). *Antisocial behavior in school: Strategies and best practices.* Pacific Grove, CA: Brooks/Cole.

Walker, H., Irvin, L., Noell, J., & Singer, G. (1992). A construct score approach to the assessment of social competence: Rationale, technological considerations, and anticipated outcomes. *Behavior Modification, 16,* 448–474.

Walker, H. M., & McConnell, S. R. (1995a). *Walker-McConnell scale of social competence and school adjustment: Elementary version.* San Diego: Singular Publishing.

Walker, H. M., & McConnell, S. R. (1995b). *Walker-McConnell scale of social competence and school adjustment: Adolescent version.* San Diego: Singular Publishing.

Walker, H., McConnell, S., Holmes, D., Todis, B., Walker, J., & Golden, N. (1983). *The Walker Social*

Skills Curriculum: The ACCEPTS *Program (A curriculum for children's effective peer and teacher skills)*. Austin: Pro-Ed.

Walker, H., & Severson, H. (1992). *Systematic screening for behavior disorders*. Longmont, CO: Sopris West.

Wolf, M. M. (1978). Social validity: The case for subjective measurement or how applied behavior analysis is finding its heart. *Journal of Applied Behavior Analysis, 11*, 203–214.

CHAPTER 12

Assessment with Brief Behavior Rating Scales

ROBERT J. VOLPE
GEORGE J. DUPAUL
Lehigh University

INTRODUCTION

Behavior rating scales have become an essential part of the psychoeducational assessment of children and adolescents. A wide variety of instruments is now available for obtaining information on how the behavior of youngsters is viewed by parents, teachers, and the children themselves. These measures can be categorized by their bandwidth, or the number of constructs or syndromes they purport to measure. Specifically, broad-band scales measure multiple syndromes or behavioral domains (e.g., internalizing and externalizing), and narrow-band scales contain items focused upon one or two behavioral domains (e.g., attention-deficit/hyperactivity disorder, or ADHD). In a typical behavioral assessment procedure, broad-band rating scales such as the Child Behavior Checklist and/or the Teacher Report Form (CBCL, TRF; Achenbach, 1991a, 1991b) are administered first, to cast a wide net of measurement across several behavioral dimensions. Then, narrow-band scales may be utilized to gather more domain-specific information. The ADHD Rating Scale—IV (DuPaul, Power, Anastopoulos, & Reid, 1998) is an example of a narrow-band scale because it measures a single syndrome (e.g., ADHD).

This chapter focuses on narrow-band rating scales completed by children and the adults who have contact with them. These instruments offer several advantages to practitioners. Several commercially available narrow-band

Handbook of Psychoeducational Assessment

rating instruments are well validated and normed. In many instances, such instruments allow the acquisition of detailed information concerning child emotions and behaviors of interest across several informants and settings, making them useful sources of diagnostic information. These instruments are also cost effective in that they are easily administered and scored. Other advantages of narrow-band scales include their utility in monitoring child behavior during treatment and their ability to assess low-frequency behaviors that are difficult to evaluate with other methods (e.g., direct observations).

The rating scales reviewed in this chapter can be used at several assessment stages. First, due to their relative brevity, they may be useful as screening instruments for specific behavioral or emotional problems. Next, once children meet screening criteria, these measures may be administered to additional informants to gather information on the behaviors of interest across settings. Finally, the instruments may also be useful for the monitoring of treatment effects.

This chapter reviews and compares three measures that have been designed to measure symptoms of child externalizing behavior: the ADHD-IV, the ADHD Symptom Checklist—4, and the Short Forms of the Conners' Revised Parent and Teacher Rating Scales. We also review and compare the following child self-reported measures of internalizing symptoms: the Child "Depression Inventory (CDI), the Revised Children's Manifest Anxiety Scale (RCMAS), the Reynolds Child Depression Scale (RCDS), and the Reynolds Adolescent Depression Scale (RADS). It is our goal to provide a quick reference source to practitioners interested in using rating scales in their clinical practices. In addition to summarizing each measure's purpose, we provide a synopsis of each measure's reliability and validity as well as a description of its standardization, administration, scoring, usability, and utility. Finally, we compare and contrast rating scales that are focused on the same class of behavior. Due to space restrictions, we limit our review to the most useful and widely studied narrow-band scales relevant to those childhood emotional and behavior problems with the highest prevalence: ADHD and related disorders, depression, and anxiety. It is important to note, however, that narrow-band rating scales are available to assess other childhood disorders and behavioral concerns (e.g., pervasive developmental disorders) that are less common (see Table 12.1).

MEASURES TO ASSESS EXTERNALIZING BEHAVIOR

Occurring in 3–6% of the school-aged population (American Psychiatric Association, 1994), ADHD is the most common childhood psychiatric disorder (Taylor, 1995). Children with ADHD are principally affected by developmentally inappropriate levels of inattention and/or overactivity-impulsivity that

TABLE 12.1
Behavior Rating Scales to Assess Childhood Disorders

Disorder	Rating Scale
Conduct Disorder	Eyberg Child Behavior Inventory (Eyberg, 1992)
	Sutter-Eyberg Student Behavior Inventory (Eyberg, 1992)
	Children's Hostility Inventory (Kazdin, Rodgers, Colbus, & Siegel, 1987)
	Interview for Antisocial Behavior (Kazdin & Esveldt-Dawson, 1986)
Autistic Disorder	Childhood Autism Rating Scale (Schopler, Reichler, & Renner, 1986)
	Autism Behavior Checklist (Krug, Arick, & Almond, 1980)
	Checklist for Autism in Toddlers (Baron-Cohen, Allen, & Gillberg, 1992)
Eating Disorders	Psychiatric Rating Scale for Anorexia Nervosa (Goldberg, Halmi, Casper, Eckert, & Davis, 1977)
	Binge Eating Scale (Gormally, Black, Daston, & Rardin, 1982)
	Eating Attitudes Test (Garner & Garfinkel, 1979)
	Eating Disorders Inventory (Garner, Olmsted, & Polivy, 1983)

must be present in two or more settings (see Table 12.2). More severe externalizing problems (e.g., Oppositional Defiant Disorder and Conduct Disorder) as well as internalizing problems commonly have been found to co-occur with ADHD (August, Realmuto, MacDonald, Nugent, & Crosby, 1996).

TABLE 12.2
Examples of Attention-Deficit/Hyperactivity
Disorder Symptoms

Inattention
 Often does not pay attention to details or makes careless errors
 Often has difficulty paying attention
 Often does not seem to listen
Hyperactivity
 Often fidgets or squirms around
 Often gets out of seat when he or she is not supposed to
 Often talks too much
Impulsivity
 Often blurts out answers to questions
 Often cannot wait turn
 Often butts in

Hence, practitioners assessing youngsters at-risk for ADHD may find themselves using narrow-band rating scales that assess both externalizing and internalizing domains.

The three measures reviewed in this section (see Table 12.3) are all psychometrically sound instruments that could aid a clinician in determining whether the frequency of ADHD symptoms displayed by a specific child is developmentally deviant for that child's age and gender (i.e., by comparing a child's scores with normative data). It should be noted, however, that narrow-band rating scales are only one component of a comprehensive multimethod evaluation of ADHD that typically includes diagnostic interviews with the parent and teacher, behavior rating scales, and direct observations of behavior (Barkley, 1998). A case study at the end of this section illustrates the use of narrow-band measures as part of a comprehensive evaluation of a child suspected of having ADHD.

TABLE 12.3
Summary of Measures to Assess ADHD and Related Disorders

	ADHD-IV	ADHD Symptom Checklist—4	Revised Conners' (S)
Authors	George J. DuPaul, Tomas J. Power, Arthur D. Anastopoulos, & Robert Reid (1998)	Kenneth D. Gadow & Joyce Sprafkin (1997)	C. Keith Conners (1997)
Publisher	The Guilford Press New York, NY www.guilford.com	Checkmate Plus, Ltd., Stony Brook, NY www.checkmateplus .com	Multi-Health Systems, Inc.. North Tonawanda, NY www.mhs.com
Copyrighted	Yes	Yes	Yes
Time to Complete	< 15 minutes	< 15 minutes	< 15 minutes
Scoring Software	No	No	Yes
Ages	5–18	3–18	3–17
Items	18	50	Parent—27, Teacher—28
Subscales	3 ADHD subtypes	3 ADHD subtypes, ODD, Peer Conflict, Stimulant Side-Effects	Oppositional, Cognitive Problems, Hyperactivity, ADHD Index
Scaling	0–3	Symptom Severity— 0–3 Symptom Cutoff—0–1	0–3

(continues)

Table 12.3—*Continued*

	Available Reliability Information		
Test-Rest	Yes	Yes	Yes
Interrater	Yes	Yes	Yes
Internal Consistency	Yes	No	Yes
Normative Data			
Parent Completed	N = 2,000	N = 1,844	N = 2,426
Teacher-Completed	N = 2,000	N = 2,715	N = 1,897
	Available Validity Information		
Construct	Yes	Yes	Yes
Discriminant	Yes	Yes	Yes
Concurrent	Yes	Yes	Yes
Predictive	Yes	Yes	No
Treatment-Sensitive	No	Yes	No

ADHD Rating Scale—IV

General Overview and Psychometric Characteristics

The home and school versions of the ADHD Rating Scale—IV (ADHD-IV; DuPaul, Power, Anastopoulos, & Reid, 1998) are 18-item questionnaires designed to gather information from parents and teachers, respectively, about child symptoms of ADHD. The items mirror the diagnostic criteria of the *Diagnostic and Statistical Manual—Fourth Edition* (DSM-IV; American Psychiatric Association, 1994), and are administered in a Likert format (e.g., "never or rarely" = 0, "sometimes" = 1, "often" = 2, and "very often" = 3). Respondents are asked to endorse each item as it best describes the target child in the past six months (or if the child is new to the teacher, since the beginning of the school year). Items on the home and school versions are identical.

The reliability and internal consistency of the ADHD-IV are generally good. Specifically, test-retest coefficients (for administrations four weeks apart) were between .88 and .90 for the three subscales of the school version and between .78 and .86 for the home version. Coefficient alphas were consistently high for both versions of the checklist (alphas ≥ .86; DuPaul, Power, McGoey, Ikeda, & Anastopoulos, 1998).

The results of exploratory and confirmatory factor analyses performed on the home and school versions of the ADHD-IV suggest that both a two-factor (e.g., Inattention and Hyperactivity/Impulsivity) and a single-factor solution (ADHD) fit the data well (DuPaul et al., 1997, 1998). Some analyses favored the two-factor solution in correspondence with the DSM-IV model.

The discriminant and concurrent validities of the ADHD-IV have been investigated and appear adequate. Scores on the ADHD-IV subscales of

Inattention and Hyperactivity/Impulsivity were found to significantly discriminate between children diagnosed with ADHD-combined type (ADHD-
COM), ADHD–inattentive type (ADHD-I), and psychiatric controls in a sample
of 92 consecutive referrals to a child psychiatric outpatient clinic (DuPaul,
Power, McGoey et al., 1998). Significant correlations have been obtained between subscales of the home version of the ADHD-IV and the Conners' Parent
Rating Scale—48 (CPRS) as well as between subscales of the school version
of the ADHD-IV and the Conners' Teacher Rating Scale—39 (CTRS; DuPaul,
Power, McGoey et al., 1998).

The predictive validity of the ADHD-IV was investigated by using a logistic regression procedure (Power et al., 1998). The relevant subscales of the
ADHD-IV were able to differentiate between ADHD diagnostic groups, as well
as between children diagnosed with ADHD and psychiatric controls. Teacher
ratings were shown to be superior discriminators of diagnostic status. However, parent ratings were also significant predictors and, when used in conjunction with teacher ratings, added to the strength of prediction. There are
no data available concerning the sensitivity of the ADHD-IV to treatment
effects.

Adequate normative data are available for the ADHD-IV (DuPaul, Anastopoulos et al., 1998; DuPaul, Power, McGoey et al., 1998). The school and home
versions were standardized on samples of 2000 children and adolescents between the ages of 4 and 20 drawn from over 20 school districts across the
United States. Each sample approximated the 1990 Census data for ethnic
group and geographic region. Scores on both versions of the ADHD-IV were
found to vary significantly by age, gender, and ethnic group. As would be expected, boys tended to receive higher ratings than girls, and older children
received lower ratings than younger children. African-American children received higher ADHD-related ratings than did Latino-American or Caucasian
children, even when the effects of socioeconomic status were statistically
controlled. These findings led the authors of the ADHD-IV to provide separate standardization data by age and gender. Due to insufficient cell size, however, they were unable to develop separate scoring data based on ethnic
background. Hence, one should exercise caution when interpreting ratings
for African-American children to minimize false positives.

Administration and Scoring

The ADHD-IV manual includes all of the materials needed to administer
and score both the home and school versions and provides permission for
the purchaser to reproduce the checklists and scoring sheets for use with
their own clients and students. The ADHD-IV is comprised of two 9-item subscales (Inattention and Hyperactivity/Impulsivity) and should take a parent
or teacher no more than 5 minutes to complete. Scoring of the ADHD-IV involves summing the values of the odd-numbered items for the Inattention
raw score, summing the even-numbered items for the Hyperactivity/Impul-

sivity raw score, and then summing these two scores to obtain the Total raw score. To obtain percentile scores, the practitioner simply selects the appropriate score sheet (e.g., Home Version for Girls), finds the appropriate column based upon subscale and age (e.g., Hyperactivity/Impulsivity, 5–7), and circles the appropriate raw score (e.g., 19). The corresponding percentile score is printed on the far right or left of the score sheet.

Usability and Usefulness

The ADHD-IV is a well-developed and validated instrument that offers several advantages in the assessment of ADHD in children and adolescents. First, the instrument can be used to obtain reliable data on the presence of ADHD-related symptoms across multiple settings, and is useful in discriminating between children with and without ADHD and between children with different subtypes of ADHD. Second, the instrument is brief, affording easy administration and scoring. Because of the brevity of the scale, it is especially well-suited to monitoring treatment effects. Unfortunately, there is heretofore little evidence for the instrument's sensitivity to treatment effects. However, the authors of the ADHD-IV do provide statistical guidelines and resources for using the instrument to monitor changes in behavior (DuPaul, Power, Anastopoulos et al, 1998). Given its brevity, this scale lends itself to repeated administrations during the course of a stimulant medication trial or to monitor behavior change due to a classroom intervention. In such cases, one would need to modify instructions about the time frame to consider when rating the child's behavior (i.e., specify a treatment time frame other than over the previous 6 months).

ADHD Symptom Checklist—IV

General Overview and Psychometric Characteristics

The ADHD-Symptom Checklist—4 (SC-4; Gadow & Sprafkin, 1997) is a 50-item parent- and teacher-completed checklist composed of four categories: (a) ADHD, (b) Oppositional Defiant Disorder (ODD), (c) the Peer Conflict Scale, and (d) the Stimulant Side Effects Checklist. Items of the ADHD and ODD categories are highly similar to individual diagnostic criteria for the corresponding disorders set forth in the DSM-IV. The SC-4 was developed for several uses. First, the SC-4 was designed as a screening instrument for the most common causes of referral (e.g., disruptive child behavior) to child psychiatric clinics and to monitor changes in these symptoms during treatment. Second, given the prescription rate of psychostimulants in children with externalizing behavior difficulties, the developers of the SC-4 provided a measure of stimulant side effects that includes three indices (Mood, Attention-Arousal, and Physical Complaints).

No internal consistency data are available for the SC-4. The test-retest reliability of the SC-4 appears adequate. Reliability coefficients for the symptom severity scores of the ADHD, ODD, and Peer Conflict categories (6-week latency) ranged from .67 to .89.

No factor analytic data are available for the SC-4. The discriminant and concurrent validities of the SC-4 have been investigated and appear adequate. With a few exceptions, scores on the SC-4 have been shown to discriminate between "normal" and clinically referred groups of children and adolescents (Sprafkin & Gadow, 1996; Gadow & Sprafkin, 1997). Supporting the concurrent validity of the SC-4, the manual reports moderate to high correlations between the SC-4 categories and commonly used checklists such as the CBCL, TRF, the Mother's Objective Measure for Subgrouping (MOMS; Loney, 1984), and the IOWA Conners' (Loney & Milich, 1982).

The predictive validity of the SC-4 was assessed by investigating the degree to which cutoff scores on various SC-4 categories agreed with relevant clinical diagnoses. The statistics of sensitivity (the degree to which a measure minimizes false negatives) and specificity (the degree to which a measure minimizes false positives) are commonly used for assessing predictive validity. Generally, the predictive validity of the parent- and teacher-completed SC-4 was moderate to high (i.e., sensitivity between .58 and .89; specificity between .57 and .94).

The treatment sensitivity of the SC-4 has been investigated in several double-blind placebo-controlled studies of stimulant medication (Gadow, Nolan, Sverd, Sprafkin, & Paolicelli, 1990; Gadow, Sverd, Sprafkin, Nolan, & Ezor, 1995). Differences in scores between doses indicate that the SC-4 is a good measure of response to stimulant medication. Furthermore, the instrument appears sensitive to several stimulant side effects.

The normative data for the SC-4 were recently expanded (Gadow & Sprafkin, 1999). According to the authors, T-scores between old and new samples are very similar; however, some differences may be noted between the manual (Gadow & Sprafkin, 1997) and the revised Score Sheets. Normative data are available on 4559 children and adolescents between the ages of 3 and 18. It should be noted that normative data for the SC-4 categories of ADHD and ODD were, with few exceptions, generated with other checklists developed by the same authors (e.g., Early Childhood Inventories and Child Symptom Inventories). Items are identical except for eight ADHD items that were shortened for the SC-4. With the exception of the preschool samples, the normative samples are smaller for the Peer Conflict scale. In general, data were gathered across a number of geographic regions; however, minorities were somewhat underrepresented for some age groups.

Administration and Scoring

Checklists, Score Summary Records, and Score Sheets for the SC-4 may be obtained with the manual as a kit, and purchased separately thereafter. Identical checklists may be used for parents and teachers, and both parent and teacher scores can be recorded on the same Score Summary Record. There are also separate Score Sheets for parent- and teacher-completed checklists, which present male and female scoring information on either side of the form.

The SC-4 should take no more than 10–15 minutes for informants to complete, which they do by recording raw category scores in the cells on the form. In using the symptom severity method of scoring, individual items are scored as follows: "Never" = 0, "Sometimes" = 1, "Often" = 2, and "Very often" = 3. Item scores from each category are then summed to obtain raw category scores. The Inattentive and Hyperactive/Impulsive scores are summed to obtain an ADHD Combined Type raw score. Separate Score Sheets are available that include tabulated T-scores. The SC-4 may also be scored using the Symptom Criterion method. Here, items are scored as follows: "Never" and "Sometimes" = 0, "Often" and "Very often" = 1. The DSM-IV specifies the number of symptoms required to meet criteria for various diagnoses, and this serves as the basis for meeting criteria for the disorders represented in the SC-4. The authors of the SC-4 provide the DSM-IV symptom count criteria on the Score Summary Sheet.

Usability and Usefulness

The SC-4 appears to be a useful measure of childhood externalizing behavior difficulties (ADHD, ODD, and Interpersonal Aggression). Given the high degree of comorbidity among childhood disruptive behavior disorders, an instrument like the SC-4 that is sensitive to both ADHD and more severe behavior problems is highly desirable. The Peer Conflict Scale and the Stimulant Side Effects Checklist appear to be useful indices of interpersonal aggression and stimulant side effects, respectively. Furthermore, data supporting the sensitivity of this instrument to treatment conditions suggest that the SC-4 is a useful instrument for monitoring child behavior. Finally, the inclusion of the Stimulant Side Effects Checklist makes the SC-4 a valuable tool in the titration of stimulant medication.

The Conners' Rating Scales—Revised (Short Form)

General Overview and Psychometric Characteristics

The parent and teacher short forms of the Conners' Rating Scales—Revised (Conners, 1997) were designed for repeated and/or brief assessment of symptoms relevant to ADHD and related disorders. These instruments are available in long or short versions for parent, teacher, and adolescent completion. The long versions will not be reviewed here because they represent broadband measures. It should be noted that only the long forms of the revised

Conners' scales contain the DSM-IV symptom subscales that may be preferred for diagnostic purposes. These subscales should not be confused with the ADHD Index that is included in the short form. The 12-item ADHD Index is not factor-derived; rather, it represents the best items for distinguishing ADHD from nonclinical children. Due to space limitations, we will restrict our review to the 27-item parent short form (CPRS-R:S) and the 28-item teacher short form (CTRS-R:S). The parent and teacher short forms contain the same subscales/indices (e.g., Oppositional, Cognitive Problems, Hyperactivity, and the ADHD Index), thus allowing easy comparisons across informants. Respondents are asked to rate behavior that has been problematic over the preceding month using a four-point Likert scale labeled with both levels of appropriateness (e.g., "Not true at all" = 0), and frequency (e.g., "Very frequent" = 3).

The test-retest reliability and internal consistency of the CPRS-R:S and CTRS-R:S have both been investigated (Conners, 1997). The internal consistencies of these instruments are good. Coefficient alphas range between .86 to .94 for the parent version and between .88 to .95 for the teacher version. The test-retest reliability (over a 6–8-week period) is somewhat variable across scales and informants, with coefficients of stability ranging between .62 to .85 for parents and between .72 and .92 for teachers. For example, the coefficient of stability for the parent-rated Oppositional subscale is low (.62), whereas the stability for the teacher ratings on the same subscale is good (.84). Conversely, the stability of the parent-rated Hyperactivity subscale is good (.85), whereas teacher-rated Hyperactivity is moderate (.72).

The Oppositional, Cognitive Problems, and Hyperactivity subscales of the CPRS-R:S and the CTRS-R:S were drawn from exploratory factor analyses of the long forms of the Conners' scales (see Conners, Sitarenios, Parker, & Epstein, 1998a, 1998b). Those items with the highest factor loadings were used in the construction of the shortened subscales. These items were then subjected to a set of confirmatory maximum likelihood analyses. Goodness of fit for both the parent and teacher versions was adequate as assessed across multiple indices (e.g., AGFI, GFI, RMS). Intercorrelations between subscales were highly similar across child gender.

Correlations between the long and short versions of the three factor-derived subscales approached 1.0. Hence, Conners (1997) performed concurrent and discriminant analyses on the long forms only. The concurrent and discriminant validity of the Conners' scales appear adequate. The Oppositional, Cognitive Problems, and Hyperactivity subscales and the ADHD Index all differed significantly in comparisons of nonclinic and ADHD groups. Correlations between the revised Conners' scales and the subscales of the CPRS-93 and the CTRS-39 indicate significant overlap across relevant constructs. For example, correlations between pertinent subscales such as CPRS-R Hyperactivity and CPRS-93 Hyperactive Immature range between .63 to .89 for parent-completed instruments, and between .71 and .88 for teacher-completed instruments.

Adequate normative data (Conners, 1997) are available for the CPRS-R:S (N = 2426) and CTRS-R:S (N = 1897). It should be noted that the majority of these data were derived from rescored long forms. Caucasians in these samples appear to be overrepresented (over 80%). Males received higher scores on the three subscales and the ADHD Index on both parent and teacher versions, and in general, younger children received higher ratings on Hyperactivity and lower ratings on Cognitive Problems. It appears, however, that the gap between boys and girls on the Hyperactivity subscale narrows as children age. Several ethnic differences were also found. Specifically, the Native-American group differed from the African-American, Hispanic, Asian, and Caucasian groups on the Oppositional subscale of the CPRS-R:S. Furthermore, teacher ratings of Hyperactivity for the African-American group were found to be significantly higher than those from the Asian and Caucasian groups, and the Asian group was found to be significantly lower than the Hispanic group. These ethnic differences should be considered in interpreting scores from these instruments due to the lack of separate normative data for various ethnic groups.

Administration and Scoring

The CPRS-R:S and the CTRS-R:S each contain the Oppositional, Cognitive Problems, and Hyperactivity subscales and the ADHD Index. These instruments should take informants between 5 and 10 minutes to complete, and just a few minutes are needed to score them using the QuickScore forms. The CPRS-R:S and CTRS-R:S are assembled in three layers. As informants endorse items on the protocol layer, their responses are also recorded on the Quick-Score layer. Adjacent to the recorded responses on the QuickScore form is a scoring grid where item scores should be recorded as indicated by shading and column heading. Appropriate item scores are then summed, and total scores may be recorded at the bottom of the scoring grid. Tables of T-scores are available on the bottom layer of the QuickScore forms. T-scores of 65 or greater are usually indicative of a clinically significant problem. Simple descriptors of each scale are presented on the back of the QuickScore form.

Usability and Usefulness

The CPRS-R:S and CTRS-R:S are abbreviated versions of arguably the most commonly used rating scales for assessing child externalizing behavior. These scales offer a time-efficient alternative to the longer instruments while maintaining a substantial degree of coverage across symptoms of externalizing behavior. Clinicians can use these scales to assess the frequency that a child is reported (by parents and teachers) to exhibit symptoms of externalizing disorders relative to the normative population. This normative comparison is important because all children exhibit behaviors associated with externalizing disturbance on occasion. Therefore, it is critical to determine the degree to which a child differs quantitatively from his or her peers. Given the choice between the long and short forms of the Conners' scales, one should choose the short form when time-efficiency is important or when one expects to administer the measure repeatedly, as for treatment evaluation (Conners, 1997). Although the CPRS-R:S and the CTRS-R:S appear to be useful in the monitoring of change, no data are currently available in this regard.

Comparison of Measures for Child Externalizing Behavior

There are a number of factors to consider when comparing the three narrow-band rating scales for the assessment of externalizing behaviors. First, the degree to which each questionnaire represents the diagnostic criteria for disruptive behavior disorders as set forth in the DSM-IV is important to consider given the use of these criteria in clinical practice. Both the ADHD-IV and the SC-4 are explicitly tied to these criteria whereas the short form of the Conners' Rating Scales is not. It should be noted, however, that the Conners' ADHD index has been empirically derived to discriminate children with ADHD from normal control children.

A second factor to consider is the balance between brevity (to facilitate practical administration) and breadth of coverage. Specifically, the ADHD-IV can be completed in a very time-efficient fashion because it contains only 18 items. However, this measure does not include items related to ODD or CD, and therefore its use is limited to the assessment of ADHD symptomatology. The SC-4 and Conners' Scales are longer but do allow evaluation of ODD and CD symptoms. Thus, when choosing among these questionnaires one must consider the nature of the referral and the degree to which broad assessment of symptoms is necessary. Moreover, when one is selecting questionnaires to assess treatment response on an ongoing basis, it is important to use a measure that is quick to complete while tapping into the most critical dimensions of potential behavior change.

Another important factor is the degree to which the questionnaire has been normed on the population of interest. For example, if one is assessing preschool-aged children, then the SC-4 or Conners' scales should be used because these have normative data for children aged 3 years and up. Alternatively, when assessing ADHD in school-aged children, the ADHD-IV may be the best choice because its normative data are most representative of the U.S. population.

Finally, it should be noted that all three of these questionnaires are convenient and easy to administer and score. Furthermore, they all have sound psychometric properties when used for their intended purposes. Given that all three measures are very practical for clinicians to use, decisions about which measure is appropriate for a given situation should be based on the factors discussed above.

Case Study: Child Exhibiting
Externalizing Behavior Difficulties

Tom is an 8-year-old third grader in a general education classroom in a public elementary school. According to his parents, Tom experienced normal cognitive and physical development until he reached kindergarten. At that time, Tom's kindergarten teacher reported that he had difficulty playing quietly, had poor attention, and had a difficult time obeying classroom rules. These problems were also reported to be problematic at home. Tom's parents reported that he often seemed to ignore their requests, was difficult to control, and was easily frustrated. His current teacher reported that Tom had been inattentive and often had a difficult time staying in his seat when required to do so. The teacher also reported that he was almost always doing things other than what he was supposed to be doing, and this was disruptive to classroom activities. He frequently appeared to have a reason to avoid work (e.g., sharpening a pencil or throwing away a scrap of paper), but appeared able to do just enough work to "get by." Currently, Tom is performing at grade level in all academic areas, but he seldom completes homework assignments, which significantly impacts his grades. Also, he is beginning to experience some difficulty in mathematics. Tom's teacher is concerned with his disruption of the classroom and its impact on other students. Furthermore, he is concerned that Tom will have more difficulty in later grades if these problems persist.

After briefly discussing the case with Tom's teacher, the school psychologist asked him to complete the Teacher Report Form (TRF; Achenbach, 1991b) as a screening instrument. On the TRF, elevated scores were obtained on both the Attention Problems and Aggressive Behaviors subscales. T scores on these scales were greater than 70 (above the 98th percentile). All other scores were within the normal range (below the 93rd percentile). Based on these scores and the teacher concerns, a multimethod assessment of ADHD appeared justified.

The next step in the assessment procedure was to interview Tom's teacher. In the interview, the teacher reported that Tom often experienced problems with attention, overactivity, and impulsivity in most school settings. Problems with oppositional or aggressive behavior were not reported to occur. Tom's teacher was also asked to complete the ADHD-IV. Tom's ratings were above the 93rd percentile on the total score as well as on the Inattention and Hyperactivity-Impulsivity scores. Additionally, 14 of the 18 DSM-IV symptoms of ADHD were endorsed as occurring at least "often." Observations conducted in Tom's classroom were consistent with the reports from Tom's teacher. Tom was significantly off-task compared to randomly observed classroom peers.

When Tom's mother was interviewed, she corroborated the teacher's reports of problems with inattention, overactivity, and impulsive behavior in the absence of significant internalizing problems, and reported that most of the symptoms of ADHD had occurred frequently since kindergarten. Tom's mother was then asked to complete the Child Behavior Checklist (CBCL; Achenbach, 1991a). Her ratings generated a significantly elevated score on the Attention Problems subscale (i.e., greater than the 95th percentile). All other scores were in the normal range and below the 93rd percentile. Scores obtained on the home version of the ADHD-IV were consistent with the teacher ratings, suggesting that Tom was exhibiting significant symptoms of ADHD across school and home settings.

Based upon these assessment results, Tom appeared to be exhibiting significant symptoms of ADHD at home and school. A treatment plan was designed by the school psychologist to include behavior modification programming across settings and a referral to Tom's physician in order to explore the utility of stimulant medication. After discussing the medication option with the physician, Tom's parents opted for a trial of stimulant medication. They asked that the school psychologist be involved in the titration process so that the effects of the medication could be properly evaluated.

Tom's response to three doses (5, 10, and 15 mg) of methylphenidate (MPH) and placebo was evaluated using multiple assessment measures, including ratings on the ADHD-IV and Stimulant Side Effects Checklist of the SC-4 as well as direct observations of Tom's classroom behavior and academic performance. Each dose condition lasted for one week. Tom and his parents, teacher, and school psychologist were blind to what dose he was taking in a given week.

Analysis of the resultant data using the Reliability Change Index for ADHD-IV ratings indicated that Tom's behavior improved from placebo at each of the three doses of MPH. However, two pieces of data led the school psychologist to recommend the 5 mg dose. First, both the observational and ADHD-IV data indicated that there was not a significant change in behavior from the 5mg to 10mg dose of MPH. Second, maternal ratings from the SC-4 indicated that there was an increase in stimulant side effects from the 5mg to 10mg dose. After the titration procedure, Tom's progress was monitored by use of observation and rating scale data each month.

MEASURES TO ASSESS ANXIOUS
AND DEPRESSIVE SYMPTOMS

Children and adolescents can exhibit significant symptoms of a number of internalizing disorders, such as Separation Anxiety Disorder, Generalized Anxiety Disorder, Major Depression, and Dysthymic Disorder (American Psychiatric Association, 1994). Although the specific nature of symptomatology may differ between children and adults (e.g., children who are depressed may exhibit a chronic irritable mood rather than a depressed mood), these disorders lead to impairment in functioning as they do in adults. Specifically, children with anxiety disorders and/or depression can experience significant difficulties with academic performance and social functioning (Callahan, Panichelli-Mindel, & Kendall, 1996). Due to the overlap of symptomatology between anxiety and depression as well as the possibility that children with externalizing disorders could also experience internalizing disturbance, it is important for clinicians to assess internalizing symptoms in many cases. In particular, self-report ratings are critical because many of the symptoms of these disorders can only be detected by the children themselves (Kazdin, 1990).

The measures reviewed in this section can be used for a number of purposes, including screening for further assessment, being part of a multimodal evaluation battery, and assessing treatment outcome (see Tables 12.4 and 12.5). A case study illustrates the use of these scales as part of a multimodal assessment of internalizing behavior.

TABLE 12.4
Summary Information for the Revised
Children's Manifest Anxiety Scale

Authors	Cecil R. Reynolds and Bert O. Richmond (1985)
Publisher	Western Psychological Services Los Angeles, CA
Copyrighted	Yes
Time to Complete	< 15 minutes
Scoring Software	No
Ages	6–19
Items	37
Scaling	Yes-No
Available Reliability Information	
Test-Retest	Yes
Interrater	No
Internal Consistency	Yes
Normative Data	N = 4,972
Available Validity Information	
Construct	Yes
Discriminant	Yes
Concurrent	Yes
Predictive	No
Treatment-Sensitive	No

TABLE 12.5
Summary of Self-Report Measures to Assess Depressive Symptoms

	Children's Depression Inventory	Reynolds Adolescent Depression Scale	Reynolds Child Depression Scale
Author	Maria Kovacs (1992)	William M. Reynolds (1989)	William M. Reynolds (1989)
Publisher	Multi-Health Systems, Inc. North Tonawanda, NY www.mhs.com	PAR Odessa, FL www.testpublisher .com	PAR Odessa, FL www.testpublisher .com
Copyrighted	Yes	Yes	Yes
Time to Complete	< 15 minutes	< 15 minutes	< 15 minutes
Scoring Software	Yes	No	No
Ages	7–17	13–18	8–12
Items	27	30	30
Subscales	Negative Mood, Interpersonal Problems, Ineffectiveness, Anhedonia, Negative Self-Esteem	Total Score	Total Score
Scaling	0–2	1–4	1–4
Available Reliability Information			
Test-Retest	Yes	Yes	Yes
Interrater	No	No	No
Internal Consistency	Yes	Yes	Yes
Normative Data	N = 1,266	N = 2,460	N = 1,620
Available Validity Information			
Construct	Yes	Yes	Yes
Discriminant	Yes	Yes	Yes
Concurrent	Yes	Yes	Yes
Predictive	No	No	No
Treatment-Sensitive	Yes	No	Yes

The Revised Children's Manifest Anxiety Scale

General Overview and Psychometric Characteristics

The Revised Children's Manifest Anxiety Scale (RCMAS; Reynolds & Richmond, 1985) is a revision of the Children's Manifest Anxiety Scale (Casteneda, McCandless, & Palermo, 1956), which was derived from an adult rating scale, the Taylor Manifest Anxiety Scale (Taylor, 1951). The RCMAS is a 37-item self-report questionnaire designed to obtain information from children concerning their feelings of anxiety across several dimensions. Items on the RCMAS are worded as short statements (e.g., "I am afraid of a lot of things") and children are asked to circle "Yes" if the statement is true of them and "No" if the item is not true of them. The checklist is headed by the nonthreatening title, "What I Think and Feel."

The test-retest reliability and internal consistency of the RCMAS appear adequate. Specifically, a Kuder-Richardson 20 alpha (an index of internal consistency for dichotomously scored items) of .85 has been obtained for the total scale (Reynolds & Paget, 1983). Coefficients of stability have ranged from .68 for elementary school children tested 9 months apart to .90 for administrations 3 weeks apart (Reynolds & Paget, 1983).

In their exploratory factor analytic study, Reynolds and Paget (1981) found a five-factor solution to be the most lucid reduction of the RCMAS items. The five factors include the 11-item Worry/Oversensitivity factor, which accounted for the most variance (42%); Physiological Anxiety (10 items); Social Concerns/Concentration (7 items); Lie Scale 1 (6 items); and Lie Scale 2 (3 items). The two lie scales can be useful in determining the degree to which children respond to items in a socially desirable manner (e.g., "I tell the truth every single time").

Although the RCMAS has been found to discriminate between groups of children with anxiety disorders and normal control groups, its ability to discriminate children with anxiety disorders from other psychiatric groups has been mixed (cf., Mattison, Bagnato, & Brubaker, 1988; Perrin & Last, 1992). The RCMAS has been found to correlate highly with the Trait anxiety scale of the State-Trait Anxiety Inventory for Children (STAIC; Spielberger, 1973), yet correlations between the RCMAS and the State scale of the same STAIC were found to be nonsignificant. Finally, little information exists on the utility of the RCMAS in the monitoring of treatment regimens.

The standardization sample for the RCMAS (N = 4972) consisted of students between 6 and 19 years old who attended 80 school districts in 13 states across all major geographic regions in the United States (Reynolds & Paget, 1983). Although efforts were made to obtain ethnic diversity in the sample, children of color appear to be underrepresented (11.8% of the total sample). Approximately 600 children in the standardization sample were in classes for children who were educably mentally retarded, learning disabled, or intellectually gifted. RCMAS scores have been found to differ by age, race, and gender. Hence, normative data are organized by these variables.

Administration and Scoring

The RCMAS was designed to be administered to children and adolescents between 6 and 19 years old. As the readability of the RCMAS is estimated by its authors to be approximately third-grade level, items should be read to younger children and children who are not fluent at the third-grade level. The instrument should take no more than 15 minutes to complete. If a child is observed marking more than one response on an item (e.g., "Yes" and "No"), which often happens when children are not sure how to respond, the child should be instructed to select the choice that best describes him or her.

Scoring the RCMAS is relatively straightforward. A transparent scoring key can be placed over the child's responses to derive 5 scores: Physiological Anxiety, Worry/Oversensitivity, Social Concerns/Concentration, Lie Scale (Lie 1 and Lie 2 combined), and Total Anxiety. Each subscale has a partially opaque column that only displays the item responses for that subscale when placed over the response area of the protocol. Items can then be summed ("Yes" = 1, "No" = 0) to obtain subscale scores.

Usability and Usefulness

The RCMAS is arguably the best known measure of general childhood distress. It is easily administered and scored, and it possesses adequate psychometric properties. However, due to mixed results in the measure's ability to discriminate between psychiatric groups, it appears to be most useful as a screening instrument. A structured psychiatric interview may be preferred for diagnostic purposes. The Lie scales of the RCMAS make it a useful tool for practitioners who wish to measure a child's tendency to respond in a socially desirable manner. Finally, normative data for the RCMAS was collected over 20 years ago and might be considered outdated. Furthermore, the normative sample is composed almost entirely of Caucasian children. Thus, clinicians should be cautious when using this instrument with children from minority backgrounds.

The Children's Depression Inventory

General Overview and Psychometric Properties

The Children's Depression Inventory (CDI; Kovacs, 1981, 1992) is a downward extension of the Beck Depression Inventory (Beck, Ward, Mendelson, Mock, & Erbaugh, 1961) for children and adolescents between 7 and 17 years old. The CDI is available in both a 27-item version, which was designed to measure cognitive, affective, and behavioral indicators of depression, and a 10-item version (CDI-S; Kovacs, 1992), which may be preferred for a quick screening instrument. The administration of the CDI and CDI-S involves the presentation of three alternative statements (e.g., "I am sad once in a while," "I am sad many times," and "I am sad all the time"). Children are asked to select the statement that best describes them within the past two weeks.

The psychometric properties of the CDI have been well studied (e.g., Finch,

Saylor, & Edwards, 1985; Kazdin, French, Unis, Esveldt-Dawson, & Sherick, 1983; Kovacs, 1981). The internal consistency and item-total score correlations appear adequate (coefficient alphas ranged between .71 to .89). Several studies have found adequate coefficients of stability for the CDI. For example, Finch et al. (1987) obtained adequate test-retest reliability coefficients for 2-week (.82), 4-week (.66), and 6-week (.67) latencies in a normative sample. However, for shorter latencies (e.g., 1 week), low stability has been found (.38) in a group of normal school children, compared to high stability (.87) for a group of psychiatric inpatients (Saylor, Finch, Baskin, Furey, & Kelly, 1984).

Several studies have investigated the factor structure of the 27-item CDI (e.g., Helsel & Matson, 1984; Saylor, Finch, Spirito, & Bennett, 1984; Weiss & Weisz, 1988; Weiss et al., 1991). At least partially due to disparate factor analytic strategies, investigators have found different numbers of factors for the CDI items (between three and eight). Based upon a set of maximum likelihood factor analyses on a normative sample of 1266 school-aged children, prior factor analytic studies, and the interpretability of factors, Kovacs (1992) chose a five-factor solution: Negative Mood, Interpersonal Problems, Ineffectiveness, Anhedonia, and Negative Self-Esteem. All of these factors have been found to be significantly intercorrelated (Kovacs, 1992).

The concurrent validity of the CDI has been studied by several investigators (e.g., Kazdin et al., 1983). The CDI has been found to correlate with other measures of depression (e.g., Weissman, Orvaschel, & Padain, 1980) and measures of other related constructs such as self-concept and hopelessness (e.g., Kazdin, French, Unis, & Esveldt-Dawson, 1983; Saylor, Finch, Baskin, Furey, & Kelly, 1984). Information concerning the discriminant validity of the CDI is mixed. Although the CDI has demonstrated the ability to discriminate depressed children from non-depressed children as identified by child interviews (Hodges, 1990), its ability to discriminate between psychiatrically diagnosed groups has been inadequate. For example, Wendel, Nelson, Politano, Mayhall, and Finch (1988), investigating the ability of the CDI to discriminate between inpatient clinic samples and a large sample of normal children, found the CDI to correctly classify 83% of all subjects. However, 100% of the inpatient children were incorrectly classified as normal. The treatment sensitivity of the CDI has been demonstrated in a study of group therapy for children of divorced parents (Garvin, Leber, & Kalter, 1991).

The standardization sample of the CDI and CDI-S consisted of 1266 children and adolescents between 7 and 16 years old from public schools in Florida (Kovacs, 1992). Although demographic data were not collected, it has been estimated that 77% of the sample was Caucasian and a relatively large percentage of the sample was middle class. No formal comparisons were made to U.S. Census data. Based upon the homogeneity of this normative sample (e.g., geographic region, race, and class), one should exercise caution in making generalizations from these data to underrepresented populations.

Administration and Scoring

The CDI and CDI-S were designed to be administered to children and adolescents between 7 and 17 years old, although normative data are limited to boys between 7 and 15 years old and girls between 7 and 16 years old. The 27-item CDI should take no more than 15 minutes for children to complete and the 10-item CDI-S no more than 5–10 minutes. Although the specific readability of the CDI has not been assessed, it may be advisable to read the items to younger children or those with reading difficulties while allowing them to follow along on their own form. One should ensure that the child is aware that he or she should mark only a single box out of the three alternatives. Occasionally, children express concern that some items do not pertain to them. In this event, one should encourage the child to mark the choice that best fits him or her. Like the revised Conners', the CDI and CDI-S use QuickScore forms, which automatically transfer child responses to the scoring layer of the protocol. The CDI/CDI-S items are scored on a 3-point scale. Next to each box on the scoring layer is a number from 0 to 2. Each item also is labeled with a letter indicating which factor it is associated with (e.g., A = Negative Mood, B = Interpersonal Problems). The scores for each item contributing to the factor in question (e.g., all the items labeled A) are summed to obtain the factor raw score. T-scores 65 or greater are considered clinically significant.

Usability and Usefulness

The CDI is the most widely used self-report rating scale to assess childhood depressive symptoms (Kazdin, 1990). Items are reflective of affective, cognitive, and behavioral symptoms associated with depression, and the CDI has demonstrated reasonable psychometric properties. The CDI is relatively easy to administer and score, and the CDI-S may be used when an especially brief measure is desired. Finally, the CDI may be a useful tool in assessing treatment efficacy, although this has not been extensively studied.

The Reynolds Child and Adolescent Depression Scales

General Overview

The Reynolds Adolescent Depression Scale (RADS; Reynolds, 1987) is a 30-item self-report questionnaire developed to measure the severity of depressive symptoms in adolescents between 13 and 18 years old. The protocol itself is labeled in a nonthreatening manner (e.g., "About Myself"). Items are presented as short statements (e.g., "I feel lonely"), and adolescents are asked to respond on a 4-point Likert scale based on frequency ("Almost never," "Hardly ever," "Sometimes," and "Most of the time"). The Reynolds Child Depression Scale (RCDS; Reynolds, 1989) is a similar 30-item self-report questionnaire designed for children between 8 and 12 years old. The first 29 items are presented as short statements; most of which are identical to the statements in the RADS. Children are asked to respond on a similar scale to the RADS ("Almost never," "Sometimes," "A lot of the time," and "All the time"). The final item presents children with 5 line-drawn faces that appear in the range from very happy to very sad; children are asked to "Fill in the circle over the face that shows how [they] feel."

Psychometric Properties of the RADS

The RADS has demonstrated good internal consistency, including alphas of .90 (Reynolds, 1987). The stability of the RADS was measured at 6-week, 3-month, and 1-year intervals in heterogeneous groups of depressed and nondepressed high-school students. Coefficients of stability ranged between .80 and .79 for 6-week and 3-month intervals, respectively, and .63 for a 1-year latency (Reynolds, 1987).

A series of factor analytic studies (Reynolds, 1987) indicate a five-factor solution for the RADS, with the majority of items loading on the first factor (Generalized Demoralization), which accounted for approximately 32% of the overall variance. The other four factors accounting for an additional 28% of the overall variance are Despondency and Worry, Somatic-Vegetative, Anhedonia, and Self-Worth. However, norms have not been developed for these individual factors.

The validity of the RADS has been supported by several methods. Consistent with the factor analytic data, item-total correlations in a sample of 2296 adolescents suggest good content validity (median $r = .53$). The concurrent validity of the RADS appears adequate. Specifically, the RADS has been compared to several other self-report depression rating scales including the Beck Depression Inventory (Beck et al., 1961), the Center for Epidemiological Studies Depression Scale (Radloff, 1977), the Self-Rating Depression Scale (Zung, 1965), and the Children's Depression Inventory (Kovacs, 1992). The RADS has been shown to discriminate between groups of adolescents with and without depression (Evert & Reynolds, 1986). Finally, a wait-list-controlled comparative treatment study of adolescents with severe depression has supported the utility of the RADS as a treatment-monitoring instrument: While the treatment groups evidenced declining RADS scores, the wait-list control group's RADS scores were relatively stable (Reynolds & Coats, 1986).

Normative data are available for 2460 7th- through 12th-graders from one senior- and two junior-high schools in an urban/suburban community in the midwestern United States. Despite the apparent overrepresentation of Caucasians (76%) and the restricted geographic sampling, Reynolds (1987) reports that the sample is well stratified in terms of age, sex, race, and socioeconomic status.

Psychometric Properties of the RCDS

The RCDS has demonstrated good internal consistency and stability (Reynolds, 1989). Specifically, coefficient alphas computed for individual grades and for the entire standardization sample were consistently high (alphas between .85 to .90). The RCDS has demonstrated good 4-week stability ($r = .85$) in a sample of 220 third- through fifth-grade students (Reynolds & Graves, 1989).

Results of a factor analytic study conducted by Reynolds (1989) indicate a five-factor solution to the RCDS items. The first factor, Despondency-Worry, accounted for 27.5% of the total variance. The four remaining factors (Generalized Demoralization-Despondency, Somatic-Vegetative, Dysphoric Mood, and Anhedonia) account for an additional 19.6% of the total variance. The results of this analysis suggest that the RCDS, like the RADS, measures several dimensions of depression.

Supporting the content validity of the RCDS, the vast majority of items (24 out of 30) were found to significantly covary as indicated by a set of item-total scale correlations (Reynolds, 1989). The concurrent validity of the RCDS has been investigated utilizing several other self-report measures of depressive symptomatology (Reynolds, 1989); for example, the RCDS was found to correlate significantly with the Children's Depression Rating Scale—Revised (Poznanski, Freeman, & Mokros, 1985) as well as with clinical interviews. The convergent validity of the RCDS has been found to correlate significantly with measures of constructs related to depression such as self-esteem and anxiety (Reynolds, Anderson, & Bartell, 1985). A study conducted by Stark, Reynolds, and Kaslow (1987) demonstrated the utility of the RCDS as a treatment outcome measure: While the two treatment groups in this study demonstrated significant declines in RCDS scores, the control group's scores were relatively stable.

Normative data for the RCDS are based upon a sample of 1620 second- through seventh-grade students from the midwestern and western United States. Grade-level normative data are only available for grades 3 through 6 due to a limited sample size in grades 2 and 7. According to Reynolds (1989), the standardization sample was heterogeneous in terms of age, sex, gender, and socioeconomic status. Approximately 71% of the sample children were Caucasian.

Administration and Scoring of the RADS and RCDS

The RADS and RCDS are available in both hand-scored and computer-scored versions, and neither instrument should take informants more than 5 to 10 minutes to complete. As with some of the instruments described above, it may be preferable to read items to young children while they follow along on their protocol. Reynolds (1987, 1989) suggested that children and adolescents be informed that there are no right and wrong answers, and that the purpose of the instrument is to assess the individual's general feelings about himself or herself. Responses should be made with a pencil so that children can change them. Both the RADS and RCDS generate a single total score. Transparent scoring keys are available for hand-scoring the RADS and RCDS. It is essential that the scoring keys be used because several items on both instruments are reverse-scored. Protocols with less than 24 items endorsed should not be considered valid. For protocols that have between 24 and 29 items endorsed, multiply the total score by 30 and divide by the number of items completed. Other validity checks are available in the manuals of these measures and should be referred to when interpreting scores. Percentile scores based on grade and gender are available in the appendices of the RADS and RCDS manuals. It is suggested that a raw score greater than 77 on the RADS or greater than 74 on the RCDS is clinically significant; however, certain critical items (e.g., those indicating self-destructive behavior) should also be examined in children and adolescents who do not meet the clinical cutoff (Reynolds, 1987, 1989).

Usability and Usefulness of the RADS and RCDS

The RADS and RCDS appear to be psychometrically sound measures of child and adolescent depressive symptomatology, and both are easily administered and scored. They seem well suited for use as screening tools, as part of a comprehensive diagnostic assessment, and for the monitoring of intervention effects.

Comparison of Measures for Depressive Symptoms

All three of the depression measures reviewed in this chapter have adequate psychometric properties, are of approximately the same length, and are easy to administer and score. The CDI has been in use for a longer period of time and consequently has been subjected to greater empirical scrutiny. Furthermore, the response format of the CDI may be easier for children to understand because it is more concrete than the anchor points used in the Likert scale on the RADS and RCDS. However, the total sum scoring of the RADS and RCDS may be more appropriate for assessing depressive symptoms given that the construct of depression in children appears to be a unitary (i.e., one-factor) phenomenon. When one examines the factor analytic results for the CDI, it appears that it is composed of one strong factor (accounting for 23% of the variance) and possibly a second factor (Negative Mood). Thus, the clinical utility of CDI factors beyond the total score and Negative Mood score may be limited. Finally, it should be noted that minority representation in the normative data of all three measures is very limited. Clinicians should use caution when using these depression measures to assess children from non-Caucasian backgrounds. Both the RADS and the RCDS have demonstrated adequate treatment sensitivity. Hence, by administering these scales before the implementation of treatment and by intervals throughout the intervention, these scales may be a source of useful information in monitoring treatment effects.

Case Study: Child Exhibiting Internalizing Behavior Difficulties

Michelle is a 10-year-old fifth-grader who was referred by her teacher to the school psychologist for academic difficulty and inattentive behavior. A review of Michelle's academic records indicated that she was an above-average student, receiving A's and B's since school entry.

An interview with Michelle's teacher revealed that Michelle's grades were average in September, but had been dropping steadily for several months. It seemed that Michelle was having great difficulty staying on task and would frequently exhibit escape behaviors (e.g., asking to go to the lavatory or for a drink of water). Over the past several weeks, Michelle began to complain of aches and pains during class tests, and her teacher was becoming concerned that Michelle appeared withdrawn and sad.

The scores on the TRF generated by Michelle's teacher showed clinically significant elevations (T scores above 70) on both the Withdrawn and Anxious/Depressed subscales.

Michelle's parents noted similar concerns during a phone interview. They reported that Michelle had become increasingly withdrawn and seemed to change activities frequently. She often appeared to be sad and did not seem to enjoy her usual play activities. Furthermore, she had been having difficulty sleeping through the night. The parental interview revealed that Michelle's parents had been experiencing marital discord since the previous summer, and Michelle's father had recently moved out of the house.

Michelle was asked to complete both the RCDS and the RCMAS. On the RCDS, Michelle responded to all 30 items, receiving a score of 89 (98th percentile). Some of the items that she endorsed as happening "a lot of the time" were "I worry about school," "I feel like crying," and "I feel my parents don't like me." Michelle's response of "sometimes" to the item "I feel like hurting myself" was considered an important issue to raise during a subsequent interview with her. On the RCMAS, Michelle received a scaled score of 13 (88th percentile) on the Physiological subscale, a 14 (92nd percentile) on both the Worry/Oversensitivity and Social Concerns subscales, and a Total Anxiety T score of 66. Examples of some of the items endorsed by Michelle that were addressed in the subsequent interview with her were "I feel alone even though people are with me," "I worry about what is going to happen," and "It is hard for me to keep my mind on my schoolwork." Michelle was interviewed by the school psychologist and reported that she was getting a lot of homework this year and that she was feeling overwhelmed. Michelle described the situation at home and said that she was worried about what would happen with her parents. She also reported feeling sad quite frequently. The issue of suicidal ideation was discussed and Michelle said she had thought about what would happen if she were to hurt herself, but these were passing thoughts with no clear plans for following through.

A curriculum-based assessment revealed that Michelle was at or close to grade level in the areas of reading, mathematics, and written expression. Thus, taken together, the assessment data suggested that Michelle was experiencing clinically significant depressive symptoms and some noteworthy anxiety disorder symptoms, all of which appeared to be the result of her home situation. These symptoms appeared to be affecting her ability to concentrate and socialize in school, which had a negative impact on her academic performance. In turn, Michelle's difficulty in keeping up with task demands in school exacerbated her symptoms of anxiety.

A treatment plan was designed to reduce task demands so that Michelle would not be overwhelmed by her class assignments and homework. It was further recommended that Michelle's parents help her to understand the marital difficulties they were experiencing and to consider family counseling.

Evaluating Children from Diverse Backgrounds

The population of children in North America is becoming increasingly diverse in terms of ethnicity and language. Thus, clinicians are now faced with the challenge of evaluating children from diverse backgrounds, and unfortunately the normative samples of many behavior rating scales do not include adequate numbers of children from non-Caucasian, non-English-speaking backgrounds. The measures reviewed in this chapter vary with respect to the degree to which their normative data are representative of the U.S. population. Some recently devised scales, such as the Conners' and the ADHD-IV, include norms that are based on nationally representative samples. Older questionnaires, like the RCMAS, have been standardized on virtually all-Caucasian samples. Thus, clinicians must be aware of the degree to which normative data are applicable when evaluating a specific child. Furthermore, even when normative data are representative, there may be systematic differences in scores between ethnic groups (e.g., higher ratings for African-Americans than Caucasians on the ADHD-IV). In such cases, clinicians should be cautious in using normative cut points. For example, a higher threshold (e.g., 98th percentile) might be used to determine the clinical significance of ADHD-IV scores for an African-American child.

Integrating Data from Multiple Informants

It is generally accepted that a thorough assessment of child psychopathology requires reports from one or more adults (e.g., mother and/or teacher) in addition to the report of the child. Efforts of combining information from multiple informants to increase diagnostic accuracy have been complicated by low correlations between types of informants (e.g., Edelbrock, Costello, Dulcan, Conover, & Kalas, 1986). The discrepancies in scores can be attributed to several factors (e.g., variance across situations and differential perceptions of behavior). How data are combined to arrive at reliable diagnostic decisions depends largely on the type of assessment one is conducting. For example, by summing responses across informants one improves sensitivity (e.g., increasing true positives), but almost always at the cost of specificity (e.g., increasing false positives). When the mission of assessment is to screen for behavior or emotional problems, this trade-off may be acceptable. Alternatively, when using rating scales to derive a clinical diagnosis, false positives are far less acceptable. In such cases, one may choose to take an optimal informant approach (e.g., Loeber, Green, Lahey, & Stouthamer-Loeber, 1989). This methodology involves selecting the most reliable informant based on age and the dimension of behavior being assessed. For example, when assessing a child in elementary school, teacher ratings may be more useful than parent ratings because teachers have more experience with school-aged children and presumably are in a better position to make normative comparisons. Unfortunately, the optimal informant approach does not fully take into consideration differences in behavior across settings. For example, a child may only exhibit behavior problems when he or she is at home. Hence, teacher reports would not be sensitive to the problems experienced by the child's family. Offord et al. (1996) suggest that child emotional and behavioral problems may best be viewed as "informant specific," and that combining data from different informants may obscure the true pattern of behavior. Thus, practitioners must decide how to handle informant discrepancies based on the context and purpose of the evaluation.

Evaluating Treatment Outcome

Several of the measures (SC-4, CDI, RADS, and RCDS) reviewed here have been studied for their sensitivity to treatment regimens. Due to their relative brevity, all of the measures reviewed here may be considered for assessing changes in child behavior. Supplied with such measures, practitioners are left with the problem of determining if a measured change is clinically significant. Fortunately, the Reliability Change Index (RCI; Jacobsen & Truax, 1991) is well suited to fulfill this need. The RCI is simply the difference between a child's pretreatment and posttreatment score, divided by the standard error of difference between the two test scores. When this value is greater than 1.96, it is unlikely that the change between administrations is due to chance ($p < .05$). Although only the ADHD-IV manual contains tables helpful in deriving RCI scores, clinicians can determine this for any of the rating scales reviewed here by using the test-retest reliability coefficient to calculate the standard error of difference (see Jacobsen & Truax, 1991, for details).

SUMMARY AND CONCLUSIONS

A number of narrow-band rating scales are available to assess the internalizing and externalizing behavior difficulties exhibited by children. All of the questionnaires reviewed in this chapter possess adequate psychometric properties and are clinically useful. In particular, these instruments are quite valuable when screening children for further assessment. Specifically, narrow-band rating scales provide clinicians with important information regarding the degree to which children exhibit behavior difficulties at a significantly higher rate or of greater severity than do other children of the same age and gender. This information is helpful because, for many of the disorders assessed by these rating scales (e.g., ADHD), one must establish that behavioral symptoms are quantitatively different from the normative population. Although these instruments also are useful for diagnostic decision making and treatment evaluation, it should be noted that rating scales should never be used in isolation for these purposes; instead, assessment methods that incorporate information from multiple sources and settings should be used to make important clinical decisions. The rating scales reviewed in this chapter can be useful in this context when supplemented with other data to give a more complete picture of a child's functioning.

The empirical underpinnings of child behavior rating scales are relatively strong and support the use of these instruments in most clinical circumstances. Nevertheless, several factors should be taken into account when interpreting scores from behavior questionnaires. The relevance of available normative data to the child population being assessed is extremely important. Specifically, some measures (e.g., RCMAS) may have normative data that are relatively outdated and that do not include adequate numbers of children from minority groups. In general, one must be cautious in using clinical cutoff scores, especially when assessing children from diverse ethnic or linguistic backgrounds. There simply are not enough data to support the strict use of percentile and cut-point scores with minority children, especially when one is concerned about overidentification of children from diverse backgrounds as disordered. When evaluating students from minority backgrounds, clinicians should use more conservative cut points (e.g., 98th percentile) for diagnostic decision making. Another possible solution is to collect data from a local sample that is representative of the population being served. This may not be practical in some circumstances but can serve as a stopgap measure until more representative normative data are available for these instruments.

Another factor to consider when interpreting the results of behavior rating scales is the nature of responses to individual items. Although one would typically place most credence in total or subscale scores, in some instances individual item scores should be examined for clinically relevant information. This is particularly true for measures of internalizing symptoms like certain items on the CDI (e.g., "I want to kill myself") and RCDS (e.g., "I feel like hurting myself"). Individual item responses may indicate problem areas that are not immediately evident when relying solely on summary scores.

Narrow-band rating scales are very useful in the assessment of disruptive and internalizing behaviors exhibited by children and adolescents. This chapter has reviewed some of the more commonly used measures employed by clinicians for screening, diagnostic, and treatment-evaluation purposes. Such scales have become more popular for clinical decision making and fortunately their use is supported by a growing body of empirical investigations. When included as part of a multimethod assessment battery, narrow-band rating scales can provide information that is both time-efficient and clinically relevant.

References

Achenbach, T. M. (1991a). *Manual for the Child Behavior Checklist/4–18 and 1991 Profile.* Burlington, VT: Univ. of Vermont Press.

Achenbach, T. M. (1991b). *Manual for the Teacher's Report Form and 1991 Profile.* Burlington, VT: Univ. of Vermont Press.

American Psychiatric Association. (1994). *Diagnostic and statistical manual for mental disorders* (4th ed.). Washington, DC: Author.

August, G. J., Realmuto, G. M., MacDonald, A. W., Nugent, S. M., & Crosby, R. (1996). Prevalence of ADHD and comorbid disorders among elementary school children screened for disruptive behavior. *Journal of Abnormal Child Psychology, 24,* 571–595.

Barkley, R.A. (1998). *Attention deficit hyperactivity disorder: A handbook for diagnosis and treatment* (2nd ed.). New York: Guilford.

Baron-Cohen, S., Allen, J., & Gillberg, C. (1992). Can autism be detected at 18 months? The needle, the haystack, and the CHAT. *British Journal of Psychiatry, 161,* 839–843.

Beck, A. T., Ward, C., Mendelson, M., Mock, J., & Erbaugh, J. (1961). An inventory for measuring depression. *Archives of General Psychiatry, 4,* 561–571.

Callahan, S. A., Panichelli-Mindel, S. M., & Kendall, P. C. (1996). DSM-IV and internalizing disorders: Modifications, limitations, and utility. *School Psychology Review, 25,* 297–307.

Castenada, A., McCandless, B., & Palermo, D. (1956). The children's form of the Manifest Anxiety Scale. *Child Development, 27,* 317–326.

Conners, C. K. (1997). *Conners' Rating Scales Revised.* North Tonawanda, NY: Multi-Health Systems.

Conners, C. K., Sitarenios, G., Parker, J. D. A., & Epstein, J. N. (1998a). The Revised Conners' Parent Rating Scale (CPRS-R): Factor structure, reliability, and criterion validity. *Journal of Abnormal Child Psychology, 26*(4), 257–268.

Conners, C. K., Sitarenios, G., Parker, J. D. A., & Epstein, J. N. (1998b). Revision and restandardization of the Conners' Teacher Rating Scale (CTRS-R): Factor structure, reliability, and criterion validity. *Journal of Abnormal Child Psychology, 26*(4), 279–291.

DuPaul, G. J., Anastopoulos, A. D., Power, T. J., Reid, R., Ikeda, M., & McGoey, K. (1998). Parent ratings of attention-deficit/hyperactivity disorder symptoms: Factor structure and normative data. *Journal of Psychopathology and Behavioral Assessment, 20,* 83–102.

DuPaul, G. J., Power, T. J., Anastopoulos, A. D., & Reid, R. (1998). *ADHD Rating Scale-IV: Checklists, Norms, and Clinical Interpretation.* New York: Guilford.

DuPaul, G. J., Power, T. J., Anastopoulos, A. D., Reid, R., McGoey, K., & Ikeda, M. (1997). Teacher ratings of attention-deficit/hyperactivity disorder symptoms: Factor structure and normative data. *Psychological Assessment, 9,* 436–444.

DuPaul, G. J., Power, T. J., McGoey, K., Ikeda, M., & Anastopoulos, A. D. (1998). Reliability and validity of parent and teacher ratings of attention-deficit/hyperactivity disorder symptoms. *Journal of Psychoeducational Assessment, 16,* 55–68.

Edelbrock, C., Costello, A. J., Dulcan, M. K., Conover, N. C., & Kalas, R. (1986). Parent-child agreement on child psychiatric symptoms assessed via structured interview. *Journal of Child Psychology & Psychiatry & Allied Disciplines*, 27(2), 181–190.

Evert, T., & Reynolds, W. M. (1986). Efficacy of a multistage screening model for depression in adolescents. Unpublished manuscript.

Eyberg, S. M. (1992). Parent and teacher behavior inventories for the assessment of conduct problem behaviors in children. In L. VandeCreek, S. Knapp, & T. L. Jackson (Eds.), *Innovations in clinical practice: A source book* (Vol. 11, pp. 261–270). Sarasota, FL: Professional Resource Exchange.

Finch, A. J., Saylor, C. F., & Edwards, G. L. (1985). Children's Depression Inventory: Sex and grade norms for normal youth. *Journal of Consulting and Clinical Psychology*, 53(3), 424–425.

Gadow, K. D., Nolan, E. E., Sverd, J., Sprafkin, J., & Paolicelli, L. (1990). Methylphenidate in aggressive-hyperactive boys: I. Effects on peer aggression in public school settings. *Journal of the American Academy of Child and Adolescent Psychiatry*, 29, 710–718.

Gadow, K. D., & Sprafkin, J. (1997). ADHD *Symptom Checklist*—4 Manual. Stony Brook, NY: Checkmate Plus, Ltd.

Gadow, K. D., & Sprafkin, J. (1999). 1999 *Revised Norms: ADHD-SC4*. Stony Brook, NY: Checkmate Plus, Ltd.

Gadow, K. D., Sverd, J., Sprafkin, J., Nolan, E. E., & Ezor, S. N. (1995). Efficacy of methylphenidate for attention-deficit hyperactivity disorder in children with tic disorder. *Archives of General Psychiatry*, 52, 444–455.

Garner, D. M., & Garfinkel, P. E. (1979). The Eating Attitudes Test: An index of the symptoms of Anorexia Nervosa. *Psychological Medicine*, 9, 273–279.

Garner, D. M., Olmsted, M. P., & Polivy, J. (1983). Development and validation of a multidimensional Eating Disorder Inventory for Anorexia Nervosa and Bulimia. *International Journal of Eating Disorders*, 2, 15–34.

Garvin, V., Leber, D., & Kalter, N. (1991). Children of Divorce: Predictors of change following preventive intervention. *American Journal of Orthopsychiatry*, 61(3), 438–447.

Goldberg, S. C., Halmi, K. A., Casper, R., Eckert, E., & Davis, J. M. (1977). Pretreatment predictors of weight change in Anorexia Nervosa. In R. A. Vigersky (Ed.), *Anorexia Nervosa* (pp. 31–42). New York: Raven Press.

Gormally, J., Black, S., Daston, S., & Rardin, D. (1982). The assessment of binge eating severity among obese persons. *Addictive Behaviors*, 7, 47–55.

Helsel, W. J., & Matson, J. L. (1984). The assessment of depression in children: The internal structure of the Child Depression Inventory (CDI). *Behavior Research and Therapy*, 22(3), 289–298.

Hodges, K. (1990). Depression and anxiety in children: A comparison of self-report questionnaires to clinical interview. *Psychological Assessment*, 2, 376–381.

Jacobsen, N. S., & Truax, P. (1991). Clinical significance: A statistical approach to defining meaningful change in psychotherapy research. *Journal of Consulting and Clinical Psychology*, 59, 12–19.

Kazdin, A. E. (1990). Assessment of childhood depression. In A. M. La Greca (Ed.), *Through the eyes of the child* (pp. 189–233). Boston: Allyn & Bacon.

Kazdin, A. E., & Esveldt-Dawson, K. (1986). The Interview for Antisocial Behavior: Psychometric characteristics and concurrent validity with child psychiatric inpatients. *Journal of Psychopathology and Behavioral Assessment*, 8, 289–303.

Kazdin, A. E., French, N. H., Unis, A. S., & Esveldt-Dawson, K. (1983). Assessment of childhood depression: Correspondence of child and parent ratings. *Journal of the American Academy of Child Psychiatry*, 22(2), 157–164.

Kazdin, A. E., French, N. H., Unis, A. S., Esveldt-Dawson, K., & Sherick, R. B. (1983). Hopelessness, depression, and suicidal intent among psychiatrically disturbed inpatient children. *Journal of Consulting and Clinical Psychology*, 51(4), 504–510.

Kazdin, A. E., Rodgers, A., Colbus, D., & Siegel, T. (1987). Children's Hostility Inventory: Measurement of aggression and hostility in psychiatric inpatient children. *Journal of Clinical Child Psychology*, 16, 320–328.

Kovacs, M. (1981). Ratings to assess depression in school-aged children. *Acta Paedopsychiatria*, 46, 305–315.

Kovacs, M. (1992). *Children's Depression Inventory Manual.* North Tonawanda, NY: Multi-Health Systems.

Krug, D. A., Arick, J., & Almond, P. (1980). Behavior checklist for identifying severely handicapped individuals with high levels of autistic behavior. *Journal of Child Psychology & Psychiatry & Allied Disciplines, 21,* 221–229.

Loeber, R., Green, S., Lahey, B. B., & Stouthamer-Loeber, M. (1989). Optimal informants on child disruptive behaviors. *Development and Psychopathology, 1,* 317–337.

Loney, J. (1984). "A short parent scale for subgrouping childhood hyperactivity and aggression." Paper presented at the meeting of the American Psychological Association, Toronto.

Loney, J., & Milich, R. (1982). Hyperactivity, inattention, and aggression in clinical practice (the IOWA Conners'). In M. Wolraich & D. K. Routh (Eds.), *Advances in developmental and behavioral pediatrics* (Vol. 3, pp. 113–147). Greenwich, CT: JAI.

Mattison, R. E., Bagnato, S. J., & Brubaker, B. H. (1988). Diagnostic utility of the Revised Children's Manifest Anxiety Scale for children with DSM-III anxiety disorders. *Journal of Anxiety Disorders, 2*(2), 147–155.

Offord, D. R., Boyle, M. H., Racine, Y., Szatmari, P., Fleming, J. E., Sanford, M., & Lipman, E. L. (1996). Integrating assessment data from multiple informants. *Journal of the American Academy of Child and Adolescent Psychiatry, 35*(8), 1078–1085.

Perrin, S., & Last, C. G. (1992). Do childhood anxiety measures measure anxiety? *Journal of Abnormal Child Psychology, 20*(6), 567–578.

Power, T. J., Doherty, B. J., Panichelli-Mindel, S. M., Karustis, J. L., Eiraldi, R. B., Anastopoulos, A. D., & DuPaul, G. J. (1998). Integrating parent and teacher reports in the assessment of ADHD. *Journal of Psychopathology and Behavioral Assessment, 20,* 57–81.

Poznanski, E. O., Freeman, L. N., & Mokros, H. B. (1985). Children's Depression Rating Scale—Revised. *Psychopharmacology Bulletin, 21,* 979–989.

Radloff, L. S. (1977). The CES-D Scale: A self-report scale for research in the general population. *Applied Psychological Measurement, 1,* 385–401.

Reynolds, C. R., & Paget, K. D. (1981). Factor analysis of the Revised Children's Manifest Anxiety Scale for blacks, whites, males, and females with a national normative sample. *Journal of Consulting and Clinical Psychology, 49*(3), 352–359.

Reynolds, C. R., & Paget, K. D. (1983). National normative and reliability data for the Revised Children's Manifest Anxiety Scale. *School Psychology Review, 12*(3), 324–336.

Reynolds, C. R., & Richmond, B. O. (1985). *Revised Children's Manifest Anxiety Scale manual.* Los Angeles: Western Psychological Services.

Reynolds, W. M. (1987). *Reynolds Adolescent Depression Scale.* Odessa, FL: Psychological Assessment Resources.

Reynolds, W. M. (1989). *Reynolds Child Depression Scale.* Odessa, FL: Psychological Assessment Resources.

Reynolds, W. M., Anderson, G., & Bartell, N. (1985). Measuring depression in children: A multi-method assessment investigation. *Journal of Abnormal Child Psychology, 13,* 513–526.

Reynolds, W. M., & Coats, K. I. (1986). A comparison of cognitive-behavioral therapy and relaxation training for the treatment of depression in adolescents. *Journal of Consulting and Clinical Psychology, 54,* 653–660.

Reynolds, W. M., & Graves, A. (1989). Reliability of children's reports of depressive symptomatology. *Journal of Abnormal Child Psychology, 17*(6), 647–655.

Saylor, C. F., Finch, A. J., Baskin, C. H., Furey, W., & Kelly, M. M. (1984). Construct validity for measures of childhood depression: Application of multitrait-multimethod methodology. *Journal of Consulting and Clinical Psychology, 52*(6), 977–985.

Saylor, C. F., Finch, A. J., Spirito, A., & Bennett, B. (1984). The Children's Depression Inventory: A systematic evaluation of psychometric properties. *Journal of Consulting and Clinical Psychology, 52*(6), 955–967.

Schopler, E., Reichler, R. J., & Renner, B. R. (1986). *The Childhood Autism Rating Scale.* Los Angeles: Western Psychological Services.

Spielberger, C. D. (1973). *Preliminary manual for the State-Trait Anxiety Inventory for Children ("How I Feel Questionnaire")*. Palo Alto, CA: Consulting Psychologists.

Sprafkin, J., & Gadow, K. D. (1996). *The Early Childhood Inventories Manual*. Stony Brook, NY: Checkmate Plus.

Stark, K. D., Reynolds, W. M., & Kaslow, N. J. (1987). A comparison of the relative efficacy of self-control therapy and behavioral problem-solving therapy for depression in children. *Journal of Abnormal Child Psychology*, 15, 91–113.

Taylor, E. (1995). Dysfunctions of attention. In D. Cicchetti & D. J. Cohen (Eds.), *Developmental psychopathology, Vol. 2: Risk, disorder, and adaptation*. New York: Wiley.

Taylor, J. A. (1951). The relationship of anxiety to conditioned eyelid response. *Journal of Experimental Psychology*, 41(2), 81–92.

Weiss, B., & Weisz, J. R. (1988). Factor structure of self-reported depression: Clinic referred children versus adolescents. *Journal of Abnormal Psychology*, 97(4), 492–495.

Weiss, B., Weisz, J. R., Politano, M., Carey, M., Nelson, W. M., & Finch, A. J. (1991). Developmental differences in the factor structure of the Child Depression Inventory. *Psychological Assessment*, 3(1), 38–45.

Weissman, M. M., Orvaschel, H., & Padain, N. (1980). Children's symptom and social functioning self-report scales: Comparisons between mothers' and children's reports. *The Journal of Nervous and Mental Disease*, 168(12), 736–740.

Wendel, N. H., Nelson, W. M., Politano, P. M., Mayhall, C. A., & Finch, A. J. (1988). Differentiating inpatient clinically diagnosed and normal children using the Children's Depression Inventory. *Child Psychiatry and Human Development*, 19(2), 98–108.

Zung, W. W. K. (1965). A self-rating depression scale. *Archives of General Psychiatry*, 12, 63–70.

PART
IV

Recent Advances
in Psychological and
Educational Assessment

CHAPTER 13

Cross-Cultural Cognitive and Neuropsychological Assessment

JOSETTE G. HARRIS
University of Colorado School of Medicine

RUBEN ECHEMENDÍA
Pennsylvania State University

ALFREDO ARDILA
Memorial Regional Hospital

MÓNICA ROSSELLI
Florida Atlantic University

The literature on the assessment of culturally diverse individuals is saturated with statistics and projections regarding the rapid growth of ethnic groups in the United States and Canada. Often in this context there is commentary on the dearth of providers who share cultural backgrounds and language with the individuals who are referred to them, and on the barriers to providing assessment and intervention services. Extreme positions are sometimes taken, such as maintaining that it is unethical to provide services when one does not share the language or culture of the referred individual, a position that ignores the fact that there is a shortage of bilingual and bicultural providers. Unfortunately, few alternatives are offered to practitioners, with the result that clinicians often default to an inadequate solution of refusing services rather than face the challenge of cross-cultural assessment. In this chapter, we hope to encourage practitioners to view the challenge of cross-cultural assessment as surmountable with the proper tools. We present for discussion a number of variables that occur in the context of culture, but

Handbook of Psychoeducational Assessment

ultimately suggest that empirical knowledge and knowledge of each individual's unique background and experiences will facilitate the assessment process and outcome.

The chapter begins with an overview of the concept of cultural values and the role of acculturation in determining "readiness" for assessment. Education and literacy, and the influence of these factors on cognitive performance, are discussed. Language and language proficiency are addressed in the context of the language used in the assessment, test selection, test adaptation, and the use of translators. Examples of specific language characteristics on cognitive performance are also provided. Finally, two case studies are presented that illustrate the ways in which the process of assessment can be conceptualized and undertaken, with the ultimate goal of improving the ecological validity of assessment results.

CULTURAL AND COGNITIVE VALUES

Cultural values and expectations have a significant influence on both the process and the outcome of cognitive and neuropsychological assessment. Culture provides specific models for ways of behaving, feeling, thinking, and communicating. In general, culture dictates what is, and what is not, situationally relevant. According to Berry (1988), cognitive values are "the set of cognitive goals which are collectively shared and toward which children are socialised in a particular society. It is essential to understand these goals, since one cannot assess how far a person has gotten unless one understands where he is going" (p. 12). As Berry has maintained, in order to understand the goals for cognitive competence in children, it is essential to understand the skills and abilities that are valued in that society. This is critically important for the accurate assessment and understanding of both normal and abnormal cognitive functioning and for the accurate interpretation of cognitive performance.

To understand the limitations of interpreting and predicting cognitive performance based on knowledge of one's culture, it is necessary to appreciate that within a given culture there are, in reality, multiple cultures and societies. For this reason, intracultural variability in cognitive performance may be as great or greater than that observed cross-culturally. The diversity found among American Indian and Alaska Native populations is a good example. There are 556 federally recognized American Indian tribes and Alaska Native entities (Bureau of Indian Affairs, 2000). Furthermore, 135 Indian and 20 Alaska Native languages have been identified (Dillard & Manson, 2000). These statistics reflect vast diversity in language, tradition, religious beliefs, and other cultural values among Indian and Alaska Native people. The diversity in tradition and, to a lesser extent, language is also evident among individuals of "Hispanic origin," who can belong to one of many races and may be identified as belonging to one or a mixture of various subgroups, each with their own cultural values and Spanish dialects (e.g., Mexican, Puerto Rican, Cuban, Dominican, Central American, South American, or Spaniard). Similar diversity exists among individuals of African origin, some of whom have long cultural and familial histories in the United States dating back to the southern slaves in the 1700s, while others have more recently immigrated from Egypt, Ethiopia, Ghana, Nigeria, Haiti, Panama, Jamaica, Trinidad, Barbados, and other Caribbean nations (U.S. Department of Commerce, 1995). Even immigrants originating from the same country, such as Vietnamese, Cambodian, and Laotian immigrants, have differing circumstances and periods of arrival as well as differing languages, making the Southeast Asian population, for example, far from homogeneous, and distinct from other Asian and Pacific Islander groups (Holzer & Copeland, 2000). Differences in socioeconomic status, education, and geographic location within cultural or ethnic groups further explain why intracultural differences may be greater than those identified between groups. Generalities aimed at describing any one broadly defined cultural group (e.g., Asian Americans) or its cultural and cognitive values may be grossly misleading or inaccurate in the individual case, and may contribute little that is constructive to the assessment process.

CULTURE AND ASSESSMENT

Cultural values and expectations are exemplified in the manner in which individuals approach a cognitive evaluation and respond to test stimuli. Many individuals who have been raised and educated in the United States have been exposed to the expectations for performance in the context of a test situation. Testing in many public school systems is introduced early in the formal education process, and the role of an examinee becomes familiar early on. Standardized testing may occur with regularity for children in the United States, while for others, such as those from some Latin American cultures, standardized testing is an unfamiliar and often unwelcome concept.

For individuals familiar with formal testing, the examiner may be readily accepted as a person of authority who is to be trusted. This may be particularly true if the examinee shares the same cultural heritage as the examiner. This may not be true, however, for examinees who have immigrated from other cultures or whose collective histories are characterized by victimization or oppression. For example, Native American and Native Alaskan populations suffered tremendous losses of people, leaders, language, and traditions when they were relocated to reservations and English-only boarding schools upon the arrival of European settlers and missionaries (Krauss, 1980; Nies, 1996). The interventions "on behalf of" Indian and Native people resulted in multifaceted, multigenerational losses, which have been handed down through the generations of their respective cultures. Consequently, examinees may have "valid" fear and distrust of both the assessment process and the examiner who purports to act in the interest of the examinee or family. Under some circumstances, parents may be fearful and suspicious of the purpose of testing, may resist an evaluation, and may directly or indirectly communicate their discomfort to their children, thus compromising performance and the validity of the evaluation. Those residing in the United States without "documented" or legal residency, for example, may be particularly fearful of any scrutiny or evaluation by those in authority. Examiners must be sensitive to these issues in testing and may consider performing an evaluation in a less structured or more informal manner. It may be necessary to meet with the child and parents over extended periods of time in order to build rapport and clarify the nature and purpose of an evaluation, the confidential nature of the evaluation, and the manner in which results will be utilized.

Acculturation

Clinicians and diagnosticians are taught to consider acculturation in determining whether an individual from one culture can be assessed using tests and norms developed with individuals from another "source" culture. Determination of the level of acculturation of the examinee may be based on superficial, informal, and somewhat limited impressions, such as whether the examinee appears to understand the conversational language of the examiner, or the examinee's length of residence in the United States. Assessing acculturation from this perspective asks the question of whether the individual is "ready" for the test. This perspective does not directly address whether the test is "ready" or appropriate for the examinee and does not reveal the presence of specific cultural values that might influence the assessment process and results. For example, speed and competitiveness are valued in some Western cultures, and it may be implicitly understood by examinees from these cultures that speed is essential to achieving optimal scores on tests. For individuals from some Latin American cultures, speed and quality may be contradictory. In these cultures, there is a social norm that good products are the result of a careful and slow process, and work is generally not to be rushed. Individuals from some tribal and Hispanic cultures may also display in test situations a style of interpersonal relatedness that includes silence, passivity, and deference. These are behaviors intended to convey respect for the person in authority (the examiner) and may occur even in response to direct questioning, particularly when personal information is solicited (Black, 1973). An examiner who is naive to these behaviors may inappropriately assume that the behaviors indicate defensiveness or evasiveness. The individual meanings of these behaviors and their relationship to traditional values are not likely to be revealed through the administration of acculturation surveys or superficial questions designed to gauge acculturation. Rather, these behaviors will be understood through exploration of the cultural values held by the examinee.

Most literature concerning the assessment of multicultural populations suggests that the first step in the assessment process is a determination of the examinee's level of assimilation or acculturation. More accurately, the first step in the assessment process should be for the clinician or diagnostician to acculturate to the examinee's culture (Malgady et al., 1987). This step includes an understanding of the cognitive abilities that are valued and trained within the culture; developmental expectations for acquisition of various cognitive competencies; cultural expectations for display of cognitive competencies and abilities; knowledge of the collective and individual history of the examinee; and knowledge of cultural values, traditions, and beliefs that will impact both the process and outcome of assessment (Berry, 1988; Dillard & Manson, 2000).

TEST TRANSLATION AND ADAPTATION

Psychologists have long been using tests developed for Western, urban, middle-class, literate people to evaluate cognitive abilities of people belonging to other cultural groups (Ardila, Rosselli, & Ostrosky-Solis, 1992). Survey data collected by Echemendía, Harris, Congett, Diaz, & Puente (1997) illustrate that the vast majority of Spanish-speaking individuals who receive neuropsychological evaluations in the United States are tested with the same tests as their English-speaking counterparts. These tests are either formally or informally translated and the results frequently are interpreted using norms from an English-speaking population, such as the population on which the original English-language measure was normed.

The literal translation of a test from the original language for use with a new target population is fraught with methodological, statistical, and theoretical problems. Literal translations are problematic because words and phrases differ in level of difficulty, familiarity, and meaning from one culture to another. Culturally specific nuances cannot be directly translated. Even seemingly "non-linguistically" based items may be problematic. For example, the use of a picture-sequencing item that depicts the changing seasons of the year may be more complex for a Latino born in Costa Rica and living in Miami than it is for a Latino living in New York. Padilla (1979) has emphasized that the adaptation of a test to a culture requires more than simply translating the instrument from one language to another; it is also necessary to adapt the new measure to the specific demands existing in the new target culture. In a comprehensive article, Geisinger (1994) states that "[the] adaptation of assessment instruments for new target populations is generally required when the new target population differs appreciably from the original population with which the assessment device is used in terms of culture or cultural background, country, and language" (p. 304).

The second step in the assessment process should be an evaluation of whether the assessment techniques, tests, and norms are suitable for the examinee. The International Test Commission has set forth guidelines (Van de Vijver & Hambleton, 1996) for translating and adapting tests, which are summarized as follows: (1) The test translation methods must minimize or avoid construct, method, and item bias; (2) a thorough knowledge and understanding of the language and culture into which a test will be translated must guide the translation process; (3) the materials, methods, and techniques of administration must be familiar to the target cultural group; and (4) the ecological validity of the test must be statistically documented to assure accurate score interpretation. Test translation is also addressed in *Standards for Educational and Psychological Testing* (American Educational Research Association, American Psychological Association, & National Council on Measurement in Education, 1999), in which Standard 9.7 states: "When a test is translated from one language to another, the methods used in establishing the adequacy of the translation should be described, and empirical and logical evidence should be provided for score reliability and the validity of the translated test's score inferences for the users intended in the linguistic groups to be tested" (p. 99).

Once translated and adapted, the validity and reliability of the new instrument must be reestablished. It is not appropriate to assume that simply because a set of measurement domains is useful in one culture that those domains will be equally useful (or similarly measured) in a different culture. The test developer must demonstrate that the new measure assesses the same characteristics as the original measure, and does so reliably, in the new culture. Similarly, once adapted, new normative data must be generated that are specific to the new culture. Translating a test and using the normative tables from the original-language version of the test, without documenting the comparability of norms, is unacceptable practice. Norms based on native English speakers either should not be used with those who speak English as a second language or results should be interpreted by in some way reflecting the level of English proficiency (American Educational Research Association et al., 1999). Geisinger (1994) cautions that a very good (and preferably empirically supported) reason must exist in order to justify the use of U.S. norms with linguistically and culturally different populations. When making decisions about test use, "Fairness of testing in any given context must be judged relative to that of feasible test and nontest alternatives" (American Educational Research Association et al., 1999, p. 73).

Table 13.1 is a select list of tests and references that may be useful in the assessment of Spanish-speaking children and adolescents. Neuropsychological batteries in Spanish are also included.

TABLE 13.1
Select List of Tests with References for Use with
Spanish-Speaking Children and Adolescents

Bilingual Verbal Ability Tests (Muñoz-Sandoval, Cummins, Alvarado, & Ruef, 1998)

Boston Naming Test (Ardila & Rosselli, 1994)

Clinical Evaluation of Language Fundamentals—3, Spanish Edition (Semel, Wiig, & Secord, 1997)

NEUROPSI (Ostrosky-Solis, Ardila, & Rosselli, 1999)

NeSBHIS (Pontón et al., 1996)

Phonologic and Semantic Verbal Fluency (Ardila & Rosselli, 1994)

Recognition of Overlapped Figures (Ardila & Rosselli, 1994)

Rey-Osterrieth Complex Figure (Ardila & Rosselli, 1994)

Sequential Verbal Memory Test (Ardila & Rosselli, 1994)

Spanish Language Assessment Procedures (Mattes, 1995)

Token Test (Ardila & Rosselli, 1994)

Wechsler Intelligence Scale for Children—Revised (Wechsler, 1983, 1993)

Wechsler Memory Scale (Ardila & Rosselli, 1994)

Wisconsin Card Sorting Test (Rosselli & Ardila, 1993)

Woodcock-Johnson—Revised in Spanish (Woodcock & Muñoz-Sandoval, 1996a, 1996b, 1996c)

Note: In addition to the measures listed above, there are a number of tests classified as non-verbal intelligence tests available from major test publishers.

EDUCATION AND COGNITIVE PERFORMANCE

Attendance of school is perhaps the most formal way that academic learning takes place in the context of culture. Despite the considerable variability across cultures found regarding both the aims and structure of schooling, the process of formal education trains certain abilities and reinforces certain attitudes in all cultures. Development of vocabulary, grammar, and syntax skills are an example of the way that formal education can facilitate the development of verbal skills and abilities. Even on relatively simple and seemingly straightforward tests, the influence of literacy and reading skills becomes apparent. Lecours et al. (1987) found that illiterate individuals tended to select one of the incorrect foils on a test of simple and complex sentence comprehension. In one example, 35% of the illiterate individuals selected a picture representing a girl running as the correct representation of the statement, "The girl walks." The authors suggested that the illiterate individuals may have considered the action of running equivalent to walking fast and that such errors might represent incomplete semantic organization related to lack of school education, not to be confused with aphasic errors. Translating verbal items from one language into another may also yield less familiar tenses or undesirable syntax, which may impact the manner in which children and adults decode and understand logical relationships.

Examiners often make the mistake of assuming that, if an individual has had limited formal education, literacy and linguistic skills understandably will be influenced but that nonverbal skills will be unaffected. Several studies have compared performance on verbal and visuospatial/nonverbal tasks in adults. For example, Ardila, Rosselli, & Rosas (1989) and Rosselli, Ardila, & Rosas (1990) found performance to be worse for illiterate persons compared with literate persons on nearly all tasks, including tests of visuospatial, memory-related, linguistic, and praxic abilities. Manley et al. (1999) found that even when illiterate subjects are matched to literate persons on years of education, illiterate individuals have more difficulty on tasks such as visual matching and recognition. Manley et al. suggested that literacy may facilitate the development of skills necessary to analyze visuospatial information or, alternatively, that linguistic skills associated with literacy may assist in mediating performance on nonverbal tasks.

The development of writing skills associated with formal education has been suggested to facilitate not only performance on visuospatial, graphomotor, and fine motor tasks, but to influence other cognitive skills as well (Deregowski, 1980; Pontius, 1989; Ardila, Rosselli, & Rosas, 1989). Harris & Cullum (2001) investigated the performance of lower- versus higher-educated subjects in a sample of Mexico-origin individuals who completed both the Digit Symbol (Wechsler, 1981) and the Symbol Digit (Smith, 1982) tests. The lower-educated individuals performed worse than the higher-educated subjects on Digit Symbol but not on Symbol Digit. One possible way of interpreting this finding is that the subjects with limited education were compromised in their graphomotor ability to make the less familiar symbol responses. The writing of digits may be less influenced by education than the drawing of figures, provided some degree of literacy is attained.

Variables such as education and cultural values, however, should not be confused with the quality of one's environment. Certainly, some ethnic minority groups have high rates of poverty and may consequently have higher rates of exposure to prenatal and postnatal complications, malnutrition, exposure to environmental toxins, and increased risk of neurocognitive trauma related to occupational hazards (see also Ostrosky-Solis et al., 1985; Amante, Vanhouten, Grieve, Bader, & Margules, 1977). All of these factors represent additional variables that may be operating in a culture or subculture and may impact cognitive performance, but they should not be confused with culture per se. It is also important to bear in mind that, in the assessment of individuals who have received little or no formal education by Western standards, the examinee may simply lack familiarity with the task demands and may in fact be able to display the skill or intellectual ability under other, more culturally relevant test conditions. Goodenough (1936) cautioned that test items and concepts should be "representative and valid samples of the ability in question, as it is displayed within a particular culture" (p. 5). It is dangerous to define knowledge or skills as formal "schooled" knowledge, because this may disregard the knowledge base otherwise defined by one's culture.

LANGUAGE AND PROFICIENCY

Language may impact assessment from a number of perspectives. For a variety of reasons, children and adults may overestimate their ability to speak English. There may be shame associated with a lack of mastery of the English language, and a risk of not being accepted by peers or by the examiner if one's true level of proficiency were discovered. Some individuals have mastered conversational English and may appear to be fluent when engaged in superficial conversation, and this may prompt the clinician to assume that the individual can be adequately tested in English. Another common mistake is to assume that, because an individual appears to possess spoken language proficiency in English, all language related skills (e.g., reading and writing) are at the same level of proficiency. Such an assumption may lead to the erroneous interpretation of variations in performance, such as erroneously finding evidence of a learning disability.

Even for bilingual individuals who appear to have mastery of both languages, fluency in the second language may be diminished when placed in a stressful situation such as an interview or evaluation (Peck, 1974). With or without a stressful situation, concepts may be less available in the second language, and words to express internal experiences or symptoms may be less accessible in the second language. Schooling language can indeed be a highly significant and decisive variable in developing a language preference as well as in determining the facility with which complex material can be discussed. Limiting an individual to one language in the assessment may limit the completeness of the communication, which has the potential of introducing error into the history-taking and testing. Monolingual assessment in either language may fail to address the need of a bilingual person to utilize both languages for effective communication. This is a complex issue to address in testing because, although it may be inappropriate to use norms based on a monolingual sample, norms for bilingual subjects are largely unavailable.

THE USE OF TRANSLATORS

The *Guidelines for Providers of Psychological Services to Ethnic, Linguistic, and Culturally Diverse Populations* (American Psychological Association, 1990) state that psychologists should interact in the language requested by the client. When an examiner does not speak the language of an examinee, translators often are included in the assessment. However, translators must be used cautiously because error can be introduced into the evaluation at many points. First, while proficient in the language of the examinee, a translator may not be educated in the particulars of that individual's culture, and may fail to communicate the nonverbal content of the communication or the emotional content that is shared between the translator and the examinee. McShane & Plas (1984) noted that in some Indian cultures there may be more reliance on nonverbal language systems than on verbal language to communicate complex "language." A lack of response to a question may reflect a cultural norm regarding the permissibility of discussing the topic and may have little to do with resistance or aggression. A skilled translator should not merely be a translator of language, but of the examinee's culture as well.

Translators also may be burdened with greater clinical responsibilities than they are trained or prepared to manage. Echemendía, Harris, Congett, Diaz, and Puente (1997) found that translators were often used in the assessment of monolingual Spanish speakers in the United States, but that the translators possessed little or no formal training in neuropsychology. When using a translator, the clinician responsible for the assessment has no direct knowledge as to the accuracy of the translation, or whether the translated information maintains the intended meaning of the original communication. If the translator has little or no training in the theories and methods of cognitive assessment, the psychologist at best may be losing valuable qualitative data, and at worst may be receiving information that has been embellished by the translator in an attempt to "help" the patient. The translator should be viewed as an extension of the clinician. It is the responsibility of the clinician to thoroughly train the translator, particularly regarding the goals of assessment, and to educate himself or herself on the complexities of cross-cultural assessment and test selection.

LINGUISTIC CONSEQUENCES IN PERFORMANCE

Specific linguistic idiosyncrasies also may directly influence performance in cognitive or neuropsychological testing. For example, formal spelling does not receive the same emphasis in Spanish as it does in English. Also, the use of spelled abbreviations is common in English, but not in Spanish. A native Spanish speaker would never read UCLA as "U-C-L-A" (or "u" "se" "ele" "a" in Spanish) but rather "ukla." Furthermore, English speakers may know the alphabet sequence better because it is essential in spelling. These factors may explain some differences between Spanish and English speakers in phonemic word fluency (Taussig, Henderson, & Mack, 1992; Rosselli et al., 2000). In tests of phonemic fluency, subjects are instructed to generate words that begin with a specific letter (Rosen, 1980). Typically, subjects are given three different letters (e.g., F, A, and S) and are given one minute for each letter to generate words. Spanish speakers tend to generate words according to phonologic similarities, disregarding spelling (e.g., *sal*, *cebolla*, and *cesped*). In most cases it is inappropriate to strictly adhere to scoring criteria when evaluating a Spanish speaker because this penalizes the examinee for choosing phonologically correct words (counting words as incorrect that are phonologically correct ["ce" or "se"] but orthographically incorrect ["C"]). It is also inappropriate to apply English-language fluency norms when evaluating performance.

The strong tendency to "spell" in English is observed even when reciting numbers. For example, in English the numbers "3, 4, 5" are typically read as "three, four, five." Spanish speakers, on the other hand, prefer to cluster numbers when presenting numbers to others (e.g., a phone number), such that "3, 4, 5" becomes "three hundred forty-five". The single-digit presentation of digit-span stimuli is less familiar to Spanish speakers and this may interfere with encoding and subsequent chunking for recall. Indeed, reduced digit-span performance has been identified in Spanish speakers (Naveh-Benjamin & Ayres, 1986; Loewenstein, Arguelles, Barker, & Duara, 1993). It also is possible that children and adults who have not achieved proficiency in English may utilize internal translation strategies to convert test stimuli into more familiar terms in an effort to improve encoding. For example, a child who hears a string of numbers in English may attempt to translate the numbers into the native language for rehearsal and then translate them back into English when providing the examiner with the response. This kind of effort reduces the availability of processing resources for other aspects of the task, such as reordering digits in reverse when performing Digit Span Backwards.

A second linguistic-related explanation for reduced digit span concerns the reduction of immediate memory span due to the longer amount of time it takes to articulate words in some languages. Baddeley, Thomson, and Buchanan (1975) first demonstrated that memory span for short words was greater than for long words. Although the number of syllables or phonemes in the stimulus may explain the effect, the effect persists when syllables and phonemes are held constant (Baddeley, Thomson, and Buchanan, 1975; Ellis & Henneley, 1980; Olazaran, Jacobs, & Stern, 1996) The more critical variables that affect the number of words that can be rehearsed in the phonological loop appear to be spoken word length or articulation time. When the technique called articulatory suppression (e.g., repeatedly saying "A-B-C-D") is used to prevent rehearsal, the word length effect is no longer evident.

It is known that languages differ in their spoken word lengths. Languages with short articulation time for words therefore are expected to make fewer demands on phonological loop resources. Studies of word or digit span in non-English languages illustrate the potential differences in span. For example, Cantonese and Chinese spans are greater than English on simple span tasks (Hoosain, 1979), and it appears there are differences between English and Spanish digit spans, with English having the greater span (Loewenstein et al., 1993; Naveh-Benjamin & Ayres, 1986).

Our own work in a recent pilot study (Harris, Adler, & Cullum, 2000) has suggested that it is important to consider test stimuli and the interaction with spoken word length for a given language. We compared performance of Spanish and English speakers on four tests of working memory, one of which we designed to be equivalent in the Spanish and English languages on spoken word length. Preliminary data analyses comparing 10 normal Spanish and 5 normal English speakers revealed significantly worse performance for Spanish speakers on the three tasks for which word length was not controlled. However, there was no difference between English and Spanish speakers on the equated task.

These very preliminary findings suggest that processing resources may be differentially affected in English versus Spanish on "simple" working memory tests and that proficiency in English also can be expected to influence available processing resources. These findings also have implications for performance on other cognitive tasks (e.g., those that rely on working memory and organizational strategies to aid encoding or learning of new information), and suggest that care must be taken to equate tasks on word length and difficulty in the assessment of cross-linguistic samples.

Word-length effects also may account for reduced semantic fluency performance found in adults who speak Spanish, compared with other languages. For example, Kempler, Teng, Dick, Taussig, and Davis (1998) compared performances of Chinese, Hispanic, and Vietnamese immigrants in their native languages on a semantic verbal fluency task (animal naming) and found that the Spanish-speaking Hispanics produced the fewest responses, even after statistically controlling for age and education. The average word length of animal names was longest in Spanish and shortest in Vietnamese. Jacobs et al. (1997) also reported fewer semantic category exemplars for Spanish compared with English speakers. While these issues have not been directly investigated in children, there is reason to expect that semantic fluency tasks given in the child's native language would yield similar findings.

CASE STUDIES

Having now reviewed some of the important considerations in cognitive and neuropsychological assessment with regard to culture, education, and language, we present two case studies as illustrations of these considerations. In the first case, relevant history and specific test results are presented to assist the clinician in formulating hypotheses and arriving at a working diagnosis. In the second, a description of specific factors likely to influence the examinee's and family's participation in the assessment process are addressed, with an example of reconceptualizing the assessment.

Case One

Reason for Referral

Maria was an 8-year, 8-month-old white Hispanic female of Mexican origin. She was referred for a neuropsychological evaluation because of learning difficulties at school. She was involved in a motor vehicle accident approximately 2.5 years prior to the evaluation. There were no medical records available concerning the accident. However, according to her parents, Maria had been unrestrained and was thrown out of the vehicle. She was initially nonresponsive but responded immediately to CPR initiated by her father. She had a right frontal laceration and numerous other abrasions on her shoulders, arms, and leg. She was taken to a local hospital and then a regional trauma center, where she was discharged after one day. Her parents described her as withdrawn and apathetic upon discharge from the trauma center but believed she had returned to her baseline personality functioning within two to three days. Her parents were unaware of any difficulties regarding language or other cognitive functions following the accident. Her neurological exam at the time of her neuropsychological evaluation was completely normal, and no sequelae from the accident were identified. Vision and hearing were also reported as normal.

Sociodemographic History

Maria was born in a large urban city in Mexico, where her parents worked in manufacturing. Maria's prenatal and birth histories were unremarkable, and she was reported to be a healthy child, attaining normal developmental milestones. There was no history of loss of consciousness or head injury aside from the car accident. Spanish was the only language spoken in the home, and consequently Maria only began to learn English when she entered preschool at the age of four. She and her parents immigrated to the United States when Maria was two, in search of a better economic life and future for Maria and her sister. Both parents completed 11 years of education in Mexico, equivalent to a high-school education in the United States.

Observations

Maria's parents reported that she had difficulty expressing herself in both English and Spanish. In kindergarten, Maria had difficulty learning to write her name and recognizing letters of the alphabet. In first grade, additional problems were identified in learning to read and understanding and following directions in English. Her third-grade teacher reported that Maria had difficulties comprehending spoken language and needed frequent repetition in order to understand what she was learning. Maria was described as frequently forgetting what she had learned. Additionally, she was described as having difficulties with spelling, the mechanics of math computations, problem solving, following simple directions, and telling time. She had problems understanding stories that were read aloud and discussed in the classroom, and she took an excessive amount of time to respond to questions, sometimes giving no response at all. She was functioning below grade level in all academic areas at the time of the evaluation.

Because her language difficulties initially appeared to be worse in English than in Spanish, she was placed in an English as a Second Language (ESL) program during first grade and remained in the program through the third grade. Maria complained of being embarrassed about going to school and did not like leaving the regular classroom to receive ESL instruction in English, math, and reading. She was aware that she had difficulties with learning compared with peers, and she at times became tearful in school. She reportedly enjoyed doing homework and reading in English at home.

Maria was evaluated by a bilingual examiner whose first language was Spanish. Maria presented for the evaluation as a pleasant, well-groomed child who was rather passive and quiet. She did not initiate any conversation with the examiner and frequently would stare quietly after being asked a question in either Spanish or English. When given extended time to respond, she would often attempt to answer a question, but at other times she required many cues and follow-up prompts in order to formulate a response. Test instructions were presented to Maria in both English and Spanish. Departure from standardized test administration method was done to give Maria the best chance of understanding test requirements. She remained motivated and persistent throughout the evaluation, but often required extra assistance, such as repeated explanation in both languages. She also tended to exhibit a trial-and-error approach to novel tasks.

Results

Maria's test results are presented in Table 13.2. Although both raw and standard scores are provided for illustrative purposes, it is the responsibility of the test user or examiner in any testing situation to know the applicability of each test to specific individuals and to employ norms appropriately (American Educational Research Association et al., 1999).

Maria's performance on the WISC-III resulted in a Verbal IQ score of 72, a Performance IQ score of 87, and a Full Scale IQ score of 77. This pattern of better Performance compared to Verbal IQ score is common among Hispanic children, especially those whose first language is Spanish. With the exception of the Verbal Comprehension index score, which was below average, Maria's index scores were in the average to low-average range.

TABLE 13.2
Case One Results

- Wechsler Intelligence Scale for Children—Third Edition
  - Full Scale IQ — 77
  - Verbal IQ — 72
  - Performance IQ — 87
  - Verbal Comprehension Index — 68
  - Perceptual Organization Index — 90
  - Freedom from Distractibility Index — 84
  - Processing Speed Index — 88

  Subtest Scaled Scores
  - Information — 6
  - Similarities — 5
  - Arithmetic — 9
  - Vocabulary — 2
  - Comprehension — 3
  - Digit Span — 5
  - Picture Completion — 9
  - Picture Arrangement — 6
  - Block Design — 9
  - Object Assembly — 9
  - Coding — 7
  - Symbol Search — 8

- Wechsler Individual Achievement Test
  Standard Scores
  - Basic Reading — 81
  - Mathematical Reasoning — 76
  - Spelling — 77
  - Reading Comprehension — 80
  - Numerical Operations — 87
  - Listening Comprehension — NA
  - Oral Expression — NA
  - Written Expression — NA

- California Verbal Learning Test

	R	z / T
Trial 1	R = 4	z = −1.0
Trial 5	R = 9	z = −0.5
Trials 1–5	R = 30	T = 40
List B	R = 6	z = 0.5
Short Delay Free Recall	R = 2	z = −2.0
Short Delay Cued Recall	R = 2	z = −3.0
Long Delay Free Recall	R = 0	z = −3.5
Long Delay Cued Recall	R = 3	z = −2.5
Recognition Hits	R = 11	z = −1.0
False Positives	R = 3	z = 0.0
Discriminability	R = 84%	z = −0.5
Perseverations	R = 0	z = −1.0
Intrusions	R = 3	z = −0.5

(continues)

Table 13.2—*Continued*

- Rey-Osterrieth Complex Figure

Copy	R = 24	z = .05
Recall	R = 16	z = −.05

- Boston Naming Test R = 21 z = −3.92
- Animal Naming R = 6 z = −2.34
- Token Test R = 48 z = −1.17

- Clinical Evaluation of Language Fundamentals—Third Edition
  Scaled Scores

Sentence structure	8
Concepts and directions	7

- Gordon Diagnostic System
  Delay Task

Efficiency ratio	R = .83	WNL

  Vigilance

Correct	R = 40	WNL
Commissions	R = 3	WNL

  Distractibility

Correct	R = 35	WNL
Commissions	R = 6	WNL

- Sensory-Perceptual Examination
  Double simultaneous visual stimulation

Right errors	R = 0	WNL
Left errors	R = 0	WNL

  Tactile finger identification

Right errors	R = 0	WNL
Left errors	L = 0	WNL

  Finger Tapping Test

Right	R = 32	WNL
Left	L = 29	WNL

Note: R = raw score, T = T score (M = 50, SD = 10), z = z score (M = 0, SD = 1), WNL = within normal limits. Qualitative levels are provided when published norms do not permit conversion.

Maria was administered two receptive language subtests from the Clinical Evaluation of Language Fundamentals—Third Edition (CELF-III) in Spanish and scored in the low-average to average range. She refused to converse in Spanish with the examiner, precluding administration of any of the expressive language subtests. Qualitative observations of subtest performance revealed that she had particular difficulty with lengthy and complex directions. She was unable to follow three-step directions and had difficulty with right-left orientation. Her ability to follow directions on the Token Test was consistent with the CELF-III. She was able to follow some multistep instructions in English but had difficulty with more complex syntax. She was administered the Boston Naming Test and asked for the names of objects in Spanish whenever she made an error in English. This did not appreciably improve her performance. There was only one item (comb) that she was able to name in

Spanish but not in English, and she was unable to name a broom in either language. Her verbal fluency skills, as assessed on the Animal Naming Test, were below average in English, and she was unwilling to attempt the task in Spanish. There was limited opportunity to observe her spontaneous language in Spanish with her parents. She exhibited some grammatical and syntactical errors, although to a lesser extent in Spanish than when she spoke in English.

Using the Gordon Diagnostic System, attention was in the normal range. Maria's verbal learning was adequate, particularly considering her verbal cognitive abilities. On the California Verbal Learning Test, she displayed an acceptable learning slope. However, following interference, her spontaneous recall was impaired, and she did not benefit from cueing. Her recognition of words presented earlier in the evaluation was in the low-average range. This pattern suggested that she was adequately encoding words but had difficulty with retrieval. Maria refused to participate in a Spanish list-learning test. Nonverbal learning and memory were evaluated as adequate. Maria's motor performance and sensory perceptual examination were within normal limits.

On academic achievement testing using the Wechsler Individual Achievement Test (WIAT), Maria's word recognition and reading comprehension skills were in the low-average range. On the Reading Comprehension subtest, she exhibited problems drawing conclusions, comparing and contrasting types of material, recognizing implied cause and effect, and remembering or recognizing details from narrative information she had just read. Spelling skills were impaired and errors were predominantly phonetic in nature. Maria's mathematical reasoning skills were also quite poor, although she was able to perform simple calculations somewhat better than word problems.

Summary

In summary, Maria demonstrated deficits in verbal and linguistic skills consistent with a mixed receptive-expressive language disorder, which did not appear to be attributable to her status as a child learning English as a second language. Her results were not consistent with a traumatic brain injury. In fact, a careful exploration of her history revealed that the language problems predated the car accident. Maria's reluctance to speak with the examiner in Spanish suggested that she was aware she would gain little advantage in Spanish, although it could also suggest that Maria was struggling with identity and acculturation issues regarding her ethnic and linguistic background.

Although the assessment was hampered by Maria's reluctance to participate in testing in Spanish, test data were supplemented by the clinician's careful history-taking and interviews with the parents and previous and current teachers. This approach supported hypothesis-testing and arrival at a working diagnosis for further evaluation. Some of Maria's deficits, such as her retrieval difficulties on the list-learning task, could be accounted for by her language dysfunction. On the other hand, Maria displayed a number of strengths that could go unrecognized in school because of the emphasis on verbal academic instruction. These strengths included intact attention, non-verbal learning and memory, and visuospatial and visuomotor skills.

Specific recommendations included a thorough speech and language evaluation in both languages to confirm the diagnosis of a language disorder. The examiner also recommended that the assessment process continue in other respects. Maria's level of intellectual functioning may have been underestimated because of a possible language disorder. Use of norms based upon English-speaking children may not be appropriate in this case, and may have been another source of variability in estimating Maria's intellectual and cognitive skills.

Case Two

Reason for Referral

Carlos was a 7-year, 8-month-old white Hispanic male of Mexican origin living in a small rural farming community. He was referred for educational testing by his homeroom teacher because of poor compliance with classroom assignments, inattentiveness, and academic underachievement, particularly in reading and spelling. According to Carlos' teacher, Carlos frequently did not respond to her questions, although he appeared to hear and comprehend them. Although he lagged behind his peers in reading and spelling, he was making some progress in his oral reading skills. His teacher was concerned, however, that when Carlos was asked questions to ascertain his understanding of reading material, he often responded that he did not know the answer. Carlos attended ESL programs for two hours per day and remained in the regular classroom for the remainder. The description of his behavior by the ESL tutor was consistent with that of his homeroom teacher.

Sociodemographic History

Little was known about Carlos' history, other than that he was born in Mexico. He attended only one grade in Mexico prior to coming to the United States with his family, who initially migrated as seasonal farm workers.

Assessment

The psychologist first recommended that the teacher, with the assistance of a translator, call Carlos' parents in order to arrange a meeting to review Carlos' school progress, prior to planning any formal assessment. This approach was recommended because of the teacher's more direct contact with Carlos and his family, compared with the psychologist, who had never met the child or his parents. With the assistance of a skilled translator who was knowledge-able about the Mexican immigrant culture and of migrant families in a neigh-boring community, the teacher arranged for a meeting. The meeting was ar-ranged and the family was encouraged to invite a friend or relative from the community to the meeting if that would be helpful to them. The teacher told the family that an individual from the school who helps evaluate the progress of students and identifies ways to help students with their learning would also be present, and provided the psychologist's name. The family was asked if they would like to have a translator present, and they agreed that this would be helpful.

Prior to meeting with the family, the psychologist consulted with individ-uals of Mexican origin and individuals actively involved in providing services to Hispanic individuals in the community, such as spiritual guidance and as-sistance services. The psychologist learned that formal education could be limited for migrant and first-generation immigrant parents in the community and that literacy could be in question. This called for careful attention to the informed consent procedure. He also learned that newly immigrated individ-uals might have undocumented residency status, which could influence the comfort level of the parents in response to working with school personnel and responding to questions regarding Carlos or the family. It would be nec-essary to reiterate the educational rights of children and to be mindful of the potential anxiety that any formal evaluation might initiate.

The parents, Carlos, and two younger siblings arrived at the meeting un-accompanied. The parents previously had had very limited contact with the school and appeared both concerned and anxious, as did Carlos. The family also had had very limited contact with the teacher, but her presence appeared to be reassuring. Care was taken to explain the purpose of the meeting and to explain that it would be helpful to understand more of Carlos' culture and educational experience in order to understand both his educational weak-nesses as well as strengths. The psychologist apologized in advance for ask-ing any questions that might touch on private matters of the family and ex-plained the relevance of such questions to understanding Carlos' skills and abilities and to clarifying the source of educational difficulties and planning interventions. The psychologist also invited questions from the parents.

The psychologist, with the assistance of the translator, learned that the family had lived in an isolated and very poor rural community in Mexico. Car-los attended a school in which books, paper, and pencils were quite limited and shared among students, who ranged in age from 6 to 10 and were all educated in the same informal classroom together. Most children in the community did not advance beyond four years of school and in fact there was no option available in their community to advance beyond six years. Car-los' mother herself had attained four years of education and his father six years. At the urging of a relative, Carlos' parents left their home in Mexico to seek a better life for their children in the United States. They first worked as seasonal migrant workers. Although Carlos' parents were very interested in his education, they were unsure of their own ability to contribute to his learning process.

The psychologist obtained a thorough history of Carlos' behavior in the home and learned that Carlos did not exhibit in the home any of the behaviors in the classroom as described by his teacher. In fact, he was quite respectful of his parents, always responded to their questions and directions in Spanish, and was quite attentive. His parents reported that Carlos liked to watch English-language television in the afternoons and would do so for extended periods of time. The parents supported this as a means for their son to gain additional exposure to the English language. They also described other age-appropriate play and interests for their child but indicated that it was necessary for Carlos to assist his mother with the care of his younger siblings in the evenings due to the long hours his father worked. Carlos' parents appeared to appreciate the focus of attention on their son and equally appreciated the opportunity to ask questions of the clinician. This provided the clinician an opportunity to explain that there was some question concerning Carlos' skill level given that his native language was Spanish, but that the clinician and Carlos' teacher hoped to better understand his strengths and weaknesses in the weeks and months to come. The meeting closed with a plan to meet again in one month to evaluate Carlos' progress.

Summary

In this example, assessment was limited to initiating a process of information gathering and acculturation of the psychologist and teacher to the background and experience of Carlos and his family, both in their native country and in their new place of residence. The psychologist determined that Carlos' formal education in Mexico had been qualitatively much different than his relatively new experience in an educational setting in his new country, and that he was still early in the process of learning expectations in his new school culture. Following the meeting with Carlos and his parents, the psychologist felt that it was too early in the educational process to evaluate Carlos with formal measures in English and that even baseline testing in Spanish would be of limited value. A plan of intervention for Carlos included assisting him to acculturate to the educational setting, assisting him with peer relationships, and reassessing his ESL plan to consider more intense tutoring and close monitoring of his progress.

CONCLUSION

The challenge of providing assessment and intervention services to culturally and linguistically diverse individuals, particularly children, clearly will continue. It is estimated that, by the year 2050, some ethnic minority groups (e.g.,

Hispanic and Asian/Pacific Islander) will increase by more than 200% from the year 2000 estimates, while others will also see sizable growth (U.S. Census Bureau, 2000). Immigration patterns for 1995–1998 indicate that approximately 20% of the immigrants admitted each year were under the age of 15, and another 33% were between the ages of 15 and 29 (U.S. Department of Justice, 1999). This trend likely will continue. Children currently constitute 31% of the Hispanic population, 27% of the American Indian/Aleut/Eskimo, 27% of the Asian/Pacific Islander, and 19% of the Black population (U.S. Census Bureau, 2000). It is unrealistic to assume that the challenge of cross-cultural assessment of children and adults can be managed by simply referring ethnic minority individuals to bicultural, bilingual clinicians and providers. A practical point is that there simply are not enough providers to match the cultural and linguistic backgrounds of examinees. An additional point, however, is that bilingual, bicultural psychologists are not immune from the cultural issues addressed in this chapter. The tools for meeting the challenge of cross-cultural assessment lie in the achievement of competence and expertise (American Psychological Association, 1992; Canadian Psychological Association, 1991), the acculturation of providers to the individual cultures of those they serve, and the expansion of the empirical knowledge base regarding cross-cultural and cross-linguistic issues in assessment.

References

Amante, D., Vanhouten, V. W., Grieve, J. H., Bader, C. A., & Margules, P. H. (1977). Neuropsychological deficit, ethnicity and socioeconomic status. *Journal of Consulting and Clinical Psychology*, 45, 524–535.

American Educational Research Association, American Psychological Association, & National Council on Measurement in Education (1999). *Standards for educational and psychological testing*. Washington, DC: American Educational Research Association.

American Psychological Association. (1990). *Guidelines for providers of psychological services to ethnic, linguistic, and culturally diverse populations*. Washington, DC: American Psychological Association.

American Psychological Association (1992). Ethical principles of psychologists and code of conduct. *American Psychologist*, 47, 1597–1611.

Ardila, A., & Rosselli, M. (1994) Development of language, memory and visuospatial abilities in 5 to 12-year-old children using a neuropsychological battery. *Developmental Neuropsychology*, 10, 97–116.

Ardila, A., Rosselli, M., & Ostrosky-Solis, F. (1992). Sociocultural factors in neuropsychological assessment. In A. E. Puente & R. J. McCaffrey (Eds.), *Psychobiological factors in clinical neuropsychological assessment*. New York: Plenum.

Ardila, A., Rosselli, M., & Rosas, P. (1989). Neuropsychological assessment in illiterates: Visuospatial and memory abilities. *Brain and Cognition*, 11, 147–166.

Baddeley, A. D., Thomson, N., & Buchanan, M. (1975). Word length and the structure of short-term memory. *Journal of Verbal Learning and Verbal Behavior*, 14, 575–589.

Berry, J. W. (1988). Cognitive values and cognitive competence among the bricoleurs. In J. W. Berry & S. H. Irvine (Eds.), *Indogenous Cognition: Functioning in cultural context*. NATO ASI Series D: Behavioural and social sciences, No. 41. Dordrecht, Netherlands: Martinus Nijhoff.

Black, M. B. (1973). Ojibwa questioning etiquette and use of ambiguity. *Studies in Linguistics*, 23, 13–29.

Bureau of Indian Affairs (2000). Answers to frequently asked questions. (On line). Available Internet: www.doi.gov/bai/tribes/entry.html.

Canadian Psychological Association. (1991). *Canadian Code of Ethics for Psychologists*. Ottawa, Ontario: Canadian Psychological Association.

Deregowski, J. B. (1980). Illusions, patterns, and pictures: A cross-cultural perspective. London: Academic Press.

Dillard, D. A., & Manson, S. M. (2000). Assessing and treating American Indians and Alaska Natives. In I. Cuéllar and F. A. Paniagua (Eds.), *Handbook of multicultural mental health*. San Diego: Academic Press.

Echemendía, R. J., Harris, J. G., Congett, S. M., Diaz, L. M., & Puente, A. E. (1997). Neuropsychological training and practices with Hispanics: A national survey. *The Clinical Neuropsychologist*, 11(3), 229–243.

Ellis, N. C., & Hennelly, R. A. (1980). A bilingual word-length effect: Implications for intelligence testing and the relative ease for mental calculations in Welsh and English. *British Journal of Psychology*, 71, 43–51

Geisinger, K. (1994). Cross-cultural normative assessment: Translation and adaptation issues influencing the normative interpretation of assessment instruments. *Psychological Assessment*, 6(4), 304–312.

Goodenough, F. (1936). The measurement of mental functions in primitive groups. *American Anthropologist*, 38, 1–11.

Harris, J. G., Adler, L. E., & Cullum, C. M. (2000). Spoken word length effects on working memory in Spanish speakers. *Journal of the International Neuropsychological Society*, 6, 246.

Harris, J. G., & Cullum, C. M. (2001). Symbol vs. digit substitution task performance in culturally and linguistically diverse populations.

Holzer, C. E., III, & Copeland, S. (2000). Race, ethnicity, and the epidemiology of mental disorders in adults. In I. Cuéllar and F. A. Paniagua (Eds.), *Handbook of multicultural mental health*. San Diego: Academic Press.

Hoosain, R. (1979). Forward and backward digit span in the languages of the bilingual. *The Journal of Genetic Psychology*, 135, 263–268.

Jacobs, D. M., Sano, M., Albert, S., Schofield, P., Dooneief, G., & Stern, Y. (1997). Cross-cultural neuropsychological assessment: A comparison of randomly selected, demographically matched cohorts of English-and Spanish-speaking older adults. *Journal of Clinical and Experimental Neuropsychology*, 19(3), 331–339.

Kempler, D., Teng, E. L., Dick, M., Taussig, I. M., & Davis, D. S. (1998). The effects of age, education, and ethnicity on verbal fluency. *Journal of the International Neuropsychological Society*, 4(6), 531–538.

Krauss, M. E. (1980). *Alaska Native languages: Past, present, and future*. (Alaska Native Language Center Research Papers, No. 4). Fairbanks: Alaska Native Language Center.

Lecours, R. L., Mehler, J., Parente, M. A., et al. (1987). Illiteracy and brain damage—1: Aphasia testing in culturally contrasted populations (control subjects). *Neuropsychologia*, 25(1B), 231–245.

Loewenstein, D. A., Arguelles, T., Barker, W. W., & Duara, R. (1993). A comparative analysis of neuropsychological test performance of Spanish-speaking and English-speaking patients with Alzheimer's disease. *Journal of Gerontology: Psychological Sciences*, 48, 142–149.

Malgady, R. G., Rogler, L. H., & Constantino, G. (1987). Ethnocultural and linguistic bias in mental health evaluation of Hispanics. *American Psychologist*, 42(3), 228–234.

Manley, J. J., Jacobs, D. M., Sano, M., Bell, K., Merchant, C. A., Small, S. A., & Stern, Y. (1999). Effect of literacy on neuropsychological test performance in nondemented, education-matched elders. *Journal of the International Neuropsychological Society*, 5(3), 191–202.

Mattes, L. J. (1995). *Spanish Language Assessment Procedures*. Los Angeles: Western Psychological Services.

McShane, D. A., & Plas, J. M. (1984). The cognitive functioning of American Indian children: Moving from the WISC to the WISC-R. *School Psychology Review*, 13(1), 61–70.

Muñoz-Sandoval, A., Cummins, J., Alvarado, C. G., & Ruef, M. L. (1998). *Bilingual Verbal Ability Tests.* Itasca, IL: Riverside.

Naveh-Benjamin, M., & Ayres, T. J. (1986). Digit span, reading rate and linguistic relativity. *Quarterly Journal of Experimental Psychology, 38,* 739–751.

Nies, J. (1996). *Native American history: A chronology of a culture's vast achievements and their links to world events.* New York: Ballantine.

Olazaran, J., Jacobs, D., & Stern, Y. (1996). Comparative study of visual and verbal short term memory in English and Spanish speakers: Testing a linguistic hypothesis. *Journal of the International Neuropsychological Society, 2,* 105–110.

Ostrosky-Solis, F., Ardila, A., & Rosselli, M. (1999). NEUROPSI: A brief neuropsychological test battery in Spanish with norms by age and educational level. *Journal of the International Neuropsychological Society, 5*(5), 413–433.

Ostrosky-Solis, F., Canseco, E., Quintanar, L., Navarro, E., Meneses, S., & Ardila, A. (1985). Sociocultural effects in neuropsychological assessment. *International Journal of Neuroscience, 27,* 53–66.

Padilla, A. M. (1979). Crucial factors in the testing of Hispanic-Americans: A review and some suggestions for the future. In R. W. Tyler & S. H. White (Eds.), *Testing, teaching and learning: Report of a conference on testing.* Washington, DC: National Institute of Education.

Peck, E. (1974). The relationship of disease and other stress to second language. *International Journal of Social Psychiatry, 20,* 128–133.

Pontius, A. A. (1989). Color and spatial error in block design in stone age Auca: Ecological underuse of occipital-parietal system in men and of frontal lobe in women. *Brain and Cognition, 10,* 54–75.

Pontón, M., Satz, P., Herrera, L., Ortiz, F., Urrutia, C. P., Young, R., D'Ellia, L. F., Furst, C. J., & Nameron, N. (1996). Normative data stratified by age and education for the Neuropsychological Screening Battery for Hispanics (NeSBHIS): Initial report. *Journal of the International Neuropsychological Society, 2,* 96–104.

Rosen, W. G. (1980). Verbal fluency in aging and dementia. *Journal of Clinical Neuropsychology, 2,* 135–146.

Rosselli, M., & Ardila, A. (1993) Developmental norms for the Wisconsin Card Sorting Test in 5- to 12-year-old children. *The Clinical Neuropsychologist, 7,* 145–154.

Rosselli, M., Ardila, A., Araujo, K., Weekes, V. A., Caracciolo, V., Pradilla, M., & Ostrosky, F. (2000). Verbal fluency and repetition skills in healthy older Spanish-English bilinguals. *Applied Neuropsychology, 7,* 17–24.

Rosselli, M., Ardila, A., & Rosas, P. (1990). Neuropsychological assessment in illiterates II: Language and praxic abilities. *Brain and Cognition, 12,* 281–296.

Semel, E., Wiig, E. H., & Secord, W. (1997). *Clinical Evaluation of Language Fundamentals—3, Spanish Edition.* San Antonio: The Psychological Corporation.

Smith, A. (1982). *Symbol Digit Modalities Test (SDMT) Manual (Revised).* Los Angeles: Western Psychological Services.

Taussig, I. M., Henderson, V. W., & Mack, W. (1992). Spanish translation and validation of a neuropsychological battery: Performance of Spanish- and English-speaking Alzheimer's disease patient and normal comparison subjects. *Clinical Gerontologist, 11*(3–4), 95–108.

U.S. Census Bureau (2000). (Online) Available Internet: *www.census.gov/www/projections/natsum*-T3 .html.

U.S. Department of Commerce (1995). *Statistical abstract of the United States.* Washington, DC: Department of Commerce.

U.S. Department of Justice Immigration and Naturalization Service. (1999, May). *Office of Policy and Planning Annual Report No. 2.* Washington, DC: Department of Justice.

Van de Vijver, F., & Hambleton, R. K. (1996). Translating tests: Some practical guidelines. *European Psychologist, 1*(2), 89–99.

Wechsler, D. (1981). *Wechsler Adult Intelligence Scale—Revised.* San Antonio: The Psychological Corporation.

Wechsler, D. (1983). *Escala de Inteligencia Wechsler Para Niños—Revisada* (EIWN-R). San Antonio: The Psychological Corporation.

Wechsler, D. (1993). *Escala de Inteligencia Wechsler Para Niños-Revisada de Puerto Rico* (EIWN-R PR). San Antonio: The Psychological Corporation.

Woodcock, R. W., & Muñoz-Sandoval, A. F. (1996a). *Batería Woodcock-Muñoz—Revisada.* Itasca, IL: Riverside.

Woodcock, R. W., & Muñoz-Sandoval, A. F. (1996b). *Batería Woodcock-Muñoz: Pruebas de Habilidad Cognitiva—Revisada.* Itasca, IL: Riverside.

Woodcock, R. W., & Muñoz-Sandoval, A. F. (1996c). *Batería Woodcock-Muñoz: Pruebas de Aprovechamiento—Revisada.* Itasca, IL: Riverside.

CHAPTER

14

Neuropsychological Assessment of Children

KEITH OWEN YEATES

Ohio State University & Children's Hospital, Columbus, Ohio

H. GERRY TAYLOR

Case Western Reserve University & Rainbow Babies and Children's Hospital, Cleveland, Ohio

INTRODUCTION AND HISTORICAL OVERVIEW

In recent years, there has been a growing interest in the neuropsychological assessment of children (Taylor & Fletcher, 1990). Many clinical neuropsychologists focus exclusively on children and adolescents (Putnam & DeLuca, 1990; Slay & Valdivia, 1988; Sweet & Moberg, 1990), and there is an extensive literature devoted specifically to the field of child neuropsychology (e.g., Baron, Fennell, & Voeller, 1995; Pennington, 1991; Reynolds & Fletcher-Janzen, 1997; Rourke, Bakker, Fisk, & Strang, 1983; Rourke, Fisk, & Strang, 1986; Spreen, Risser, & Edgell, 1995; Yeates, Ris, & Taylor, 2000).

The history of child neuropsychology can be divided into three eras. The first, which has been called the medical era, lasted until about 1940 (Kessler, 1980). This era involved observations of children with various medical conditions by physicians who theorized about possible relationships between the status of the central nervous system and behavior. This era was hampered by the anecdotal nature of clinical reports.

The second era of child neuropsychology began around the time of World War II, when A. A. Strauss, Heinz Werner, and their colleagues began using experimental techniques to study the behavior of children with purported brain injuries. They also coined the term "minimal brain injury" to describe a cluster of behaviors that they believed were generally characteristic of brain-injured children (Strauss & Lehtinen, 1947; Strauss & Werner, 1941). This era was hampered by the limited knowledge base and methods available for assessing brain function in children. Clinicians often assumed that the presence of cognitive or behavioral deficits characteristic of children with documented brain injury were indicative of brain abnormalities, even in children without any known injury (Fletcher & Taylor, 1984).

The advent of modern neuroimaging technology and other advances in cognitive neuroscience signaled the beginning of the third and current era of child neuropsychology. This era involves a more sophisticated approach to the study of brain-behavior relationships, not only in children with neurological disease, but also in those with other systemic medical illnesses, developmental disorders such as learning disabilities and attention deficit disorder (ADD), and psychiatric disorders (Dennis & Barnes, 1994; Fletcher, 1994).

The current era of child neuropsychology is characterized by broader conceptual models of neuropsychological assessment (Bernstein & Waber, 1990; Taylor & Fletcher, 1990; Yeates & Taylor, 1998). These models capitalize on the existing knowledge base in developmental psychology (Fischer & Rose, 1994; Welsh & Pennington, 1988) and on recent advances in developmental cognitive neuroscience (Diamond, 1991; Elman et al., 1996; Johnson, 1997; Tager-Flusberg, 1999; Temple, 1997). According to these conceptual models, the goal of neuropsychological assessment is not simply to document the presence of cognitive deficits and their possible association with known or suspected brain impairment. The goal, rather, is to describe cognitive and behavioral functioning and relate it both to biological, brain-based constraints and to environmental forces in a way that enhances children's adaptation.

This chapter provides a general introduction to the neuropsychological assessment of school-age children and adolescents. We begin by describing four general principles that help to conceptualize neuropsychological assessment. We then describe neuropsychological assessment procedures, discuss some common patterns of results and associated interpretive hypotheses, and present an illustrative case study. We next discuss the benefits and limitations of neuropsychological assessment, and examine its reliability and validity. Finally, we conclude with comments regarding the future prospects for neuropsychological assessment.

PRINCIPLES OF
NEUROPSYCHOLOGICAL ASSESSMENT

We believe that the neuropsychological assessment of children and adolescents is not defined by specific test instruments, which are simply tools that should evolve substantially over time. Instead, child neuropsychological assessment is based on a broad conceptual foundation and knowledge base regarding brain-behavior relationships that can be applied to enhance children's adaptation. Recent models of child neuropsychological assessment (Bernstein, 2000; Bernstein & Waber, 1990; Taylor & Fletcher, 1990; Yeates & Taylor, 1998) share several general principles that reflect this belief.

Adaptation

The first principle is that the major goal of neuropsychological assessment is to promote children's adaptation, rather than to document the presence or location of brain damage or dysfunction. Adaptation results from interactions between children and the contexts in which they develop. In other words, adaptation reflects the functional relationship between children and their environments. Failures in adaptation, such as poor school performance or unsatisfactory peer relationships, are usually why children are brought to the attention of clinical neuropsychologists. To be useful, neuropsychological assessment must explain failures in adaptation and facilitate future outcomes, not only in the immediate contexts of school and home but also in terms of long-term adaptation to the demands of adult life.

Brain and Behavior

The second principle is that an analysis of brain-behavior relationships is a complex undertaking that can provide insights into children's adaptation. Simplistic notions of localization have been superseded by more dynamic models involving the interaction of multiple brain regions (Cummings, 1993; Derryberry & Tucker, 1992; Mesulam, 1998). Neuropsychology has begun to move beyond the uncritical application of adult models of brain function to children (Fletcher & Taylor, 1984). The assessment of brain-behavior relationships in children must take into account many factors, such as the child's age and particular medical or developmental disorder, the specific cognitive skills and behaviors assessed, and the nature of the documented or hypothesized brain impairment (Dennis, 1988).

Context

The third principle is that environmental contexts help to constrain and determine behavior. Neuropsychologists cannot determine whether brain impairment contributes to failures of adaptation without examining the environmental variables that also influence behavior. An assessment of the situational demands placed on the child is necessary to rule out alternative explanations for adaptive failures. More broadly, neuropsychological assessment not only must measure specific cognitive skills, but also must determine how children apply these skills in their specific environments. By examining how children's cognitive and behavioral profiles match the contextual demands of their environments, neuropsychologists can characterize the developmental risks facing children, and thereby make more informed recommendations for intervention (Bernstein, 2000; Bernstein & Waber, 1990).

Development

The final guiding principle is that assessment involves the measurement of development across multiple levels of analysis. Brain development is characterized by multiple processes (e.g., cell differentiation and migration, synaptogenesis, dendritic arborization and pruning, myelinization), each with its own timetable (Nowakowski, 1987). Although less is known about developmental changes in children's environments, there is nevertheless a natural history of environments characteristic of most children in our culture (Holmes, 1987). Cognitive and behavioral development results from the joint interplay of these biological and environmental timetables (Greenough & Black, 1992), and involves the emergence, stabilization, and maintenance of new skills such as language abilities, as well as the loss of earlier ones such as primitive reflexes (Dennis, 1988).

Summary

The neuropsychological assessment of children requires a model that acknowledges the role played by developmental changes in brain, behavior, and context as determinants of children's adaptation. Failures in adaptation frequently result from asynchronies between different developmental timetables (e.g., biological and environmental) that result in mismatches between children's competencies and the situational demands with which they must cope. The expression of brain impairment can vary substantially as a function of factors such as the developmental timing of a brain lesion, the age at which a child is assessed, and the environmental demands and resources impinging on a child (Taylor et al., 1995).

METHODS OF NEUROPSYCHOLOGICAL ASSESSMENT

The four general principles outlined above—adaptation, brain and behavior, context, and development—provide a foundation for the specific methods of assessment used by child neuropsychologists. Although neuropsychological assessment is usually equated with the administration of a battery of tests designed to assess various cognitive skills, in actual practice most neuropsychologists draw on multiple sources of information and do not rely solely on the results of psychological tests. The most typical combination of methods involves the collection of historical information, behavioral observations, and psychological testing, which together permit a broader and more detailed characterization of neuropsychological functioning.

History

The careful collection of historical information using structured questionnaires and parent interviews is an essential part of neuropsychological assessment. A thorough history clarifies the nature of a child's presenting problems, and also can help to determine if a child's presenting problems have a neuropsychological basis or if they are related primarily to psychosocial or environmental factors. A detailed history begins with simple demographic information, such as a child's age, sex, and race, but extends to a variety of other topics, including birth and early development, past or current medical involvement, family and social circumstances, and school history.

Birth and Developmental History

Neuropsychologists typically inquire about a mother's pregnancy, labor, and delivery, as well as about the child's acquisition of developmental milestones. Information about such topics is useful in identifying early risk factors as well as early indicators of anomalous development. The presence of early risk factors or developmental anomalies makes a stronger case for a constitutional, or neuropsychological, basis for a child's failures in adaptation. For example, perinatal complications such as prematurity and low birthweight are often associated with later neuropsychological deficits (Taylor, Klein, & Hack, 2000).

Medical History

A child's medical history often contains predictors of neuropsychological functioning, the most obvious of which are documented brain abnormalities or insults. For instance, closed-head injuries during childhood can compromise cognitive and behavioral function (Yeates, 2000). Other aspects of a child's medical history can be linked in a more indirect fashion to neuropsychological deficits. For example, chronic ear infections are occasionally linked with cognitive delays, due perhaps to the effects of the infections on hearing during language acquisition (Kavanagh, 1986). Another critical piece of medical information is whether the child is taking any medications. Anticonvulsants (Trimble, 1987), stimulants (Brown & Borden, 1989), and other psychotropic medications (Cepeda, 1989) are especially likely to affect children's performance on tests of cognitive skills.

Family and Social History

Neuropsychologists typically collect information regarding the family's history of learning and attention problems, language disorder, psychiatric disturbances, and neurological illnesses. A positive family history can signal a biological foundation for later neuropsychological deficits (Lewis, 1992). A review of family history should also attend to socioeconomic factors. Parental education and occupation are related to the developmental stimulation and learning opportunities provided for children, as well as to later childhood intellectual functioning (Yeates, MacPhee, Campbell, & Ramey, 1983).

Information regarding peer relationships and a child's capacity for sustained friendships is also extremely important in neuropsychological assessment. Poor social skills are sometimes associated with nonverbal learning problems, and may be linked with a particular neuropsychological profile (Rourke, 1989). In other instances, difficulties with peer relationships may be a sign of the psychological distress that is secondary to other difficulties, such as academic failure (Taylor, 1988).

School History

A complete school history includes information regarding current grade and school placement, any history of grade repetition or special education services, and the results of any prior testing. Information about school history is usually available from parents, but also should be sought from school personnel. School reports often corroborate parental information, but sometimes provide new or even contradictory information.

If a child has been referred for special education services in the past, the timing of those services often serves as a clue to the nature of a child's academic difficulties (Holmes, 1987). The results of prior testing can be compared to the child's current test performance to assess change or stability in neuropsychological functioning across time. Descriptions of educational interventions are also valuable, as they can help to gauge the academic demands placed on a child as well as the nature of available support. Information about previous services is also needed to make practical recommendations, if only to avoid repeating interventions that have already failed.

Behavioral Observations

Behavioral observations are the second critical source of information for child neuropsychologists. Behavioral observations are critical for interpreting the results of neuropsychological testing (Kaplan, 1988) and for judging the adequacy of certain skills that are less amenable to being measured by standardized testing. A child's behavior is often noteworthy when it requires the examiner to alter his or her usual responses (Holmes, 1988). For instance, changes in the clinician's style of speaking may be one signal that the child has a language disorder.

Rigorous observation extends across several domains of functioning. A typical list of domains includes mood and affect; motivation and cooperation; social interaction; attention and activity level; response style; speech, language, and communication; sensory and motor skills; and physical appearance.

Mood and affect often color the entire assessment process. If a child is depressed and withdrawn, or angry and oppositional, then he or she is likely to be difficult to engage in testing. A lack of cooperation does not necessarily invalidate psychological testing, but it may influence the interpretation of test results. In some cases, a lack of motivation may reflect brain impairment. A child who is compliant but unenthusiastic, who follows directions but does not initiate many actions spontaneously, may be demonstrating signs of frontal lobe pathology (Stuss & Benton, 1984). Alternatively, a lack of enthusiasm about testing, or even outright resistance, often characterizes children with learning disabilities.

Observations of social interactions with parents and the examiner are useful as well. For instance, a child who interacts appropriately with parents but is socially awkward or even inappropriate with the examiner may have a subtle nonverbal learning disability that only becomes evident in unfamiliar settings (Rourke, 1989).

A child's capacity to regulate attention and activity level also warrants appraisal. Observations of inattention and motor disinhibition during an evaluation provide important information regarding the capacity to regulate behavior under the stress of performance demands. Another strategy for assessing self-regulation is to observe a child's responsiveness to various contingencies designed to increase on-task behavior.

A child's response style or approach to tasks is likewise important. Qualitatively different errors on the same task have been associated with different types of cognitive deficits or brain pathology (Kaplan, 1988). For instance, a child who orients individual blocks incorrectly on a block design task may have a different underlying impairment than a child who does not maintain a square arrangement of the blocks. More generally, a child's responses to different test demands offer valuable clues regarding the nature of the child's cognitive deficits. Observations of a child's response style also can reveal strategies that the child uses to compensate for specific neuropsychological deficits.

Speech, language, and communication skills are also deserving of close observation. Language disorders often are associated with failures in the acquisition of basic academic skills. Neuropsychologists usually monitor the ease with which children engage in spontaneous conversation, their level of comprehension, the quality of their language expression in terms of both grammatical/syntactic form and lexical/semantic content, and the occurrence of more pathognomonic errors such as naming problems and paraphasias. Even when speech is fluent and language expression is appropriate, children may display deficits in pragmatic language, such as poor discourse skills, an inability to maintain a topic of conversation and engage in reciprocal turn-taking, and a lack of appreciation for paralinguistic features such as intonation, gesture, and facial expression (Dennis & Barnes, 1993).

Gross disturbances in sensory and motor functioning may interfere with the standardized administration of psychological tests. These disturbances also are important because of the purported association between neurological "soft signs" and cognitive functioning (Shaffer, O'Connor, Shafer, & Prupis, 1983; Taylor, 1987). Asymmetries in sensory and motor function can sometimes assist with the localization of brain dysfunction, and also may provide support for the notion that a child's adaptive difficulties have a neurological basis.

The final category of observation is physical appearance. Physical dysmorphology is frequently associated with specific neuropathological syndromes. The more mundane aspects of a child's appearance, such as their size, dress, and hygiene, can likewise be important. For example, being taller than one's peers is typically an advantage, especially for boys, and may buffer children from the potential negative psychosocial consequences of neuropsychological deficits, whereas being smaller than one's peers may increase the risk of adverse social interactions.

Psychological Testing

Psychological testing is the third source of information on which child neuropsychologists rely, and the source most often equated with neuropsychological assessment. Formal testing permits normative comparisons, and also provides a standardized context for making qualitative observations of response styles and problem-solving strategies.

Some child neuropsychologists administer standardized test batteries, such as the Halstead-Reitan Neuropsychological Test Battery (Reitan & Wolfson, 1992a) or NEPSY (Korkman, Kirk, & Kemp, 1998). Other neuropsychologists administer fixed batteries using tests drawn from various sources. In still other cases, neuropsychologists adopt a flexible approach to assessment, and select tests for each individual patient based on specific referral questions. Each approach has its own strengths and weaknesses (Fletcher, Taylor, Levin, & Satz, 1995). Table 14.1 lists some of the tests commonly used by child neuropsychologists.

Regardless of whether a neuropsychologist administers a fixed battery or adopts a more flexible approach to test selection, most test batteries are selected to assess several core neurobehavioral domains: general cognitive

TABLE 14.1

Selected List of Tests Commonly Used in Child Neuropsychological Assessment

Test domain/Test name	Age range (years)
General neuropsychological test batteries	
Halstead-Reitan Neuropsychological Test Battery for Older Children	
(Reitan & Wolfson, 1992a)	9 to 15
NEPSY—A Developmental Neuropsychological Assessment	
(Korkman, Kirk, & Kemp, 1998)	3 to 12
Reitan-Indiana Neuropsychological Test Battery (Reitan & Wolfson, 1992b)	5 to 8
General cognitive ability	
Cognitive Assessment System (Naglieri & Das, 1997)	5 to 17
Differential Abilities Scale (Elliott, 1990)	2.6 to 17
Stanford-Binet Intelligence Scale—Fourth Edition	
(Thorndike, Hagen, & Sattler, 1986)	2 to adult
Wechsler Abbreviated Scale of Intelligence (Psychological Corporation, 1999)	6 to adult
Wechsler Adult Intelligence Scale—Third Edition (Wechsler, 1997a)	16 to adult
Wechsler Intelligence Scale for Children—Third Edition (Wechsler, 1991)	6 to 16
Wechsler Preschool and Primary Scales of Intelligence—Revised	
(Wechsler, 1989)	3 to 7
Memory abilities	
Children's Memory Scale (Cohen, 1997)	5 to 16
California Verbal Learning Test (Delis, Kramer, Kaplan, & Ober, 1994)	5 to 16
Test of Memory and Learning (Reynolds & Bigler, 1994)	5 to 19
Wechsler Memory Scale—Third Edition (Wechsler, 1997b)	16 to adult
Wide Range Assessment of Memory and Learning (Sheslow & Adams, 1990)	4 to adult
Language skills	
Boston Naming Test (Kaplan, Goodglass, & Weintraub, 1983)	5 to 13
Clinical Evaluation of Language Fundamentals—Third Edition	
(Semel, Wiig, & Secord, 1995)	6 to 21
Neurosensory Center Comprehensive Examination for Aphasia	
(Spreen & Benton, 1969)	6 to 13
Peabody Picture Vocabulary Test—Fourth Edition (Dunn & Dunn, 1997)	2.6 to adult
Test of Language Competence (Wiig & Secord, 1989)	5 to 18
Visual-perceptual and visual-motor skills	
Benton Visual Retention Test—Fifth Edition (Benton, 1992)	8 to adult
Developmental Test of Visual-Motor Integration—Fourth Edition	
(Beery, 1996)	2 to 18
Hooper Visual Organization Test (Western Psychological Services, 1983)	5 to 13
Judgment of Line Orientation Test (Benton, Sivan, Hamsher, Varney, &	
Spreen, 1994)	7 to 14
Rey-Osterrieth Complex Figure (Bernstein & Waber, 1996)	5 to 18
Attention and executive functions	
Gordon Diagnostic System (Gordon, 1996)	4 to 16
Children's Category Test (Boll, 1992)	5 to 16
Contingency Naming Test (Taylor, Albo, Phebus, Sachs, & Bierl, 1987)	6 to 17
Test of Variables of Attention (Greenberg & Dupuy, 1993)	4 to adult
Tower of London (Anderson, Anderson, & Lajoie, 1996; Krikorian, Bartok, &	
Gay, 1994)	7 to 13

(continues)

Table 14.1—*Continued*

Test domain/Test name	Age range (years)
Trail Making Test (Reitan & Wolfson, 1992a)	9 to adult
Wisconsin Card Sorting Test (Heaton, Chelune, Talley, Kay, & Curtiss, 1993)	6.6 to adult
Motor skills	
Bruininks-Oseretsky Test of Motor Proficiency (Bruininks, 1978)	4.6 to 14.5
Finger Tapping Test (Reitan & Wolfson, 1992a, 1992b)	5 to adult
Grooved Pegboard (Matthews & Klve, 1964)	5 to adult
Purdue Pegboard (Gardner & Broman, 1979)	5 to 15
Academic skills	
Comprehensive Test of Phonological Processing (Wagner, Torgeson, & Rashotte, 1999)	5 to adult
Kaufman Test of Educational Achievement (Kaufman & Kaufman, 1997)	6 to adult
Peabody Individual Achievement Test—Revised (Markwardt, 1992)	5 to adult
Test of Word Reading Efficiency (Torgeson, Wagner, & Rashotte, 1999)	6 to adult
Test of Written Language—Third Edition (Hammill & Larsen, 1996)	7.5 to 17
Wechsler Individual Achievement Test (Psychological Corporation, 1992)	5 to 19
Wide Range Achievement Test—Third Edition (Wilkinson, 1993)	5 to adult
Woodcock-Johnson Tests of Achievement—Revised (Woodcock & Mather, 1989)	5 to adult
Adaptive behavior	
Scales of Independent Behavior—Revised (Bruininks, Woodcock, Weatherman, & Hill, 1996)	0 to adult
Vineland Adaptive Behavior Scales (Sparrow, Balla, & Ciccetti, 1984)	0 to 18
Behavioral adjustment	
Behavior Assessment System for Children (Reynolds & Kamphaus, 1992)	2.6 to 18
Child Behavior Checklist (Achenbach, 1991)	2 to 18
Conners' Rating Scales—Revised (Conners, 1997)	3 to 17
Personality Inventory for Children—Revised (Wirt, Seat, Broen, & Lachar, 1990)	3 to 16

ability; language abilities; visuoperceptual and constructional abilities; learning and memory; attention and executive functions; corticosensory and motor capacities; academic skills; and emotional status, behavioral adjustment, and adaptive behavior. In the following sections, we describe examples of tests and briefly examine the rationale and limitations of measurement in each domain.

General Cognitive Ability

General cognitive ability is usually assessed using standardized intelligence tests, such as the Wechsler Intelligence Scale for Children—Third Edition (WISC-III; Wechsler, 1991; see also Chapter 1), the Stanford-Binet Intelligence Scale—Fourth Edition (Thorndike, Hagen, & Sattler, 1986), or the Differential Abilities Scale (Elliott, 1990; see also Chapter 3). Intelligence tests are well-standardized measures that assess a broad range of cognitive skills. These tests typically have excellent psychometric properties in terms of both reliability and validity (Sattler, 1992). They provide an estimate of a child's overall functioning, which can be useful in justifying placement recommendations in clinical practice.

On the other hand, intelligence tests are not, as often supposed, measures of learning potential. Moreover, the tests were designed primarily to predict academic achievement, and in many cases their subtests were not developed to assess distinct or unitary mental abilities. Intelligence tests also fail to measure many important skills, as reflected in the robust relationship between academic achievement and neuropsychological test performance, even after IQ is controlled statistically (Taylor, Fletcher, & Satz, 1982). Thus, intelligence tests are helpful in neuropsychological assessment, but they do not capture all relevant cognitive abilities.

Some attempts have been made to develop or modify standardized intelligence tests to be more informative neuropsychologically. For instance, the Cognitive Assessment System (Naglieri & Das, 1997; see also Chapter 2) is predicated on a Lurian model of neuropsychological functioning. Similarly, the modifications that are incorporated in the WISC-III as a Process Instrument (WISC-III PI; Kaplan, Fein, Kramer, Delis, & Morris, 1999) permit a more detailed analysis of the cognitive components of a child's test performance, and are based on the so-called process approach to neuropsychological assessment (Kaplan, 1988). Neither of these tests, however, examines the full breadth of neurocognitive skills of interest to most neuropsychologists.

Language Abilities

The study of aphasia was one of the driving forces in the growth of neuropsychology. Thus, when testing language abilities, child neuropsychologists often draw on aphasia batteries such as the Neurosensory Center Comprehensive Examination of Aphasia (Gaddes & Crockett, 1975; Spreen & Benton, 1969) or associated tests such as the Boston Naming Test (Kaplan, Goodglass, & Weintraub, 1983; Yeates, 1994). Neuropsychologists also make use of other tests used by speech pathologists, such as the Clinical Evaluation of Language Fundamentals—Third Edition (Semel, Wiig, & Secord, 1995). The goal typically is to assess functions such as comprehension, repetition, naming, and other receptive and expressive skills.

Language skills are a critical determinant of academic success and social competence, and children with learning disorders and brain injuries frequently display language deficits (Ewing-Cobbs, Levin, Eisenberg, & Fletcher, 1987). Performance on language measures, however, often reflects skills other than those that the tests purport to assess. For example, attention problems rather than comprehension deficits may interfere with a child's ability to follow oral directions, and cultural differences rather than retrieval problems may hamper performance on a picture naming test. As is often true in neuro-psychological assessment, the interpretation of language test performance must take into account competencies in other domains.

Most formal language tests do not tap the communication skills that are of particular relevance to a child's adaptive functioning. Specifically, there is a paucity of measures designed to assess pragmatic language skills such as discourse, the ability to maintain a topic of conversation and engage in re-ciprocal turn-taking, and the understanding of paralinguistic features such as intonation, gesture, and facial expression (Dennis & Barnes, 1993). As al-ready noted, pragmatic language is typically assessed through observation of informal conversations with children or through qualitative analysis of lan-guage samples provided on other tasks, such as the Vocabulary subtest of the WISC-III or story recall measures on tests of verbal memory.

Visuoperceptual and Constructional Abilities

Tests of nonverbal skills typically are of two sorts. One sort draws on visuo-perceptual abilities without requiring any motor output, and the other de-mands constructional skills and involves motor control and planning. Com-mon tests of visuoperceptual skills include the Hooper Visual Organization Test (Kirk, 1992; Western Psychological Services, 1983) and the Judgment of Line Orientation Test (Benton, Sivan, Hamsher, Varney, & Spreen, 1994). Tests of constructional skills include the Developmental Test of Visual-Motor Integration (Beery, 1996), the Rey-Osterrieth Complex Figure (Bernstein & Waber, 1996), and the Block Design and Object Assembly subtests of the WISC-III.

Nonverbal deficits predict poor performance in certain academic do-mains, particularly arithmetic, and also are associated with a heightened risk for psychosocial maladjustment, including poor peer relationships (Rourke, 1989). In addition, nonverbal deficits are common in children with brain injuries and other acquired neurological insults, suggesting that nonverbal skills are especially vulnerable to being affected by brain damage in children (Taylor, Barry, & Schatschneider, 1993). Tests of nonverbal abilities also draw on other skills, however, such as attention and organization, and many of the tests demand substantial motor dexterity. Thus, test interpretation must take into account a child's overall neuropsychological test profile.

Learning and Memory

Despite the obvious importance of learning and memory for children's adap-tation, and especially their school performance, there were until recently few instruments available for assessing these skills. Fortunately, a variety of measures now are available, including the California Verbal Learning Test—Children's Version (Delis, Kramer, Kaplan, & Ober, 1994), the Children's Mem-ory Scale (Cohen, 1997), the Test of Memory and Learning (Reynolds & Bigler,

1994), and the Wide Range Assessment of Memory and Learning (Sheslow & Adams, 1990).

Children with brain impairment typically do not demonstrate the dense amnesia characteristic of adults with neurological disorders such as Alzheimer's disease, but they do show distinct deficits on tests of learning and memory (Yeates, Blumenstein, Patterson, & Delis, 1995; Yeates, Enrile, Loss, Blumenstein, & Delis, 1995). Tests of children's learning and memory only recently have begun to reflect advances in the neuroscience of memory (Squire, 1987; Butters & Delis, 1995), however, and substantially more research is needed to examine their predictive validity (Loring & Papanicolau, 1987). Clinically, performance on tests of memory and learning is multiply determined. For example, story recall is affected by children's language competencies and attention skills. Once again, test interpretation cannot proceed without a broader understanding of a child's abilities.

Attention

Attention is a multidimensional construct that overlaps with the domain of executive functions discussed below (Mesulam, 1981; Mirsky, Anthony, Duncan, Ahearn, & Kellam, 1991; Taylor, Schatschneider, Petrill, Barry, & Owens, 1996). Neuropsychologists typically assess various aspects of attention, such as vigilance, selective and divided attention, the ability to shift set, and cognitive efficiency (Cooley & Morris, 1990). Relevant tests include the Gordon Diagnostic System, one of several continuous performance tests (Grant, Ilai, Nussbaum, & Bigler, 1990); the Contingency Naming Test (Taylor, Albo, Phebus, Sachs, & Bierl, 1987); the Trail Making Test (Reitan & Wolfson, 1992a); and the Arithmetic, Digit Span, Coding, and Symbol Search subtests from the WISC-III (Wechsler, 1991).

Attention problems are a common reason for referral to child neuropsychologists, and are central to the diagnosis of attention-deficit/hyperactivity disorder (ADHD; Barkley, 1990). However, the relationship between formal tests of attention and the behaviors about which parents and teachers complain is modest at best (Barkley, 1991). The weak relationship reflects the complex nature of attention as a cognitive construct (Cooley & Morris, 1990), as well as the multifactorial nature of behavioral problems such as inattention and hyperactivity. Despite their lack of diagnostic utility, tests of attention remain an important component of neuropsychological assessment. The tests permit assessment of the cognitive construct of attention, which not only moderates performance on many other psychological tests but also is selectively affected by early brain insults (Taylor, Hack, & Klein, 1998).

Executive Functions

Executive functions are involved in the planning, organization, regulation, and monitoring of goal-directed behavior (Denckla, 1994). The assessment of these skills and related abilities, such as problem solving and abstract reasoning, has often been conducted informally, by examining the quality of performance on tests in other measurement domains. More recently, tests have been developed specifically to assess executive functions. Such tests include the Wisconsin Card Sorting Test (Heaton, Chelune, Talley, Kay, & Curtiss, 1993), the Tower of London (Anderson, Anderson, & Lajoie, 1996; Krikorian, Bartok, & Gay, 1994), and the Children's Category Test (Boll, 1992).

Executive functions are a critical determinant of a child's adaptive functioning. Deficits in executive functions are ubiquitous in children with documented brain dysfunction, as well as in those with developmental learning disorders. Despite recent research devoted to clarifying the relevant constructs and their assessment, however, the nature of executive function in children remains uncertain (Levin et al., 1991; Taylor et al., 1996; Welsh, Pennington, & Groisser, 1991). Of particular concern in the context of clinical assessment is the paucity of studies examining the ecological validity of purported measures of executive function.

Corticosensory and Motor Capacities

Tests of corticosensory and motor capacities usually involve standardized versions of components of the traditional neurological examination. Relevant corticosensory skills include finger localization, stereognosis, graphesthesia, sensory extinction, and left-right orientation. A variety of standardized assessment procedures are available to assess corticosensory skills (Benton et al., 1994; Reitan & Wolfson, 1992a, 1992b). In the motor domain, tests such as the Grooved Pegboard (Matthews & Kløve, 1964), Purdue Pegboard (Rapin, Tourk, & Costa, 1966), and Finger Tapping Test (Reitan & Wolfson, 1992a, 1992b) typically are used to assess motor speed and dexterity, although batteries such as the Bruininks-Oseretsky Test of Motor Proficiency (Bruininks, 1978) are also available. In addition, tests of oculomotor control, motor overflow, alternating and repetitive movements, and other related skills are often used to assess "soft" neurological signs (Denckla, 1985).

Tests of corticosensory and motor capacities are sensitive to neurological disorders and can provide useful confirmatory evidence of localized brain dysfunction. These tests also may help to predict learning problems in younger children and to differentiate older children with different types of learning disorders (Casey & Rourke, 1992). However, many children perform well on sensory and motor tasks despite clear evidence of learning disorders or neurological impairment. Moreover, the assessment of sensory and motor abilities often is hampered by inattention or poor cooperation, especially among young children.

Academic Skills

Academic underachievement is one of the most common reasons that children are referred for neuropsychological assessment. Several test batteries are available for assessing academic achievement, including the Wide Range Achievement Test—Third Edition (Wilkinson, 1993), the Woodcock-Johnson Tests of Achievement—Revised (Woodcock & Mather, 1989; see also Chapter 5), the Wechsler Individual Achievement Test (The Psychological Corporation, 1992; see also Chapter 6), Kaufman Test of Educational Achievement (Kaufman & Kaufman, 1997), and the Peabody Individual Achievement Test—Revised (Markwardt, 1992).

The assessment of academic skills provides information on the nature and severity of underachievement. Selective problems in achievement, such as deficits in reading but not math, can provide evidence of specific learning disabilities. Thus, achievement test results often are used to determine whether a child is eligible for special education services, and may also carry more specific treatment implications. However, patterns of performance on standardized achievement tests afford limited insight into the cognitive processes underlying underachievement.

Recently, the assessment of academic skills has begun to incorporate the measurement of the specific cognitive processes that underlie those skills. For example, the assessment of reading now often includes measures of phonological awareness and rapid naming (Torgeson, Wagner, & Rashotte, 1999; Wagner, Torgeson, & Rashotte, 1999; see also Chapter 7). Similarly, the assessment of math may include measures of math fact retrieval and an analysis of arithmetic procedural errors (Sokol, Macaruso, & Gollan, 1994; Temple, 1991; see also Chapter 8). In the future, this broader approach also may be incorporated in the assessment of other pertinent academic abilities, such as study habits and the use of strategies for remembering and problem solving.

Emotional Status, Behavioral Adjustment, and Adaptive Behavior

Adaptive failures frequently occur in domains other than academic performance. These failures may be manifest in psychological distress, inappropriate or otherwise undesirable behavior, or deficits in everyday functioning, including poor daily living skills or social skills. A wide variety of formal checklists are available to assess emotional status and behavioral adjustment, including the Child Behavior Checklist (Achenbach, 1991; see also Chapter 10), the Behavior Assessment System for Children (Reynolds & Kamphaus, 1992; see also Chapter 9), the Personality Inventory for Children (Wirt, Seat, Broen, & Lachar, 1990), and the Conners' Rating Scales—Revised (Conners, 1997). Rating scales also are available to assess various aspects of adaptive behavior, such as the Scales of Independent Behavior—Revised (Bruininks, Woodcock, Weatherman, & Hill, 1996), as are detailed semistructured interview procedures, such as the Vineland Adaptive Behavior Scales (Sparrow, Balla, & Ciccetti, 1984).

The assessment of emotional and behavioral adjustment and of adaptive functioning is crucial. A careful analysis of deficits in adjustment and adaptive behavior can help to define the mismatch between a child's neuropsychological profile and the environmental demands placed on the child. However, the relationship between neuropsychological skills and adjustment problems or deficits in adaptive behavior is complex. For example, premorbid behavior problems and adaptive deficits may increase the risk of traumatic brain injury. Adjustment problems and adaptive difficulties also may be an indirect result of the frustration associated with consistent failures to cope with environmental demands. In other cases, behavioral difficulties or adaptive deficits may be a more direct manifestation of neuropsychological deficits (Rourke & Fuerst, 1991).

CLINICAL INTERPRETATION
OF ASSESSMENT RESULTS

The final step in assessment involves the integration of historical information, behavioral observations, and test results. The integration of these diverse sources of data results in a diagnostic formulation of a child's presenting problems from a neuropsychological perspective. Treatment recommendations follow from this formulation, based on impressions regarding the reasons for the child's current adaptive problems and predictions regarding the adaptive risks anticipated in the future.

The process by which neuropsychologists integrate diverse pieces of information is difficult to describe in explicit terms. Indeed, the ability of neuropsychologists to utilize the myriad pieces of information generated in neuropsychological assessment has been called into question (Dawes, Faust, & Meehl, 1989). Research on clinical judgment suggests that clinicians rely on a limited amount of information in their decision making and cannot use additional information when it is available to them (Garb, 1998). Nevertheless, systematic research indicates that neuropsychologists can use the information they gather to generate diagnostic formulations in a reliable fashion (Brown, Del Dotto, Fisk, Taylor, & Breslau, 1993; Waber, Bernstein, Kammerer, Tarbell, & Sallan, 1992).

Neuropsychologists attempt to integrate historical information, behavioral observations, and test results by searching for converging findings that are consistent with current knowledge regarding brain function in children and the nature of cognitive-behavioral relationships across development (Bernstein, 2000; Bernstein & Waber, 1990). Neuropsychologists typically evaluate test results in terms of level of performance on each task, pattern of performance across tasks, and strategies or processes used to attempt each task. However, diagnostic formulations do not depend solely on an analysis of test scores, but instead involve the integration of multiple sources of data in light of a broad conceptual foundation and knowledge base.

For clinical purposes, brain function is usually defined in general terms, with reference to the three primary neuroanatomic axes: left-hemisphere/right-hemisphere; anterior/posterior; and cortical/subcortical (Bernstein, 2000; Bernstein & Waber, 1990). The three-axis model is used as a organizational heuristic that helps to integrate the data gleaned from neuropsychological assessment, including test results, behavioral observations, and historical information. The overarching concerns of the neuropsychologist are whether the findings can be interpreted in terms of brain-behavior relationships and whether they can be determined to have a neurological basis. Whether or not the findings raise concerns about actual brain damage is a distinct issue.

Certain patterns lend themselves to specific interpretations (Baron, 2000). For instance, a constellation of specific delays in the acquisition of language milestones, poor performance on language and reading tests, configurational approaches on constructional tasks, and right-sided sensorimotor deficits might be conceptualized as implicating the left hemisphere, without necessarily assuming that there is any focal brain lesion. In contrast, the presence of language and reading deficits in isolation would be more difficult to interpret, because isolated deficits in those domains have many other potential explanations, such as a lack of appropriate environmental stimulation.

Similarly, a long-standing history of difficulties with attention and organization in school and at home, a disinhibited response style, and poor performance on tests of attention and executive functions, expressive language, complex constructional skills, processing speed, and fine-motor skills might be interpreted as implicating the brain's frontal-subcortical axis. This interpretation would gain credence if functions usually associated with posterior brain regions (e.g., receptive language, visuoperceptual, and corticosensory skills) were intact. In contrast, the interpretation would be more difficult to entertain if the findings were characterized by more generalized impairment.

Frequently, the findings from a neuropsychological assessment are interpreted only in terms of whether they are likely to have a biological or constitutional basis, because they do not lend themselves to more specific brain-related interpretations. For instance, a family history of reading problems increases the likelihood that a child's own reading problems have a genetic basis, but does not necessarily suggest relatively greater involvement of any particular brain system. Similarly, unexpectedly low performance across a variety of neuropsychological domains may suggest a biological basis for a child's adaptive difficulties, but generalized impairment usually does not support more specific brain-related interpretations.

In addition to making brain-related interpretations of their findings, neuropsychologists employ the knowledge base about cognitive and behavioral development to characterize what Taylor and Fletcher (1990) refer to as "behavior-behavior" relationships. For example, neuropsychologists may draw distinctions between verbal and nonverbal skills, perceptual input and behavioral output, or automatic and effortful processing. Similarly, they may correlate reading disabilities with deficits in phonological awareness or arithmetic disabilities with poor visuospatial skills.

After constructing a diagnostic formulation, neuropsychologists typically evaluate the fit between a child's neuropsychological profile and the child's environmental context. The child's current adaptive failures can then be explained in terms of a poor fit, and the nature of the poor fit can be used to forecast the risks faced by the child in the future. The assessment of risk must take into account both a child's neuropsychological profile and the particular features of the child's environment, including his or her family, school, and community (Rourke, Fisk, & Strang, 1986). Recommendations for management do not arise directly from test results, but instead from an evaluation of the risks associated with neuropsychological profiles and environmental demands.

CASE STUDY

To illustrate neuropsychological assessment procedures, we present the case study of "John," a 7-year, 1-month-old white male. John sustained a closed-head injury in a motor vehicle accident about 3 years prior to being referred for a neuropsychological evaluation. He was referred to the senior author by the attorney representing him in litigation regarding the circumstances of his injury. The attorney wished to document John's current neuropsychological functioning, the relationship of the neuropsychological findings to his head injury, and the implications of the findings for his quality of life.

Relevant information was obtained from hospital medical records, including two previous neuropsychological evaluations, and through an interview with John's mother. She also completed the Scales of Independent Behavior—Revised and the Child Behavior Checklist. John's special education teacher completed the Teacher's Report Form. This information was supplemented by detailed observations of John's behavioral repertoire and his performance on a variety of psychological tests, the results of which are listed in Table 14.2.

At the time of the evaluation, John lived with his parents and sister in a middle-class home. Family history was significant for the appearance of seizures, migraine headaches, learning problems, and depression in the extended maternal family. Birth history was unremarkable. Developmental milestones were acquired within normal limits.

Medical history was unremarkable until John sustained a severe closed-head injury in the motor vehicle accident when he was 4 years of age. Neuroimaging documented widespread injuries in the subcortical and cortical regions of the brain, predominantly in the anterior regions (see Figure 14.1). John was in a coma for several days after the accident. After regaining consciousness, he demonstrated a left-sided partial paralysis and left-sided

TABLE 14.2
Case Study Test Results

Wechsler Intelligence Scale for Children—Third Edition

Full Scale IQ	95		
Verbal Scale IQ	90		
Performance Scale IQ	102		
Verbal Comprehension Index	93		
Perceptual Organization Index	99		
Freedom from Distractibility Index	90		
Processing Speed Index	104		
Subtest scaled scores:			
Information	7	Picture Completion	9
Similarities	11	Picture Arrangement	9
Arithmetic	6	Block Design	10
Vocabulary	7	Object Assembly	11
Comprehension	10	Coding	12
Digit Span	10	Symbol Search	9

NEPSY—A Developmental Neuropsychological Assessment

Language core (St)	95		
Visuospatial core (St)	124		
Attention/executive function core (St)	85		
Sensorimotor core (St)	82		
Subtest scaled scores:			
Phonological Processing	8	Tower	6
Speeded Naming	10	Auditory Attention and Response Set	10
Comprehension of Instructions	10	Visual Attention	8
Sentence Repetition	8	Fingertip Tapping	7
Verbal Fluency	6	Imitating Hand Positions	5
Design Copying	15	Visuomotor Precision	11
Arrows	14		

Children's Memory Scale

Visual Immediate Index (St)	100		
Visual Delayed Index (St)	94		
Verbal Immediate Index (St)	88		
Verbal Delayed Index (St)	91		
General Memory Index (St)	90		
Attention/Concentration Index (St)	94		
Learning Index (St)	106		
Delayed Recognition Index (St)	97		
Subtest scaled scores:			
Stories Immediate	6	Dot Locations Learning	12
Stories Delayed	7	Dot Locations Long Delay	11
Stories Delayed Recognition	9	Faces Immediate	8
Word Pairs Learning	10	Faces Delayed	7
Word Pairs Long Delay	10	Numbers	10
Word Pairs Delayed Recognition	10	Sequences	8

Wide Range Achievement Test—Third Edition

Reading (St)	81		
Spelling (St)	77		
Arithmetic (St)	97		

Boston Naming Test

Total correct	R: 20	T: 18	

California Verbal Learning Test

List A, trial 1	R: 1	$z: -2.5$	
List A, trial 5	R: 5	$z: -1.5$	
Total list A, trials 1–5	R: 16	T: 25	

(continues)

Table 14.2—*Continued*

List B	R:	2	z:	−1.5
Free recall short delay	R:	2	z:	−2.0
Cued recall short delay	R:	3	z:	−2.0
Free recall long delay	R:	3	z:	−2.0
Cued recall long delay	R:	3	z:	−2.0
Recognition hits	R:	9	z:	−1.5
False positives	R:	2	z:	−0.5
Discriminability	R:	82%	z:	−0.5
Perseverations	R:	1	z:	−1.0
Intrusions	R:	22	z:	+1.0

Hooper Visual Organization Test
Total correct	R:	17	T:	34

Gordon Diagnostic System
Delay task
Total correct	R:	40	T:	50
Efficiency ratio	R:	.77	T:	47

Wisconsin Card Sorting Test
Categories completed	R:	6	WNL
% conceptual responses	R:	73	St: 113
% perseverative errors	R:	9	St: 115
Failures to maintain set	R:	3	WNL

Children's Category Test
Total errors	R:	16	T:	54

Sensory-Perceptual Examination
Double-simultaneous visual stimulation
Right errors	R:	0	WNL
Left errors	R:	0	WNL

Tactile finger identification
Right errors	R:	3	Impaired
Left errors	R:	4	Impaired

Finger Tapping Test
Right	R:	31	T:	57
Left	R:	23	T:	43

Grooved Pegboard
Right	R:	42"	T:	49
Left	R:	88"	T:	25

Scales of Independent Behavior—Revised
Motor (St)	115
Social Interaction & Communication (St)	117
Personal Living (St)	133
Community Living (St)	102
Broad Independence (St)	119

Child Behavior Checklist
Parent
Total T	42
Internalizing T	43
Externalizing T	38

Teacher
Total T	31
Internalizing T	36
Externalizing T	39

Note: R = raw score, T = T score (M = 50, SD = 10), Sc = Scaled score (M = 10, SD = 3), St = Standard score (M = 100, SD = 15), z = z score (M = 0, SD = 1), WNL = within normal limits. Qualitative levels are provided when published norms do not permit conversion.

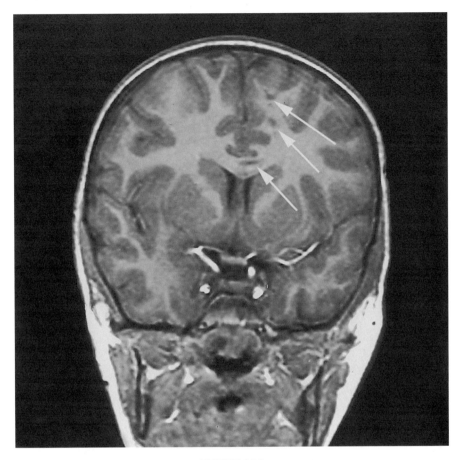

FIGURE 14.1

Coronal MRI scan showing lesions in left frontal lobe and corpus callosum of brain in child with severe closed-head injury at age 4 (see white arrows).

visual neglect. He was transferred to a rehabilitation program 1 week after his injury, and discharged about 1 month later.

John attended a parochial preschool program for 2 years, and also attended kindergarten in a parochial school. He had difficulty expressing himself in class and acquiring early school-related skills. He participated in speech/language therapy and also received private tutoring for his academic skills. Because of his academic difficulties, John's parents transferred him to public school for first grade. At that time, he began to receive special education services under the Traumatic Brain Injury (TBI) classification. John also continued participating in speech/language therapy and private academic tutoring.

John was completing first grade in a local public school system. He received most of his academic instruction in a resource room. His teacher described his academic performance as far below grade level in language arts, and at grade level in mathematics, social studies, and science. She described John as a hard worker with a positive attitude, and characterized him as responsible, helpful, attentive, motivated, friendly, and an excellent role model.

John's mother reported that the provision of special education services had resulted in a significant improvement in John's academic performance. She stated that his attention had improved, but that he remained more forgetful than his peers. John's mother also described improvements in his personality and behavior. He was less withdrawn than before, and he socialized more readily with other children. He was not as anxious or easily frustrated.

John had participated in two previous neuropsychological evaluations. The first one took place about 1 month after his head injury. At that time, his IQ was below average. He displayed deficits in nonverbal skills and motor output. By contrast, his language skills were generally secure. A second evaluation was completed about 1 year after the injury. At that time, John's IQ remained below average. He displayed deficits in verbal and nonverbal memory, as well as in executive functions such as attention, behavioral regulation, and abstraction. His psychomotor speed was also below average. In contrast, his language skills, visuoperceptual skills, and constructional abilities were generally intact, as was his corticosensory functioning.

During testing, John interacted appropriately with the examiner. He approached testing more cooperatively than he had previous evaluations, and he was motivated to perform well. His attention was generally well sustained, at least in the structured, one-on-one testing sessions. His activity level was not well regulated, however, and he was quite fidgety. In addition, his response style was disinhibited. For instance, he tended to begin responding before task instructions were completed.

Spontaneous conversation was not difficult to elicit. In conversation with John, his comprehension was intact. His language expression was appropriate in form and content, without overt aphasic errors. His speech was clearly articulated and intelligible. His language pragmatics were intact, aside from occasional interruptions of the examiner, which were secondary to his disinhibition. John also demonstrated a satisfactory appreciation of paralinguistic features such as gesture, intonation, and facial expression.

John's physical appearance was unremarkable, as were his gait and balance. His graphomotor skills were still somewhat insecure. He preferred his right hand for writing and drawing. He employed an awkward tripod grip, but produced legible print.

Test results are presented in Table 14.2. Overall performance on the WISC-III was average, and reflected substantial improvement compared to the previous neuropsychological evaluation. All four index scores were in the average range, and they did not differ significantly. Several qualitative observations were noteworthy on the WISC-III. Latencies to response were longer than expected on Information. Definitions on Vocabulary frequently included nonessential information, and in several cases he received no credit despite apparent word knowledge. John was able to repeat a maximum of five digits forward and three backward on Digit Span. He frequently made irrelevant comments during Picture Arrangement. He used his right hand almost exclusively during Block Design. He was unable to complete any Block Design items that did not include internal guidelines, and he broke the square matrix on such items.

Formal language testing revealed expressive deficits that were more pronounced than during the previous neuropsychological evaluation. John performed adequately on tests assessing comprehension and repetition. His phonological skills also were intact. In contrast, he displayed mild to moderate deficits on measures of confrontation naming and rapid word generation.

Verbal memory was hampered by retrieval deficits. On a word-list learning task and a story recall task, delayed recall was below average, but recognition was average, suggesting retrieval difficulties. Performance was average on a paired-associates learning task.

Nonverbal skills were intact, and somewhat improved compared to previous testing. John performed average on tests of spatial judgment and drawing skills, but somewhat below average on a test of perceptual recognition. Nonverbal memory was intact, again representing some improvement compared to previous testing. John performed at an average level on tests of facial memory and spatial location memory.

Tests of executive functions revealed persistent deficits in focused attention and planning, with some improvement in abstract reasoning. John displayed some difficulties on complex measures of sustained attention and response inhibition, one of which had to be discontinued. He performed at an average level on measures of working memory and response speed, as well as on measures of concept formation and cognitive flexibility. His planning skills were in the low-average range.

Tests of sensorimotor functioning revealed persistent deficits. John demonstrated bilateral errors in tactile finger recognition. Simple motor speed was intact, but complex motor speed fell below expectations on the left side. Manual coordination was below average bilaterally. Graphomotor skill was average.

On tests of academic skills, John's performance continued to be poorer than expected in reading and spelling, despite some improvement in word recognition. Arithmetic skills had improved substantially.

John's mother described his overall adaptive functioning as in the high-average range. She characterized John's motor skills and social/communication skills as in the high-average range, his personal living skills as above average, and his community living skills as average. She did not report significant maladaptive behavior.

John's mother and special education teacher rated his behavioral adjustment. Neither of them reported a significant overall level of behavioral disturbance or any significant elevations on specific problem scales.

In summary, the evaluation indicated that general intellectual functioning was average. Within that context, the neuropsychological protocol revealed specific deficits in expressive language and verbal memory, as well as more general deficits in certain executive functions, including focused attention, response inhibition, and planning. Deficits in sensorimotor skills also were evident bilaterally. In contrast, nonverbal skills were generally intact, as were some other executive functions, such as cognitive flexibility and abstraction.

From a neuropsychological perspective, the findings suggested relatively greater deficits in functions usually associated with left-hemisphere and anterior brain regions. In other words, the deficits in expressive language, verbal memory, and reading and spelling implicated the left hemisphere, while those in focused attention, response inhibition, and planning implicated the frontal-subcortical axis.

Compared to previous evaluations, the findings reflected substantial improvement in overall cognitive ability. Improvements also were apparent in specific cognitive functions, including nonverbal skills and abstraction. Academic skills also had improved, especially in arithmetic. By contrast, expressive language skills had shown a relative decline, and verbal memory remained poorer than expected. Executive functions were less globally impaired than they were in previous evaluations, but deficits in attention and planning still were apparent.

Thus, despite improvements over time, John continued to show persistent neuropsychological deficits that probably were attributable to his head injury. His neuropsychological profile reflected the sorts of deficits in memory and executive functions that commonly occur following severe traumatic brain injuries (Yeates, 2000). In John's case, his neuropsychological deficits also were consistent with the multifocal lesions documented by neuroimaging.

Because of his persistent deficits, John continued to be at-risk for learning problems in school. His expressive language and verbal memory difficulties were likely to hamper his participation in classroom activities, limit his retention of novel information, and slow his acquisition of basic academic skills. In addition, because of his deficits in executive functions, his work was likely to be inefficient and disorganized.

The risks associated with John's neuropsychological profile extended to his psychosocial adjustment. Children with traumatic brain injuries often demonstrate difficulties such as poor judgment, emotional lability, and behavioral disinhibition. These difficulties can create behavior management problems for parents and other adult caregivers, and can also interfere with peer relationships.

Fortunately, several factors were working in John's favor. His overall cognitive ability was average, as were many of his specific cognitive skills. In addition, John's behavior had improved significantly over time, and he no longer displayed the adjustment problems that were apparent soon after his injury. Moreover, his adaptive functioning was in the high-average range.

Based on these considerations, the neuropsychologist made recommendations for the provision of ongoing special education services. Specific suggestions included a combination of classroom accommodations and individualized instruction in academic skills. Based on his medical history, John was felt to qualify for special education services under the TBI classification.

Because of John's deficits in attention and executive functions, it was recommended that he be seated near his instructor and preferably where there were few potential distractions. Teachers were encouraged to monitor him closely to ensure that he stayed on task and used appropriate strategies to complete tasks. They also were encouraged to remind him to "stop and think" before responding to task demands. In addition, it was suggested that he would benefit from a reduction in time constraints, so that he was not penalized for the inefficiency that sometimes characterized his work.

Specific accommodations also were suggested to address John's deficits in expressive language. It was recommended that verbal instruction be supplemented with graphic materials, demonstrations, and models, and that John be presented with other hands-on experiences to capitalize on his relatively stronger nonverbal skills. It also was suggested that classroom discussions be broken into small groups to give him a greater opportunity to participate, and that John be encouraged to demonstrate his knowledge nonverbally, through multimedia projects, drama, and other related means that do not depend entirely on oral communication.

Additional accommodations were suggested because of John's difficulties with verbal memory. He was likely to need more repetition and review of unfamiliar material. Teachers were encouraged to present novel information in close relationship to previous lessons, to help link it to what John already knew. It also was suggested that John was likely to benefit from various forms of cueing, to help overcome his retrieval difficulties. On formal testing, for instance, he would probably perform better on multiple-choice, true-false, and matching items than on short answer or essay questions, which require spontaneous recall. In addition, it was recommended that John be taught simple mnemonic techniques (e.g., rehearsal) to help improve recall.

Along with classroom accommodations, John warranted specialized instruction in reading and writing. Based on current research (Fletcher & Lyon, 1998), it was recommended that he be taught to read using a structured multisensory approach that emphasized phonological skills, but that also included substantial practice in the application of those skills while reading actual text. It was further suggested that writing be taught using a systematic approach that included separate instruction in the mechanics of writing and in composition. John also was likely to benefit from being taught to use word-processing software, which can make the process of revision less onerous and can assist with the mechanical aspects of writing.

Finally, teachers and school personnel were encouraged to seek additional information regarding the educational implications of traumatic brain injuries. Recommended resources included *Head Injury in Children and Adolescents*, published by Clinical Psychology Publishing (Begali, 1992); the *Educator's Manual*, published by the Brain Injury Association (Savage & Wolcott, 1995); and *Traumatic Brain Injury in Children and Adolescents*, published by Pro-Ed (Tyler & Mira, 1999).

At the time of the evaluation, John did not appear to require substantial additional support outside of school. The personality and behavior changes that he displayed previously had largely resolved. The improvement probably reflected both recovery from the brain injury and the salutary effects of the special education assistance he had been receiving on his academic performance.

BENEFITS AND LIMITATIONS OF
NEUROPSYCHOLOGICAL ASSESSMENT

Neuropsychological assessment can provide several advantages compared to traditional psychoeducational testing. Neuropsychological test batteries are generally broader in scope and more in-depth than traditional batteries, and hence provide a more thorough and detailed description of a child's cognitive strengths and weaknesses. Traditional psychoeducational testing, for example, often does not include measures of memory or executive functions, despite the potential importance of such measures as predictors of academic performance and other adaptive outcomes.

Neuropsychological assessment also can play a critical role in clarifying the etiology of a child's adaptive difficulties. Neuropsychologists are trained specifically to determine whether behavior arises as a result of brain impairment or from other causes such as various environmental factors. Additionally, neuropsychological assessment can help to resolve diagnostic uncertainties. For example, traumatic brain injuries are associated with deficits in attention, memory, and executive functions (Yeates, 2000). The detection of deficits in those domains in a child with documented head trauma increases the likelihood that the child suffered a traumatic brain injury. Finally, neuropsychological assessment can have substantial prognostic value. For instance, the severity of neuropsychological deficits associated with traumatic brain injury predicts longer-term adaptive outcomes.

Thus, child neuropsychologists are distinguished by their ability to characterize children's cognitive functioning in considerable detail and to render complex etiological, diagnostic, and prognostic judgments, especially as the judgments are related to brain function. These clinical judgments depend on neuropsychologists' expertise and knowledge base rather than the tests that they use. Indeed, many of the tests mentioned in this chapter can be used by psychologists from other specialties to broaden their assessment repertoire, even if their training does not prepare them to make neuropsychological inferences.

The aforementioned benefits suggest that neuropsychological assessment is indicated when children have medical or neurological disorders that are likely to affect their adaptive functioning. Neuropsychological assessment also is likely to be useful for children with developmental or psychiatric disorders who warrant more in-depth assessment than that afforded by traditional psychoeducational testing. Finally, it warrants consideration when children display learning difficulties, behavior problems, or other adaptive failures that are suspected of having a biological basis.

Despite its virtues, neuropsychological assessment is subject to at least two limitations. First, the relevance of assessment results to children's functional adaptation remains unclear. The ecological validity of neuropsychological assessment is receiving increased attention (e.g., Sbordone & Long, 1995), but there still is much to learn, particularly in terms of outcomes other than academic achievement. Relevant areas for future research will include the prediction of social competence, daily living skills, and long-term vocational attainment.

Second, the contention that neuropsychological test findings contribute to more effective educational planning also has little empirical support (Reschly & Graham, 1989). There have been few experimental research studies designed to test the hypothesis that children with distinct neuropsychological profiles profit from different instructional techniques (Lyon & Flynn, 1991). However, recent studies of different types of reading instruction have been based in part on neuropsychological analyses of the cognitive processes involved in reading, and provide a template for future research that extends to other academic skills and adaptive domains.

RELIABILITY AND VALIDITY OF NEUROPSYCHOLOGICAL ASSESSMENT

Psychological tests are evaluated in terms of essential psychometric properties such as reliability and validity. A review of the reliability and validity of the specific tests used in neuropsychological assessment is beyond the scope of this chapter (for comprehensive reviews, see Lezak, 1995; Spreen & Strauss, 1998). A reasonable synopsis, however, is that the psychometric properties of neuropsychological tests often are poorly documented, even for some of the most widely used instruments, such as the Halstead-Reitan Neuropsychological Test Battery (Reynolds, 1989; Brown, Rourke, & Cicchetti, 1989; Leckliter, Forster, Klonoff, & Knights, 1992).

A concern that extends beyond the psychometric properties of specific tests is the reliability and validity of the neuropsychological assessment process as a whole (Matarazzo, 1990). In other words, the integrity of the assessment enterprise depends on the consistency with which neuropsychologists interpret test results and the extent to which the results of neuropsychological assessments are related both to underlying neurological impairment and to children's adaptive functioning. The key questions are: Can clinicians agree on the nature of a child's neuropsychological profile, and does that profile have both neurological and ecological validity (Taylor & Schatschneider, 1992)?

Two recent studies examined the consistency with which child neuropsychologists interpret test results. Brown et al. (1993) asked three neuropsychologists to rate the functioning of normal and low-birthweight children in seven neuropsychological domains: intelligence; auditory-perceptual/language functioning; visual perceptual/visuomotor functioning; haptic perceptual functioning; memory; attention; and global functioning. Raters were blind to each other's ratings and to birthweight status. The results revealed good to excellent agreement between raters, with intraclass correlations of ratings within domains ranging from .53 to .85.

Another investigation examined the ability of clinicians to make reliable neuropsychological diagnoses (Waber et al., 1992). Two judges were asked to make neuropsychological diagnoses based on test data and behavior ratings derived from assessments of children treated for either acute lymphoblastic leukemia or Wilm's tumor. The former disease is likely to be associated with central nervous system impairment, but the latter is not. Neuropsychological diagnoses were structured in terms of the three axes of brain function described above. For each axis, raters were asked if a localizing discrimination could be made and, if so, in what direction (i.e., left or right hemisphere, anterior or posterior, cortical or subcortical). Raters were blind to each other's ratings and to medical diagnosis. The reliability of neuropsychological diagnoses was also satisfactory in this study. The results from these two studies suggest that clinicians can make reliable ratings of neuropsychological test performance and its presumed neural substrates.

The validity of neuropsychological assessment was examined by Taylor and Schatschneider (1992). They wanted to determine if neuropsychological test results were related to the integrity of the central nervous system and if the results also would predict adaptive outcomes such as academic skills and behavioral adjustment. Their sample consisted of 113 school-age children who had been hospitalized early in life with *Haemophilus influenza* type b meningitis. The children's medical records pertaining to their acute-phase illness provided measures of the degree of brain insult (e.g., presence/absence of neurological complications). Social variables also were assessed (e.g., family socioeconomic status). The children were administered a neuropsychological test battery, which included measures of academic skills, and their parents provided ratings of behavioral adjustment and adaptive behavior. Even after controlling for social factors, acute-phase medical variables accounted for a significant proportion of variance in performance on a variety of neuropsychological tests. Similarly, although social factors accounted for a significant proportion of variance in functional outcomes, significant additional variance was explained by neuropsychological test results.

Thus, the results indicated that child neuropsychological assessment is sensitive to neurological insult, even when it occurs at a time far removed from the actual assessment. The results also indicated that neuropsychological test performance predicts meaningful variations in children's academic skills, behavioral adjustment, and adaptive functioning. Interestingly, the tests that were most sensitive to neurological insult were not always the same as those that were most predictive of functional outcomes. Effective neuropsychological assessment depends on the selection of tests with both neurological and ecological validity. Neurological validity is necessary to determine whether cognitive deficits are related to variations in brain status, whereas tests with ecological validity have more immediate implications for clinical management.

PROSPECTS FOR NEUROPSYCHOLOGICAL ASSESSMENT

The interest in and demand for neuropsychological assessment likely will continue to grow. In the future, neuropsychologists are increasingly likely to integrate their assessments with the results of neuroimaging (Bigler, 1994). The correlation of volumetric neuroimaging analyses with neuropsychological functioning already has provided interesting insights into brain-behavior relationships during childhood and adolescence. The relevance of neuroimaging to neuropsychological assessment is likely to remain relatively obscure, however, unless the brain can be studied "on line," in terms of its functional activity. As functional magnetic resonance imaging and related techniques become more widely available, the integration of assessment and imaging should become more feasible.

Child neuropsychologists also are likely to pay increasing attention to the environment as a determinant of children's neuropsychological functioning. Detailed analyses of the tests that comprise neuropsychological assessment batteries can help clarify how different test characteristics, including the manner in which they are administered, affect performance. At a more macroscopic level, examination of children's environments is critical in determining how those environments constrain and moderate neuropsychological functioning. In this regard, procedures for evaluating children's environments also warrant consideration by clinicians (Friedman & Wachs, 1999; Wachs & Plomin, 1991).

The dynamic nature of the interaction between brain, behavior, and context during childhood and adolescence highlights the importance of a developmental approach to child neuropsychology (Dennis & Barnes, 1993). In clinical practice, neuropsychological tests developed for use with adults often have been applied unthinkingly to children, as have adult models of brain-behavior relationships. In the future, child neuropsychologists will seek a rapprochement with both developmental neuroscience (Diamond, 1991; Elman et al., 1996; Johnson, 1997; Tager-Flusberg, 1999; Temple, 1997) and developmental psychology (Fischer & Rose, 1994; Welsh & Pennington, 1988). Contributions from those disciplines will provide the foundation for a more precise characterization of children's neuropsychological functioning in their everyday environments.

References

Achenbach, T. M. (1991). *Integrative guide for the* 1991 CBCL/4–18, YSR, *and* TRF *profiles*. Burlington, VT: Univ. of Vermont Department of Psychiatry.

Anderson, P., Anderson, V., & Lajoie, G. (1996). The Tower of London test: Validation and standardization for pediatric populations. *The Clinical Neuropsychologist*, 10, 54–65.

Barkley, R. A. (1990). *Attention deficit hyperactivity disorder: A handbook for diagnosis and treatment*. New York: Guilford.

Barkley, R. A. (1991). The ecological validity of laboratory and analogue assessment methods of ADHD symptoms. *Journal of Abnormal Child Psychology*, 19, 149–178.

Baron, I. S. (2000). Clinical implications and practical applications of child neuropsychological evaluations. In K. O. Yeates, M. D. Ris, & H. G. Taylor (Eds.), *Pediatric neuropsychology: Research, theory, and practice* (pp. 439–456). New York: Guilford.

Baron, I. S., Fennell, E., & Voeller, K. (1995). *Pediatric neuropsychology in the medical setting*. New York: Oxford Univ. Press.

Beery, K. E. (1996). *Developmental Test of Visual-Motor Integration—Fourth Edition*. Parsipanny, NY: Modern Curriculum.

Begali, V. (1992). *Head injury in children and adolescents: A resource and review for school and allied professionals* (2nd ed.). Branton, VT: Clinical Psychology.

Benton, A. L. (1992). *Benton Visual Retention Test—Fifth Edition*. San Antonio, TX: The Psychological Corporation.

Benton, A. L., Sivan, A. B., Hamsher, K. deS., Varney, N. R., & Spreen, O. (1994). *Contributions to neuropsychological assessment: A clinical manual* (2nd ed.). New York: Oxford Univ. Press.

Bernstein, J. H. (2000). Developmental neuropsychological assessment. In K. O. Yeates, M. D. Ris, & H. G. Taylor (Eds.), *Pediatric neuropsychology: Research, theory, and practice* (pp. 405–438). New York: Guilford.

Bernstein, J. H., & Waber, D. P. (1990). Developmental neuropsychological assessment: The systemic approach. In A. A. Boulton, G. B. Baker, & M. Hiscock (Eds.), *Neuromethods: Vol. 17, Neuropsychology* (pp. 311–371). New York: Humana Press.

Bernstein, J. H., & Waber, D. P. (1996). *Developmental scoring system for the Rey-Osterrieth Complex Figure*. Odessa, FL: Psychological Assessment Resources.

Bigler, E. D. (1994). Neuroimaging and neuropsychological assessment. In C. R. Reynolds (Ed.), *Cognitive assessment: A multidisciplinary perspective* (pp. 1–34). New York: Plenum.

Boll, T. (1992). *Children's Category Test manual*. New York: The Psychological Corporation.

Brown, G., Del Dotto, J. E., Fisk, J. L., Taylor, H. G., & Breslau, N. (1993). Analyzing clinical ratings of performance on pediatric neuropsychology tests. *The Clinical Neuropsychologist*, 7, 179–189.

Brown, R. T., & Borden, K. A. (1989). Neuropsychological effects of stimulant medication on children's learning and behavior. In C. R. Reynolds & E. Fletcher-Janzen (Eds.), *Handbook of clinical child neuropsychology* (pp. 443–474). New York: Plenum.

Brown, S. J., Rourke, B. P., & Cicchetti, D. V. (1989). Reliability of tests and measures used in the neuropsychological assessment of children. *The Clinical Neuropsychologist*, 3, 353–368.

Bruininks, R. H. (1978). *Bruininks-Oseretsky Test of Motor Proficiency*. Circle Pines, MN: American Guidance Service.

Bruininks, R. H., Woodcock, R. W., Weatherman, R. F., & Hill, B. K. (1996). *Scales of Independent Behavior—Revised comprehensive manual*. Chicago: Riverside Publishing.

Butters, N., & Delis, D. C. (1995). Clinical assessment of memory disorders in amnesia and dementia. *Annual Review of Psychology, 46,* 493–523.

Casey, J. E., & Rourke, B. P. (1992). Disorders of somatosensory perception in children. In I. Rapin & S. J. Segalowitz (Eds.), *Handbook of neuropsychology* (Vol. 6): *Child neuropsychology* (pp. 477–494). Amsterdam: Elsevier.

Cepeda, M. L. (1989). Nonstimulant psychotropic medication: Side effects on children's cognition and behavior. In C. R. Reynolds & E. Fletcher-Janzen (Eds.), *Handbook of clinical child neuropsychology* (pp. 475–488). New York: Plenum.

Cohen, M. J. (1997). *Children's Memory Scale manual*. San Antonio, TX: The Psychological Corporation.

Conners, C. K. (1997). *Conners' Rating Scales—Revised technical manual*. North Tonawanda, NY: Multi-Health Systems.

Cooley, E. L., & Morris, R. D. (1990). Attention in children: A neuropsychologically based model for assessment. *Developmental Neuropsychology, 6,* 239–274.

Cummings, J. L. (1993). Frontal-subcortical circuits and human behavior. *Archives of Neurology, 50,* 873–880.

Dawes, R. M., Faust, D., & Meehl, P. E. (1989). Clinical versus actuarial judgment. *Science, 243,* 1668–1674.

Delis, D. C., Kramer, J. H., Kaplan, E., & Ober, B. A. (1994). *Manual for The California Verbal Learning Test for Children*. New York: The Psychological Corporation.

Denckla, M. B. (1985). Revised neurological examination for soft signs. *Psychopharmacology Bulletin, 21,* 733–800, 1111–1124.

Denckla, M. B. (1994). Measurement of executive function. In G. R. Lyon (Ed.), *Frames of reference for the assessment of learning disabilities* (pp. 117–142). Baltimore: Paul H. Brookes.

Dennis, M. (1988). Language and the young damaged brain. In T. Boll & B. K. Bryant (Eds.), *Clinical neuropsychology and brain function: Research, measurement, and practice* (pp. 85–123). Washington, DC: American Psychological Association.

Dennis, M., & Barnes, M. (1993). Oral discourse skills in children and adolescents after early-onset hydrocephalus: Linguistic ambiguity, figurative language, speech acts, and script-based inferences. *Journal of Pediatric Psychology, 18,* 639–652.

Dennis, M., & Barnes, M. (1994). Developmental aspects of neuropsychology: Childhood. In D. Zaidel (Ed.), *Handbook of perception and cognition* (pp. 219–246). New York: Academic Press.

Derryberry, D., & Tucker, D. M. (1992). Neural mechanisms of emotion. *Journal of Clinical and Consulting Psychology, 60,* 329–338.

Diamond, A. (1991). Some guidelines for the study of brain-behavior relationships during development. In H. Levin, H. Eisenberg, & A. Benton (Eds.), *Frontal lobe function and dysfunction* (pp. 189–211). New York: Oxford Univ. Press.

Dunn, L. M., & Dunn, L. M. (1997). *Peabody Picture Vocabulary Test-Fourth Edition*. Circle Pines, MN; American Guidance Service.

Elliott, C. (1990). *Differential Abilities Scale administration and scoring manual*. San Antonio, TX: The Psychological Corporation.

Elman, J. L., Bates, E. A., Johnson, M. K., Karmiloff-Smith, A., Parisi, D., & Plunkett, K. (1996). *Rethinking innateness: A connectionist perspective on development*. Cambridge, MA: MIT Press.

Ewing-Cobbs, L., Levin, H. S., Eisenberg, H. M., & Fletcher, J. M. (1987). Language functions following closed-head injury in children and adolescents. *Journal of Clinical and Experimental Neuropsychology, 9,* 575–592.

Fischer, K. W., & Rose, S. P. (1994). Dynamic development of coordination of components in brain and behavior: A framework for theory and research. In G. Dawson & K. W. Fischer (Eds.), *Human behavior and the developing brain* (pp. 3–66). New York: Guilford.

Fletcher, J. M. (1994). Afterword: Behavior-brain relationships in children. In S. H. Broman & J. Grafman (Eds.), *Atypical cognitive deficits in developmental disorders: Implications for brain function* (pp. 297–326). Hillsdale, NJ: Erlbaum.

Fletcher, J. M., & Lyon, G. R. (1998). Reading: A research-based approach. In W. Evers (Ed.), *What's gone wrong in America's classrooms* (pp. 49–90). Stanford, CA: Hoover Institution Press.

Fletcher, J. M., & Taylor, H. G. (1984). Neuropsychological approaches to children: Towards developmental neuropsychology. *Journal of Clinical Neuropsychology, 6,* 39–56.

Fletcher, J. M., Taylor, H. G., Levin, H. S, & Satz, P. (1995). Neuropsychological and intellectual assessment of children. In H. I. Kaplan & B. J. Saddock (Eds.), *Comprehensive textbook of psychiatry* (Vol. 1, 6th ed.) (pp. 581–601). Baltimore: Williams & Wilkins.

Friedman, S. L., & Wachs, T. D. (Eds.) (1999). *Measuring environment across the life span.* Washington, DC: American Psychological Association.

Gaddes, W. H., & Crockett, D. J. (1975). The Spreen-Benton aphasia tests: Normative data as a measure of normal language development. *Brain and Language, 2,* 257–280.

Garb, H. N. (1998). *Studying the clinician: Judgment research and psychological assessment.* Washington, DC: American Psychological Association.

Gardner, R. A., & Broman, M. (1979). The Purdue Pegboard: Normative data on 1334 school children. *Journal of Clinical Psychology, 1,* 156–162.

Gordon, M. (1996). *The Gordon Diagnostic System.* DeWitt, NY: Gordon Systems.

Grant, M. L., Ilai, D., Nussbaum, N. L., & Bigler, E. D. (1990). The relationship between continuous performance tasks and neuropsychological tests in children with attention deficit hyperactivity disorder. *Perceptual and Motor Skills, 70,* 435–445.

Greenberg, L. M., & Dupuy, T. R. (1993). *Test of Variables of Attention.* Los Alamitos, CA: Universal Attention Disorders.

Greenough, W. T., & Black, J. E. (1992). Induction of brain structure by experience: Substrates for cognitive development. In M. R. Gunnar & C. A. Nelson (Eds.), *The Minnesota symposia on child psychology: Vol. 24, Developmental behavioral neuroscience* (pp. 155–200). Hillsdale, NJ: Erlbaum.

Hammill, D. D., & Larsen, S. C. (1996). *Test of Written Language—Third Edition.* Austin: Pro-Ed.

Heaton, R. K., Chelune, C. J., Talley, J. L., Kay, G. G., & Curtiss, G. (1993). *Wisconsin Card Sorting Test manual, revised and expanded.* Odessa, FL: Psychological Assessment Resources.

Holmes, J. M. (1987). Natural histories in learning disabilities: Neuropsychological difference/environmental demand. In S. J. Ceci (Ed.), *Handbook of cognitive, social, and neuropsychological aspects of learning disabilities* (pp. 303–319). Hillsdale, NJ: Erlbaum.

Holmes, J. M. (1988). History and observations. In R. Rudel (Ed.), *Assessment of developmental learning disorders: A neuropsychological approach* (pp. 144–165). New York: Basic Books.

Johnson, M. H. (1997). *Developmental cognitive neuroscience.* Cambridge, MA: Blackwell.

Kaplan, E. (1988). A process approach to neuropsychological assessment. In T. Boll & B. K. Bryant (Eds.), *Clinical neuropsychology and brain function: Research, measurement, and practice* (pp. 125–168). Washington, DC: American Psychological Association.

Kaplan, E., Fein, D., Kramer, J., Delis, D., & Morris, R. (1999). *Wechsler Intelligence Scale for Children—Third Edition as a Process Instrument manual.* San Antonio, TX: The Psychological Corporation.

Kaplan, E., Goodglass, H., & Weintraub, S. (1983). *Boston Naming Test (Revised 60-item version).* Philadelphia: Lea & Febiger.

Kaufman, A. S., & Kaufman, N. (1997). *Kaufman Test of Educational Achievement—Normative update.* Circle Pines, MN: American Guidance Service.

Kavanagh, J. F. (Ed.) (1986). *Otitis media and child development.* Parkton, MD: York.

Kessler, J. W. (1980). History of minimal brain dysfunctions. In H. E. Rie & E. D. Rie (Eds.), *Handbook of minimal brain dysfunction: A critical view.* New York: Wiley.

Kirk, U. (1992). Evidence for early acquisition of visual organization ability: A developmental study. *The Clinical Neuropsychologist, 6,* 171–177.

Korkman, M., Kirk, U., & Kemp, S. (1998). *NEPSY, A Developmental Neuropsychological Assessment, manual.* San Antonio, TX: The Psychological Corporation.

Krikorian, R., Bartok, J., & Gay, N. (1994). Tower of London procedure: A standard method and developmental data. *Journal of Clinical and Experimental Neuropsychology, 16,* 840–850.

Leckliter, I. N., Forster, A. A., Klonoff, H., & Knights, R. M. (1992). A review of reference group data from normal children for the Halstead-Reitan Neuropsychological Test Battery for Older Children. *The Clinical Neuropsychologist, 6,* 201–229.

Levin, H. S., Culhane, K. A., Hartmann, J., Evankovich, K., Mattson, A. J., Harward, H., Ringholz, G., Ewing-Cobbs, L., & Fletcher, J. M. (1991). Developmental changes in performance on tests of purported frontal lobe functioning. *Developmental Neuropsychology, 7,* 377–395.

Lewis, B. A. (1992). Pedigree analysis of children with phonology disorders. *Journal of Learning Disabilities, 25,* 586–597.

Lezak, M. D. (1995). *Neuropsychological assessment* (3rd. ed.). New York: Oxford Univ. Press.

Loring, D. W., & Papanicolau, A. C. (1987). Memory assessment in neuropsychology: Theoretical considerations and practical utility. *Journal of Clinical and Experimental Neuropsychology, 9,* 340–358.

Lyon, G. R., & Flynn, J. M. (1991). Educational validation studies of subtypes of learning-disabled readers. In B. P. Rourke (Ed.), *Neuropsychological validation of learning disability subtypes* (pp. 233–242). New York: Guilford.

Markwardt, F. C. (1992). *Peabody Individual Achievement Test-Revised manual.* Circle Pines, MN: American Guidance Service.

Matarazzo, J. D. (1990). Psychological assessment versus psychological testing: Validation from Binet to the school, clinic, and courtroom. *American Psychologist, 45,* 999–1017.

Matthews, C. G., & Kløve, H. (1964). *Instruction manual for the Adult Neuropsychology Test Battery.* Madison, WI: Univ. of Wisconsin Medical School.

Mesulam, M-M. (1981). A cortical network for directed attention and unilateral neglect. *Annals of Neurology, 10,* 309–325.

Mesulam, M-M. (1998). From sensation to cognition. *Brain, 121,* 1013–1052.

Mirsky, A. F., Anthony, B. J., Duncan, C. C., Ahearn, M. B., & Kellam, S. G. (1991). Analysis of the elements of attention: A neuropsychological approach. *Neuropsychology Review, 2,* 109–145.

Naglieri, J., & Das, J. P. (1997). *Cognitive Assessment System administration and scoring manual.* Chicago: Riverside.

Nowakowski, R. S. (1987). Basic concepts of CNS development. *Child Development, 58,* 568–595.

Pennington, B. F. (1991). *Diagnosing learning disorders: A neuropsychological framework.* New York: Guilford.

Psychological Corporation. (1992). *Wechsler Individual Achievement Test manual.* San Antonio, TX: Author.

Psychological Corporation. (1999). *Wechsler Abbreviated Scale of Intelligence.* San Antonio, TX: Author.

Putnam, S. H., & DeLuca, J. W. (1990). The TCN professional practice survey: Part I. General practices of neuropsychologists in primary employment and private practice settings. *The Clinical Neuropsychologist, 4,* 199–244.

Rapin, I., Tourk, L. M., & Costa, L. D. (1966). Evaluation of the Purdue Pegboard as a screening test for brain damage. *Developmental Medicine and Child Neurology, 8,* 45–54.

Reitan, R. M., & Wolfson, D. (1992a). *Neuropsychological evaluation of older children.* South Tuscon, AZ: Neuropsychology Press.

Reitan, R. M., & Wolfson, D. (1992b). *Neuropsychological evaluation of young children.* South Tucson, AZ: Neuropsychology Press.

Reschly, D. J., & Graham, F. M. (1989). Current neuropsychological diagnosis of learning problems: A leap of faith. In C. R. Reynolds, & C. Fletcher-Janzen (Eds.), *Handbook of clinical child neuropsychology* (pp. 503–520). New York: Plenum.

Reynolds, C. R. (1989). Measurement and statistical problems in neuropsychological assessment of children. In C. R. Reynolds, & C. Fletcher-Janzen (Eds.), *Handbook of clinical child neuropsychology* (pp. 147–166). New York: Plenum.

Reynolds, C. R., & Bigler, E. D. (1994). *Test of Memory and Learning examiner's manual.* Austin: Pro-Ed.

Reynolds, C. R., & Fletcher-Janzen, E. (Eds.). (1997). *Handbook of clinical child neuropsychology* (2nd ed.). New York: Plenum.

Reynolds, C. R., & Kamphaus, R. W. (1992). *Behavior Assessment System for Children manual.* Circle Pines, MN: American Guidance Service.

Rourke, B. P. (1989). *Nonverbal learning disabilities: The syndrome and the model.* New York: Guilford.

Rourke, B. P., Bakker, D. J., Fisk, J. L., & Strang, J. D. (1983). *Child neuropsychology: An introduction to theory, research, and clinical practice.* New York: Guilford.

Rourke, B. P., Fisk, J. L., & Strang, J. D. (1986). *Neuropsychological assessment of children: A treatment-oriented approach.* New York: Guilford.

Rourke, B. P., & Fuerst, D. R. (1991). *Learning disabilities and psychosocial functioning.* New York: Guilford.

Sattler, J. M. (1992). *Assessment of children* (3rd ed., revised). San Diego: Jerome M. Sattler.

Savage, R. C., & Wolcott, G. F. (Eds.) (1995). *An educator's manual: What educators need to know about students with brain injury* (3rd ed.). Washington, DC: Brain Injury Association.

Sbordone, R. J., & Long, C. J. (Eds.) (1995). *Ecological validity of neuropsychological testing.* Delray Beach, FL: St. Lucie Press.

Semel, E., Wiig, E. H., & Secord, W. (1995). *Clinical Evaluation of Language Fundamentals—Third Edition manual.* New York: The Psychological Corporation.

Shaffer, D., O'Connor, P. A., Shafer, S. Q., & Prupis, S. (1983). Neurological "soft signs": Their origins and significance. In M. Rutter (Ed.), *Developmental neuropsychiatry* (pp. 144–163). New York: Guilford.

Sheslow, D., & Adams, W. (1990). *Wide Range Assessment of Memory and Learning administration manual.* Wilmington, DE: Jastak.

Slay, D. K., & Valdivia, L. (1988). Neuropsychology as a specialized health service listed in the National Register of Health Service Providers in Psychology. *Professional Psychology: Research and Practice, 19,* 323–329.

Sokol, S. M., Macaruso, P., & Gollan, T. H. (1994). Developmental dyscalculia and cognitive neuropsychology. *Developmental Neuropsychology, 10,* 413–441.

Sparrow, S. S., Balla, D. A., & Ciccetti, D. V. (1984). *Vineland Adaptive Behavior Scales.* Circle Pines, MN: American Guidance Service.

Spreen, O., & Benton, A. L. (1969). *Neurosensory Center Comprehensive Examination for Aphasia—1977 revision.* Victoria, BC: Univ. of Victoria Press.

Spreen, O., Risser, A. H., & Edgell, D. (1995). *Developmental neuropsychology.* New York: Oxford Univ. Press.

Spreen, O., & Strauss, E. (1998). *A compendium of neuropsychological tests: Administration, norms, and commentary* (2nd ed.). New York: Oxford Univ. Press.

Squire, L. R. (1987). *Memory and brain.* New York: Oxford Univ. Press.

Strauss, A. A., & Lehtinen, L. (1947). *Psychopathology and education of the brain-injured child.* New York: Grune & Stratton.

Strauss, A. A., & Werner, H. (1941). The mental organization of the brain-injured mentally defective child. *American Journal of Psychiatry, 97,* 1194–1203.

Stuss, D. T., & Benton, D. F. (1984). Neuropsychological studies of the frontal lobes. *Psychological Bulletin, 95,* 3–28.

Sweet, J. J., & Moberg, P. J. (1990). A survey of practices and beliefs among ABPP and non-ABPP clinical neuropsychologists. *The Clinical Neuropsychologist, 4,* 101–120.

Tager-Flusberg, H. (Ed.) (1999). *Neurodevelopmental disorders.* Cambridge, MA: MIT Press.

Taylor, H. G. (1987). The meaning and value of soft signs in the behavioral sciences. In D. E. Tupper (Ed.), *Soft neurological signs: Manifestations, measurement, research, and meaning* (pp. 297–335). New York: Grune & Stratton.

Taylor, H. G. (1988). Learning disabilities. In E. J. Mash & L. G. Terdal (Eds.), *Behavioral assessment of childhood disorders* (2nd ed., pp. 402–450). New York: Guilford.

Taylor, H. G., Albo, V. C., Phebus, C. K., Sachs, B. R., & Bierl, P. G. (1987). Postirradiation treatment outcomes for children with acute lymphocytic leukemia. *Journal of Pediatric Psychology, 12,* 395–411.

Taylor, H. G., Barry, C., & Schatschneider, C. (1993). School-age consequences of *Haemophilus influenzae* Type B meningitis. *Journal of Clinical Child Psychology, 22,* 196–206.

Taylor, H. G., Drotar, D., Wade, S., Yeates, K. O., Stancin, T., & Klein, S. (1995). Recovery from traumatic brain injury in children: The importance of the family. In S. Broman & M. Michel (Eds.), *Traumatic brain injury in children.* New York: Oxford Univ. Press.

Taylor, H. G., & Fletcher, J. M. (1990). Neuropsychological assessment of children. In M. Hersen

& G. Goldstein (Eds.), *Handbook of psychological assessment* (2nd ed., pp. 228–255). New York: Plenum.

Taylor, H. G., Fletcher, J. M., & Satz, P. (1982). Component processes in reading disabilities: Neuropsychological investigation of distinct reading subskill deficits. In R. N. Malatesha & P. G. Aaron (Eds.), *Reading disorders: Varieties and treatments*. New York: Academic Press.

Taylor, H. G., Hack, M., & Klein, N. (1998). Attention deficits in children with <750 gm birth weight. *Child Neuropsychology*, 4, 21–34.

Taylor, H. G., Klein, N., & Hack, M. (2000). School-age consequences of <750 g birth weight: A review and update. *Developmental Neuropsychology*, 17, 289–321.

Taylor, H. G., & Schatschneider, C. (1992). Child neuropsychological assessment: A test of basic assumptions. *The Clinical Neuropsychologist*, 6, 259–275.

Taylor, H. G., Schatschneider, C., Petrill, S., Barry, C. T., & Owens, C. (1996). Executive dysfunction in children with early brain disease: Outcomes post *Haemophilus Influenzae* meningitis. *Developmental Neuropsychology*, 12, 35–51.

Temple, C. M. (1991). Procedural dyscalculia and number fact dyscalculia: Double dissociation in developmental dyscalculia. *Cognitive Neuropsychology*, 8, 155–176.

Temple, C. M. (1997). *Developmental cognitive neuropsychology*. East Sussex, UK: Psychology Press.

Thorndike, R. L., Hagen, E. P., & Sattler, J. M. (1986). *Stanford-Binet Intelligence Scale* (4th ed.). Chicago: Riverside.

Torgeson, J. K., Wagner, R. K., & Rashotte, C. A. (1999). *Test of Word Reading Efficiency examiner's manual*. Austin: Pro-Ed.

Trimble, M. R. (1987). Anticonvulsant drugs and cognitive function: A review of the literature. *Epilepsia*, 28 (supplement 3), 37–45.

Tyler, J. S., & Mira, M. P. (1999). *Traumatic brain injury in children and adolescents: A sourcebook for teachers and other school personnel* (2nd ed.). Austin: Pro-Ed.

Waber, D. P., Bernstein, J. H., Kammerer, B. L., Tarbell, N. J., & Sallan, S. E. (1992). Neuropsychological diagnostic profiles of children who received CNS treatment for acute lymphoblastic leukemia: The systemic approach to assessment. *Developmental Neuropsychology*, 8, 1–28.

Wachs, T. D., & Plomin, R. (Eds.) (1991). *Conceptualization and measurement of organism-environment interaction*. Washington, DC: American Psychological Association.

Wagner, R. K., Torgeson, J. K., & Rashotte, C. A. (1999). *Comprehensive Test of Phonological Processing examiner's manual*. Austin: Pro-Ed.

Wechsler, D. (1989). *Wechsler Preschool and Primary Scales of Intelligence—Revised*. San Antonio, TX: The Psychological Corporation.

Wechsler, D. (1991). *Wechsler Intelligence Scale for Children—Third Edition*. San Antonio, TX: The Psychological Corporation.

Wechsler, D. (1997a). *Wechsler Adult Intelligence Scale—Third Edition*. San Antonio, TX: The Psychological Corporation.

Wechsler, D. (1997b). *Wechsler Memory Scale—Third Edition*. San Antonio, TX: The Psychological Corporation.

Welsh, M. C., & Pennington, B. F. (1988). Assessing frontal lobe functioning in children: Views from developmental psychology. *Developmental Neuropsychology*, 4, 199–230.

Welsh, M. C., Pennington, B. F., & Groisser, D. B. (1991). A normative-developmental study of executive function: A window on prefrontal function in children. *Developmental Neuropsychology*, 7, 131–149.

Western Psychological Services. (1983). *Hooper Visual Organization Test—1983 edition*. Los Angeles: Author.

Wiig, E. H., & Secord, W. (1989). *Test of Language Competence-Expanded Edition*. San Antonio, TX: The Psychological Corporation.

Wilkinson, G. S. (1993). *Wide Range Achievement Test—Revision 3 manual*. Wilmington, DE: Jastak Associates.

Wirt, R. D., Seat, P. D., Broen, W. E., & Lachar, D. (1990). *Personality Inventory for Children—Revised*. Los Angeles: Western Psychological Services.

Woodcock, R., & Mather, N. (1989). *Woodcock-Johnson Tests of Achievement—Revised standard and supplemental batteries*. San Antonio, TX: The Psychological Corporation.

Yeates, K. O. (1994). Comparison of developmental norms for the Boston Naming Test. *The Clinical Neuropsychologist, 8*, 91–98.

Yeates, K. O. (2000). Closed-head injury. In K. O. Yeates, M. D. Ris, & H. G. Taylor (Eds.), *Pediatric neuropsychology: Research, theory, and practice* (pp. 92–116). New York: Guilford.

Yeates, K. O., Blumenstein, E., Patterson, C. M., & Delis, D. C. (1995). Verbal learning and memory following pediatric closed-head injury. *Journal of the International Neuropsychological Society, 1*, 78–87.

Yeates, K. O., Enrile, B. E., Loss, N., Blumenstein, E., & Delis, D. C. (1995). Verbal learning and memory in children with myelomeningocele. *Journal of Pediatric Psychology, 20*, 801–815.

Yeates, K. O., MacPhee, D., Campbell, F. A., & Ramey, C. T. (1983). Maternal IQ and home environment as determinants of early childhood intellectual competence: A developmental analysis. *Developmental Psychology, 19*, 731–739.

Yeates, K. O., Ris, M. D., & Taylor, H. G. (2000). *Pediatric neuropsychology: Theory, research, and practice.* New York: Guilford.

Yeates, K. O., & Taylor, H. G. (1998). Neuropsychological assessment of older children. In G. Goldstein, A. Puente, & E. Bigler (Eds.), *Human brain function, assessment and rehabilitation: Vol. III, Neuropsychology* (pp. 35–61). New York: Plenum.

Dynamic Assessment of Learning Potential

DAVID TZURIEL
Bar-Ilan University, Israel

INTRODUCTION

Dynamic assessment has been found to be an efficient approach to identify learning processes, learning potential, specific cognitive functions, and mediation strategies required for the enhancement of learning potential (e.g., Campione & Brown, 1987; Feuerstein, Rand, & Hoffman, 1979; Guthke & Wingenfeld, 1992; Haywood, 1997; Haywood & Tzuriel, 1992a; Lidz, 1987, Lidz & Elliott, 2000; Resing, 1997; Swanson, 1995; Tzuriel, 1992a, 1997a, 1998, 2000b, 2000c; Vygotsky, 1978).

Dynamic assessment (DA) and *static testing* have been used in the literature to refer to different modes of evaluating individuals' cognitive capacities. DA refers to an assessment of thinking, perception, learning, and problem solving by an active teaching process aimed at modifying cognitive functioning. The major idea in DA is to observe and measure change criteria as predictors of future learning. *Static testing*, on the other hand, refers to measurement of a child's response without any attempt to intervene in order to change, guide, or improve the child's performance. The conceptualization behind using change criteria is that measures of modifiability are more closely related to the teaching processes by which the child is taught how to process information than are static measures of intelligence. In other words, the teaching strategies used in DA are more closely related to learning processes in school and to other life contexts than are standardized static methods.

DA differs from conventional static tests in its goals, processes, instruments, test situation, and interpretation of results (Feuerstein et al., 1979; Grigorenko & Sternberg, 1998; Haywood & Tzuriel, 1992a; Tzuriel, 1998, 2000b, in press; Tzuriel & Haywood, 1992). Several arguments have been raised against standardized static tests; the most frequent one is that they are inadequate to reveal the cognitive capacities of children who come from culturally different populations and children with learning difficulties (e.g., Hessels & Hamers, 1993; Tzuriel, 1998, 2000b, in press; Vygotsky, 1978). In Haywood's (1997) words: "The most frequent complaint is that they are not uniformly valid across ability levels, ages, and ethnic groups" (p. 103).

Criticism of Standardized Static Tests

Tzuriel (1998, 2000b, in press) has summarized four major criticisms that have been raised with respect to the use of static tests:

(a) While standardized psychometric tests provide information on children's intellectual performance, they typically do not provide important information about learning processes, specific cognitive functions, and teaching strategies that would facilitate learning. Psychologists and educational practitioners need to know not only about the actual level of performance, but also what a child might achieve with an adult's guidance, metacognitive processes that could facilitate learning, and the nature of learning processes.

(b) Low level of performance, as revealed in standardized static tests and in academic achievements, very frequently falls short of revealing the learning potential of children. This problem is sharpened among children coming from disadvantaged social backgrounds or children with learning difficulties. Many children perform poorly on standardized tests, not due to low intellectual ability but due to various reasons such as lack of opportunities for learning experiences, cultural differences, specific learning difficulties, and traumatic life experiences. Recent studies on the effects of schooling on performance of Piagetian-type tasks demonstrated that a high variability in performance has been attributed to familiarity with materials and concepts, rather than to ability (Rogoff & Chavajay, 1995). Some writers (e.g., Cole, 1990) argue that concrete operational thinking is not influenced by schooling but by the ability to understand the language of testing and the presuppositions of the testing situation itself. Very frequently standardized tests contribute to confusion between ability and efficiency. Children with a high level of intelligence or abstract ability might perform poorly on a test because they are inefficient in dealing with certain types of tasks presented, especially when performance within a time limit and awareness to amount of invested efforts are required.

(c) Another criticism is that standardized tests do not provide clear descriptions of the cognitive processes involved in learning or specific recommendations for prescriptive teaching and remedial learning strategies. The idea of assessment of processes rather than the end products of learning has been suggested since the beginning of the twentieth century (e.g., Binet, 1909; Thorndike, 1926). Only in the 1970s, with the introduction of Vygotsky's (1978) theory and Feuerstein's (1979) ideas to modern psychology, was there a growth of interest, elaboration, and the spread of the idea of DA.

The lack of specific description of learning processes often creates a communication gap between psychologists and teachers who have incongruent expectations about testing goals. For example, in psychological reports there frequently is a statement describing the gap between the verbal and performance subscale scores of the WISC-III, but no specific recommendation about what exactly to do about it. What kind of training does the child need and how exactly should it be done? How can we ensure transfer of learning from that cognitive domain to classroom performance? The description of the psychometric properties of the individual's functioning does not provide the necessary information on learning processes that are required to bring about improvement of intellectual functioning.

Utley, Haywood, and Masters (1992) have remarked in regard to this point that the principal use of psychometric IQ test is *classification*, with the aim of giving differential treatment for individuals differing in level and/or pattern of intelligence. Such a classification not only has limited value, but also may have negative effects. First, the *manifest* cognitive performance shown by the IQ test does not necessarily reflect individual differences in *latent* intelligence. Second, even if it does, it is highly questionable whether individuals with the same IQ have similar characteristics and needs that would necessitate similar treatment. On the contrary, practical experience shows that even children who are virtually identical in terms of age, gender, and IQ show markedly different behavior, cognitive or affective, and therefore require different teaching approaches.

(d) Another major criticism is that psychometric tests do not relate to nonintellective factors, which can influence individuals' cognitive performance. Many researchers showed that non-intellective factors (e.g., intrinsic motivation, need for mastery, locus of control, anxiety, frustration tolerance, self-confidence, accessibility to mediation) are no less important in determining children's intellectual achievements than are "pure" cognitive factors (Tzuriel, Samuels, &

Feuerstein, 1988). Cognitive functioning and motivational-affective factors were conceived as inseparable, representing two sides of the same coin (Haywood, 1992). As will be shown later, DA is conceived as a holistic assessment approach that permits observation of individuals on cognitive, affective, and behavioral levels as well as the interrelation among these levels of functioning.

The problems of standardized tests are magnified when used with mentally retarded (MR) or learning disabled individuals. These individuals very frequently have difficulties understanding the nature and requirements of the standard tasks; therefore, their performance on those tasks does not necessarily reflect inability. In some cases, removal of some obstacles to conceptualize the nature of the tasks (Haywood, 1997), inhibition of impulsivity, and/or provision of extra time to process the information (Tzuriel, in press) improves their performance significantly. Haywood (1997) has already clearly shown that the validity of standardized tests for MR persons does not lie in what these persons can do but in identifying what they presumably cannot do. Empirical support has been found in studies showing lower prediction of school achievement by standardized tests in cases of persons with MR than in persons without MR. Furthermore, DA procedures, although not designed primarily for prediction, have been found to be better predictors of school achievement among persons with MR than in persons without MR (Haywood, 1997; Tzuriel, 2000c). The role of nonintellective factors, which are integrated within the DA approach, is especially important with MR individuals whose personality or motivational problems interfere with their cognitive performance on standardized tests (e.g., Haywood & Switzky, 1986; Paour, 1992).

The main purpose of this chapter is to present the effectiveness of DA with various educational and clinical groups and describe its use in evaluation of cognitive intervention programs aimed at improvement of "learning how to learn" skills. DA has been used extensively in my developmental research of the effects of parent-child mediated learning strategies on children's cognitive modifiability. These studies are not reported here and the reader is referred to reviews of these studies reported elsewhere (Tzuriel, 1999, 2000b, in press).

The DA approach was influenced by two theories: Vygotsky's (1978) sociocultural theory, especially the concept of the *zone of proximal development* (ZPD), and Feuerstein et al.'s (1979) *mediated learning experience* (MLE) theory. Both theories emerged as a response to needs to include sociocultural factors in understanding of cognitive development and learning potential. In the following section, these two theories, which serve as the basis of the DA approach, are presented. The theoretical section is followed by two sections concerning the empirical foundation of DA; one is focused on educational perspectives and the second on evaluation of cognitive education programs. The educational perspective section includes a case study of a child with slight learning difficulties who was administered static assessment and DA. Finally, a conclusion section discusses integrative perspectives and gives suggestions for future development.

THEORETICAL BACKGROUND OF DYNAMIC ASSESSMENT: VYGOTSKY AND FEUERSTEIN

Vygotsky's Sociocultural Theory

Perhaps the major reason for the interest in Vygotsky's work in the West is his contribution to the understanding of the social origins of cognitive processes and the conceptual foundation of DA. According to Vygotsky's sociocultural theory, in order to understand an individual's cognitive development one should understand the individual's social, cultural, and historical background. The origins of a child's higher mental functions derive from social interactions with more experienced adults or peers who guide the child towards higher levels of competency. Any function of a child's development appears twice, first at the social level and then, via an internalization process, on the psychological level. The internalization process is gradual, starting with help from an experienced adult or peers. As children take gradually more initiative, the adults modify their guidance. The children finally become independent in self-regulating their learning process, with the adults having only a supportive function.

The ZPD was defined as the difference between a child's "actual developmental level as determined by independent problem solving" and the higher level of "potential development as determined through problem solving under adult guidance or in collaboration with more capable peers" (Vygotsky, 1978, p. 86). Using the ZPD concept, Vygotsky suggested that children might perform above the limits of their initial capability when supported by an experienced adult. All higher planning and organizing functions in development appear first on the interpersonal plane of social interaction and subsequently on the intrapersonal plane of individual cognitive functioning.

Vygotsky distinguished between three types of mediated activities: material tools, psychological tools, and human beings (Kozulin, 1990). *Material tools*, which have an indirect effect on human psychology, change with historical progress and affect the developing child by putting new demands on human mental processes. *Psychological tools*, which mediate the child's own psychological processes, include written, numerical, notational, and other sign systems. The psychological tools, mediated by culturally determined systems of symbols, can transform an individual's experience from a concrete one to an abstract one. Vygotsky (1978) argued that a radical change in the thinking of educationally deprived and culturally different persons could be effected by the introduction of symbolic psychological tools. The *human being* as mediator helps the developing individual to internalize cognitive functions that appear first on a social level and to acquire the meaning of actions (Vygotsky, 1978).

Contemporary researchers (e.g., Kozulin, 1990; Rogoff, 1990; Wood, 1989) have suggested that at least two characteristics of effective social interaction are important: intersubjectivity and scaffolding. *Intersubjectivity* refers to a process whereby two learning partners negotiate a mutual understanding of a task and how to proceed with its solution. It involves mutual adjustments to the perspective of the other participant in the interaction. In a DA situation, for example, the examiner may point out to the child the links between a new task and a familiar one that the child already knows. *Scaffolding* refers to a process by which an experienced partner changes the degree and quality of support provided to the less skilled partner as he or she becomes more proficient (Wood, 1989). For example, when the child has little notion of how to proceed in solving a problem, the parent or teacher might break the task into manageable units and call the child's attention to specific features. As the child's competency grows, the parent gradually withdraws his or her support and encourages the child to take independent steps toward mastery and self-regulation.

Vygotsky argued that measurement of the individual's potential for development is just as important as measuring the actual level of development. The importance of ZPD was illustrated by comparing two children of the same mental age who show a different performance pattern when they are given mediation (i.e., asked leading questions, given examples, and shown how to solve the problems). One of the children could solve problems that were two years above his or her age, whereas the other solved problems that were only a half-year above his or her actual developmental level. In spite of their equal manifested performance levels, their immediate potential development was sharply different. Vygotsky, who was involved in heated discussions regarding the merit of using standard intelligence testing, argued that interpreting test results (IQ) as a reflection of children's abilities is misleading. The reason is that in reality children's performance reflects their entire socioeducational history and is not limited to inner factors.

Vygotsky's approach has inspired several researchers who developed DA techniques such as the learning test (e.g., Guthke & Wingenfeld, 1992) and the graduated prompt procedure (e.g., Brown & Ferrara, 1985; Campione & Brown, 1987; Resing, 1997).

The *learning test* is a diagnostic method in which examiners record to what extent individuals are able to improve their test performance if they are provided with feedback, prompts, or even complete training programs between a pretest and a posttest. Guthke and Wingenfeld (1992) tried to be faithful simultaneously to both the psychometric demands for objectivity and to measurement of the individual's ability to learn. The intervention within the testing procedure is based on Gal'perin's (1966) theory of systematic formation of mental actions and concepts. According to Gal'perin, teaching is perceived as a psychological experiment, the goal of which is to bring the student to a new, higher level of development. Guthke and Wingenfeld's learning test methodology also was influenced by the theory of activity from Soviet psychology (Leontiev & Luria, 1964). According to the activity theory, mental processes and characteristics are conceived of as products of human activity with particular emphasis on the concept of age- and situation-specific dominant activity. Examiners are required in their diagnostic procedures to include activities that predominate in a given age range and in everyday life situations—much similar to the principle of ecological validity in Western psychology. The assessment of children therefore should be focused on learning as their dominant activity and not merely on the results of their learning.

Similarly, the principle behind the *graduated prompt* procedure (Campione & Brown, 1987) is basically to help subjects gradually until they solve the problem. The amount of aid needed in order to solve the problem is taken as an indication of the subject's ZPD. Once a particular problem is solved, another version of the problem is given, and the number of prompts required to solve the new problem is taken as an indication of transfer of learning. It should be noted that, unlike other DA approaches (e.g., Carlson & Wiedl, 1992; Guthke & Wingenfeld, 1992), the outcome measure in the graduated prompt approach is not the amount of improvement in performance but rather the amount of mediation needed to reach a specified criterion. The implication is that one can infer how much additional help is needed to transfer the learned principles to novel situations. The outcome measures for this approach are the sums of the total number of hints given at each of the testing phases (i.e., initial learning, maintenance, and transfer). A profile of the outcome measure is taken as an indication of the child's ZPD. It is assumed that a child with a broad ZPD profits more from mediation and needs less help than a child with a narrow ZPD. Brown and Ferrara (1985) argued that, in addition to the importance of the graduated prompts, the assessment of ZPD should entail *task analysis* and *transfer of learning*. These aspects coincide with contemporary theories of learning and cognition. An understanding of task components and their transfer helps in selecting the series of graduated prompts and in designing appropriate methods for assessing efficiency of learning and transfer. Transfer of learning is considered to be especially important in academic situations, in which instruction is often incomplete and ambiguous. Campione and Brown suggested that the ratio of learning (i.e., number of graduated prompts) to transfer (i.e., the distance of application of knowledge from original example) should be viewed as a measure of individual differences.

Feuerstein's Structural Cognitive Modifiability and Mediated Learning Experience (MLE) Theory

The *structural cognitive modifiability* theory (Feuerstein et al., 1979) is based on two basic assumptions. The first one is that individuals have the unique capacity to modify their cognitive functions and adapt their functioning to changing demands. According to this assumption the responsibility for the individual's modifiability shifts from the assessed or treated individual to the examiner or mediator. Cognitive modifiability is considered possible irrespective of three conditions considered as barriers to change: etiology of the individual's learning problems, age of the individual, and severity of condition. Structural cognitive modifiability was defined by three characteristics: permanence, pervasiveness, and centrality. *Permanence* refers to the endurance of the cognitive changes across time and space. *Pervasiveness* is related to a "diffusion" process in which changes in one part (e.g., perceptual system) affect the whole (e.g., memory processes, abstraction capacity). *Centrality* reflects the self-perpetuating, autonomous, and self-regulating nature of cognitive modifiability.

The second basic assumption is that cognitive modifiability is best explained by MLE interactions. MLE *interactions* are defined as a process in which parents or substitute adults interpose themselves between a set of stimuli and the child and modify the stimuli for the developing child. In mediating the world to the child, the adult may use different strategies such as alerting the child's attention (e.g., changing the frequency, order, and intensity of presented stimuli), giving them meaning (e.g., "How beautiful is this flower"), and transcending the concrete aspects of the situation (e.g., "This type of flower grows in the spring time"). In a DA context the examiner uses mediation principles by focusing the child on important aspects of the problem, labeling objects and relations, and explaining the rules and strategies for solving a specific problem. The examiner assesses the level of internalization of these learned rules and strategies by observing how the individual solves other problems of increased level of complexity, novelty, and abstraction.

The mediator relates not only to cognitive factors but also to emotional and motivational aspects by arousing the child's curiosity, vigilance, and challenge. From a cognitive perspective the mediator tries to improve and/or create in the child the cognitive functions required for temporal, spatial, and cause-effect relationships. As the MLE processes are gradually internalized by the child, they become an integrated mechanism of change within the child. Adequate MLE interactions facilitate the development of various cognitive functions, learning set, mental operations, metacognitive functions (e.g., strategies, reflective thinking), and need systems. The acquired and internalized MLE processes allow developing children to later use them in other contexts independently, to benefit from learning experiences, to self-mediate in new learning situations, and to modify their own cognitive system. The MLE strategies provided by examiners within the test situation help to facilitate children's learning processes, to identify deficient cognitive functions, and, at the end of the process, to provide recommendations for intervention and development of cognitive structures.

Feuerstein conceived MLE interactions as a *proximal* factor that explains in-dividual differences in learning and cognitive modifiability. Factors such as organic deficit, poverty, socioeconomic status, and emotional disturbance are considered to be *distal* factors, which might correlate with learning ability, but they affect learning ability only through the proximal factor of MLE. Feu-erstein, Rand, and Rynders (1988) suggested 12 criteria of MLE. The first five criteria were operationalized in studies of infants and young children (e.g., Klein, 1988; Tzuriel, 1998, 1999, in press) and are described here. The first three criteria (Intentionality and Reciprocity, Meaning, and Transcendence) are considered as necessary and sufficient for an interaction to be classified as MLE. For a detailed description of all MLE criteria, see Feuerstein et al. (1979, 1988).

(a) *Intentionality and Reciprocity* are characterized by efforts to create in the child a state of vigilance, and to facilitate an efficient registration of the information (input phase), an adequate processing (elaboration phase), and an accurate responding (output phase). The Reciprocity component is of crucial importance to the quality and continuation of the mediational process. The mediated child who reciprocates to the mediator's behavior enables the mediator to adjust his or her mediation and continue the process efficiently. Intentionality and Reciprocity are observed, for example, when a mediator intentionally focuses the child's attention on an object and the child responds overtly to that behavior.

(b) *Mediation of Meaning* refers to interactions in which the mediator tries, when presenting a stimulus, to emphasize its importance by expressing interest and by pointing to its worth and value. Media-tion of meaning can be expressed nonverbally by body gestures, facial expressions, tone of voice, rituals, and repetitive actions. Verbally, mediation of meaning can be expressed by illuminating a current event, activity, or learned context, relating it to past or cur-rent events, and emphasizing its importance and value. Children, who experience and internalize this interaction, will later seek mean-ing for novel stimuli and will initiate attachment of meaning to new information rather than passively waiting for meaning to come.

(c) In *Mediation for Transcendence* the mediator goes beyond the concrete context or the immediate needs of the child and tries to reach out for general principles and/or goals that are not bound to the "here and now" or the specific and concrete aspects of the situation. In daily life situations the parent, who is usually the main mediation agent, might use spontaneous events to teach strategies, rules, and principles in order to generalize to other situations. In formal teaching situations the teacher might mediate rules and principles that govern a problem or a learned subject and show how they are generalized to other school subjects or daily life situations. In a DA context the examiner mediates the rules and strategies for solving a specific problem and assesses the level of internalization of these rules and strategies to other problems of increased level of complexity, novelty, and abstraction. Although mediation for Transcendence depends on the first two criteria, the combination of all three criteria becomes a powerful vehicle for the development of cognitive modifiability and the widening of the individual's need system.

(d) In *Mediation of Feelings of Competence* the mediator initially arranges the environment to ensure the child's success and interprets the environment in a manner that conveys to the child an awareness of the capability of functioning independently and successfully. This is done in various ways such as reorganizing aspects of the environment (e.g., graduating levels of task difficulty), providing opportunities for success, interpreting the meaning of success, and rewarding the child for attempts to master and cope effectively with the situation. The mediator provides feedback not only to successful solutions but also to partially successful performances and attempts at mastery.

(e) In *Mediation for Regulation of Behavior* the mediator regulates the child's responses, depending on the task's demands as well as on the child's behavioral style, by either inhibiting impulsive tendencies or by accelerating behavior. The mediator can analyze the task components, inhibit the child's acting-out behavior, delay immediate gratification, focus on task characteristics, and elicit metacognitive strategies. Mediation for Regulation of Behavior is of critical importance in helping the child register information accurately, and it affects the whole process of mental operations.

The MLE theory has produced practical tools for diagnosis and intervention programs, the most known of which are the *Learning Propensity Assessment Device* (LPAD; Feuerstein, Rand, Haywood, Kyram, & Hoffman, 1995), *Instrumental Enrichment* (Feuerstein, Rand, Hoffman, & Miller, 1980), *Bright Start* (Haywood, Brooks, & Burns, 1986), *Cognitive Network* (COGNET; Greenberg, 1990), *Cognitive Modifiability Battery* (CMB): *Assessment and Intervention* (Tzuriel, 1995a, 2000c, in press), The Peer-Mediation Program (Shamir & Tzuriel, 1999), and *More Intelligent and Sensitive Child* (MISC; Klein, 1996). The focus of this paper is diagnostic tools.

EDUCATIONAL PERSPECTIVES OF DYNAMIC ASSESSMENT RESEARCH

This section first portrays qualitative aspects of DA by describing the case study of an adolescent boy who failed a conventional group test. Following the case study is a discussion of several key issues and questions from a research perspective.

Case Study: A Child with an Impulsive Tendency

Jacob, a 13-year-old boy, was referred for DA after repeated failures to enroll in a secondary high school. His family lives in a developing small town in Israel and comes from middle socioeconomic status (SES). As one of the requirements for enrolling to a secondary high school, Jacob was administered a conventional group test at a well-known institute for vocational counseling in Jerusalem. The test findings revealed that Jacob was at the 4th to 6th percentile across several domains of the test. Consequently Jacob was rejected from several schools and referred to a vocational school considered to be appropriate for children with mild mental retardation. The parents could not accept this referral, as they knew their child to be a smart and resourceful boy, creative in problem solving, full of initiative activities around the house, and with a rich social life. His academic achievements were adequate, indicating an appropriate level of understanding. All of these factors did not justify the level of education assigned to him.

The parents referred Jacob first to a psychologist, who began to test him by using the WISC-R. However, after 15 minutes Jacob showed signs of stress, began to cry, complained about the need to be tested again, and ran away from the testing room. Following this session, the psychologist diagnosed the child as having an emotional instability and referred the parents and the child to a psychiatrist. In a later interview with the parents they reported deep despair because they received the impression that from one helping agent to another the child's situation became worse. The father commented sarcastically, "I guess that the next step is to hospitalize the child." Following the advice of another psychologist, the parents decided to take Jacob in for DA.

In the first session, which took about two hours, Jacob was initially very suspicious and depressed, but within 30 minutes he showed more confidence and his overall emotional mood changed. Jacob was given several tests from the Learning Propensity Assessment Device (LPAD; Feuerstein et al., 1979). It was immediately clear that Jacob was an intelligent child and a fast learner. He could immediately grasp new cognitive principles, worked systematically in gathering information, and applied the newly acquired principles to novel and more complex problems. The main deficient cognitive functions revealed were impulsivity in gathering the information (input phase), impulsivity in choosing the right answer after correct verbal anticipation (output phase), deficient verbal tools for helping to register information, and deficient need for accuracy in data gathering. These deficiencies were significantly improved after an intervention aimed at enhancement of self-regulated behavior, learning a few task-specific concepts and terms, and developing awareness of the importance of accuracy and precision. These deficiencies could easily explain his failure in the first group test administered in the vocational counseling institute. That test, which was composed of a set of multiple-choice questions, requires fine distinctions among several alternatives, paying attention to specific verbal terms that provide cues about the correct answer, and choice of the best answer after considering very similar alternatives. For children who have these kinds of cognitive deficiencies, the multiple-choice type of test is disastrous because it requires exactly the cognitive functions that are deficient. It should be noted that these cognitive functions are not indicative of a child's ability for abstraction and understanding but rather of poor learning habits, behavioral tendencies, and attitudes toward learning. It seems that the low score achieved by Jacob on the group test did not reflect his true level of functioning, but rather a behavioral tendency to react impulsively, a lack of learning opportunities to learn verbal tools, and poor mediation in the family for accuracy and precision.

As a result of the DA testing Jacob was referred for cognitive intervention aimed at remediation of the specific deficiencies. The psychological report sent to the secondary high school strongly recommended to accept him on the premise that, by the time that school started (6 months from the testing date), a cognitive intervention program would be implemented to prepare Jacob for school activities. Jacob received the planned intervention for six months (three hours a week) and showed significant progress. He was eventually accepted to the secondary high school and graduated successfully. Today, ten years after the testing, Jacob is serving in the army in a responsible job and planning to go to college. It should be noted that acceptance to the secondary high school was not automatic upon receiving the psychological report. There was need for a special meeting with school staff members to explain the DA results and the prognosis based on them, as well as to negotiate the terms for acceptance.

Jacob's case exemplifies many of the problems and difficulties psychologists and educators face when dealing with DA findings. These difficulties include understanding the goals of DA, the specific diagnostic procedures, the translation of findings into intervention processes, and the educational and socioemotional implications of the assessment.

One of the main issues regarding DA is to what degree learning processes within the test situation improve the performance of children coming from diverse ability groups, cultural backgrounds, SES groups, and children with learning difficulties. It was expected that children who had not been exposed to adequate mediation in the past, because of internal or external reasons, would benefit more from the mediation given in the DA procedure than would children who had relatively rich learning experiences. It should be noted that very frequently the distinction between SES level, cultural difference, and learning difficulty is not possible. Nevertheless, the following section presents research focused on DA as related to socioeconomic level, cultural difference, and mental handicap. In order to facilitate understanding of cognitive processes involved in DA, several of the DA measures are described with a focus on indications of cognitive modifiability.

DA in Different SES Level and Ability Level Groups

Previous research has shown generally that standardized intelligence scores underestimate the cognitive ability of individuals coming from low SES levels and that DA provides information that could not be achieved by static tests (see, e.g., Brown & Ferrara, 1985; Hamers, Hessels, & Pennings, 1996; Hessels, 1997; Lidz & Thomas, 1987; Resing, 1997; Tzuriel, 1989; Tzuriel & Haywood, 1992). Tzuriel and Klein (1985) showed that advantaged and disadvantaged children scored 69% and 64%, respectively, on the *Children's Analogical Thinking Modifiability* test (CATM; Tzuriel & Klein, 1985), as compared to 39% and 44%, respectively, on the *Raven's Colored Progressive Matrices* (RCPM; Raven, 1956). These findings were replicated with hearing and deaf preschool children (Tzuriel & Caspi, 1992).

Shochet (1992) used DA as a group test to predict the success of black undergraduate students in South Africa. The criterion measures were the number of credits and the average grade achieved at the end of the first year. The students were divided into low and high modifiable groups on the basis of the Deductive Reasoning Test (Verster, 1973), which was adapted as a DA predictive measure. The results revealed significant prediction of the criterion measures among the low modifiable students ($r = .55$ for Credits) as compared to negative prediction among the high modifiable students ($r = -.22$ for Credits). Shochet explained the findings by suggesting that the low modifiable students were less susceptible to being modified during a period of one year, hence the higher correlation between the modifiability measure and the achievement criterion. The negative correlation in the high modifiable students indicates that what was being measured in the static test was not a reflection of their skills in the range of the cognitive area being tested. Shochet's conclusion was that the static test was invalid for predicting achievement of the more modifiable disadvantaged students. This study raises the issue of the construct validity of static tests such as the SAT and part of the GRE as aptitude tests rather than as achievement tests.

Using a different approach and different predictive and criterion variables, Campione and Brown (1987) and Brown and Ferrara (1985) found in their studies that students of lower ability, as compared with higher ability students, require more instruction to reach a learning criterion and need more help to show transfer. In a series of studies, Brown and Ferrara (1985) used different tasks. In their first study, they used a letter completion task (alphabetical progression task) that required understanding of several rules. The problems were presented initially to a group of third and fifth graders to be solved independently, much like a standard test. In the next step the researchers introduced a set of standardized graduated prompts increasing in level of explicitness. The first prompt was a subtle hint whereas the final step was direct teaching of the problem's solution. The extent of the ZPD was empirically translated into the number of prompts needed to solve the first problem versus the second problem, and so on. A child revealing a wide ZPD was one who reduced the number of prompts needed from one trial to another, or in other words showed effective transfer of a new solution across similar problems. The findings showed, as expected, that the fifth graders learned more quickly (i.e., needed less hints) than the third graders, and that high-IQ children required about three-fourths the number of hints needed by the average-IQ children to reach a criterion of learning. What is more important with regard to the difference between static assessment and DA is that a good number of children (about one-third) had a learning speed that was not predicted by their IQ level. The authors reported also that more prompts were needed to solve the far transfer problems than the maintenance and near transfer problems. Interactions of grade and IQ level with breadth of transfer showed that more prompts were needed for the third graders and for the low-IQ level children than for the fifth graders and the high-IQ level children. IQ level did not predict the degree of transfer for about one-third of the children. Comparison of speed of learning with degree of transfer showed that about one-third of the subjects did not conform to the slow learning/low transfer and fast learning/high transfer patterns.

When learning speed and transfer level profiles were broken down by IQ level, it was found that the IQ of almost 50% of the children did not predict learning speed and/or degree of transfer. The findings revealed five learning profiles: (a) *slow*: slow learners, narrow transferors, low IQ, (b) *fast*: fast learners, wide transferors, high IQ, (c) *reflective*: slow learners, wide transferors, (d) *context-bound*: fast learners, narrow transferors, and (e) *high scores*: fast learners, wide transferors, low IQ.

In a second study, Brown and Ferrara (1985) posed the question whether these profiles are consistent across domains. For this purpose the authors used the letter-completion task and a progressive matrices task, both of which involve inductive reasoning but were different in modality of presentation (verbal versus figural). The subjects were EMR students (mean IQ = 70) who were classified by the above five learning profiles. The findings revealed that the correlation for number of hints required to reach learning criteria on both tasks was .66. The correlation for performance on maintenance/transfer tasks, however, was more domain-specific, as reflected by the lower correlation of .39. Another finding was that for number of hints, 76% of the children displayed the same learning status on both tasks. On maintenance/transfer criteria, 43% were identical on both tasks but 52% shifted from one to the opposite status.

In two other studies (Campione & Brown, 1987), change scores on the RCPM were predicted by ability (IQ) and dynamic (measures of learning and transfer) tests. The change scores were the residual gain calculated by the pre- to postteaching performance. The DA measures were simplified forms of the progressive matrices and a series completion task. The findings showed that the learning and transfer measures predicted the residual gain scores above and beyond the measures of ability.

Tzuriel and Klein (1985, 1987) explored the effects of mediation in a DA context with kindergarten children identified as being advantaged, disadvantaged, having needs for special education, or as MR. The kindergarten children were 5 to 6 years old, whereas the last group was composed of older MR children with a mental age (MA) equal to kindergarten level. Before discussing the results, the CATM test is briefly described. The children were administered a DA measure for young children (the CATM) and a static test, the RCPM.

The purpose of the CATM is to test cognitive modifiability and use of higher-order concepts and operations. The operation of analogy has been considered by many authors as a powerful tool for a wide range of cognitive processes and as a principal operation for problem solving activities (e.g., Goswami, 1991; Holyoak & Thagard, 1995). The CATM test is composed of 14 items for each phase of administration (preteaching, teaching, and postteaching), and 18 colored blocks are used to present and solve the analogies. The CATM items, graduated in level of difficulty, require a relatively higher level of abstraction and various cognitive functions. During the teaching phase, the child is mediated to (a) search for relevant dimensions required for the analogical solution, (b) understand transformational rules and analogical principles, (c) search systematically for correct blocks, and (d) improve efficiency of performance. Examples of two analogical problems are presented in Figure 15.1.

In order to solve the problems the child has to infer the relation between the first two blocks and transfer it to the second pair of blocks. In the second problem the child has to understand the concept of "opposite" (in the first pair the yellow on top goes to bottom and the blue in bottom goes to top). In addition, the task requires systematic exploratory behavior, simultaneous consideration of several sources of information, need for accuracy, and control of impulsivity.

The CATM can be administered in one of two versions: clinical/educational and measurement/research. In the measurement/research version, preteaching and postteaching phases are given without mediation, and the child's responses are scored. A short-term but intensive mediation is given in the time between the tests, and responses are recorded and scored. In the clinical/educational version, no scores are given, and assessment refers mainly to qualitative aspects of the child's performance. The qualitative aspects refer to the amount and nature of mediation needed to solve a problem, the level of task difficulty in relation to the child's solution, behavioral tendencies that affect the child's cognitive responses, and affective-motivational (nonintellective) factors that affect performance. Mediation is adapted to the child's level, and parallel items are presented only after the child shows mastery level. Once the child shows adequate mastery, it is possible to move to a higher level of difficulty.

Tzuriel and Klein's findings showed that the highest gains from pre- to

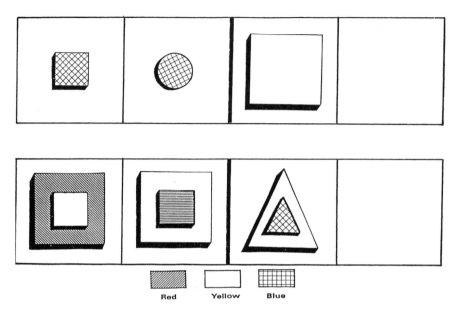

FIGURE 15.1
Example problems from the CATM test.

postteaching phases were found among children identified as disadvantaged and advantaged as compared to children with needs for special education and MR children, who showed small gains. The MR group, however, showed significant improvement when a "partial credit" scoring method was applied (i.e., credit given for each correctly solved dimension of color, size, and shape). This last finding indicates that the MR group has a difficulty in integration of all sources of information and therefore showed modifiability only when the "partial credit" method was used.

Lidz and Thomas (1987) and Tzuriel (1989) further confirmed the effectiveness of DA with young children from different SES levels. Lidz and Thomas (1987) administered the Preschool Learning Assessment Device (PLAD) to an experimental group composed of 3- to 5-year-old Head Start preschool children, mostly black and Hispanic. The experimental children were compared to control children who had experience with the same materials but without mediation. The PLAD is based on the MLE approach and Luria's (1976) neuropsychological theory as elaborated by the Das, Naglieri, and Kirby (1994) PASS model (Planning, Arousal, Simultaneous, Successive). The testing procedure is basically a test-intervention-retest model using readiness tasks for 3- to 5-year-old preschool children. The testing procedure is anchored to the Triangles subtest of the Kaufman Assessment Battery for Children (K-ABC; Kaufman & Kaufman, 1983). The tasks include human figure drawing, building steps with cubes, and copying parquetry designs. The authors reported that the mediated children showed higher gains as compared to the control children, who showed no change. Significant strong correlations also were reported between the magnitude of gains and a social competency measure.

A question raised by Tzuriel (1989) was whether the effects of mediation, found with children coming from disadvantaged families, are more articulated in difficult as compared to easy tasks. This question was studied with a group of disadvantaged (N = 54) and advantaged (N = 124) children in kindergarten and grade 1. The children were administered a DA test—the Children's Inferential Thinking Modifiability (CITM; Tzuriel, 1989, 1992b)—and a static measure (RCPM).

The objectives of the CITM are to assess young children's ability to solve problems that require inferential thinking as well as their ability to modify their performance following a process of mediation. The CITM is composed of four sets of problems for preteaching, teaching, postteaching, and transfer phases. Content analysis of the CITM tasks reveals that it is a strategy-dependent test with relatively complex and abstract problems, in Piagetian terms. An example problem (B6) is presented in Figure 15.2.

In item B6, three houses with black, blue, and white roofs are presented at the top of the page. The child is instructed to place cards with pictures into the appropriate houses at the top of the page. To solve the problem the child is presented with three rows at the bottom of the page, with each row containing part of the information. The rules are that, in each row, the objects on the left should enter the houses with patchworks to the right. In the first row, the Bed and the Flower should go into the houses with lines (white and blue); it is not known at this stage which object goes to which house. In the second row, the Bed and Boat should go into the houses with lines (black and white). Similar to the first row, it is not known which object goes to which house. In the third row, either the Boat or the Leaf should enter the house with lines (black). In order to solve the problem one should compare the lines and make several analytic inferences. This inferential task requires systematic exploratory behavior, control of impulsivity, spontaneous comparative behavior, planning, inferential-hypothetical ("iffy") thinking, and simultaneous consideration of several sources of information. The operations required for solving the task are related to negation-negative inference ("the chair is not in the red house and not the blue house"), and inductive reasoning. Cronbach-alpha reliability coefficients of the preteaching, postteaching, and transfer phases are .82, .82, and .90, respectively (Tzuriel, 1992b). The validity of the CITM has been established in several developmental and educational studies (e.g., Samuels, 1998; Tzuriel, 1989; Tzuriel & Eran, 1990; Tzuriel & Weiss, 1998).

The findings have showed higher pre- to postteaching improvements for disadvantaged than for advantaged children (Tzuriel, 1989). The degree of improvement of the disadvantaged children over the advantaged children was higher in the medium- and high-complexity level problems than in the low-complexity level problems. These results verify what is known clinically—

B6

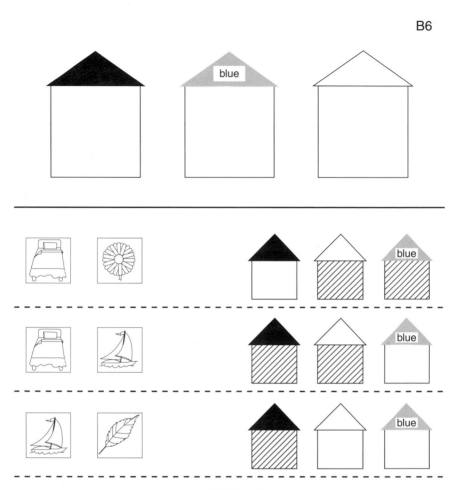

FIGURE 15.2
Example item (B6) from the CITM test.

that mediation is most effective and therefore most needed in complex and/ or abstract tasks. While the higher gains of the disadvantaged children over the advantaged children also might be contributed to by a ceiling effect, the magnitude of gains indicates that mediation is more effective with children who have a lower initial performance level.

The effectiveness of DA with children of low SES was shown also on older children in grades 7–9, using the Set Variations II (SV-II) test from the LPAD (Feuerstein, Rand, Haywood, Kyram, & Hoffman, 1995) administered as a group DA test (Tzuriel & Feuerstein, 1992). It should be noted that Jensen (1980) considers tasks such as those in SV-II as representing Level II of thinking and, therefore, essentially untrainable. The SV-II was administered to advantaged and disadvantaged students (N = 749) in three experimental conditions: High Teaching (HT), Low Teaching (LT), and No Teaching (NT). The Raven Standard Progressive Matrices (RSPM) was administered as a static test to all groups twice, once before and once two weeks after the treatment. The initial scores on this test were used to classify subjects into three levels of initial performance.

The findings showed that performance on the SV-II was higher for: (a) subjects who received the higher level of teaching, (b) subjects who had initially high performance (based on RSPM initial score), and (c) socially advantaged subjects as compared to those from disadvantaged families. Another finding indicated that the difference between advantaged and disadvantaged children was much lower in the HT condition than in the LT condition. The results of this study indicate, in general, the invalidity of the RSPM scores in representing an individual's "psychometric intelligence," especially for low-performing groups, and that with the relatively short intervention procedure given in group DA situations one can achieve much higher performance. The fact that the second administration of the RSPM was two weeks after the intervention strengthens the argument that the changes were not superficial or temporary but represented a solid phenomenon.

The differences between children coming from low and middle SES groups were studied recently using the Children's Seriational Thinking Modifiability test (CSTM; Tzuriel, 1995b). The CSTM test is a DA measure designed for 3- to 5-year-old children. It is based mainly on operation of seriation, although other operations related to comparisons and quantitative relations are included as well. The CSTM allows the assessment of cognitive modifiability in a domain considered to be prerequisite for further mathematical skills (Ginsburg, 1977) and transitive relations (Kingma, 1983). The CSTM is composed of unique problems that require both an arrangement of stimuli on a certain continuum and the controlling for one or more dimensions that are embedded within the same set of stimuli. In several of the items, for example, the examinee is required first to order the set according to one dimension (e.g., size) while trying to avoid interference of other dimensions within the given set. An example from the CSTM is presented in Figure 15.3.

Figure 15.3 shows the ordering of the horses according to the two dimensions embedded in the problem (size and number). The cards are presented in a mixed order, and the child is asked to order them; no instructions are given as to how to order. If the child experiences difficulties, he or she is given the term of the first dimension (e.g., number) and mediated how to make the order. After mastering one dimension the child is asked to reorder by a different dimension, and the same mediation procedure is repeated whenever necessary. The child's ability to shift from one order to another and to control for irrelevant information when focusing on the target dimension indicates an inclination for flexibility and self-regulation of behavior.

A study on a sample of disadvantaged (N = 69) and advantaged (N = 62)

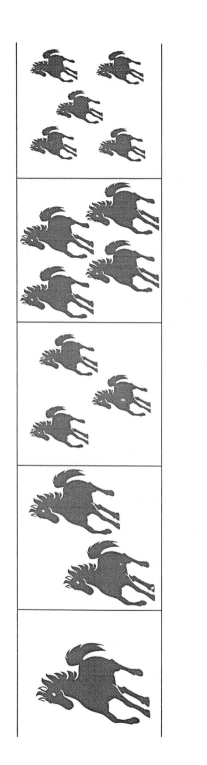

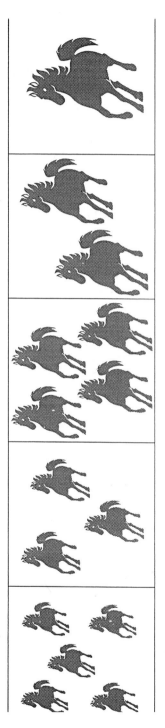

FIGURE 15.3

The horses problem from the CSTM test.

kindergarten children showed that the disadvantaged children achieved initially lower scores than advantaged children did but significantly improved their performance from the pre- to postteaching phase and narrowed the gap with the advantaged group. Similar to previous findings (Tzuriel, 1989), the pre- to postteaching gains were more articulated in problems with a high level of complexity (e.g., containing more dimensions in one set) than in problems with a low level of complexity.

Dynamic Assessment of Children with Mental Handicap, Developmental Delay, and Specific Learning Difficulties

In one of the first extensive clinical studies, Samuels, Tzuriel, and Malloy-Miller (1989) administered a battery of eight tests from the LPAD to four groups of children: learning disabled (LD), learning disabled with attention deficit disorder (LD/ADD), educable mentally handicapped (EMH), and normally achieving children. In addition to performance scores three types of data were collected: *deficient cognitive functions* (i.e., deficient spatial orientation, deficient comparative behavior), *type and amount of mediation* (i.e., restraint of impulsivity, metacognitive questioning), and *nonintellective factors* (i.e., accessibility to mediation, frustration tolerance). All data were videotaped during both training and testing phases and later rated on rating scales. The findings showed that the performance scores of the normally achieving children and LD children were similar. Both groups did not have difficulties on the LPAD tests. The LD/ADD group, however, had significantly lower scores than the normally achieving children and the LD children on all tests. The EMH group showed the poorest performance on all tests but also showed significant gains on every test with mediation prior to responding. Group differences were reduced when a score of correct answers with mediation prior to response was computed.

The findings on the deficient cognitive functions showed that a higher percentage of LD/ADD children were rated with deficient cognitive functions than the LD children. This finding was consistent across all categories. The highest percentage of children rated as deficient was found in the EMH group. Interestingly, the group differences are primarily in degree of deficiency rather than in kind. Comparison of training to testing phase showed, as expected, a consistent drop in the percentage of children rated as deficient, with the exception of language and communication categories, which remained high for all three groups.

The findings on mediation showed that the EMH group required the greatest amount of mediation, followed by the LD/ADD group. The LD group required less mediation than the LD/ADD or EMH groups, except in mediation for competence, which was given more extensively to the EMH group than to the other groups. The categories of prompting, focusing, promoting metacognitive awareness, teaching rules and strategies, and mediation of competence were the most frequently required mediations for the EMH group and, to a lesser degree, the LD/ADD and LD groups. The normal achieving group required minimal mediation.

Of most importance are the findings showing that the gains of the EMH group, following mediation, as well as their ability to deal with abstract formal operational tasks, could not have been predicted by their standard WISC-R scores. The authors reported also that, while the WISC-R scores could have predicted the general performance pattern among the groups across all LPAD tests, this was not the case for the LD and LD/ADD groups. Both groups showed similar performance on the WISC-R but demonstrated consistent differences in performance on the LPAD tests. The LD group consistently made more errors, exhibited more deficient cognitive functions, and required more mediation to perform effectively. The authors concluded that the LPAD provides useful information about children with learning difficulties that is not readily apparent from static assessment, and that the information can change clinicians' and teachers' views about children's learning potential.

Similar findings were reported by Rutland and Campbell (1995) with a group of learning disabled and nondisabled children who were administered a spatial orientation task (i.e., locating an object within a large-scale maze environment using a map). All children were taught by the graduated prompt approach. The findings showed that, while IQ and pretest scores contributed 25% to the variance of the pre- to posttest improvement, DA measures accounted for 31% of the variance, and that predictive validity among learning disabled children was higher than among non-disabled children.

The effectiveness of DA was demonstrated extensively on different samples of young children showing various learning difficulties (Burns, 1991; Reinharth, 1989; Missiuna & Samuels, 1989; Tzuriel & Klein, 1985). Reinharth (1989), for example, using a sample of developmentally delayed children, showed that experimental children who received mediation improved their pre- to posttest scores and continued to improve their performance in a follow-up phase more than a control group. Reinharth's findings contradict previous findings with kindergarten children identified as needing special education (Tzuriel & Klein, 1985) who did not show an improvement on the CATM test after a mediation phase.

Missiuna and Samuels (1989) tried to explain why these children showed no pre- to posttest improvement by referring to the type of mediation required for this group. Their arguments were that the mediation given in Tzuriel and Klein's (1985) study was standardized (i.e., given similarly to each child without taking into account the unique difficulties of the specific tested individual) and that children needing special education are especially sensitive to the type of mediation given to them. Missiuna and Samuels also argued that mediation that is tailored to the children's specific needs is more effective than the mediation given regularly in the teaching phase of the DA procedure. In a replication study, they introduced two adjustments. First, learning disabled children in kindergarten were assigned randomly to treatment conditions of either "instruction" or "mediation." "Instruction" was similar to the original teaching phase in that the children received the same nonprescribed mediation. The "mediation" condition, however, was tailored to the unique difficulties demonstrated by the child during assessment (e.g., attention span, labeling, and self-regulation). Second, the CATM was administered twice with no mediation in between in order to rule out practice effects and familiarity with test problems. Their findings showed no practice effect, as evidenced by the lack of improvement between the two administrations. The main findings, however, showed that the handicapped children who received mediation significantly improved their scores, whereas the "instruction" group showed no change. Thus, the minor improvement of the "instruction" group replicated Tzuriel and Klein's (1985) results with the special education group, using the regular mediation.

The modifiability of the special education group was demonstrated more impressively with use of the "partial credit" scoring method than with the "all-or-none" method. This result might be explained by the difficulties of the children in simultaneously considering and integrating all three types of information (color, shape, and size). Also, the "mediation" group required significantly more time to solve the postteaching problems than did the "instruction" group, a result that was explained by better control of impulsivity and awareness of different options for problem solving strategies. Missiuna and Samuels (1989) concluded that mediation in DA should be tailored to children's unique learning difficulties in order to reveal their learning potential.

The utility of DA also was demonstrated in a study carried out in Canada by Samuels, Killip, MacKenzie, and Fagan (1992) with a group of kindergarten children with learning disabilities. The children were given the CATM (dynamic) and the RCPM and PPVT-R (static). An outcome-unobtrusive measure of regular versus special education class attendance, taken two years later, showed that only the CATM postteaching score significantly predicted class attendance. Children attending regular classes had higher CATM postteaching scores than did children who ended up attending special education classes. This result supported the notion that postmediation scores are better predictors of future learning than is initial performance on a static measure.

The importance of DA with learning disabled children was demonstrated also by Resing (1997) on groups of second-grade children coming from classes of slow-learning, learning disabled, and regular education students. Resing designed a learning potential test based on two inductive reasoning

tests: exclusion and verbal analogies (i.e., Pencil : Writing :: Mouth : _____).
These tests were taken from the Revised Amsterdam Kindergarten Intelligence Test (RAKIT; Bleichrodt, Drenth, Zaal, & Resing, 1984). The inductive reasoning tests were chosen because of their centrality in theories of intelligence, their central role in cognitive development, and the frequency with which a variety of tasks are solved by inductive and analogical reasoning processes. The test was administered by the graduated prompt technique. Learning potential was defined by the number of hints necessary to reach a specified amount of learning and the amount of transfer on various tasks defined. A system of graduated prompts was designed using metacognitive hints ("What do you have to do?"), cognitive hints ("What is the relation between pencil and writing?"), and training steps, each of which was composed of several graduated steps. Resing's findings showed that learning disabled and slow-learning children needed twice and three times, respectively, as many hints as children coming from mainstream education. The learning potential test revealed, as expected, more qualitative information about the child's cognitive functioning (e.g., type of hints needed, type of strategies used) than did the static test performance. Both learning potential scores had significant additional predictive value for school performance. Resing (1997) concluded that the learning potential tests are of most importance when there are doubts about the child's real intelligence level because of cultural background or disadvantaged educational history.

Application of DA with Culturally Different Children

Assessment of culturally different children is of great theoretical and practical importance. Theoretically, DA can shed light on the influence of cultural factors on children's cognitive modifiability and learning processes. For example, three of the crucial issues are the role of mediation in a specific culture as a determinant of *cognitive plasticity* (i.e., modifying cognitive structures as a response to environmental demands), internalization of novel cultural *symbolic mental tools* with transition from one culture to another, and development of resiliency in coping with cultural conflicts. Practically, DA can provide information regarding specific educational practices of culturally different groups, and adequate cognitive intervention programs aimed at narrowing academic gaps among these groups.

Culturally different children might show low performance in standardized tests because of language differences and/or lack of learning opportunities. DA can go beyond these difficulties and provide a better understanding of the basic learning processes and learning potential. Cross-cultural research showed DA to be more accurate than standardized tests in revealing children's cognitive abilities (Guthke & Al-Zoubi, 1987; Hessels & Hamers, 1993; Kaniel, Tzuriel, Feuerstein, Ben-Shachar, & Eitan, 1991; Skuy & Shmukler,

1987; Tzuriel & Kaufman, 1999; Vygotsky, 1978). The reason is that the interactive nature of the test allows undeveloped cognitive capacities to mature and provides the possibility to observe learning processes and to go beyond the children's manifested cognitive performance.

Hessels and Hamers (1993) and Hessels (1997) carried out extensive studies in the Netherlands on samples of Moroccan and Turkish minority children who were compared to Dutch school-age children. Both studies used a language-free test of learning potential. The test is based on a short-term learning test model (Guthke & Wingenfeld, 1992) and is composed of five subtests: classification, number series, figurative analogies, word-object association (recognition and naming), and syllable recall. The first three subtests address inductive reasoning. Achievements on all five subtests are age related, sensitive to individual differences, and substantially correlated with school achievement. The findings showed that, although the minority groups scored lower than the native Dutch children on standardized IQ tests, there were no differences on the DA measure. No difference was found in the predictive power of static and DA measures. In the later study, Hessels (1997) found that children who scored low on the standard test scored low, average, or even high on the LEM. About 10–15% of the minority children and 10% of the Dutch children were labeled as intellectually impaired, whereas their learning potential scores were average or above average. Prediction of academic gains in classroom settings showed that the learning potential scores were better predictors of academic achievements than were static scores, and that higher prediction was found among children with high learning potential than among children with average learning potential.

Tzuriel and Kaufman (1999) demonstrated the efficiency of DA with a group of grade 1 Ethiopian immigrants to Israel compared to a group of Israeli-born grade 1 children. The question was how to assess the immigrants' learning potential in view of the fact that their cognitive scores on static tests were low and that standard testing procedures inaccurately reflected this population's cognitive functioning. It should be noted that the Ethiopian immigrants had to overcome a "civilization gap" in order to adapt to Israeli society. This issue transcends the specific context of the Ethiopian immigrants, both theoretically and pragmatically. The main hypothesis of this study was that many of these immigrants would reveal cultural difference but not *cultural deprivation* (i.e., when the child lacks parental mediation in his or her own culture), and therefore that they would reveal high levels of modifiability within a DA situation. The Ethiopian group was compared to the group of Israeli-born children on the RCPM and on two young children's DA measures (the CATM and the CITM). The findings for the CITM are described in Figure 15.4.

Figure 15.4 shows an initial superiority on the CITM preteaching scores of the Israeli-born group over the Ethiopian group. The Ethiopian children, however, improved their performance more than the Israeli children and

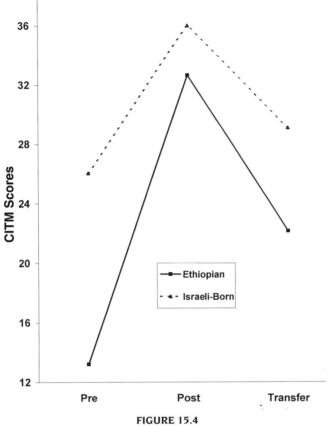

FIGURE 15.4

The CITM scores among Ethiopian and Israeli-born children.

closed the gap in the postteaching performance. The gap between the two groups was even narrower in the transfer phase, which consists of more difficult problems. Similar results were found also on the CATM, which taps a different cognitive domain. Thus, in spite of the initial superiority of the Israeli-born children in every test, after a short but intensive teaching process the Ethiopian group significantly narrowed the gap. These findings are similar to those reported previously on older Ethiopian children (Kaniel et al., 1991) and to findings in other countries showing smaller differences between minority and mainstream groups after a mediation given within a DA process (i.e., Skuy & Shmukler, 1987). Unlike the initial group difference on the inferential domain of the CITM, the performance on a rather simple domain—the Free-Recall subtest—showed no significant difference. The lack of inferiority of the Ethiopian children on this task probably reflects the Ethiopian's culture of oral learning and rote learning strategies. Correlation analyses showed that the Free-Recall score was significantly correlated with the RCPM score only in the Ethiopian group. This result was explained by the Ethiopian children's tendency to use similar cognitive processes in solving both tasks, as compared to the Israeli-born children's tendency to apply different processes.

A striking finding was the improvement of the Ethiopian-born children on the CITM Classification subtest. The Classification subtest is composed of 24 pictures divided into six categories. The child is asked to classify the pictures he or she has been already exposed to in the previous inferential test. After initial performance, a short teaching phase is given, followed by a parallel posttest. The teaching phase is composed of a short (1–2 min.) explanation of the concept of a group, with demonstration of one category. The findings showed drastic improvement among the Ethiopian group (from .70 to 9.00) as compared to the Israeli-born group (from 10.20 to 12.00). Although these findings should be taken cautiously because of the group differences in standard deviations and because of a ceiling effect, it nevertheless indicates very substantial differences between the two groups in their basic approach to the classification task. The very low initial performance of the Ethiopian children was explained as a result of the lack of familiarity with classification tasks rather than to a lack of ability. These results coincide with cross-cultural research findings indicating that individuals in many non-Western nations classify items into functional rather than taxonomic categories (e.g., Luria, 1976; Scribner, 1984; Sharp, Cole, & Lave, 1979).

Dynamic Assessment of Children with Language Deficits

DA has been adapted by several researchers, especially speech-language pathologists, to provide a valid means for the assessment of reading difficulties and for differentiating children with language differences from children with language disorders (e.g., Jeffrey, 1997; Peña & Gillam, 2000; Sharoni & Greenfeld, 1999). Peña and Gillam (2000) showed, for example, with a group of low SES children that cognitive strategies, rather than intervention materials, influenced gains on a labeling task in a DA procedure. Sharoni and Greenfeld (1999) developed an integrative model for remedial teaching of reading that combines three approaches: the cognitive strategies involved in reading, the mediated learning approach, and cognitive behavior strategies. Sharoni and Greenfeld applied this model in a seminar for teachers as well as in a clinic for assessment and remedial teaching of reading difficulties. In a single case study the authors reported the effectiveness of their paradigmatic integrative approach with both college students who learned teaching processes and with children diagnosed in the clinic. Using a clinical approach, Jeffrey (1997) and Jeffrey and Tzuriel (1999) demonstrated the efficient use of the Cognitive Modifiability Battery (CMB; Tzuriel, 1995a, 2000c) to assess and intervene with children showing language difficulties. The CMB tasks were used to identify various difficulties such as definition of verbal categories, memory deficits, number concepts, directionality, grammatical markers of comparison (e.g., bigg*est*), self-talk strategies, and limiting of options strategies. In all of these areas the CMB tasks were used to "bridge" newly acquired concepts to letter formation, directionality of letters, and word formation. In conclusion, the clinical use of DA in content-related domains and the research in this area are relatively scarce, but the novel attempts for applications are promising.

Prediction of School Achievements
by Dynamic Assessment Measures

One of the problems in predicting school achievements by DA as compared to static tests is that the academic achievement scores are usually measured in a static way, thus giving priority to static tests. In spite of this methodological difficulty, several studies have reported the superiority of postteaching scores over preteaching or static tests in predicting school achievements (Lidz & Greenberg, 1997; Tzuriel, Kaniel, Kanner, & Haywood, 1999; Tzuriel, in press). Lidz and Greenberg (1997) used a modified dynamic measure of the Cognitive Assessment System (CAS; Das & Naglieri, 1997) with a group of first graders in a rural school, half of whom were Native Americans. Lidz and Greenberg reported that a significant relationship existed between cognitive processes (i.e., attention, planning, simultaneous, and successive) and school achievements. Reading scores correlated higher with the posttest than with the pretest scores. Furthermore, lower-functioning students improved their functioning from pre- to posttest phase more than higher-functioning students.

Similar results were reported by Tzuriel et al. (1999) with a group of grade 1 children who had participated in the Bright Start program in kindergarten. The prediction pattern was compared to a comparison group of children who participated in a general skills program. Both groups received reading comprehension and math tests one year after the end of the intervention as well as the RCPM and two DA measures (CATM and Complex Figure). The findings showed that reading comprehension was significantly predicted by the RCPM in both the experimental ($R^2 = .19$) and the comparison group ($R^2 = .26$). Math scores were predicted in the experimental group far more powerfully by the CATM postteaching (dynamic) than by the RCPM (static); both measures predicted 47% of the variance. In the comparison group, math was predicted by the CATM postteaching score alone ($R^2 = .54$).

Similar findings were reported (Tzuriel, 2000c) on a sample of first graders who were administered the CMB, reading comprehension, and math tests.

The findings showed that reading comprehension was predicted by the post-teaching Seriation and postteaching Analogies subtests of the CMB; both tests predicted 45% of the variance. This finding was explained by the fact that the Analogies test taps an abstraction domain, which is closer to reading comprehension than is Seriation. Seriation, on the other hand, characterizes the individual's ability to learn task-specific strategies, which is a cognitive function related to the technical skills required in reading.

The findings for math showed that it was predicted by the postteaching Seriation and preteaching Reproduction of Patterns subtests of the CMB; both scores explained 57% of the variance. Detailed task analysis of these domains showed that both tests require precision and accuracy, a cognitive function that is required in math performance. In addition, Seriation requires systematic exploratory behavior and learning of task-specific strategies, which together characterize successful performance in math.

In conclusion, the findings of all studies indicate that the postteaching scores are more powerful than static tests in predicting academic achievement scores. It is assumed that, if academic performance were measured dynamically, prediction by dynamic tests would be much higher than what has been found so far.

USE OF DYNAMIC ASSESSMENT IN EVALUATION OF COGNITIVE EDUCATION PROGRAMS

DA has also been used in evaluation of the efficacy of several cognitive education programs, all based on the MLE theory: the Instrumental Enrichment program (Feuerstein, Rand, Hoffman, & Miller, 1980), the Bright Start (Haywood, Brooks, & Burns, 1986, 1992; Tzuriel et al., 1999; Tzuriel, Kaniel, Zeliger, Friedman, & Haywood, 1998), the Structured Program for Visual-Motor Integration (Tzuriel & Eiboshitz, 1992), and the Cognitive Modifiability Battery (Lauchlan & Elliott, 1997; Tzuriel, 1995a, 2000c). Given that one of the major goals of the cognitive education programs is to teach "learning to learn," it was essential to use DA, in which change and improvement criteria could be assessed. In the following sections I describe first the Complex Figure test that was used as the "far transfer" measure of the effects of cognitive education program. Following this I describe some applications of DA to evaluate several cognitive education programs.

The Complex Figure test was originally developed by Rey (1959), elaborated later as a DA measure by Feuerstein et al. (1979), and adapted for young children by Tzuriel and Eiboshitz (1992). The test was used in several cognitive education programs as a criterion measure and is described here briefly.

The Complex Figure test, presented in Figure 15.5, is composed of five

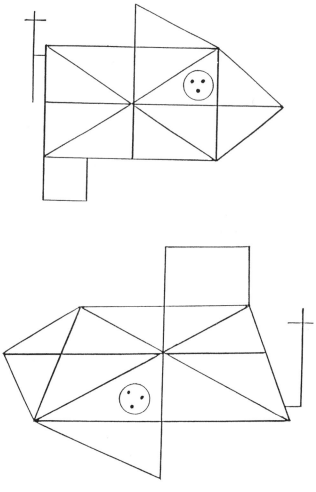

FIGURE 15.5
The Complex Figure test (versions for young children).

phases. In the first phase (Copy-I), the child is asked to copy the figure. In the second phase, the child is asked to draw the figure from memory (Memory-I). In the Teaching (mediation) phase that follows, the child is taught how to gather the information systematically, to plan the construction (i.e., drawing first the major lines and then the secondary lines, going in clockwise order), and to pay attention to precision, proportions, and the quality of lines. A second copy phase (Copy-II) and a second memory phase (Memory-II) are administered exactly as in the first two phases. Comparison of copy and memory phases—before and after teaching—provides information about the cognitive modifiability of the child's performance.

The Bright Start Program

The Bright Start program contains seven cognitive instructional units used with small groups and addresses fundamental aspects of preschool children's cognitive functioning: Self-Regulation, Number Concepts, Comparison, Role-Taking, Classification, Sequences and Patterns/Seriation, and Letter-Shape Concepts/Distinctive Features (Haywood et al., 1986, 1992). A basic component of the Bright Start program is mediational teaching style, which is characterized by mediating basic thinking skills, generalized meanings of the children's experiences, and metacognitive processes.

Bright Start, when applied systematically with young disadvantaged and/or handicapped children, is expected to increase learning effectiveness through acquisition of cognitive, motivational, and metacognitive prerequisites to learning of academic content, and to prepare young children for school learning. The Bright Start program was evaluated in two studies uing a DA approach (Tzuriel et al., 1998, 1999). In the first study (Tzuriel et al., 1999), the effectiveness of Bright Start was investigated with a sample of kindergarten children who participated in the program for 10 months. This experimental group was compared to a parallel group of children who received a basic skills program. All children were administered first the static and then the DA measures, before and after the intervention. The DA measures were the CATM and the Complex Figure tests. The Complex Figure test was conceptualized as a "far-transfer" test because the Bright Start contains no visual-motor component. The Complex Figure test, however, requires cognitive functions that were taught in the program in different modalities (e.g., planning, regulation of behavior, need for accuracy, and systematic exploratory behavior).

The findings indicate that the experimental group made more changes from pre- to postintervention than the comparison group on the Cognitive Development test (Simpson, 1985), the CATM preteaching, and the Complex Figure preteaching test (Copy-I and Memory-I). In spite of the relatively lower performance level of the experimental children, they succeeded in closing the gap with the comparison group after the intervention. Of most importance are the results of the Complex Figure test, which requires fine visual-motor integration skills—skills that were not part of the Bright Start program, which was heavily based on verbal interactions. A follow-up study carried out in grade 1 showed that the experimental group scored not only higher than did the control group but also showed higher pre- to postteaching improvement.

Similar findings were reported with a sample of kindergarten children who received only the Classification and Seriation units of the Bright Start program (Tzuriel et al., 1998). The findings indicated that, while both groups performed about the same before the program on Visual Memory and Concept Formation tests (static), the experimental group showed higher improvement than did the control group after the intervention. Findings on the CATM and the Complex Figure tests (dynamic) given after the intervention showed that the experimental group made greater pre- to postteaching changes than did the control group. The Complex Figure findings indicated transfer effects due to the fact that they tap a different domain than what is taught in the Bright Start program.

The replication of results across the two studies might suggest that, unlike skills-based programs, the treatment effects of cognitive education programs can be integrated across skill domains within individuals' cognitive systems. Bright Start does not include any specifically visual-motor exercises; rather, the whole program is based on visual presentation of stimuli, discussion of strategies for solving problems, metacognitive processes, verbal dialogues, social interactions, and logical analyses of situations and problems. In spite of the verbal-logical nature of the program, the experimental children in both studies were able to generalize from the mediational experiences and perform much better than the control groups.

Structured Program of Visual Motor Integration (SP-VMI)

More evidence for the utility of the use of DA is reported in regard to the SP-VMI (Tzuriel & Eiboshitz, 1992). This program is composed of a combination of MLE processes and the practice of visual-motor tasks aimed at enhancing VMI skills. A group of randomly selected disadvantaged and special education preschool children were randomly assigned to experimental (N = 60) and control (N = 30) groups and were given static and DA measures before and after the intervention. The experimental children received the SP-VMI for about three months (12 hours of intervention), whereas the control group participated in a general motor skills program. The major comparison in this study was between gain scores achieved on the Complex Figure before and after the intervention. The results indicated significant improvement of the experimental over the control group on most static tests and on the Complex Figure gain score. The experimental group showed a significant increase in gain after the intervention, whereas the control group showed a slight decrease, a result that was explained by the more difficult version of the Complex Figure test given after the intervention. In all studies, DA measures were found to be more useful as criterion measures of cognitive education programs than were static measures.

The Cognitive Modifiability Battery (CMB): Assessment and Intervention

Tzuriel (1992a, 1998, in press) has long suggested using DA instruments interchangeably for assessment and intervention. A practical application of this idea was designed in the CMB (Tzuriel, 1995a, 1997b, 2000c), which is aimed at diagnosing and treating deficient cognitive functions, various cognitive operations, and problem-solving strategies. The CMB was developed primarily for students in kindergarten through grade 3, but it can be used also with older children who have learning difficulties. The CMB is composed of four plates and 64 wooden blocks (in red, green, blue, and yellow). Each of the four plates contains nine "windows" (arranged in a 3 × 3 pattern) and small removable wooden squares that cover the windows, thereby creating different patterns of open windows as required for the different CMB tasks.

The CMB is composed of five subtests, each tapping a different area of cognitive functioning: Seriation, Reproduction of Patterns, Analogies, Sequences, and Memory. An example item from the Sequences (Level II) subtest (Transfer section) is shown in Figure 15.6.

In Sequences (Level II), the child is presented with four plates; all outside windows are open. The examiner places colored blocks on the first three plates, and the child must complete the blocks in the fourth plate. In order to solve the Transfer problem presented in the figure (TRNS9-B), the child has to grasp the systematic way by which the blocks change color, number, height, and position. The blue and the yellow blocks change positions from one plate to the next in a counterclockwise direction, whereas the red and green blocks change positions clockwise. In addition, all blocks increase in height from one plate to another, but the position of blocks within the windows is constant.

The CMB has been used in several educational and developmental studies that have not yet been published (Jeffrey, 1997; Lauchlan & Elliot, 1997; Tzuriel, 1997b, 2000c), but initial reports show a strong relation to various educational and developmental variables. Lauchlan and Elliott (1997) used the CMB as an intervention instrument with severely learning disabled children aged 8–9 years, and Jeffrey (1997) used the CMB as a diagnostic and treatment instrument with young children showing developmental delays and speech and language pathologies. Jeffrey (1997) used it also with older children who showed a low level of cognitive performance. Jeffrey found, for example, that difficulties of directionality (e.g., confusion of mirror imaging) and deficiencies in visual transport and/or mental representation were related to acquisition of written language and school achievement. Clinical experience showed significant improvement of linguistic skills as a result of intervention aimed at remediation of various deficient cognitive deficiencies by the CMB.

The CMB was administered as a DA test to a sample of 91 kindergarten children and 96 grade 1 children (Tzuriel, 2000c). Principal factor analysis with varimax rotation on the CMB subtest scores revealed five independent factors, which explained 71.8% of the variance. The factors paralleled almost completely to the five CMB subtests, a result that indicates the separation of the subtests as representing different cognitive domains.

TRNS9-B

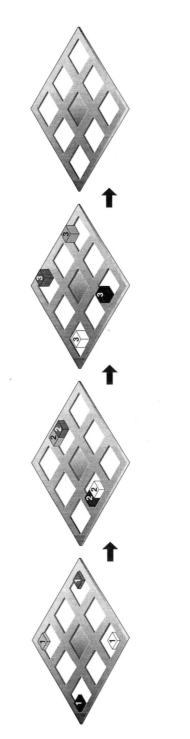

FIGURE 15.6

Example problem from the CMB Sequences Level-II Subtest (transfer phase).

Comparison of Different Mediational Strategies in DA

A promising line of research is related to differential effects of teaching strategies within DA on cognitive performance. Burns (1991), for example, showed with high-risk kindergarten children that the mediated learning approach was associated with higher cognitive performance and higher transfer scores than was either the graduated prompt or static testing procedure.

Peña and Gillam (2000) compared direct instruction, mediated learning, and hybrid methods for instructing children about labeling on a sample of low SES preschool children, the majority of whom came from culturally and linguistically diverse backgrounds. Their findings indicated that the effect size of the direct intervention gain was approximately half as large as the effect size for the hybrid group, and more than three times smaller than the effect size for the mediated learning group. The mediated learning approach was most effective because it involves an understanding of transcendent rules for labeling beyond specific context. These findings are consistent with earlier theory and research (e.g., Missiuna & Samuels, 1989; Rogoff, 1990; Tzuriel, 1998) about the importance of using mediation within the child's zone of proximal development.

Dynamic Assessment and
Reflectivity–Impulsivity Dimension

Clinical experience in DA shows that impulsivity affects cognitive processing in a pervasive way across various cognitive domains and phases of mental activity. Impulsivity relates to a cognitive/behavioral style rather than to the individual's abstraction ability. Very frequently impulsivity and ability are confounded, especially in timed tests. The effects of impulsivity on cognitive functioning as well as change of impulsivity level after intervention were investigated in several studies (Tzuriel, 1997b, 2000a; Tzuriel & Schanck, 1994). Tzuriel and Schanck (1994) showed that reflective children perform better in problem-solving tasks than impulsive children or even children who have a fast and accurate style as measured by the Matching Familiar Figures Test (MFFT; Kagan, 1965). It was shown also that experimental children who were administered two DA tests (CATM and CITM) had changed their cognitive style from pre- to postteaching toward reflectivity, whereas the control children displayed no change. The findings indicate that a reflective cognitive style is very effective in determining abstract thinking skills. The educational implications of these findings are that one should concentrate on the level of accuracy and on inhibition of the tendency to respond quickly, rather than the frequently used approach of encouraging fast answers. These findings were replicated by Tzuriel (1997b) on a sample of kindergarten to third-grade students using the CMB.

The effects of mediation on impulsivity and prediction of math achieve-ments by process-oriented measures of impulsivity were investigated re-cently with a group of grade 1 children using the Seria-Think Instrument (Tzuriel, 2000a). The Seria-Think Instrument is a novel DA measure aimed at assessing and teaching children a variety of arithmetic skills based on the op-eration of seriation, in combination with mastery of the math skills of addi-tion and subtraction. The Seria-Think Instrument is composed of a wooden block with three rows of holes (five holes in each row), a set of cylinders vary-ing in length, and a measuring rod divided equally into several units. In the first row the depth of holes is fixed, in the second row the depth of holes in-creases progressively, and in the third row the depth of holes is in a mixed or-der. The tasks involve insertion of the cylinders inside the holes in order to get lines of cylinders with (a) equal height, (b) an increasing height, and (c) a decreasing height. The instructions are to try to solve the problems with as few insertions of the cylinders into the holes as possible but with a possibil-ity to use the measuring rod as many times as the child wishes. To solve the problems, the child has to calculate the depth of the holes and the height of the cylinders, compare the height of the cylinders and the depth of holes, and plan which cylinder goes into which hole. The problems require several cog-nitive functions, the most important of which are regulation of impulsivity, planning behavior, systematic exploratory behavior, simultaneous consider-ation of few sources of information, needs for accuracy, and control of trial and error behavior. The Seria-Think yields three measures: performance level, as indicated by the accuracy of the solution; number of insertions, which in-dicates the efficiency level; and the number of measurements of the depths, which indicates planning behavior.

Children in experimental and control groups were administered pre- and postteaching phases on the Seria-Think. The experimental group received mediation for regulation of behavior with special focus on planning, compar-ing, and computing (i.e., measuring the depth of holes and length of cylin-ders, adding, and subtracting), whereas the control group received free-play manipulative experience with no mediation. Following the Seria-Think, both groups received a content-related math test. The findings clearly indicated that, from pre- to postteaching, the experimental children decreased signifi-cantly their number of insertions and concurrently increased their number of measurements. The control group, on the other hand, showed about the same response pattern before and after the treatment. Of most importance is the result indicating that both process-oriented measures were significant in differentiating between the experimental and control groups; the combi-nation of both characterizes the dimension of reflectivity versus impulsivity. The findings showed also that math score was predicted in the experimental group by postteaching number of insertions ($R^2 = .19$)—the fewer insertions the child used in the postteaching phase the higher was the math score. In the control group, the math score was predicted by the post-teaching number of measurements and post-teaching performance ($R^2 = .54$)—the higher the score on both variables the higher was the math score. In both groups the postteaching scores were more accurate in predicting the math scores than were the preteaching scores.

The results of all three studies show consistently that an impulsive inclination is detrimental to cognitive performance, and that even having an accurate mode of processing does not guarantee efficient cognitive functioning if it is not accompanied by a slow information-processing tempo. These findings have important implications for the validity of static measures of intelligence, especially the timed tests, which encourage children to work quickly. Static tests that rest heavily on timed factors tend to constrain efficiency and ability. Impulsive children frequently manifest a lower level of cognitive performance in spite of their relatively high learning potential and/or abstraction level. Their low performance might be interpreted as low ability rather than as low efficiency. The findings might have implications for teaching procedures in the school system and for societal values that encourage speed over accuracy, and efficiency over depth of processing and comprehension.

CONCLUSION

The research evidence presented in this paper validates DA as a more accurate and useful approach for measuring individual's cognitive abilities and relating them to various educational and intervention variables than the static test approach. Current research with various clinical groups shows that children's performance in a DA context is a more accurate indicator of their learning potential than performance on a static test. The lower the cognitive performance level of the child, the more effective is the mediation given for modifying his or her performance. Cross-cultural studies using DA with minority and learning disabled children have shown higher predictive value of school performance than have standard static tests. Similarly, DA was found more useful than static assessment when applied in cognitive education programs aimed at teaching children systematic data gathering, problem-solving strategies, and "how to learn."

The use of DA in different settings and groups also has proved its efficiency as a powerful intervention procedure. The integrative blend of assessment and intervention is novel in view of the fact that over recent decades each activity was separated, conceptually and methodologically. Another aspect of the DA approach is that it offers an optimistic view of the individual as a problem-solving thinker who possesses much higher ability than what is manifested in other testing approaches.

In spite of the efficacy of DA there are some unresolved problems related to cost-effectiveness, level of training, reliability and validity, and integration of assessment and intervention. The cost-effectiveness considerations relate to the fact that DA takes much more time to administer than static tests and requires more skill, better training, more experience, and greater investment of efforts. School psychologists may ask themselves, "How can we afford testing a child for 6–8 hours when the case load is high and the time required for DA exceeds the maximal 2–3 hours given for each case?" Policy makers surely will ask why they should invest in methods that require several times as many hours from the psychologists as do present methods. More evidence should be presented for the effectiveness of DA, especially in relation to popular criterion measures of school achievements (e.g., reading comprehension and math). The answer to the question of DA's effectiveness and worth lies in what one considers the major goal of the assessment. If the goal is to provide a quick and economical device to scan a child's current difficulties and predict his or her future performance, then static tests are more useful than DA tests. If the goal is to reveal a child's learning potential and learning processes and, as a result, to prescribe specific learning strategies, then DA seems to be a better approach. To some degree the goal of the DA approach is to refute the prediction of the static test approach. The distinction between static and DA goals derives from different philosophical perspectives. Feuerstein et al. (1979) referred to the differences between the static and DA approaches as a difference between the passive-acceptant and the active-modifying approaches, respectively.

The challenge of DA, then, is to be certain that the information derived is worth the investment required to get it, and that the information then is used in a way that results in educational benefits for the tested child. Proponents of DA frequently mention the argument that society at large and the individual, in particular, benefit in the long run (and often in the short run) from DA. A short, "instant" assessment might be cheaper in the short run but is superficial, wasteful, and less effective in the long run. DA, on the other hand, is lengthier and more expensive but provides in-depth and qualitatively better results, which ensure accurate future intervention procedures. Psychologists, educators, and policymakers should be convinced first that the information derived from DA is worth the investment, and that the information obtained then will then be used in a way that will have an impact on specific learning strategies and academic achievements.

Several intriguing issues have opened up a new field for further research. One of the main issues is: To what extent is cognitive modifiability generalized across domains? This issue has not only theoretical importance but also carries with it practical implications for the designing of tests and mediational procedures. In several studies carried out at Bar-Ilan University, we found that different measures of cognitive modifiability did not correlate significantly at kindergarten age, but with increasing age there was a tendency for increased correlations—a phenomenon that is attributed to the development of metacognitive skills with age. The increasing metacognitive processes helped children to benefit from mediation in one domain and transfer whatever has been learned to another domain. Metacognition had a consolidating effect by bridging cognitive modifiability across different domains.

The results of several studies support the argument that DA measures are more accurate than static measures in assessment of cognitive intervention programs (Tzuriel et al., 1999), especially when the aim is to evaluate "learning how to learn" skills and cognitive modifiability. My argument is: If the declared goal of the intervention is to teach children how to learn, the outcome measures should tap precisely that goal. The outcome measures should be assessed dynamically; change criteria and cognitive modifiability indicators should be the focus of evaluation. It is surprising, therefore, that many intervention programs aimed at modifying learning skills do not use DA as a primary outcome measure.

Two major unresolved issues that should be researched further are the reliability and validity of DA. One of the objectives of DA is to change the individual's cognitive functioning within the testing context so as to produce internal "unreliability." Reliability then can be assessed by interrater comparisons (Tzuriel, 1992a). The psychometric properties of the tests can be examined by group administration of the DA measures, as actually was done by several researchers (e.g., Kaniel et al., 1991, Tzuriel & Schanck, 1994). The group DA results, besides providing information about the psychometric properties of the tests, have been found to be crucial for indicating prescriptive teaching and educational strategies for the integration of students into educational systems.

Interrater agreement of DA tests have been studied intensively by Samuels et al. (1989) and Tzuriel and Samuels (2000) with learning disabled and EMH groups. These authors showed, for example, that the overall interrater percentage of agreement for rated deficient cognitive functions was 87.6% and for type of mediation was 91.6%. For different cognitive tasks, a different profile of deficient cognitive functions has been observed and different types of mediation can be applied. In spite of these findings more research is needed to verify the reliability of judgments made with DA procedures.

Validity is a major concern for any test and especially for DA, which has been claimed to be a more accurate measure of learning potential than static tests. Validation of DA is much more complex than validation of a static test, for several reasons. First, DA has been claimed to have a broader scope of goals such as assessing initial performance, deficient cognitive functions, and type and amount of mediation, nonintellective factors, and different parameters of modifiability. Each of these dimensions requires a different criterion; some of them might overlap. Second, many concepts within the MLE theoretical framework applied extensively in assessment and intervention still require empirical validation (e.g., the distinction among deficient cognitive functions of the input, elaboration, and output phases of the mental act). It is important to validate which deficient cognitive functions are more easily observed than others, and in what kind of task domain. One of the problems in validating DA is the need to develop a criterion variable that is derived from a cognitive intervention. The criterion validity of DA should be tested against criteria that match the nature of the testing, namely with changes in other domains (e.g., school achievements, cognitive changes on other tests). This requires implementing a cognitive education program that is aimed at bringing about these changes. Because a main objective of many programs is to teach children how to learn and to be independent in developing their learning potential, it follows that exactly this ability of learning how to learn should be assessed as a primary effect in a program's evaluation. Unfortunately, not many studies concentrate on this aspect of validity. Many investigators have used standard normative tests of general intelligence to assess children's stores of knowledge, and they have sometimes regarded the results as indicators of learning potential.

The main validation of DA should refer to prediction of aspects that are not predicted by static test results. Future research should tap questions such as the effects of failure and success in test items on subsequent performance, the effects of nonintellective factors on cognitive change, and the utility of specific mediation strategies on both cognitive and motivational factors.

A major criticism of DA relates to the relatively high prediction of school achievement by static test scores. The literature is replete with evidence showing a strong relation between IQ and school achievement. For example, Fraser, Walberg, Welch, and Hattie (1987) carried out a meta-analytic study based on 2575 studies to support the relationship between IQ and academic achievement. The massive data set in this case showed a familiar IQ-achievement correlation of .71. This means that nearly 50% of the variance in learning outcomes for students was explained by differences in psychometric IQ. This indeed is a crowning achievement for psychometrics. My argument is that, although no one argues that ability is uncorrelated with achievement, three extremely important questions remain: (a) What happened to the other 50% of the achievement variance?, (b) When IQ predicts low achievement, what is necessary to defeat that prediction?, and (c) What factors influencing the unexplained variance can help us to defeat the prediction in the explained variance?

One of the practical problems that psychologists often encounter when testing children coming from a different culture is how to differentiate, on an individual level, between those who manifest low level of functioning as a result of cultural difference and those that also have experienced cultural deprivation (i.e., deprived of mediation in their own culture). In this respect the DA approach offers an alternative that is superior over the static approach not only for its differential diagnostic value but also for its potential prescriptive remediation of deficiencies and enhancement of learning processes. On a broader sociohistorical scale DA can open opportunities for investigating cognitive change processes as a function of specific mediational procedures, implementation of learning contexts, and use of mental operations across cultures. What is important is not so much *what* children know or do but rather *how* they learn, and how they modify their cognitive structures as a function of mediational processes. Most important in further research is for research-ers to look at children's cognitive modifiability indices as a function of spe-cific cultural components that enhance mediation and change processes within families, classrooms, and more extensively in broader social circles. DA has much to offer examiners who want to understand what is limiting the child's performance and what may be helpful for facilitating higher levels of performance (Feuerstein et al., 1979; Haywood, 1997; Tzuriel, 1997a, 1998)

Haywood and Tzuriel (1992b) concluded that, in spite of the difficult prob-lems mentioned,

> interactive approaches to psychoeducational assessment appear to offer useful and even rich alternatives to standardized, normative assessment. The DA approaches appear to offer the possibility of more adequate assessment of handicapped per-sons (e.g., mentally retarded, sensory impaired, emotionally disturbed persons) and persons with learning disabilities, than do standardized, normative tests. They appear also to offer the possibility of some solution to "nondiscriminatory" assessment and educational programming for persons in minority ethnic groups and those in "trans-cultural" status: immigrants and those with language differences. (pp. 56–57)

Grigorenko and Sternberg (1998), in their extensive review of dynamic test-ing, concluded that it is difficult to argue that DA "clearly has proved its use-fulness and has shown distinct advantages over traditional static testing rela-tive to the resources that need to be expanded" (p. 105). They admit, however, that DA has suggested interesting paradigms as well as promising findings, and that in the future DA will prove to be a valuable resource to the psycho-logical profession. Grigorenko and Sternberg suggested that, in order to make DA studies more compelling, certain requirements are needed. One of these requirements is definition of DA as an independent tradition of testing in psychology, in terms of better distinction of goals and methodologies. On a small-scale level the requirements are to conduct studies with larger pop-ulations, to validate DA against educational and professional criteria, and to replicate findings beyond different laboratories and specific methodologies.

My conclusion, based on educational and intervention research with young children, is more positive than Grigorenko and Sternberg's conclusion. Some of the research discussed in this paper probably was not familiar to them, as well as developmental research that provides further support for the utility of DA (a detailed review of the developmental line of research is given in Tzuriel, 1999). I believe that DA already has established itself as a separate branch in the psychology of assessment, especially in circles that are involved in the practice of education rather than in circles that are research oriented. I agree, however, with Grigorenko and Sternberg's requirements for defining DA as an independent tradition of testing in psychology, in terms of better distinction of goals and methodology, and in regard to the need for studies with larger populations, for validation of DA against educational and professional criteria, and for replication of findings beyond different laboratories and specific methodologies.

References

Binet, A. (1909). *Les idees modernes sur les enfants* [Modern concepts concerning children]. Paris: Flammerion.

Bleichrodt, N., Drenth, P. J. D., Zaal, J. N., & Resing, W. C. M. (1984). *Revisie Amsterdamse kinder intelligentietest* [Revised Amsterdam child intelligence test]. Lisse: Swets & Zeitlinger.

Brown, A. L., & Ferrara, R. A. (1985). Diagnosing zones of proximal development. In J. V. Wertsch (Ed.), *Culture, communication, and cognition: Vygotskian perspectives.* Cambridge, MA: Cambridge Univ. Press.

Burns, S. (1991). Comparison of two types of dynamic assessment with young children. *The International Journal of Dynamic Assessment and Instruction, 2,* 29–42.

Campione, J. C., & Brown, A. (1987). Linking dynamic assessment with school achievement. In C. S. Lidz (Ed.), *Dynamic assessment* (pp. 82–115). New York: Guilford.

Carlson, J. S., & Wiedl, K. H. (1992). The dynamic assessment of intelligence. In H. C. Haywood & D. Tzuriel (Eds.), *Interactive assessment* (pp. 167–186). New York: Springer-Verlag.

Cole, M. (1990). Cognitive development and formal schooling: The evidence from cross-cultural research. In L. C. Moll (Ed.), *Vygotsky and education* (pp. 89–110). Cambridge, UK: Cambridge Univ. Press.

Das, J. P., & Naglieri, J. A. (1997). *Das and Naglieri: The Cognitive Assessment System.* Chicago: Riverside.

Das, J. P., Naglieri, J. A., & Kirby, J. R. (1994). Assessment of cognitive processes: The PASS theory of intelligence. Boston: Allyn & Bacon.

Feuerstein, R., Hoffman, M. B., Jensen, M. R., & Rand, Y. (1985). Instrumental enrichment: An interventional program for structural cognitive modifiability: Theory and practice. In J. W. Segal, S. F. Chipman, & R. Glaser (Eds.), *Thinking and learning skills* (Vol.1). Hillsdale, NJ: Erlbaum.

Feuerstein, R., Rand, Y., Haywood, H. C., Kyram, L., & Hoffman, M. B. (1995). *Learning Propensity Assessment Device—Manual.* Jerusalem: The International Center for the Enhancement of Learning Potential (ICELP).

Feuerstein, R., Rand, Y., & Hoffman, M. B. (1979). *The dynamic assessment of retarded performers: The learning potential assessment device: Theory, instruments, and techniques.* Baltimore: University Park Press.

Feuerstein, R., Rand, Y., Hoffman, M., & Miller, R. (1980). *Instrumental Enrichment.* Baltimore: University Park Press.

Feuerstein, R., Rand, Y., & Rynders, J. E. (1988). *Don't accept me as I am.* New York: Plenum.

Fraser, B. J., Walberg, H. J., Welch, W. W., & Hattie, J. A. (1987). Synthesis of educational productivity research. *International Journal of Educational Research, 11,* 145–252.

Gal'perin, P. Ya. (1966). K Ucheniui ob interiorizatsii [Toward the theory of interiorization]. *Voprosy Psikhologii, 6,* 20–29.

Ginsburg, H. (1977). *Children's arithmetic: The learning process.* New York: Van Nostrand.

Goswami, U. (1991). Analogical reasoning: What develops? A review of research and theory, *Child Development, 62,* 1–22.

Greenberg, K. H. (1990). Mediated learning in the classroom. *International Journal of Cognitive Education and Mediated Learning, 1,* 33–44.

Grigorenko, E. L., & Sternberg, R. J. (1998). Dynamic testing. *Psychological Bulletin, 124,* 75–111.

Guthke, J., & Al-Zoubi, A. (1987). Kulturspezifische differenzen in den Colored Progressive Matrices (CPM) und in einer Lerntestvariante der CPM [Culture-specific differences in the Colored Progressive Matrices (CPM) and in learning potential version of the CPM]. *Psychologie in Erziehung und Unterricht, 34,* 306–311.

Guthke, J., & Wingenfeld, S. (1992). The learning test concept: Origins, state of the art, and trends. In H. C. Haywood & D. Tzuriel (Eds.), *Interactive assessment* (pp. 64–93). New York: Springer-Verlag.

Hamers, J. H. M., Hessels, M. G. P., & Pennings, A. H. (1996). Learning potential in ethnic minority children. *European Journal of Psychological Assessment,* 12, 183–192.

Haywood, H. C. (1992). The strange and wonderful symbiosis of motivation and cognition. *International Journal of Cognitive Education and Mediated Learning,* 2, 186–197.

Haywood, H. C. (1997). Interactive assessment. In R. Taylor (Ed.), *Assessment of individuals with mental retardation,* (pp. 108–129). San Diego: Singular Publishing.

Haywood, H. C., Brooks, P. & Burns, S. (1986). Stimulating cognitive development at developmental level: A tested non-remedial preschool curriculum for preschoolers and older retarded children. In M. Schwebel & C. A. Maher (Eds.), *Facilitating cognitive development: Principles, practices, and programs* (pp. 127–147). New York: Haworth.

Haywood, H. C., Brooks, P. H., & Burns, S. (1992). *Bright Start: Cognitive curriculum for young children.* Watertown, MA: Charles Bridge.

Haywood, H. C., & Switzky, H. (1986). Intrinsic motivation and behavior effectiveness in retarded persons. In N. R. Ellis & N. W. Bray (Eds.), *International review of research in mental retardation* (Vol. 14, pp. 1–46). New York: Academic Press.

Haywood, H. C., & Tzuriel, D. (Eds.) (1992a). *Interactive assessment.* New York: Springer-Verlag.

Haywood, H. C., & Tzuriel, D. (1992b). Epilogue: The status and future of interactive assessment. In H. C. Haywood & D. Tzuriel (Eds.), *Interactive Assessment* (pp. 504–507). New York: Springer-Verlag.

Hessels, M. G. P. (1997). Low IQ but high learning potential: Why Zeyneb and Moussa do not belong in special education. *Educational and Child Psychology,* 14, 121–136.

Hessels, M. G. P., & Hamers, J. H. M. (1993). A learning potential test for ethnic minorities. In J. H. M. Hamers, K. Sijtsma, & A. J. J. M. Ruijssenaars (Eds.), *Learning potential assessment.* Amsterdam: Swets & Zeitlinger.

Holyoak, K. J., & Thagard, P. (1995). *Mental leaps: Analogy in creative thought.* Cambridge, MA: MIT Press.

Jeffrey, I. (July, 1997). The Cognitive Modifiability Battery—Assessment and Intervention: Clinical perspectives of a language therapist. Paper presented at the 6th Conference of the International Association for Cognitive Education (IACE), Stellenbosch, South Africa.

Jeffrey, I., & Tzuriel, D. (1999). The Cognitive Modifiability Battery (CMB): Applications of a dynamic instrument in speech language therapy. Unpublished paper, School of Education, Bar-Ilan University.

Jensen, A. R. (1980). *Bias in mental testing.* New York: Free Press.

Kagan, J. (1965). Individual differences in the resolution of response uncertainty. *Journal of Personality and Social Psychology,* 2, 154–160.

Kaniel, S., Tzuriel, D., Feuerstein, R., Ben-Shachar, N., & Eitan, T. (1991). Dynamic assessment, learning, and transfer abilities of Jewish Ethiopian immigrants to Israel. In R. Feuerstein, P. S. Klein, & A. Tannenbaum (Eds.), *Mediated learning experience.* London: Freund.

Kaufman, A. S., & Kaufman, N. L. (1983). *Kaufman Assessment Battery for Children: Administration and scoring manual.* Circle Pines, MN: American Guidance Service.

Kingma, J. (1983). Seriation, correspondence, and transitivity. *Journal of Educational Psychology,* 75, 763–771.

Klein, P. S. (1988). Stability and change in interaction of Israeli mothers and infants. *Infant Behavior and Development,* 11, 55–70.

Klein, P. S. (Ed.). (1996). *Early intervention: Cross-cultural experiences with a mediational approach.* New York: Garland.

Kozulin, A. (1990). *Vygotsky's psychology: A biography of ideas.* Cambridge, MA: Cambridge Univ. Press.

Lauchlan, F., & Elliott, J. (July, 1997). The use of the Cognitive Modifiability Battery (CMB) as an intervention tool for children with complex learning difficulties. Paper accepted for presentation at the 6th Conference of the International Association for Cognitive Education (IACE), Stellenbosch, South Africa.

Leontiev, A. N., & Luria, A. R. (1964). Die psychologischen Anschauungen L. S. Wygotskis. Einfuhrung. [The psychological views of L. S. Vygotsky: Introduction]. In L. S. Vygotsky (Ed.), *Denken und Sprechen* (pp. 1–33). Berlin: Akademie-Verlag.

Lidz, C. S. (Ed.). (1987). *Dynamic assessment*. New York: Guilford.

Lidz, C. S., & Elliott, J. (Eds.). (2000). *Dynamic assessment: Prevailing models and applications*. Greenwich, CT: JAI Press.

Lidz, C. S., & Greenberg, K. H. (1997). Criterion validity of group dynamic assessment procedure with rural first grade regular education students. *Journal of Cognitive Education, 6*, 89–100.

Lidz, C. S. & Thomas, C. (1987). The Preschool Learning Assessment Device: Extension of a static approach. In C. S. Lidz (Ed.), *Dynamic assessment* (pp. 288–326). New York: Guilford.

Luria, A. R. (1976). *The working brain* (B. Haigh, Trans.). New York: Basic Books.

Missiuna, C., & Samuels, M. (1989). Dynamic assessment of preschool children in special education with special needs: Comparison of mediation and instruction. *Remedial and Special Education 5*, 1–22.

Paour, J.-L. (1992). Induction of logic structures in mentally retarded: An assessment and intervention instrument. In H. C. Haywood & D. Tzuriel (Eds.), *Interactive assessment* (pp. 119–166). New York: Springer-Verlag.

Peña, E. D., & Gillam, R. B. (2000). Outcomes of dynamic assessment with culturally and linguistically diverse students: A comparison of three teaching methods. In C. S. Lidz and J. Elliott (Eds.), *Dynamic Assessment: Prevailing models and applications* (pp. 543–575). New York: JAI/Elsevier Science.

Raven, J. C. (1956). *Guide to using the Colored Progressive Matrices, Sets A, Ab, and B*. London: H. K. Lewis.

Reinharth, B. M. (1989). Cognitive modifiability in developmentally delayed children. Unpublished doctoral dissertation, Yeshiva University, New York.

Resing, W. C. M. (1997). Learning potential assessment: The alternative for measuring intelligence? *Educational and Child Psychology, 14*, 68–82.

Rey, A. (1959). *Test de copie et de réproduction de mémoire de figures géométriques complexes* [Test of copying and memory reproduction of geometric figures]. Paris: Centre de Psychologie Appliqué.

Rogoff, B. (1990). *Apprenticeship in thinking*. New York: Oxford Univ. Press.

Rogoff, B., & Chavajay, P. (1995). What's become of research on the cultural basis of cognitive development? *American Psychologist, 50*, 859–877.

Rutland, A., & Campbell, R. (1995). The validity of dynamic assessment methods for children with learning difficulties and nondisabled children. *Journal of Cognitive Education, 5*, 81–94.

Samuels, M. T. (1998). Tzuriel, D. Children's Inferential Thinking Modifiability Test. *Journal of Psychoeducational Assessment, 16*, 275–279.

Samuels, M. T., Killip, S. M., MacKenzie, H., & Fagan, J. (1992). Evaluating preschool programs: The role of dynamic assessment. In H. C. Haywood & D. Tzuriel (Eds.), *Interactive assessment* (pp. 251–271). New York: Springer-Verlag.

Samuels, M., Tzuriel, D., & Malloy-Miller, T. (1989). Dynamic assessment of children with learning difficulties. In R. T. Brown & M. Chazan (Eds.), *Learning difficulties and emotional problems* (pp. 145–166). Calgary, Alberta: Detselig.

Scribner, S. (1984). Studying working intelligence. In B. Rogoff & J. Lave (Eds.), *Everyday cognition: Its development in social context* (pp. 9–40). Cambridge MA: Harvard Univ. Press.

Shamir, A., & Tzuriel, D. (June, 1999). Peer-mediation with young children: The effects of intervention on children's mediational teaching style and cognitive modifiability. Paper presented at the International Conference of the International Association for Cognitive Education (IACE), Calgary, Alberta, Canada.

Sharoni, V., & Greenfeld, T. (1999). Applications of dynamic assessment and mediated learning principles in a reading remedial workshop: Case study. In D. Tzuriel (Ed.), *Mediated learning experience: Theory applications and research* (pp. 121–141). Haifa: Ach and the International Center for Enhancement of Learning Potential.

Sharp, D., Cole, M., & Lave, J. (1979). Education and cognitive development: The evidence from experimental research. *Monographs of the Society for Research on Child Development*, 44 (1–2, Serial No. 178).

Shochet, I. M. (1992). A dynamic assessment for undergraduate admission: The inverse relationship between modifiability and predictability. In H. C. Haywood & D. Tzuriel (Eds.), *Interactive assessment* (pp. 332–355). New York: Springer Verlag.

Simpson, S. (1985). *Test for assessment of preschool children*. Ramat-Gan, Israel: Bar-Ilan University.

Skuy, M., & Shmukler, D. (1987). Effectiveness of the Learning Potential Assessment Device for Indian and "colored" South Africans. *International Journal of Special Education*, 2, 131–149.

Swanson, H. L. (1995). Using the cognitive processing test to assess ability: Development of a dynamic assessment measure. *School Psychology Review*, 24, 672–693.

Thorndike, E. L. (1926). *Measurements of intelligence*. New York: Teachers College Press.

Tzuriel, D. (1989). Inferential cognitive modifiability in young socially disadvantaged and advantaged children. *International Journal of Dynamic Assessment and Instruction*, 1, 65–80.

Tzuriel, D. (1992a). The dynamic assessment approach: A reply to Frisby and Braden. *Journal of Special Education*, 26, 302–324.

Tzuriel, D. (1992b). *The Children's Inferential Thinking Modifiability (CITM) test—Instruction manual*. Ramat-Gan, Israel: School of Education, Bar Ilan University.

Tzuriel, D. (1995a). *The Cognitive Modifiability Battery (CMB): Assessment and Intervention—Instruction manual*. Ramat-Gan, Israel: School of Education, Bar Ilan University.

Tzuriel, D. (1995b). *The Children's Seriational Thinking Modifiability (CSTM) Test—Instruction manual*. Ramat-Gan, Israel: School of Education, Bar-Ilan University.

Tzuriel, D. (1997a). A novel dynamic assessment approach for young children: Major dimensions and current research. *Educational and Child Psychology*, 14, 83–108.

Tzuriel, D. (July, 1997b). The Cognitive Modifiability Battery (CMB): Assessment and Intervention. Presentation at the 6th Conference of the International Association for Cognitive Education (IACE), Stellenbosch, South Africa.

Tzuriel, D. (1998). *Cognitive modifiability: Dynamic assessment of learning potential* (in Hebrew). Tel Aviv: Sifriat Poalim.

Tzuriel, D. (1999). Parent-child mediated learning transactions as determinants of cognitive modifiability: Recent research and future directions. *Genetic, Social, and General Psychology Monographs*, 125, 109–156.

Tzuriel, D. (2000a). The Seria-Think instrument: A novel measure for assessment and intervention in seriational-computational domain. *School Psychology International*, 20, 173–190.

Tzuriel, D. (2000b). Dynamic assessment of young children: Educational and intervention perspectives. *Educational Psychology Review*, 12, 385–435.

Tzuriel, D. (2000c). The Cognitive Modifiability Battery (CMB)—Assessment and Intervention: Development of a dynamic assessment instrument. In C. S. Lidz and J. Elliott (Eds.), *Dynamic assessment: Prevailing models and applications* (pp. 355–406). New York: JAI/Elsevier Science.

Tzuriel, D. (in press). *Dynamic assessment of young children*. New York: Plenum.

Tzuriel, D., & Caspi, N. (1992). Dynamic assessment of cognitive modifiability in deaf and hearing preschool children. *Journal of Special Education*, 26, 235–252.

Tzuriel, D. & Eiboshitz, Y. (1992). A structured program for visual motor integration (SP-VMI) for preschool children. *Learning and Individual Differences*, 4, 104–123.

Tzuriel, D., & Eran, Z. (1990). Inferential cognitive modifiability as a function of mother-child mediated learning experience (MLE) interactions among Kibbutz young children. *International Journal of Cognitive Education and Mediated Learning*, 1, 103–117.

Tzuriel, D., & Feuerstein, R. (1992). Dynamic group assessment for prescriptive teaching: Differential effect of treatment. In H. C. Haywood & D. Tzuriel (Eds.), *Interactive assessment* (pp. 187–206). New York: Springer-Verlag.

Tzuriel, D., & Haywood, H. C. (1992). The development of interactive-dynamic approaches for assessment of learning potential. In H. C. Haywood & D. Tzuriel (Eds.), *Interactive assessment* (pp. 3–37). New York: Springer-Verlag.

Tzuriel, D., Kaniel, S., & Kanner, A., & Haywood, H. C. (1999). The effectiveness of Bright Program in kindergarten on transfer abilities and academic achievements. *Early Childhood Research Quarterly*, 114, 111–141.

Tzuriel, D., Kaniel, S., Zeliger, M., Friedman, A., & Haywood, H. C. (1998). Effects of the Bright Start program in kindergarten on use of mediated learning strategies and children's cognitive modifiability. *Child Development and Care*, 143, 1–20.

Tzuriel, D., & Kaufman, R. (1999). Mediated learning and cognitive modifiability: Dynamic assessment of young Ethiopian immigrants in Israel. *Journal of Cross-Cultural Psychology*, 30, 364–385.

Tzuriel, D., & Klein, P. S. (1985). Analogical thinking modifiability in disadvantaged, regular, special education, and mentally retarded children. *Journal of Abnormal Child Psychology*, 13, 539–552.

Tzuriel, D., & Klein, P. S. (1987). Assessing the young child: Children's analogical thinking modifiability. In C. S. Lidz, (Ed.), *Dynamic assessment* (pp. 268–282). New York: Guilford.

Tzuriel, D., & Samuels, M. T. (2000). Dynamic assessment of learning potential: Inter-rater reliability of deficient cognitive functions, type of mediation, and non-intellective factors. *Journal of Cognitive Education and Psychology*, 1, 41–64.

Tzuriel, D., Samuels, M. T., & Feuerstein, R. (1988). Non-intellective factors in dynamic assessment. In R. M. Gupta & P. Coxhead (Eds.), *Cultural diversity and learning efficiency: Recent developments in assessment* (pp. 141–163). London: NFER—Nelson.

Tzuriel, D., & Schanck, T. (July, 1994). Assessment of learning potential and reflectivity-impulsivity dimension. Paper presented at the 23rd International congress of Applied Psychology, Madrid, Spain.

Tzuriel, D., & Weiss, S. (1998). Cognitive modifiability as a function of mother-child mediated learning interactions, mother's acceptance-rejection, and child's personality. *Early Childhood and Parenting*, 7, 79–99.

Utley, C. A., Haywood, H. C., & Masters, J. C. (1992). Policy implications of psychological assessment of minority children. In H. C. Haywood & D. Tzuriel (Eds.), *Interactive assessment* (pp. 445–469). New York: Springer-Verlag.

Verster, J. M. (1973). Test administrators' manual for Deductive Reasoning Test. Johannesburg, South Africa: National Institute for Personnel Research.

Vygotsky, L. S. (1978). *Mind in society*. Cambridge, MA: Harvard Univ. Press.

Wood, D. J. (1989). Social interaction as tutoring. In M. H. Bornstein & J. S. Bruner (Eds.), *Interaction in human development*. Hillsdale, NJ: Erlbaum.

Index